PREFACE

On <u>Historical</u> occasions, Questions of Right and Wrong, Justice and Injustice, will naturally arise, and may be put to Youth, which they may debate . . . . They will . . . be sensible to the use of <u>Logic</u>, or the Art of Reasoning to <u>discover</u> Truth, and of Arguing to <u>defend</u> it, and <u>convince</u> Adversaries.

- Benjamin Franklin, 1749

Franklin's proposal for the education of youth in Pennsylvania captures the essential elements of Bicentennial Youth Debates: utilizing debate as a vehicle for youth to examine questions of value in an historical context. The appropriateness of the involvement of youth in a program commemorating the American Revolution becomes apparent when one realizes the role that youth played in that Revolution: Andrew Jackson was thirteen when he fought in the Battle of Hanging Rock; Nathan Hale had reached only his twentieth year when he was hanged; Alexander Hamilton at nineteen was staff aide to General Washington; James Monroe, like a great many of his contemporaries, was eighteen when he first entered battle; and both Betsy Ross and Molly Pitcher were in their mid-twenties when they acted out their parts in the American Revolution. One historian has concluded that "the younger men were the activists that could be depended upon. . . ." Roughly half the nation was under sixteen years of age in 1776.

Two streams—the historical role of debate in American life and the contribution of debate to the individual—unite to make debate a fitting vehicle for examining Bicentennial issues. John Adams, writing in July of 1776, proclaimed the decision to declare independence the greatest question "which ever was debated in America, and a greater perhaps, never was nor will be decided among men. . . ." Disputations, widely employed in the early colleges and universities at the time of the American Revolution, were an important academic exercise in which the student would put forth a proposition, affirm or deny it, and respond to questions. Some of the disputation topics prior to the Revolution are illustrative: "all power of making laws and inflicting penalties is derived from the people"; "anyone who takes liberty from another is unworthy to enjoy his own liberty"; and "unjust laws often impel man to make revolution." The testing of ideas by argument has always been central to the American experience. Webster, Calhoun, Lincoln, Darrow, Dirksen and Kennedy are merely representative of our rich tradition of great public advocacy. Student participants

in debate gain historical insight, critical thinking ability and research and communication skills.

The occasion of our two hundredth year of national existence places us at a crossroads. We should look back and reflect on where we have been and what has guided us; we should look ahead and imagine where we are going and what propels us. It is fitting, therefore, that we focus on critical historical and value questions.

Bicentennial Youth Debates, a project of the Speech Communication Association, supported by a grant from the National Endowment for the Humanities, offers every young person throughout the nation an opportunity to join in a meaningful commemoration of our 200th year. Officially recognized by the American Revolution Bicentennial Administration, BYD is a national program operating in all fifty states and the District of Columbia.

Our national heritage is the focus of the American Issues Forum from which BYD topics have been derived. Historical and value questions receive attention; our form of government, the rights of individuals and the obligations of society are only a few of the areas addressed. The nine "Issues" into which this volume is divided are the American Issues Forum monthly topics. Debate, extemporaneous and persuasive topics indicated in the introductory pages of the nine segments of this book have been developed from the specific weekly AIF questions.

In competitive events, each participating institution will conduct three events—Lincoln-Douglas Debate, Extemporaneous Speaking and Persuasive Speaking. Representatives in each of these events will proceed to the next contest level. Students will advance through District, Sectional and Regional competition to a final National conference. The events will be judged by members of civic organizations, community leaders, professional educators and a broad spectrum of interested citizens.

The BYD Community Program provides the opportunity for an ongoing dialogue between members of the community and young people who will be tomorrow's opinion leaders. In addition to scheduling participants before specific organizations, public meetings and town forums will be held.

The *BYD Issue Analysis* is designed to aid participants as they prepare for the three BYD events. Each of the nine major topic areas is divided into three questions that correspond to the three BYD events: Lincoln-Douglas Debate, Persuasive Speaking and Extemporaneous Speaking. Each of the twenty-seven topics is treated in three ways: an introductory essay raises basic questions and provides historical context for the area discussed; excerpted documents give the flavor of the issues as they were actually discussed at the time and interpretations placed on events by later analysts; selected bibliographies provide a basis for further investigation of the issues. Those preparing on a specific question should take note of relevant material to be found in other topics. These materials do not provide the answers to hard questions of American history and values; rather, we have sought to expose many of the questions needing answers. Events are subject to many interpretations; the brevity of this volume precluded an airing of all views. We expect this to happen as debates take place across the nation. Although Bicentennial Youth Debates is a project of the Speech Communication Association and supported by a grant from the National Endowment for the Humanities, any views expressed in this material do not necessarily reflect those of NEH or SCA.

It is our intent that Bicentennial Youth Debates and this volume will be the impetus for vigorous debate and discussion by Americans of all ages about issues that matter. Indeed, we hope that debate may be revitalized as a form for focusing questions and reaching decisions critical to America's future.

Richard C. Huseman, Director
James I. Luck, Associate Director

ACKNOWLEDGEMENTS

We would be remiss, indeed, if we failed to seize this opportunity to extend our personal thanks and acknowledge the program's indebtedness to a number of key contributors. The National Endowment for the Humanities provided the initial stimulus and on-going financial support fundamental to BYD's existence. The Speech Communication Association's commitment and national membership network were indispensable in implementing the program. Our liaisons with these organizations, Armen Tashdinian and Stan Turesky of NEH's Office of Planning and Analysis, and William Work, SCA's Executive Secretary, have supplied valuable suggestions and support.

We are particularly grateful to the members of the National Advisory Council: Joseph L. Block, National Merit Scholarship Corporation; William F. Buckley, Jr., Editor, *National Review*; Walter Cronkite, CBS News Correspondent; Arthur J. Goldberg, Former U.S. Supreme Court Justice; Barry Goldwater, U.S. Senator; Patricia Roberts Harris, former Ambassador to Luxembourg; Barbara Jordan, U.S. Representative; George Meany, President, AFL-CIO; Francine I. Neff, Treasurer of the United States; Dean Rusk, former Secretary of State. Early endorsements by these outstanding Americans with their good counsel enhanced the nature and reach of the program.

Participation by other leaders in education, industry, government, labor and the professions widened involvement in the project. Nationwide participation is reflected in the membership of the Council for Development and Community Involvement and Forensic Leadership Council.

BYD Regional Directors, often at considerable personal sacrifice, took mid-year leaves from teaching to develop and coordinate activities in their areas. The implementation of the BYD was accomplished by the eight Regional Directors: Irene Matlon, Northeast Region; David Horn, Mid-Atlantic Region; Lannie Katzman, Central Region; John Bloodworth, Southeast Region; John Crain, Southwest Region; Steve Davis, Mid-West Region; Donald Ritzenhein, North-Central Region; Louis W. Cockerham, Pacific Region. The task of the Regional Directors would have been an impossible one without the assistance of their respective secretaries: Eileen Locke, Jeanette Clark, Jacqueline Ellis, Vicki Chambers, Kathleen Dawson, Kerry Horan, Jenny Juodvalkis and Alma Rushing.

The volunteer work of 187 Sectional Coordinators, 2,552 District Coordinators and many thousands more school and community coordinators made the program a reality for young people.

This volume benefited from the work of many dedicated and talented people. The nucleus responsible for generating and reviewing topics, essays, documents and bibliographies included Gerald E. Ledford, Jr., James W. Paulsen, Joan Darby, Saul Benjamin and Michael W. Naylor. Each helped shape the final document. Other significant contributors, leaving their imprint as well, include: Robert McCabe, Michael Manley, Linda Listrom, Kenneth Simon, Madeleine Clarke, Philip Zelikow and Bruce Bosley. P. Jane Padgett typed the manuscript. Stu McMichael worked tirelessly coordinating our printing efforts.

Others in the national office who have made important contributions to the total project include: Harvey Silver (Information and Development), Virginia A. Everett (Administrative Assistant), Sandra Bryant, Larry Penley, Uday K. Lama, Evelyn Schindler, Joyce Howard, Bob Pease and Faith LaSalle. Special notes of appreciation are due Pam Martinson (Project Manager), and Marvin Isgur (Regional Coordinator). Marvin developed project administrative materials and coordinated regional activities. Pam coordinated public relations, managed project finances and applied her abundant energy whenever and wherever it was needed to ensure the program's success.

R.C.H.
J.I.L.

TABLE OF CONTENTS

ISSUE I
A NATION OF NATIONS

LOCAL EVENTS—HIGH SCHOOL ISSUE
September 27—November 1, 1975

DEBATE   *Resolved: That the "melting pot" metaphor is an historical fiction.*

PERSUASIVE   *My Country, right or wrong?*

EXTEMPORANEOUS   *Out of Many, One*

1. *The American Indian: Is this land his land?*
2. *What impact do the Puritans still have on our lives today?*
3. *Does America have "second class citizens?"*
4. *The settlement of America: For wealth or principles?*
5. *To what extent have today's regional divisions resulted from the patterns of settlement during the Colonial Period?*
6. *Has the Americanization process deprived the nation of valuable contributions of immigrant peoples?*
7. *Have the causes of America's racial problems chiefly been economic in nature?*
8. *Contributions of Black Americans: An overlooked chapter in American history?*
9. *Were immigrant migrations responsible for keeping alive the American dream?*
10. *Would America's industrial supremacy have been possible without open immigration?*
11. *America's immigrants: Did they find what they had hoped for?*
12. *Ethnic neighborhoods in America: Have they been assets or liabilities?*
13. *Why historically did most Americans come to put loyalty to country above loyalty to native state?*
14. *What's unique about American character?*

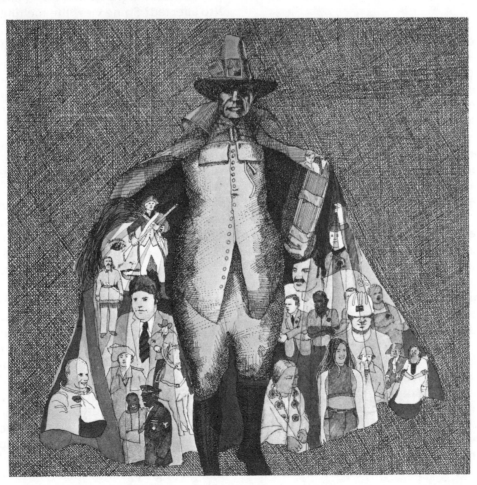

RESOLVED: THAT THE "MELTING POT" METAPHOR IS AN HISTORICAL FICTION.

Introductory Essay

It is the fire of God round his Crucible. There she lies—the great Melting Pot—listen! Can't you hear the roaring and the bubbling? There gapes her mouth—the harbour where a thousand mammoth feeders come from the end of the world to pour in their human freight. Oh, what a stirring and seething! Celt and Latin, Slav and Teuton, Greek and Syrian, black and yellow, [Jew and Catholic]. Yes, East and West, North and South . . . Now the Great Alchemist melts and fuses them with his purging flame! Here shall they all unite to build the Republic of Man and the Kindgom of God.

Israel Zangwill
The Melting Pot.
A Drama in Four Acts

The "melting pot"—one of the most enduring metaphors—describes the integration of immigrant groups into American society. The idea that something magical about the New Land would transform the French aristocrat and German peasant alike into sturdy republicans has, for many, struck sympathetic chords. Although the precise words "melting pot" were introduced in this century by Israel Zangwill's 1909 play, similar language and the concept had been long in use. J. Hector St. John de Crevecoeur wrote in 1782 that "here [in America] individuals of all nations are melted into a new race of men." Later Frederick Jackson Turner described the frontier as a "crucible" where "the immigrants were Americanized, liberated, and fused into a mixed race, English in neither nationality nor characteristics."

The "melting pot" is by no means universally accepted as an accurate or desirable description of the assimilation process. In fact, even Zangwill's play was widely criticized in this regard. A reviewer in *The Forum* vigorously denied the notion that the immigrants of the early 1900's were still shaping America. He expressed great concern over "the indiscriminate commingling of alien races on our soil" and vehemently denied the idea that "the scum and dregs" of Europe could enrich America. In 1926, another writer declared flatly that "if we must have a symbol for race mixture, much more accurate than the figure of the melting pot is the figure of the vil-

lage pound." Nor was the concern limited to bigots. A German American newspaperman expressed the distaste of many immigrants for the metaphor when he wrote that the play was "simply a mixture of insipid phrases and unhistorical thinking" and was "just the contrary of that toward which we strive." To many foreign-born citizens, the "melting pot" required too great a sacrifice; they felt that they could participate in American society while still maintaining their cultural and ethnic identity.

The "melting pot" has no precisely assigned meaning. In fact, a large part of the reason why it enjoys such lasting popularity is its ambiguity. According to its account immigrants are put into the "melting pot" and something happens, but what? Is it only the immigrants that are changed or is society also affected? Some view the melting pot as containing all citizens, old and new, so that when a new culture is stirred in, it enriches and changes the entire mixture. Others see American society as the container and the melting pot as a crucible that boils away the impurities until the final product is someone "just like everybody else." During an early Ford Motor Company pageant, presented by members of its school for immigrant employees, a huge pot was placed center stage. The immigrants, wearing native costumes and cards identifying them by country, disappeared into the pot from one side and emerged on the other side dressed in identical business suits, singing the national anthem, and (one observer claimed) each one carrying an Eversharp pencil in his pocket. Even opponents of immigration have accepted the metaphor, arguing only that the raw materials were of such low quality that an acceptable product could no longer be expected or, as in the case of one West Coast columnist, suggesting that something should be done about the "yellow froth" on the pot. Since there is such a variety of different and often contradictory interpretations of the "melting pot" metaphor it is possible that one of the focal points of controversy in any debate on this topic will be the validity of the definition chosen by the affirmative speaker. Certainly, though, the interpretation of the "melting pot" metaphor should include the peaceful interaction and assimilation of immigrant groups into society, with the new groups at least accepting the fundamental goals and values of that society.

Finally, many scholars disagree not on the definition of the "melting pot," but its applicability to history. Some argue it has never worked; some that it has worked better on certain groups than others; and still others claim that it worked once, but certainly does no longer. Pointing to the change in character of immigration in the 1880's and legislation beginning in 1924, they argue that there are today visible signs of a different kind of immigration and different attitudes toward the foreign-born. How are we to judge the historical truth of the metaphor? One must begin with a general knowledge of historical trends in immigration.

Immigration problems and policies existed even before the founding of this country. Land companies and foreign governments encouraged settlement both for profit and to establish the claims of their respective nations to the ownership of the regions. By the Revolution, America contained not only English, Scotch and Irish immigrants, but very substantial minorities of Germans (the "Pennsylvania Dutch") as well as members of the former colonies of New Netherlands and New Sweden. The colonists considered substantial immigration important to the economic growth of America and one of the complaints of the signers of the Declaration of Independence was that King George III "has endeavoured to prevent the population of these States; for that reason obstructing the laws for the Naturalization of Foreigners; refusing to pass others to encourage their migrations hither, and raising the conditions of new Appropriations of Lands." Of the fifty-six signers of the Declaration, eighteen were of non-English stock and eight were foreign-born. One immigrant, West Indian Alexander Hamilton, played a decisive role in the establishment of many of our nation's institutions. In popular usage, however, a somewhat arbitrary distinction has emerged; settlers arriving before 1776 are identified as "colonists," and those arriving later are called "immigrants." The distinction is important in some social circles, one author quoting a book on genealogy which states: "It is a relief to know that all members of the ---- family were safely in America before the Revolution."

Immigration, halted temporarily by the Revolution, continued at a moderate rate. Generally, the newcomers were welcomed, but some groups created serious misgivings. With the outbreak of the French Revolution a large number of aristocrats and royalist sympathizers, as well as over 10,000 refugees from a black revolt in Santo Domingo, settled in the United States. The monarchical leanings of these refugees worried the Anti-Federalists who were already disturbed at the aristocratic pretentions of the Hamiltonians. Ironically, it was not this influx but the arrival of radical French elements—

Girondists and Jacobins—that finally aroused enough concern to pass exclusionary acts—the Alien and Sedition Acts of 1798, which gave the President arbitrary powers to expel aliens suspected of subversive activites. Although they were never used, the Acts induced several shiploads of French refugees to seek other ports. These Acts, combined with the war between England and revolutionary France, and later between Great Britain and the United States, brought immigration to a temporary halt.

The signing of the Treaty of Ghent signaled the beginning of the first great wave of immigration. Census figures in 1790 showed that the nation had only four million inhabitants, not nearly enough to provide the labor needed for the widening frontier and the demands of growing industries. Consequently, the policy of government as well as the private sector was to encourage immigration—with the result that from the end of the War of 1812 to the beginning of the Civil War foreign immigration alone added another five million citizens. The first immigration act passed by Congress, in 1819, was designed to improve the conditions of passage, as were similar acts in 1847, 1848, and 1855. Improved conditions at sea through laws forcing bonding and setting fines for unsanitary conditions on ships, the rise of established ship lines such as the Black Ball and Cunard Lines, and unsettled conditions in Europe combined to produce a flood of immigrants: Norwegians and Dutch in the wake of severe crop failures, Irishmen during the potato famine, and Germans in the aftermath of the unsuccessful Revolution of 1848. The Castle Gardens immigration depot in New York was soon established to deal with this mass migration.

Although the government officially encouraged immigration not all Americans were enthusiastic. Isolated outbursts of anti-immigrant feeling were commonplace, with perhaps the worst example occurring in Philadelphia in 1844. Irish Catholic children in that city were permitted to forgo the Protestant religious instruction which was at that time part of public education. The apparent Papist interference in "American" matters caused a riot in May of 1844 that continued for days and gutted several blocks of the Irish section of the city. The unwise decision to hold a Fourth of July parade dedicated to the riot's dead triggered another outbreak of violence in which fighting between state militiamen and rioters resulted in thirteen dead, over 50 wounded, and a general exodus of Catholics from the city.

This kind of violence was universally condemned, but resistance to immigration gained respectability in the political arena. The most prominent movement was the Supreme Order of the Star-Spangled Banner, organized in New York in 1850. It was a secret fraternity-style organization with elaborate rituals and oaths. When questioned about their group, members invariably replied "I don't know' or "I know nothing," in consequence of which they acquired the popular title of "Know-Nothings." At the height of their power, 1854, they elected six governors and 75 congressmen and in 1856 ran a candidate named Millard Fillmore for the Presidency. Their aims may be judged best from an oath they required all candidates for office to take:

> That you will not vote nor give your influence to any man for any office in the gift of the people unless he be an American-born citizen, in favor of Americans ruling America, nor if he be a Roman Catholic. You will, when elected or appointed to an official station, conferring on you the title to do so, remove all foreigners, aliens, or Roman Catholics from office or place in your gift.

Fortunately, the demise of the party was as rapid as its rise, and it soon disappeared as an organized force, although anti-Catholicism has been much slower to disappear from the political scene.

In 1818, Congress made what one writer called "certainly one of the most important decisions . . . in the first half-century of America's existence." Irish associations had petitioned the legislature for a large grant of land on which to settle the Irish poor from Eastern cities. The Congress refused to sell blocks of land for such purposes, greatly limiting the possibility of nationally conscious European communities on the frontier and thus giving legislative expression to the principle of the melting pot.

The Civil War produced great changes in the status of immigrants in the United States. Most importantly, the war served (as all wars since have served) as a powerful assimilating factor. "Native" Americans, who claimed special treatment because their grandfathers had fought to create the nation, were placed on a par with the rawest immigrants who were fighting to preserve it. The manpower demands and industrial activity occasioned by the war prompted organized efforts to recruit immigrants to serve in the army and in industry. Additionally, the departure of the Southern legislators from the U.S. Congress allowed passage of an act prohibiting slave trade with the Orient, as well as the Homestead Act of 1862, which put citizens and aliens on an equal basis in the settling of public lands.

In 1882, the first federal immigration laws barred lunatics, idiots, convicts, and persons who seemed unable to support themselves. In the same year, Congress also passes the Chinese Exclusion Act, after pressure from the far Western states. In 1876, the California legislature had studied the "Oriental problem." One member summed up the findings by saying "the Chinese are inferior to any race God ever made. These people have got the perfection of crimes of 4,000 years. I believe the Chinese have no

souls to save, if they have, they are not worth saving." This anti-Chinese sentiment was institutionalized in a new California constitution, which barred Chinese from voting, employment by any corporation, or from employment on public works, and later resulted in national law. 1882 is also used by many historians as a convenient dividing line between "old" and "new" immigration. Prior to this time most immigration had been from Great Britain and the northwestern European countries; after 1882, it was to be predominantly southeast European races and nationalities.

In general, this new wave of immigrants was much harder to assimilate. Since they settled largely in cities there was a greater tendency for national groups to cluster, creating ethnic neighborhoods like New York's "Little Italy," where a newly-arrived immigrant could spend his entire life with no compelling reason to learn English, much less learn "The American Way." This tendency of immigrant groups to cluster, to speak their own languages, and practice their strange customs led to widespread suspicion among native Americans and even among earlier immigrants. In 1886, the Statue of Liberty was dedicated, with an inscription in part reading "Give me your tired, your poor, your huddled masses yearning to breathe free . . ." In the same year, six immigrants and one native were sentenced to death in Chicago for complicity in the "Haymarket Affair"—an anarchist bombing that killed and maimed many Chicago policemen trying to control a work strike. Although the guilt of those sentenced was questionable, the message was clear to most Americans: immigrants are anarchists, and anarchists are dangerous. Newspapers angrily denounced the "long-haired, wild-eyed, bad-smelling, atheistic, reckless foreign wretches." The Italians also suffered because the public equated every Italian with the Mafia. In 1891, eleven Italian immigrants were lynched in New Orleans on the suspicion that they were responsible for the murder of that city's police superintendent. The Italian government formally protested, and the Secretary of State, James G. Blaine, tactlessly replied that "We have never received orders from any foreign power, and shall not begin now. It is a matter of indifference what persons in Italy think of our institutions." Although the dispute was eventually settled peacefully, the temporary removal of the Italian ambassador and rumors that Italian warships were steaming toward America did not promote better relations with the Italian community.

Formal groups of the period emphasized the growing public sentiment against immigration. The late 1880's and early 1890's brought the return of anti-Catholicism in the form of the American Protective Association, which singled out the recent arrivals because of their predominantly Roman Catholic composition. At its zenith, the APA claimed to control several states and over a hundred members of

Congress. In 1894, the Immigration Restriction League, which was to be the leader in the restrictionist movement, was formed. In its ideology, it drew a distinction between the "old" immigration and the "new," suggesting that the desirable qualities possessed by the former group were lacking in the latter. This organization was considerably more broad-based since it did not limit its support by a specifically anti-Catholic stance. The resurgence of the Ku Klux Klan in 1915 was also a product of the growing fear of foreigners.

World War I was effectively the end of the "immigrant century." The restrictionist movement at home and the isolationist attitude in foreign policy culminated in an emergency immigration restriction law in 1921 and more permanent legislation in 1924. It is probable that immigration would have tapered off anyway; recurring economic depressions made America a less attractive place and European governments, mindful of the possibility of another major war, had begun to treat emigrants from their nations less as surplus population and more as a source of military manpower. These facts, however, do not detract from the significance of the exclusionary legislation. The National Origins Act, with its discriminatory racial and ethnic quotas, constituted an explicit national denial of faith in America as a melting pot. Legislation since that date has tended to modify the more obviously racist exclusions as well as, in some cases, liberalizing admission criteria, but none has changed the basic restrictive character of immigration law. More recently immigrant groups have been admitted under special legislation: the "displaced persons" following World War II, the Hungarian freedom fighters, the Korean refugees, and most recently, the Vietnamese. Some have been largely assimilated into American society; others, like the Cuban exiles, have formed their own society. An independent subject worthy of investigation is the detention of the Japanese-Americans during the Second World War. Does their deprivation of civil rights constitute the ultimate denial of the "melting pot," or should it be dismissed as an unfortunate manifestation of wartime hysteria—with the true temper of the nation shown by the widespread public shame expressed at the treatment of the Nisei in the war's aftermath?

What, then, is the true account of the history of immigration to the United States? Consider the remarkable fabric from which the contemporary American scene is woven. Ours seems a single Nation, and yet also a nation of many nations: a people, that is, whose roots have no single parentage. Each region contains peoples of remarkably different pasts; each city has within its own boundaries, numerous enclaves of people whose speech, myths, political expectations and cultural ways fit no simple mold, answer to no ready formula.

It would seem that the very character of this diversity rules out drawing any single neat explanation as to the manner in which a national character is formed. And yet, much has been experienced in common. Surely, one might suggest, the very industrialization which became increasingly the economic mode of the nation could not but work to affect a narrowing of diverse heritages, and the making for a uniform experience among the many immigrants who arrived in the New Land. Against this, however, one could easily enlist doubts. For how much, really, have immigrants changed? Perhaps a person's past is the most intractable, unyielding part of his nature. If so, then perhaps those who have suggested the now commonplace metaphor have been misled by the mere appearances of integration. And one could, further, consider the experiences of other nations confronted with rapid growth in their population. It may be, as one recent commentator has observed, that ethnicity is essentially "unmeltable." From the web of such competing possibilities comes evidence with which to test the metaphor.

Excerpted Documents

Is "melting pot" a useful metaphor?

Francis J. Brown, Staff Associate — American Council on Education, *One America*, 1952, p. 4.

The melting pot is only a myth; America will continue to be a nation of heterogenous peoples, but a nation richer in its heritage by the very fact of its variability. The problem is not that of seeking to establish a common mold for all, even if this were possible, but rather that of finding ever more effective ways in which each variant may be increasingly aware of its integral relationship to the composite pattern of American life.

Nathan Glazer, *Immigration and the United States*, 1956, pp. 58-59.

. . . the "melting pot" described the reality of assimilation which has characterized, to some extent, and in every period, each one of the ethnic groups migrating to this country. The "nation of nations" described one reality for the earlier period of our history: those homogenous colonies to be found principally on the Great Plains, but to some extent everywhere in the country, which maintained the immigrant's language, religion, and culture. Today the "nations" that make up America no longer find much justification in the maintenance of language, religion, and culture: they are private or subconscious "nations" held together only by a nostalgia which does not dare to become an ideology, a frame of mind which itself has no organic relation to their Old World past but is a reaction to the conditions of twentieth-century America.

Francis J. Brown, Staff Associate — American Council on Education, and Joseph C. Roucek, Chairman, Department of Sociology — University of Bridgeport, *One America*, 1952, pp. ix-x.

America, made up of peoples from every nation of the world, has attained and maintained an internal unity that was the bitterest disappointment to those abroad who believed that first- or even second-generation "native sons" would remain true to the "homeland." True, Bundist organizations sprang up, seditious material was published, and a resultant mass trial of those who sought to undermine the loyalty of men in the armed forces became necessary. The number of persons engaged in such activities is insignificant, however, in comparison with the millions of their countrymen who have kept the faith with America. Our allies have been their allies, and our enemies, their enemies, though tied by bonds of language, of culture, and of blood to a nation with which we were at war. In the changing alignments of war, this loyalty has meant for many of foreign birth or foreign stock an abrupt shift and the acceptance of attitudes contrary to old-world patterns. In a very real sense, they have demonstrated in the acid test of war that they are Americans.

Melvin Steinfield, Assistant Professor of History — San Diego Mesa College, *Cracks in the Melting Pot; Racism and Discrimination in American History*, 1970, p. 317.

The Melting Pot is obsolete. It had long ago outlived its usefulness, but it is manifestly obsolete today. Aroused members of ethnic minorities are seeking equality under the law and nondiscrimination in society; but they are also attempting to preserve the many elements of their individual cultures without having to conform to the cultural dictates of the majority. They regard Anglo-Saxon culture less than lovingly, and they know that they were never fully accepted by WASP society anyway, even when they wanted to assimilate.

Melvin Steinfield, Assistant Professor of History — San Diego Mesa College, *Cracks in the Melting Pot; Racism and Discrimination in American History*, 1970, pp. 317-318.

The historical record shows that the Melting Pot was one of those ideas that just hasn't worked out. Racism and discrimination are part and parcel of American life, and are likely to remain so in the years to come. It would be unjustifiable optimism and frivolous irresponsibility to delude ourselves into believing that there are significant trends away from racism. For every white . . . who led marches through the streets in favor of open housing in 1968, there are hundreds of whites who take their stand among those who would preserve the sacred right of the homeowner to discriminate. If it is difficult to emerge from the decade of the 1960's with any type of optimism about the future of American ethnic relations, it is virtually impossible to image that the resurrection of the Melting Pot can ever take place in the forseeable future.

John F. Kennedy, *A Nation of Immigrants*, 1964, p. 67.

Only in the case of the Negro has the melting pot failed to bring a minority into the full stream of American life. Today we are belatedly, but resolutely, engaging in ending this condition of national exclusion and shame and abolishing forever the concept of second-class citizenship in the United States.

Donald Keith Fellows, Professor of Geography — San Fernando Valley State College, *A Mosaic of America's Ethnic Minorities*, 1972, p. v.

The United States has often been regarded as the melting pot of the world—meaning, of course, that immigrants from other countries and Americans in minority racial or ethnic groups lose their unique self-identity, their culture and their heritage, and become submerged by the overpowering dominance of what has come to be called the "American way of life." While many individuals from a great number of different ethnic groups have gone their separate ways and have blended into the dominant society, others have found themselves unable or unwilling to do so. Anyone who has lived in one of the large metropolitan areas of the United States has witnessed the variety of ethnic, racial and religious groups which are still separated from the mainstream of American life.

Melvin Steinfield, Assistant Professor of History — San Diego Mesa College, *Cracks in the Melting Pot; Racism and Discrimination in American History*, 1970, p. 275.

At the end of the Johnson administration, in 1968, the President's National Advisory (Kerner) Commission on Civil Disorders warned of the imminent danger of America's moving toward two separate societies. Early in 1969 an independent report issued by the Urban Coalition and Urban America, Inc., entitled *One Year Later*, found virtually no progress toward ending the white racism which the Kerner report indicted. By the end of the 1960's it was clear that the myth of the Melting Pot was shattered because the last-ditch effort to keep it together had failed resoundingly. America was coming apart at the seams.

Carl Wittke, *We Who Built America*, 1964, p. xi.

Until the close of the First World War, the gates to the United States stood open and almost unguarded, and although American politics have never been altogether free of nativism, the American people as a whole offered a generous welcome to those who wanted to throw in their lot with them. Indeed, as the late E.D. Adams once pointed out, it was the immigrants who "led America to expand the vision of her democracy into a haven of refuge, where all the races of the world might share in her peace and prosperity." Here was a "melting pot" for all the world, and for centuries one of the most compelling convictions of the American people was the thought that their country was destined to become the mother of a mighty race.

Did the "melting pot" succeed with early immigrants?

John Quincy Adams (as Secretary of State, in a letter to the Baron von Furstenwaether), in *Minorities in a Changing World*, 1967, p. 398.

They [immigrants to America] come to a life of independence, but to a life of labor—and, if they cannot accommodate themselves to the character, moral, political, and physical, of this country with all its compensating balances of good and evil, the Atlantic is always open to them to return to the land of their nativity and their fathers. To one thing they must make up their minds, or they will be disappointed in every expectation of happiness as Americans. They must cast off the European skin, never to resume it. They must look forward to their posterity rather than backward to their ancestors; they must be sure that whatever their own feelings may be, those of their children will cling to the prejudices of this country.

Milton M. Gordon, *Minorities in a Changing World*, 1967, p. 396.

Political differences with ancestral England had just been written in blood; but there is no reason to suppose that these men looked upon their fledgling country as an impartial melting pot for the merging of the various cultures of Europe, or as a new "nation of nations," or as anything but a society in which, with important political modifications, Anglo-Saxon speech and institutional forms would be standard. Indeed, their newly won victory for democracy and republicanism made them especially anxious that these still precarious fruits of revolution should not be threatened by large influx of European peoples whose life experiences had accustomed them to the bonds of despotic monarchy.

Ralph Waldo Emerson, 1845, in *Minorities in a Changing World*, 1967, pp. 401-402.

Man is the most composite of all creatures . . . Well, as in the old burning of the Temple at Corinth, by the melting and intermixture of silver and gold and other metals a new compound more precious than any, called Corinthian brass, was formed; so in this continent,—asylum of all nations,—the energy of Irish, Germans, Swedes, Poles, and Cossacks, and all the European tribes,—of the Africans, and of the Polynesians, —will construct a new race, a new religion, a new state, a new literature, which will be as vigorous as the new Europe which came out of the smelting pot of the Dark Ages, or that which earlier emerged from the Pelasgic and Etruscan barbarism.

Benjamin Franklin (letter to Peter Collinson), May 1753, in *Historical Aspects of the Immigration Problem*, 1969, p. 416.

I am perfectly of your mind, that measures of great temper are necessary with the Germans; and am not without apprehensions that, through their indiscretion, or ours, or both, great disorders may one day arise among us. Those who come hither are generally the most stupid of their own nation, and, as ignorance is often attended with credulity when knavery would mislead it, and with suspicion when honesty would set it right; and as few of the English understand the German language, and so cannot address them either from the press or the pulpit, it is almost impossible to remove any prejudices they may entertain.

J. Hector St. John de Crevecoeur, *Letters from an American Farmer*, 1782, in *Immigration, the American Mosaic*, 1966, p. 113.

What then is the American, this new man: He is either European, or the descendant of an European, hence a strange mixture of blood which you will find in no other country. I could point out to you a family whose grandfather was an Englishman, whose wife was Dutch, whose son married a French woman, and whose present four sons have now four wives of different nations. He is an American, who leaving behind him all his ancient prejudices and manners, receives new ones from the new mode of life he has embraced, the new government he obeys, and the new rank he holds. He becomes an American by being received in the broad lap of our great Alma Mater. Here individuals of all nations are melted into a new race of men, whose labours and posterity will one day cause great changes in the world.

Samuel F. B. Morse, *Journal of Commerce*, 1835, in *Historical Aspects of the Immigration Problem*, 1969, pp. 448-449.

Few, out of the great cities, are aware what sophistry has of late been spread among the more ignorant class of foreigners, to induce them to clan together, and to assert what they are pleased to call their rights. The ridiculous claim to superior privileges over native citizens, which I have noticed, is a specimen . . . Already has the influence of bad councils led the deluded emigrant, particularly the Irish emigrant, to adopt such a course as to alienate from him the American people. Emigrants have been induced to prefer such arrogant claims, they have nurtured their foreign feelings and their foreign nationality to such a degree and manifested such a determination to create and strengthen a separate and a foreign interest, that the American people can endure it no longer, and a direct hostile interest is now in array against them.

Republican National Platform of 1864, in *The Immigration Problem*, 1948, p. 47.

Foreign immigration, which in the past has added so much to the wealth, development of resources, and increase of power to the nation—the asylum of the oppressed of all nations, should be fostered and encouraged by a liberal and just policy.

George Hedley, *The Immigration Problem*, 1948, p. 16.

. . . a breath of caution was to frost upon the alien atmosphere at an early date. So great was the concentration of Germans in Pennsylvania that Ben Franklin was moved to comment upon the possible need for interpreters in the State Assembly. Washington was not convinced of the wisdom of unrestricted immigration. Jefferson felt the need of discouraging the influx from monarchial countries. Congressman Otis of Massachusetts in 1797 stated upon the floor of the House that "it is no longer" good policy "to admit foreigners."

Was the "new wave" of immigrants impossible to assimilate?

Mary Antin, *They Who Knock at Our Doors*, 1914, p. 123.

The only reason the mill is grinding so slowly is that the miller is overworked and the hopper is choked. We are letting a few do the work we should all be helping in. At the settlements, devoted young men and women are struggling with classes that are too large, or turning away scores of eager children, and their fathers and mothers, too, because there are not enough helpers; and between classes they spend their energies in running down subscribers, getting up exhibitions to entice the rich men of the community to come and have a look at their mission and drop something in the plate.

Konrad Bercovici, a European traveler in America in 1919, in *Immigration, The American Mosaic*, 1966, pp. 159-160.

I strolled over Third Avenue [in New York] into Mulberry Street. I was in Sicily at one end of the street and in Piedmont at the other end. The very same odor of fried fish I had tried to escape in Naples assailed my nostrils. The very same impudent cries of the Genoese fish-seller greeted my ears. From one end of the street to the other not a word of English except the vilest curses. . . . It was all Italian. It was Italy, with separate provinces and dialects . . . On the corner of the street stood a policeman. I was tempted to ask him "Please, where is America?" But he stared me out of my wits.

I walked out of Mulberry Street and fell into the Greek quarter. It looked more like some side street of Stamboul. Cafes every ten feet. . . .

I soon came into the Jewish quarter. Here and there a sign in another language than Hebrew. I wandered into the Syrian quarter on Washington Street. Beautiful laces and heavy brocades in the store windows. . . . It was Smyrna or Jaffa or the Port of Athens. A young, barefooted boy sold a newspaper printed in the Arabic language which was eagerly bought by every one . . .

For days and days I searched for Americans, but the only thing American I saw was the dollar . . .

John F. Kennedy, *A Nation of Immigrants*, 1964, p. 58.

One New York newspaper had these intemperate words for the newly arrived Italians: "The flood gates are open. The bars are down. The sally-ports are unguarded. The dam is washed away. The sewer is choked . . . the scum of immigration is viscerating upon our shores. The horde of $9.60 steerage slime is being siphoned upon us from Continental mud tanks."

James Bryce, *The American Commonwealth*, 1888, in *Immigration, The American Mosaic*, 1966, p. 157.

What strikes the traveller, and what the Americans themselves delight to point out to him is the amazing solvent power which American institutions, habits and ideas exercise upon new-comers of all races. The children of Irishmen, Germans, and Scandanavians are far more like native Americans than prevalent views of heredity would have led us to expect; nor is it without interest to observe that Nature has here repeated on the Western continent that process of mixing Celtic with Germanic and Norse blood which she began in Britain more than a thousand years ago.

Jethro K. Lieberman, *Are Americans Extinct?*, 1968. p. 61.

Cried Representative MacLafferty: "For God's sake, you men who know what the colored problem means, not only to the white man but to the colored man, stand with us in this. We will not forget if you do." Mr. Miller of Washington summed it up: "The Japanese cannot be made Americans. The native-born are Japanese heart, blood, and soul. They never yield to the American idea of things. In their hearts, they owe a superior allegiance to the Mikado. Their national sentiment is fixed, their faith is pledged. There is no such thing in truth as an American-Japanese; he is a Japanese, simon-pure, every inch of his body, every drop of his blood."

Henry Cabot Lodge, 1888, in *Immigration and the United States*, 1956, p. 62

Let us be done with British-Americans and Irish-Americans and German-Americans, and so on, and all be Americans . . . if a man is going to be an American at all, let him be so without any qualifying adjective.

William M. Floyd, National Commander — Veterans Association, before the Committee on the Judiciary, June 6, 1947, in *The Immigration Problem*, 1948, pp. 107-108.

The United States is no longer the melting pot of a hundred years or more ago. That was recognized in 1921 before there was any restriction on immigration. The hard-working, honest, and industrious people who came to this country from northern Europe in earlier years, eager to adopt the principles and institutions of America as their own and become Americans in fact, were giving way to immigrants from southern and eastern Europe and from Russia. The latter began entering the country at something more than a million each year. By 1914 they comprised more than half of our total population increase. A large percentage of this element were undesirables in anything resembling comparison with former immigrants.

David Bowers, *Foreign Influences in American Life*, 1944, p. 42

In the later nineteenth century, when the character of immigration changed, the cordiality of the welcome cooled as many people began to doubt whether widely heterogeneous peoples could indeed be transformed into creditable Americans. It began to be said that the melting pot failed to melt, and ultimately restrictive legislation put an end to the whole movement.

Did immigrants function as distinct political groups?

George M. Stephenson, Professor of History — University of Minnesota, *A History of American Immigration, 1820-1924*, 1926, p. 103.

The evils of foreign-born suffrage were undoubtedly great in the cities of the East, where immigrants were naturalized wholesale and herded to the polls by ward-heelers, native and foreign. The immigrants to some extent considered themselves a separate class, and their prejudices were carefully nursed by demagogues and self-seekers. Urged by foreign-language newspapers and their leaders, the naturalized Americans showed a disposition to exercise the privilege of the ballot box as citizens. On certain issues they voted in a body.

Martin Stalding, *Miscellanea*, 1855, in *Historical Aspects of the Immigration Problem*, 1969, pp. 471-472.

Much has been said and written of late years about the "foreign vote." Both parties, on the eve of elections, have been in the habit of courting "foreigners" who have thus, against their own choice and will, been singled out from the rest of the community and placed in a false and odious position by political demagogues for their own vile purposes. That they have been thus severed from their fellow-citizens and insulted with the compliment of their influence as a separate body, has not been so much their fault, as it has been their misfortune. From the successful party they have generally received—with a few honorable exceptions—little but coldness, after the election; while from the party defeated, they have invariably received nothing but abuse and calumny. So they have been, without their own agency, placed between two fires, and have been caressed and outraged by turns.

Senator John B. Thompson (Whig, Kentucky), 1808, in *A History of American Immigration*, 1820-1924, 1926, p. 123.

The first thing you see these president-aspirants do . . . is to start out a demagoging; and, sir, he draws himself up; he is not an American at all; his father was an Irishman, and his mother a Dutchman [laughter]. That is the beginning of it. Then though he has no respect for religion . . . the next thing we hear he is making the sign of the cross to catch Catholics [laughter].

Francis J. Brown, Staff Associate — American Council on Education, *One America*, 1952, p. 22.

. . . contrary to the popular conception that there is such a thing as a "German" vote or mentality, there are no Germans, Czechoslovaks, Poles, or other minority groups living in America, that are characterized by definite and singular characteristics applicable to each group member. It is impossible to speak about such minorities in terms of their collective names without noting that each cluster is subdivided into numerous socially stratified classes and castes, disintegrated and frequently in conflict with one another in terms of their differences.

Parke Goodwin, *Putnam's Monthly*, January 1855, in *Historical Aspects of the Immigration Problem*, 1969, pp. 802-802.

It cannot be denied that, for some years now, both whigs and democrats have prostrated themselves before the alien voters, in a servile and disgraceful way. Holding the balance of power, as the latter did, between the two parties, there was no end to the concessions . . . No ticket was a complete ticket which did not contain a sop, in the shape of a candidate to the Irish interest or the German interest, and the suppleness with which senators and governors bent themselves in that direction set new lessons in the art of fawning—gave new formulas for the preparation of adroit lies.

Does the "melting pot" affect the second generation?

Julius Drachsler, Assistant Professor of Economics and Sociology — Smith College, *Democracy and Assimilation*, 1920, p. 79.

. . . the fatal disease gnawing at the vitals of the immigrant community is the "diluted" second generation. Silently, under the roof of every immigrant home there is going on a death struggle between two worlds, two cultures, two civilizations . . . In the same family circle different tongues are spoken, different newspapers and books are read, different foods are eaten, different manners and customs observed.

Stoyal Cristowe, Bulgarian immigrant, quoted in *Immigration and Assimilation*, 1933, pp. 636-637.

Despite the readiness and zeal with which I tossed myself in the melting pot I am still not wholly an American, and never will be. It is not my fault. I have done all I could. America will not accept me. I shall always be the adopted child, not the real son, of a mother that I love more than the one that gave me birth. It is hard for a man with ingrained native traits and characteristics to remake himself in the course of one generation. There is still something outlandish about me; mannerisms and gestures that must strike as odd one born and bred here; tints and nuances in my speech that must betray my foreign birth soon after I open my mouth to speak. I once believed that America demanded complete surrender from those who adopted it as their mother. I surrendered completely. Then I discovered that America wanted more—it wanted complete transformation, inward and outward. That is impossible in one generation.

Marcus Lee Hansen, *The Immigrant in American History*, 1940, p. 93.

The appearance of the second generation has always marked a new chapter in the history of any immigrant stock. The Norwegian father considered his children Norwegians; the children considered themselves Americans. In reality they were neither. They were experiencing a transition stage characterized by an exaggerated

Americanism which obscured the cultural values they had imbibed from their immigrant surroundings. With the point of view of the older generation the younger had no sympathy; and upon reaching maturity the son hastened to throw off every distinctive feature that had set the father apart from his American neighbors. "Old fashioned" was the inclusive charge directed against the parents—old fashioned in speech, in dress, in methods of work and in standards of conduct.

Minnesota Chronicle and Register, September 23, 1850, in A History of American Immigration, 1820-1924, 1926, p. 101.

[The public school] takes the child of the exile of Hungary, of the half-starved emigrant from the Emerald Isle, and of the hardy Norwegian, and places them on the same bench with the offspring of those whose ancestors' bones bleached upon the fields of Lexington . . . As the child of the foreigner plays with his school fellow, he learns to whistle "Yankee Doddle" and sing "Hail Columbia," and before he leaves the school-desk for the plough, the anvil or the trowel, he is as sturdy a little republican as can be found in the land.

Selected Bibliography

Abbott, Edith. *Historical Aspects of the Immigration Problem*. New York: Arno Press and the New York Times, 1969.

Antin, Mary. *They Who Knock at Our Gates*. Boston: Houghton Mifflin Co., 1914.

Barron, Milton L., ed. *Minorities in a Changing World*. New York: Knopf, 1967.

Bernard, William S., ed. *American Immigration Policy: A Reappraisal*. New York: Harper and Brothers, 1950.

Blegen, Theodore C., ed. *Land of Their Choice: The Immigrants Write Home*. Minneapolis: University of Minnesota Press, 1955.

Bowers, David F. *Foreign Influences in American Life*. Princeton, N.J.: Princeton University Press, 1944.

Brown, Francis J., And Roucek, Joseph C., eds. *One America*. Englewood Cliffs, N.J.: Prentice-Hall, Inc., 1952.

Commager, Henry Steele, ed. *Immigration and American History*. Minneapolis: University of Minnesota Press, 1961.

Divine, Robert A. *American Immigration Policy, 1924-1952*. New Haven: Yale University Press, 1957.

Drachsler, Julius. *Democracy and Assimilation*. New York: The Macmillan Company, 1920.

Duncan, H.G. *Immigration and Assimilation*. Boston: D.C. Heath & Co., 1933.

Garraty, John A. *The American Nation: A History of the United States*. New York: Harper & Row, 1966.

Glazer, Nathan, and Moynihan, Daniel Patrick. *Beyond the Melting Pot: The Negroes, Puerto Ricans, Jews, Italians, and Irish of New York City*. Cambridge, Massachusetts: The M.I.T. Press and the Harvard University Press, 1963.

Gleason, Philip. "The Melting Pot: Symbol of Fusion or Confusion." *American Quarterly*, (Spring, 1964).

Gordon, Milton M. *Assimilation in American Life: The Role of Race, Religion, and National Origins*. New York: Oxford University Press, 1955.

Handlin, Oscar, ed. *Immigration as a Factor in American History*. New York: Prentice-Hall, 1959.

Hansen, Marcus Lee. *The Immigrant in American History*. New York: Harper & Row, 1940.

Hansen, Marcus Lee. *The Atlantic Migration, 1607-1860*. Cambridge: Harvard University Press, 1940.

Higham, John. *Strangers in the Land*. New Brunswick: Rutgers, 1955.

Jaworski, Irene D. *Becoming American*. New York: Harper & Row, 1960.

Jones, Maldwyn Allen. *American Immigration*. Chicago: University of Chicago Press, 1960.

Kennedy, John F. *A Nation of Immigrants*. New York: Harper & Row, 1964.

Kraus, Michael. *Immigration, The American Mosaic*. Princeton, N.J.: D. Van Nostrand Co., 1966.

Laski, Harold J. *The American Democracy: A Commentary and an Interpretation*. New York: The Viking Press, 1948.

Lieberman, Jethro K. *Are Americans Extinct?* New York: Walker and Co., 1968.

Novak, Michael. *The Rise of the UnMeltable Ethnics*. New York: Collier-MacMillan, 1972.

Peters, Clarence A., ed. *The Immigration Problem*. New York: H.W. Wilson Co., 1948.

Schlesinger, Arthur M. Jr., and White, Morton, eds. *Paths of American Thought*. Boston: Houghton Mifflin Co., 1963.

Schlesinger, Arthur M. Jr., *Paths to the Present*. New York: The Macmillan Co., 1949.

Smith, William C. *Americans in the Making: The Natural History of the Assimilation of Immigrants*. New York: Appleton-Century, 1939.

Steinfield, Melvin, ed. *Cracks in the Melting Pot; Racism and Discrimination in American History*. Beverly Hills: Glencoe Press, 1970.

Stephenson, George M. *A History of American Immigration, 1820-1924*. Boston: Ginn & Co., 1926.

Tyler, Poyntz. *Immigration and the United States*. New York: H.W. Wilson Co., 1956.

Wittke, Carl. *We Who Built America*. Cleveland, Ohio: The Press of Western Reserve University, 1964.

Ziegler, Benjamin Munn, ed. *Immigration: An American Dilemma*. Boston: D.C. Heath & Co., 1953.

MY COUNTRY, RIGHT OR WRONG?

Introductory Essay

Today's bumper sticker slogans "America—Love It or Leave It" and "America—Change It or Lose It!" reflect much of the controversy long associated with the exclamation "My Country, Right or Wrong!" Serious questions about the moral foundations of the state are involved. For centuries men have divided into those who would give primacy to the state and those who would give primacy to something higher, whether divinity or individual conscience, in laying down the moral law. Men also differ over what one should do when the state violates the moral law. Many believe that one should pursue legitimate avenues, such as the elective process or the courts, until these are exhausted and then abide with the result. A few maintain that one should further resist through civil disobedience. The country began, of course, with a revolution when the people objected so strongly to the wrongs of the state that they proposed a new state. At least one time since (the Civil War) a large part of the country felt that more than civil disobedience was necessary.

Defining what the exclamation has meant and now means may prove to be the most difficult problem for the speaker. Is it rant? Emotional outcry? Or does it mask the view that the effort to alter particular policies and laws, no matter how wrong these may be, should not become a threat to the system of law itself? The speaker might well begin his preparation with such classic works as Plato's "Crito" and Thoreau's "Civil Disobedience." In the "Crito," Socrates rejects his friends' proposal that he escape the death penalty unjustly imposed on him by the Athenian court; Socrates distinguishes between the unjust misuse of the laws by those who accused and judged him and the just system of law itself which the individual is obligated to uphold. Escape would undermine that system, for what would happen to the state if individuals submitted to the laws only when convenient? For Socrates the system of law itself is the moral foundation of the state. Echoes of this view can be heard throughout American history. Rufus Choate, a Massachusetts lawyer, for example, declared in a famous letter in 1856 that the law is "the absolute justice of the State." In "Civil Disobedience," however, Thoreau claims that the individual conscience is the moral foundation of the state. Thoreau recognizes that there are unjust laws and that the system of law itself does not necessarily embody justice. When the state gears the system of law to expedience so that it threatens justice, then justice must be restored at any cost. Until that time, the individual must withdraw his support and allegiance. Therefore Thoreau refused to pay his poll tax and spent a night in jail in order to protest the government's war on Mexico and its tolerance of slavery. Thoreau's view clearly echoes a long tradition of religious and secular appeal to higher law, from Aquinas through Calvin to Americans like Channing and Emerson, and it would be echoed for decades by the New England anarchists like Benjamin Tucker, who also refused to pay his poll tax in 1875.

Frequently the exclamation "My country, right or wrong!" has been applied simultaneously to foreign crises and domestic conflicts. How has the meaning of the exclamation changed with reference to different events in American history, for example, Shay's Rebellion in 1786, the Underground Railroads in the 1840's and 50's, the Suffragettes, Coxey's Army of the Unemployed in 1894, the Labor Movement, and the Anti-War Movement in recent years? Has the exclamation had different meanings for a war that seems to pose an immediate threat to the country, a distant war that does not, domestic disputes when the law explicitly runs counter to the dissenter's position, when the law is nebulous, or when there is no applicable law, when the redress is available through legitimate avenues, when redress is not available, and so forth? Would the exclamation mean the same thing for a Black living before the Civil War and for a Black living after *Brown v. Board of Education* and the *Civil Rights Act*? Would it mean the same thing for a miner seeking better working conditions before unionization and legal protection for the right to strike and for one now? Would it mean the same thing for the Quaker who applies for Conscientious Objector status because he is affiliated with a religion historically opposed to war and for someone disavowing religious affiliation who applies for that status because he is opposed to violence on moral and philosophical grounds? What meaning would it have had for the Japanese Americans who were relocated in special camps during WW II? What meaning does it have for the Chicano? What meaning does it have for the American Indian?

It may be that the exclamation "My country, right or wrong!" has been shouted most vigorously during wartime. Dissenters have been equally vigorous. Horace Greeley, the American journalist, opposing the war with Mexico, insisted that no American is obligated to support an unjust or immoral war:

People of the United States! Your rulers are precipitating you into a fathomless abyss of crime and calamity! Why sleep you thoughtless on its verge, as though this was not your business, or Murder could be hid from the sight of God by a few flimsy rags called banners?

While America's year-long encounter with France during the Napoleonic Wars drew modest dissent from Republicans, the War of 1812 with England was perhaps the most unpopular war in American history. The Congressional Declaration of War passed by 79-49 vote in the House and a 19-13 vote in the Senate. In New England, dissenters argued that the war would damage their manufacturing trade with Great Britain and would weaken the only European nation capable of defeating Napoleon. All of the New England Governors except Gilman of New Hampshire, regularly refused to subscribe to government bonds unless President Madison promised to negotiate immediately for a peace settlement. Governor Strong of Massachusetts conducted a secret mission to obtain a separate peace with Great Britain. John Lowell of Massachusetts initiated a movement for a new union to be composed only of the thirteen original states, and his proposal was endorsed by every Boston Federalist paper.

In 1846 the United States declared war on Mexico over the Texas-Mexico boundary. The United States drew the boundary at the Rio Grande River while Mexico drew it at the Nueces River. Whigs protested that the United States did not have a legitimate claim to the territory and that the war was an imperialist venture to acquire additional room for the extension of slavery. Despite their disapproval, Whigs continued to vote supplies and resolutions of thanks to the Generals. In a strong act of protest in August of 1846, Whig senators attempted to attach a rider to an administration bill; the Wilmot Proviso specified that territory acquired from the war would not be open to slavery, but it was defeated, as were later attempts to attach similar riders to legislation.

In the North, the Civil War encountered opposition. The Republicans lost heavily in the 1862 Congressional elections, and the 1864 Democratic Platform declared that the war had been a failure. In contrast, the Spanish-American War was popular. Americans were too caught up in the clamor for empire and the hysteria over the *Maine* to appraise the war critically. After Admiral Dewey had defeated the Spanish fleet at Manila, the United States became the new colonial power in the Philippines. On February 4, 1899, hostilities broke out between the United States and the Philippines. Many opposed this war as inhumane and imperialistic. Veteran Edward Atkinson attempted to distribute anti-war pamphlets to members of the armed forces; when he was unable to procure the necessary mailing list, he instead mailed copies to Admiral Dewey and other prominent military officers. Eventually 135,000 pamphlets were distributed to the civilian population. Congress extensively investigated the American wartime atrocities which had left 200,000 Philippinos dead.

Little American dissent was heard in either of the world wars. Dissent in World War I came primarily from socialist and ethnic groups who were pacifist or opposed American intervention in European affairs. The Japanese bombing of Pearl Harbor and the German and Italian Declarations of War against the United States virtually eliminated opposition to World War II. Similarly, there was little opposition to the Korean War which was fought during a period of intense anti-Communism in the United States and which was apparently justified as a multilateral effort to defend the United Nations Charter.

The Vietnam War, however, sparked intense opposition and resulted in some of the largest demonstrations and marches for peace that the country has ever seen, culminating in a nationwide student strike that closed campuses all over the country during the Cambodian invasion in the spring of 1970.

The question remains, just what are a citizen's obligations to the country in wartime? Conscription during a war (and amnesty afterwards) have been major points of contention. In the *Selective Draft Law Cases* of 1918, the Supreme Court ruled that Congress had the power to enact a draft law under Article 1 Section 8 of the Constitution which gives Congress the power to declare war and raise and support armies. It is possible, however, that the framers of the Constitution never intended to give the federal government the power to force citizens into the military.

England provided the colonies with a tradition of distrust for the military and opposition to conscription. The "Agreement of the People" which passed the House of Commons in 1648 declared that "constraining any of us to serve in the wars is against our freedom and therefore we do not allow it. . ." Because both Charles II and James II had used the army to defy English law and infringe upon the rights of the people, the 1689 Declaration of Rights provided "That the raising or keeping a standing army within the kingdom in time of peace unless it be with the consent of Parliament is against the law. . ."

The experiences of England under Charles II and James II greatly affected colonial attitudes toward the military, and colonial limits upon the military were similar to those imposed by Great Britain. Prior to the Revolution there was no colonial army.

Instead, every colonist owned a weapon, and this armed citizenry constituted the militia. A citizen could be required to participate in training sessions, but no member of the militia was actually required to fight during hostilities; the militia could only be used for defensive purposes, and no citizen fought outside his own colony. During the Revolution, the Continental Congress created a regular army, but continued to demonstrate its distrust of the military by requiring regular reports from commanding officers and retaining the authority to appoint all officers. The Continental Congress also enacted a draft statute. The statute did not give the Army the power to draft men directly. Instead, the Army regularly gave each state a quota of men to supply through the militia. A state could refuse the Army's request, and any individual chosen by his state could avoid military service by paying a small fine or finding a man to serve in his place. George Washington proposed a direct draft in 1777, 1778, and again in 1780, but Congress refused his request on the grounds that the state could better safeguard individual rights and that a direct draft would give too much power to the military.

The question of military obligation and conscription brings with it the question of conscientious objectorship. Long before the United States was formed, the Quakers and other minorities refused support for the military in any way. At first the colonies persecuted them; later the colonial legislatures granted them exemption from military duty, but sometimes required them to pay tax to provide a substitute. Pacifists frequently declined even to pay the tax. When the country was formed, James Madison proposed a Bill of Rights that included the principle of permanent exemption of conscientious objectors ("no person religiously scrupulous of bearing arms shall be compelled to render military service in person"). This plank, however, was not adopted, perhaps because no draft was foreseen. During the Civil War, pacifists were at times tortured, but some were offered alternate service. In WWI, alternate service became the standard option, for the conscientious objector, but he had to perform this service in a special camp under military supervision. Those who refused to co-operate with the military were sent to Leavenworth and Alcatraz. The conscientious objector fared better in WW II. The Civilian Public Service Camps were supervised by church-appointed administrators rather than the military. Throughout this period, conscientious objectorship was defined strictly in religious terms; usually only those who were members of a religious group historically opposed to all war could receive this status. Since the Korean War, the courts have grown sympathetic to the nonreligious objector. While Congress still seems to demand belief in a Supreme Being, the courts seem willing to recognize any "sincere belief" which "fills the same

place" in one's life as the belief in God does in an orthodox religious man's life (the crucial case being *United States vs. Seeger*, 1965). During the Vietnam War, the question of selective objectorship, that is, objection to particular unjust or immoral wars rather than to all war, has gained importance, but such objection has not yet been legally sanctioned. Although the country has tended to be suspicious of the conscientious objector, it has gradually but clearly admitted that a higher law may in some cases overrule military obligation.

The uneasy national conscience over the wisdom and morality of the Vietnam conflict has also been visited by a perennial specter—the question of amnesty for dissidents. There have been thirty-seven acts of amnesty during American history, many of which related to war. In 1794 President Washington granted amnesty to participants in the Whiskey Rebellion, and President Madison granted amnesty to those who deserted during the War of 1812. There were 18 acts of amnesty during the Civil War. By the amnesty declaration of 1868 all those who had committed treason could receive amnesty if they took an oath of allegiance to the United States; the only exception to this proclamation were those in civil or military jails. Amnesty laws passed in 1872, 1884, and 1896 restored the civil rights of those who had been disenfranchised by the Fourteenth Amendment. Complete universal amnesties were granted following the Spanish-American War and the Philippine Insurrection. There was only limited amnesty following World War I. Under an Act of Congress in 1912 deserters lost their citizenship. In 1924 President Coolidge granted amnesty to approximately one hundred military personnel who had deserted after the armistice. In 1933 FDR granted citizenship to draft evaders and deserters who had completed their sentences. After World War II an amnesty board was established to grant amnesty on a case by case basis. Of 15,000 draft evaders and deserters, 1,523 eventually received amnesty. President Truman granted amnesty for those who deserted between July 14, 1945 and June 25, 1950 and were court martialed or dishonorably discharged. Recently, President Ford granted amnesty to draft evaders and deserters from the Vietnam War who were willing to work for several years in public service jobs. In short there has been some form of amnesty granted after every major American war, but often amnesty has only been available to a limited number of people.

So too may international law influence military obligation. The United States has always recognized international law which governs the conduct of nations during war. During the American Revolution, military courts were established to judge the laws of war, and in 1863 President Lincoln approved the War Department's "Instructions for the Government Armies of the United States" which prescribed rules of conduct towards inhabitants of hostile countries, prisoners of war, and spies. The Fourth Hague Convention of 1907 was the first significant international effort to codify the laws of war. Participant nations agreed that enemy soldiers who surrender should not be killed, military forces should not pillage captured cities, and a nation should not use weapons which cause unnecessary suffering. The Geneva Conventions of 1929 and 1949 established standards for humane treatment of prisoners of war. During World War II, the United States, Great Britain, France, and the Soviet Union signed the London Charter and agreed to establish an international tribunal to preside over the trials of war criminals. The trials which followed in Nuremberg and Tokyo defined three broad categories of international crimes: crimes against the peace, or waging a war of aggression; crimes against humanity; and crimes of war. The rulings of these tribunals were eventually incorporated in the Army Manual, "The Law of Land Warfare."

Historically, soldiers have been expected to disobey orders which command them to commit illegal acts. As early as 1804, United States Supreme Court Chief Justice Marshall argued that a soldier had the duty to disobey unlawful orders, and the first American court case upholding Marshall's position arose following the War of 1812. Bevans, a marine, had been ordered to guard the *Independence* in Boston Harbor and to bayonet anyone who bothered him. When a passerby insulted the marine, Bevans speared him with a bayonet. The United States Supreme Court ruled that Bevans should have disobeyed his orders, and found the marine guilty of murder. Following the Civil War, Major Henry Wirz, former commander of the Confederate prison camp at Andersonville, was tried for the murder of over 14,000 prisoners of war. The camp had not provided any shelter for many prisoners, prisoners had been forced to drink from a stream polluted with corpses and human waste, and thousands had starved. Wirz claimed that he was following the orders of General John H. Winder who was in charge of all the Confederate prison camps. The military tribunal rejected this defense, however, and found Wirz guilty of murder. German officers on trial at Nuremberg also claimed that they were following the orders of superior officers when they violated international law. The Nuremberg tribunal ruled that the German defendants could not escape conviction by claiming the defense of superior orders, although the existence of such orders could be taken into account in reducing the severity of punishment. Most of the men who were convicted at Nuremberg were high level commanders or government officials, and therefore a soldier in the field who violates international law may not be convicted if he can prove that he was following the order of a superior officer. The United States courts have adhered to the principles established at Nuremberg. For example, during the Vietnam War, Captain Howard Levy refused to provide medical training for Green Berets, because he believed that they would use the information to commit war crimes. During Levy's court martial, Colonel Earl Brown ruled that "if the defense can prove that the United States is committing war crimes in Vietnam as a matter of policy, it will acquit the doctor." This burden and the consequences of a failure to sustain it rest with the soldier who elects to disobey.

How critical an element of the social contract is a universal and unfailing adherence to the laws and policies of the state by all its members? Should individual conscience or religious belief supercede the dictates of the state? In short. . ."my country right or wrong?"

Excerpted Documents

The moral foundation of the state.

Sophocles, *Antigone*, translated by Dudley Fitts and Edward Fitzgerald, 1939, p. 203.

Creon:
And yet you dared defy the law.

Antigone:

                        I dared.
It was not God's proclamation. That final Justice
That rules the world below makes no such laws.

Your edict, King, was strong,
But all your strength is weakness itself against
The immortal unrecorded laws of God.
They are not merely now: they were, and shall be,
Operative for ever, beyond man utterly.

Plato, "Crito," translated by Hugh Tredennick, *The Collected Dialogues of Plato,* 1961, p. 36.

Socrates: ...Both in war and in the law courts and everywhere else you must do whatever your city and your country command, or else persuade them in accordance with universal justice, but violence is a sin even against your parents, and it is a far greater sin against your country.

What shall we say to this, Crito—that what the laws say is true, or not?

Crito: Yes, I think so.

Immanuel Kant, *Critique of Practical Reason,* translated by Lewis White Beck, 1956, p. 136.

It follows of itself that, in the order of ends, man (and every rational being) is an end-in-himself, i.e., he is never to be used merely as a means for someone (even for God) without at the same time being himself an end, and that thus the humanity in our person must itself be holy to us, because man is subject to the moral law and therefore subject to that which is of itself holy, and it is only on account of this and in agreement with this that anything can be called holy. For this moral law is founded on the autonomy of his will as a free will, which by its universal laws must necessarily be able to agree with that to which it subjects itself.

Henry David Thoreau, "Civil Disobedience," *Walden and Civil Disobedience,* edited by Owen Thomas, 1966, pp. 225, 228.

. . .a government in which the majority rule in all cases cannot be based on justice, even as far as men understand it. Can there not be a government in which majorities do not virtually decide right and wrong, but conscience?—in which majorities decide only those questions to which the rule of expediency is applicable? Must the citizen ever for a moment, or in the least degree, resign his conscience to the legislator? Why has every man a conscience, then? I think that we should be men first, and subjects afterward. It is not desirable to cultivate a respect for the law, so much as for the right. The only obligation which I have a right to assume, is to do at any time what I think is right....

This people must cease to hold slaves, and to make war on Mexico, though it cost them their existence as a people.

Leo Tolstoy, *Tolstoy's Writings on Civil Disobedience and Non-Violence,* 1967, pp. 100, 103.

. . .patriotism is chiefly impossible today because, however much we may have endeavored during eighteen hundred years to conceal the meaning of Christianity, it has nevertheless leaked into our lives and controls them to such an extent that the dullest and most unrefined of men must see today the complete incompatibility of patriotism with the moral law by which we live....

Patriotism is slavery.

Martin Luther King, *Why We Can't Wait,* 1963, pp. 84-85.

A just law is a man-made code that squares with the moral law or the law of God. An unjust law is a code that is out of harmony with the moral law. To put it in the terms of Saint Thomas Aquinas: An unjust law is a human law that is not rooted in eternal and natural law.

Harrop A. Freeman, Professor of Law—Cornell University, "Pacifism and Law," in *The Critique of War,* **pp. 290-292.**

Civil disobedience is sometimes the *only* legal procedure to raise constitutional and other legal issues. It may be required by law itself as the Nuremburg principles require an American to refuse participation in the Vietnam War if that war is against the established principles of international law. Civil disobedience may be a form of free speech (like picketing) protected by the First Amendment; it may be the assertion of the validity of a higher law over a lesser law (federal constitution over city trespass law); it may even be a challenge to a previously upheld law, recognizing that legal principles do change through continuous dialogue *(Brown v. Board of Education,* 347 U.S. 483 [1954], overruling *Plessy v. Ferguson,* 163 U.S. 537 [1896] on segregation). Much of this argument has already been accepted by the U.S. Supreme Court and the highest courts of other countries....

Often set off against any right of civil disobedience is a certain concept of the rule of law. It is argued that law is to be distinguished from politics: politics is the place for debate; law is not the place for debate. Once law is enacted or adopted it must be supreme; therefore *all* law must be obeyed—bad law as well as good law. Law is absolute so that obedience to it must be absolute. Any rule of law stated in this way is equivalent to the defense of war and patriotism as "my country, right or wrong." This cannot be the true concept of rules of law. It does not square with the history of the development of law. It is disproved by the thousands of cases that reach the courts each year and the very profession of lawyers engaged in challenging and avoiding laws.

Historical dissent
in domestic issues.

Samuel Gompers, in *American Labor Leaders: Personalities and Forces in the Labor Movement,* **1962, p. 99.**

Show me a country in which there are no strikes and I'll show you that country in which there is no liberty. The state, when it has interfered with industrial affairs, has become the greatest tyrant in the world.

Matthew Woll, Labor Leader and friend of Gompers, in *American Federationist* **editorial, in** *American Labor Leaders: Personalities and Forces in the Labor Movement,* **1962, p. 103.**

The strike is a legitimate weapon by which the workers may secure their industrial rights against employers, but when abused and perverted and used to attack the community so that chaos and disruption may paralyze the arm of government, it then becomes an instrument of anarchy and revolution and carries with it more harm than good to all concerned.

Carleton H. Parker, I.W.W. Organizer, in *American Labor Leaders: Personalities and Forces in the Labor Movement,* **1962, p. 281**

You ask me why the I.W.W. is not patriotic to the United States. If you were a bum without a blanket; if you had left your wife and kids when you went West for a job and had never located them since; if your job never kept you long enough in one place to qualify you to vote; if you slept in a busy, sour bunkhouse, and ate food just as rotten as they could give you and get by with it;...if every person who represented law and order and the nation beat you up, railroaded you to jail, and the good Christian people cheered and told them to go to it, how the hell do you expect a man to be patriotic?

Robert T. Hall, *The Morality of Civil Disobedience,* **1971, p. 31.**

The civil rights movement of the past decade or so was launched in late 1955 in Montgomery, Alabama when Mrs. Rosa Parks, a Negro, refused to give up her seat on the bus to a white man. She was arrested, convicted of violating the segregation law, and fined ten dollars. The organization of the Montgomery Improvement Association under the leadership of Dr. Martin Luther King, Jr. and the bus boycott which followed set a pattern for the massive effort to secure equal rights for black people in the United States which was to preoccupy the country for so many years. . . .

The action of Mrs. Parks and that advocated by Dr. King exemplify the most basic form of civil disobedience, violation of a law which is itself considered morally unjust... Those who gave aid to Jews in Nazi Germany were directly disobedient, that Dr. Benjamin Spock and the Rev. William Sloane Coffin, Jr. were directly disobedient when they advocated refusal of induction into military service, and that the men of the seminary community at Oberlin, Ohio in the 1850s were directly disobedient when they released fugitive slaves from the local jail. The agents in each of these actions objected to the law itself as immoral.

Robert T. Hall, *The Morality of Civil Disobedience*, 1971, p. 113.

In a characteristically strong statement, Mr. Justice Douglas wrote, "The right to defy an unconstitutional statute is basic in our scheme. Even when an ordinance requires a permit to make a speech, to deliver a sermon, to picket, to parade, or to assemble, it need not be honored when it is invalid on its face."

Wartime dissent
in American history.

James Reston, Journalist, *The Artillery of the Press: Its Influence on American Foreign Policy*, 1966, p. 94.

The newspapers didn't help the country much, in my view, by taking a "my country right or wrong" attitude when Presidents Kennedy and Johnson began slipping into the war in Viet Nam. It is difficult to see how we can get a clear picture of the world as it is if we see it only from our own side, like a football game, and do not challenge the national assumptions that we can do almost anything anywhere in the world.

Horace Greeley, 19th Century Journalist, in *The Newsmongers*, 1973, p. 157.

"Our Country, Right or Wrong," is a maxim as foolish as Heaven-daring. If your country be wrong . . . it is madness, it is idiocy, to wish or struggle for her success in the wrong; for such success can only be more calamitous than failure, since it increases our Nation's guilt.

Samuel Eliot Morison, Professor of History—Harvard University, *Dissent in Three American Wars*, 1970, p. 11.

Francis Blake, state senator from Worcester, delivered a glowing eulogy of Great Britain, declaring that if our Constitution permitted embargoes, he preferred the British, "monarchy and all." Samuel Fessenden of New Gloucester, Maine, announced that "it was time to take our rights into our own hands....We ought to establish a custom house by law, and the sooner we come at issue with the general government the better." One who heard this speech wrote that "these ravings of a political maniac were received with manifest applause." But, he adds, Harrison Gray Otis threw cold water upon them.

Frank Freidel, Professor of History—Harvard University, *Dissent in Three American Wars*, 1970, p. 95.

The Philippine Insurrection, like other unpopular wars, raised the question whether or not objectors should have the right to dissent. One of those who commented most interestingly upon this question at the time was Mark Twain. He had responded with vigorous horror to suppression of the Filipinos, bitterly writing that the American flag should have "the white stripes painted black and the stars replaced by the skull and cross-bones." A short while later he heard a clergyman publicly attack him. "He said that if I had my just deserts I should be. . .dangling from a lamp-post somewhere. . .He hadn't anything personal against me, except that I was opposed to the political war, and he said I was a traitor." Then Twain insisted, "It would be an entirely different question if the country's life was in danger, its existence at stake; then. . .we would all come forward and stand by the flag, and stop thinking about whether the nation was right or wrong; but when there is no question that the nation is any way in danger, but only some little war away off, then it may be that on the question of politics the nation is divided, half-patriot and half-traitors, and no man can tell which from which."

The draft.

L. Friedman, Professor of Law, "Conscription and the Constitution: The Original Understanding," *Michigan Law Review,* **June 1969, p. 1547.**

The militia is therefore to be composed of Citizens of the States, who retain all their rights and privileges as citizens, who when called into service by the United States are not to be "fused into one body"—nor confounded with the Army of the United States, but are to be called out as the militia of the several states. . .and consequently commanded by the officers appointed by the State. It is only in that form or organization that they are recognized in the Constitution as a military force.

Daniel Webster, Senate Debate on the 1812 War Draft, in *Michigan Law Review,* **June, 1969, pp. 1542-1543.**

Is this, sir, consistent with the character of a free government? Is this civil liberty? Is this the real character of our Constitution? No, sir, indeed it is not. The Constitution is libelled, foully libelled. The people of this country have not established for themselves such a fabric of despotism. They have not purchased at a vast expense of thier own treasure and their own blood a Magna Charta to be slaves. Where is it written in the Constitution. . . that you may take children from their parents, and parents from their children, and compel them to fight the battles of any war in which the folly or the wickedness of government may engage it?

L. Friedman, Professor of Law, "Conscription and the Constitution: The Original Understanding," *Michigan Law Review,* **June, 1969, p. 1519.**

The only mention of the draft at the Convention was by Edmund Randolph, a leading Federalist figure and proponent of the Constitution, who denied that the new government should have that power. It is inconceivable that staunch Antifederalists like Elbridge Gerry, who strongly opposed the creation of any standing army, would not have raised the loudest protest about any general power to draft by the federal government if they had thought that it was contained within the general grant of authority "to raise and support armies." All that was given by the grant, therefore, was the power to organize and enlist a federal, professional army which—the delegates thought—would consist of a limited number of garrison troops. That power was given grudgingly, only in the light of the severe hardship Congress had experienced during the Revolution in depending solely on the states for manpower and military supplies. But the door was opened for that limited purpose only.

War crimes and international law.

Guenther Lewy, Professor of Political Science, *Political Obligations and Civil Disobedience,* **1972, p. 405.**

So one critic writes: International law is not in position to protect individuals, wherever they may be, against a domestic law which is illegal from the point of view of international law. According to general legal principles, it therefore cannot expect the individuals to expose themselves to such a risk. For the individual, always and everywhere, national law precedes international law. He has to obey the national law even where it compels him to violate international law.

United States Supreme Court, *Selective Draft Law* **Cases, 245 U.S. 379-80. (1914).**

In the Colonies before the separation from England, there cannot be the slightest doubt that the right to enforce military service was unquestioned and that practical effect was given to the power in many cases. Indeed the brief of the Government contains a list of Colonial acts manifesting the power and its enforcement in more than two hundred cases. . .[I]t is indisputable that the States in response to the calls made upon them [by the Continental Congress] met the situation when they deemed it necessary by directing enforced military service on the part of the citizens. In fact the duty of the citizen to render military service and the power to compel him against his consent to do so was expressly sanctioned by the constitutions of at least nine of the States.

L. Friedman, Professor of Law, "Conscription and the Constitution: The Original Understanding," *Michigan Law Review,* Vol. 67, June, 1969, p. 1503.

The American colonial leaders were steeped in this anti-military tradition; the available evidence indicates that they were extremely sensitive to the dangers of a professional army and that they saw clearly the distinction between regular forces and the armed citizenry composing the militia. They were also conscious of the fact that no general compulsory conscription law for the regular army was in force in England during the eighteenth century.

Guenther Lewy, Professor of Political Science, *Political Obligations and Civil Disobedience,* 1972, p. 395.

When Francis Gary Powers was asked by the presiding judge of the Soviet military tribunal trying him for espionage whether he had not considered the possibility that his U-2 flight might provoke armed conflict, the captured pilot answered, "The people who sent me should think of these things. My job was to carry out orders. I do not think it was my responsibility to make such decisions."

Telford Taylor, U.S. Chief Counsel—Nuremberg, *Nuremberg and Vietnam: An American Tragedy,* 1970, p. 40.

It is only necessary to consider the rules on taking prisoners in the setting of the Second World War to realize the enormous saving of life for which they have been responsible. Millions of French, British, German and Italian soldiers captured in Western Europe and Africa were treated in general compliance with The Hague and Geneva requirements and returned home at the end of the war. German and Russian prisoners taken in the eastern front did not fare nearly so well and died in captivity by the millions, but many survived. Today there is surely much to criticize about the handling of prisoners on both sides of the Vietnam war, but at least many of them are alive, and that is because the belligerents are reluctant to flout the laws of war too openly.

Telford Taylor, U.S. Chief Counsel—Nuremberg, *Nuremberg and Vietnam: An American Tragedy,* 1970, p. 44-45.

There are rigid, absolute formulations, such as the statement of Chief Justice Taney in 1851 that: "It can never be maintained that a military officer can justify himself for doing an unlawful act, by producing the order of his superior." More realistic judicial assessments, however, recognized that often the subordinate is in no position to determine the legality or illegality of the order, and that the very nature of military service requires prompt obedience. "While subordinate officers are pausing to consider whether they ought to obey, or are scrupulously weighing the evidence of the facts upon which the commander-in-chief exercises the right to demand their services," Justice Story observed in 1827, "the hostile enterprise may be accomplished." Twenty-five years later Justice Curtis made much the same point in a case where the soldier was sued for false arrest: "I do not think the defendant was bound to go behind the order, apparently lawful, and satisfy himself by inquiry that his commanding officer proceeded upon sufficient grounds. To require this would be destructive of military discipline and of the necessary promptness and efficiency of the service.

Amnesty.

Douglas Jones and David Raish, Professors of Law, Selective Service and Amnesty, Hearings before the Subcommittee on Administrative Practice and Procedures, 92d Congress, 2d session, 1973, p. 476.

Not only are there numerous precedents for amnesty in United States history, but the historic role of this nation is that of a free land to which exiles from other lands have frequently turned; it would be ironic for such a nation to bar its exiles from returning to free and productive life in the United States.

New York Times, Nov. 24, 1946, p. 8.

The private conscience is one of democracy's most precious possessions. Indeed, the liberty allowed it is a basic test of whether or not democracy exists in a nation. We believe President Truman will be amply justified and supported, even by the veterans who bore the brunt of the battle, if he grants the amnesty petition. General McNarney . . . ordered 4,000 prisoners in the American zone in Germany released. If we can forgive our enemies in this way surely we can forgive our fellow citizens who honestly could not accept the majority view in time of war.

Jonathan Davis, Professor of History—Eastern Kent State College, *Selective Service and Amnesty,* **Hearings before the Subcommittee on Administrative Practice and Procedure, 92d Congress, 2d session, 1973, reprinted from "Treatment of Confederates by Lincoln and Johnson," 1959.**

General Sherman states in his *Memoirs* that he asked Lincoln at City Point on March 27-28, 1865 "What was to be done with the rebel armies when defeated? And what was to be done with the political leaders? . . . Should we allow them to escape?" Sherman says that "All he wanted of us was to defeat the opposing armies, and to get the men composing the confederate armies back to their homes and in their shops. As for Jefferson Davis, he was hardly at liberty to speak his mind fully, but he estimated that he ought to clear out "escape the country" only it would not do for him to say so openly.

George Washington, *Selective Service and Amnesty,* **Hearings before the Subcommittee on Administrative Practice and Procedure, 92d Congress, 2d session, 1973, p. 435.**

It may be laid down as a primary position, and the basis of our system, that every citizen who enjoys the protection of free government owes not only a portion of his property, but even his personal services to the defense of it.

Cardinal Cushing, in *Selective Service and Amnesty,* **Hearings before the Subcommittee on Administrative Practice and Procedure, 92d Congress, 2d session, 1973, p. 436.**

Would it be too much to suggest that we empty our jails of all the protesters—the guilty and the innocent—without judging them; call back from the border and around the world the young innocent men who are called deserters; drop the cases that are still awaiting judgement on our college youth? Could we not do all of this in the name of life, and with life, hope?

Hugo L. Black, Supreme Court Justice, in *Selective Service and Amnesty,* **Hearings before the Subcommittee on Administrative Practice and Procedure, 92d Congress, 2d. session, 1973, p. 439.**

When [America] begins to send its dissenters to jail, the liberties indispensable to its existence must be fast disappearing.

Selected Bibliography

Adickes, R. "Constitutional Validity of the Draft." *Southern California Law Review,* 46 (1973), 385.

Adler, Gerald J. "Targets in War: Legal Considerations." *Houston Law Review,* 8 (1970), 1.

Bernstein, J.L. "Conscription and the Constitution: The Amazing Case of *Kneedler v. Lane.*" *ABA Journal,* 53 (August 1967), 708.

Brendan, Francis Brown, and Keenan, Joseph Berry. *Crimes Against International Law.* Washington: Public Affairs Press, 1950.

Broderick, Francis L. and Meier, August, eds. *Negro Protest Thought in the Twentieth Century.* Indianapolis: Bobbs-Merrill, 1965.

Burns, A.L. "Must Strategy and Conscience Be Disjoined?" *World Politics,* 17 (1965), 681.

Cohen, Carl. *Civil Disobedience: Conscience, Tactics, and the Law.* New York: Columbia University Press, 1971.

D'Amato, Anthony A.; Gould, Harvey L.; and Woods, Larry D. "War Crimes and Vietnam: The Nuremberg Defense and the Military Service Resister." *California Law Review,* 57 (1969), 1055.

Deutsch, Kenneth, and Smith, Michael P. *Political Obligation and Civil Disobedience.* New York: Thomas Y. Crowell Co., 1972.

Dorsen, N., and Rudovsky, D. "Some Thoughts on Dissent, Personal Liberty, and War." *ABA Journal,* 54 (1968), 752.

Dunbar, N.C.H. "Problems of Superior Orders in the Law of War." *Judicial Review,* 63 (1951), 247.

Engelbrecht, Helmuth Carol. *Revolt Against War.* New York: Dodd, Mead, and Co., 1937.

Falk, Richard A. *Law, Morality, and War in the Contemporary World.* New York: Praeger, 1963.

Finn, James, ed. *A Conflict of Loyalties.* New York: Western Publishing Co., 1968.

Freeman, H.A. "Constitutionality of Direct Federal Military Conscription." *Indiana Law Journal,* 46 (1971), 333.

Freeman, H.A. "An Historical Justification and Legal Basis for Amnesty Today." *Law and Social Order,* (1971).

Friedman, L. "Conscription and the Constitution: The Original Understanding." *Michigan Law Review,* 67 (1969), 1493.

Gandhi, Mohandas K. *Non-Violent Resistance.* Compiled and edited by Bharatan Kumarappa. New York: Schocken Books, 1961.

Gigon, Henri. *Ethics of Peace and War.* London: Burns, Oats, and Washborne Ltd., 1935.

Glasser, I. "Judgement at Fort Jackson: The Court Martial of Captain Howard B. Levy." *Law in Transition Quarterly,* 4 (September, 1967), 123.

Hall, Robert T. *The Morality of Civil Disobedience.* New York: Harper and Row, 1971.

Hopkins, G.E. "Bombing and the American Conscience During World War II." *Historian,* 28 (1966), 451.

Jones, Douglas, and Raish, David. "American Deserters and Draft Evaders: Exile Punishment or Amnesty?" *Harvard International Law Journal,* 13 (1972), 88.

Kelsen, Hans. "Will the Judgement of the Nuremberg Trial Constitute a Precedent in International Law?" *International Law Quarterly,* 1 (1947), 153.

King, Martin Luther. *Stride Toward Freedom.* New York: Ballantine Books, 1958.

Knoll, Erwin, and McFadden, Judith. *War Crimes and the American Conscience.* New York: Holt, Rinehart, and Winston, 1970.

Ladd, Everett C. *Negro Political Leadership in the South.* Ithaca, New York: Cornell University Press, 1968.

Lowell, Abbott Lawrence. *Public Opinion in War and Peace.* Cambridge: Harvard University Press, 1923.

Malbin, M.J. "Conscription, the Constitution, and the Framers: An Historical Analysis." *Fordham Law Review,* 40 (1972), 805.

Meckler, Alan M., and O'Sullivan, John. *The Draft and Its Enemies: A Documentary History.* Urbana: University of Illinois Press, 1974.

Morgan, E.S. "Puritan Ethic and the American Revolution." *William and Mary Quarterly,* 24 (January 1967), 3rd supp., 3.

Murdock, Eugene. *Patriotism Limited, 1862-65; The Civil War Draft and the Bounty System.* Kent, Ohio: Kent State University Press, 1967.

"Nuremberg, U.S.A." *Economist,* 223 (1967), 916.

O'Brien, W.V. "Selective Conscientious Objection, and International Law." *Georgetown Law Journal,* 56 (1968), 1080.

"Panel: The Nuremberg Trials and Objection to Military Service in Vietnam." *American Society of International Law Proceedings,* 63 (1969), 140.

Peck, James. *Freedom Ride.* New York: Simon and Schuster, 1962.

Perkins, D. "Dissent in Time of War." *Virginia Quarterly Review,* 47 (September 1971), 161.

Ramsey, Paul. *The Just War: Force and Political Responsibility.* New York: Scribner, 1968.

Rayback, Joseph C. *A History of American Labor.* New York: Macmillan, 1959.

Redgrove, Herbert Stanley. *The Indictment of War.* London: C.W. Daniel Ltd., 1919.

Rohr, John Anthony. *Prophets without Honor: Public Policy and the Selective Conscientious Objector.* Nashville: Abingdon Press, 1971.

Schlissel, Lillian, ed. *Conscience of America.* New York: Dutton, 1968.

Shultz, George P., and Coleman, John R. *Labor Problems: Cases and Readings.* New York: McGraw-Hill Book Co., Inc., 1959.

Sibley, Mulford, and Jacob, Philip E. *Conscription of Conscience: The American State and the Conscientious Objector, 1940-47.* Ithaca, New York: Cornell University Press, 1952.

"Symposium: The Draft, the War, and Public Protest." *George Washington University Law Review,* 37 (1969), 433.

Taylor, Telford. *Nuremberg and Vietnam: An American Tragedy.* Chicago: Quadrangle Books, 1970.

Thomas, Norman M. *The Conscientious Objector in America.* New York: B.W. Huebsh, Inc., 1923.

Tolstoy, Leo. *Tolstoy's Writings on Civil Disobedience and Non-Violence.* New York: Bergman Publishers, 1967.

Useem, Michael. *Conscription, Protest, and Social Conflict: The Life and Death of a Draft Resistance Movement.* New York: Wiley, 1973.

Veysey, Laurence, ed. *Law and Resistance: American Attitudes toward Authority.* New York: Harper and Row, 1970.

Walzer, Michael. *Obligations: Essays on Disobedience, War, and Citizenship.* Cambridge: Harvard University Press, 1970.

Wells, D.A. "How Much Can a Just War Justify?" *Journal of Philosophy,* 66 (1969), 819.

Woodward, Beverly. "Nuremberg Law and the U.S. Courts." *Dissent,* (April, 1969), 128.

Zashin, Elliot M. *Civil Disobedience and Democracy.* New York: The Free Press, 1972.

OUT OF MANY, ONE

Introductory Essay

These States are the amplest poem,
Here is not merely a nation but
a teeming Nation of nations.
-- Walt Whitman

The Revolutionary period of our history holds a special attraction for Americans. In a very large part, the character and destiny of our nation was hammered out on the forge of the Revolution. Yet in giving the Revolution and the events surrounding it their well-deserved recognition, we often neglect another force which shaped the American nation—the immigrants. One of the major complaints of the colonists, vocalized in the Declaration of Independence, was that King George III had attempted to curb the influx of immigrants in order to stifle the economic growth of the colonies. It is particularly appropriate, then, on the anniversary of our country's creation, to consider the roles of immigrants and other minority groups in the growth of the United States.

America, even before the Revolutionary War, was not a homogenous nation. The majority (almost two-thirds of the white population) were of English extraction, but substantial minorities of Germans, Dutch, French, and Scandinavians were also present. From the end of the War of 1812 to the beginning of the First World War (a period often referred to as the "immigrant century"), however, the addition of over 35 million immigrants radically changed the "mix." Although it is hard to determine precisely, statisticians and historians in the 1920's estimated that about 49% of the population was of immigrant ancestry, and only 51% of all colonial stock combined. One report noted further that "the birth rate of the population [from immigrant stock] is higher than that representing [colonial roots]." Why did the immigrants come and why did they stay? What did they contribute to the American economy and American culture? Have they helped to shape the American character? How do blacks and Indians fit into American history? These are some of the questions facing a contemporary commentator.

Why did the immigrant come? What would impel a peasant, living on and farming the same land his great-grandfather had owned, who had never been more than twenty miles from his village church, to sell his belongings, leave his native country behind and head for a new land about which he knew little more than the name? There is no simple, universal answer; and for such momentous decisions in the lives of the persons involved, probably no two answers were exactly the same. Yet some generalizations can and have been drawn, and the most common of these is that immigrants came for political or religious reasons. The visualization of America as a refuge for the oppressed, a haven for the man of unpopular convictions, is an appealing and useful likeness. From the Pilgrims to the Vietnamese refugees, peoples fleeing persecution form a recurrent theme. Lord Baltimore established Maryland as a refuge for Catholics in 1634. Twenty years later, shiploads of Jews fleeing the Portuguese Inquisition arrived in New Amsterdam. Religious persecution drove Quakers from England, Mennonites from Germany and Huguenots from France, all to America. Ironically, the French Revolution caused not only many royalists but later some of the quarreling revolutionary forces to take up residence in America. In the Twentieth Century, refugees from Nazi Germany, displaced persons in the wake of the Second World War, Hungarian "freedom fighters," Korean and Cuban exiles, as well as the Vietnamese have sought refuge in this country. America has been proud of her role as an asylum for those "yearning to breathe free." In 1836, thirty-six sections of land in Illinois were enthusiastically offered to refugees of the Polish Revolution. Reports of pogroms in 1906 led an indignant Congress to adopt a resolution reading in part "that the people of the United States are horrified by the report of the massacre of Hebrews in Russia on account of their race and religion, and that those bereaved thereby have the hearty sympathy of this country." The message did not go unnoticed—258,000 Jews from Eastern Europe arrived in 1907 alone. Certainly, America's religious and political freedom attracted many millions of immigrants.

Yet these are only millions out of tens of millions who immigrated, most of whose religious beliefs were conventional and political convictions were not at issue. What force impelled these immigrants to seek a new life in America? For many, the answer was the opportunity for personal advancement. Europe was a continent where land was the mark of a rich man and people were a surplus commodity; America had seemingly limitless tracts of virgin soil lacking only population. Even before the Revolution, many sought economic advancement on the American frontier. One of the stated purposes of the colony of Virginia was to "fetch treasure" and the settlement of the Carolinas was conducted as a business venture by a group of English nobility. Periods of great immigration coincided with economic troubles in Europe—expulsion of Irish tenants, crop failures in Germany and the Netherlands, the potato famine. Equally significant, immigration was greatest during times of economic boom here. Emigration has exceeded immigration only once—a six-year period in the depths of the Great Depression. But economic motives were often understated by the immigrants. Even the rawest immigrant, fresh off the Liverpool steamer, knew the proper answer to the question "Why did you come to America?" A truthful answer—that he came to improve his economic lot—would be seen as a threat to the job of every American citizen. If, on the other hand, he replied that he had come to take advantage of the wonderful laws and institutions of this country, he would be assured a warm welcome.

Did the immigrants find what they were looking for? The obvious answer, of course, is "Yes." That so many came serves as eloquent testimony. Certainly, all who came did not have the option of returning; many had spent their last penny and indebted themselves for years merely to buy steerage room on a westward-bound vessel. Yet it was very hard to be a failure in America. A German farmer might sell his land, spend two-thirds of the proceeds for passage to this country, and still be able to buy a farm four times the size of his original holding with the remainder. Social structure was fluid and the man who began a pauper could amass considerable wealth. Examples of such successful immigrants as Andrew Carnegie, Alexander Graham Bell, and publisher Joseph Pulitzer were repeated many times on a smaller scale. Early arrivals wrote to their friends and relatives at home, and the cheerful tone was reflected in the continuing stream.

There was a darker side as well. Large numbers of immigrants did not even survive the voyage to the "Promised Land." In 1818, for instance, a Dutch vessel began a voyage from the Netherlands with 1200 passengers. 115 bodies were sent ashore before the ship even left port, and sickness at sea forced the ship back to Amsterdam with another 300 dead. Nor was this an isolated incident—medical statistics report 20,000 deaths from illness occurred aboard ship in 1847 alone. The first federal laws regulating immigration were an attempt to alleviate this problem. The hazards awaiting the immigrant did not end when he reached port, either. "Sharpers," thieves, and "white slavers" took their toll of the unsuspecting. Economic opportunity was often not as readily accessible as the immigrant imagined, and many ended their days in the crowded tenements of the same city where they had first landed. Some immigrants simply could not cope with the difference between what they expected and what they found. Others could not accept their loss of status: persons who had held high positions in their native land now found themselves looked down upon; intellectuals were forced to accept menial labor because they did not have a working knowledge of the English language. Even the religious did not always find the freedom from persecution they expected. Minority religious groups, from the Quakers (several were hanged in Boston) to the Catholics, the Jews, the Mormons, and the Jehovah's Witnesses, have all suffered periods of discrimination and histility in the United States.

Not all of this disillusionment and heartbreak was unavoidable. Immigrants were often recruited by steamship agents and propagandists for industrial concerns whose descriptions of the opportunities available in America could not have been fulfilled save in Paradise itself. Some immigrants threw away all cooking utensils on sighting the shoreline, confident that new sets would be available for the asking, while others were puzzled at the absence of money lying in the gutters. The less scrupulous steamship companies deliberately recruited immigrants who stood little chance of making good in the New World, reasoning that there was more profit to be made in round trip passage. Establishment of information offices in major foreign ports, efforts by other governments and the activities of numerous immigrant aid societies reduced such abuses.

What did the immigrants contribute to American growth? Many had nothing but bitter memories of the old country and embraced American culture with such fervor that they were described as being "more American than the Americans." Others were not adverse to maintaining the traditions of their homeland, but abandoned their folkways from fear of public ridicule. Those, however, who sought to maintain the traditions of their native countries made many positive contributions to American culture. American cooking gained from the introduction of such dishes as goulash, chile, sauerkraut, filet mignon, the Spanish omelet, and ravioli. German immigrants introduced symphonic orchestras and the Italians the opera. The austere Puritan Sabbath was challenged by the Germans, who had been accustomed to Sunday as a day for picnicking, drinking, and dancing. Over the long term, the immigrants won out, contributing to such American institutions as the "Sunday drive," but there were some short-term failures. One of these occurred in Wisconsin, when a local newspaper berated the immigrants for desecration of the Sabbath and editorially warned them to "behave like respectable Americans if they wanted to enjoy the privileges of the country." When the immigrant church sided with the newspaper, parishioners innocently asked how something which was accepted by God in the old country could be a sin in the new. The minister adroitly explained that anything that brought the church into disrepute with its neighbors was a sin.

More visible than their cultural contributions were the contributions of the immigrants to the economy of America. New arrivals were willing to take any type of work, and thus filled many essential jobs that the native Americans were not interested in. Immigrant labor built the railroads, dug the canals and mined the Pennsylvania coal that fueled factories also dependent on immigrant labor. In a nation where population was the most vital national asset, every immigrant was valuable. During the Civil War immigrants were actively recruited for factories and the Army. In 1864, Congress even passed the Contract Labor Law, permitting businesses to advance passage money to immigrants otherwise unable to come to America.

Their contributions to America's economic welfare were not universally appreciated, however. Whenever an economic depression threw "native" workers out of jobs, they were quick to single out the immigrant as the source of their economic woes. Riots were caused by resentment of the Irish in the 1840's and the Germans in the 1850's. Ironically, both these groups joined their former persecutors in decrying the Italian influx later in the century. At first, labor unions had little use for the immigrants, who were often used as "scabs" to break the power of union organization. Unions were able to secure the repeal of the Contract Labor Law in 1885 with passage of the Foran Act forbidding anyone from encouraging "the importation or migration of aliens . . .under contract or agreement . . . to perform labor or service of any kind in the United States." Ironically immigration probably worked to labor's advantage in the long run; immigrants familiar with European unions were quick to realize the advantages of extending the system to the United States, and many became heavily involved in the labor movement.

Economic competition bred racial and religious intolerance. The arrival of millions of immigrants from Southeast Europe led to such organizations as the American Protective Association of the 1890's and a revived Ku Klux Klan after World War I, both of which mixed economic arguments with anti-Catholicism. An influx of hundreds or thousands of Jews in the early 1900's not only created fear among the laboring class, but inspired opponents to proclaim that "from all over the world, the Children of Israel are flocking to this country, and plans are on foot to move them from Europe en masse . . . to empty upon our shores the very scums and dregs of the Parasite race." Perhaps the most disturbing example is that of the Chinese, originally welcomed to California to farm because most whites were concentrating on mining. By 1870, 90% of all agricultural labor

in California was Chinese. They were vital to the welfare of the state and were praised as being "our most orderly and industrious citizens," "the best immigrants in California," "thrifty," "sober," "inoffensive," and "law-abiding." By 1859, however, the mines were beginning to play out, and whites began to compete for Chinese jobs. By the fall of 1867 both major political parties in California had anti-Chinese planks in their campaign platforms. During this interval, the character of the Chinese had so magically and quickly deteriorated that they were now "a distinct people," "unassimilable," whose very existance "lowered the plane of living." They "shut out white labor," were "deceitful and vicious," were now "inferior from a mental and moral point of view, immeasurably lower than the Indian, for instance."

In all fairness, though, it is possible that economics bred discrimination in other ways. Almost the only jobs open to immigrants were on the lower end of the social spectrum and their original economic status may in itself have engendered discrimination. It is even possible that race prejudice against blacks likewise is rooted partially in economics. A severe labor shortage forced the importation of slaves and the eventual equation of "black" with the lowest position in society undoubtedly did nothing to improve race relations.

Many of the regional characteristics of our nation today are reflections of economic history. When the United States was primarily agricultural, immigrants followed the advance of the frontier. Ill-adapted to the conditions of the raw wilderness, they were rarely found among the woodsmen or fur traders, nor among the pioneer settlers. In general, they formed a second wave of settlement, buying cleared land from the early settler who wanted to move further on. An immortal couplet, conveying both fact and the imprint of vicious cultural prejudices, describes the advance:

Across the plains where once there roamed
the Indian and the Scout
The Swede with alcoholic breath
sets rows of cabbage out.

The rise of industrialism changed the main flow of migration and later immigrant groups moved into the great industrial cities of the North, forming major ethnic sections in Eastern cities. Welshmen and Poles settled near the Pennsylvania coal fields, and the Irish followed the New Brunswick timber trade. The South, unlike other sections of the nation, attracted few immigrants. Blacks filled all the menial positions that the newly arrived citizens could compete for, and immigrant guidebooks warned against the region because of the high initial costs of establishing a plantation. Consequently, the white population of the South today is largely of colonial stock.

Having examined the contributions of the immigrant peoples, it is also appropriate to explore the place in American history of the blacks, "the unwilling immigrants, and the Indians, the only really "native" Americans. From the beginning of our nation's history, these two groups have been treated as exceptions to the rule. Black slaves were imported from the African continent to serve as common laborers because the colonial system of importing indentured servants was deficient. As soon as a man completed servitude he sought higher status and left to start his own farm. Slavery as an institution flourished in the antebellum South, and few seriously questioned it. Even the Civil War, which resulted in the eventual elimination of slavery, was not fought primarily for that purpose. Lincoln on occasion had to restrain field commanders who took it on themselves to free the slaves. The New York draft riots were as much protests against blacks as they were against the draft laws.

The freed slaves after the Civil War saw many of their newly found rights cleverly repealed by state law and could expect little relief in the courts. Some fled to the North, meeting a mixed reaction of sympathy and resentment at their infringement on "white" jobs. Those heading West found a more favorable reception. Two black cavalry and two black infantry regiments fought with distinction in the Indian wars, and many found jobs as cowhands. The Twentieth Century has been frustrating for the blacks in many ways, but has generally marked a substantial advance toward equality.

The story of the Indian is considerably different. Numbering anywhere from the most extreme estimates of 8 to 100 million when the colonists first arrived, they had no place in the society created by the settlers. Slavery was impractical, and coexistence impossible, because the one thing the Indian had was the very thing the colonists wanted—land. The Indians had to be evicted; that eviction is the tragic theme of our frontier saga. Unlike the black, who was despised, the Indian generally earned the grudging respect of the whites. European travelers and some Americans extolled the virtues of the "Noble Redman," but the inevitable armed conflicts caused much bitterness among Western settlers. Atrocities committed by whites at Sand Creek and

Wounded Knee were condemned by many in the East, but Westerners generally agreed with Colonel J. M. Chivington's orders to his men during the Sand Creek massacre to "kill and scalp all, big and little—nits make lice." Some influential officials, among them General Philip Sheridan, Grant's cavalry commander, defended the Indians. "We took away their country and their means of support, broke up their mode of living, their habits of life, introduced disease and decay among them and it was for this and against this that they made war. Could anyone expect less?" Graft among Indian agents and the siting of reservations in inhospitable environments contributed to the decimation of the Indian. Well-meaning sympathizers improved some conditions, but mistakenly attempted to integrate the Indians into American life as small farmers and break up tribal life.

The cultural diversity that is America issued from our immigrant tradition. Centuries of immigrants have reinforced faith in the American dream; too, the newcomers have encouraged the restless, moving spirit that marked the death of loyalty to state and the strengthening of loyalty to nation. The average newcomer, often unaware of the existence of smaller political subdivisions such as "states," was inclined to treat such distinctions lightly; he had come to America, not Massachusetts or Ohio, and his goal was to be a citizen of the United States, not Indiana. Given an opportunity, immigrants demonstrated on the field of battle that although their loyalty may not have been that of birth, it was at least as strong as that of the native born. While softening the restrictive Puritan morality, the immigrant endorsed, preserved, and strengthened the work ethic: work was the key to advancement in society, work provided the economic security missing in the home country, and work was not only available for, but was universally demanded of the immigrant. Pride in ethnic ancestry has recently found new spokesmen, and no longer is the immigrant expected to completely submerge his own identity in an amorphous whole. In this way, the mosaic which is America promises future enrichment.

Excerpted Documents

Reasons for immigration.

Joseph Gaer and Ben Siegel, *The Puritan Heritage*, 1964, pp. 18-19.

If America's first English settlers, at Jamestown, were motivated by mercantile rather than religious reasons, just the reverse was true for this handful of their impoverished countrymen. The Pilgrim saga represents not only man's conquest of nature, but also his self-conquest in search of an ideal.

John F. Kennedy, *A Nation of Immigrants*, 1964, pp. 10-11.

The first wave of settlement came with the colonists at Jamestown in 1607 and at Plymouth in 1620. It was predominantly English in origin. The urge for greater economic opportunity, together with the desire for religious freedom, impelled these people to leave their homes. Of all the groups that have come to America, these settlers had the most difficult physical environment to master, but the easiest social adjustment to make. They fought a rugged land, and that was hard. But they built a society in their own image, and never knew the hostility of the old toward the new that succeeding groups would meet.

Henry Pratt Fairchild, *Immigration*, 1913, p. 145.

The natural causes of immigration at the present time lie primarily in the superiority of the economic conditions in the United States over those in the countries from which the immigrants come. Modern immigration is essentially an economic phenomenon. Religious and political causes have played the leading part in the past, and still enter in as contributory factors in many cases. But the one prevailing reason why the immigrant of today leaves his native village is that he is dissatisfied with his economic lot, as compared with what it might be in the new world.

Francis J. Brown, Staff Associate—American Council on Education, *One America*, 1952, pp. 8-9.

With the rapid industrial expansion that came with the recovery from the panic of 1873, it was apparent that a horde of cheap labor was necessary to hew our forests, mine our coal and minerals, lay the ribbons of steel across our far-flung continent, and tend the tireless wheels of industry. America then became the great "melting pot," the haven of the oppressed, and the escape from war-torn Europe. Agents traveled through village and country spreading the gospel of freedom and plenty . . . For nearly half a century this need for cheap labor continued, and America remained the pot of gold at the end of the rainbow.

Immigrant contributions.

John F. Kennedy, *A Nation of Immigrants*, 1964, p. 66.

Significant as the immigrant role was in politics and in the economy, the immigrant contribution to the professions and the arts was perhaps even greater. Charles O. Paullin's analysis of the *Dictionary of American Biography* shows that, of the eighteenth- and nineteenth-century figures, 20 percent of the businessmen, 20 percent of the scholars and scientists, 23 percent of the painters, 24 percent of the engineers, 28 percent of the architects, 29 percent of the clergymen, 46 percent of the musicians and 61 percent of the actors were of foreign birth—a remarkable measure of the impact of immigration on American culture.

Edward Corsi, Former United States Immigration Commissioner, *Immigration and the United States*, 1956, p. 86.

From the earliest days of the Republic, the immigrant helped to create employment by introducing new industries. The chemical industry was introduced into Delaware by the French. The Swiss and French were the first watchmakers. Tanning was introduced by the Germans; the glove industry by the Scotch. The clothing industry was founded here by the Germans, Austrians, Russians and Italians. The wine industry in this country was largely the work of Italian immigrants.

William M. Floyd, National Commander—Veterans Association, before the House Judiciary Committee, June 6, 1947, *The Immigration Problem*, 1948, p. 108.

It was during the period from about 1891 to 1920 that gangsterism, anarchism, communism, which is not far removed from anarchy, and subversive activities generally began to get a foothold. This, together with an unrestricted flow of immigration, created a disquieting and menacing situation . . . It is not difficult to visualize what the future of the United States would have been had not the Immigration Act of 1924 shut off a large part of the source of potential revolution by force and violence.

Edward Corsi, Former United States Immigration Commissioner, *Immigration and the United States,* **1956, pp. 86-87.**

Without the manpower supplied by immigration, the process of industrial growth and development would have been long delayed. The German, Scandinavian, and southern European groups followed the pioneers westward to cultivate the undeveloped land. The railroads were pushed toward the Pacific by the work of the Irish, the Poles, the Italians, while in the far west the Chinese lent a hand. Coal was dug and iron ore mined by the Hungarians, the Poles, and other immigrants from Central Europe. Much of the work that went into our highway system, our canals and our shipbuilding was performed by immigrant labor. The great expansion of American industry that took place in the last decades of the nineteenth and the early part of the twentieth century would have been impossible without the muscles and brains of new Americans.

U. S. President's Commission on Immigration and Naturalization, *Whom We Shall Welcome,* **1953, pp, 23-24.**

Immigration brought wealth to the United States, many billions of dollars. The immigrants did not bring this wealth in their baggage—many arrived penniless and in debt—but in their skills, their trades, and their willingness to work. In his testimony to the Commission, Dr. Louis I. Dublin [a statistician] pointed out that a young adult immigrant of 18 years today is worth to the Nation at least $10,000, since that is what it costs to raise the average American. The average net worth of such a person to the economy of the United States falls between $30,000 and $80,000, depending on his potential earning power. Throughout our history immigrants have in this way represented additional wealth to our country.

Report of the Senate Committee on Agriculture, 1864 (38th Congress, 1st Session, No. 56), *A History of American Immigration, 1820-1924,* **1926, pp. 135-136.**

The advantages which have accrued heretofore from immigration can scarcely be computed. Such is the labor performed by the thrifty immigrant that he cannot enrich himself without contributing his full quota to the increase of the intrinsic greatness of the United States. This is equally true whether he work at mining, farming, or as a day laborer on one of our railroads.

John F. Kennedy, *A Nation of Immigrants,* **1964, p. 69.**

In the Constitutional Convention James Madison noted, "That part of America which has encouraged them [the immigrants] has advanced most rapidly in population, agriculture and the arts." So, too, Washington in his Thanksgiving Day Proclamation of 1795 asked all Americans "humbly and fervently to beseech the kind Author of these blessings . . . to render this country more and more a safe and propitious asylum for the unfortunate of other countries."

U. S. President's Commission on Immigration and Naturalization, *Whom We Shall Welcome,* **1953, p. 26.**

Whether immigration was cause or effect, it is true today, as it was in Revolutionary times, that the richest regions are those with the highest proportion of recent immigrants . . . . The per capita incomes are highest in regions with a high percentage of recent foreign stock, lowest where immigrants are few. Immigrants went to the regions where there was demand for labor as expressed in high wages. In turn their industry, their skills and their enterprise were major factors in the economic development that has made these regions prosperous.

John F. Kennedy, *A Nation of Immigrants,* **1964, p. 53.**

To the influence of the German immigrants in particular—although all minority groups contributed—we owe the mellowing of the austere Puritan imprint on our daily lives. The Puritans observed the Sabbath as a day of silence and solemnity. The Germans clung to their concept of the 'Continental Sunday' as a day, not only of churchgoing, but also of relaxation, of picnics, of visiting, of quiet drinking in beer gardens while listening to the music of a band.

Regional characteristics.

Niles Carpenter, U.S. Census Bureau, *Immigrants and Their Children*, 1927, p. 42.

It is well to remember that there are certain areas, notably in the 'old South,' where infusions of foreign blood have been almost negligible and where, excepting the possibility of unions between negroes and white persons, the old American stock continues to breed practically 'pure.'

George M. Stephenson, Professor of History—University of Minnesota, *A History of American Immigration, 1820-1924*, 1926, p. 99.

The Irish congregated in the manufacturing cities of the East. The Germans, possessed of more money, went in large numbers to the West, where they became valuable additions to the agricultural population; but many of them settled in New York, Cincinnati, St. Louis, Philadelphia, Baltimore, Milwaukee, and other cities. In the urban centers hostility to the foreign-born was much greater than in the rural districts. Naturally economic competition was stronger in the cities.

Niles Carpenter, U.S. Census Bureau, *Immigrants and Their Children*, 1927, pp. 42-43.

The old colonial stock has by no means been overwhelmed by the foreign element. It is true that the population of 100 years hence will be ethnically very different from that which witnessed the founding of the Republic, yet the older stock appears to have withstood remarkably well the initial shock of the foreign invasion, to be still the dominant racial element, and to be on the way to accomplishing a gradual absorption of the various immigrant breeds. Whether the native American type could continue indefinitely to hold its own if a reversal of conditions should bring about for another two or three decades an immigrant wave comparable in volume to that which ended in 1914 is, however, quite another matter.

Mary Antin, *They Who Knock at our Gates*, 1914, p. 63.

If rural New England today shows signs of degeneracy, it is because much of her sinew and bone departed from her long ago. Some of the best blood of New England answered to the call of "Westward ho!" when the empty lands beyond the Alleghenies gaped for population, while on the spent farms of the Puritan settlements too many sons awaited the division of the father's property.

Niles Carpenter, U.S. Census Bureau, *Immigrants and Their Children*, 1927, p. 15.

The percentage of foreign born in the total population ranges all the way from 0.8 per cent in the East South Central States to 25.5 per cent in the New England States. The individual States show an even wider divergence, namely, from 29 per cent for Rhode Island to 0.3 per cent for North Carolina . . . . In the Northeast there is a large accumulation of immigrant stock; in the South and Southwest this element assumes almost negligible proportions. Between these two extremes stand the Middle West and the Far West, the latter slightly in the lead.

Blacks and Indians.

Rayford W. Logan, Howard University, *One America*, 1952, p. 39.

As late as 1947 Arnold J. Toynbee was repeating a statement that millions of American school children—black as well as white—had been taught in school, namely, "The Black races alone have not contributed positively to any civilization—as yet." Such a statement reveals an ignorance not only of the history of Ancient and Medieval Ethiopia, of Ghana, Melle and Songhay but also of the contributions of Negroes to American civilization. These contributions include virtually every facet of American life.

Rayford W. Logan, Howard University, *One America*, 1952, p. 35.

The position of the Negro in American society and thought today has advanced beyond the fondest dreams of even the most articulate of the so-called radicals at the beginning of the century. Most Negroes face the future with hope and optimism instead of gloom and despair. More Americans than ever before in the history of the United States are demanding that Negroes be treated as first-class citizens. Part of this almost unbelievable change has been due to the American Creed; part to the consequences of two world wars and the Cold War and part to the efforts of Negroes themselves.

Robert F. Heizer, University of California, *One America*, 1952, p. 30.

In the historical development of the American nation the influence of the Indian upon the "national conscience" has been important. Although Indian slavery does not weigh on the American conscience, the treatment of the aborigines through the Colonial and westward expansion periods is something Americans now deplore. The Indian has always had his enemies and his champions, and it is the humanitarian view that has finally prevailed. The attitude of the Indian Affairs administration may be partly an attempt to compensate for earlier injustices. Whether this be admitted or not, the Americans now feel that the Indian is being treated considerately, a comforting thought that makes most of us believe our actions are consistent with the American ideal.

Robert E. Park, Professional Lecturer—University of Chicago, and Herbert A. Miller, Professor of Sociology—Oberlin College, *Old World Traits Transplanted*, 1969, pp. 263-264.

Every country has a certain amount of culturally undeveloped material. We have it, for instance, in the Negroes and Indians, the Southern mountaineers, the Mexicans and Spanish-Americans, and the slums. There is a limit, however, to the amount of material of this kind that a country can incorporate without losing the character of its culture. For example, the "three R's" represent our minimum of cultural equipment, and we are able to transmit this much to practically everybody. With this equipment the individual is able to penetrate any sphere of life; without it he cannot move upward at all.

Robert C. Day, "The Emergence of Activism as a Social Movement," *Native Americans Today: Sociological Perspectives*, 1972, p. 506.

"Custer Had It Coming!" "Red Power!" "Indians Discovered America!" "Kemo Sabe Means Honky!" The slogans on bumpers, telephone poles, and student note-books announce to white Americans that after more than a century of silent anger and hostile passivity, the original American is astir, seeking new ways of solving the "white problem." The new voices of Indian militancy make it clear that Indians are fed up with silence, poverty, and the agencies of white power that have made the Indian an alien in his own land.

Alvin M. Josophy, Jr., Editor—The American Heritage Book of Indians, *Red Power: The American Indian's Fight for Freedom*, 1971, p. 236.

. . . a larger proportion of America's Indians are [probably] living off the reservation than ever before in our history. Some authorities even estimate that more Indians are living in cities and towns than are remaining on the reservation. Of those American Indians who are now dwelling in urban areas, approximately three-fourths are living in poverty.

Commission on the Rights, Liberties and Responsibilities of the American Indian, *The Indian, America's Unfinished Business*, 1966, p. 10.

Ostensible familiarity with the English language and the adoption of white manners and customs by no means demonstrates that the Indian also adopts the white man's ethics. He may only be aping the ways of a society alien to him. Below the surface he may still form judgements based on tribal usages. As a case in point, he may lack the necessary urge for individual initiative and reject a competitive life despite his verbal acceptance of the white man's ways. The absence of adequate words in his language to convey the meanings of many concepts, values, and institutions further complicates the difficulty of communication between the two races.

31

Stuart Levine, Chairman of the American Studies Program—University of Kansas, and Nancy Lurie, Professor of Anthropology—University of Wisconsin, *The American Indian Today*, 1968, p.3.

Although Indians have a great many problems and grievances, they do not for the most part, like to be associated with the Civil Rights Movement . . . Some young Indian people put it this way: The aims of the Civil Rights Movement are good, but seem to concern only Negro rights . . . .The Indian case is subtly different from that of the Negro . . . [T]he Negro, by and large, wants a fair share in the general culture. The Indian wants to remain special.

Stuart Levine, Chairman of the American Studies Program—University of Kansas, and Nancy Lurie, Professor of Anthropology—University of Wisconsin, *The American Indian Today*, 1968, p. 5.

Indian people . . . in no sense threaten national well-being. Indian values and ideals are not especially incompatible with national norms. And Indian cultures have always adapted extremely well to change when they have been given anything like a fair chance to make a go of the new situation. Their societies can be altered quite radically without losing their essentially Indian structure and flavor.

The Puritan influence.

George M. Stephenson, Professor of History—University of Minnesota, *The Puritan Heritage*, 1952, p. 267.

Twentieth-century America appears to have lost the Puritan heritage. A generation whose "literature" is more akin to the licentiousness of the press which ridiculed the Puritans in England, whose "movies" revel in the filth of the muckrake, whose radio and television programs serve a fare of vulgarity, and whose mechanism has degraded the superior man and has enhanced the power of the inferior man, is incapable of understanding a religious movement whose appeal is to the "remnant," to those who are conscious of the brevity of human life and recognize the spiritual life as the one great reality.

Marcus L. Hansen, *The Immigrant in American History*, 1940, p. 99.

Puritanism has appeared as an explanation in the most unexpected places. The reform campaigns that periodically overrun municipal administrations are presented, not as a plain revolt of civic decency, but as a sudden reawakening of the primitive American conscience. Candidates for office must expect traits of character that have absolutely no bearing upon official fitness to be exposed to public view. In the past, at least, clergymen have exercised a remarkable influence in determining the availability of men who desired political preferment, and the "Methodist vote" and the "Baptist vote" have been angled for as consistently as the vote of the farmers or laborers.

Joseph Gaer and Ben Siegel, *The Puritan Heritage*, 1964, p. 13.

Much of what is now recognized as distinctively American in thought, culture, and tradition is derived essentially from four very different sets of values. These begin with seventeenth-century Puritanism, and go on to the eighteenth-century fusion of liberalism, federalism, and the Southern aristocratic code. Then follow nineteenth-century New England transcendentalism and, finally, the western frontier's "rugged individualism." Most historians agree that, of all these influences, Puritanism has proved the most sustained. Not to understand Puritanism, they insist, is not to understand America.

Contributions to the American spirit.

Jethro K. Lieberman, *Are Americans Extinct?*, 1968, p. 198.

If two words could summarize America, they would be "activity" and "freedom." More than to anything else, Americans point with pride to their land of ceaseless creating and building, carried on by a free and spirited people. Without the central fact of immigration, it would be difficult to conceive that either of these conditions could have been fulfilled in the New World.

George M. Stephenson, Professor of History—University of Minnesota, *A History of American Immigration, 1920-1924*, 1926, p. 134.

The immigrants were strongly attached to the Federal government. In their native lands they thought of America in terms of the United States. They knew little of the rivalries and jealousies between the American states, and they had not resided here long enough to form a special attachment to any state. Moreover, their naturalization made them first of all citizens of the United States, and their title to the public lands had been obtained from the Federal government.

John F. Kennedy, *A Nation of Immigrants*, 1964, p. 67.

Immigration plainly was not always a happy experience. It was hard on the newcomers, and hard as well on the communities to which they came. When poor, ill-educated and frightened people disembarked in a strange land, they often fell prey to native racketeers, unscrupulous businessmen and cynical politicians. Boss Tweed said, characteristically, in defense of his own depredations in New York in the 1870's, "This population is too hopelessly split into races and factions to govern it under universal suffrage, except by bribery, or patronage, or corruption."

Jethro K. Lieberman, *Are Americans Extinct?*, 1968. p. 202.

Senator Ervin did raise a point in criticism which we would do well to heed: When we get oratorical and emotional, he said, we say we want the tired and poor and despised, but we really take the brilliant and energetic only. Our preference system is effectively geared to keep out the lone, rude immigrant of our simpler days. Although America is a nation of immigrants, we are becoming increasingly less an immigrant society and the dangers from becoming too homogenous should be contemplated. When the nation drew inward on itself, fearing the outside conspiracies that loomed everywhere, and forgetting its transplanted origins, hysterical legislation threatened the premises of American democracy. "Internal security" laws cannot flourish where optimism prevails, and optimism demands a look at the path from which we have come to know the path toward which we are going.

Jethro K. Lieberman, *Are Americans Extinct?*, 1968, p. 198.

American "know-how" is not some mysterious hereditary quirk of peoples indigenous to the Western Hemisphere; it is a by-product of a pragmatic people who have a job to do and who fervently believe that their children will have a better life than they. This was a contribution of the immigrant and it developed because they were immigrants who grasped the enormous potential of the willingness to abide change. It is not at all coincidental that the mounting despair of Negroes in the late 1960's springs from the one group in America which did not freely emigrate and which has not been allowed to realize its potential.

Michael Krans, Professor of History—City College of New York, *Immigration, The American Mosaic*, 1966, pp. 103-104.

The American immigration story is a compound of myth and reality. The reality was the heartbreak of quest defeated, satisfaction with modest achievement, or glittering success in the New World. But to the Old World the myth was larger than success or failure. It encompassed nothing less than the creation of a new order of man in a new promised land.

Selected Bibliography

Antin, Mary. *They Who Knock At Our Gates*. Boston: Houghton Mifflin Co., 1914.

Bahr, Howard M.; Chadwick, Bruce A.; and Day, Robert C., eds. *Native Americans Today: Sociological Perspectives*. New York: Harper & Row, 1972.

Barron, Milton L., ed. *Minorities in a Changing World*. New York: Knopf, 1967.

Bernard, William S., ed. *American Immigration Policy: A Reappraisal*. New York: Harper & Brothers, 1950.

Brown, Francis J., and Roucek, Joseph C., eds. *One America*. Englewood Cliffs, N.J.: Prentice-Hall, 1952.

Carpenter, Niles. *Immigrants and Their Children*. 1920 Census Monograph. Washington, D.C.: U.S. Government Printing Office, 1927.

Commission on the Rights, Liberties, & Responsibilities of the American Indian. *The Indian, America's Unfinished Business*. Norman: University of Oklahoma Press, 1966.

Eaton, Allen H. *Immigrant Gifts to American Life*. New York: Russell Sage Foundation, 1932.

Erickson, Charlotte. *American Industry and the European Immigrant, 1860-1885*. Cambridge: Harvard University Press, 1957.

Fairchild, Henry Pratt. *Immigration*. New York: The Macmillan Co., 1913.

Fellows, Donald Keith. *A Mosaic of America's Ethnic Minorities*. New York: John Wiley & Sons, 1972.

Gaer, Joseph, and Siegel, Ben. *The Puritan Heritage: America's Roots in the Bible*. New York: New American Library, 1964.

Garraty, John A. *The American Nation: A History of the United States*. New York: Harper & Row, 1966.

Gordon, Milton M. *Assimilation in American Life: The Role of Race, Religion, and National Origins*. New York: Oxford University Press, 1955.

Hansen, Marcus Lee. *The Immigrant in American History*. New York: Harper & Row, 1940.

Jones, Maldwyn A. *American Immigration*. Chicago: University of Chicago Press, 1960.

Josephy, Alvin M., Jr. *Red Power: The American Indian's Fight for Freedom*. New York: American Heritage Press, 1971.

Kennedy, John F. *A Nation of Immigrants*. New York: Harper & Row, 1964.

Kraus, Michael. *Immigration, The American Mosaic*. Princeton, N.J.: D. Van Nostrand Co., 1966.

Laski, Harold J. *The American Democracy: A Commentary and an Interpretation*. New York: The Viking Press, 1948.

Levine, Stuart, and Lurie, Nancy Oestreich, eds. *The American Indian Today*. Deland, Florida: Everett Edwards, 1968.

Lieberman, Jethro K. *Are Americans Extinct?* New York: Walker & Co., 1968.

Mikulski, Barbara. "Who Speaks for Ethnic America?" *New York Times*. September 29, 1970, p. 43.

Park, Robert E., and Miller, Herbert A. *Old World Traits Transplanted*. New York: Arno Press and the New York Times, 1969.

Peters, Clarence A., ed. *The Immigration Problem*. New York: H.W. Wilson Co., 1948.

Schlesinger, Arthur M. Jr., *Paths to the Present*. New York: The Macmillan Co., 1949.

Schlesinger, Arthur M. Jr., and White, Morton, eds. *Paths of American Thought*. Boston: Houghton Mifflin Co. 1963.

Steinfield, Melvin, ed. *Cracks in the Melting Pot; Racism and Discrimination in American History*. Beverly Hills: Glencoe Press, 1970.

Stephenson, George M. *A History of American Immigration, 1820-1924*. Boston: Ginn & Co., 1926.

Stephenson, George M. *The Puritan Heritage*. New York: The Macmillan Co., 1952.

Tyler, Poyntz. *Immigration and the United States*. New York: H.W. Wilson Co., 1956.

U.S. President's Commission on Immigration and Naturalization. *Whom We Shall Welcome*. Washington: U.S. Government Printing Office, 1953.

Wittke, Carl. *We Who Built America*. Cleveland, Ohio: Western Reserve University Press, 1964.

Ziegler, Benjamin Munn, ed. *Immigration: An American Dilemma*. Boston: D.C. Heath & Co., 1953.

ISSUE II
THE LAND OF PLENTY

LOCAL EVENTS—COLLEGE AGE ISSUE
September 27—November 1, 1975

DEBATE   *Resolved: That urbanization has lowered the quality of American life.*

PERSUASIVE   *The American Frontier: Crucible of our National Character?*

EXTEMPORANEOUS   *The Sprawling City*

1. *How has urbanization affected the core values of the American people?*
2. *The colonizers of Boston and Philadelphia sought to build cities that would be examples to the world. Have out urban centers met their goals?*
3. *What's American about American cities?*
4. *Thomas Jefferson said he never wanted to see the day when a majority of Americans lived in cities. Was that statement wise?*
5. *Are cities the new frontier?*
6. *Big city "bosses" through the years: democrats or dictators?*
7. *Can traditional values of local self-government be made relevant to large urban communities?*
8. *From Plymouth to "new towns": Why haven't planned communities ever caught on in America?*
9. *The ownership of land: Is it still a noble goal?*
10. *Has our form of government seriously underrepresented urban interests?*
11. *What can't cities provide?*
12. *How has urbanization affected the prospects for equality of opportunity?*
13. *How has mechanization of food production influenced patterns of urbanization?*
14. *Have American political institutions traditionally reflected an anti-urban bias?*
15. *How has urbanization changed our utilization of energy resources?*

RESOLVED: THAT URBANIZATION HAS LOWERED THE QUALITY OF AMERICAN LIFE.

Introductory Essay

Our most philosophical President, Thomas Jefferson, viewed large cities as virtual reservoirs of evil. In large urban centers, Jefferson saw disease, the perversion of nature, a fundamental threat to democracy, a dearth of aesthetics, and dangerous disparities of wealth. Not cities and manufacturing, but an idyllic America of small, independent, largely self-sufficient farms was considered the best way to restrict government encroachments on individual liberty and to foster the pursuit of happiness. This agrarian vision, which crystallized attitudes prevalent in Jefferson's day, had a profound impact on America's view of her cities in subsequent ages. Elements of it may be found in the Southern defense of rural life both before and after the Civil War, in the Populist revolt in the late Nineteenth Century, in the agricultural and housing programs of the New Deal, and in the modern passion for low-density suburban living. Americans have been unable to overcome a deep current of antipathy toward city life even as urban existence has become the national norm. A study of poetry from the period 1876 to 1905 revealed the symbols associated with the city. Images were solidly negative: cities were portrayed as ugly, artificial, overcompetitive, and given to every manner of vice. Paradoxically, this was the period in which the city was rising most swiftly toward dominance in American life.

What does "urbanization" mean? Dictionary definitions are not especially helpful. They direct attention to the idea of a city. What constitutes a city? The Census Bureau has relied since 1790 on the definition of a city as a settlement of 2500 or more. Few people think that places where a few thousand townfolk congregate have "urban problems" in the same sense that, say, Chicago or Los Angeles have urban problems. Yet the commonly cited statistic— that 70% of the U. S. population lives in urban areas —reflects the Census Bureau definition. In fact, today around half of the U.S. population lives in either rural areas or in cities with a population of under 50,000. (Some of these small cities are really suburbs of large cities, though the extent to which such satellites share the hardships of their giant neighbors is unclear.)

And how are we to understand assertions about ... "The quality of American life"? Is the quality of life measured by its order and tranquility, or by its opportunity and challenge? By its simplicity, or its sophistication? One who prizes simplicity, order and tranquility will probably find rural life more appealing than the person who prefers diversity.

There are compelling alternatives to consider. The affirmative speaker may choose to defend the resolution by demonstrating the shortcomings of urbanization, even though the historical inevitability of urbanization may be granted. It can be suggested that America could realistically have chosen another historical path. Our rich anti-urban tradition provides several possibilities, including: the Jeffersonian ideal; versions of communitarian living, which attracted great attention throughout the Nineteenth Century; and planned decentralization of industry and population advocated by various reformers. An examination of the origins of our contemporary scene will be essential to its critical and rhetorical assessment.

Our modern cities bear only a limited resemblance to their infant namesakes. The most striking difference is sheer size. In the absence of a technology to build tall buildings, the city did not rise far above the earth; in the absence of modern transportation systems, the city could not sprawl outward. At the start of the Revolution, Philadelphia was the largest U.S. city with less than 40,000 inhabitants. (The other cities in the top five were New York, with 25,000; Boston with 16,000; Charleston with 12,000; and Newport with 11,000.) In 1790 the first Census disclosed that the nation was 95% rural.

The Industrial Revolution did not invade the United States until well into the 1800's. Hence, the cities were fairly small commercial centers, dominated by a middle class of shopkeepers, tradesmen, and artisans. The separation of industry and urban life at this time is demonstrated by the fact that in 1820 about 12% of the nation's labor force was employed in manufacturing and construction, but the population of the major cities and their suburbs was only 3.7% of the American total. (The primitive state of that industry which did exist is suggested by the estimate that the entire horsepower potential of the country's industrially employed steam engines in 1838 was equivalent to that of 200 contemporary American automobiles.) The cities have always had wealth and political influence disproportionate to their population. The events leading to the Revolution, for example, took place largely in Boston, Philadelphia, and other cities. But the tentacles of a modern industrialized society had begun to reach outwards, past the traditional confines of the other cities.

American cities grew fastest in the period before the Civil War; the larger cities typically doubled or tripled in size. But with the advent of industrialization, a real transformation of the landscape took place. In the 1880's, the U.S. became the world's foremost economic power. A reflection of the meaning of this for the cities was the doubling in size of over one hundred cities during the decade. The Great Lakes, the Ohio River valley, and a few areas of the South and far West now competed with the East coast as centers of urbanization. By 1890, the population was one-third urban.

These rapid changes reflect historical developments. National transportation systems integrated the economy, spurring commerce and enabling farmers to feed city dwellers. Railroad track mileage continued to be laid at a startling pace from the time of its introduction in the 1830's until near the end of the century. Steamboats and canals augmented the railroads. Industrial growth created expanded job opportunities, while making population density a physical possibility through architectural and civil engineering developments. The rapid growth of the cities was accounted for by an influx of 25 million new immigrants, most of whom settled in urban areas; the migration of many thousands of rural folk to the city; and a 35% growth in the existing urban populations, attributable chiefly to improved public health and sanitation measures.

Among the consequences of this growth was the development of huge slums in larger cities, frequently inhabited by immigrants. Partly to escape the ugliness and social problems of the poor central city, the wealthy began to move toward the outskirts of the urban areas. Development of the frontier was a somewhat unexpected consequence of urbanization. Through a process historian Richard Wade has called "urban imperialism," small towns and large cities alike developed commercial markets in their rural hinterlands. Mutual benefits followed for the farmer, who was provided with a place to barter his products, and the urban businessman, who could expect to make profits on the goods he sold and perhaps even on land speculation.

The Progressive Era saw the continued growth of existing cities. The nation was one-half urban by 1920; its largest city was New York, then the world's second largest with over two million people. Both Chicago and Philadelphia topped the one million mark. Only the South, which remained three-quarters rural, resisted the trend toward city life. One major development of the era was the reform of corrupt administrations of many cities. New and more

honest leadership in Toledo, Cleveland, St. Louis, Denver, and Milwaukee, among other places, replaced corrupt bosses. Many cities attempted permanent institutional reform through the establishment of the city manager plan. This trend continued, so that by 1940 this reform had been adopted by 450 cities. Another trend was the amelioration of some of the worst poverty conditions in the slums. General economic prosperity benefitted the poor through more and better paying employment. In Cincinnati, for instance, one-fourth of the population of the Basin tenement area left between 1910 and 1930.

The Great Depression disrupted a great many patterns of American life, among them the trend toward urbanization. In 1932, the flow from farm to city was reversed for one of the few times in American history. In addition, the immigration which contributed so much to urban expansion had been greatly slowed by legislation during the twenties. Yet the national die had already been cast; the nation was over half urban, and one-third of the population lived in cities of 100,000 or more. The development of surburban areas, greatly facilitated by the flexibility of automobile and truck transportation for commuters and businesses, created almost 100 metropolitan regions. Then as today, the suburbs were characterized by a degree of fragmentation that frustrated regional cooperation and hampered planning.

The end of World War II released considerable demand for housing, which was satisfied partly through funds provided under the GI Bill. A tremendous flight from the central city to the less dense suburbs followed. Between 1940 and 1950, a staggering 2.3 million people, or 12% of the population, moved out of the twelve largest central cities. Poor people, especially blacks, took their place. Between 1940 and 1960, the percentage of U.S. blacks living in the South dropped from 72% to 54%, and one-half of all blacks lived in "inner cities." The improvement in the quality of urban housing during the 1950s was vast; half of substandard urban housing was restored during this decade.

The convulsive decade of the 1960's saw racial riots in most major U.S. cities, broad-scale social programs generated partly as a response to the urban violence, and then restrictions on these programs in the face of mounting fiscal demands from the Vietnam war. The War on Poverty of the mid-sixties was further restricted by Republican administrations since 1969, which have sought to emphasize local and state responsibility for social programs.

During the past two centuries, the quality of urban life has been attacked in almost every aspect. No claims have been advanced with greater vehemence than the psycho-social arguments that the city is an unhealthy place in which to live and grow. The development of the social sciences during the last hundred years has added greater objective understanding and precision to these criticisms. A standard description of the modern city might approximate the following. City life tends to increase the interdependence of individuals at the same time that it depersonalizes human contacts; its symbols are the assembly line, the department store, and the apartment building. The stabilizing influences of the family and religion are seriously weakened by competing claims of a wide variety of contacts with different lifestyles, ethnic groups, and religions. A "dehumanization" occurs, leaving the individual with a feeling of isolation and rootlessness.

This condition has been used to explain in whole or in part a number of social disorders. Urban crime is said to be the result of a breakdown of internalized moral constraints, in addition to other factors such as the greater opportunity for crime in densely packed areas. Crime has worried city dwellers since the earliest days of the nation. De Tocqueville in the 1830's found the growth of great cities "a real danger which threatens the future security of the democratic republics of the New World," due to the threatened and actual violence of the urban poor. During the period of rapid urbanization in the 1880's, the prison inmate population in the U.S. increased 50%, while the homicide rate tripled. Most of the imprisoned were children of the slums. More recently, FBI statistics have shown that cities of 250,000 or more have several times as much major crime as rural areas in virtually every category of offense.

The isolation of inner life in the city and the increased stress of high-density living have also been used to explain the higher rates of mental illness in the city, alcoholism and other forms of drug addiction and suicide.

Racial and ethnic problems have often found their most serious expressions in urban areas. The concentration of poor minority groups in ghetto areas has always been viewed as explosive, all too often with good reason. Serious rioting occured in such places as Charleston, Louisville, Cincinnati, New York, and New Orleans, among others, in the Nineteenth Century. Historian Richard Wade has concluded that the most important underlying causes of this urban violence included the dislocations surrounding the rapid growth of cities; loose, shifting social structures; and a large number of transients in the population, such as seamen and teamsters.

If the psycho-social case against the cities seems formidable, an inspection of the opposing point of view reveals useful conflicting evidence. First, many of the problems attributed to urban areas in general apply mostly to large industrial cities. Are small cities also impersonal, lacking in values, reliant on external controls? It can be noted that at least two social problems—crime and suicide—appear to be related in generally linear fashion to increasing population. This means that the larger the city, the larger the rate of crime or suicide.

A defense of certain values, furthermore, can be used to deny the picture of the city presented above. If urban employment leaves something to be desired, it does offer greater material well-being and greater time for recreation than farm work. Greater density of population leads to more recreational, cultural, and educational opportunities than are feasible in rural areas. Further, even if many daily contacts are impersonal, friendship is not rendered impossible in the city; certainly there are more groups and individuals from which to choose potential friends. The closeness of rural people might even be viewed as an undesirable intrusion on privacy. Whether the loss of support from family and religion constitutes a problem or not depends upon one's convictions and justification of such institutions; it may be claimed that an individual ought to develop his own character, without the excessive interference or overprotection of others.

Political problems, as well as psycho-social ones, have plagued the cities throughout American history. The most serious and certainly the most publicized threat to municipal government has probably been corruption. Jefferson's morbid statement that "The mobs of great cities add just so much to the support of pure government, as sores do to the strength of the human body" was for a time confirmed by events. The noted British historian James Bryce wrote in his 1888 classic, *The American Commonwealth*, "There is not a city with a population exceeding 200,000 where the poison germs have not sprung into a vigorous life; and in some of the smaller ones, down to 70,000, it needs no microscope to note the results of their growth." He deemed municipal government" the one conspicuous failure of the United States." Unscrupulous men gained control of city governments from coast to coast; often by popular vote. This was made possible by a general public disinterest in such an apparently unimportant level of government; the utility of dependable local "machines" to national political parties; the ability of local bosses to ingratiate themselves to large immigrant groups through provision of such vital services as jobs, food in hard times, and help with the law; and so forth. The notorious Tweed ring in New York, one of the worst examples, pocketed virtually all of the $70 million in debt they compiled for New York City in three years.

Another political handicap of American cities has traditionally been fragmentation of authority. The same metropolitan area may overlap several independent townships, counties, or even states. The general pattern, moreover, has been to fragment political authority even within a single jurisdiction, providing limited independent revenue-raising and policy-making powers to such groups as school boards and municipally-controlled utilities. Such a system disrupts regional planning, fosters irrational patterns of urban growth, and probably reduces the ability of local government to provide effective social services. However, it should be recognized that the bewildering complexity of local government reflects a large degree of conscious design. The ability of the individual to be heard in his community has been valued more by Americans than the extension of governmental authority, which increases collective power by sacrificing individual power.

Concentration of immigrant and racial groups in closely knit neighborhoods has been viewed by some as disruptive of democratic institutions. Urban growth has been in large measure the result of immigration, which brought over 30 million people to U.S. shores between 1815 and 1915. After 1880 the level of immigration dramatically increased as southern and eastern Europeans came to dominate the influx. The strangeness, clannishness, and often desperate poverty of the new immigrants worried many people, including many who were responsible and unprejudiced in their judgments. However, positive aspects of ethnic neighborhoods often were overlooked at the time. In a real sense, the cities have been America's melting pot, with ethnic neighborhoods serving as a point of transition for those from alien cultures. New York's Lower East Side illustrates the process of assimilation. Until the 1870's, the area was primarily a German and Irish neighborhood; by 1910 it had become a Jewish ghetto; and today blacks and Puerto Ricans inhabit the section. Neighborhoods of poverty in the area were expanding; there were no parks, no playgrounds, just tenement after tenement so primitive that the introduction of the infamous "dumbell" style of tenement improved living conditions. Population density reached one-half million per square mile, the highest congestion the world has ever known. Yet the Irish, the Germans, and the eastern European Jews were able to escape such conditions while newer and poorer ethnic groups took their place.

The cities have also been held responsible for a number of economic problems. Widespread industrial development and city life have gone hand in hand since the mid-nineteenth century. Disparities of wealth in the cities have always existed, but certainly the industrial city exacerbated the extremes of poverty and riches. Another problem associated with urbanization and especially industrialization has been environmental damage. Air and water pollution and problems in waste disposal have been aggravated by concentration of population. These problems have sometimes been shockingly acute. For example, New York as late as 1857 had no sewers for almost three-fourths of the city; 24 million gallons of sewage accumulated each day in yards, alleys, gutters, and streets.

It is important to place these problems in perspective, however. First, rural areas are not immune to poverty, through rural poverty is less concentrated and visible. As late as 1960, to provide one indication, three-fourths of deteriorating or dilapidated housing was located outside cities of 100,000 or more. Neither is rural industry more concerned with environmental protection than urban industry. Secondly, the economic difficulties of the cities are in large measure the result of societal value choices that only partly relate to urbanization. If industrialization created the slums, it also made America the wealthiest nation on earth—and not just a few capitalists shared in this wealth. The urban poor could tolerate their condition, insofar as their hopes for improvement were occasionally consummated. Government action might have reduced or eliminated urban poverty, but not until well into the Twentieth Century have Americans accepted even limited national efforts; it remained the individual's responsibility to extricate himself from poverty. The ethic of self-improvement, spawned in Puritan tracts, grew with the cities eventually encompassing the attitudes of newly-minted Americans. In an analogous way, government could have long ago begun to limit ecological damage caused by increasing urbanization. Recent federal and state actions have gone a long way toward controlling air and water pollution, although we have never been more urbanized. Similarly, the ugliness of many cities—a factor mentioned by virtually every critic of urbanization—is within the control of urban residents, if only they value beauty enough to pay for it.

Undeniably, urban areas have become the center of American civilization. Optimistic observers have welcomed this development, pointing to the vitality, the concentration of talent, the spectacular evidence of man's power over nature, the culture, and the range of experience available in cities. One statistical study in the Nineteenth Century found that communities of 8,000 or more gave birth to almost twice as many noted people as their share of the population would account for. Those interested in the arts have known that the cities have provided the audience and the financial support necessary for cultural achievements. The wealth of the cities has dazzled many in the way that the poverty of the cities has appalled others. The shortcomings of the cities have been viewed as more transitory than their advantages by urban boosters.

Americans have long been attracted by the advantages to be had in the life of a vigorous city, but their lives have often been abused by the harsher realities found there. We may not yet be completely comfortable with this tension, nor pleased to realize the frailties of some of our dreams. But while the agrarian myth may capture our hearts, our prospects seem tied to the city.

Excerpted Documents

Is city life preferable
to rural life?

Walt Whitman, 1870, in *Urban America: A History With Documents*, 1974, p. 198.

The splendor, picturesqueness, and oceanic amplitude and rush of these great cities, the . . . lofty new buildings, facades of marble and iron, of original grandeur and elegance of design, with the masses of gay color, the preponderance of white and blue, the flags flying, the endless ships, the tumultuous streets, Broadway, the heavy, low, musical roar, hardly ever intermitted, even at night; the jobbers' houses, the rich shops, the wharves, the great Central Park, and the Brooklyn Park hills, . . . the assemblages of the citizens in their groups, conversations, trades, evening amusements . . . these, I say, and the like of these, completely satisfy my senses of power, fulness, motion, etc., and give me, through such senses . . . a continued exaltation and absolute fulfilment.

Mark Twain, 1867, in *Urban America: A History With Documents*, 1974, p. 198.

. . . I have at last, after several months' experience, made up my mind that . . . [New York] is a splendid desert — a domed and steepled solitude, where a stranger is lonely in the midst of a million of his race. A man walks his tedious miles through the same interminable street every day, elbowing his way through a buzzing multitude of men, yet never seeing a familiar face, and never seeing a strange one the second time. . . . Every man seems to feel that he has got the duties of two lifetimes to accomplish in one, and so he rushes, rushes, rushes, and never has time to be companionable — never has any time at his disposal to fool away on matters which do not involve dollars and duty and business.

George Tucker, Professor of Political Economy and Moral Philosophy—University of Virginia, *Progress of the United States in Population and Wealth*, 1843, p. 127.

The growth of cities commonly marks the progress of intelligence and the arts, measures the sum of social enjoyment, and always implies increased mental activity, which is sometimes healthy and useful, sometimes distempered and pernicious. If these congregations of men diminished some of the comforts of life, they augmented others: if they are less favorable to health than the country, they also provide better defenses against disease, and better means of cure. From causes both physical and moral, they are less favorable to the multiplication of the species. In the eyes of the moralist, cities afford a wider field both for virtue and vice; and they are more prone to innovation, whether for good or evil.

Report of the Urbanism Committee to the National Resources Committee, *Our Cities: Their Role in the National Economy*, 1937, p. vi.

There is liberty of development in isolation and wide spaces, but there is also freedom in the many-sided life of the city where each may find his own kind. There is democracy in the scattered few, but there is also democracy in the thick crowd with its vital impulse and its insistent demand for a just participation in the gains of our civilization. There is fertility and creation in the rich soil of the broad countryside, but there is also fertility and creativeness in forms of industry, art, personality, emerging even from the city streets and reaching toward the sky.

Willard Glazier, *Peculiarities of American Cities*, 1884, p. 332.

(Pittsburg) is the domain of Vulcan, not Pluto. Here, in this gigantic workshop, in the midst of the materials of his labor, the god of fire, having left his ancient home on Olympus, and established himself in this newer world, stretches himself beside his forge, and sleeps the peaceful sleep which is the reward of honest industry. Right at his doorway are mountains of coal to keep a perpetual fire upon his altar; within the reach of his outstretched grasp are rivers of coal oil; and a little further away great stores of iron for him to forge and weld, and shape into a thousand forms and at his feet is the shining river, an impetuous Mercury, ever ready to do his bidding. Grecian mythology never conceived of an abode so fitting for the son of Zeus as that which he has selected himself on this western hemisphere. And his ancient tasks were child's play compared with the mighty ones he has undertaken to-day.

William Jennings Bryan, Speech accepting nomination of the 1896 Democratic National Convention for the Presidency, Chicago.

. . .the great cities rest upon our broad and fertile praries. Burn down your cities and leave our farms, and your cities will spring up again as if by magic; but destroy our farms and the grass will grow in the streets of every city in the country.

Herbert J. Muller, *The Uses of the Past*, 1952.

The rise of the city has been the historic sign of a society on the march; it stimulated further adventure by bringing people together, pooling their efforts, promotes change by exchange, enlarging the world through contact with other peoples and cities. The great city became the center of unrest and disorder because it remained the center of creative activity.

Daniel J. Elazar, "Are We A Nation of Cities?," *A Nation of Cities: Essays on America's Urban Problems*, 1966, pp. 100-101.

It is generally known by now that suburbia has become the equal of small-town America as the symbol of the country's grass roots and the fountainhead of what is distinctive about "the American Way of Life." This is so regardless of whether suburbia is praised or condemned for its role. The popular literature defending suburbia and that attacking it are both strongly reminiscent of the popular literature devoted to small-town America two to four generations ago. If some see virtue in the small community — whether it is typified by a predominantly small-town society or a predominantly suburban society — others see ignorance, provincialism, decadence, and even corruption in the same locale. If the latter speak loudly with words, the former are speaking louder with their feet.

Report of the Urbanism Committee to the National Resources Committee, *Our Cities: Their Role in the National Economy*, 1937, p. vi.

The faults of our cities are not those of decadence and impending decline, but of exuberant vitality crowding its way forward under tremendous pressure—the flood rather than the drought. The city is both the great playground and the great battleground of the Nation—at once the vibrant center of a world of hectic amusement lovers and also the dusty and sometimes smoldering and reddened area of industrial conflict. It is the cities that must meander the ambiguous and shifting boundaries between recreation and vice, not only for their own citizens but for some of their visitors as well. It is the cities that must deal with the tragic border lines of order and justice in bitter industrial struggles.

What are the processes
and causes of urbanization?

John Adams, in *The Earliest Diary of John Adams*, 1966, p. 99.

Am returned from Boston, and according to my Promise . . . beginning to write you a Discription or a History of what I saw, and heard, & . . .

My Eyes were entertained with Objects, in every figure and Colour of Deformity . . . My Ears were ravished with every actual or imaginable sound, except harmonious sounds . . . The fragrance of the Streets, were a continual feast to my Nostrils. — Thus Pleasure entered all my senses, and roused in my Imagination, scenes of still greater tumult, Discord, Deformity, and filth. . . .

But all this is the dark side. — In reward of this Pain, I had the Pleasure to sit and hear the greatest Lawyers, orators, in short the greatest men, in America, harranging at the Bar, and on the Bench. I had the Pleasure of Spending my Evenings with my friends in the . . . Joys of serene sedate Conversation, and perhaps it is worth my while to add, I had the Pleasure of seeing a great many, and of feeling some very [pretty] Girls.

Henry Hartwell, James Blair, and Edward Chilton, *Large and True Account of the Present State of Virginia,* **1697, in** *Urban America: A History With Documents,* **1974, p. 19.**

. . . as to . . . natural advantages [Virginia] is one of the best . . . But . . . if we inquire for well-built towns, for convenient ports and markets [it is] one of the poorest, miserablest, and worst countries in all America . . . No doubt [this] is chiefly to be imputed to the first wrong measures that were taken in not seating themselves in towns . . .

For want of towns, markets, and money, there is but little encouragement for tradesmen and artificers . . . The merchants . . . are subject to great inconveniences in the way of their trade, which might be avoided if they had towns, markets, and money . . .

Samuel P. Hays, Professor of History—University of Pittsburgh, *The Response to Industrialism: 1885-1914,* **1957, p. 95.**

By 1900 [immigrants] constituted about 40 percent of the population of the twelve largest cities in the country; another 20 percent were second generation. Each succeeding wave of immigration out-numbered the previous one: the first, between 1820 and 1860 reached approximately five million, the second, between 1860 and 1890, thirteen and one-half million, and the third, between 1900 and 1930, almost nineteen million. Between 1820 and 1930 over thirty-seven and one-half million people came to America in one of the largest and most significant migrations in the world's history.

Stephen Thernsdrom, Associate Professor of History—Brandeis University, "Urbanization, Migration, and Social Mobility in Late Nineteenth-Century America," *Urban America in Historical Perspective,* **1970, p. 194.**

The urbanization of late nineteenth-century America took place at a dizzying pace. Chicago, for instance, doubled its population every decade but one between 1850 and 1890, growing from 30,000 to over a million in little more than a generation. And it was not merely the conspicuous metropolitan giants but the Akrons, the Duluths, the Tacomas that were bursting at the seams; no less than 101 American communities grew by 100% or more in the 1880's.

F. J. Kingsbury, "The Tendency of Man to Live in Cities," *Journal of Social Science,* **November 1895.**

. . . within a very recent period three new factors have been suddenly developed which promise to exert a powerful influence on the problems of the city and country life. These are the trolley, the bicycle, and the telephone. It is impossible to forsee at present just what their influence is to be on the question of the distribution of population; but this much is certain, that it adds from five to fifteen miles to the radius of every large town.

It is by such apparently unimportant, trifling, and inconspicuous forces that civilization is swayed and moulded in its evolutions and no man can forsee them or say whether they lead . . .

David Montgomery, Professor of History—University of Pittsburgh, "The Working Classes of the Pre-Industrial American City, 1780-1830," *Labor History,* **Winter 1968, p. 4.**

Most manufacturing [between 1780 and 1830], in other words, was carried on outside of the major cities. By 1820 some 12 percent of the nation's labor force was engaged in manufacturing and construction, and 28 percent in all non-agricultural occupations, but at that time the residents of these cities and their contiguous suburbs totalled only 356,452, or 3.7 percent of the American people.

DeWitt Clinton, Governor of New York, *A View of the Grand Canal,* 1825, pp. 20-21.

The most fertile and extensive regions of America will avail themselves of [the Erie Canal] for a market. All their surplus productions, whether of the soil, the forest, the mines, or the water, their fabrics of art and their supplies of foreign commodities will concentrate in the city of New York, for transportation abroad or consumption at home. Agriculture, manufactures, commerce, trade, navigation, and the arts, will receive a correspondent encouragement. That city will, in ths course of time, become the granary of the world, the emporium of commerce, the seat of manufacturers, the focus of great moneyed operations, and the concentrating point of vast, disposable, and accumulating capitals, which will stimulate, enliven, extend, and reward the exertions of human labour and ingenuity, to all their processes and exhibitions. And, before the revolution of a century, the whole island of Manhattan, covered with habitations and replenished with a dense population, will constitute one vast city.

Has urbanization engendered
significant social problems?

The New York Independent Reflector, January 18, 1753.

Another Consequence of their clustering into Towns, is Luxury — a great and mighty Evil, carrying all before it, and crumbling States and Empires, into slow, but inevitable Ruin. . . It is almost impossible for a Number of People, and absolutely so, if they are idle, to live together, but they will very soon attempt to out vie each other, in Dress, Tables, and the like. This is the Case in the Massachusetts-Bay: Let a Man enter one of their Country Churches, and he will be struck with the Geiety of Ladies, in Silks and Lawn. . . . Boston is their pattern, and too, too closely imitated. . . . perhaps it may deserve the serious Consideration, of their *Society for the Promotion of Industry,* and *Employment of the Poor,* whether the first Step they took, should not be, to dissipate their Towns, and multiply the Number of their Farms.

B. O. Flower, *Civilization's Inferno, or, Studies in the Social Cellar,* 1893, pp. 23-24.

It is difficult to over-estimate the gravity of the problem presented by those compelled to exist in the slums of our populous cities, even when considered from a purely economic point of view. From the midst of this commonwealth of degredation there goes forth a moral contagion, scourging society in all its ramifications, coupled with an atmosphere of physical decay — an atmosphere reeking with filth, heavy with foul odors, laden with disease. In time of any contagion the social cellar becomes the hot-bed of death, sending forth myriads of fatal germs which permeate the air for miles around, causing thousands to die because society is too short-sighted to understand that the interest of its humblest member is the interest of all. The slums of our cities are the reservoirs of physical and moral death, an enormous expense to the state, a constant menace to society, a reality whose shadow is at once colossal and portentous. In time of social upheavals they will prove magazines of destruction; for, while revolution will not originate in them, once let a popular uprising take form and the cellars will re-inforce it in a manner more terrible than words can portray. Considered ethically, the problem is even more embarrassing and deplorable; here, as nowhere else in civilized society, thousands of our fellow-men are exiled from the enjoyments of civilization, forced into life's lowest stratum of existence, branded with that fatal word, "scum." If they seek to rise, society shrinks from them; they seem of another world; they are driven into the darkness of a hopeless existence and viewed much as were lepers in olden times.

Kenneth T. Jackson and Stanley K. Schultz, *Cities in American History,* 1972, p. 46.

[During the Colonial period, city] residents confronted some of the basic problems that have continued to plague urban dwellers down to the present. Congested housing, the dangers of fire, the ravages of disease, pollution in the streets and in the air, crime and inadequate police forces—such social problems are as old as our cities themselves. Only the nature of the collective urban response has changed over time.

Charles Abrams, *The City is the Frontier*, 1965, p. 354.

Every industrializing nation must go through a period of slum formation, and the United States is no exception.

Samuel M. Jones, Mayor of Toledo, "The New Patriotism: A Golden Rule Government for Cities," *Municipal Affairs Magazine*, September, 1899, p. 455.

The ethics of the wild beast, the survival of the strongest, shrewdest and meanest, have been the inspiration of our materialistic lives during the last quarter or half century. This fact, in our national history, has brought us to-day face to face with the inevitable result. We have cities in which a few are wealthy, a few are in what may be called comfortable circumstances, vast numbers are propertyless, and thousands are in pauperism and crime. Certainly, no reasonable person will contend that this is the goal that we have been struggling for; that the inequalities that characterize our rich and poor represent the ideas that the founders of this republic saw when they wrote that "All men are created equal."

Josiah Strong, *Our Country: Its Possible Future and Its Present Crisis*, 1885, pp. 128-130.

The city is the nerve center of our civilization. It is also the storm center. . . .

It is the city where wealth is massed; and here are the tangible evidences of it piled many stories high. Here the sway of mammon is widest, and his worship the most constant and eager. Here are luxuries gathered — everything that dazzles the eye, or tempts the appetite; here is the most extravagant expenditure. Here, also, is the *congestion* of wealth severest. . . . here . . . are the *ennui* of surfeit and the desparation of starvation. The rich are richer, and the poor are poorer, in the city than elsewhere; and, as a rule, the greater the city, the greater are the riches of the rich and the poverty of the poor.

Edward Banfield, Professor of Political Science—Harvard University, *The Unheavenly City: The Nature and Future of our Urban Crisis*, 1968, p. 6.

Most so-called urban problems are more characteristic of rural and small-town places than of cities. We have been conditioned to associate 'slums' with 'cities,' but in 1960 74 percent of all deteriorating and 81 percent of all dilapidated housing was *outside* cities of 100,000 or more in population, and 60 percent of all families in substandard housing lived outside metropolitan areas. The situation is similar in other matters.

ic* The New York Independent Reflector*, January 18, 1753.

It appears, Sir, from the most accurate Calculation, that we have in this City, at least a Thousand Dogs: I do not mean of the human kind; for the Extirpation of those, would prove such an Augean Stable, as to require a Labour perfectly Herculean. The Dogs I intend, are that real canine Species, which, with their dismal Howlings, disturb the Repose of the Healthy, break the interrupted Slumbers of the Sick, add fresh Horrors to the Night and render it perilous to traverse our Streets after the Sun is sunk beneath our Horizon. . . .

Henry George, *Social Problems*, 1883, p. 12.

. . . . let the policeman's club be thrown down or wrested from him and the fountains of the great deep are opened, and quicker than ever before chaos comes again. Strong as it may seem, our civilization is evolving destructive forces. Not desert and forest, but city slums and country roadsides are nursing the barbarians who may be to the new what the Hun and Vandal were to the old.

Report of the President's Commission on Law Enforcement and Administration of Justice, *The Challenge of Crime in a Free Society,* **1967, p. 6.**

Warring on poverty, inadequate housing, and unemployment, is warring on crime. A civil rights law is a law against crime. Money for schools is money against crime. Medical, psychiatric, and family-counseling services are services against crime. More broadly and most importantly, every effort to improve life in America's ''inner cities'' is an effort against crime.

Carl Feiss, Planning and Urban Renewal Consultant, "Progress and Poverty—1965 Version," *Law and Contemporary Problems,* **Winter 1965, p. 193.**

All of our housing and renewal programs stem from a sixty-five year old war on poverty beginning with the great work of Robert de Forest and Laurence Veiller, *Slums and Housing,* published in 1900. This and the impassioned pleas of Jacob Riis before World War I, the devoted lives of Jane Addams, Lilian D. Wald, Marie Simkovitch, the multitude of settlement house workers, child labor reformers, labor leaders seeking minimum wage laws and equitable working conditions, George Ford and Lawson Purdy fighting for minimum housing standards; these and countless more are among the precursors of the present attack on poverty. This history of these people and the movements they led are unsung in the school history books . . . . The battle is still being fought, so far the longest and least successful war of our history.

Thomas Jefferson, in *Urban America: A History With Documents,* **1974, pp. 482-483.**

I think our governments will remain virtuous for centuries as long as they are agricultural. When the get piled upon one another in large cities, as in Europe, they will become as corrupt as in Europe.

Irving Kristol, "The Negro in the City," in *A Nation of Cities: Essays on America's Urban Problems,* **1966, pp. 48-49.**

No one acquainted with the historical record can fairly doubt that American cities such as Boston and New York were much nicer places to live in before the immigrant mobs from Western Europe descended upon them in the 1830's and 40's. Our conventional history textbooks — sensitive to the feelings (and to the political power) of yesterday's immigrants, who are by now important people — tend to pass over this point in silence.

Has the growth of cities harmed the American political system?

Herbert Webb, *The Movement for Good Government in the United States, An Address Delivered Before the Men's Patriotic Guild,* **May 3, 1894 (Pamphlet).**

It would seem clear, then, that Bad City Government may be found existing very generally over the country, justifying the criticism of Mr. Bryce, the author of the 'American Commonwealth,' that the government of American cities is the one conspicuous failure in the United States. . .

Now, [the question of Good City Government] asks whether small bands of disciplined mercenaries are to prey upon public office, to falsify election returns, to bribe or intimidate voters, to be guilty of gross dishonesty, and yet retain office; whether great corporations are justified in purchasing legislation, in employing the machine as an agency for permanently corrupting politics in order that their ends may be the more effectually served; whether city franchises which are worth many million dollars to taxpayers shall be given by bribed City Councilmen to corporations for the asking?

Lincoln Steffens, first and greatest of the "Muckrakers," *The Shame of the Cities,* **1904, pp. 120-121.**

If a city treasurer runs away with $50,000 there is a great halloo about it. In St. Louis the regularly organized thieves who rule have sold $50,000,000 worth of franchises and other valuable municipal assets. This is the estimate made for me by a banker, who said that the boodlers got not one-tenth of the value of the things they sold, but were content because they got it all themselves. And as to the future, my boodling informants said that all the possessions of the city were listed for future sale, that the list was in existence, and that the sale of these properties was only postponed on account of accident—the occurrence of Mr. Folk.

Henry Ford Jones, "Municipal Corruption," *Political Science Quarterly,* **December 1904, p. 676.**

The growth of an extra-legal system of connecting the disconnected functions of government for administrative purposes certainly entails corruption, but it does not follow that under such circumstances it is disadvantageous although founded upon venality. Our ordinary system of municipal government is so opposed to all sound principles of business organization that it is highly creditable to our practical capacity for government that we are able to work at all. The graft system is bad, but it is better than the constitutional system as established by law.

Selected Bibliography

Anderson, Nels. *Industrial Urban Community.* New York: Meredith Corporation, 1971.

Anderson, Nels, and Lindeman, Eduard. *Urban Sociology.* New York: Alfred A. Knopf, 1928.

Banfield, Edward C. *The Unheavenly City: The Nature and Future of Our Urban Crisis.* Boston: Little, Brown, & Co., 1968.

Bartholomew, Harland. *Land Uses in American Cities.* Cambridge, Massachusetts: Harvard University Press, 1955.

Callow, Alexander B. Jr., ed. *American Urban History: An Interpretive Reader with Commentaries.* Fair Lawn, New Jersey: Oxford University Press, 1969.

Duhl, Leonard, ed. *The Urban Condition: People and Policy in the Metropolis.* New York: Simon and Schuster, 1963.

Feiss, Carl. "Progress and Poverty—1965 Version." *Law and Contemporary Problems,* 30 (Winter, 1965), 193.

Gilchrist, David T., ed. *Growth of Seaport Cities, 1790-1825.* Charlottesville: University Press of Virginia, 1967.

Glaab, Charles N. *The American City: Documentary History.* Homewood, Illinois: Dorsey Press, 1963.

Glaab, Charles N., and Brown, A. Theodore. *History of Urban America.* Riverside, New Jersey: MacMillan and Company, 1967.

Goodall, Leonard E. *American Metropolis.* Columbus, Ohio: Charles E. Merrill Publishing Co., 1968.

Gottman, Jean. *Megalopolis: Urbanized Northeastern Seabord of United States.* Cambridge: MIT Press, 1961.

Green, Constance M. *American Cities in Growth of the Nation.* New York: Harper and Row Publishers, Inc., 1967.

Green, Constance M. *Rise of Urban America.* New York: Harper and Row Publishers, Inc., 1965.

Griffith, Ernest S. *History of American City Government.* New York: Da Capo Press, Inc., 1938.

Griffith, Ernest S. *Modern Development of City Government in United Kingdom and United States.* Washington, D.C.: Macgrath Publishing Co., 1969.

Hauser, Philip M., and Schnore, Leo F., eds. *Study of Urbanization.* New York: John Wiley & Sons, Inc., 1965.

Hoover, Dwight W. "The Diverging Paths of American Urban History," *American Quarterly,* 20 (Summer Supplement, 1968), 296.

Jackson, Kenneth T., and Schultz, Stanley K., eds. *Cities in American History.* New York: Alfred A. Knopf, 1972.

Jacobs, Jane. *Death and Life of Great American Cities.* Westminster, Maryland: Modern Library, Inc., 1961.

Jacobs, Jane. *Economy of Cities.* Westminster, Maryland: Random House, 1969.

Krischner, Don S. *City and Country: Rural Responses to Urbanization in the 1920's.* Westport, Connecticut: Greenwood Press, Inc., 1970.

Lynch, Kevin. *The Image of the City.* Cambridge, Massachusetts: MIT Press, 1960.

McKelvey, Blake, *Emergence of Metropolitan American, 1915-1966.* New Brunswick, New Jersey: Rutgers University Press, 1968.

McKelvey, Blake. *Urbanization of America, 1860-1915.* New Brunswick, New Jersey: Rutgers University Press, 1963.

Madden, Carl H. "On Some Indications of Stability in the Growth of Cities in the United States." *Economic Development and Cultural Change,* 4 (1955-56), 236.

Madden, Carl H. "Some Spatial Aspects of Urban Growth in the United States." *Economic Development and Cultural Change,* 4 (1955-56), 371.

Mohl, Raymond A., and Betten, Neil, eds. *Urban America in Historical Perspective.* New York: Weybright and Talley, 1970.

Morrissett, Irving. "The Economic Structure of American Cities." *Papers and Proceedings of the Regional Science Association,* (1958), 239.

Mumford, Lewis. *Interpretations and Forecasts.* New York: McGraw-Hill, 1973.

Northam, Ray M. "Declining Urban Centers: 1940-1960." *Annals* (of the Association of American Geographers), 53 (1963), 50.

Pred, Allan. *Spatial Dynamics of U.S. Urban Growth, 1800-1914.* Cambridge, Massachusetts: MIT Press, 1970.

Schlesinger, Arthur M. *Rise of the City.* New York: Franklin Watts, Inc., 1933.

Schmitt, Peter J. *Back to Nature: The Arcadian Myth in Urban America.* Fair Lawn, New Jersey: Oxford University Press, 1969.

Schnore, Leo F., ed. *The New Urban History: Quantitative Explorations by American Historians.* Princeton: Princeton University Press, 1974.

Still, Bayrd. *Urban America: A History With Documents.* Boston: Little, Brown & Co., 1974.

Strong, Josiah. *Twentieth Century City.* New York: Arno Press, 1970 (reprint of 1898 edition).

Taylor, George R. "American Urban Growth Preceding the Railway Ages." *Journal of Economic History,* 27 (1967), 309.

Thernstrom, Stephan. *Poverty and Progress: Social Mobility in a Nineteenth Century City.* Cambridge, Massachusetts: Harvard University Press, 1964.

Thernstrom, Stephan, and Sennett, Richard, eds. *Nineteenth-Century Cities: Essays in the New Urban History.* New Haven: Yale University Press, 1969.

Vance, Rupert B., and Demerath, Nicholas J., eds. *Urban South.* Plainview, New York: Books for Libraries, Inc., 1954.

Weber, Adna F. *Growth of Cities in the Nineteenth Century.* Ithaca, New York: Cornell University Press, 1963.

Writh, Louis. "Urbanism as a Way of Life." *American Journal of Sociology,* 44 (July, 1938), 1.

THE AMERICAN FRONTIER: CRUCIBLE OF OUR NATIONAL CHARACTER?

Introductory Essay

In 1893, Frederick Jackson Turner, a relatively unknown professor at the University of Wisconsin, presented a paper to a convention of the American Historical Association. Entitled "The Significance of the Frontier in American History," Turner's hypothesis rocked the academic establishment. This rather brief paper assured his reputation, and has been called our most important historical work. Turner's ideas have been subjected to continuing debate, but a large number of scholars still agree with his basic thesis: "American history has been in a large degree the history of the colonization of the Great West. The existence of an area of free land, its continuous recession, and the advance of American settlement westward, explain American development." Though rich in controversy, Turner's vision of the growth of the Republic remains a legacy of considerable importance.

How, then, are we to understand the idea of America's frontier? Even the definition of a frontier is open to interpretation, running the gamut from a certain state of mind or way of viewing things to the Census Bureau's "two inhabitants per square mile of land," with representatives from all points in between: the western fringe at any point in time, where civilization meets barbarism, and so on. To add to the confusion, settlement was generally incremental: first the fur trader, then the hunter, the cattleman, and the pioneer farmer. Additionally, the advance of civilization did not occur in convenient blocks or orderly time spans, but in whirls and eddies: the opening of land following the Louisiana Purchase and Mexican War; the Homestead Act, its amendments and related legislation; the waves of immigration from Europe and Scandinavia; the discovery of gold in California and silver in Colorado and Nevada; as well as Eastern fashion in apparel, from beaver to buffalo to seal. The definition chosen and the emphasis placed on particular periods and phases of settlement will color one's approach to this subject.

What qualities are peculiar to the American character? Is there anything that distinguishes an American generically from a citizen of any other nation in the world? Most would agree that there are certain "American" qualities, but there is much disagreement on what those qualities are. Characteristics that occur more frequently and more intensely in America than in other countries, according to some observers, are an aggressive sense of nationalism, coupled with blind faith in democratic principles; a brash minimization of social distinctions and intolerance of ceremony; an abiding distrust of authority; an attitude of profligacy in the use of natural resources; and a boundless faith in the future and in the power of each individual to control his destiny.

It is simplistic to claim that the frontier by itself molded the American character. The people who settled the frontier region retained many elements of their national and ethnic heritage, as evidenced by communities that even today retain their Scandinavian and European customs and language. The same frontier environment that produced Jackson and Lincoln nurtured river pirates and lynch law. Yet one should not conclude that there has been no frontier influence on the American spirit—the frontier's contribution is strong and continuing.

In general, life in the new lands encouraged an increased sense of nationalism. The most vehement advocates of a weak national government were largely members of the original thirteen colonies and Texas, a state which had enjoyed a period as an independent nation before entering the Union. The frontier states were much more favorable to the national government. While the federal government was created by the thirteen original states, the frontier states owed their origin to the grace of Congress. Furthermore, there were compelling practical considerations. The national government controlled land sales, communication, and most importantly, defense. The stationing of troops on the frontier to protect settlers from Indian attack was the primary necessity of pioneer life. In short, the services provided by the federal government were of sufficient importance to override the natural tendency to prefer the more personal forms of local governmental bodies.

The frontier also contributed to American government by accenting and augmenting democratic principles. The frontier was an equalizer of men. An immigrant could build a cabin as easily as the son of Boston society, and a wealthy man had no natural advantage over a poor man in firing a rifle. The political arena was open to anyone who wanted to enter, and the "log cabin to White House" ideal was literally true. While the common man was not always elected to office, few had a chance who did not at least profess to be of common stock. During most of the time of Western settlement, the mark of a respectable man was simply land ownership, a requirement that could be easily fulfilled on the frontier.

These trends in government were strengthened by the fact that the frontier gave its people a chance to constantly experiment. Every township needed a charter, and every state a constitution. The change in attitudes worked by the frontier found easy avenues for concrete expression, and the constitutions of frontier states showed this through provisions for expansion of suffrage, increased numbers of elective posts, reduced qualifications for office, and so on. The more established states also felt the impact. The suggestive power of the frontier innovations, coupled with the loss of population experienced by the older states, forced modifications and adjustments in their own attitudes toward government.

The picture is not this simple, of course. While the frontier was an equalizer, it did not eliminate class differences. Men tried to recreate European fashions. Traditional titles and social rank were looked down upon, but many a frontiersman was proud to be called "Judge" or "Colonel," apellations that did not depend on any judicial or military experience. And while there were many innovations in state constitutions, significant segments of them were carbon-copies from other states. In general, however, the frontier unquestionably exerted a democratizing influence.

The frontier also encouraged an increased sense of self-reliance. The American ideal of the "rugged individualist" had its roots in our frontier heritage. In part, this was a natural selection process. The West initially attracted men who were able to exist without all the trappings and protection of organized society, men who were able to spend many months with very little human contact. The perils of frontier life served to quickly weed out those who could not measure up to these standards. The West, having a less formal social organization, made fewer demands on an individual's beliefs and behavior. The environment of the frontier was a seedbed of individualism.

There is another side to the coin, however. While the dangers of the frontier rewarded individualism, they also necessitated an increased sense of community spirit. Frontiersmen were quick to band together for collective defense against hostile Indians, as well as to perform functions an individual could not effectively accomplish: floating a load of furs down the Missouri, journeying to a salt lick, or raising a cabin.

The relative scarcity of human contact, the need for working together, and the constant reorganization of communities altered the concept of friendship. It became necessary to size up a stranger quickly and accurately and to form almost immediate friendships. This habit of spontaneous friendship still persists in our society, and is sometimes mistaken by foreigners for a lack of sincerity. Actually, it is a part of the same tradition as "Western hospitality."

The frontier also nurtured one of the most uniquely American characteristics—a boundless optimism, combined with a firm belief in the ability of the individual to direct his own fate. The discouraged and disheartened did not make the journey to unsettled lands. The privations that all settlers endured required a firm conviction that the end result would be well worth the effort. In large part, the frontier justified that conviction. The American frontier offered large tracts of amazingly fertile land, boundless forests, and abundant mineral resources. Anyone willing to invest the requisite work could confidently expect a huge return for his effort.

The opportunities available on the frontier gave rise to a very materialistic outlook on life, an earthy practicality at the expense of aesthetic considerations. In the early years, at least, the frontier did not attract the poet, the dreamer, or the intellectual so much as it did persons seeking wealth from the California mines, rich land, or vast quantities of fur. The rough conditions of the frontier demanded hard labor and material instincts. This system of priorities still finds expression today in the greater respect paid the "hard-headed businessman" as opposed to intellectuals. The frontier rewarded a materialistic temper, and the immense physical resources of the West seemed to offer no obstacles nor end to profit.

Concomitant with this materialistic attitude was a disregard for the preservation of natural resources. This perspective was understandable. The frontier was so enormous that there seemed to be no limit to its bounty. Overhunting, excessive timber cutting, and poor farming practices had no immediate ill effects. There was always more virgin land waiting. It was not uncommon for a settler to "wear out" three or four farms in a lifetime, and fur traders would regularly "trap out" a region. The long-term damage done to America is incalculable. Over-grazing in conjunction with the Winter of 1886 led to the virtual destruction of large portions of the cattle business. Poor land management contributed to the "dust bowls" of the 1930's; overhunting removed the beaver from large portions of the country, almost eliminated the buffalo and alligator, and exterminated the passenger pigeon, to name only a few of the better-known examples. But even this regrettable frontier influence on the American character has a bright side; the frontier legacy and nostalgia provide a large portion of the current impetus for conservation.

The frontier was also conducive to the American traits of innovation and risk-taking. Packing up one's family and moving West was the ultimate gamble, and those attracted to the frontier were much more willing to try new ideas and take greater risks than their Eastern counterparts. Given this attitude, it is easy to understand how the professional gambler's place in society advanced as one went further West. Although classed with the dregs of society in the East, one author maintains that in the frontier West, the professional gambler was exceeded in prestige only by the physician, and was far more respectable than the lawyer. The continuing novelty of the frontier experience and the unique problems it presented served as a continuing challenge to ingenuity. The requirements of ranching on the Great Plains, for instance, led to the adaptation of windmills, deep well-drilling techniques, and barbed wire. The vast distances involved stimulated development of better train systems and provided an immediate use for the telegraph. The frontier was both an incitement to thought and a ready market for innovations.

The frontier also had a role in the reduction of race prejudice. The individualistic, freedom-loving frontiersman found it hard to countenance the institution of slavery, and the prevalence of raw democracy confirmed his misgivings. In addition, there was little economic use for slaves, and for frontiersman could thus condemn the institution with little fear of economic loss. The rise of the cattle empires at the close of the Civil War promoted racial equality. Top cowhands were at a premium, and with many of the experienced Texas cowboys black or Mexican-American, trail bosses could not afford the luxury of prejudice. Fully a third of the Western cowboys were black or chicano. Many black familes settled in the West, and the Army stationed two black Army regiments (the 9th and 10th U.S. Cavalry) on the frontier. The enviable performance of these "buffalo soldiers" as they were called by the Indians, earned the respect of many. As a result, the black faced less prejudice on the frontier than anywhere else in the nation.

Prejudices, of course, run deep. The irrational hatred of many settlers toward the "redskins," had distinct racial overtones, and although black cowboys got equal pay, they were often assigned the dirtiest jobs. The emerging West witnessed outbursts of senseless violence against Chinese railroad workers and miners. The attitude of many Westerners was summed up by the fabled Judge Roy Bean, the "Law West of the Pecos," when dismissing a case against a cowboy accused of shooting a Chinese worker. Bean, after surveying a few tattered law books, remarked that he'd be damned if he could find any law against killing a Chinaman.

Many authors claim that American violence and the large number of people killed by firearms can be traced to our frontier heritage. Guns were an integral part of American frontier life. They were necessary to hunt game as well as to defend a homestead from Indian raids. The cowboy found so much value in the revolver for defense, food, and killing rattlesnakes and "varmints" that he developed the habit of wearing it continuously. The rough nature of frontier life increased the probability of violence and the constant availability of firearms worsened the consequences. Sociologist Bradford Smith believes that this heritage still manifests itself in American behavior. "This violence," he said, "has continued in such aspects of life as gangsterism, race riots, corrupt politics, union racketeering and the violent political attack."

Finally, the student might choose to examine the contribution of the frontier to America's literary heritage. Innumerable novels, movies, and television shows have been based on the frontier. The westward movement in history coincided with the romantic movement in literature. Beginning with James Fenimore Cooper, and continuing with Ned Buntline, Zane Grey, and Max Brand a romanticized conception of the frontier played a prominent part in literature. The rise of the silver screen brought us Tom Mix, Gary Cooper, and John Wayne. The perennial popularity of the West as a literary theme says a great deal about the American character.

The frontier contributed to the formation of the American character, but many scholars question whether it plays a role today. Even as early as 1890, the Superintendent of the Census reported that "the unsettled area has been so broken by isolated bodies of settlement that there can hardly be said to be a frontier line . . . It cannot, therefore, any longer have a place in the census reports." Frederick Jackson Turner himself believed that this development would set in motion a new series of forces, and that the influence of the frontier was waning. Franklin D. Roosevelt reflected this view when he declared:

> Our last frontier has long since been reached . . . Equality of opportunity as we have known it no longer exists . . . Our task now is not the discovery or exploitation of natural resources or necessarily producing more goods. It is the sober, less dramatic business of administering resources and plants already in hand, . . . of distributing wealth and products more equitably, of adapting existing economic organizations to the service of the people . . .

Embedded in the often inarticulate corridors of our collective past, the idea of a frontier retains a deep hold on our imagination and hopes. Historians and diplomats alike point to American expansionism, the Spanish-American War, the Panama Canal, the renewed interest in international affairs as attempts to find new frontiers. More recently, the space program's popularity is a Twentieth Century manifestation of the frontier vision. Some political scientists see frontier goodwill in American foreign aid programs. Political leaders still find the frontier attractive to voters, with John F. Kennedy entitling his legislative program the "New Frontier." William Faulkner wrote that the past is never dead, it's not even past. Our frontier past held the promise of future dreams. No Census Bureau proclamation can take away that promise, or limit the ability of the American people to find new frontiers.

Excerpted Documents

The frontier.

Nelson Keyes, *The American Frontier: Our Unique Heritage,* 1954, p. 12.

. . . one of the unique features of our heritage is the continuing influence of the frontier as it recurred time after time, and in area after area across the broad waist of North America. It was more than a "melting pot," and actually a long series of refiner's furnaces, burning the dross from older cultures and transmuting the remainder into a bright new metal with excellent characteristics. It was in the white heat of the frontier that American character was patterned and formed.

Ray Allen Billington, "Introduction," *The Significance of the Frontier in American History,* 1963, p. 2.

Timothy Dwight, President of Yale, saw no reason in 1821 to take Western expansion seriously. To him pioneers were merely social misfits—"too idle, too talkative, too passionate, too prodigal, and too shiftless to acquire either property or character." Another dyed-in-the-wool New Englander, Oliver Wendell Holmes, found amusement in comparing a typical Boston Brahmin with his "inelegant," "uncouth," "coarse," and "clumsy" counterpart in the West.

Kent Steckmesser, *The Westward Movement: A Short History,* 1969, p. 403.

Television has added a further dimension to the myth. The proliferation of westerns on the new medium in the mid-1950s caused a severe depression in the market for both western novels and run-of-the-mill western movies. Many of the TV series have exploited actual historical figures, notably Wild Bill Hickok, Wyatt Earp, and Daniel Boone. The longest-running series has been Gunsmoke, featuring Sheriff Matt Dillon of Dodge City. Tourists continually ask for information about this individual, and the Kansas Historical Society must regretfully advise that "no police officer of this name ever served in early Dodge City." Thus does the line between history and fable become blurred in the popular mind.

Walker Wyman and Clifton Kroger, *The Frontier in Perspective,* 1957, p. 231.

To the outside world there is a closer association of the Indian with the image of America than perhaps we are aware of. For example, Cooper's *The Last of the Mohicans* is not only read by every American schoolchild, it has been said to be the best known American novel in the world. So too, *Hiawatha,* Longfellow's poetic image of the Indian, is widely read and translated in other countries. Ivan Bunin, the Russian poet and novelist, "is probably as well recognized for his translation of *Hiawatha* as for any of his original works."

Walker Wyman and Clifton Kroger, *The Frontier in Perspective,* 1957, p. 231.

Our contacts with the Indians have affected our speech, our economic life, our clothing, our sports and recreations, certain indigenous religious cults, many of our curative practices, folk and concert music, the novel, poetry, drama, even some of our basic psychological attitudes, and one of the social sciences, anthropology.

William Hollon, *Frontier Violence: Another Look*, 1974, p. x.

. . . our folklore tends to support the image of Americans as tough, aggressive, and unafraid—real go-getters who tamed the wild frontier and never lost a war. "Winning is not just important, it's everything!" Success depends upon aggressiveness, whether on the football field, in the used-car lot, or behind the desk in the Oval Office of the White House. This may be why the frontier outlaw has endured so long in literature and legend. He went out and got what he wanted with his own two hands, frequently by violent means. His deeds, real and imaginary, have served as a culturally valid metaphor of how we have viewed ourselves.

Allen C. Bogue, *Turner and the Sociology of the Frontier*, 1968, p. 92.

In *Modern Homesteaders,* the social anthropologist, Evon Vogt, has studied a New Mexican community which was established in the early 1930's by settlers who left the main current of southwestern migration to California and sought to carve out homes for themselves on the Pueblo Plateau to the south of Gallup. To a far greater extent than any other community discussed here, the circumstances under which "Homestead" was founded paralleled frontier conditions during the nineteenth century.

. . .Vogt's central concern was with the values, or more precisely the value orientations, of the residents. In the behavior of the homesteaders, "these revealed themselves as a strong stress upon *individualism* . . .; an accent upon . . . *hopeful mastery over nature* . . .; an emphasis upon the *future* . . ."

Thomas D. Clark, *Frontier America*, 1969, p. 4.

In its broader meaning the history of the frontier is the account of the molding of people of diverse origins and motives into a fairly homogeneous national group. In its more localized implications, it is the story of thousands of individuals, tiny communities, counties, towns, and sections making primitive beginnings and growing into mature and permanent political, economic, and social institutions.

Thomas D. Clark, *Frontier America*, 1969, p. 22.

In the latter half of the twentieth century there are still discernible underlying influences of frontier origin in national society, politics, and economics. In large measure American folk nostalgia is frontier based. Much of the national literature and historical writings treat western themes, and scholars continue to search for basic facts and sources and to apply fresh interpretations to the pioneering era of American history. So long as the memory of the great pioneer experience remains bright, or historians probe searchingly into the past, the westward movement will remain an important element of our history.

Ray Allen Billington, *Westward Expansion*, 1974, p. 654.

The rosy optimism with which the people of the United States contemplate the future has long been recognized as distinct. The frontiersman was a confirmed optimist and with good reason; life in a new land where progress was the order of the day, where continuous improvement was inevitable, encouraged the belief that tomorrow would surely be better than today. Nowhere was the "go-ahead" spirit better exemplified than in the successive Wests of the nineteenth century; with unbounded resources awaiting exploitation, with a continent to be robbed of its riches,with speculation in the air, pioneers were cockily confident of a better future as they hurried to reach the pot that they knew to be at the end of the rainbow. Faith in the future was a built-in by-product of frontier abundance.

Ray Allen Billington, *Westward Expansion*, 1974, p. 653.

The creation of wealth by the continuing exploitation of successive layers of natural resources, and the steady flow of that wealth eastward, helped engender a state of mind in which material progress became the sole objective of many people. Money was the talisman that would open the door to elevated social status, the key to political influence, the portal to cultural magnificence. Money, to many frontiersmen and to many Americans after them, was the primary objective in life. Materialistic attitudes, long associated with the United States by the citizens of other lands, are traceable in part to frontier affluence.

Ray Allen Billington, *American Heritage*, April 1958, p. 89.

Some statesmen and scholars have rebelled against what they call Turner's "Space Concept of History," with all that it implies concerning the lack of opportunity for the individual in an expansionless land. They insist that modern technology has created a whole host of new "frontiers"—of intensive farming, electronics, mechanics, manufacturing, nuclear fission, and the like—which offer diverse outlets to individual talents.

Ray Allen Billington, *American Heritage*, April 1958, p. 89.

Harry Truman envisaged his "Truman Doctrine" as a device to extend and defend the frontiers of democracy throughout the globe. While popular belief in the superiority of America's political institutions was far older than Turner, that belief rested partly on the frontier experience of the United States.

Ray Allen Billington, *Westward Expansion*, 1974, p. 660.

The end of the era of westward expansion, although most notable in its effect on the farmer, was not without influence on other aspects of American life. One immediate result was to strengthen popular support for the nation's newly launched imperialistic foreign policy. To say that the vanishing frontier was alone responsible for the jingoism of the 1890's would be a gross exaggeration; improved transportation facilities, the demand of industrialists for markets, the export of surplus capital abroad, and the example set by European nations were all equally important. Yet, for the man on the street, there was a direct connection between the Census Bureau's announcement of 1890 and the need for overseas possessions. With opportunity drawing to a close within the nation's borders, he reasoned, the government's duty was to provide areas for exploitation elsewhere. Hence he gave enthusiastic approval as his leaders grabbed Puerto Rico and the Philippines from Spain in 1898, added the Hawaiian Islands and other Pacific possessions during the next years, muscled Panama from Colombia in 1903, and extended American rule over the Caribbean during the next decade. To many Americans these lands were new frontiers, waiting development by a new type of pioneer from the United States.

Nationalism.

Frederick Jackson Turner, *The Significance of the Frontier in American History*, 1963, p. 51.

Mobility of population is death to localism, and the western frontier worked irresistibly in unsettling population. The effects reached back from the frontier and affected profoundly the Atlantic coast and even the Old World.

Frederick Jackson Turner, *The Significance of the Frontier in American History*, 1963, p. 50.

It was this nationalizing tendency of the West that transformed the democracy of Jefferson into the national republicanism of Monroe and the democracy of Andrew Jackson. The West of the War of 1812, the West of Clay, and Benton, and Harrison, and Andrew Jackson, shut off by the Middle States and the mountains from the coast sections, had a solidarity of its own with national tendencies. On the tide of the Father of Waters, North and South met and mingled into a nation. Interstate migration went steadily on—a process of cross-fertilization of ideas and institutions.

Ray Allen Billington, *Westward Expansion*, 1974, p. 655.

. . . nationalism was heightened by the frontier habit of moving about, which lessened local attachments, and by the partnership between state and national governments needed to build roads and canals, dispose of the public domain, and in many other ways care for the needs of an expanding people. The ardent nationalism that characterized the United States during the nineteenth century, and that persists today in more sophisticated form, was in part a product of the pioneering experience.

Ray Allen Billington, *Westward Expansion*, 1974, p. 654.

The presence along the frontiers of unique opportunities for self-improvement similarly accentuated other traits that are today considered typically American. One was the distinctive form of individualism that Europeans still associate with those reared in the United States. To the pioneer, every man was a self-dependent individual, fully capable of caring for himself without the aid of society. If he fell by the wayside he had only himself to blame, for he had not taken proper advantage of his opportunities. Hence the frontier was distrustful of governmental meddling with affairs of the individual. The successful man should be let alone to achieve greater success; the unsuccessful should not be pampered for he could succeed if he tried.

Social leveling.

Thomas D. Clark, *Frontier America*, 1969, p. 14.

It was hard to maintain artificial social stratification where one's human contacts were limited and where differences in economic conditions remained undefined. Because of this condition, frontier society more often than not found a common level where one man was socially as acceptable as another.

Thomas D. Clark, *Frontier America*, 1969, p. 4.

When settlers came in contact with woods, prairies and plains, they started life anew at elementary levels. Social and economic advances were almost always achieved from the same simple beginnings. The frontier was the place of trail and ground breaking in new country, and of establishing afresh social and political institutions. Settlers coming into contact with the vast areas of virgin lands and mineral resources behaved much alike, whether in the pine lands cotton belt or the mountainous gold diggings.

Ray Allen Billington, *Westward Expansion*, 1974, p. 650.

. . . in the successive Wests, the relatively propertyless individual had a better chance to improve his social and economic status than in the heavily populated Easts, whether as farmer, merchant, professional man, or speculator. There he found comparatively unutilized resources as well as a plastic social order that had not yet been solidified by the passage of time. One gave him an improved opportunity to amass wealth and property, the other, a chance to rise in society on a scale unrivaled elsewhere. Class lines existed along the frontiers, but they were less firmly drawn, and more easily breached, than in older communities.

Frederick Paxson, *History of the American Frontier*, 1924, p. 97.

In few communities have wealth, station in life, education, or refined taste brought less immediate profit to their possessor than on the frontier. It was as hard for the rich as for the poor to build the cabin, clear the cornfield, extract the first unwilling crop, and raise the children through the perils of childhood. There were few things that money could buy, in the form of either goods or service; and small leisure for the enjoyment of intellectual or social pleasure. There was grinding labor for all who made life go. The occupations at any stage of its development were identical for every family on a new frontier. The necessity to live the common life made them resentful of the pretensions of persons who tried to live it differently. In their minds the distinctions of the older States that were based on property or station lost much of their significance. Economic and social equality were hard facts that they could not evade.

Frederick Paxson, *History of the American Frontier*, 1924, p. 96.

Civilization is founded upon the subordination of individual aspiration and accomplishment to the common good, but not many men have loved the giving up that this entails. Along the frontier, men came to accept the idea of equality with greater ease than usual, because as they looked around them, they saw men equal.

William Katz, *The Black West*, 1971.

A recent study by historian Kenneth W. Porter indicates that black cowboys probably suffered less because of discrimination than almost any other occupation open equally to black and white at the time anywhere in the nation. Many black cowboys were hired, according to a white cowpuncher, "to do the hardest work around an outfit"—as bronco-busters. Very few rose to the position of foreman or trail boss, but there was also no discrimination in their wages. Sleeping arrangements often found ranch owner, trail boss, black and white cowboys in the same shack or under the same blankets.

William Katz, *The Black West*, 1971.

The black cowboys found less discrimination out on the trail than in town, more equality back on the ranch than in the frontier communities that were springing up everywhere. Generally speaking, the less stable a community, particularly if it had no women, the more equality if offered its black cowboys. The arrival of "civilization" and white women meant that the racial bars were about to be erected. Perhaps that is why many a black cowboy enjoyed life on the open plains more than city visits, and headed further west as frontier communities became stabilized.

Ray Allen Billington, *Westward Expansion*, 1974, p. 10.

Scandinavians and Germans in Wisconsin found no barriers before them, but Mexicans in the southwestern borderland were denied the right to own slaves, hold equal jobs, or attend school. Frontiering did not automatically wipe out the class distinctions of prejudices carried westward by the pioneers; it did allow a greater number (including many aliens) to step aboard the escalator, and it did offer a hand up to easterners who had been handicapped by improper lineage or social position.

Democracy.

Allen C. Bogue, *Turner and the Sociology of the Frontier*, 1968, p. 92.

. . . there was a greater degree of political participation on the frontier than in older communities. This resulted from the efforts of individuals to gain status through leadership in a relatively unstructured society, from the effort to establish group ties, and from the greater relative significance of the economic rewards of politics in the frontier community.

Frederick Jackson Turner, *The Significance of the Frontier in American History*, 1963, p. 51.

The frontier States that came into the Union in the first quarter of a century of its existence came in with democratic suffrage provisions, and had reactive effects of the highest importance upon the older States whose peoples were being attracted there. An extension of the franchise became essential. It was *western* New York that forced an extension of suffrage in the constitutional convention of that State in 1821; and it was *western* Virginia that compelled the tide-water region to put a more liberal suffrage provision in the constitution framed in 1830, and to give to the frontier region a more nearly proportionate representation with the tide-water aristocracy. The rise of democracy as an effective force in the nation came in with western preponderance under Jackson and William Henry Harrison, and it meant the triumph of the frontier—with all of its good and with all of its evil elements.

Ray Allen Billington, *Westward Expansion*, 1974, p. 652.

The Wests also showed a tendency to extend the elective process to a wide range of officials; governors, legislators, school-board members, and even judges were chosen by the people. Later in the nineteenth century the newer states of the West pioneered in bringing legislation under popular control with such devices as the initiative, referendum, and recall. Even more pronounced was the tendency of frontier communities to award governing posts to ordinary citizens who had risen from the ranks.

Frederick Paxson, *History of the American Frontier*, 1924, p. 252.

The first scattered farmers of a region knew that they were to become leaders in local and county government; that improvements would surely come; that statehood was inevitable. The mature men were entitled to believe that the senatorial toga might descend upon them; and they brought up their boys in the belief that any of them might be President. The American worship of the self-made man has been founded in this general knowledge that most Americans in the beginning were self-made.

Thomas D. Clark, *Frontier America*, 1969, p. 19.

The frontier was not, of course, the birthplace of the common man, but in few regions in history has he thrived so well. Every man was a potential officeholder who could advance as far as the voters would let him. He was most tender on the subject of taxation, of legislation that discriminated against his section and of certain general national policies.

Individualism.

Frederick Jackson Turner, *The Significance of the Frontier in American History*, 1963, p. 51.

. . . the frontier is productive of individualism. Complex society is precipitated by the wilderness into a kind of primitive organization based on the family. The tendency is anti-social. It produces antipathy to control, and particularly to any direct control. The tax gatherer is viewed as a representative of oppression.

Ray Allen Billington, *American Heritage*, April 1958, p. 87.

. . . the abundant resources and the greater social mobility of frontier areas did instill into frontiersmen a uniquely American form of individualism. Even though they may be sheeplike in following the decrees of social arbiters or fashion dictators, Americans today, like their pioneer ancestors, dislike governmental interference in their affairs. "Rugged individualism" did not originate on the frontier any more than democracy or nationalism did, but each concept was deepened and sharpened by frontier conditions.

Neighborliness.

William Hollon, *Frontier Violence: Another Look*, 1974, p. 212.

Sir Rose Lambert Price, an Englishman who traveled extensively throughout the United States in the 1870's, observed that he had never met with more kindness, hospitality, and respect for the rights of others than in the American West: "Never once . . . in the meanest ranche [sic] or the most primitive mining camp did I ever experience the slightest discourtesy or lack of kindness." Another Englishman wrote that "Even the rough western men, the hardy sons of the Indian frontier, accustomed from boyhood to fighting for existence, were hospitable and generous to a degree hard to find in more civilized life.

Nelson Keyes, *The American Frontier: Our Unique Heritage,* **1954, p. 11.**

Men sought the frontiers here not only for land, but also for freedom. As long as one's neighbors' chimneys were not too close, individualism could grow to be pretty rugged. Men and women thrown largely upon their own resources learned to be self-sufficing as well as self-sustaining, and in some instances might carry such sufficiency to rather unfortunate ends. But with frequent threats from the displaced natives close at hand, or from a capricious nature overhanging their efforts, there was almost always present some call for co-operative action. There were times when neighbors either stood together and both weathered the storm, or they ran the rather certain risk of perishing separately.

Resource waste.

Thomas D. Clark, *Frontier America,* **1969, p. 19.**

Frontiersmen . . . were economically prodigal. With ax and torch they slashed through the forests. Soils were dredged of their fertility, deep gullies gashed the face of the earth, and impoverished homesteads were deserted when the owners moved away. An old frontier adage said that many a man had buried three wives and had worked the fourth down to skin and bones, that he had gutted three farms, and that he was growing gullies on the fourth. To their lasting discredit, many frontiersmen prostituted nature's bounty. They developed profligate habits which were shameful in the eyes of frugal foreigners. Many of the charges of prodigality made against Americans have arisen from abuse of the continent's land resources.

Ray Allen Billington, *Westward Expansion,* **1974, p. 654.**

The American tradition of wastefulness is traceable to the pioneering experience. The frontiersman had a dual reason to scorn conservation of the natural wealth about him: resources were so plentiful that not even the most fevered imagination could picture their depletion, and wealth could be gained more rapidly by their exploitation than by their preservation. So pioneers slaughtered the virgin forests, raped the mineral wealth, and mined the fertility from the soil with no thought of posterity; this was the road to fortune, not scrimping and conserving. The conservationist cause has been preached with some success in the twentieth-century United States, but among the people the habit of wastefulness persists. The United States is today the land of the no-deposit-no-return bottle, the beer can, the disposable tissues.

Work ethic.

Ray Allen Billington, *Westward Expansion,* **1974, p. 653.**

Hard work was the gospel of frontiersmen. With wealth the certain destination of all who labored, and with every pioneer community measuring its progress toward civilization by the dedication of its inhabitants, there was no place in pioneer life for the sluggard or the lazy. All must labor for the common good no less than the personal good; those who would not had no place in the social order and were pushed aside. Although machines and automation have in the twentieth century usurped many of the tasks formerly assigned to men, this attitude persists in the United States. The prolonged siesta of other lands, the leisurely luncheons, the hour-long teas, are unknown; only the recently introduced "coffee break" has intruded on the routine of dedicated labor.

Thomas D. Clark, *Frontier America,* **1969, p. 15.**

To fail to comprehend the place of grinding, sweaty, devitalizing labor is to fail to understand the most important source of economic success on the frontier. Work became a habit of the settler, and throughout American history it has remained a national virtue—whether in the field behind a plow, or in a store behind the counter.

To this extent the frontier adopted the old Puritan trait of glorifying labor. To gain a stake on the frontier usually required an enormous expenditure of energy.

Selected Bibliography

Allen, Harry Cranbrook. *Bush and Backwoods: A Comparison of the Frontier in Australia and the United States.* East Lansing: Michigan State University Press, 1959.

American Heritage. *Book of the Pioneer Spirit.* New York: American Heritage Publishing Company, 1959.

Babcock, Clarence Merton. *The American Frontier: A Social and Literary Record.* New York: Holt, Rinehart & Winston, 1965.

Barraclough, G. "Metropolis and Macrocosm." *Past and Present,* 3 (May, 1954).

Bartlett, Richard A. *The New Country: A Social History of the American Frontier, 1776-1890.* New York: Oxford University Press, 1974.

Billington, Ray Allen. *The American Frontier.*Washington, D.C.: Service Center for Teachers of History (American Historical Association), 1958.

Billington, Ray Allen. *America's Frontier Heritage.* New York: Holt, Rinehart & Winston, 1966.

Billington, Ray Allen. *The Frontier Thesis: Valid Interpretation of American History?* New York: Holt, Rinehart & Winston, 1966.

Billington, Ray Allen. "How the Frontier Shaped American Character." *American Heritage,* 9 (April, 1958).

Billington, Ray Allen. *The Westward Movement in the United States.* Princeton: Van Nostrand, 1959.

Boynton, Percy Holmes. *The Rediscovery of the Frontier.* New York: Greenwood Press, 1968.

Clark, Thomas D. *Frontier America; The Story of the Westward Movement.* New York: Scribner, 1959.

Clark, Thomas D. *Three American Frontiers: Writings of Thomas D. Clark.* Lexington: University of Kentucky Press, 1968.

Froneck, Thomas. *Voices from the Wilderness: The Frontiersman's Own Story.* New York: McGraw-Hill, 1974.

Gard, Wayne. *Frontier Justice.* Norman, Oklahoma: University of Oklahoma Press, 1949.

Gobrice, Ralph Henry. *The Lure of the Frontier: A Story of Race Conflict.* New York: Yale University Press, 1929.

Greenway, John. *Australia: The Last Frontier.* New York: Dodd Mead, 1973.

Hofstadter, Richard. *Turner and the Sociology of the Frontier.* New York: Basic Books, 1968.

Hollon, William Eugene. *Frontier Violence: Another Look.* New York: Oxford University Press, 1974.

Jordan, Philip Dillon. *Frontier Law and Order: Ten Essays.* Lincoln, Nebraska: University of Nebraska Press, 1970.

Katz, William Loren. *The Black West.* Garden City, N.Y.: Doubleday, 1971.

Keyes, Nelson Beacher. *The American Frontier: Our Unique Heritage.* New York: Hanover House, 1954.

Klose, Nelson. *A Concise Study Guide to the American Frontier.* Lincoln, Nebraska: University of Nebraska Press, 1964.

Nash, Roderick. *Wilderness and the American Mind.* New Haven: Yale University Press, 1973.

Parish, John C. *The Persistence of the Westward Movement and Other Essays.* Berkeley: University of California Press, 1945.

Paxson, Frederic L. *When the West is Gone.* New York: Holt, 1930.

Sharp, Paul F. "Three Frontiers: Some Comparative Studies of Canadian, American, and Australian Settlement." *Pacific Historical Review,* 24 (November, 1955).

Simonson, Harold Peter. *The Closed Frontier: Studies in American Literary Tragedy.* New York: Holt, Rinehart & Winston, 1970.

Smith, Bradford. *Why We Behave Like Americans.* Philadelphia: J.B. Lippincott Company, 1957.

Steckmesser, Kent L. *The Westward Movement: A Short History.* New York: McGraw-Hill, 1969.

Taylor, George Roger, ed. *The Turner Thesis Concerning the Role of the Frontier in American History.* Boston: Heath and Company, 1956.

Tocqueville, Alexis de. *Democracy in America.* New York: Knopf, 1945.

Tryon, Warren Stenson. *A Mirror for Americans: Life and Manners in the United States, 1790-1870, As Recorded by American Travelers.* Chicago: University of Chicago Press, 1952.

Turner, Frederick Jackson. *Frontier and Section.* Englewood Cliffs, N.J.: Prentice-Hall, Inc., 1961.

Turner, Frederick Jackson. *The Frontier in American History.* New York: Holt, Rinehart & Winston, 1966.

Turner, Frederick Jackson. *The Significance of the Frontier in American History.* New York: Ungar, 1963.

Wade, Richard D. *The Urban Frontier: The Rise of Western Cities, 1790-1830.* Cambridge: Harvard University Press, 1959.

Wallace, Henry A. *New Frontiers.* New York: Rexnal and Hitchcock, 1934.

Webb, Walter Prescott. *Divided We Stand: The Crisis of a Frontierless Democracy.* New York: Farrar and Rinehart, 1937.

Westemeyer, Ina Faye. *Westward Movement: A Book of Readings on Our Changing Frontiers.* New York: Appleton-Century, 1939.

Wyman, Walker Demarquis, and Kroger, Clifton B. *The Frontier in Perspective.* Madison: University of Wisconsin Press, 1957.

THE SPRAWLING CITY

Introductory Essay

Men have dreamed for centuries of ideal cities, even the city of God, but have succeeded in building only mortal cities that display the full range of human experience, from the finest artistic and intellectual achievements to the worst forms of degradation and suffering. For Theodore Parker, cities were "the fireplaces of civilization whence light and heat radiated out into the dark world." For Thomas Jefferson, cities were sores sapping the strength of the body politic. While Jefferson's agrarian view has tended to dominate American attitudes toward cities, most Americans now live in them and defend their worth while they deal with their problems.

But what is a city? The Bureau of the Census defines a city as a settlement of 2500 people or more; according to this definition, 70% of the population of the United States now live in cities. Such a definition may have been adequate at the time of the Declaration of Independence when Philadelphia, with about 30,000 people, was a big city. Today when metropolitan areas consisting of a nuclear city surrounded by satellites have well over a million people, we may need to distinguish between kinds of cities in order to differentiate their advantages and disadvantages. A metropolis (mother city) is generally construed as a major city and its environs. A metropolitan area, according to the Bureau of the Census, has a population of 50,000 or more. The terms megalopolis and conurbation were created specifically for the "unique cluster of metropolitan areas of the Northeastern seaboard of the United States." All of these terms attempt to describe what is popularly called the "urban sprawl," the creeping growth of a large nuclear city until it absorbs outlying towns, villages, and countryside; the resulting maze of densely populated urban sections, sparsely populated open sections, and moderately populated suburban sections weave city and country together into a new whole. Some experts believe this worldwide phenomenon may be as significant for civilization as the settlement of nomadic tribes around the Mediterranean. No ancient city could compete in size with an average modern metropolis. Rome had little more than three quarters of a million people, and even by 1800 no western city had surpassed the million mark. By 1900, however, eleven western metropolises had over a million people. Thirty years later, twenty seven metropolises had over a million,

and cities of a hundred thousand proliferated. In the United States, nearly half the population now live in urban areas of one million or more. As Charles Abrams notes, "The city has become the frontier."

Amid the various descriptions of cities posited by political scientists, economists, geographers, sociologists, anthropologists, and historians, two factors stand out: the city as a body of heterogeneous individuals drawn from all over the country in order to work together, and the city as the source and disseminator of culture and technology. What had been separate functions in an agrarian society become concentrated inside the city walls into a single "organism." Originally the city had been designed to represent the cosmos, to unite heaven and earth, whether by means of ziggurats or cathedrals. Historically the city has at least united multitudes from a given countryside through a process of what Lewis Mumford calls "implosion." But now, as Mumford observes, cities seem to develop through "explosion," and this characteristic may reflect the most fundamental changes of our era: "We live in fact in an exploding universe of mechanical and electronic invention, whose parts are moving at a rapid pace ever further and further away from their human center, and from any rational, autonomous human purposes. This technological explosion has produced a similar explosion in the city itself: the city has burst open and scattered its complex organs and organizations over the entire landscape."

American cities were susceptible to this explosiveness from the start. Lacking the historical roots of European cities where layer upon layer of walls and buildings dictated growth patterns, American cities could unfold freely. They were all, in a sense, "new towns." Unfortunately, efforts to control this unfolding were usually stymied by speculators who were more concerned with profits and expedience than with community welfare. In Washington, a real estate syndicate engaged in disastrous dealings that undermined Pierre Charles L'Enfant's overall planning. In Philadelphia, capitalists subverted William Penn's proposal for parks and boulevards. Most American cities underwent similar experiences which would exact a high cost in the decades that followed.

American cities also benefited from rich resources that seemed to promise endless possibilities for expansion. While European cities were sometimes stifled amid villages all feeding on the same limited countryside, American cities could reach into great hinterlands. As the seaboard cities competed to develop these regions, settlements in the west "spearheaded" the frontier, as Richard C. Wade has shown, forcing a re-examination of Frederick Jackson Turner's thesis that the frontier has been the determining factor in American history. By 1800, the ground had been broken for every important city in the Northwest, except Chicago, Milwaukee, and Indianapolis. As the Nineteenth Century advanced, the extension of railroads and the mechanization of agriculture prompted the explosion of cities as industrial centers. Raw materials could be brought, and goods sent, over longer distances, and fewer farmers cultivating less land could provide more food than ever before. While the cities spread across the abandoned farms, the dislocated rural population joined the foreign immigrants pouring into the cities to become laborers.

The rapid and unregulated growth of cities inevitably gave rise to serious practical problems that inhibited the civilized life the city was supposed to offer. Many problems, such as transportation deficiencies, could be corrected through technology. Architectural innovations and the invention of the elevator soon got the city off the ground. Other problems, like inadequate sanitation, were far more serious since they threatened life itself. In the muddy unpaved streets, hogs, dogs, geese, rats, and even vultures rummaged through refuse and carrion. What they ignored contaminated water supplies. By the middle of the Nineteenth Centruy, major cities like New York had constructed sewers for only about a fourth of the residents. Slums were breeding grounds for typhoid, typhus, dysentery, cholera, and, in the South, yellow fever. Disease was for a long time considered to be God's scourge of the wicked, but as the germ theory gained adherents, demands for realistic measures were made. The turning point came in 1883 with the isolation of the microorganism responsible for cholera. By the end of the Nineteenth Century, most cities had proper sanitation facilities and water purification systems.

A more complex problem was the inextricable knot of poor health, poverty, crime, and degradation that afflicted, and still afflicts, the slum, threatening the principle of equality of opportunity that the city hoped to fulfill. In midcentury New York ragpickers and bonegatherers scratched the streets for a living in "Rag-Pickers Paradise." An investigating committee was greeted by the odor of boiled bones and baskets of putrifying calves' heads. By 1893, over half of New York's population lived in tenements, but strong housing codes were not enacted until the Twentieth Century. Even then, new slums appeared. Harlem, for example, was trans-

formed into a world famous slum during the great Black migration of the 1920's. Not only did Blacks confront minimal employment opportunities and high rents, they were exposed to high rates of disease and death (42% higher than the rest of the city from 1923 to 1927). The infant mortality rate was particularly high, and rickets (resulting from malnutrition) was common among children. Snake oils, herbs, and magic couldn't cure these ills, nor could incomplete and unenforced laws. While urban renewal in recent years has helped, it has not fully eliminated these problems. It might, of course, be argued that progress is being made since the earlier waves of Eastern European immigrants generally escaped to better lives and since some Blacks now seem to be doing the same. Just where the Blacks are moving, whether to better or worse conditions, is still controversial.

Meanwhile the city's political problems have posed a complicated threat to the democratic principles of government the city is obligated to uphold. Within the city, conflict of jurisdictions and fragmentation of authority have hampered action while the multiplicity of issues and candidates often has confused the voter. The kind of decentralized local government that works well in the village can become a hindrance in the city. Corruption, of course, has been the most significant political problem. New York's Tweed Ring, Philadelphia's Gas Ring, St. Louis' Butler Machine, Kansas City's Pendergasts, and San Francisco's "Blind Boss" Buckley emerged as types of bad government, but they also performed some necessary functions that the city had neglected. Bosses bound the rapidly expanding city together with a communications network capable of getting jobs done (including the sordid ones); they furthermore provided welfare for the immigrant poor and prepared them to succeed or at least to survive in America. However, graft and disruption of the elective process spurred reformists to seek new techniques of city government, professionalization of public servants, and "home rule" freeing the city from the rural dominated state legislature.

In recent years, a host of other problems have assailed the city; pollution, energy, and mass transportation are daily news topics. More difficult to treat, the psychological and social malfunctions accelerate as the city expands. *Mechanization, depersonalization, isolation* and *fragmentation* are abstractions commonly used to describe what the sociologist likes to call *anomie* or the social void. While the strictly organized system of interdependence threatens to turn human beings into tools of technology and of each other, the "repressed energies" threaten to erupt in anything from alcoholism to riots. The high urban crime rate is often explained in these terms. Whether man's mind forged manacles, or economic and historical conditions are to blame has been the subject of debate for several centuries, but little has been done other than to trust in improvements of material well-being as a pacifier. Long before megalopolis, Melville recognized the possible conclusion of this "dehumanization" in *Bartleby, The Scrivener*. Bartleby, screened in a cubicle with a small window looking out a brick wall on Wall Street, finally refuses to perfom any task with the polite phrase "I would prefer not to," until he even refuses to live.

If the city should succeed in mitigating these problems, then its value as a center of civilization may become meaningful for everyone. Certainly the city has its appeal—at its best offering diversity, stimulation, and opportunity. Educational and cultural centers thrive in the city. Men of achievement, according to statistics, seem more likely to come from the city. One investigation found that "the main factors in producing scientific and other forms of intellectual performance seem to be density of population, wealth, opportunity, and institutions and social traditions and ideals." Furthermore, as Arthur Schlesinger argues, the city has been a major moving force in American democracy. The eastern cities instigated and organized the struggle for independence. Schlesinger also observes that the city played a crucial part in realizing the Jeffersonian goal of public education, in promoting public health, and in protecting free speech: "It was townsfolk who led in founding schools and colleges. The protracted battle to establish innoculation as a preventive against smallpox was fought out in the cities. The first great victory for freedom of the press was won by a Philadelphia lawyer defending a New York editor." Particularly striking is Samuel Stouffer's 1954 study indicating that urban residents are far more tolerant of dissenting minorities than rural residents. Urban residents also participate more actively in elections

Reformist criticism of the city's failures to mitigate its problems often has been couched in optimistic language pointing to the city's potential, but an older tradition of criticism is more pessimistic. In this era of the camper, the suburb, and the back to nature cereal, no one should be surprised to find that agrarian values have attracted many of the best minds that our culture has begotten. The city has repeatedly been condemned as a source of disease, corruption, artificiality, loss of innocence, and personal isolation, all summed up in the archetype of the underworld. The country, on the other hand, has received a vigorous philosophical defense that can still be heard through the current sentimental parodies. Remembering the pastoral tradition that goes back to Hesiod, Thomas Jefferson maintained that the farmer is the economic, political, and moral mainstay of the state: "The proportion which the aggregate of the other classes of citizens bears in any state to that of its husbandmen is the proportion of its unsound to its healthy parts." Not only would

the work on a farm keep one physically and morally healthy, the ownership of a farm would make one self-sufficient and independent. Because Jefferson feared the city as a source of corruption ("the mobs of great cities add just so much to the support of pure government as sores to the strength of the human body"), he hoped that the yellow fever epidemics would have the beneficial result of discouraging the expansion of cities. Jefferson's use of disease imagery to denigrate cities is not just a figure of speech; it is based on the prevailing theory that disease arose from miasmas and manifested itself in both physical and moral symptoms. This view underlies most Nineteenth Century criticism of urban life and curiously anticipates the Twentieth Century view that such ills as crime, suicide, alcoholism and drug addiction are products not merely of isolated causes in individual cases but of the entire economic and social milieu. During the Napoleonic Wars, Jefferson of course did concede the necessity of industrialization when the danger of overdependence on Europe for manufactured goods became apparent, but he later returned to his initial agrarian position.

This position would be reiterated by other major figures like James Madison, Andrew Jackson, and William Jennings Bryan who exclaimed in his 1896 Cross of Gold Speech: "The great cities rest upon our broad and fertile prairies. Burn down your cities, and leave our farms, and your cities will spring up again as if by magic, but destroy our farms and the grass will grow in the streets of every city in the country." Eventually, reformers diluted Jefferson's criticism with other ingredients, even prejudice. Josiah Strong, for example, saw the city as "a serious menace to our civilization" because of its congestion of "dangerous elements": immigrants, Romanism, intemperance, poverty, socialism, crime, and irreligion. The persistence of these anti-urban attitudes in this century has been identified as a major factor in politics, particularly in the defeat of Al Smith in the 1928 presidential election. From the rural standpoint, Smith had everything against him: association with New York's Tammany machine, Catholic immigrant descent, and a "wet" stance toward prohibition.

Under the influence of the agrarian view, a searching critique of both urban and rural existence has occasionally been written, exposing the possibility of limitations inherent in human life that simply manifest themselves differently under city and country conditions. Thoreau, for example, found men in the city, the town, and the country all enslaved by their attitudes and their labor. In the city man is enslaved by the machine that promised to free him. In the country man is enslaved by the property that Jefferson hoped would give him self-sufficiency. Everywhere, Thoreau concluded, "The mass of men lead lives of quiet desperation." This observation is reflected in such works as Sherwood Anderson's *Winesburg, Ohio* where a small mid-western town turns people into "grotesques," their only escape being to the city, but the city, as Theodore Dreiser's *Sister Carrie* reveals, can threaten destruction precisely through the enticing artifice it offers on all sides or it can isolate the one who succeeds in reaching the top, in either case producing painfully distorted human beings.

The extreme prophecies may well be Whitman's proclamation that all men would unite as one in America and Henry Adam's apprehension that bombs would explode. Whitman found excitement and vitality in New York; he loved the faces, the glances, the talk, the reality of life in all its phases. Garcia-Lorca found cancer and hysteria; he loved the sufferers, the crabs, the glass of the metropolitan nightmare. There have been a few bombs, but the city still spirals into the countryside.

Excerpted Documents

From village to megalopolis: definition and development of the city.

Lewis Mumford, Social Historian, *The City in History: Its Origins, Its Transformations, and Its Prospects*, 1961, p. 30.

From its origins onward, indeed, the city may be described as a structure specifically equipped to store and transmit the goods of civilization, sufficiently condensed to afford the maximum amount of facilities in a minimum space, but also capable of structural enlargement to enable it to find a place for the changing needs and the more complex forms of a growing society and its cumulative social heritage. The invention of such forms as the written record, the library, the archive, the school, and the university is one of the earliest and most characteristic achievements of the city.

Hans Blumenfeld, Lecturer in Urban and Regional Planning—University of Toronto, "The Modern Metropolis," *Scientific American*, September, 1965.

To sum up, the modern metropolis differs from the traditional city in several crucial respects: (1) it combines the function of central leadership with the function of providing the main bulk of material production and services; (2) its population is up to 10 times larger than that of the biggest preindustrial city; (3) with modern fast transportation, which has increased its commuting radius about tenfold, it is up to 100 times larger in area than the biggest city of former times; (4) it is neither city nor country but a complex of urban districts and open areas; (5) its residential and work areas are no longer combined in one place but are located in separate districts; (6) its workers have high mobility in the choice of jobs and occupations.

Jean Gottmann, French Geographer, *Megalopolis: The Urbanized Northeastern Seaboard of the United States*, 1961, p.5.

. . .the old distinctions between rural and urban do not apply here anymore. Even a quick look at the vast area of Megalopolis reveals a revolution in land use. Most of the people living in the so-called rural areas, and still classified as "rural population" by recent censuses, have very little, if anything, to do with agriculture. In terms of their interests and work they are what used to be classified as "city folks," but their way of life and the landscapes around their residences do not fit the old meaning of urban.

Charles Abrams, *The City is the Frontier*, 1965, p.3.

In our own era, the world's cities are witnessing their greatest surge in man's history. Everywhere hordes of people are leaving the hinterlands in quest of the city's opportunities, its excitements, and its way of life. From 1800 to 1900, the proportion of people living in cities with more than 20,000 people leaped from 2.4 percent to 21 percent. Our civilization is becoming urban, and the advance into cities is one of the most spectacular social phenomena of our time. The city has become the frontier.

Charles N. Glaab, Historian, *The American City: A Documentary History*, 1963, p. 34.

Efforts in America to establish planned communities, whether large or small, have conflicted with the pressures created by an expansive capitalistic economy. In the struggle between the speculator and the architect, the planner, or the visionary, the speculator has ordinarily won. The founding of the national capital is a case in point. During the years in which Washington was being built, real-estate holders in the District of Columbia were involved in decisions and continually tried to alter the plan for the city made by the French engineer, Pierre Charles L'Enfant.

James Mease, *The Picture of Philadelphia Giving an Account of its Origin, Increase and Improvements*, 1811, p. xi, in *The American City: A Documentary History*, 1963, p. 37.

Upon some subjects he [William Penn] has forborn to speak, because he found that in considering them he could not be moderate. He will only mention one; the public squares:—the prostitution of which, in the thickly settled parts of the city, and the neglect to enclose and plant the rest, in order to prepare for the comfort and health of a population, rapidly increasing, loudly call for reprehension:—European nations will hear with astonishment, that out of the five squares, expressly set apart , by the benevolent founder of the city, for the purpose of public walks, and the salutary recreation of future generations, not one has been exclusively appropriated to its destined object!—that parts of some of them have been applied to the most injurious uses; and that even an open space near the Delaware, in the southern part of the city, also left for general benefit, has been rented for a board yard.

Report of the Urbanism Committee to the National Resources Committee, *Our Cities: Their Role in the National Economy*, 1937, p. 46, in *The American City: A Documentary History*, 1963, p. 454.

While during the colonial period there was evidence of building restrictions and some indication of an interest in community design, the subsequent irresistible expansion and the undaunted spirit of private enterprise swept most of these away. Laws designed to curb the greed and heedlessness of the individual owner and speculator in the interests of order health, safety, and public welfare were allowed to lapse and were resuscitated only when it was too late to repair most of the damage that had been done through generations of neglect.

Jean Gottmann, French Geographer, *Megalopolis: The Urbanized Northeastern Seaboard of the United States*, 1961, p. 218.

In the nineteenth century, migrations between rural and urban areas followed the typical pattern of "push off the land" and "pull of the cities." A profitable expansion of agricultural production required more machines and chemicals and fewer hands, and displaced farm workers were attracted to cities by new jobs in industry and by a life that was more glamorous and definitely easier, especially for the womenfolk. This pattern still applies today to migrations from the agricultural lands of the Great Plains to the metropolitan areas of the United States, . . .

Poverty, disease, and death in the city.

Charles N. Glaab, Historian, *The American City: A Documentary History*, 1963, pp. 115-116.

In 1857 there were. . . only 158 miles of sewers constructed in the near 500 miles of New York streets, leaving three fourths of the city, including most of the slum areas, without facilities. Other cities, with a few exceptions such as Baltimore, were little better off. A Cincinnati Board of Health report of 1865 told, for example, of a two-story house containing 102 persons for whom only one privy was provided. Under these circumstances, diseases, particularly those communicated through contaminated water, could be expected to flourish, and they did. Outbreaks of typhoid, dysentery, and typhus were continual in the poorer sections of cities. In New York's sixth ward—which encompassed the notorious Five Points district—the death rate was nearly three times that of the city as a whole.

State of New York, *Report of the Select Committee Appointed to Examine the Condition of Tenant Houses in New York and Brooklyn*, Assemb. Doc. 205, March 9, 1857, in *The American City: A Documentary History*, 1963, pp. 271-272.

But why extend the catalogue? or why attempt to convey to the imagination by words, the hideous squalor and deadly effluvia; the dim, undrained courts oozing with pollution; the dark, narrow stairways, decayed with age, reaking with filth, overrun with vermin; the rotted floors, ceilings begrimed, and often too low to permit you to stand upright; the windows stuffed with rags? or why try to portray the gaunt, shivering forms and wild ghastly faces, in these black and beetling abodes. . .

Gilbert Osofsky, *Harlem: The Making of a Ghetto*, 1963, in *American Urban History: An Interpretive Reader with Commentaries*, 1969, pp. 250-251.

Whatever the causes of Harlem's health problems—and medical investigators continue to search for all the answers—a good deal can be laid at the door of slum environment. Urban reformers consistently showed a high correlation between poverty and congestion on the one hand and disease and mortality on the other . . . working-class families in old-law tenements (pre-1901) died at a higher-rate than those in newer houses; poverty led to the consumption of the cheapest foods, and this in turn fostered diseases of poor diet; working mothers died more readily in childbirth than unemployed women; and so on.

Nathan S. Caplan and Jeffery M. Paige, "A Study of Ghetto Rioters," *Scientific American*, (August, 1968), p. 21.

The survey data support the blocked-opportunity theory. One is led to conclude that the continued exclusion of Negroes from American economic and social life is the fundamental cause of riots. This exclusion is a result of arbitrary racial barriers rather than lack of ability, motivation or aspiration on the part of Negroes, and it is most galling to young Negroes who perceive it as arbitrary and unjust.

One important question remains to be answered: "Why do they riot now?" After all, the opportunity structure has been closed for 100 years. Our data suggest that Negroes who riot do so because their conception of their lives and their potential has changed without commensurate improvement in their chances for a better life.

Thomas Merton, *The Seven Story Mountain*, 1970, pp. 417-418.

Here in this huge, dark, steaming slum, hundreds of thousands of Negroes are herded together like cattle, most of them with nothing to eat and nothing to do. All the senses and imagination and sensibilities and emotions and sorrows and desires and hopes and ideas of a race with vivid feelings and deep emotional reactions are forced in upon themselves, bound inward by an iron ring of frustration: the prejudice that hems them in with its four insurmountable walls. In this huge cauldron, inestimable natural gifts, wisdom, love, music, science, poetry are stamped down and left to boil with the dregs of an elementally corrupted nature, and thousands of souls are destroyed by vice and misery and degradation, obliterated, wiped out, washed from the register of the living, dehumanized.

What has not been devoured, in your dark furnace, Harlem, by marihuana, by gin, by insanity, hysteria, syphilis?

Martin Luther King, *Federal Role in Urban Affairs*, Hearings before the Subcommittee on Executive Reorganization of the Committee on Government Operations, U.S. Senate, December 14-15, 1966, in *Political Power and the Urban Crisis*, 1969, p. 451.

American cities are not the City of God nor the City of Man, They contain the residues of exploitation, of waste, of neglect, of indifference. The poor and the discriminated huddle in the big cities—the poorhouses of the welfare state—while affluent America displays its new gadgets in the crisp homes of suburbia. Will we move to provide a moral balance in American life and give priority to the disinherited? Or shall we continue our token attention?

Arthur M. Schlesinger, Historian, *Paths to the Present,* **1949, in** *American Urban History: An Interpretive Reader with Commentaries,* **1969, p. 36.**

Americans had developed their political institutions under simple rural conditions; they had yet to learn how to govern cramped populations. Preyed upon by unscrupulous men eager to exploit the expanding public utilities, municipal politics became a byword for venality. As Francis Parkman wrote "Where the carcass is, the vultures gather together." New York's notorious Tweed Ring denoted a sickness that racked Philadelphia, Chicago, St. Louis, Minneapolis and San Francisco as well. "With very few exceptions," declared Andrew D. White, "the city governments of the United States are the worst in Christendom—the most expensive, the most inefficient, and the most corrupt."

Though an irate citizenry succeeded now and then in "turning the rascals out," the boss and the machine soon recovered control. Nevertheless, the good-government campaigns ventilated the abuses of municipal misrule and aroused the humane to the worsening plight of the urban poor.

Alexander B. Callow, Jr., Historian, *The Tweed Ring,* **1966, in** *American Urban History: An Interpretive Reader with Commentaries,* **1969, pp. 330-331.**

For five years the Tweed Ring had led a great treasury raid. The power of the Ring, like the tentacles of a great octopus, encircled city government, the courts, the police, the underworld, and the State legislature. The command centers of political power from the Governor to the Board of Aldermen were controlled by the Ring and its lieutenants. The Ring ruled over an empire of patronage with thousands of the faithful on the city payrolls. Tammany Hall had been remodeled into an awesome political machine, supported by the immigrant and the native poor, and sustained on election day by a horde of Tammany warriors, repeaters, and corrupt election officials who made a mockery out of the power of the ballot. No wonder Boss Tweed could ask the reformer, "What are you going to do about it". . .

The Tweed Ring . . . reinforced complacency by giving something to everyone: city advertising to the press, special favors to businessmen, state aid to charitable and religious organizations, jobs and food to the poor. Tweed through his business connections and Hall through his clubs ingratiated themselves in the upper branches of society, while Sweeny and Connolly, seasoned ward leaders, were effective in the rank and file.

George Washington Plunkitt, Tammany Boss, as "interviewed" by reporter William L. Riordan, *Plunkitt of Tammany Hall,* **1905, in** *The American City: A Documentary History,* **1963, pp. 378-379.**

Everybody is talkin' these days about Tammany men growin' rich on graft, but nobody thinks of drawin' the distinction between honest graft and dishonest graft. There's all the difference in the world between the two. Yes, many of our men have grown in politics. I have myself. I've made a big fortune out of the game, and I'm getting richer every day, but I've not gone in for dishonest graft—blackmailin' gamblers, saloon-keepers, disorderly people, etc.—and neither has any of the men who have made big fortunes in politics.

There's an honest graft, and I'm an example of how it works. I might sum up the whole thing by sayin':"I seen my opportunities and I took 'em."

Francis E. Rourke, Political Scientist, "Urbanism and American Democracy," *Ethics,* **74 (July, 1964), in** *American Urban History: An Interpretive Reader with Commentaries,* **1969, pp. 377-378.**

In its manifestations in the early part of this century, the antagonism toward cities was reinforced by two independent developments which exercised a major influence upon the course of American politics, the nativist movement and the drive for national prohibition. Early nativist sentiment was, as John Higham has shown in his *Strangers in the Land,* largely an urban rather than a rural phenomenon. The hostility toward immigrants was initially strongest in the areas where native Americans most frequently rubbed elbows with newcomers from other countries—in the great cities of the East. By the turn of the century, however, the antagonism toward the foreign-born had come to be centered in rural areas, where it blended with and helped to harden the historic

65

agrarian prejudice against the city. The "foreign" character of American cities became one of their major liabilities in rural America—the region most aroused by the wave of nativist sentiment which swept the country in the years following World War I. Speaking of the role of the Ku Klux Klan during this period, Higham writes: "Significantly, the Klan's home was not in the great cities. Its strength came chiefly from the towns, from the villages, and from the ordinarily tranquil countryside."

W. Stull Holt, Historian,"Some Consequences of the Urban Movement in American History," *Pacific Historical Review,* **(November, 1953), in** *American Urban History: An Interpretive Reader with Commentaries,* **1969, pp. 47-48.**

For years all political activity in New York State has had meaning only when interpreted in terms of New York City versus up-state. In Illinois politics has been a reflection of the antagonism between Chicago and downstate. The same situation is duplicated widely. In state after state the split between urban and rural groups is the dominant theme and in many cases the words are the same. There is scarcely a state where the urban population has not just grounds for complaining of the rotten borough system that prevails. Some citizens of Cook County, Illinois, tried in 1946 to secure corrective action by legal means. In a suit they complained that Cook County, which meant Chicago, with 52 percent of the population of the state had only nine of the twenty-five seats in Congress. The Supreme Court rejected their plea by a vote of four to three. . .

The districts had been established in 1901 on the basis of the census of 1900 and there had been no redistricting in the subsequent forty years in spite of shifts in population. The local political tensions symbolized in this fashion are sometimes as important in determining who is to be elected to the Senate or to Congress as are national party labels and are often the decisive factor in deciding nominations for office within the party.

Psychological and social malfunctions in the city.

Arthur M. Schlesinger, Historian, *Paths to the Present,* **1949, in** *American Urban History: An Interpretive Reader with Commentaries,* **1969, pp. 36-37.**

Masses of people reared in a rustic environment had suddenly to adapt themselves to the frantic urban pace. One outcome was a startling growth of neurasthenia, a word coined by Dr. George M. Beard of New York in his work *American Nervousness* (1881), which traced the malady to the hurry and scurry, the din of the streets, the frenzied struggle for existence, the mental excitements and endless distractions. From the ranks of the high-strung, Mary Baker Eddy gathered most of her converts to the new religion of Christian Science, and for much the same reason townsfolk now gave enthusiastic support to organized sports. Flabby muscles unfitted most persons for direct participation but they compromised by paying professional contestants to take their exercise for them. If, as a magazine writer said, nervousness had become the "national disease of America," baseball, partly as an antidote, became America's national game.

Louis Wirth, Sociologist, "Urbanism as a Way of Life," *The American Journal of Sociology,* **(July, 1938), in** *American Urban History: An Interpretive Reader with Commentaries,* **1969, pp. 494-495.**

The contacts of the city may indeed be face to face, but they are nevertheless impersonal, superficial, transitory, and segmental. The reserve, the indifference, and the blasé outlook which urbanites manifest in their relationships may thus be regarded as devices for immunizing themselves against the personal claims and expectations of others.

The superficiality, the anonymity, and the transitory character of urban-social relations make intelligible, also, the sophistication and the rationality generally ascribed to city-dwellers. Our acquaintances tend to stand in a relationship of utility to us in the sense that the role which each one plays in our life is overwhelmingly regarded as a means for the achievement of our own ends. Whereas, therefore, the individual gains, on the one hand, a certain degree of emancipation or freedom from the personal and emotional controls of intimate groups, he loses, on the other hand, the spontaneous self-expression, the morale, and the sense of participation that comes with living in an integrated society.

Hans Blumenfeld, Lecturer in Urban and Regional Planning—University of Toronto, "The Modern Metropolis," *Scientific American*, September, 1965, in *American Urban History: An Interpretive Reader with Commentaries*, 1969, p. 171.

The most persistent accusation against the metropolis is that it has dissolved the family and neighborhood ties that existed in the small town and has produced anomie: the absence of any values or standards of behavior. This is questionable. A number of sociological studies in metropolises of North America and western Europe have shown that family ties remain very much alive and that a considerable amount of informal community organization can be found even in their slums.

Max Picard, *The World of Silence*, translated by Stanley Goodman, 1952, pp. 210-211.

It is as though the last residuum of silence were to be destroyed; as though an order had been made for a census of the residue of silence in every person and in every house, and for that residue to be exterminated, as an enemy.

Aeroplanes scour the sky for the silence encamped behind the clouds. The propeller beats are like so many blows against the silence.

The great cities are like enormous reservoirs of noise. Noise is manufactured in the city, just as goods are manufactured. The city is the place where it is always kept in stock, completely detached from the object from which it came. It broods over the city and falls down on men and things.

But in the night, when the lights are out, the streets seem like the shafts down which the noise has fallen and in which it has disappeared. Men and things doze wearily, as they are no longer filled with the noise. People roam along by the houses like shadows, and the walls of the houses seem like the front walls of enormous dilapidated and disintegrated tombs.

In sleep, however, with their ears on the pillow, men seem to be listening to the depths of the earth, to the vanished noise or perhaps to the vanished silence.

The great city is a fortress against the silence, around which destruction hovers in its feverish activity. There is a striving towards destruction, a search for death, a search for the silence after death.

Values and goals of the city.

Arthur Schlesinger, *The Rise of the City, 1878-1898*, 1933, in *American Urban History: An Interpretive Reader with Commentaries*, 1969, p. 187.

In America in the eighties urbanization for the first time became a controlling factor in the national life. Just as the plantation was the typical product of the *antebellum* Southern system and the small farm of the Northern agricultural order, so the city was the supreme achievement of the new industrialism. In its confines were focused all the new economic forces: the vast accumulations of capital, the business and financial institutions, the spreading railway yards, the gaunt smoky mills, the white-collar middle classes, the motley wage-earning population. By the same token the city inevitably became the generating center for social and intellectual progress. To dwell in the midst of great affairs is stimulating and broadening; it is the source of a discontent which, if not divine, is at least energizing. In a populous urban community like could find like; the person of ability, starved in his rural isolation, might by going there find sympathy, encouragement and that criticism which often refines talent into genius.

Arthur Schlesinger, *Paths to the Present*, 1949, in *American Urban History: An Interpretive Reader with Commentaries*, 1969, p. 37.

The cities, re-enacting their role of the "fireplaces of civilization"—Theodore Parker's phrase—provided compelling incentives to cultural achievement, multiplying colleges, public libraries and publishing houses and founding art museums, art schools and conservatories of music. A Henry James might still find Europe an intellectually more congenial milieu, but William Dean Howells, Mark Twain and Joel Chandler Harris discovered the needed stimulus at home; and the same held true of all or nearly all the leading painters, sculptors, architects, composers, playwrights and scholars.

Francis E. Rourke, Political Scientist, "Urbanism and American Democracy," *Ethics*, (July, 1964), in *American Urban History: An Interpretive Reader with Commentaries*, 1969, p. 384.

Recent research in the general area of political behavior has also tended to refute the assumption that there is any necessary antipathy between the growth of cities and the vitality of the democratic process. In terms of some of the more obvious yardsticks that might be used to measure commitment to the norms of democracy, the urban citizen very often shows up much better than his rural counterpart. This is true, for example, with respect to two of the central attributes of democratic citizenship, an acceptance of the right of minorities to dissent from majority opinion, and an interest in the affairs of government as evidenced by participation in elections.

Hinton R. Helper, *The Impending Crisis of the South: How to Meet It*, 1857, in *The American City: A Documentary History*, 1963, pp. 168-169.

What would England be without London? What would France be without Paris? What would Turkey be without Constantinople? Or, to come nearer home, what would Maryland be without Baltimore? What would Louisiana be without New Orleans? What would South Carolina be without Charleston? Do we ever think of these countries or states without thinking of their cities also? If we want to learn the news of the country, do we not go to the city, or to the city papers? Every metropolis may be regarded as the nucleus or epitome of the country in which it is situated; and the more prominent features and characteristics of a country, particularly of the people of a country, are almost always to be seen within the limits of its capital city. Almost invariably do we find the bulk of floating funds, the best talent, and the most vigorous energies of a nation concentrated in its chief cities; and does not this concentration of wealth, energy, and talent, conduce, in an extraordinary degree, to the growth and prosperity of the nation? Unquestionably. Wealth develops wealth, energy develops energy, talent develops talent.

Report of the Urbanism Committee to the National Resources Committee, *Our Cities: Their Role in the National Economy*, 1937, p. vi, in *The American City: A Documentary History*, 1963, p. 451.

The city has seemed at times the despair of America, but at others to be the nation's hope, the battleground of democracy. Surely in the long run, the Nation's destiny will be profoundly affected by the cities which have two-thirds of its population and its wealth. There is liberty of development in isolation and wide spaces, but there is also freedom in the many-sided life of the city where each may find its own kind. There is democracy in the scattered few, but there is also democracy in the thick crowd with its vital impulse and its insistent demand for a just participation in the gains of our civilization. There is fertility and creation in the rich soil of the broad countryside, but there is also fertility and creativeness in forms of industry, art, personality, emerging even from the city streets and reaching toward the sky.

John F. Kennedy, *Federal Role in Urban Affairs*, Hearings before the Subcommittee on Executive Reorganization of the Committee on Government Operations, U.S. Senate, August 15-16, 1966, in *Political Power and the Urban Crisis*, 1969, p. 475.

The city is not just housing and stores. It is not just education and employment, parks and theaters, banks and shops.It is a place where men should be able to live in dignity and security and harmony, where the great achievements of modern civilization and the ageless pleasures afforded by natural beauty should be available to all.

The agrarian critique of the city.

Thomas Jefferson, *The Writings of Thomas Jefferson*, edited by Andrew A. Lipscomb and Albert E. Bergh, 1904, Vol. 10, p. 173.

(Jefferson to Rush, September 23, 1800)

When great evils happen I am in the habit of looking out for what good may arise from them as consolations to us, and Providence has in fact so established the order of things, as that most evils are the means of producing some good. The yellow fever will discourage the growth of great cities in our nation, and I view great cities as pestilential to the morals, the health and the liberties of man. True, they nourish some of the elegant arts, but the useful ones can thrive elsewhere, and less perfection in the others, with more health, virtue and freedom, would be my choice.

Benjamin Rush, *Letters of Benjamin Rush,* edited by L. H. Butterfield, 1951, Vol. 2, p. 821.

(Rush to Jefferson, October 6, 1800)

I agree with you in your opinion of cities. Cowper the poet very happily expresses our ideas of them compared with the country. "God made the country—man made cities." I consider them in the same light that I do abscesses on the human body, viz., as reservoirs of all the impurities of a community.

James Madison, *The Writings of James Madison,* edited by Gaillard Hunt, 1906, Vol. 6, pp. 96-98.

The life of the husbandman is pre-eminently suited to the comfort and happiness of the individual . . . The extremes both of want and of waste have other abodes. 'Tis not the country that peoples either the Bridewells or the Bedlams. These mansions of wretchedness are tenanted from the distresses and vices of overgrown cities.

Alexis de Tocqueville, *Democracy in America,* 1835, p. 289.

I look upon the size of certain American cities, and especially on the nature of their population, as a real danger which threatens the future security of the democratic republics of the New World; and I venture to predict that they will perish from this circumstance, unless the Government succeeds in creating an armed force, which, while it remains under the control of the majority of the nation, will be independent of the town population, and able to repress its excesses.

Ralph Waldo Emerson, "Culture," *The Selected Writings of Ralph Waldo Emerson,* 1940, p. 729.

Whilst we want cities as the centres where the best things are found, cities degrade us by magnifying trifles. The countryman finds the town a chop-house, a barber's shop. He has lost the lines of grandeur of the horizon, hills and plains, and with them sobriety and elevation. He has come among a supple, glib-tongued tribe, who live for show, servile to public opinion. Life is dragged down to a fracas of pitiful cares and disasters.

Selected Bibliography

Abrams, Charles. *The City Is the Frontier.* New York: Harper and Row, 1965.

Callow, Alexander B. Jr. *The Tweed Ring.* New York: Oxford, 1966.

Callow, Alexander B. Jr., ed. *American Urban History: An Interpretive Reader With Commentaries.* London: Oxford University Press, 1969.

Caplan, Nathan S., and Paige, Jeffrey M. "A Study of Ghetto Rioters." *Scientific American,* (August, 1968), 15.

Diamond, William. "On the Dangers of an Urban Interpretation of History." *Historiography and Urbanization.* Edited by Eric F. Goldman. Baltimore: The Johns Hopkins Press, 1967.

Elazar, Daniel J. *Cities of the Prairie: The Metropolitan Frontier and American Politics.* New York: Basic Books, Inc., 1970.

Glaab, Charles, N., ed. *The American City: A Documentary History.* Homewood, Illinois: The Dorsey Press, 1963.

Glaab, Charles N., and Brown, A. Theodore. *A History of Urban America.* New York: The Macmillan Company, 1967.

Gottman, Jean. *Megalopolis: The Urbanized Northeastern Seaboard of the United States.* Cambridge, Massachusetts: MIT Press, 1961.

Green, Constance McLaughlin. *American Cities in the Growth of the Nation.* New York: Harper and Row, 1957.

Green, Constance McLaughlin. *The Rise of Urban America.* New York: Harper and Row, 1965.

Isenberg, Irwin, ed. *The City In Crisis.* New York: The H. W. Wilson Company, 1968.

McKelvey, Blake. *The Urbanization of America, 1865-1915.* Rutgers, New Jersey: The State University Press, 1963.

Marx, Leo. *The Machine In the Garden: Technology and the Pastoral Ideal in America.* New York: Oxford University Press, 1964.

Mohl, Raymond A., and Betten, Neil, eds. *Urban America In Historical Perspective.* New York: Weybright and Talley, 1970.

Mumford, Lewis. *The City In History: Its Origins, Its Transformations and Its Prospects.* New York: Harcourt, Brace and World, Inc., 1961.

Osofsky, Gilbert. *Harlem: The Making of a Ghetto.* New York: Harper and Row, 1966.

Ostrogorski, Mosei. *Democracy and the Organization of Political Parties of The United States.* Vol. 2 Edited and abridged by Seymour Martin Lipset. New York: Doubleday Anchor Paperback, 1964.

Rourke, Francis E. "Urbanism and American Democracy." *Ethics,* 74 (July, 1964), 255.

Rossi, Peter H.; Berk, Richard A.; and Eidson, Bettye K. *The Roots of Urban Discontent: Public Policy, Municipal Institutions, and the Ghetto.* New York: John Wiley & Sons, 1974.

Schlesinger, Arthur M. *The Rise of the City, 1878-1898.* New York: MacMillan, 1933.

Schlesinger, Arthur M. "The City in American Civilization." *Paths to the Present.* New York: Macmillan, 1949.

Shank, Alan, ed. *Political Power and the Urban Crisis.* Boston: Holbrook Press, Inc., 1969.

Strauss, Anselm L., ed. *Images of the American City.* Glencoe, Illinois: Free Press, 1961.

Strauss, Anselm L., ed. *The American City: A Sourcebook of Urban Imagery.* Chicago: Aldine Publishing Company, 1968.

Turner, Frederick Jackson. *The Frontier in American History.* New York: Henry Holt and Co., 1920.

Turner, Ralph E. "The Industrial City: Center of Cultural Change." *The Cultural Approach to History.* Edited by Cardine F. Ware. New York: Columbia University Press, 1940, 228.

The Urbanism Committee, Report to the National Resources Committee. *Our Cities: Their Role in the National Economy.* Washington, D.C.: U.S. Government Printing Office, June, 1937.

The Urbanism Committee, Report to the National Resources Committee. *Urban Government.* 2 vols. Washington, D.C.: U.S. Government Printing Office, 1939.

Vance, Rupert B., and Demerath, Nicholas J., eds. *The Urban South.* Chapel Hill: The University of North Carolina Press, 1954.

Wade, Richard C. *The Urban Frontier: The Rise of Western Cities, 1790-1830.* Cambridge, Massachusetts: Harvard University Press, 1959.

Wade, Richard C. *The Urban Frontier: Pioneer Life in Early Pittsburgh, Cincinnati, Lexington, Louisville, and St. Louis.* Chicago: University of Chicago Press, 1964.

Walker, Robert H. "The Poet and the Rise of the City." *Mississippi Valley Historical Review,* (June, 1962), 85.

Warner, Sam Bass Jr. *The Urban Wilderness: A History of the American City.* New York: Harper and Row, 1972.

Weber, Adna F. *The Growth of Cities in the Nineteenth Century.* Ithaca: Cornell University Press, 1963.

White, Morton and Lucia. *The Intellectual Versus the City.* Cambridge, Massachusetts: Harvard University Press, 1962.

Wilson, William H. *Coming of Age: Urban America, 1915-1945.* New York: John Wiley and Sons, Inc., 1974.

ISSUE III
CERTAIN INALIENABLE RIGHTS

DISTRICT EVENTS—HIGH SCHOOL ISSUE
November 15—December 20, 1975

DEBATE   *Resolved: That extremism in the defense of liberty is no vice.*

PERSUASIVE   *The Press: Reporter or Maker of History?*

EXTEMPORANEOUS   *Equal Protection Under the Law*

1. *Can we have equal rights for minorities when the majority rules?*
2. *Impartial peers or community prejudice: Have American juries helped or hurt the cause of equality before the law?*
3. *America's lawmakers: Have they been the voice of the people or the tools of special interests groups?*
4. *Has the American system of jurisprudence been unfairly balanced in favor of the rights of defendants in criminal cases?*
5. *Money and politics: Could a man of modest means — an Abe Lincoln — be elected today?*
6. *The legal profession in American history: Force for equality or tool of the powerful?*
7. *Has minority group violence hindered the quest for equality of opportunity?*
8. *How are today's demands for sexual equality rooted in America's past?*
9. *To what extent have changes in the law reduced racial prejudice?*
10. *"All men are created equal": How has the meaning of this self-evident truth changed?*
11. *Has the education of American youth been the most important factor in increasing equality of opportunity?*
12. *How have the electronic media affected basic American freedoms?*
13. *Should the pledge of alligiance be changed to read "... seeking liberty and justice for all" instead of "... with liberty and justice for all?"*

RESOLVED: THAT EXTREMISM IN THE DEFENSE OF LIBERTY IS NO VICE.

Introductory Essay

When Barry Goldwater accepted the Republican nomination for President in 1964 he stated emphatically, "Extremism in the defense of liberty is no vice . . . moderation in the pursuit of justice is no virtue." His words generated much post-convention criticism from those who saw them as a slap at the moderate wing of the Republican party and from others who saw them as the basis for a dangerous foreign policy. Amidst the controversy, their real meaning in the context of his acceptance speech was lost. The candidate's speech had one central theme, the preservation of liberty both at home and abroad: "We must, and we shall, set the tide running again in the cause of freedom." He believed that the American tradition of liberty was endangered by such domestic problems as criminal violence, political corruption, and the aimlessness of youth, and by the foreign threat of Communism and the governments it controlled—"the enemies of every man on earth who is or wants to be free." Goldwater's belief that extremism can be justified by a threat to liberty has been shared by many Americans throughout the nation's history. Indeed, the very birth of the Republic was an uncompromising struggle to attain freedom from Britain's attempts to restrict liberty in the colonies.

"Extremism" and "liberty" have broad potential usages; unless these two terms are clearly defined and used consistently, a dialogue on this question is likely to suffer from a lack of clash of ideas or to lack the precision necessary for solid judgment. Unlike the pharmacist, we offer no prescriptions; but we do hope to raise some useful questions. "Extremism," at its broadest, can encompass virtually any activity not participated in by the bulk of the American people—forceful words; the organization of protest demonstrations, groups, or political parties; civil disobedience; or armed, violent resistance to authority. How would the definition chosen for "extremism" influence the areas to be discussed? Are some forms of extremism justified, while others are not?

"Liberty" also requires definition. Does the curtailment of *any* liberty justify extremism? An anarchist advocates the elimination of government and other institutional infringements on liberty. Thoreau thought, "that government is best which governs least" could be improved if restated "that govern-

ment is best which governs not at all." But anarchism—often attributed to those who oppose the existing order—has not been especially popular in the United States; "my country, right or wrong!" has held greater sway. Clashes over freedom of religion, freedom of assembly, freedom to uphold unpopular political views, freedom to vote, and many others have spawned extremist reactions in American history. If opposition to all government is unreasonable, is opposition to a particular law of a basically just government also unreasonable? What liberties are worth defending with which forms of extremism?

The agent of extreme action to defend liberty may be either the individual, the group, or the state. The individual may resist the encroachments of government on liberty, as when certain individuals participated in acts of civil disobedience challenging segregation laws in the South during the 1960's. Groups have used extreme measures to defend their liberties many times in U.S. history; an example is the near-warfare in mining areas of the Rockies and Pennsylvania around the turn of the Twentieth Century by unions fighting mine operators. The state may defend liberty through extremism by combatting totalitarian forces, as in World War II; but it may also restrict liberty temporarily during crisis as a means of safeguarding the exercise of freedom in the longer run, taking such extreme action as the suppression of radical views following World War I.

There is a central tension in the issues of the resolution: to what extent must our actions be limited by the rule of law and other formal restraints, and to what extent can we justify exceptions to the rules in the name of a higher morality? America attempts to balance the common good with the greatest exercise of individual freedom. The balance of powers, federalism, and the Bill of Rights are examples of attempts to write protections against tyranny over individuals and groups into the structure of government. At the same time, restrictions on freedom for the common good abound—taxation, conscription into military service, registration of automobiles, and thousands of other examples trivial and profound.

Those who support extremism in the defense of liberty are likely to place greater faith in their own individual conscience than in the "passions of the mob" or, in the case of a nation-state, in their own policies than in international law or opinion. Those arguing against extremism look to the consequences of acts—particularly the disruption of local governance and the generation of international hostilities.

Any discussion of extremism in the defense of liberty must consider the historical precedent of the American Revolution, since liberty was the fundamental premise on which the new nation was founded. The colonists' attitude toward politics and government was shaped by the root assumption that they, as Englishmen, shared in a unique inheritance of liberty. They believed that the English, though often threatened by despots, had managed for a longer period than any other people to maintain a tradition of the successful control of power and of those evil tendencies of human nature that would hinder its proper use. And while it was unusual, it was no accident because buttressing and giving official expression to this tradition was the English "constitution." Before the problems began between England and the colonies in the 1760's, John Adams referred to the English "constitution" as "the most perfect combination of human powers in society which finite wisdom has yet contrived for the preservation of liberty." It had only one officially sanctioned goal—the attainment of liberty—and if the rights and privileges embedded in it were, in any way, threatened, historical precedents in English history required extreme actions to safeguard those constitutional liberties.

The word "constitution" and the concept behind it, argues Bernard Bailyn, was of central importance to the colonists' political thought, and their whole understanding of the American Revolution rested upon it. In the decade after 1763 and the Stamp Act crisis, the colonists believed they saw emerging from "the welter of events surrounding the question of Parliament's jurisdiction in America a pattern whose meaning was unmistakable." What they perceived was a deliberate assault against liberty both in the colonies and in England, which had as its final goal the destruction of the English "constitution." The report of the Boston Town Meeting to its Assembly Representatives in 1770 read: "A series of occurrences, many recent events, . . . afford great reason to believe that a deep-laid and desperate plan of imperial despotism has been laid and partly executed, for the extinction of all civil liberty . . . . the august and once revered fortress of English freedom, the BRITISH CONSTITUTION, seems fast tottering into fatal and inevitable ruin." And it was precisely this perception of the challenge to their liberty as a usurpation of the English "constitution" which imparted a logic to the American cause and propelled the colonists into revolution against their mother country.

Thomas Jefferson purposely worded the Declaration of Independence to provide official sanction for taking extreme and revolutionary actions in the defense of liberty. Declaring that all men are endowed by their creator with inherent and inalienable rights and that governments are instituted among men to protect these rights and derived their powers exclusively from the consent of the governed, Jefferson asserted that "whenever any form of Government becomes destructive of these ends, it is the Right of the People to alter or abolish it and to institute a new government, laying its foundations on such principles . . ." And in a direct reply to British authorities, who viewed the revolutionaries solely as extremists with no regard for the law, he declared: ". . . when a long train of abuses and usurpations begun at a distinguished period and pursuing invariably the same object, evinces a design to reduce them under absolute despotism, it is their Right, it is their Duty to throw off such a Government and to provide the new guards for their future security . . ." The notion that the right of rebellion was as inalienable a right as "life, liberty and the pursuit of happiness" was the real legacy of the American Revolution and the aspect which, forever, differentiated it from all that had come before. Seen in this light, then, there is little doubt that the Founding Fathers believed their act of rebellion to be both extreme and necessary to preserve the colonists' liberty as they understood and remembered it before it was jeopardized by the mother country.

After the Revolution, the framers of the Constitution, in an attempt to protect future generations from the abuses and usurpations which they had just experienced, sought to perpetuate a philosophy which centered not on the authority of government, but rather on the rights of each member of society. Their First Amendment spelled out five areas in which citizens were to be free from governmental interference: "Congress shall make no law respecting an establishment of religion, or prohibiting the free exercise thereof; or abridging the freedom of speech, or of the press, or the right of people peaceably to assemble, and to petition the government for a redress of grievances." Subsequent amendments which prohibited unreasonable searches, which asserted that no citizen need be a witness against himself, and which guaranteed the due process of law for all, further reinforced this profound respect for the rights of the individual. By denying government the power to interfere in these critical areas of individual choice, the Founding Fathers, in the words of one Supreme Court Justice, intended to keep those areas "from the vicissitudes of political controversy, to place them beyond the reach of majorities and officials and to establish them as legal principles to be applied by the courts." And as such, the Constitution served as a charter not to protect the rights of the majority, but rather to encompass the views of the unorthodox and nonconformist and as an important protection against unjust and oppressive conduct on the part of the people themselves. Although its implementation may have been less than the Founding Fathers envisioned, nevertheless, their document reflected those views, which justified the rebellion and formed the basis for "the two contrasting concepts of constitutionalism that have remained characteristic of England and America ever since."

The passage of time has, for the most part, lent validity to that judgment. As Harold Taylor, former President of Sarah Lawrence College, has written:

> Our greatest strength as a country lies in the fact that we have a diversity of opinion and a diversity of people. We can absorb and use ideas of all kinds provided we keep ourselves in a situation in which every idea can have public expression . . . What marks our history from that of other countries is in the way we have been able to avoid orthodoxy, to remain openminded and flexible, to absorb radical ideas in the flow of social process and put them to work when needed.

The vital link between the free expression of extreme and minority views and the preservation of the democratic order throughout American history has been the political process and the two-party system. Bernard Crick has written: "Politics is a way of ruling divided societies without undue violence" and the hallmark of the two-party system in America has been its pluralism, its toleration of extreme and minority viewpoints as long as they do not threaten the common goal of the maintenance of democratic values.

There has also evolved a tradition in America for the articulation of extreme views, which fall outside the mainstream of American politics. Surfacing most frequently as third party political movements, this tradition has often had a purging effect on the political process and forced the two major parties to incorporate many of their extreme views into their own party platforms. This was the case with the three major extremist movements of the Nineteenth Century: the Anti-Masons, the Know-Nothings, and the Populists. All three believed that the democratic order and values were being threatened by elements in American society. The Anti-Masonic party, which peaked during the late 1820's, warned the nation against the Masons, an infidel society whose members were "at war with Christianity" and plotting against democracy. The Know-Nothing party of the 1850's warned the nation against the threat to liberty posed by the continued unrestricted flow of immigrants to America. And the Populists during the 1890's warned the people that they had been deprived of the nation's wealth by greedy and selfish businessmen and that control of the government should be returned to the people. Not all extremist movements throughout American history have spawned third parties, but, nevertheless, organizations such as the anti-Catholic American Protective Association, the white-supremacist Ku Klux Klan, and the reactionary John Birch society have all had a significant impact on the political process and have often dominated the local arena.

While the articulation of extreme views has been encouraged and even officially sanctioned by the political process throughout American history, the taking of extreme actions in defense of liberty and the democratic order has been much more controversial. In his farewell address to the new nation, President George Washington admonished his countrymen against the dangers of "those overgrown military establishments which under any form of government are inauspicious to liberty and which are to be regarded as particularly hostile to republican liberty." His words have reminded all leaders since of that ambiguous, but necessary relationship between the democratic order and the measures deemed necessary for its physical defense. As a result, all extreme actions taken in defense of that order, including military policies and actions, have been judged in terms of their effect upon those fundamental values which they are intended to protect and perpetuate.

Those actions in the defense of collective liberty, which have created the greatest public furor and concern, have been those directly attacking individual liberties. Such actions as the passage of the Alien and Sedition Acts during the presidency of John Adams, the suppression of habeas corpus proceedings during the Civil War, the restrictions on liberty during the first World War, the Palmer raids against aliens and dissenters in the early 1920's, and the McCarthy era's witch hunt for American Communists all were taken in the belief that by so doing our national security was enhanced and the democratic order was prevented from being undermined at home. However, these extreme measures in the cause of national security have been accepted as temporary restrictions on individual liberty, associated with transient emergencies. Nonetheless, "extremism in the defense of" collective liberty or nationhood has been at odds with extremism in the defense of individual liberty. This fundamental conflict must be resolved by an advocate of the general proposition.

This concept of extreme actions in the defense of liberty took on an additional dimension when the United States assumed a position of world leadership in the Twentieth Century and the overriding political challenge was not only the preservation of liberty in America, but also the extension of freedom to the rest of the world. Ever since President

Woodrow Wilson identified American intervention in the first World War with the higher cause of freedom in his famous Fourteen Points, which urged freedom of the seas, the self-determination of all nations and an international collective security system to keep peace and safeguard liberty, American foreign policy has been inextricably tied to the world-wide defense of freedom. During the last fifty years extreme action by the United States outside our boundaries has been justified by a threat to the preservation of our democratic system. As Barry Goldwater wrote in 1962, concerning the menace of the Communist ideology: "The objective of American foreign policy must be to protect the security and integrity of Americans and thereby help establish a world in which there is the largest possible measure of freedom and justice. . . ." The belief in a common threat to the cause of liberty has been of primary importance in the acceptance by the American public of extreme actions taken in its defense around the world, and when that consensus evaporates, as it did in the case of the Vietnam war, such actions become evidence of the abuse and arrogance of power and are themselves viewed as antithetical to the preservation of liberty.

The distinguished American historian, Oscar Handlin, has written that "the preservation of liberty is the preeminent problem of our times" and that the danger to liberty lies in the gradual erosion of individual rights: ". . . traditional freedoms are less in danger of any sudden overthrow than in gradually being bartered or traded for something else on which the people place a higher current value." The defense of liberty was, and still is, central to the American experience, and our society continues to cherish both the right to hold extreme views and the right to take extreme actions in support of commonly held democratic values. J. William Fulbright, in his book, *The Arrogance of Power,* claims that Twentieth Century Americans are emotionally and intellectually handicapped when confronted with social revolutions in the third world because even though we are not a revolutionary society" . . . a national mythology, cultivated in Fourth of July speeches and slick publications, . . . holds that we are . . ." On the other hand, Senator Goldwater sees a continuity in our beliefs and in our acts: "Patrick Henry said it in a few ringing words two hundred years ago, and his 'Give me liberty or give me death' rings just as true today."

Excerpted Documents

The nature of liberty.

George Bernard Shaw, "An Apology for Freedom of the Press," *Works,* **9th ed., Vol. III, 1845.**

It is not possible to make the ordinary moral man understand what toleration and liberty really mean. He will accept them verbally with alacrity, even with enthusiasm, because the word toleration has been moralized by eminent Whigs: but what he means by toleration is toleration of doctrines that he considers enlightened, and by liberty, liberty to do what he considers right: that is, he does not mean toleration or liberty at all; for there is no need to tolerate what appears enlightened or to claim liberty to do what most people consider right. Toleration and liberty have no sense or use except as toleration of opinions that are considered damnable, and liberty to do what seems wrong.

Baron de Montesquieu, "In What Liberty Consists," *The Spirit of Laws,* **1878 (trans.), p. 161.**

It is true, that in democracies the people seem to do what they please; but political liberty does not consist in unrestrained freedom. In governments, that is in societies directed by laws, liberty can consist only in the power of doing what we ought to will, and in not being constrained to do what we ought not to will.
We must have continually present to our minds the difference between independence and liberty. Liberty is a right of doing whatever the laws permit; and if a citizen could do what they forbid, he would no longer be possessed of liberty, because all his fellow-citizens would have the same power.

Ernst Freund, Professor of Jurisprudence—University of Chicago, *Police Power: Public Policy and Constitutional Right,* **1904, p. 509.**

As the freedom of religion would have no meaning without the liberty of attacking all religion, so the freedom of political discussion is merely a phrase if it must stop short of questioning the fundamental ideas of politics, law and government. Otherwise every government is justified in drawing the line of free discussion at those principles or institutions, which it deems essential to its perpetuation—a view to which the Russian government would subscribe.

It is the essence of political liberty that it may create disaffection or other inconvenience to the existing government, otherwise there would be no merit in tolerating it.

John Stuart Mill, English Philosopher, *On Liberty*, 1859, p. 70.

The only freedom which deserves the name, is that of pursuing our own good in our own way, so long as we do not attempt to deprive others of theirs, or impede their efforts to obtain it. Each is the proper guardian of his own health, whether bodily, or mental and spiritual. Mankind are greater gainers by suffering each other to live as seems good to themselves, than by compelling each to live as seems good to the rest.

Barry M. Goldwater, Senator from Arizona, *Why Not Victory? A Fresh Look at American Foreign Policy*, 1962, p. 120.

The only real disarmament will come when the cause for arms is removed. In our case that cause is communism. In the Soviets' case, that cause is the free world. Does anyone believe that they will voluntarily give up their gains and their objectives? Does anyone believe that we will give up our way of life and settle for peace under slavery? Those few among us who, because of a paralyzing fear of death itself, would rather be "red than dead" need a lesson in history. The idea of freedom cannot be stamped out by the scratch of a pen. Patrick Henry said it in a few ringing words two hundred years ago, and his "Give me liberty or give me death" rings just as true today.

Is extremism necessary?

William Ellery Channing, American Preacher and Author, "The Abolitionists," *Works*, 11th ed., Vol. 2, 1849, p. 161.

The progress of society depends on nothing more than on the exposure of time-sanctioned abuses, which cannot be touched without offending multitudes, than on the promulgation of principles which are in advance of public sentiment and practice, and which are consequently at war with the habits, prejudices, and immediate interests of large classes of the community.

Abraham Lincoln, *First Inaugural Address*, March 4, 1861.

If by the mere force of numbers a majority should deprive a minority of any clearly written constitutional right, it might, in a moral point of view, justify revolution—certainly would if such a right were a vital one . . . A majority held in restraint by constitutional checks and limitations, always changing easily with deliberate changes of popular opinions and sentiments, is the only true sovereign of a free people . . .

John Stuart Mill, English Philosopher, *On Liberty*, 1859, p. 52.

The dictum that truth always triumphs over persecution is one of those pleasant falsehoods which men repeat after one another till they pass into commonplaces, but which all experience refutes. History teems with instances of truth put down by persecution. If not suppressed forever, it may be thrown back for centuries. To speak only of religious opinions: the Reformation broke out at least twenty times before Luther, and was put down.

Our Founding Fathers:
Precedent for revolution.

Charles Evans Whittaker and William Sloane Coffin, Jr., Associates of the American Enterprise Institute for Public Policy Research, *Law, Order, and Civil Disobedience*, 1967, p. 37.

To keep things in perspective, it would help I think if Americans were to recall that our Puritan Fathers came to this country precisely because they refused to surrender their conscience to the state; and that many Americans whom we now hail as heroes were in their generation notorious lawbreakers.

Martin Luther King, Jr., "Letter From the Birmingham Jail," 1963, in *On Civil Disobedience*, 1968, p. 67.

Of course, there is nothing new about this kind of civil disobedience. It was evidenced sublimely in the refusal of Shadrach, Meshach and Abednego to obey the laws of Nebuchadnezzar, on the ground that a higher moral law was at stake. It was practiced superbly by the early Christians, who were willing to face hungry lions and the excruciating pain of chopping blocks rather than submit to certain unjust laws of the Roman Empire. To a degree, academic freedom is reality today because Socrates practiced civil disobedience. In our own nation, the Boston Tea Party represented a massive act of civil disobedience.

Henry David Thoreau, "Civil Disobedience," February 1848, in *On Civil Disobedience*, 1968, p. 14.

All men recognize the right of revolution; that is, the right to refuse allegiance to, and to resist, the government, when its tyranny or its inefficiency are great and unendurable. But almost all say that such is not the case now. But such was the case, they think, in the Revolution of '75 . . . when a sixth of the population of a nation which has undertaken to be the refuge of liberty are slaves, and a whole country is unjustly overrun and conquered by a foreign army, and subjected to military law, I think that it is not too soon for honest men to rebel and revolutionize. What makes this duty the more urgent is the fact, that the country so overrun is not our own, but ours is the invading army.

Thomas Jefferson, in *America Radical Thought: The Libertarian Tradition*, 1970, p. 15.

We have had 13 states independent 11 years. There has been one rebellion. That comes to one rebellion in a century & a half for each state. What country before ever existed a century & half without a rebellion & what country can preserve it's liberties if their rulers are not warned from time to time that their people preserve the spirit of resistance? Let them take arms. . . . What signify a few lives lost in a century or two? The tree of liberty must be refreshed from time to time with the blood of patriots & tyrants. It is it's natural manure.

Students for Democratic Society, "The Port Huron Statement," *American Radical Thought: The Libertarian Tradition*, 1970, p. 361.

We would replace power rooted in possession, privilege, or circumstance by power and uniqueness rooted in love, reflectiveness, reason, and creativity. As a *social system* we seek the establishment of a democracy of individual participation, governed by two central aims: that the individual share in those social decisions determining the quality and direction of his life; that society be organized to encourage independence in men and provide the media for their common participation.

Extremists and social change.

Merton C. Dillon, Professor of History—Ohio State University, *Dissent: Explorations in the History of American Radicalism*, 1968, p. 86.

It is not clear, however, that—despite all their [the Abolitionists] decades of effort before, during, and after the Civil War—they ever succeeded in transmitting their principles to more than a small part of their contemporaries. Indeed, when slavery finally was abolished—an accomplishment often credited to abolitionists—the event followed more upon the actions of southern leaders and the accidents of war than from the moral regeneration of the nation. From this point of view the abolitionists' record was one of persistent failure, and their heirs, who have felt impelled to struggle in the same irrepressible conflict, have of necessity inherited their predecessor's revolutionary role.

Melvin Dubovsky, Professor of History—University of Massachusetts, *Dissent: Explorations in the History of American Radicalism*, 1968, p. 199.

By fighting for free speech in Spokane, Fresno, Missoula, Sioux City, and Minot (among other cities), the IWW proved to long-brutalized migratories that authority could be defeated through direct action and passive resistance. Taking to the streets in defense of their civil liberties, Wobblies courted arrest, and those arrested were quickly replaced on soap boxes by other free-speech speakers. Wobblies flooded the jails, paralyzed the courtrooms, and strained the purses of the cities they confronted. Most civic authorities, unable to cope with such passive resistance on a mass scale, succumbed to IWW demands; but some authorities, like San Diego's, dealt with the IWW "menace" by methods later made infamous in Mussolini's Italy and Hitler's Germany.

The validity and impact of political pluralism.

Waldemer Read, *Great Issues Concerning Freedom*, 1962, p. 9.

Our greatest strength as a country lies in the fact that we have a diversity of opinion and diversity of people. We can absorb and use ideas of all kinds provided we keep ourselves in a situation in which every idea can have public expression. What has given this country's thought its vitality in the past is the continued struggle of men and women to gain acceptance for their own views, and the continual push of a variety of minority opinions. What marks our history from that of other countries is the way in which we have been able to avoid an orthodoxy, to remain open-minded and flexible, to absorb radical ideas in the flow of social process and to put them to work when they are needed.

Herbert J. Storing, Professor of Political Science—University of Chicago, "The Case Against Civil Disobedience," in *On Civil Disobedience*, 1968, p. 102.

The heart of [Martin Luther King's] definition is that "Any law that uplifts human personality is just. Any law that degrades human personality is unjust" . . . the important point is that to the extent that the demands of justice are obscure the gound for civil disobedience is weakened and the need for political deliberation and political working out of the answers is strengthened.

Henry U. Jaffa, Professor of Political Philosophy—Claremont Graduate School, "Reflections on Thoreau and Lincoln: Civil Disobedience and the American Tradition," in *On Civil Disobedience*, 1968, p. 38.

But why, it may be asked, should the majority principle be the one to decide the common concerns of fellow-citizens? The answer is that unanimity is impossible, and the majority principle is the only direct reflection of the original equality of natural rights of the members of the political association.

Lynd Staughton, Professor of History—Yale University, *Dissent: Explorations in the History of American Radicalism*, 1968, p. 22.

The inalienable right of revolution, on the other hand, was available only to majorities. It was "the people" (in Maryland and Massachusetts), "the community" (in Pennsylvania), and, more precisely, "a majority of the community" (in Virginia) that alone could alter, reform, or abolish government. The literature of the Revolution, as Thad Tate has written, "described resistance as a right exercised only by decision of the community, never on the initiative of the individuals."

Arthur M. Schlesinger, Jr., Historian, *The Crisis of Confidence: Ideas, Power and Violence in America*, 1969, p. 35.

Democracy requires consent—it insists, that is, that a majority of the electorate eventually be persuaded that one course is preferable to another. If men or mechanisms were infallible, there would be no need for such persuasion. But, because they are not, the discipline of consent is indispensable to civilized society. The discipline of consent means that policies must triumph not through the divine right of kings or of a "democratic educational dictatorship" but through making sense to a majority of the people; and the condition of bringing a majority along is the best guarantee that policies relate, not to private fantasy or personal power, but to the greatest good of the greatest number.

Martin Luther King, Jr., "Letter from the Birmingham Jail," 1963, in *On Civil Disobedience*, 1968, p. 66.

You express a great deal of anxiety over our willingness to break laws. This is certainly a legitimate concern. Since we so diligently urge people to obey the Supreme Court's decision of 1954 outlawing segregation in the public schools, at first glance it may seem rather paradoxical for us consciously to break laws. One may well ask: "How can you advocate breaking some laws and obeying others?" The answer lies in the fact that there are two types of laws: just and unjust. I would be the first to advocate obeying just laws. One has not only a legal but a moral responsibility to obey just laws. Conversely, one has a moral responsibility to disobey unjust laws. I would agree with St. Augustine that "an unjust law is no law at all."

Seymour Lipset, Professor of Government—Harvard University, and Earl Raab, Professor of Government—University of California, Berkeley, *The Politics of Unreason*, 1970, p. 437.

The history of right-wing extremism in the United States has been a record of association with religious-group bigotry. Although, since World War II, most right-wing extremist groups have so far either played down or formally opposed overt expressions of such sentiments, the fact remains that their political tendencies attract many bigots. Robert Welch has frequently discussed the problem he faces from Birch Society members who attempt to press that organization in an anti-Semitic direction. The various Jewish defense organizations have reported many incidents involving the presence of well-known anti-Semites at meetings of rightist groups which themselves are not anti-Semitic. The 1960 election campaign bore eloquent witness to the continuation of anti-Catholic prejudice. Any effort to evaluate the potential for various forms of extremist politics in the United States must take into account the continued existence of bigotry against these religious groups.

Extremism as a hindrance to justice.

Arthur M. Schlesinger, Jr., Historian, *The Crisis of Confidence: Ideas, Power and Violence in America*, 1969, p. 167.

Professor William Appleman Williams of Wisconsin, whose own historical writing stimulated this generation of student radicals, ended by calling them "the most selfish people I know. They just terrify me . . . . They say, 'I'm right and you're wrong and you can't talk because you're wrong.' " At Columbus SDS was prepared, as a liberal professor put it, to "exact a conformity that makes Joe McCarthy look like a civil libertarian."

Arthur M. Schlesinger, Jr., Historian, *The Crisis of Confidence: Ideas, Power and Violence in America*, 1969, p. 34.

A limited amount of collective violence may stimulate the process of democratic change; but, if the left, through the cult of the deed, helps create an atmosphere which destroys the process of democracy itself, the only winners will be those who use violence best, and they will be on the right.

Abraham Lincoln, "The Perpetuation of Our Political Institutions," January 27, 1938, in *On Civil Disobedience*, 1968, p. 3.

When men take it in their heads to day, to hang gamblers, or burn murderers, they should recollect, that, in the confusion usually attending such transactions, they will be as likely to hang or burn some one, who is neither a gambler nor a murderer as one who is; and that, acting upon the example they set, the men of tomorrow, may and probably will hang or burn some of them by the very same mistake.

Herbert Storing, Professor of Political Science—University of Chicago, "The Case Against Civil Disobedience," in *On Civil Disobedience*, 1968, p. 116.

. . . the law rests on and encourages habitual law-abidingness, the "taking for granted" of the justice of the law and its title to obedience. If mere habituation threatens freedom, sound habituation provides its necessary foundation. The man who seeks his freedom in a resistance to law as law will find instead anarchy or, more likely, paralysis. It is only through command, enforcement, and habituation that the law of the liberal regime performs one of its most admired functions, to provide the basis for political deliberation and political education.

Martin Luther King, Jr., "Letter from the Birmingham Jail," 1963, in *On Civil Disobedience*, 1968, p. 71.

The Negro has many pent-up resentments and latent frustrations, and he must release them. So let him march; let him make prayer pilgrimages to the city hall; let him go on freedom rides— and try to understand why he must do so. If his repressed emotions are not released in nonviolent ways, they will seek expression through violence; this is not a threat but a fact of history.

Martin Luther King, Jr., "Letter from the Birmingham Jail," 1963, in *On Civil Disobedience*, 1968, p. 68.

Actually, we who engage in nonviolent direct action are not the creators of tension. We merely bring to the surface the hidden tension that is already alive. We bring it out in the open, where it can be seen and dealt with. Like a boil that can never be cured so long as it is covered up but must be opened with all its ugliness to the natural medicines of air and light, injustice must be exposed, with all the tension its exposure creates, to the light of human conscience and the air of national opinion before it can be cured.

Should freedom of speech be restricted?

Theodore Roosevelt, Message to Congress, U.S. Senate Document No. 426, 60th Congress, 1st Session, 1906.

The anarchist is the enemy of humanity, the enemy of all mankind, and his is a deeper degree of criminality than any other . . . No paper here or abroad should be permitted circulation in this country if it propagates anarchistic opinions.

James Mill, English Historian and Philosopher, *Liberty of the Press*, 1825.

How can you point out a line where passionate language begins, dispassionate ends? The effect of words upon the mind depends upon the associations which we have with them. But no two men have the same association with the same words. A word which may excite strains of emotion in one breast, will excite none in another. A word may appear to one man a passionate word, which does not appear so to another.

Herbert Spencer, English Philosopher, *Principles of Ethics*, Vol. II, 1900, p. 143.

Evidently such proposals to limit the right of free speech, political or religious, can be defended only by making the tacit assumption that whatever political or religious beliefs are at the time established, are wholly true; and since this tacit assumption has throughout the past proved to be habitually erroneous, regard for experience may reasonably prevent us from assuming that the current beliefs are wholly true.

Mr. Justice Holmes, dissenting (Brandeis concurring), *Abrams v. United States*, 1919, 250 U.S. 616.

Every year, if not every day, we have to wager our salvation upon some prophecy based upon imperfect knowledge. While that experiment is part of our system I think that we should be externally vigilant against attempts to check the expression of opinions that we loathe and believe to be fraught with death, unless they so imminently threaten immediate interference with the lawful and pressing purposes of the law that an immediate check is required to save the country . . .

United States Supreme Court, *Scheneck v. United States*, 1909, 249 U.S. 47.

When a nation is at war many things that might be said in time of peace are such a hindrance to its effort that their utterance will not be endured so long as men fight, and that no Court could regard them as protected by any constitutional right . . . We admit that in many places and in ordinary times the defendants in saying all that was said in the circular would have been within their constitutional rights.

William Ellery Channing, American Preacher and Author, "The Present Age," *Works,* **11th ed., Vol. 6, 1949, p. 149.**

We have lived to hear the strange doctrine, that to expose the measures of rulers is treason; and we have lived to see this doctrine carried into practice. The cry has been that war is declared, and all opposition should therefore be hushed. A sentiment more unworthy of a free country could hardly be propagated. If the doctrine be admitted rulers have only to declare war and they are screened at once from scrutiny.

George Sutherland, Associate Justice—U. S. Supreme Court, *Constitutional Power and World Affairs,* **1919, pp. 98-99.**

Everything that he (the citizen) has or is, or hopes to be—property, liberty, life—may be required. In time of peace, an attempt to interfere with the least of these would be, and ought to be, resisted to the utmost. In time of war, when the nation is in deadly peril, every freeman who prizes the boon of enduring liberty, will lay them all, freely and ungrudgingly, upon the sacrificial altar of his country.

Selected Bibliography

Bailyn, Bernard. *The Ideological Origins of the American Revolution.* Cambridge, Mass.: Harvard University Press, 1967.

Bailyn, Bernard. *The Ordeal of Thomas Hutchinson.* Cambridge, Mass.: Harvard University Press, 1974.

Bell, Daniel, ed. *The Radical Right.* Garden City, New York: Doubleday and Co., 1963.

Carleton, William G. *The Revolution in American Foreign Policy: The Global Range.* New York: Random House, 1963.

Coffin, William Sloane Jr., and Liebman, Morris I. *Civil Disobedience: Aid or Hindrance to Justice?* Washington, D.C.: American Enterprise Institute for Public Policy Research, 1973.

Cohen, Carl. *Civil Disobedience: Conscience, Tactics, and the Law.* New York: Columbia University Press, 1971.

Davis, David Brion, ed. *The Fear of Conspiracy: Images of Unamerican Subversion from the Revolution to the Present.* Ithaca, New York: Cornell University Press, 1971.

Demaris, Ovid. *America the Violent.* New York: Cowles Book Co., 1970.

Dolbeane, Kenneth; Dolbeane, Patricia; and Hadley, Jane. *American Ideologies: The Competing Political Beliefs of the 1970's.* Chicago: Markham Publishing Co., 1973.

Douglas, William O. *Points of Rebellion.* New York: Random House, 1970.

Fortas, Abe. *Concerning Dissent and Civil Disobedience.* New York: World Publishing Co., 1968.

Fulbright, J. William. *The Arrogance of Power.* New York: Random House, 1966.

Gabriel, Ralph Henry, and Wood, William. *In the Defense of Liberty.* New Haven, Conn.: Yale University Press, 1928.

Goldwater, Barry M. *Why not Victory? A Fresh Look at American Foreign Policy.* New York: McGraw-Hill, 1962.

Goldwin, Robert A. *On Civil Disobedience: American Essays, Old and New, by Abraham Lincoln and Others.* Chicago: Rand McNally, 1969.

Golembiewski, Robert T. *The New Politics: Polarization or Utopia?* New York: McGraw-Hill, 1970.

Green, Gilbert. *The New Radicalism: Anarchist or Marxist?* New York: International Publishers, 1971.

Graham, Hugh Davis. *The History of Violence in America: Historical and Comparative Perspectives.* New York: F.A. Praeger, 1969.

Hall, Robert. *The Morality of Civil Disobedience.* New York: Harper and Row, 1971.

Handlin, Oscar and Mary. *The Dimensions of Liberty.* Cambridge, Mass.: Harvard University Press, 1961.

Hofstadter, Richard, and Wallace, Mike, eds. *American Violence: A Documentary History.* New York: Knopf, 1970.

Kiefer, Howard E., and Munitz, Milton K. *Ethics and Social Justice.* Albany: State University of New York Press, 1970.

Levy, Leonard. *Jefferson and Civil Liberties.* Cambridge, Mass.: Harvard University Press, 1963.

Lipset, Seymour Martin, and Raab, Earl. *The Politics of Unreason: Right Wing Extremism in America, 1790-1970.* New York: Harper and Row, 1970.

Lynd, Staughton, *Intellectual Origins of American Radicalism.* New York: Pantheon Books, 1968.

McCarthy, Eugene. *A Liberal Answer to a Conservative Challenge.* New York: MacFadden, 1964.

Madden, Edward H. *Civil Disobedience and Moral Law in Nineteenth Century American Philosophy.* Seattle: University of Washington Press, 1968.

Maier, Pauline. *From Resistance to Revolution: Colonial Radicals and the Development of American Opposition to Britain, 1765-1776.* New York: Vintage Books, 1974.

Marcuse, Herbert. *An Essay on Liberation.* Boston: Beacon Press, 1968.

Marshall, Charles Burton. *American Foreign Policy as a Dimension of the American Revolution.* Distinguished Bicentennial Lecture Series. Washington, D.C.: The American Enterprise Institute, 1974.

Morley, Felix, ed. *The Necessary Conditions for a Free Society.* Princeton, New Jersey: Van Nostrand, 1963.

Pinkney, Alphonso. *The American Way of Violence.* New York: Random House, 1972.

Preston, William Jr. *Aliens and Dissenters: Federal Suppression of Radicals, 1903-1933.* New York: Harper Torchbooks, 1963.

Redekop, John Harold. *The American Far Right: A Case Study of Billy James Hargis and the Christian Crusade.* Grand Rapids, Michigan: William B. Eerdmans Publishing Co., 1968.

Rose, Thomas. *Violence in America: A Historical and Contemporary Reader.* New York: Random House, 1969.

Roy, Ralph Lord. *Apostles of Discord.* Boston: Beacon, 1953.

Royster, Vermont. *The American Press and the Revolutionary Tradition,* Distinguished Bicentennial Lecture Series. Washington, D.C.: The American Enterprise Institute, 1974.

Schlesinger, Arthur M. Jr. *The Crisis of Confidence: Ideas, Power and Violence in America.* Boston: Houghton Mifflin, 1969.

Schuman, Samuel L., comp. *Law and Disorder: The Legitimation of Direct Action as an Instrument of Social Policy,* The Franklin Memorial Lectures, Vol. XIX. Detroit, Michigan: Wayne State University Press, 1971.

Sherwin, Mark. *The Extremists.* New York: St. Martin's, 1963.

Silverman, Henry J., ed. American Radical Thought: *The Libertarian Tradition.* Lexington, Mass.: Heath, 1970.

Smith, Duane, and Gerberding, William. *The Radical Left: The Abuse of Discontent.* Boston: Houghton Mifflin, 1970.

Students for Democratic Society. *The Port Huron Statement.* Chicago: SDS, 1966.

Taylor, Karl K., and Soady, Fred. W. Jr. *Violence: An Element of American Life.* Boston: Holbrook Press, 1972.

Teodori, Missimo, ed. *The New Left: A Documentary History.* Indianapolis: Bobbs-Merrill, 1969.

Tucker, Robert W. *The Radical Left and American Foreign Policy.* Baltimore: Johns Hopkins Press, 1971.

Turner, William W. *Power on the Right.* Berkeley: Ramparts Press, 1971.

Whittaker, Charles Evans, and Coffin, William Sloane Jr. *Law, Order, and Civil Disobedience.* Washington: American Enterprise Institute for Public Policy Research, 1967.

Wiebe, Robert H. *The Segmented Society: An Introduction to The Meaning of America.* New York: Oxford University Press, 1975.

Wood, Gordon S. *Revolution and the Political Integration of the Enslaved and Disenfranchised,* Distinguished Bicentennial Lecture Series. Washington, D.C.: The American Enterprise Institute, 1974.

Young, Alfred Fabian, ed. *Dissent: Explorations in the History of American Radicalism.* Dekalb, Ill.: Northern Illinois University Press, 1968.

Zinn, Howard. *Disobedience and Democracy: Nine Fallacies on Law and Order.* New York: Random House, 1968.

THE PRESS: REPORTER OR MAKER OF HISTORY?

Introductory Essay

Thomas Jefferson, who suffered as much as any President at the ink-stained hands of editorial assassins, commented to his friend, John Norwell: "To your request of my opinion of the manner in which a newspaper should be conducted, so as to be the most useful, I should answer: by restraining it to true facts and sound principles only. Yet I fear such a paper would find few subscribers." Jefferson's observation neatly encapsulated the dilemma that has historically confronted American journalists. The oft-quoted credo of a good reporter has been the "five W's—Who, What, When, Where, and Why. Proponents of this doctrine held that "the only safe thing in a newspaper...was a fact. The reporter's duty was to supply his readers with the cold, hard, barren details of what had happened—and with nothing more." Challenged on a philosophical level by Curtis MacDougall's 1938 textbook *Interpretative Reporting*, the ideal had been pragmatically denied long before by publishers who recognized that "dull" newspapers sold few copies, by printers more conscious of the need to "scoop" opposition tabloids than to check the accuracy of a rumor, and by editors unable to resist the political forum that the American newspaper offered its owner. In consequence, the influence of the press in both molding public opinion and recording public actions has been considerable.

With remarkably accurate foresight, colonial administrators attempted to prevent the infusion of printers into the new lands, suspecting the profession's ability to subvert the lawful authority. John Buckner was reprimanded in 1682 "for printing the laws of 1680, without his excellency's license," and William Bradford had similar troubles in Pennsylvania. Less than a decade earlier, Sir William Berkeley, governor of Virginia, expressed thanks that the colony had avoided free schools and printing presses, and added: "God keep us from both," while the royal governor of New York was instructed to "allow no printing press in the colony." By 1690, however, an English immigrant named Benjamin Harris printed America's first newspaper, *Publick Occurences Both Foreign and Domestick*, in Boston. Only one issue was published, as the government of the colony felt the paper contained "Reflections of a very high nature" and also "sundry doubtful and uncertain Reports." A later journalistic endeavor, presid-ed over by the local postmaster, contained little of offense to the Massachusetts Bay authorities, but little of interest to any one else. In consequence, it enjoyed a rather lackluster existence. More popular, and more controversial, was the *New England Courant*, edited by talented, English-trained printer James Franklin, who brought out the *Courant's* first issue in 1718. Stung by the paper's jibes at the ministry, Cotton Mather confided to his diary that "The Town is become almost a Hell upon Earth, a City full of Lies."

Newspapers found fertile soil for expansion in America. The relatively permissive climate, the highly literate population, and the avid interest in world affairs provided pioneer printers a ready audience. La Rouchefoucauld observed that in New England, all the people "from the landlord down to the housemaid ...all read two newspapers a day." On the eve of the Revolution, Royalist printer Ambrose Serle wrote to Lord Dartmouth that:

> One is astonished to see with what avidity they [the colonial newpapers] are sought after, and how implicitly they are believed, by the great bulk of the People...Government may find it expedient, in the Sum of Things, to employ this popular Engine.

The American press, as Serle astutely observed, had great potential power, but it was not to be exercised on behalf of the Crown.

Parliament's attempt to reduce the national debt through measures such as the Stamp Act gained few friends in the American newspaper community. Benjamin Franklin protested that the law "will affect the Printers more than anybody, as [the tax]...will go near to knock up one Half [the price]." Printer James Parker, who had planned to start a newspaper in New Jersey, complained "of the Killing Stamp, [that] has struck a deadly blow to all my Hopes on that Head." The impact of the law was minimal, as many methods were found to "elude the chains forged for us." Some papers were published without the printer's name and other publications dropped their regular titles, giving them more comfortable tax status as handbills. A few continued publication as usual, noting blandly that there was no stamped paper to be found—a situation caused by intimidation of stamp agents by angry colonials.

Rendered ineffectual, the Stamp Act was soon repealed. The colonial press did not limit itself to passive resistance to matters directly concerning journalism, however. In Boston, the haven of "foul-mouthed Trumpeters of Sedition," Samuel Adams and other radicals in the "Loyal Nine" contributed inflammatory articles to Benjamin Edes' *Gazette,* referred to by Governor Bernard as "an infamous weekly paper which has swarmed with libells of the most atrocious kind." The Governor attempted to curtail the paper's record-breaking circulation with formal libel charges, the grand jury refused to indict. "The misfortune is," the Governor fumed, "that seven eighths of the people read none but this infamous paper." Tory Peter Oliver was later to state that "Independence, it is true, was declared in Congress in 1776, but it was settled in Boston, in 1768, by Adams and his Junto."

By the outbreak of actual hostilities, the colonial press was solidly for the insurgents. It was dangerous to be otherwise, as laggards and strays found, to their discomfort. John Mein, a Scotsman whose clever attacks on Adams made him intolerable to the patriots, was eventually forced to leave the country. A friend reported that "Mr. Mein. . .is so obnoxious to the People. . .that he's oblig'd to go arm'd, and 'tis but a few nights since that two Persons who resembled him pretty much were attack'd. . .and would in all probability have lost their lives if the Mistake had not been timely discover'd." Two other Tory newspapers in Boston ceased publication within a week of the battles of Lexington and Concord, and the last one expired as the British evacuated the city. Of the seventy papers published during the Revolution, fifteen had Royalist leanings at some time. Generally, they prospered only when the Brittish forces were comfortably close at hand. Typical of the wavering loyalties of some printers were the actions of James Rivington of New York. Originally a luke-warm patriot, Rivington tried to chart a neutral course and ended with a wrecked printing shop. Angered, he turned against the rebels and showed himself willing to print any type of lie or half-truth which could discredit the revolutionaries. When he saw that the war appeared to be going for the colonials, however, he ingratiated himself with General Washington by sending out of the city "such communications as he knew would be interesting to the commanders of the American armies."

The influence of the majority of the newspapers weighed heavily for the colonials, but perhaps more important was the work of pamphleteer Tom Paine. Paine's *Common Sense,* published in the winter of 1775-1776, presented cogent arguments for separation and challenged "the warmest advocate of reconciliation to show a single advantage this continent can reap by being connected with Great Britain." Over one hundred and twenty thousand copies were sold in three months. His first *Crisis* paper,

published in the *Pennsylvania Journal* December 19, 1776 stated that "he that stands it now, deserves the love and thanks of man and woman. Tyranny, like Hell, is not easily conquered. . ." This paper, ordered by Washington to be read to his army the day before his attack on Trenton, was credited by some as a major factor in the colonial victory. Overall, an American historian of the 1790's believed that "in establishing American independence, the pen and press had merit equal to that of the sword."

Newspapers likewise played a crucial role in the establishment of a constitution for the new nation. The proposed document was reasonably short, as constitutions go, and every newspaper in the United States printed it in full. Washington wrote to a friend that "Much will depend. . .upon literary abilities, and the recommendation of it [the Constitution] by good pens should be. . .publickly afforded in the Gazettes." The cooperation of the newspapers in providing a forum for discussion of the document produced results that startled even the proposal's strongest advocates; within thirteen months, eleven states had ratified the Constitution.

Bitter controversy between Jefferson and Hamilton over the nation's future was reflected in newspapers of the period. Many were political organs that made no attempt at objectivity. In the first issue of the *Porcupine Gazette,* a strongly Federalist sheet, editor William Cobbett announced that "Professions of impartiality I shall make none. They are always useless, and are besides perfect nonsense." Opposing him was Philip Freneau's *National Gazette,* which attacked all of Hamilton's major measures, and of which Jefferson later said "His paper has saved our Constitution which was galloping fast into monarchy, and has been checked by no one means so powerfully as by that paper." With the *Gazette* stood Benjamin Franklin Bache (familiarly referred to as "Lightning Rod Junior") and the *General Advertiser,* which accused Washington of overdrawing his salary, reprinted forged letters, and vigorously opposed Jay's treaty. Bache's bitter diatribes did not cease even with Washington's farewell address; instead, he used the occasion to remark that "If ever there was a period of rejoicing this is the moment." Bache's death likewise did not lessen the ire of his Federalist adversaries. *Russell's Gazette* of Boston said "The memory of this scoundrel cannot be too highly execrated." The widespread use of "gutter journalism" led a more sedate publication to complain that "the papers are overrunning with electioneering essays, squibs, and invectives."

Jefferson was somewhat at a loss to deal with the press of what has been called the Dark Ages of American journalism. By the end of his second term, he had concluded that "Nothing can now be believed which is seen in a newspaper. Truth itself becomes suspicious by being put into that polluted vehicle." The Jackson-Adams campaign dwelt as much on the candidates' wives, ancestry, and moral attitudes as it did on their qualifications for the Chief Magistry. Jackson, opposed by two-thirds of the newspapers in the nation, sought to remedy that situation as President; no less than 57 journalists were given federal appointments. The heyday of political newspapers was to continue until 1860, when Lincoln refused to pick an official party journal and the Government Printing Office was established, almost eliminating printing-contract patronage.

Newspapers found other concerns to fill their columns. Sectional conflicts were magnified in partisan journals and fiery editorials accelerated the drift toward war. Most prominent of the Northern abolitionists was Horace Greeley who mirrored the Southern determination to allow "no more humiliation, no more truckling under." Some observers have named Greeley's *Tribune* as the chief influence responsible for freeing the slaves, although Garrison's *Liberator* and *Uncle Tom's Cabin*, a novel written by Harriet Beecher Stowe and published by the *National Era*, undoubtedly also played a large part. Ralph Waldo Emerson reported after a lecture tour of the Midwest that "Greeley does the thinking for the whole West, at $2 per year for his paper." Attempting to make, not only report, history in these troubled times was not without its perils. Radical Abolitionist editor William Lloyd Garrison, who warned his opposition "I am in earnest. I will not equivocate. I will not excuse. I will not retreat an inch. And I will be heard." had his voice. . .forever stilled by mob violence. Greeley advised his office staff that "Several pistols will be bought. . .I will stand any chances to be horsewhipped and pistolled."

The inevitable conflict gave journalists a chance to try their hand at war reporting. Although the Confederacy had effective censorship, the North had virtually free and often dangerously accurate reporting. A border paper accused Cincinatti journals of printing information which had "delayed and thwarted our armies, caused the death of our soldiers." General Sherman wrote during the Vicksburg campaign that "The only two really successful strokes out here have succeeded because of the absence of the newspapers, or by throwing them off the trail." Southern newspapers, plagued by poor communications and shortage of newsprint, had comparatively little influence on the conduct of the war. Editorials and commentary in Northern publications had more telling effect. Prentice's *Journal* is given much of the credit for persuading Kentucky not to secede. Greeley's *Tribune* urged the Federal troops "Forward to Richmond! Forward to Richmond! The rebel Congress must not be allowed to meet there on the 20th of July! BY THAT DATE THE PLACE MUST BE HELD BY THE NATIONAL ARMY!" The actual effect of the editorial is problematical,

but jeering crowds and Greeley himself blamed it for the premature union campaign and the subsequent Bull Run disaster.

Newspapers of the post-war period tried many devices to increase circulation. One of the most effective means, and one which ultimately had a great impact on American life, was the increasing image of the press as an agent for social and political reform. In 1871, the New York *Times* uncovered the Tweed ring, a venal web of corruption that controlled New York City, when former Sheriff James O'Brien gave the newspaper the City Controller's records, which he had secretly acquired before leaving office—records the brilliant satirical cartoonist Thomas Nast and the *Times* used to full advantage. A year later, the New York *Sun* discovered corruption in the United States Postal Department. The St. Louis *Democrat* exposed a whiskey ring organized to deprive the government of tax revenues. Jacob Riis, an immigrant reporter, dealt with slum living in his 1890 book, *How the Other Half Lives. McClure's*, from 1902 to 1904, published Ida Tarbull's "History of the Standard Oil" series, which led to a 1911 breakup of that company into 37 segments. *Collier's* followed with the "Great American Fraud," detailing the false claims of many drugs and revealing some with poisonous (and unlisted) ingredients. In combination with the 1906 publication of Upton Sinclair's *The Jungle*, this series generated public pressure which resulted in the Pure Food and Drugs Act of 1906.

Some publications, most notably William Randolph Hearst's *Journal*, capitalized on public fascination with sex and crime and even went beyond mere reporting to detection and apprehension of criminals. The *Journal* was responsible for the solution of several cases, and Hearst claimed his reporters constituted "a detective force at least as efficient as that maintained at public expense by this or any other city." James Gordon Bennett, Jr., owner of the New York *Herald*, was equally successful with "stunts." Perhaps his greatest coup was the dispatch of reporter Henry M. Stanley to Africa to find Livingstone. Bennett kept Stanley in the field after his historic encounter with Dr. Livingstone, and the reporter eventually traversed the continent, traced the Congo River to its source, and organized the Congo Free State. Bennett summed up his journalistic philosophy by saying "I *make* news." One of the more blatant examples of this tendency was his "wild animal hoax," November 9, 1874. On that day, the entire front page of the *Herald*, was given over to a description of the escape of all the animals from the Central Park Zoo including "terrible scenes of mutilation" and a vivid description of Governor Dix shooting a Bengal tiger in the streets. Readers who did not bother to read to the very end of the article barricaded themselves inside their houses or stood on their front steps with loaded guns. Circulation skyrocketed.

In a far more serious vein, newspapers used sensationalizing techniques to promote and popularize the war with Spain. Hearst sent a team of reporters and artists to Cuba to cover the possible outbreak of hostilities. An apocryphal story of the period has it that artist Frederic Remington wired his employer, expressing doubt that any war would occur. Hearst reportedly fired back the response "Please remain. You furnish the pictures, and I'll furnish the war." Although the story may not be true, the sentiment was valid. Hearst published stories calculated to arouse public fervor. A Hearst reporter rescued the pretty niece of an insurgent leader from a Havana jail and arranged a series of receptions in the United States calculated to arouse sympathy for the rebel cause. In another journalistic coup, the *Journal* acquired a letter stolen from the Spanish minister in Washington in which he called President McKinley a "low politician." The printing of the De Lome letter aroused considerable public indignation, which had not yet died down when the *Journal* unhesitatingly pinned the mysterious *Maine* explosion on the hapless Spaniards. Hearst was denied permission to organize a regiment, but *Journal* reporters played a part in the conduct, as well as the reporting, of the campaign. Correspondent James Creelman led an attack on a small Spanish fort, and Hearst himself captured twenty-six frightened and demoralized Spanish soldiers during the Battle of Guantanamo Bay. Nor was the *Journal* alone in this; Richard Harding Davis, representing the *Herald* and *Scribner's*, figured prominently in the fighting at Las Guasimas, and won the approval of Colonel Roosevelt. Governor Sadler of Missouri declared that it was unnecessary for the U.S. Army to fight the war, proposing instead to send Hearst with five hundred reporters to free Cuba. Ironically, a modern historian suggests that "the 'ifs' of history are usually more amusing than profitable, but there seems to be [a] great probability. . .that if Hearst had not challenged Pulitzer to a circulation contest at the time of the Cuban insurrection, there would have been no Spanish-American War."

The Twentieth Century has witnessed great changes in the press. Newspaper consolidations and chains became commonplace. The United Press in 1882 and the Associated Press in 1900 provided vehicles for cooperation among newspapers. The U.P. suffered embarrassment by "making history" prematurely and erroneously on two notable occasions, declaring the end of both World Wars some days in advance of the actual cessation of hostilities.

Newspapers, which had long held a virtual monopoly on news in America, encountered stiff competition in the Twentieth Century. The first public radio station began broadcasting in 1920, but by 1923 over five hundred commercial transmitters crowded the airwaves, bringing the dubious blessings of baseball, elections, and jazz into every prosperous American's home. Television got off to a slower start: the first experimental television studio was established in 1920, but the demands of war production prevented the emergence of the medium as a major competitor until the late 1940's. The new media were heralded as great advances in journalistic objectivity. No longer did a reader have to rely on a summary of a speech or an abbreviated report of a political convention. Now he could hear the speech or see the convention in his own home.

The innate ability of the new media to present newsworthy events more accurately and fairly has not eliminated possibilities and consequences of bias, however, but has replaced the banner headline and flaming editorial with more subtle, but equally effective devices. A newsman, no matter what his personal beliefs, who selects a few minutes of material for presentation from many hours of film, almost inevitably distorts his subject matter in some way. A video broadcast shows only what the camera's lens was focused on. And the careless comment of a nationally known news personality gains credibility simply by its source. Former Vice President Spiro Agnew, in probably the single most famous attack on television objectivity, suggested in a November 1969 speech at Des Moines, Iowa, that "a raised eyebrow, an inflection of the voice, a caustic comment dropped in the middlle of a broadcast can raise doubts in a million minds about the veracity of a public official or the wisdom of a Government policy." A week later, in an address at Montgomery, Alabama, he included one of America's leading newspapers in his criticism:

> If a theology student in Iowa should get up at a PTA luncheon in Sioux City and attack the President's Vietnam policy, my guess is that you would probably find it reported somewhere in the next morning's issue of the *New York Times*. But when 300 Congressmen endorse the President's Vietnam polity the next morning it is apparently not considered news fit to print.

The response of the majority of the media was predictable. The New York *Times* editorialized that Agnew had "undermined the basic principle of freedom of speech on the air waves." David Schoenbrun, former Chief Washington Correspondent with CBS, warned: "I heard speeches like the Vice President's a year ago in Prague." *The New Republic* regarded the speech "a brutal, blatant demand by the Administration in power for friendlier treatment" and David Brinkley indicated that "when politicians are criticized they blame it on bias, sinister plots, and lack of objectivity. Objectivity means agreement." Although later events indicate that Agnew's speech was probably part of a wider antimedia campaign by the Nixon Administration, it undeniably struck an exposed nerve among broadcasters, and the generally favorable public response to the Vice Presient's comments indicate that he was not alone in his conclusions. The years to come will undoubtedly bring further advances in communication technology, but if history is any guide, the questions of the proper role for media that plagued colonial governors will continue unabated.

Excerpted Documents

The power of the press.

Benjamin Franklin, *The New-England Courant,* in *The Newsmongers,* 1973, p. 24.

I am . . . a mortal Enemy to arbitrary Government and unlimited power. I am naturally very jealous for the Rights and Liberties of my Country; and the least appearance of an Incroachment on those invaluable Priviledges, is apt to make my Blood boil exceedingly.

John Tebbel, Professor of History—New York University. *A Compact History of the American Newspaper,* 1963, p. 78.

Yet the wisest men realized the indispensability of the press, whatever its faults. Jefferson had upheld its freedom. Adams had not answered it in kind. Washington, whose personal sufferings were the most severe because of his character, had canceled most of his newspaper subscriptions when he left the Presidency, but he renewed many of them in the quiet of Mount Vernon. On the night before he died, he sat up until nine o'clock reading the newspapers, and his last utterance on any public matter that last evening was to argue "with some degree of asperity" about something he had read in the paper.

Joseph Dennie, "On Newsmongers," *The Lay Preacher,* 1817.

In America, the impertinent eagerness for news should be scolded or laughed into moderation. The country gentleman, at peace on his farm, asks for translations from the Paris *Moniteur,* absurdly anxious for the welfare of Frenchmen, skipping over the carcass of their king and country. . . Ye querists, ye quidnuncs, check your impertinent curiosity. Devote not life to hearing and telling new things. If ye have business, mind it; are you fasters of families, stay at home. Your heads are too shallow to contain the myriads of novel ideas ye wish. Action, not tattle, is the business of life.

Thomas Jefferson, in *The Opinionmakers,* 1965, p. 3.

The basis of the government being the opinion of the people, the very first object should be to keep that right: and were it left to me to decide whether we should have a government without newspapers or newspapers without a government, I should not hesitate a moment to prefer the latter.

Horace Greeley, quoted by Edwin Emery, Professor of Journalism—University of Minnesota, *The Press & America: An Interpretive History of the Mass Media,* 1972, p. 165.

But the world does move, and its motive power under God is the fearless thought and speech of those who dare to be in advance of their time—who are sneered at and shunned through their days of struggle as lunatics, dreamers, impracticables and visionaries; men of crotchets, vagaries, and isms. They are the masts and sails of the ship to which conservatism answers as ballast. The ballast is important—at times indispensable —but it would be of no account if the ship were not bound to go ahead.

President Dwight D. Eisenhower, speaking in Stockholm, in *The Opinionmakers*, 1965, p. 13.

Before anybody gets the chance to ask, I want to make clear that the remark about Sweden's high rates of suicide and alcoholism which I made in Chicago some years ago was based on what I had then recently read in an American magazine.

Joseph Pulitzer, quoted by Edwin Emery, Professor of Journalism—University of Minnesota. *The Press & America: An Interpretive History of the Mass Media*, 1972, p. 307.

. . . every issue of the paper presents an opportunity and a duty to say something courageous and true; to rise above the mediocre and conventional; to say something that will command the respect of the intelligent, the educated, the independent part of the community; to rise above fear of partisanship and fear of popular prejudice.

Journalistic objectivity.

The *New Yorker Magazine*, December 6, 1969, in *The News Twisters*, 1971, p. 19.

There is nothing in the Constitution that says the press has to be neutral. Nor, for that matter, is there anything that says it has to be objective, or fair, or even accurate or truthful, desirable though these qualities are. For who is to be the judge: The press is simply free, and its freedom, like any other freedom, has to be absolute in order to be freedom. It is free to print any information it wants to print, and to write from any point of view whatsoever.

Democratic Review, April, 1852, Vol. 30, p. 362.

[Referring to frontier newspapers:] Every particular locality is the garden spot of the Union; every little community is the most energetic and intelligent; every State the most patriotic, and every city a true exemplar of public virtue.

Ben H. Bagdikian, *The Effete Conspiracy*, 1972, Introduction.

Freud explained various human hang-ups by traumas in early life which led to reversion to infantile sexuality and Oedipus complexes. Newspaper publishers are peculiarly vulnerable to analogous complaints. Early in every publisher's career there comes a traumatic moment when he realizes that most of the reporters he is paying seem to be Democrats, which for a Republican publisher is like a man discovering that his son likes boys better than girls. This throws the publisher into a state of ideological panic, with regression to infantile economics and politics of such a primitive kind that his editorials thereafter embarrass his conservative idols such as Milton Friedman and Arthur Burns.

Elmer Davis, News Analyst—ABC, *The Press in Perspective*, edited by Ralph Carey, 1963, p. 61.

Yet those who have official positions are likely to be so taken, still. Consider Senator McCarthy; not a single one of his charges has ever been proved, most of them have been pretty conclusively disproved in public hearings—yet he can repeat those same charges and still get space in the papers, sometimes on the front page. And not always merely in papers which find him a useful stick with which to beat the political opposition; very often in papers whose editors may know that this is old stuff, may know that none of it has been proved and much of it has been refuted, yet who feel that if a United States Senator keeps on saying it, it would not be objective to refuse to print it.

Vice President Spiro Agnew, Speech at Des Moines, Iowa, November 13, 1969.

I'm not asking for Government censorship or any other kind of censorship. I'm asking whether a form of censorship already exists when the news that 40 million Americans receive each night is determined by a handful of men responsible only to their corporate employers and is filtered through a handful of commentators who admit to their own set of biases.

Arthur M. Schlesinger, Jr., "The Historian and History," *Foreign Affairs*, **April, 1963, p. 493.**

As for newspaper or magazine accounts, they are sometimes worse than useless when they purport to give the inside history of decisions; their relation to reality is often considerably less than the shadows in Plato's cave. I have too often seen the most conscientious reporters attribute to government officials views the exact opposite of which the officials are advocating within the government to make it possible for me to take the testimony of journalism in such matters seriously again.

James M. Lee, Director, Department of Journalism—New York University, *History of American Journalism*, **1917, p. 402.**

A more liberal policy in the matter of making corrections or offering apologies, adopted by newspapers all over the country marked the passing of the so-called infallibility of the press. Even such a conscientious editor as Samuel Bowles, of *The Republican*, of Springfield Massachusetts, always hesitated to make corrections in his paper. The story is told that a man whose death had been recorded in *The Republican* appeared before the editor and demanded a correction. Upon being told the policy of the paper, he exclaimed, "But I am not dead, as you can see." To this the editor replied, "We cannot print a correction, but as your case demands some attention, we will bring you back to life by putting your name in the birth column." Whether this story be fact or fiction, it recorded an attitude taken by many newspaper publishers before the Period of Social Readjustment.

Robert P. and Dale R. Newman, University of Pittsburgh, *Evidence*, **1969, p. 151.**

On a typical newspaper, aside from writing editorials, an editor usually confines himself to polishing and refining copy coming from the field; the story published is basically a product of the man at the scene of the story. With *Time*, the reverse is true. Copy filed from reporters in the field is primarily stimulus to editorial imagination. Testimony on this point from defectors from the magazine is unanimous.

Arthur Krock, Journalist, *The Consent of the Governed*, **1971, in** *President Nixon and The Press*, **1972, p. 10.**

The "new American liberals" have infiltrated the press—as well as the electronic media—so deeply, and are so busy looking for material on which they can base charges of "suppression," that publishers fear the outcry sure to follow the omission or responsible editing of even rabid commentaries from a writer the liberals claim as their own.

Declaration of Policy of the *New York World*, **1908, in** *History of American Journalism*, **1917, p. 402.**

[As a result of exposure of a largely fictitious news story:]

The World aims to be accurate. It aims to be fair and just to every person who reads it and to every person whose name it prints.

Accuracy and fair play are inseparable in journalism. Inaccuracy often means injury to innocent persons. A newspaper's influence is measured by the number of people who read it AND BELIEVE IN IT.

The words "accuracy and fair play" sum up the law of libel. If what is published is true and fair, the writer need not worry about the libel law, civil or criminal.

Lowell Thomas, Radio Broadcaster, 1970, in *President Nixon and the Press*, **1972, p. 8.**

I have spent my life in the communications world and I have discovered that perhaps 95% of all those involved, reporters, editors and so on, are definitely to the left.

Cabell Phillips, Staff—New York Times, in *The Opinionmakers*, 1965, p. 13.

The bars, lounges, and dining tables of the National Press Club have been a kind of alchemists retort in which thousands of Washington stories have been distilled, synthesized, or even induced out of the thin but susceptible air.

Herbert Brucker, *Communication is Power*, 1973, p. 197.

"FEW AMERICAN institutions are as free from responsible and systematic analysis as the American press. The press, which performs the role of reporter and critic for other institutions, has been reluctant to undertake self-analysis."
That comment, made by a study group reporting in 1969 to Milton Eisenhower's National Commission on the Causes and Prevention of Violence, must have been the understatement of the year. Whenever anyone directs Juvenal's question *Quis custodiet ipsos custodes?* toward the press, the press answers that there isn't going to be any guardian over the guardians of the press.

The media and politics.

Reverend Samuel Miller, 1785(?), in *The Newsmongers*, 1973, p. 55.

Never, it may be safely asserted, was the number of political journals so great in proportion to the population of a country as at present in ours. Never were they, all things considered, so cheap, so universally diffused, and so easy of access.

Nikolai Lenin, Speech in Moscow, 1920, in *The Artillery of the Press: Its influence on American Foreign Policy*, 1966, p. 1.

Why should freedom of speech and freedom of press be allowed? Why should a government which is doing what it believes to be right allow itself to be criticized? It would not allow opposition by lethal weapons. Ideas are much more fatal things than guns. Why should any man be allowed to buy a printing press and disseminate pernicious opinions calculated to embarrass the government?

James Reston, Journalist, *The Artillery of the Press: Its Influence on American Foreign Policy*, 1966, p. 5.

The eighteenth-century American pamphleteers not only helped write the Constitution, but thought—with considerable justification—that they created the Union. They believed that government power was potentially if not inevitably wicked and had to be watched, especially when applied in secret and abroad, and they wrote the rules so that the press would be among the watchers.

John Tebbell, Professor of History—New York University. A compact History of the American Newspaper, 1963.

In these papers and others Lincoln was referred to by such common epithets as "a slang-whanging stump speaker," "half-witted usurper," "mole-eyed," "the present turtle at the head of government," "the head ghoul at Washington," and others even less complimentary. There was not a major paper Lincoln could depend on, except the *New York Times* and Samuel Bowles' Springfield (Mass.) *Republican*. Greeley was unpredictable. Bryant was offensively moral. Bennett could never be counted upon. The Springfield (Ill.) *Daily State Journal* was the only newspaper in the country, according to Robert S. Harper, the modern authority on the subject, which never wavered in its admiration for the President.

Edwin Emery, Professor of Journalism—University of Minnesota, *The Press & America: An Interpretive History of the Mass Media*, 1972, p. 389.

In April 1901, the *Journal* declared editorially that "if bad institutions and bad men can be got rid of only by killing, then the killing must be done." Two months before, on February 4, Ambrose Bierce had written a quatrain for the *Journal* which read:

> The bullet that pierced Goebel's breast
> Can not be found in all the West;
> Good reason, it is speeding here
> To stretch McKinley on his bier.

Goebel was Governor Goebel of Kentucky, a victim of an assassin. When in September, 1901, President McKinley was fatally wounded by anarchist, the offending lines in the *Journal* were recalled, along with the Hearst paper's continual assaults upon McKinley. Hearst found it advantageous to change the name of his morning New York paper to the *American*. But the incident was to haunt him for the rest of his life.

William L. Rivers, *The Opinionmakers*, 1965, p. 5.

The party press dominated political journalism from the beginning of the Jefferson Administration. The President had other favorites—he once wrote to William Dunne, editor of the wild *Aurora,* asking for "an exact list of the prosecutions of a public nature against you, & over which I might have control"—but Smith's *National Intelligencer* was the dominant source of Presidential news. It was an efficient system. There were no Presidential press conferences, and no Presidential interviews. Other editors were forced to rely for information on partisans like Smith.

The press in war.

Frank Luther Mott, University of Missouri, *American Journalism*, 1950, p. 330.

The heading "IMPORTANT—IF TRUE" was common in all papers. The Baltimore *Sun,* during the first few weeks of hostilities, headed a front-page colums "RUMORS AND SPECULATIONS" and published the following editorial paragraph:

> Rumors of every kind multiply. Every hour gives rise to the most extravagant reports. . . . The press North and South seems to have entered upon a war of crimination and recrimination, and instead of calming the excitement and allaying unfounded prejudices, to rejoice in adding to the excitement of the moment. The importance of the condition thus pointed out by the *Sun* in the formation of a belligerent public opinion can scarcely be exaggerated.

***Chicago Inter-Ocean*, February 14, 1898.**

[Referring to the General Manager of the Associated Press:]

> 'Tis Then Field Marshall Melville Stone
> Rides in his Martial car,
> And Makes, with genius all his own,
> Our Sunday Morning war.

Theodore Draper, *The Dominican Revolt*, 1968, p. 146.

It is not often that journalists can be said to have saved the honor of their country. This was, I believe, one of those very rare occasions. Tad Szulc, Barnard L. Collier, Dan Kurzman, James Nelson Goodsell, Philip Geyelin, Bert Quint of CBS, and others, made one feel proud of and grateful for a free press without which the moral and political disaster would have been infinitely greater. When they were struggling against the greatest odds to get the truth and make it known, no public figure was able or willing to speak out against the inconsistencies, contradictions, and outright misrepresentations. In this Dominican crisis, the best and worst of American journalism were manifested—but the worst is far less a stranger than the best.

Arthur M. Schlesinger, *Prelude to Independence: Newspaper War on Britain,* 1764-1776, 1966.

In "Lines on Mr. Rivington's new engraved King's Arms to his *Royal Gazette*," Satan commended the editor,

Since under my banners so bravely you fight,
Kneel down!—for your merits I dubb you a knight,
From a passive subaltern I bid you to rise
The Inventor as well as the Printer of lies.

New York Evening Post, February 19, 1898.

Nothing so disgraceful as the behavior of two of these newspapers [the *Journal* and the *World*] this week has been known in the history of American journalism. Gross misrepresentation of the facts, deliberate invention of tales calculated to excite the public, and wanton recklessness in the construction of headlines which even outdid these inventions, have combined to make the issues of the most widely circulated newspapers firebrands scattered broadcast throughout the country. . . . It is a crying shame that men should work such mischief simply in order to sell more papers.

James Reston, Journalist, *The Artillery of the Press: It's Influence on American Foreign Policy,* 1966, p. 94.

It was a jingoistic American press that whooped us into the Spanish-American War and then, having helped extend our commitments all the way to the Phillippines, confirmed isolationism as the first article of faith.

New York Tribune, March 9, 1898.

Up to this point the war has been a glorious success, as will be seen by the billboard announcements of the increased circulation of the newspapers which have carried it on. If, as now seems probable, its ravages can be confined to Printing House Square, and Spain is "licked" right here with blood-red extras without resorting to shot and shell, it will be the greatest triumph ever achieved by large type and a liberty-loving press.

The press and social reform.

Edward Scripps, Editor—Cincinnati Post quoted by Edwin Emery, Professor of Journalism—University of Minnesota, *The Press & America: An Interpretive History of the Mass Media,* 1972, p. 379.

I have only principle, and that is represented
by an effort to make it harder for the rich to
grow richer and easier for the poor
to keep from growing poorer.

Vice President Spiro Agnew, Speech at Des Moines, Iowa, November 13, 1969.

It must be recognized that the networks have made important contributions to the national knowledge—for news, documentaries and specials. They have often used their power constructively and creatively to awaken the public conscience to critical problems. The networks made hunger and black lung disease national issues overnight. The TV networks have done what no other medium could have done in terms of dramatizing the horrors of war. The networks have tackled our most difficult social problems with a directness and an immediacy that's the gift of their medium. They focus the nation's attention on its environmental abuses—on pollution in the Great Lakes and the threatened ecology of the Everglades.

John Tebbel, Professor of History - New York University. *A Compact History of the American Newspapers,* **1963, p. 153.**

The progress the South has made in the past century toward the better industrial life Watterson and Grady [Henry Grady of the Atlanta *Constitution* & Henry Watterson of the *Louisville Courier-Journal*] dreamed for it must be attributed at least in part to the kind of leadership they provided in a period of crisis. The role their newspapers played, and are playing now, in the creation of a new South is one of the best examples extant of the press truly acting in the public interest.

Edwin Emery, Professor of Journalism—University of Minnesota, *The Press & America: An Interpretive History of the Mass Media,* **1972, p. 406.**

The most common criticism of the muckrakers and the crusaders of this period has been that many of them offered nothing but protests against the injustices and inadequacies of American economic and political life. They aroused discontent, they exposed corruption and greed, they pointed to the inevitable growth of corporations and trusts, but they had few constructive solutions to offer, few alternatives to suggest. So the criticism runs, with some validity, although it should be tempered by the realization that the noisy, persistent radical often prods more cautious people into making needed reforms which keep society in balance.

James Reston, Journalist, *The Artillery of the Press: It's Influence on America Foreign Policy,* **1966, p. 69.**

Within the nation, reporters have a powerful influence on local and national issues. The local editor is usually a respected leader on community issues. The television reports of racial strife in the American South undoubtedly aroused the conscience of millions of viewers and helped produce the nationwide protest movement and the legislation that transformed the legal position of the American Negro in the mid-1960s.

R.E. Wolseley, Lecturer in Journalism—Northwestern University, "Newspaper Editors are Sissies," *Commonweal,* **July 29, 1938.**

Today a thousand causes go unpublicized in the majority of American newspapers. . . How about a few really big drives against munitions makers who profit from the deaths of Japanese, Chinese, and several kinds of Spaniards? Or a campaign against lynch law? Against waste of natural resources by private business as well as by government? Against Frank Hague's facism? Against municipal corruption in dozens of cities?

Selected Bibliography

Archer, G.L. *Big Business and Radio.* New York: The American Historical Co., Inc., 1939.

Archer, G.L. *History of Radio.* New York: The American Historical Co., Inc., 1938.

Bagdikan, Benjamin H. "Grass Roots Press," *Harper's Magazine,* 229 (1964), 102.

Bagdikian, Benjamin H. *The Effete Conspiracy and Other Crimes of the Press.* New York: Harper & Row, 1972.

Barnouv, Erik. *History of Broadcasting in the United States.* New York: The Vanguard Press, 1941.

Barrett, James Wyman. *Joseph Pulitzer and His World.* New York: Oxford University Press, 1941.

Bent, Silas. *Newspaper Crusaders; A Neglected Story.* New York: McGraw Hill, 1939.

Bogart, Leo. *Age of Television.* New York: F. Ungar Publishing Co., 1958.

Cook, Fred J. *The Muckrakers: Crusading Journalists Who Changed America.* Garden City, New York: Doubleday, 1972.

Dinsmore, Herman H. *All the News That Fits.* New Rochelle, New York: Arlington House, 1969.

Emery, Edwin. *The Press and America: An Interpretive History of Journalism.* Englewood Cliffs, N.J.: Prentice Hall, 1972.

Friedenthal, Jack H., and Medalie, Richard J. "Impact of Federal Regulation of Political Broadcasting." *Harvard Law Review,* 72 (1959), 445.

Friendly, Fred. *Due to Circumstances Beyond Our Control.* New York: Random House, 1967.

Hulteng, John L. *The Fourth Estate: An Informal Appraisal of the News and Opinion Media.* New York: Harper and Row, 1971.

Jones, Robert W. *Journalism in the United States.* New York: E.P. Dutton and Co., 1947.

Keogh, James *President Nixon and the Press.* New York: Funk & Wagnalls, 1972.

Kobre, Sidney. *The Press and Contemporary Affairs.* Tallahassee: Florida State University Press, 1957.

Kobre, Sidney. *The Yellow Press and the Guilded Age.* Tallahassee: Florida State University Press, 1964.

Lee, Alfred McClung. *The Daily Newspaper in America: The Evolution of a Social Instrument.* New York: The MacMillan Co., 1937.

McGaffin, William. *Anything but the Truth: The Credibility Gap; How the News is Managed in Washington.* New York: Putnam, 1968.

MacNeil, Robert. *People Machine: Influence of Television on American Politics.* New York: Harper and Row, 1958.

Mott, Frank L. *American Journlism: A History, 1690-1960.* New York: MacMillan, 1962.

Mott, Frank L. *American Journalism.* New York: The MacMillan Co., 1941.

Mott, Frank L. *A History of American Magazine.* Cambridge: Harvard University Press, 5 vols., 1930-68.

Mott, Frank L. *Jefferson and the Press.* Baton Rouge: Louisiana State University Press, 1943.

Mott, Frank L. *The News in America.* Cambridge: Harvard University Press, 1952.

Nevins, Allan. *American Press Opinion, Washington to Coolidge: A Documentary Record of Editorial Leadership and Criticism, 1785-1927.* Boston: Heath, 1928.

Newman, Robert P., and Newman, Dale R. *Evidence.* Boston: Houghton Mifflin Co., 1969.

Peterson, Theodore. *Magazines in the Twentieth Century.* Urbana: University of Illinois Press, 1964.

Pollard, James Edward. *The Presidents and the Press.* New York: MacMillan, 1947.

Reston, James B. *The Artillery of the Press; Its Influence on American Foreign Policy.* New York: Harper & Row, 1967.

Rivers, William. *The Opinionmakers.* Boston: Beacon Press, 1965.

Rutland, Robert A. *The Newsmongers.* New York: Dial Press, 1973.

Schiller, Herbert I. *Mass Communication and American Empire.* New York: A.M. Kelley, 1969.

Schlesinger, Arthur Meir. *Prelude to Independence: The Newspaper War on Britain, 1764-1776.* New York: Knopf, 1958.

Semonche, John E. "The American Magazine of 1906-1915: Principle vs. Profit." *Journalism Quarterly,* 40 (1963), 36.

Siepman, Charles A. *Radio, Television, and Society.* New York: Oxford, 1950.

Singleton, Marvin K. *H. L. Mencken and 'American Mercury' Adventure.* Durham, N.C.: Duke University Press, 1962.

Skornia, Harry J. *Television and the News: A Critical Appraisal.* Palo Alto: Pacific Books, 1968.

Smith, James Steel. "America's Magazines: Missionaries of Culture." *Journalism Quarterly,* 43 (1966), 449.

Stewart, Donald. *Opposition Press of the Federalist Period.* Albany: State University of New York Press, 1969.

Swanberg, W. *Citizen Hearst: A Biography of William Randolph Hearst.* New York: Scribner, 1961.

Tebbel, John. *Compact History of the American Newspaper.* New York: Hawthorn Books, 1969.

Tebbel, John. *The American Magazine: A Compact History.* New York: Hawthorn Books, 1969.

Wilkerson, Marcus Manley. *Public Opinion and the Spanish-American War: A Study in War Propaganda.* Baton Rouge: Louisiana State University Press, 1932.

Winkler, John Kennedy. *William Randolph Hearst, An American Phenomenon.* New York: Simon and Schuster, 1928.

EQUAL PROTECTION UNDER THE LAW

Introductory Essay

More than any other concept, the notion of the fundamental equality of men underlaid the American Revolution. In 1828 Edward Corbett used the occasion of a Fourth of July speech to espouse the common conviction that, on that day

The momentous experiment was commensed, by which the world and posterity were to be taught, how far a nation of men can be trusted with self-government. . . . The day when, for the first time in the world a numerous people was ushered into the family of nations, organized on the principle of the political equality of all the citizens.

The stated purpose of the Declaration of Independence was to explain to the world community the grievances of the American colonists, but Thomas Jefferson's proclamation of the self-evident truth that "all men are created equal" was directed to the more immediate problem of persuading the domestic audience, Jefferson himself terming it "an expression of the American mind." The response was overwhelmingly favorable. The better-educated could find confirmation for this belief in the political philosophy of Eighteenth-Century liberalism—Hobbes, Montesquieu, and especially Locke, who maintained

There [is] nothing more evident than that creatures of the same species and rank, promiscuously born to all the same advantages of nature and the use of the same faculties, should also be equal one amongst another without subordination or subjection. . . .

Perhaps more important than current philosophy, at least among the less politically conscious of the colonists, was the influence of biblical precepts. The importance of the Bible cannot be exaggerated; often the only book owned by a family, it was for many the primary source of knowledge, and the sole arbiter of moral issues. Saint Paul's teachings that in the communion of the universal church "there is neither Jew nor Greek, there is neither bond nor free, there is neither male nor female; for ye are all one in Jesus Christ," did not go unheeded by the American people.

The ultimate independence of the colonies and the establishment of a nation formally committed to the principles of political equality did not resolve differing opinions as to the true meaning and nature of equality — as two centuries of legislation and the nation's bloodiest conflict were to bear witness.

Division of opinion was not slow to emerge. The sole reference to individual rights in the Articles of Confederation of 1781 was "The free inhabitants of each of these states, paupers, vagabonds, and fugitives from justice excepted." The national Constitution reflected, in many of its provisions, doubts about the true meaning of equality.

The general spirit of the Constitution is egalitarian, as evidenced by its very first words "We the People" and the establishment of representative government and the rule of law. The proposed judicial system was steeped in egalitarian beliefs. Reliance on judges appointed by the Crown had been one of the objectionable aspects of the colonial system of justice. The complicated rules and practices of courts aroused widespread suspicion of the legal profession. In fact, the number of lawyers involved in writing the Constitution was, to some, the strongest indictment of the document. The solution was widespread availability of trial by jury, injecting the common man into a position of responsibility in the legal process. The Zenger case had shown the institution's capacity to resist tyrannic rule, and one of the complaints against King George III was that he had deprived the colonists "in many cases of the benefits of trial by jury."

Exceptions to the egalitarian framework of the Constitution, however, were numerous. Political necessity forced the framers to accept human slavery; in apportioning members of Congress a slave was considered three-fifths of a person. This contradiction of the Compromise of 1787 with the "self-evident" truths of 1776 prompted George Mason's refusal to sign the document, and inspired his fight against ratification in the Virginia legislature. Other constitutional provisions mitigated against popular representation: the President was to be selected indirectly by an Electoral College composed of the better elements of the nation, members of the Supreme Court were not elected at all, but appointed by the President, and the Senate was selected by state legislatures — the last a repudiation of Locke's stress on fair and equal representation on the basis of population rather than geographic units. The only portion of the government originally under popular control was the House of Representatives, and even that decision was made with considerable trepidation. Gouverneur Morris warned that "the time is not distant when this country will abound with [industrial workers] ... will such men be the secure and faithful Guardians of Liberty?" and John Mercer found no part of the proposal so objectionable as "the mode of election by the people. The people cannot know and judge of the character of candidates. The worst possible choice will be made." Ironically, "the people" who were able to overcome both constitutional and state restrictions on the franchise numbered only 120,000—about one-thirtieth of the population. Even so, the United States had the most liberal suffrage provisions of any nation in the world. Legislative treatment of the slighted groups since that time has largely been an attempt to reconcile the Constitution with the Declaration of Independence or, as the vice-chairman of the U.S. Commission on Civil Rights put it: "Declaration of the equality of all men under law was revolutionary, but its realization in practice and experience has been evolutionary."

The rise of political parties, the growth of sectional and economic conflicts, and the demands of the emergent West all contributed to expansion of the franchise, as older states abandoned restrictions and the new refused to adopt them. Tennessee's admission to the Union in 1796 made it the last new state with property qualifications. Jefferson's tenure as president and the following period of "Jacksonian Democracy" injected egalitarian concepts into the functioning of government. In his now-famous veto of the bank bill, Jackson deplored the fact that "the rich and the powerful too often bend the acts of government to their selfish purpose." The growth of democratic principles in the political arena was so marked that, by 1835, de Tocqueville could observe that "the gradual development of the principle of equality is, therefore, a providential fact... it is universal, it constantly eludes all interference, and all events as well as all men contribute to its progress."

Much earlier than de Tocqueville's visit, however, a serious national rift had developed. In debate over admission of Missouri into the Union in 1821, Northerners evoked the egalitarian principles of the Declaration of Independence in an effort to preclude slave-holding in the Western territories. Southerners responded by pointing to the status of blacks in the North. "Where is the State in the Union in which the emancipated negro has been admitted to the enjoyment of equal rights with the white population? I know of none." Representative McLane's challenge was echoed in the Senate by Richard Johnson of Kentucky: "If your humanity has conquered your prejudice, till you know no color,

where are your magistrates, your governors, your representatives, of the black population?"

The slavery question was temporarily avoided by the Missouri compromise, but another "minority group," comprising a little over one-half of the populace, began to stir. During the 1820's and 1830's a number of visiting foreign lecturers promoted the idea of rights for women. In 1838, Sarah Grimke's *Letters on the Equality of the Sexes* became the first major contribution by an American. Attacking the biblical arguments for the subjugation of women, she claimed that "whatsoever it is morally right for a man to do, it is morally right for a woman to do." Grimke's largely theological arguments were followed in 1844 by Margaret Fuller's *Women in the Nineteenth Century*. Her claim of intellectual equality enjoyed much greater popular success: "If you ask me what offices they [women] may fill, I reply— any. I do not care what case you put; let them be sea captains if you will." Beginning in 1836, several state legislatures considered legislation to safeguard women's property. Initially, the women allied themselves with the abolitionist movement. In 1840, however, the American Anti-Slavery Society split over the issue of allowing women to hold office. Eight years later a group of feminists, led by several women who had recently been excluded from an international abolitionist conference, met at Seneca Falls, New York. They adopted a "declaration of Sentiments" that mimicked the Declaration of Independence, adding the words "and women" to the proposition that all men are created equal, and substituting for the list of grievances against George III an indictment of man's inhumanity to women.

These efforts were to be eclipsed, however, by the brilliance of the clash over slavery. A number of intellectual and literary figures attacked the idea of equality for the Negro. Albert Taylor Bledsoe, professor of mathematics at the University of Virginia, branded the argument against slavery drawn from the Declaration of Independence "the seventeenth fallacy of the abolitionist." He added "it were much nearer the truth to say that all men have an equal right...to have their wills restrained by law." Rufus Choate, a Massachusetts lawyer, referred to "the glittering and sounding generalities of natural right which make up the Declaration of Independence," while it was denounced on the floor of the U.S. Senate as a "self-evident lie." Chancellor Harper termed the principles of the Declaration "false, sophistical or unmeaning," and George Fitzhugh summed up the views of many Southerners toward Jefferson by naming him "the genius of innovation, the architect of ruin, the inaugurator of anarchy."

In 1856, as the nation reached a critical juncture in its history, all eyes turned to the state of Illinois, where a series of verbal battles were being fought between "The Little Giant" — Senator Stephen A. Douglas, guiding spirit of the Kansas-Nebraska bill and presidential hopeful — and a lanky, relatively-unknown frontier lawyer with abolitionist leanings. Speaking to crowds of up to 20,000, with shorthand reporters telegraphing the speeches to the leading newspapers of the nation, their positions were known to almost every literate person in the country. Lincoln had been disturbed at the political trend away from egalitarianism, and had earlier written a friend that he was afraid that "when the Know-Nothings get control [the Declaration] will read 'all men are created equal, except negroes and foreigners and Catholics.'" In the debates, Douglas moved within earshot of that conclusion.

> No man can vindicate the character, motives, and conduct of the signers of the Declaration of Independence except upon the hypothesis that they referred to the white race alone, and not to the African; when they declared all men to have been created equal; that they were speaking of British subjects on this continent being equal to British subjects born and residing in Great Britain.

Lincoln, although he urged moderation on the slavery issue and freely admitted he was not sure what was an acceptable solution to the controversy, left few doubts regarding his basic view of the Declaration.

> I think the authors of that notable instrument intended to include *all* men, but ... not... *in all respects.* They did not mean to say all were equal in color, size, intellect, moral developments, or social capacity. ... but that all possessed "certain inalienable rights, among which are life, liberty, and the pursuit of happiness." This they said, and this they meant.

Lincoln admitted that the Declaration did not attempt to correct the human inequalities of that time, but concluded that the writers "meant simply to declare the right, so that enforcement of it might follow as fast as circumstances should permit."

The Illinois legislature returned Douglas to the Senate and Lincoln to the shambles of his Illinois law practice. But the Republican party and, in 1860, the nation did not forget this man. Nor did the South. Lincoln stated after his victory that he had "never had a feeling, politically, that did not spring from the sentiments embodied in the Declaration of Independence." Dixie legislators responded to his election with other, far different, declarations.

Half a million lives were lost in a bloody, fratricidal struggle, that was popularly viewed as confirming a national commitment to equality. In the post-war period, egalitarian principles made great inroads in the nation's political life. The growing popularity of party primaries, which made their debut in 1890,

involved the citizenry more directly in the selection of their representatives. The general prosperity and opportunities for advancement created a popular feeling that success was due to effort and luck, not innate superiority.

Controversy over theories of equality was reflected in the treatment afforded minority groups. Blacks had been given the franchise, but considerable doubt over whether they could wisely use it remained in some corners. The Southern states devised ingenious ways of disenfranchising the blacks: poll taxes, residency requirements, literacy qualifications, and the "grandfather clause"—which exempted from rigorous voting tests anyone whose grandfather had been able to vote. Coincidentally, this excluded virtually all blacks. Although the Congress initially attempted to protect them, and the courts occasionally struck down a particularly odious requirement (the grandfather clause was outlawed in 1915), the South emerged victorious. Under the Compromise of 1876, federal controls were lifted in exchange for electoral support, signalling a virtual abandonment of any commitment to Negro suffrage. Public opinion had also shifted. The New York *Tribune,* once an abolitionist voice, now said that blacks had been given "ample opportunities to develop their own latent capacities" but had instead shown themselves to be "idle, ignorant and vicious."

Immediately after the war, the Radical Republicans had passed the Civil Rights Act, and amendments to the Freedmen's Bureau Act. They also proposed the Fourteenth Amendment, ratified in 1868 which provided that "No state shall... deprive any person of life, liberty, or prosperity, without due process of law; nor deny to any person within its jurisdiction the equal protection of the laws." The intent of Congress was clear, but the record of the Supreme Court was one of systematic contraction and virtual annulment of the law. Almost the only expansion of the Amendment's scope was the Court's decision that the equal protection clause also applied to corporations. Of the equal protection cases heard by the Supreme Court, over three-quarters dealt with legislation affecting economic interests. In the Civil Rights Act of 1875, Congress attempted to secure for all persons "the full and equal enjoyment of the accomodations, facilities and privileges of inns, public conveyances, ... theaters, and other places of public amusement. . . ." A series of decisions in 1883 invalidated portions of the law. In one of these Justice Bradley observed: "there must be some stage in the process of his [the Negro's] elevation when he takes the rank of a mere citizen, and ceases to be the special favorite of the laws. . . ." Earlier, a case decided in 1873 had concluded that the Fourteenth Amendment added nothing to "the rights of one citizen against another." This restrictive attitude culminated in the 1896

Plessy v. Ferguson decision. Homer Plessy, a black, sought to challenge segregated seating on railroad cars. The Courts denied his arguments in what one scholar described as "a compound of bad logic, bad history, bad sociology, and bad constitutional law." Justice Brown spoke for the majority when he said that "the Fourteenth amendment. . . could not have been intended to abolish distinctions based upon color, or to enforce social, distinguished from political, equality. . . ." Modern viewers remember better Justice Harlan's vigorous dissent, which proclaimed "Our Constitution is color blind and neither knows nor tolerates classes among citizens. In respect of civil rights all citizens are equal before the law."

Women had devoted themselves wholeheartedly to the abolitionist movement, but felt deserted in the war's aftermath. National attention was focused on the black, not the woman, and Reconstructionists wished to fight only one battle at a time. Even Frederick Douglas, a strong supporter of women's rights, felt that this was "the Negro's hour," and the Fourteenth Amendment enshrined sex discrimination by specifically referring to "male citizens." The woman's movement gradually gained momentum, however. Wyoming in 1859 had been the first state to grant female suffrage, followed by Utah in 1870. By 1912, only 9 states, all of them in the West, had enfranchised women. A New York state referendum in 1915 failed, but the suffragists converted the wives of Tammany Hall politicans to their cause and succeeded in a second try two years later. The New York law prompted similar legislation in other states, and in 1918, a federal amendment was introduced in the Congress. A dramatic two-year battle culminated in a 49 to 47 ratifying vote in the Tennessee legislature. The deciding ballot was cast by 24-year-old Harry Burns, the youngest member of the state's legislature, whose mother had written him, "Hurrah! And vote for suffrage and don't keep them in doubt. . . . Don't forget to be a good boy and help Mrs. Catt [a prominent suffragette] put 'rat' in ratification."

The Twentieth Century has marked substantial progress toward the ideals of the Declaration. A 1913 constitutional amendment substituting popular vote for the traditional legislative appointment system transformed the Senate from a conservative "rich man's club" to what many feel is the more liberal and responsive half of the Congress. Judicial interpretation of the equal protection clause also contributed to a more representative government, in the 1964 case of *Reynolds v. Simms.* The plaintiffs argued that the failure of Alabama to reapportion since 1901 meant that less than one-quarter of the state's population could elect a majority of the legislature. In invalidating the apportionment system, the court established the constitutional right under the Fourteenth Amendment of equality of representation—the "one man, one vote" rule. Congress also contributed to equality of representation with passage of the Voting Rights Act of 1965, barring voting tests, including the literacy requirement. A 1966 Supreme Court case also attacked wealth as a requirement for voting. Explaining the Court's prohibition of a $1.50 Virginia state poll tax, Justice Douglas wrote that "to introduce wealth or payment of a fee as a measure of a voter's qualifications is to introduce a capricious or irrelevant factor. The degree of discrimination is irrelevant."

Before 1954, the equal protection clause had been of secondary importance to the Supreme Court, which tended to favor use of the due process provision of the Fourteenth Amendment. In that year, however, the landmark decision in *Brown v. Board of Education of Topeka* was the capstone of an edifice of decisions slowly repudiating *Plessy.* Justice Warren summarized the Court's view: "we conclude that in the field of public education the doctrine of 'separate but equal' has no place. Separate educational facilities are inherently unequal." The Court also stated that education was the most important function of state governments. "Today it is a principal instrument in awakening the child to cultural values. . . and in helping him to adjust normally to his environment." Segregationist hopes that the Court would confine itw new doctrine to education were shattered as subsequent decisions struck down separation on buses, in public housing, recreational facilities, and other areas.

Has America reached the goal of the signers of the Declaration of Independence? Certainly the nation has made much progress toward reducing the inequities of our society. But flaws in our legal system still distort the ideal of equal justice. Mass production of court cases has caused legal scholar Edward L. Barnett, Jr., to deplore the "scant regard for human dignity and the worth of the individual." Widespread use of plea bargaining encourages the innocent to confess their guilt and rewards the guilty with lighter sentences. Statistics indicate that the poor have less chance for pre-trial release on their own recognizance, are more likely to be found guilty, and are more often sent to jail. Judge Marvin E. Frankel condemns judicial discretion in sentencing as "a wild array of. . . judgements without any semblance of the consistency demanded by the ideal of equal justice." Lawyers are not immune from criticism; a committee appointed by the New Jersey Supreme Court in 1972 reported a "diminishing concern for the integrity of the profession," and a 1973 Harris poll that ranked confidence showed that Americans relegate lawyers to a relatively low position among occupational groups. There are many hopeful signs, however. The Supreme Court seems to be moving from equality of opportunity toward equality of results (as is the Congress with such legislation as the Equal Pay Act) and a series of recent court decisions has demonstrated judicial concern for the problems of the indigent caught up in our legal machinery. Public-interest law firms are also becoming a major force. When de Tocqueville concluded *Democracy in America*, he ended with a warning:

> The nations of our time cannot prevent the conditions of men from becoming equal, but it depends upon themselves whether the principle of equality is to lead them to servitude or freedom, to knowledge or barbarism, to prosperity or wretchedness.

The commitment to equality has not yet been fulfilled, but its quest has been one of the noblest facets of our national life.

Excerpted Documents

Equality and the law.

Bernard Schwartz, Professor of Law—Columbia University, *The Fourteenth Amendment*, 1970, p. 106.

... [M]en utter and use the words of equality within the framework of their own moral and political conceptions. The recital in the Declaration of Independence is marvelously inspiring: that all men are created equal and that they are endowed by their Creator with certain inalienable rights among which are life, liberty and the pursuit of happiness. But the sad truth is that for that age, "All men" did not mean *all* men. It did not include slaves. It did not really include all freedmen, or women, or Indians.

Morroe Berger, *Equality By Statute: The Revolution in Civil Rights*, 1967, p. 3.

Law, it is clear, can work both ways. It can sustain inequality, as it has done in the South and in some ways in the North, or it can sustain equal rights, as it has been doing increasingly in the last quarter century. Many opponents of laws against inequality argue that discrimination, based upon personal attitudes and tastes, cannot be altered by law. The two Eisenhower Administrations lent a skeptical note of this sort to the 1950s, seeking other remedies because, as the President put it to newpapermen when asked about a federal bill directed against discrimination in employment: "I believe there are certain things which are not best handled by punitive or cumpulsory law." The defenders of inequality, nevertheless, have strongly relied upon law; they have used law to defend their own values and have then sought to deny its power to defend other values. The position that law cannot promote equality implies that where law is not backed by the community it is futile and where law is backed by the community it is unnecessary. Such an absurd view excludes law entirely; it simply ignores the real problem of the effective limits of legal controls in specific situations.

William J. Brennan, Jr., Associate Justice of the Supreme Court of the United States, "Landmarks of Legal Liberty," *The Fourteenth Amendment*, 1970, p. 2.

It is true that, in the first half century of its [the Fourteenth Amendment's] existence, its function as a document of human freedom lay dormant; it was employed instead as a weapon by which to censor and strike down economic regulatory legislation of the States. This was in step with the compromise which settled the Hayes-Tilden Presidential election of 1876. That compromise postponed the enforcement of the Fourteenth Amendment in behalf of the Negro, a result furthered by the decisions of the Supreme Court which invalidated the Civil Rights Act of 1875 and held that separate but equal facilities satisfied the demands of the equal protection clause. In the last half century, however, the construction and application given the amendment by the federal judiciary has put it back on the track, and it has come into its own.

Education and opportunity.

Michael Parenti, *Democracy for the Few*, 1974, p. 32.

From their earliest grade school days Americans are taught privatized, competitive methods of accomplishment. One's peers are potentially one's enemies; their successes can cause us envy and anxiety, and their failures bring secret feelings of relief. The ability or desire to work collectively with others of the same social group or class is much retarded. Competitive efforts are primarily directed against those of the same class or those below, a condition that suits the interests of those at the top.

Winthrop P. Jordan, *White Over Black: American Attitudes toward the Negro 1550-1812*, 1968, p. 355.

The most eloquent and prophetic plea for Negro education came from James Sullivan of Boston, a wealthy, prominent lawyer and Democratic politican and founding member of the American Academy of Arts and Sciences . . . :

> But there is, in my mind, this resource; and I am obliged to think that it is the only one in the case, and that a very slow one. As there is no way to eradicate the prejudice which education has fixed in the minds of the white against the black people, otherwise than by raising the blacks, by means of mental improvements, nearly to the same grade with the whites, the emancipation of the slave in the United States of America must be slow in its progress, and ages must be employed in the business. The time necessary to effect the purpose must be as extensive, at least, as that in which slavery has been endured here. The children of the slaves must, at the public expence, be educated in the same manner as the children of their masters, being at the same schools, etc, with the rising generation, that prejudice, which has been so long and inveterate against them on account of their situation and colour, will be lessened within thirty or forty years.

Nancy Reeves, *Womankind: Beyond the Stereotypes*, 1971, p. 19.

Even in advanced education, now available to women more or less without discrimination, is counterfeit equality, for open doors without opportunities might as well be closed.

Henry J. Abraham, Professor of Political Science—University of Pennsylvania, *Freedom and the Court*, 1967, p. 242.

The sentiments and prejudices of large sections of the people in the North as well as in the South, die hard—if indeed they die at all. And government, under the Constitution the great line-drawer in the absence of voluntary action, must always be cautious lest it move too far in advance of those sentiments and prejudices. For full enforcement of the civil rights of all, there must be mutual trust and respect—and although government can accomplish much to promote trust and respect, it cannot ultimately be a substitute for the slow, hard process of education.

Sexual equality.

Nancy Reeves, *Womankind: Beyond the Stereotypes*, 1971, p. 18.

Hidden obscurely in the ballyhoo is the sobering truth that 85 per cent of the top professional and technical jobs in the United States today are still held by men. This results, as the Report of the President's Commission on the Status of Women points out, in a low proportion of women in public office, since "few women possess the practical experience obtained at middle and upper levels of administrative and executive responsibility" and consequently lack the public visibility that would be the basis for such posts. So, fifty years after the passage of the Nineteenth Amendment, there are thirteen women in the 92nd Congress, with the pattern more or less the same at other levels of government. Clearly, the presence of a few commoners in the castle does not make a revolution.

Jean Murphy and Susan D. Ross, Hays Civil Liberties Fellows—New York University, "Liberating Women—Legally Speaking." *With Justice for Some: An Indictment of the Law by Young Advocates*, 1970, p. 131.

Achieving equality for women is, of course, far more than a legal problem. Oppression is basically a social, not a legal fact. To end it, women must reject the roles imposed on them by society and assert themselves as equals. Yet, as evidenced by the black struggle for equality in the last two decades, law can be effective in eliminating some kinds of discriminatory behaviour immediately and legal efforts can serve as a catalyst for political organization and individual change.

Eugene V. Hecker, *A Short History of Womens Rights*, 1914, pp. 151-152.

From a speech of the Rev. Knox-Little at the Church of St. Clements in Philadelphia in 1880: "God made himself to be born of a woman to sanctify the virtue of endurance; loving submission is an attribute of a woman; men are logical, but women, lacking this quality, have an intricacy of thought. There are those who think women can be taught logic; this is a mistake. They can never by any power of education arrive at the same mental status as that enjoyed by men, but they have a quickness of apprehension, which is usually called leaping at conclusions, that is astonishing. There, then, we have distinctive traits of a woman, namely, endurance, loving submission, and quickness of apprehension. Wifehood is the crowning glory of a woman. In it she is bound for all time. To her husband she owes the duty of unqualified obedience. There is no crime which a man can commit which justifies his wife in leaving him or applying for that monstrous thing, divorce."

Thomas Paine, 1775, in *Sisterhood Is Powerful*, 1970, p. 6.

Even in countries where they may be esteemed the most happy, [women are] constrained in their desires in the disposal of their goods, robbed of freedom and will by the laws, the slaves of opinion, which rules them with absolute sway and construes the slightest appearances into guilt; surrounded on all sides by judges who are at once tyrants and their seducers.

Minority violence.

Bernard Schwartz, Professor of Law—Columbia University, *Statutory History of the United States*, 1970, p. 12.

Using the techniques of nonviolent protest, the civil rights demonstrators soon dramatized the moral issues involved and focused the attention of the country on the illegal resistance of the South to vindication of the rights so plainly decreed in the Constitution itself. The result was a massive demand for correction, growing in intensity as racial incidents multiplied, which all but forced the legislative and executive branches into action.

Richard Maxwell Brown, *American Violence*, 1970, p. 1.

Violence has formed a seamless web with the most positive episodes in American history: the birth of the nation (Revolutionary violence), the freeing of the slaves and the preservation of the Union (Civil War violence), the occupation of the land (Indian wars), the stabilization of frontier society (vigilante violence), the elevation of the farmer and the laborer (agrarian and labor violence), and the preservation of law and order (police violence). The patriot, the humanitarian, the nationalist, the pioneer, the farmer, the laborer, and the capitalist have all used violence as an ignoble means to a noble end. Goal-oreinted in nature, American violence has often been conservative in its assertion of community values and defensive of the interest of established social and economic blocs and local groups. Rising elements like the urban Irish, the laboring masses, and ghetto blacks have also employed violence to gather larger shares of the privileges and benefits of American society.

H. L. Neiburg, "Uses of Violence," *Civil Strife in America: A Historical Approach to the Study of Riots in America*, 1972, p. 225.

The threat of violence, and the occasional outbreak of real violence (which gives the threat credibility) are essential elements in conflict resolution not only in international, but national communities. Individuals and groups, no less than nations, exploit the threat as an everyday matter. This fact induces flexibility and stability in democratic institutions and facilitates peaceful social change . . . . Violence and the threat of violence . . . is an underlying, tacit, recognized, and omnipresent fact of domestic life, of which democratic politics is sometimes only the shadow-play. It is the fact that instills dynamism to the structure and growth of the law, the settlement of disputes, the process of accommodating interests, and that induces general respect for the verdict of the polls.

Bernard Schwartz, Professor of Law—Columbia University, *Statutory History of the United States,* **1970, p. 12.**

... the increasing militancy of the Negro protest movement, and the intransigence which it continued to meet, soon convinced both the executive and legislative branches that much more was necessary. Presidential blandness on the civil rights issue gave way in 1963 to leadership which induced the Congress to enact the most-far-reaching civil rights laws (those of 1964, 1965, and 1968) since Reconstruction days.

William J. Chambliss, Professor of Sociology—University of California at Santa Barbara, and Robert B. Seidman, Professor of Law—University of Wisconsin, *Law, Order and Power,* **1971, p. 70.**

In recent years television and newspapers have brought to the attention of the middle classes the violence that periodically erupts in the slums of major cities. The responses of legislation have been diverse. A few measures have been taken which are aimed at relieving the conditions presumed to lead to the riots in the first place. More have been aimed at increasing the penalties for rioting.

Robert Dahl, Professor of Political Science—Yale University, *Pluralist Democracy in the United States: Conflict and Consent,* **1967, p. 111.**

...it seems to have been widely assumed at the [Constitutional] Convention that the House of Representatives would be the driving force in the system; that the peoples representatives would be turbulent and insistent; that they would represent the majorities and would be indifferent to the rights of minorities; that the people would be the winds driving the ship of state and their representatives would be the sails, swelling with every gust.

Robert Dahl, Professor of Political Science—Yale University, *Pluralist Democracy in the United States,* **1967. p. 169.**

The main objective of presidential leadership is to build a stable and dominant aggregation of minorities with a high probability of winning the Presidency and one or both houses of Congress.

Alexis de Tocqueville, *Democracy In America,* **1835.**

If ever the free institutions of America are destroyed, that event may be attributed to the omnipotence of the majority, which may at some future time urge the minorities to desperation and oblige them to have recourse to physical force. Anarchy will then be the result, but it will have been brought about by despotism.

Marian D. Irish and James W. Prothro, *The Politics of American Democracy,* **1965, p. 55.**

The ambiguity of democratic theory stems largely from an apparent conflict between *majority rule* and the equally basic principle of *minority rights.* In its extreme form, majoritarianism holds that the majority view is always right; in less extreme form, that it must always be followed, right or wrong. But democracy holds some freedoms to be "unalienable rights," beyond the reach even of majority preference. Since absolute truth has been revealed to no one, the majority is quite capable of making mistakes.

Robert Dahl, Professor of Political Science—Yale University, *Pluralist Democracy in the United States,* **1967, p. 169.**

Generally speaking, policy at the national level is the outcome of conflict, bargaining, and agreement among minorities; the process is niether minority rule nor majority rule but what might better be called *minorities* rule, where one aggregation of minorities achieves policies opposed by another aggregation.

Politics and elites.

Neil MacNeil, "The House Confronts Mr. Kennedy," *Fortune*, January 1962, pp. 71-72.

There emerged then one significant difference between Senators and Representatives (after the institution of popular vote for Senators): Senators' constituencies were entire states; Representatives' were fractionalized districts. In time this difference switched the bias of the Senate from conservative to liberal, for it made Senators subject to a twentieth-century phenomenon, the "bullet vote" of the activist political minorities—labor unions, racial groups, and religious-ethnic organizations. These minorities, usually concentrated in cities, can make their influence felt only on those Representatives in the House who come from urban districts. In the Senate, however, they hold a power beyond their actual numbers.

William J. Chambliss, Professor of Sociology—University of California at Santa Barbara, and Robert B. Seidman, Professor of Law—University of Wisconsin, *Law, Order and Power*, 1971, p. 65.

In all societies, regardless of how the interest groups vary in number, those which are most likely to be effective are the ones that control the economic or political institutions of the society. The most influential groups will of course be those which control both. As a consequence, legislation typically favors the wealthier, the more politically active groups in the society. Not surprisingly, in America this means the managers and owners of large corporations and mammoth business complexes will enjoy more success in getting laws passed which benefit them than will the "average citizen" or, in more extreme contrast, the unemployed resident of a slum. It seems to be the case that two things characterize laws passed which superficially seem inimical to the best interests of the powerful. First, some laws are passed primarily as a token gesture to assuage some group that has the capacity to disrupt the ongoing process. Secondly, laws which are passed under these conditions are rarely if ever enforced with the same vigor as characterizes the enforcement of those laws which are in the best interests of persons in positions of power.

Robert Dahl, Professor of Political Science—Yale University, *Pluralist Democracy in the United States*, 1967, p. 130.

One of the most palpable facts of life in American society (as, indeed, in all large societies) is that most resources are unequally distributed. Yet it does not follow that Congressmen are invariably responsive to small groups with large resources. . . . there is at least one resource that is distributed equally in most states in the North: the legal right to vote. To a Congressman who wants to be re-elected—and few Senators and Representatives do not—one vote counts just as much as another. . . . Other things being equal, therefore, the Congressman will be more responsive to two potential votes than one, more eager to win the votes of a group of one thousand voters (whose other political resources may be very slender) than a group of one hundred voters (whose political resources may be very large).

Professor V. O. Key, Harvard University, *Politics, Parties, and Pressure Groups*, 1964, p. 515.

The cynical view that a campaign contribution is equivalent to a bribe at times indubitably matches the facts. Yet the significance of money in politics can be grasped only by a view that places party finance in the total context of the political process. It is probably fair enough to conclude that men of wealth on the whole use money in politics to protect what they regard as their interests. Their votes are few in a regime of popular government and they build their political defenses by the use of money. Others have votes; they have money. The two are, if not in perpetual conflict, always potentially at loggerheads.

Reinhard H. Luthin, Professor of History—Columbia University, *The Real Abraham Lincoln*, 1960, p. 217.

Lincoln's Illinois workers performed highly adroit services in attracting key delegations to their favorite. Judge Davis promised the supporters of Senator Simon Cameron that their favorite, the unsavory Pennsylvanian, would be tendered a Cabinet post if Lincoln were nominated and elected President, should the Cameron delegates go for Lincoln in the balloting. The Lincoln men gave a similar pledge to Caleb B. Smith of Indiana, head of the Hoosier delegation, if that State's delegates would go into Lincoln's camp.

Bernard Schwartz, Professor of Law—Columbia University, *Statutory History of the United States,* **1970, p. 5.**

. . . the Jacksonian program called for legislation designed to curb corporations, monopolies, and special privileges. For, as Jackson warned, "unless you become more watchful . . . and check this spirit of monopoly and thirst for exclusive privileges, you will, in the end, find that the mot important powers of Government have been given or bartered away, and the control over your dearest interests has passed into the hands of these corporations.

The judicial system.

Chief Justice Warren E. Burger, Speaking at the National Conference on the Judiciary, Williamsburg, Virginia, March 12, 1971.

Man can tolerate many shortcomings of his existence, but history teaches us that great societies have foundered for want of an adequate system of justice—and by that I mean justice in its broadest sense.

Cotton Mather, *Bonifacius—An Essay upon the Good that is to be Devised and Designed by those who Desire to Answer the Great End of Life and to Do Good while they Live,* **1710.**

(From the first American address to lawyers) Sirs, be prevailed withal to keep constantly a Court of Chancery in your own Breast. . . . This Piety must Operate very particularly in the Pleading of Causes. You will abhor, Sir, to appear in a Dirty Cause. If you discern that your Client has an Unjust Cause, you will faithfully advise him of it. You will be Sincerely desirous that Truth and Justice may take place. You will speak nothing which shall be to the Prejudice of Either. You will abominate the use of all unfair Arts to Confound Evidence, to Browbeat Testimonies, to Suppress what may give Light in the Case. . . .There has been an old Complaint, That a Good Lawyer seldom is a Good Neighbor. You know how to Confute it, Gentlemen, by making your Skill in the Law, a Blessing to your neighborhood.

Abraham Lincoln, in *Why Justice Fails,* **1973, p. 14.**

Discourage litigation. Persuade your neighbors to compromise whenever you can. Point out to them how the nominal winner is often a real loser—in fees, expenses and waste of time. As a peacemaker, the lawyer has a superior opportunity of being a good man. Never stir up litigation. A worse man can scarcely be found than one who does this. Who can be more nearly a fiend than he who habitually overhauls the register of deeds in search of defects of titles, whereupon to stir up strife and put money in his pocket? A moral tone ought to be enforced in the profession which would drive such men out of it.

Federal District Court Judge John P. Fullam, in *The Other Government: The Unseen Power of Washington Lawyers,* **1973.**

The antitrust field I think is an area where lawyers, perhaps without realizing it, come closest to the very limits of what is ethically proper. . . . On the defendant's side they are closer to the line in actually advising clients to cover up criminal activity. [Judging from] some of the essays I have read in the *Antitrust Law Journal,* if you took out the word "antitrust" and substituted "prostitution" or "narcotics," you would think that the lawyer would be disbarred if he put into practice the views expressed.

Alexander Hamilton, in *Pluralist Democracy in the United States,* **1967, p. 148.**

. . .By a limited Constitution, I understand one which contains certain specified exceptions to the legislative authority; such, for instance, as that it shall pass no bills of attainder, no ex-post-facto laws, and the like. Limitations of this kind can be preserved in practice no other way than through the medium of courts of justice, whose duty it must be to declare all acts contrary to the manifest tenor of the Constitution void. Without this, all the reservations of particular rights or privileges would amount to nothing.

John Galloway, Adjunct Assistant Professor of Political Science—Hunter College, *The Supreme Court and the Rights of the Accused*, 1973, p. 82.

Miranda has led to increased scrutiny as to the value of confessions in obtaining convictions and reducing crime. Many studies indicate that the importance of confessions has been exaggerated by the public and the police.

Justice Tom Clark, *Mapp v. Ohio*, 367 US 643, 1961.

The ignoble shortcut to conviction left open to the state tends to destroy the entire system of constitutional restraints on which the liberties of the people rest. Having once recognized that the right to privacy embodied in the 4th Amendment is enforceable against the states, and that the right to be secure against rude invasions of privacy by state officers is, therefore, constitutional in origin, we can no longer permit that right to remain an empty promise. Because it is enforceable in the same manner and to like effect as other basic rights secured by the due process clause, we can no longer permit it to be revocable at the whim of any police officer who, in the name of law enforcement itself, chooses to suspend its enjoyment. Our decision, founded on reason and truth, gives to the individual no more than that which the Constitution guarantees him, to the police officer no less than that to which honest law enforcement is entitled, and, to the courts, that judicial integrity so necessary in the true administration of justice. . . .

The media and freedom.

Herbert Brucker, Stanford University, *Communication Is Power*, 1970, p. 353.

. . .a democratically and professionally controlled press is the best we can hope for. It would, as far as possible, close the gap between today's increasingly intricate public issues and public underinformation about those issues. It would take us as far toward an ideal journalism as fallible man can go, as long as he is faced with our existing journalistic technology and its increasing demand for larger and larger amounts of capital.

Senator J. W. Fulbright, August 4, 1970, in *Communication Is Power*, 1973.

Communication is power, and exclusive access to it is a dangerous, unchecked power.

Herbert Marcuse, *One Dimensional Man*, 1964, p. 8.

Our insistence on the depth and efficacy of these controls is open to the objection that we overrate greatly the indoctrinating power of the "media," and that by themselves the people would feel and satisfy the needs which are now imposed upon them. The objection misses the point. The preconditioning does not start with the mass production of radio and television and with the centralization of their control. The people enter this stage as preconditioned receptacles of long standing; the decisive difference is in the flattening out of the contrast (or conflict) between the given and the possible, between the satisfied and the unsatisfied needs. Here, the so-called equalization of class distinctions reveals its ideological function. If the worker and his boss enjoy the same television program and visit the same resort places, if the typist is attractively made up as the daughter of her employer, if the Negro owns a Cadillac, if they all read the same newspaper, then this assimilation indicates not the disappearance of classes, but the extent to which the needs and satisfactions that serve the preservation of the Establishment are shared by the underlying population.

Herbert Brucker, Stanford University, *Communication Is Power*, 1970, p. 1.

A republic in which the people are the ultimate source of power must strive constantly, in the face of inevitable change, to democratize its communications.

Selected Bibliography

Abernathy, M. Glenn. *Civil Liberties Under the Constitution.* New York: Dodd, Mead, & Co., 1972.

Bedau, Hugo A., ed. *Justice and Equality.* Englewood Cliffs, N.J.: Prentice-Hall, 1971.

Berger, Morroe. *Equality by Statute: The Revolution in Civil Rights.* Garden City, N.Y.: Doubleday, 1967.

Bloomstein, Morris, *Verdict: The Jury System.* New York: Dodd, Mead, & Co., 1972.

Brown, Richard M., ed. *American Violence.* Englewood Cliffs, N. J.: Prentice-Hall, 1970.

Catt, Carrie C., and Shuler, Nettie. *Woman Suffrage and Politics.* Seattle: University of Washington Press, 1923.

Chroust, Anton-Hermann. *The Rise of the Legal Profession in America.* Norman: University of Oklahoma Press, 1965.

Cohen, Norman S., ed. *Civil Strife in America: A Historical Approach to the Study of Riots in America.* Hinsdale, Ill.: The Dryden Press, 1972.

Coleman, James S. *Equality of Educational Opportunity.* Washington: U.S. Government Printing Office, 1966.

Connery, Robert H. *Urban Riots: Violence and Social Change.* New York: Random House, 1968.

Cornish, W.R. *The Jury.* London: The Penguin Press, 1968.

Cortner, Richard C., and Lytle, Clifford M. *Modern Constitutional Law: Commentary and Case Studies.* New York: The Free Press, 1970.

Downie, Leonard Jr. *Justice Denied: The Case for Reform of the Courts.* New York: Praeger, 1971.

Ferguson, E. James, ed. *The Random House Reader in American History: Essays on the National Past, 1607 to the Present.* New York: Random House, 1970.

Fleming, Donald, and Baylyn, Bernard, eds. *Law in American History.* Boston: Little, Brown & Co., 1971.

Gans, Herbert J. *More Equality.* New York: Pantheon Books, 1973.

Goedecke, Robert. *Change and the Law.* Tallahassee: Florida State University Press, 1969.

Goldberg, Arthur J. *Equal Justice: The Warren Era of the Supreme Court.* Evanston, Ill.: Northwestern University Press, 1971.

Green, Mark J. *The Other Government: The Unseen Power of Washington Lawyers.* New York: Grossman Publishers, 1973.

Green, Mark J.; Fallows, James M.; and Zwick, David R. *Who Runs Congress?* New York: Grossman Publishers, 1972.

Grimes, Alan P. *Equality in America: Religion, Race, and the Urban Majority.* New York: Oxford University Press, 1964.

Gunther, Gerald, and Dowling, Noel T. *Constitutional Law.* Mineola, N.Y.: The Foundation Press, 1970.

Harris, Robert J. *The Quest for Equality: The Constitution, Congress, and the Supreme Court.* Baton Rouge: Louisiana State University Press, 1960.

Harrell, Mary Ann, and Jones, Stuart E. *Equal Justice Under Law: The Supreme Court in American Life.* Washington: Foundation of the Federal Bar Association, 1965.

Irish, Marian D., and Prothro, James W. *The Politics of American Democracy.* Englewood Cliffs, N.J.: Prentice-Hall, 1968.

Jaffa, Harry V. *Equality and Liberty: Theory and Practice in American Politics.* New York: Oxford University Press, 1965.

Joiner, Charles W. *Civil Justice and the Jury.* Englewood Cliffs, N.J.: Prentice-Hall, 1962.

Kalven, Harry, Jr., and Zeisel, Hans. *The American Jury.* Chicago: University of Chicago Press, 1966.

Kirby, James C. Jr. *Congress and the Public Trust: Report of the Association of the Bar of the City of New York Special Committee on Congressional Ethics.* New York: Atheneum, 1970.

Kraditor, Aileen S. *Up from the Pedestal.* Chicago: Quadrangle Books, 1968.

Lakoff, Sanford A. *Equality in Political Philosophy.* Cambridge: Harvard University Press, 1964.

Lowi, Theodore J. *Legislative Politics, U.S.A.* Boston: Little, Brown, & Co., 1962.

Mason, Alpheus T., and Beaney, William M. *American Constitutional Law: Introductory Essays and Selected Cases.* Englewood Cliffs, N.J.: Prentice-Hall, 1968.

Meier, August, and Rudwick, Elliott, eds. *The Making of Black America: Essays in Negro Life and History.* New York: Atheneum, 1969.

Myers, Henry A. *Are Men Equal? An Inquiry into the Meaning of American Democracy.* Ithaca, N.Y.: Great Seal Books, 1955.

Rubenstein, Richard E. *Rebels in Eden: Mass Political Violence in the United States.* Boston: Little, Brown, & Co., 1970.

Schwartz, Bernard, ed. *The Fourteenth Amendment: Centennial Volume.* New York: New York University Press, 1970.

Seymour, Whitney J. Jr. *Why Justice Fails.* New York: William Morrow & Co., 1973.

Sloan, Irving J. *Our Violent Past.* New York: Random House, 1970.

Ten Broek, Jacobus. *Equal Under Law.* New York: Collier Books, 1965.

Tremain, Rose. *The Fight for Freedom for Women.* New York: Ballentine Books, 1973.

Truman, David B. *The Congress and America's Future.* Englewood Cliffs, N.J.: Prentice-Hall, 1965.

U.S. Commission on Civil Rights. *With Liberty and Justice for All.* Washington: U.S. Government Printing Office, 1959.

Van den Haag, Ernest. *Political Violence and Civil Disobedience.* New York: Harper & Row, 1972.

Warren, Charles. *A History of the American Bar.* Boston: Little, Brown, & Co., 1911.

Wasserstein, Bruce, and Green, Mark J., eds. *With Justice for Some: An Indictment of the Law by Young Advocates.* Boston: Beacon Press, 1970.

ISSUE IV
A MORE PERFECT UNION: THE AMERICAN GOVERNMENT

DISTRICT EVENTS—COLLEGE AGE ISSUE
November 15—December 20, 1975

DEBATE Resolved: That American political parties have been dominated by socioeconomic elites.

PERSUASIVE Is Federalism Obsolete?

EXTEMPORANEOUS "In Congress Assembled ...": A Representative Legislature

1. Should we return to a one-house Congress?
2. Has the Congressional Seniority System benefitted or hindered the nation?
3. Has the election of Representatives from specific districts helped or impeded their ability to legislate on national affairs?
4. Should the Founding Fathers have reserved for Congress the judicial power to interpret the Constitution?
5. What should be the role of compromise in Congress?
6. Throughout American history, has Congress mainly represented the interests of the rich and powerful?
7. Has Congress been too large to adequately perform its Constitutional functions?
8. Why didn't the Founding Fathers allow Senators to be directly elected by the people?
9. Should Congressmen follow their personal judgment or heed the opinions of their constituents?
10. Did Congress work more effectively in America's past?
11. Should the Founding Fathers have chosen a Parliamentary form of government?
12. Has Congress tradionally played too small a role in American foreign policy?
13. Should the executive, legislative, and judicial branches of government be coequal?
14. Has the committee system helped or hindered Congressional performance?

RESOLVED: THAT AMERICAN POLITICAL PARTIES HAVE BEEN DOMINATED BY SOCIOECONOMIC ELITES.

Introductory Essay

In 1796, the outgoing President, George Washington, issued a solemn warning in his farewell speech to the nation:

All combinations and associations, under whatever plausible character, with the real design to direct, control, counteract, or awe the regular deliberation and action of the constituted authorities are . . .of fatal tendency. They serve to organize faction, to give it an artificial and extraordinary force; to put in the place of the designated will of the Nation, the will of a party; often a small but artful and enterprising minority of the community. . .However combinations or associations of the above description may now and then answer popular ends, they are likely, in the course of time and things, to become potent engines, by which cunning, ambitious and unprincipled men will be enabled to subvert the Power of the People. . .

Present-day historians looking back on Washington's admonitions, however, point out an irony—Washington's statement against factions was in itself partisan. The President's comments were directed against the supporters of Jefferson, viewed by Washington as a faction dedicated to upsetting the government. Washington was unable to realize that his friends within the administration, on whose behalf the statement was made (in fact, Hamilton drafted this portion of the farewell address), would also be viewed in future years as a political party.

Whatever Washington's prejudices, his statement raises a fundamental question. What constitutes a political party? And deeper still, who runs America? A textbook, not surprisingly, will recite a textbook's definition. "An organization that has as its basic purpose controlling the choice of governmental personnel and policies." But an important ambiguity arises when we attempt to examine the degree and level of organization and commitment. Should one include the voters who do not participate in party activities but who consistently "vote the party line," the non-affiliated but reliable contributer, committees formed to aid a particular candidate or cause rather than the party in general, and individuals who contribute to more than one party? A party structure

fluid enough to allow the existence of such groups as "Young Republicans for Kennedy" and "Democrats for Goldwater" admits of no simple definition. It is clear that the description chosen by a contestant in any particular debate will have a major influence on the issues important in that round.

Other terms are subject to interpretation. "Socioeconomic elite" seems straightforward enough, referring to the upper stratum of society. The upper ten percent of the American people have incomes roughly equal to those of the lower fifty percent combined. Available evidence indicates that such an income distribution has been the pattern in the United States. The situation is more complex, however. America has a strong democratic tradition. Most people do not identify themselves with an elite (or, for that matter, a lower-class group). A Gallup poll has reported that 88% of the population consider themselves as "middle class" while only 6% identified with either the upper or lower classes. A *Fortune* survey reported similar findings. Can anyone be a member of an elite who does not think of himself as a member of an elite? It would seem that the very concept of elitism entails a particular outlook or attitude. Even using this working definition, however, embarrassing questions might be raised: How does one square elitist behavior as evidence of elitism with the fact that, for instance, many rank-and-file Republicans identify strongly with the basic tenets of their party, and yet possess neither great wealth nor high social status? An elitist attitude need not be caused by an elitist background; neither wealth nor poverty precludes a commitment to an elitist view of things political. At the same time, one can hold elitist attitudes and, in fact, have no real power at all.

Finally, the term "dominated" itself deserves examination. What, in short, can be taken as evidence of domination? Any of the following criteria can be scrutinized: Policies adopted as a political platform, information regarding the sources of a campaign's financing, the nature and relation of the structure of the party being considered, and others.

Many judgments of value will present themselves, for the question of whether the political process *should* be governed by elites is basically the question of whether democracy is a workable form of government. The topic is factually worded, however, and the question of propriety will not be discussed, unless a participant can impute value to "dominate" or interpret the proposition as a whole in a value framework. In addition, values might enter a debate obliquely. For instance, a negative participant might argue that the democratic ideal is so grounded in American tradition that any attempt at elitist rule has been discouraged by popular revulsion at the polls; that even if socioeconomic elites predominate, they dare not dominate. It could be countered by offering conflicting attitudes held by the American voter: admiration for success, the self-made man, the Puritan ethic—all of which would balance the democratic ideal and encourage elite dominance.

Further research will uncover an abundance of sociological work on the class structures of current political parties. While the most recent elections deserve a place in any complete analysis, they deserve no greater place than any other historical time span. An argument about the effects the preferential primary has had on political parties has merit, but its impact is limited by the fact that for most of this nation's history, primaries did not exist. Obviously, then, a sense of historical perspective is critical.

The United States came into being without political parties and there was no great enthusiasm for acquiring them. The experiences of the framers of the Constitution with the Whig and the Tory parties in England (both controlled by the aristocracy) did not make the party system attractive. As an alternative, the Constitution set up the electoral college system, which both nominated and elected the President and Vice-President. The development of parties was further impeded by the fact that most of the men who could lead parties already held responsible positions in the government and, thus, possessed enough personal influence that they had no need to rely on group support. Within the government, however, two opposing camps developed: the Federalists, masterminded by the aristocratic secretary of the treasury, Alexander Hamilton (who preferred to be called "Chancellor of the Exchequer"), and the Jeffersonian-Republicans, named for their leader. Party animosity smouldered during Washington's tenure, and broke into flame when he left office. The election of 1796 was hotly contested, with the Anti-Hamilton candidates, Jefferson and Burr, losing by a margin of only three electoral votes to Adams and Pinckney, the Federalist nominees. Some question whether these were actually political parties, noting that they more strongly resembled factions and personal followings. Certainly there was no true electoral base for either party. Yet they were sensitive to popular feeling. The Democratic-Republicans used the charge of "monarchism" which gave Jefferson the Presidency in 1800. The policies of the Democratic-Republicans in this period were also favorable to the farmers and small businessmen.

The election of Jefferson began a period of dominance for Jefferson's party (later known as the Democrats) that did not end until the Civil War. The Democrats owed much of their success to the fact that they tried to broaden their base of support and include as many segments of society as possible. The demise of the Federalists, who did not attempt to broaden their appeal, was inevitable, and the country moved into a short period of one-party dominance, the "Era of Good Feelings." Even with the attempts to broaden representation, the first truly popular vote was not held until 1828, when Jackson, a man of the people (at least compared to the dynasty of Virginia aristocrats) was elected. That election was also the first time the presidential electors were chosen mainly by the voters, rather than state legislatures. During this time it also became customary for an elector to vote according to the wishes of those who elected him, rather than to act as an independent agent, as implied in the Constitution. This development was essential both to the parties (who had little incentive to appeal to the public if the public did not have the final choice) and to increased citizen participation in the electoral process.

During the same period, the number of people able to vote increased greatly. Originally, only freeholders could vote. This limited the franchise to about 800,000 (with the most liberal interpretation) of 4,000,000 citizens, and though far more liberal than other nations at that time, still slanted participation to the higher socioeconomic brackets. The expansion of suffrage had a two-fold effect. It democratized the political process and forced political parties to broaden their appeal. But at the same time it necessitated increased party organization and control. Thus, as the parties grew larger, the number of real leaders became fewer. Concurrent with this, the nominating convention replaced the caucus. Political tasks that had been delegated to a handful of the party elite were now carried out in the open by increasingly larger numbers of delegates from the rank-and-file. Participation and actual control became increasingly distinct. To participate might be a sign of democracy, but to participate may simply be licking envelopes; the real decisions are made elsewhere. Party bosses soon appeared on the scene, and while the conventions provided entertainment and a feeling of involvement, many of the real decisions were made in the "smoke-filled rooms."

Against Jackson stood the Whigs. They opposed many of his policies and enraged his populist instincts. But while they were able to break the Democratic hegemony twice—electing Harrison and Taylor, both popular war heroes, to the Presidency, they could not amass a lasting national constituency.

Their roots were essentially regional, spawned in the rocky earth of New England. Bound to a limited merchant and professional class, their future was compromised by the growth of the new nation. They never managed to adjust completely.

The rise of the Republican Party backed by anti-slavery interests and the identification of the Democrats with secession contributed to a period of Republican dominance that lasted from Lincoln's election in 1860 to 1932; a 72-year period punctuated by only two Democratic presidents. The Democrats maintained strong sectional interests in the South, initiating a period of one-party rule in the Cotton Belt that only recently seems to be ending. The expansion of suffrage by the inclusion of black, female and immigrant voters necessitated broader party bases. In part, the Republicans responded by homestead laws, measures favorable to workingmen. And they were not above reminding the newly enfranchised blacks as to whom they owed their freedom.

Having secured their positions as the two main parties, both the Democrats and the Republicans fell, for a time, into a kind of complacency. Blinded by their successes, they failed to fully appreciate the emergence of a growing national constituency. This was recognized by groups with more particular interests, and soon the political landscape was littered with innumerable "spokesmen" for this or that cause or issue. Together with the continuing growth of the labor movement, American political activity took on new dimensions. Many interest groups began to work outside the organized parties, supporting instead individual legislators sympathetic to their interest. These groups included the National Farmers Union and the Federation of Organized Trade. Minor political parties, including the Populists and the Socialists, made their appearance, advocating wide reforms. They were not widely successful in the traditional political arena, but were nonetheless able to influence a great deal of reform legislation. A graduated income tax, the Federal Trade Commission, and food and drug inspection were some of the accomplishments of reform pressure on the major parties.

The reform influence extended to politcal party organization as well as policies. Many people associated the evils of society with big business and powerful men and advocated a democratization of the political system. That influence impressed itself on the parties in a number of ways. Among these were the primaries. Beginning in Wisconsin in 1905, they spread to over one-half the states in ten years. Although, by and large, the results of the primaries were not binding, they were still a potent force in the convention. Even though the popularity of primaries has waned, a poor showing can still have a major influence on a candidate's chances, as Kennedy and Humphrey found, to their respective joy and dismay, in West Virginia in 1960.

American politics today has accepted a picture, not altogether adequate, of the composition and intention of its major political parties. Democrats, so the account reads, are liberal and apt to emphasize the problems and needs of the disadvantaged. Republicans, on the other hand, are bound to the monied interests of business and the corporate world. They are essentially Conservatives. During this period, the composition of the two parties also stabilized. Although one could find members of almost any socioeconomic stratum in either party, the Republicans draw disproportionate business and professional support, while the Democrats find their adherents in the middle and lower classes, organized labor, and minority groups.

What is particularly important is the manner in which these national parties grew. For while the enlarging franchise required a party to address itself to ever-broader assessments of issues, the very fact that they were confronting an increased electorate encouraged the tightening of internal party machinery. To govern at all became an enterprise of efficiently organizing a mass of people and energy. As the eminent French political scientist Robert Michels wrote in 1915, "every party. . .becomes divided into a minority of directors and a majority of directed." Both parties have attempted to appeal to as many people as possible forcing their positions to trend to the middle. At the same time, the views of substantial minorities from the ends of the political spectrum are ignored.

Parties, of course, require financial resources. The influence of money has not been simply limited to policies of spending; politics itself has been significantly affected by pressure groups and influential individual financiers. Campaign coffers are filled with more than silver: there is always the danger that promises, unlawful promises, have been exchanged for the desired coin. One should not, however, suppose this merely a contemporary phenomenon. Although mutlimillion dollar campaign budgets are relatively new, campaigning has always been a financial burden. Will Roger's observation that "politics has got so expensive that it takes a lot of money to get beat with" was as true in the 1830s as it was in the 1930s. Some of the Founding Fathers died bankrupt, and Lincoln had some very lean years. A representative to the Virginia House of Burgesses from Fairfax County prior to the Revolution listed campaign expenses of "28 gallons of rum, 50 gallons of rum punch, 34 gallons of wine, and 46 gallons of beer." The investment, averaging a quart and one-half of refreshments per registered voter, paid off. He later became the nation's first president.

The costs of campaigning, as well as the sacrifice of time and money necessary to work actively in the party structure, has resulted in a disproportionate number of wealthy candidates. It is also reflected in the socioeconomic makeup of party officials.

Orignially, the candidate and his friends were expected to finance the campaign out of their own pockets. As this became impractical, the spoils system afforded the party in power a chance to collect money from all who held patronage jobs. Over time this became systematized to the extent that government employees were often expected to contribute a set percentage of their salaries to the party. This was brought to a halt by the Pendleton Act of 1883, banning financial contributions by civil servants. Increased numbers of voters pyramided campaign costs, and soon big business became a major source of support. Certainly, large campaign contributions would indicate the presence of a socioeconomic elite. The numerous historical examples of modified party policies and other manifestations of *quid pro quo* clearly suggest that large contributors can dominate party organization.

Sometimes the system appears to work in reverse, however. Attempts by parties to solicit contributions have often approached blackmail, and may have inspired business contributions more from a motive of self-defense than a desire to dominate a party. Populist or grass-roots political movements have partially avoided this situation. Sometimes a party will make a conscious effort to solicit small contributions, as in the Goldwater and Wallace campaigns. Finally, much campaign money seems to be given merely in order to be on the winning side. In heavily Democratic states the big money goes to Democratic candidates, and in Republican areas, the reverse occurs.

The role of minor parties in the political system should also be noted. In general, minor parties have formed when the existing parties have refused to address a major issue or have alienated a substantial minority. They sometimes make a good showing, but rarely achieve high political office. Exceptions to this, however, include Roosevelt's "Bull Moose" Party, which made a very strong bid for the presidency, and the Republican Party, which assumed the position vacated by the Whigs.

Third parties have, in some cases, stood for a rejection of "politics as usual." If they begin to represent substantial portions of the electorate, one or both of the major parties have generally adopted their position. This was true with the Abolitionist and Liberty parties prior to the Civil War, and with the Populist party at the turn of the century. Perhaps the clearest example of a minor party serving to diminish elitist influence in government is that of the first third party—the Anti-Masons. The entire focus of their campaigns was that an aristrocratic elite—members of the Masonic Order—were in control of the government. (They were largely correct. Many of the Founding Fathers were Masons.) Anti-Masonist pressure induced many politicians to disavow their membership, and persuaded others to at least appear to be members of the common classes.

Looked at from another viewpoint, however, third parties are simply a manifestation of special and even limited interests. They often died for lack of funding, and in the eyes of many political scientists, represent not an adaptation of the party system but an abandonment and denial of that system.

Have American political parties been dominated by socioeconomic elites? The answer depends both on the meanings given "socioeconomic elites" and "domination," and to the interpretation that is placed on historical events. Only when the boundaries have been fixed and the terrain inspected can a conclusion be adduced.

Excerpted Documents

Has elite dominance been evident in party personnel and candidates?

Kenneth Dolbeare, University of Washington, and Murray Edelman, University of Wisconsin, *American Politics, Policies, Power and Change,* **1971, p. 218.**

The social backgrounds of men in major governmental positions have always been highly unrepresentative of the population as a whole. Despite notable exceptions, the historical pattern has been for key government positions to be filled from the pool that we have just described. This is confirmed by a variety of emipirical studies. They show that political decisionmakers are quite disproportionately white anglo-saxon Protestants with high incomes, many of whose families have been active in politics for generations. Their occupations are almost entirely the upper-status ones, principally the law. Although they make up less than one percent of the adult population, lawyers usually constitute about 60 percent of the two houses of the Congress and all of the justices of the Supreme Court; lawyers constituted 70 percent of all Presidents, Vice-Presidents, and Cabinet members between 1877 and 1934.

Marian D. Irish, Professor of Government—Florida State University, and James W. Prothro, Professor of Political Science—University of North Carolina, *The Politics of American Democracy*, 1965, p. 40.

The explanation of this upper- and upper-middle class domination of important political offices lies not in any "ruling-class" plot but in certain evident features of American society. First, only those at the upper level of the social scale are likely to enjoy the money, experience, and contacts required for active political life. Second, some occupations possess a greater degree of what social scientists call "role dispensability." Whereas the doctor or architect would find his professional competence impaired if he became preoccupied with politics, political activity is actually an advantage in the profession of the law; hence the lawyer's dominancance in public office. Third, opportunities for rising to positions offering status, money, and leisure are highly unequal, with those who start nearer the top having a great advantage. Finally, as members of a stratified society with recognized symbols of success, even those citizens at the lower levels tend to prefer people of established "worth" as their representatives.

Charles Mayo and Beryl Crowe, *American Political Parties*, 1967, p. 75.

. . .even in the lower houses of the state legislatures, we draw about 85 percent of our legislators from the top 14 percent of the labor force as measured by occupational stratification.

Kenneth Dolbeare, University of Washington, and Murray Edelman, University of Wisconsin, *American Parties, Policies, Power and Change*, 1971, p. 219.

Donald Matthews' study of members of the U.S. Senate during the period 1947-1957 found that 84 percent of the 180 senators involved had gone to college (at a time when only 14 percent of the white population over 25 had done so) and that 53 percent had been to law school. Sixty-three percent of the Democrats were lawyers, 45 percent of the Republicans; 17 percent of the Democrats were businessmen and 45 percent of the Republicans. The other occupations represented were those of the farmer, professor, and other professionals such as minister or physician. There were no representatives of any blue collar occupation, only one woman, and no blacks. The senators came from families of the upper and middle class, as measured by their fathers' occupations.

Thomas R. Dye, Florida State University, and L. Harmon Zeigler, University of Oregon, *The Irony of Democracy*, 1970, p. 183.

In essence, power in American parties tends to rest in the hands of those who have the time and the money to make it a full time or nearly full time occupation. Party activists—consisting of no more than 3 or 4 percent of the adult population—can decide what product is to be offered to political consumers (the party in the electorate).

Michael Parenti, State University of New York at Albany, *Democracy for the Few*, 1974, p. 149.

The weeding out of political deviants is carried on *within as* well as outside the major parties. It begins long before the election campaign and involves social forces that extend beyond the party system. First, the acceptable candidate must be born or educated into the middle or upper class, displaying the linguistic skills and social styles of a bourgeois personage. This requirement effectively limits the selection to business and professional people. Then he must express opinions of a kind that win the support of essentially conservative community leaders, party bosses and other established interests. Finally the aspiring candidate must have large sums of money of his own or access to those who do. As one Senator remarked: "The fundamental problem is that the ability to raise money starts the screening-out process. If you can't get the money, you don't get the nomination." On election day, John Coleman reminds us, "the voters will have their choice between *two* such carefully chosen candidates. But the real election in which the candidates compete for the backing of business and of its representatives in the parties and the press has already occured."

William Ebenstein, Professor of Political Science—University of California at Santa Barbara, *American Democracy in World Perspective*, 1967, p. 355.

Due to defects in certain primaries and to the failure of every leading presidential contender to enter each primary, preferential primaries are meaningful in no more than five or six states. As presidential hopefuls commonly enter only those primaries they believe they can win, in only a few states are the voters able to indicate a choice among the leading contenders in either party. For instance, in 1964 only in three states were Republican voters able to choose among the leading aspirants, and Johnson had no serious opposition in any state. Among other criticisms of the preferential primaries are the following: they are expensive and give an advantage to individuals with large funds; they exhaust prospective candidates; they may be decided on local and not on national issues; and a defeat in an early primary may eliminate a potential presidential nominee.

Richard Hofstadter, Professor of History—Columbia University, *The Idea of a Party System*, 1969, p. 85.

...notable Republican partisans like Madison, Jefferson, and Monroe were quite sincere in charging that many of their leading opponents favored monarchy and would scheme for its restoration, perhaps in some thinly disguised form under a "consolidated" state.

The charge was, though sincere also opportune: since the Revolution the tide of American opinion had set in firmly and irresistibly against monarchy and all its attendant institutions and practices, and any party that could be successfully saddled with secret monarchical preferences would carry a fatal burden. If the Federalists were indeed opponents of republicanism, then they were, by American canons, in a sense and to a degree an illegitimate party. If they believed in monarchy and in restricting popular government, then, no matter how properly they may have at first come into their power, the use they intended to make of it violated the general republican consensus upon which the Constitution had been based, and thus represented a betrayal of the common understanding at the outset. Madison's use of such phrases as "the influence of money and emoluments," "the terror of military force," "hereditary power," and the like, and charges in a companion essay about the desire of his opponents "to pervert the limited government of the Union into a government of unlimited discretion" on the part of those "who avow or betray principles of monarchy and aristocracy" substantiate this view of his intent.

Richard Hofstadter, Professor of History—Columbia University, *The Idea of a Party System*, 1969, p. 240.

In origin the Regency men were middle class or lower middle class, often self-made men or the sons of self-made men, moderately prosperous and respected, but (with the exception of Dix) not rich during their early years, and not connected to the leading families of the state. Three of them—Croswell and Butler besides Van Buren—were the sons of tavernkeepers, and the others characteristically went from farms to small-town law offices. Few Regency men had advanced formal education.

William Nisbet Chambers, Professor of History—Washington University, *American Political Behavior: Historical Essays and Readings*, 1974, p. 226.

Those who would succed in American politics *found it necessary—in the face of mass suffrage and general political participation—to deal with, mobilize, and shape into a power-base broad elements of a mass electorate and public.* The task called in effect for party-like structure—for an array of leaders cadre, and actives who could undertake sustained appeals to public opinion and employ effective campaigning techniques and for the performance of basic party functions.

William Ebenstein, Professor of Political Science—University of California at Santa Barbara, *American Democracy in World Perspective*, 1967, p. 355.

...presidential primaries provide the opportunity for individuals, like Dwight Eisenhower and John Kennedy, who are not necessarily the choice of the party leaders, to prove their popularity with the voters. Hence, presidential primaries have been instrumental in the nomination of candidates who might not otherwise have been nominated.

Hugh A. Bone, Professor of Political Science—University of Washington, *American Politics and the Party System*, 1971, p. 12.

An electoral party facilitates citizen participation and recruitment of persons for public office. It helps certain party activists attain some of their goals, such as public office, policy objectives, or recognition. Persons with ambitions of this kind who are outside the structure very often find the party a mechanism for accomplishment and indeed may find their objectives achievable only by becoming active in the party.

Has elite dominance been reflected in party policies?

Michael Parenti, State University of New York at Albany, *Democracy for the Few*, 1974, p. 144.

When magnified by partisan rhetoric, the differences between the parties appear worrisome enough to induce many citizens to vote—if not *for* then *against* someone. While there is no great hope that the party of their choice will do much for them, there persists the fear that the other party, if allowed to take office, or remain in office, will make things even worse. This lesser-of-two-evils approach is perhaps the most important inducement of voter participation.

Austin Ranney and Willmore Kendall, Political Scientists, *American Government and Politics*, 1971, p. 266.

Almost from the moment of their establishment, the legislative and congressional caucuses drew a heavy barrage of unfavorable criticism, mainly from the Jacksonian Democrats within the Republican party, who denounced the caucuses as aristocratic, immoral, and oversusceptible to manipulation by the "wire pullers". . .

Thomas R. Dye, Florida State University, and, L. Harmon Zeigler, University of Oregon, *The Irony of Democracy*, 1970, p. 177.

There is a great deal of truth to the "Tweedledum and Tweedledee" image of American political parties. American parties do, in fact subscribe to the same fundamental political ideology. Both the Democratic and the Republican parties have reflected prevailing elite consensus on basic democratic values—the sanctity of private property, a free enterprise economy, individual liberty, limited government, majority rule, and due process of law.

Michael Parenti, State University of New York at Albany, *Democracy for the Few*, 1974, p. 143.

"The rigidity of the two-party system is, I believe, disastrous," added Lippmann. "It ignores issues without settling them, dulls and wastes the energies of active groups, and chokes off the protests which should find a civilized expression in public life." That scathing judgment has stood the test of time. Today the two parties are still more ready to blur than clarify political issues, adopting stances that seldom move beyond conventional formulas. Electoral contests, supposedly providing democratic heterodoxy, have generated a competition for orthodoxy. In politics, as in economics, competition is rarely a safegurad against monopoly and seldom a guarantee that the competitors will offer the consumer a substantive choice.

Harold Bruce, Professor of Political Science—Dartmouth College, *American Parties and Politics*, 1927, p. 38.

One of America's most cherished ideals, however much unrealized it may be today is that of social democracy and the absence of social strata. Any effort, therefore, to thwart the operation of this principle by establishing parties designed to include and represent only certain groups must necessarily meet much opposition.

William Ebenstein, Professor of Political Science—University of California at Santa Barbara, *American Democracy in World Perspective*, 1967, p. 319.

Jefferson realized, as did later successful party leaders, that to win national elections a party must appeal to a broad cross section of the major segments of the population and that this can be accomplished only by advocating policies that represent the interests of these individuals and groups. In his inaugural address in 1801,

Jefferson announced that his administration favored not only the "encouragement of agriculture," but also "commerce as its handmaid." Thus, while recognizing the primacy of agriculture in his time, he understood the importance of gaining support from the commercial interests.

Walter Volkomer, Professor of Political Science—City University of New York, *American Government*, 1972, p. 299.

No matter what their "official" ideological stance, both political parties tend to support broad programs that will appeal to economically and politically diverse segments of the population—farmers, industrialists, blue-collar workers, professionals, and so on. On the issue of civil rights, for example, a party platform will often be constructed so as to gain black support, without offending or alienating those who are prejudiced against blacks.

William Nisbet Chambers, Professor of History—Washington University, *American Political Behavior: Historical Readings and Essays*, 1974, p. 220.

Party politics also reduced the differential advantages in power that had fallen to well-placed individuals and groups. Farmers, small traders, artisans, members of low-status religious groups, many intellectuals, reformers, even aliens found in the Jeffersonian Republican party a representative of their interests, perspectives opinions, and rights, as against the demands of larger property, ascribed position, high respectability, and established influence. The existence of two parties in competition provided a meaningful option between Federalist and Republican perspectives, policies, and leaders, and voters quickly learned to make use of the choice the parties put before them. Thus, in an open political system, the first modern political parties brought such important gains in democracy as representation, substantial participation, and choice.

Richard Hofstadter, Professor of History—Columbia University, *The Idea of a Party System*, 1969, p. 75.

The structural features of American society were exceptionally favorable to a moderate course of political development. Property was widely diffused. The political public was a large one, resting in part upon this propertied base and in part upon a generous suffrage. Relatively speaking, it was a literate public, and a large portion of it was accustomed to taking part in political life. It was proud of its rights, alert to violations of them, and suspicious of authority. Leadership and officeholding, of course, were largely in the hands of a patrician class —it seems hardly accurate to call it an aristocracy—and yet between the patrician leaders and the voting citizens there usually existed a fair degree of confidence, mutual respect, and accommodation. Colonial history had its record of class resentments, class conflicts, and even rebellions, but it had left no legacy of class hatred nor any fixed patterns of class hostilities.

Daniel Mazmanian, Brookings Institution, *Third Parties in Presidential Elections*, 1974, p. 136.

The emergence of significant third parties depends on the coincidence of four factors: severe national conflict over a few very important issues, a period of "crisis politics"; division of the electorate on one or more of these issues into at least one intense and estranged minority and a broad majority; rejection or avoidance of the position of the minority by both major parties, causing alienation of the minority; and a politician or political group willing to exploit the situation by initiating a new party. Such a combination assures an appreciable third-party vote.

Daniel Mazmanian, Brookings Institution, *Third Parties in Presidential Elections*, 1974, p. 136.

The ten third parties most significant in U.S. presidential elections, beginning with the Anti-Masons of 1832 and including the American Independent party of 1968, burst upon the national scene, amassing an appreciable number of popular votes, and then withered away in a fashion that is now predictable. It should be assumed that, in the future, significant third parties will follow the same pattern.
Third parties have provided important, sometimes crucial, access to the electoral arena for voting minorities.

George Thayer, *Who Shakes the Money Tree?*, 1973, p. 32.

The rising costs of campaigning in the 1840's and 1850's forced many aspirants for high office to turn to men of wealth for funds. It was in this period of American history that the bonds between political and economic interests were first forged. They are bonds that have not weakened at all over the following 130 years.

William Ebenstein, Professor of Political Science—University of California at Santa Barbara, *American Democracy in World Perspective*, 1967, p. 330.

From the election of Lincoln "the center of gravity of wealth" has been in the Republican party. The GOP dominated national politics during the period of spectacular business growth, and since that time business generally has been associated with the Republican party. President Eisenhower, after leaving office, once remarked that the Republicans have been referred to as the "party of business" and he personally was "proud of the label." His Secretary of Defense, Charles E. Wilson, former head of General Motors, made a statement that drew fire from many quarters—"what is good for General Motors is good for the nation."

Hugh A. Bone, Professor of Political Science—University of Washington, *American Politics and the Party System*, 1971, p. 36.

Powerful Western interests including cattle, lumber, land, and mineral barons attached themselves to the Republican party, which was glad to bestow on them portions of the public domain. Homestead legislation helped the more humble and adventurous, and they too, appreciated the federal beneficence. President Lincoln's administration created the first Department of Agriculture, and farmers appreciated this friendly recognition of their interests. The very considerable transportation industry voted for a party willing to subsidize a railroad to the Pacific Ocean, a link between the West and the East.

Seymore Martin Lipset, *Political Man*, 1960, p. 311.

The evidence compiled by various social scientists indicates that the men of wealth and economic power in America have *never* given more than minority support to the Democrats.

George Thayer, *Who Shakes the Money Tree?*, 1973, p. 48.

The behavior of such men as Penrose, Quay and Cameron, which was imitated time and time again by thousands of lesser politicians of all parties at all political levels, eventually produced a reaction among the voters. Their behavior had much to do with the passage of the Pendleton Act in 1883, and was responsible, at least in part, for the growth in electoral strength of both the Populists and the Progressives.

Has party membership been elitist?

Seymore Martin Lipset, *Political Man*, 1960, p. 303.

The emphasis on "classlessness" in American political ideology has led many European and American political commentators to conclude that party divisions in America are less related to class cleavages than they are in other Western countries. Polling studies, however, belie this conclusion, showing that in every American election since 1936 (studies of the question were not made before then), the proportion voting Democratic increases sharply as one moves down the occupational or income ladder.

William Ebenstein, Professor of Political Science—University of California at Santa Barbara, *American Democracy in World Perspective*, 1967, p. 317.

The formation of the first two parties may be attributed to Alexander Hamilton, the first Secretary of the Treasury, and Thomas Jefferson, the first Secretary of State. Hamilton, who lived in New York City, was the founder and acknowledged leader of the Federalist party. An exponent of the principle that "the rich, the wellborn, and the good" should rule, Hamilton advocated a government based on strong executive leadership, centralized power, and policies beneficial to the business and commercial community. Although Washington attempted to be nonpartisan, he came to accept the policies of his Secretary of State.

Seymour Martin Lipset, *Political Man*, 1960, p. 318.

Recent research by sociologists and historians has clarified some aspects of American politics which do not seem to fit a "class" interpretation of American history, like the fact, already noted, that the wealthier classes and their parties, the Whigs and Republicans, were more antislavery than the Democrats who were supported by the lower classes. Contemporary studies of political attitudes indicate that it is necessary to distinguish between so-called economic liberalism (issues concerned with the distribution of wealth and power) and noneconomic liberalism (issues concerned with civil liberties, race relations and foreign affairs). The fundamental factor in noneconomic liberalism is not actually class, but education, general sophistication, and probably to a certain extent psychic security. But since these factors are strongly correlated with class, noneconomic liberalism is positively associated with social status (the wealthier are more tolerant), while economic liberalism is inversely correlated with social status (the poor are more leftist on such issues).

Seymour Martin Lipset, *Political Man*, 1960, p. 310.

Alexis de Toqueville: "I do not assert that the ostensible purpose or even that the secret aim of American parties is to promote the rule of aristocracy in the country; but I affirm that aristocratic or democratic passions may be easily detected at the bottom of all parties, and that, although they escape a superficial observation, they are the main points and soul of every faction in the United States."

Hugh A. Bone, Professor of Political Science, University of Washington, *American Politics and the Party System*, 1971, p. 29.

Even before the Revolutionary War, Virginia had a democratic party under the leadership of Patrick Henry. It consisted of back-country small farmers, land-hungry squatters, tobacco growers, Western trappers, and diverse unorganized small proprietors and slave owners. Opposed to the ratification of the Constitution, the party came to be called Anti-Federalists, who challenged the coastal communities supporting the Constitution. The Anti-Federalists were not coordinated into a national party but offered the potential of protest especially against Alexander Hamilton's financial policies.

William Nisbet Chambers, Professor of History—Washington University, *American Political Behavior: Historical Readings and Essays*, 1974, p. 219.

It is thus possible to speak of the Republicans not only as a modern party, but as a "popular" party, in the sense of a party grounded in and sensitive to a broad and durable base in the population or electorate.

Harold Bruce, Professor of Political Science—Dartmouth College, *American Parties and Politics*, 1927, p. 37.

In describing the composition of American parties it may be said that, in general, the parties do not follow class lines but cut down through the social strata in such a way that no party can be said to be composed of a certain social group. This is not a denial of the fact that certain social and economic groups may be identified with certain parties but is a statement of the fact that class parties, as such, do not exist in this country.

Selected Bibliography

Agar, Herbert. *The Price of Union*. Boston: Houghton Mifflin, 1966.

Barber, James Alden. *Social Mobility and Voting Behavior*. Chicago: Rand-McNally, 1970.

Benson, Lee, et. al. *American Political Behavior: Historical Essays and Readings*. New York: Harper and Row, 19747

Binkley, Wilfred Ellsworth. *American Political Parties, their Natural History*. New York: Khopf, 1958.

Bone, Hugh Alvin. *American Politics and the Party System*. New York: McGraw-Hill, 1971.

Borden, Martin. *Parties and Politics in the Early Republic, 1789-1815*. London: Routledge and K. Paul, 1968.

Borden, Morton, ed. *Political Parties in American History*. New York: Putnam, 1973.

Bottomore, T. B. *Elites and Society*. Baltimore: Penguin, 1970.

Broder, David S. *The Party's Over, the Failure of Politics in America*. New York: Harper and Row, 1972.

Bruce, Harold Rozelle. *American Parties and Politics; History and Role of Political Parties in the United States*. New York: H. Holt and Company, 1932.

Chambers, William N. *Political Parties in a New Nation: the American Experience, 1776-1809*. New York: Oxford University Press, 1963.

Charles, Joseph. *The Origins of the American Party System; Three Essays*. Williamsburg, Va.: Institute of Early American History and Culture, 1956.

Clubb, Jerome M. *Electoral Change and Stability in American Political History*. New York: Free Press, 1971.

Cunningham, Noble E. *The Jeffersonian Republicans in Power, Party Operations, 1801-1809*. Chapel Hill: University of North Carolina Press, 1963.

Cunningham, Noble E. *The Making of the American Party System, 1789-1809*. Englewood Cliffs, N.J.: Prentice-Hall, 1968.

David, Paul Theodore. *Party Strength in the United States, 1872-1970*. Charlottesville, Va.: University Press of Virginia, 1972.

Dobson, John M. *Politics in the Gilded Age: A New Perspective on Reform*. New York: Praeger, 1972.

Dolbeare, Kenneth, and Edelman, Murray. *American Politics, Policies, Power, and Change*. Lexington, Mass.: D. C. Heath, 1971.

Durerger, Maurice. *Party Politics and Pressure Groups; A Comparative Introduction*. Translated by David Wagoner. New York: Crowell, 1972.

Dye, Thomas R., and Zeigler, L. Harmon. *The Irony of Democracy*. Belmont, Calif.: Wadsworth Publishing Co., 1970.

Ebenstein, William, et. al. *American Democracy in World Perspective*. New York: Harper and Row, 1967.

Goodman, Paul. *Federalists vs. the Jeffersonian Republicans*. New York: Holt, Rinehart and Winston, 1967.

Haynes, Frederick E. *Social Politics in the United States*. New York: AMS Press, 1970.

Hesseltine, William B. *Third Party Movements in the United States*. Princeton, N.J.: Van Nostrand, 1962.

Hofstadter, Richard. *The Idea of a Party System*. Berkeley and Los Angeles: University of California Press, 1969.

Jones, Charles. *The Republican Party in American Politics*. New York: Macmillan, 1965.

Irish, Marian D., and Prothro, James W. *The Politics of American Democracy*. Englewood Cliffs, N.J.: Prentice-Hall, 1965.

Ladd, Everett Carll. *American Political Parties, Social Change and Political Response*. New York: Norton, 1970.

Lipset, Seymour Martin. *Political Man, the Social Bases of Politics*. Garden City, N.Y.: Doubleday, 1960.

McCormick, Richard Patrick. *The Second American Party System, Party Formation in the Jacksonian Era*. Chapel Hill, N.C.: University of North Carolina Press, 1966.

Mayo, Charles G., and Crowe, Beryl L. *American Political Parties, a Systematic Perspective*. New York: Harper and Row, 1967.

Mazmanian, Daniel A. *Third Parties in Presidential Elections*. Washington, D.C.: The Brookings Institution, 1974.

Moe, Ronald C., and Schultze, William A. *American Government and Politics, Selected Readings*. Columbus, Oh.: Charles E. Merrill, 1971.

Morgan, Howard Wayne. *From Hayes to McKinley, National Party Politics, 1877-1896*. Syracuse, N.Y.: Syracuse University Press, 1969.

Nash, Howard P. *Third Parties in American Politics*. Washington, D.C.: Public Affairs Press, 1959.

Oath, Samuel Peter. *The Boss and the Machine; a Chronicle of the Politicians and Party Organizations*. New Haven, Conn.: Yale University Press, 1921.

Parenti, Michael. *Democracy for the Few*. New York: St. Martin's Press, 1974.

Risjord, Norman, ed. *The Early American Party System*. New York: Harper and Row, 1969.

Saloma, John, and Sontag, Frederick. *Parties*. New York: Vintage, 1972.

Schlesinger, Arthur M., ed. *History of U.S. Political Parties*. New York: Chelsea House Publishers in association with R. R. Bowker, 1973.

Silberg, Joel H. *The Transformation of American Politics, 1840-1860*. Englewood Cliffs, N.J.: Prentice-Hall, 1967.

Sorauf, Francis Joseph. *Party Politics in America*. Boston: Little, Brown, 1972.

Thayer, George. *Who Shakes the Money Tree?* New York: Simon and Schuster, 1973.

Volkomer, Walter. *American Government*. New York: Appleton-Century-Crofts, 1972.

Wolfe, Alan. *The Seamy Side of Democracy*. New York: David McKay, 1973.

Yearley, Clifton K. *The Money Machines: The Breakdown and Reform of Governmental and Party Finance in the North, 1860-1920*. Albany, N.Y.: State University of New York Press, 1970.

IS FEDERALISM OBSOLETE?

Introductory Essay

The American government is, at least theoretically, a federal system of government. That is, individual states formed a federation, maintaining independent jurisdiction over their populaces in certain matters of governing, while granting authority in certain other matters to a national government — the federal government. The topic "Is Federalism Obsolete?" questions the extent to which there has been and should be a centralization of power in the federal government. Obviously, the balance of power between the federal and state governments can shift. S.P. Aiyar of the University of Bombay pointed out:

Its [the Constitution's] federalism now is very different in spirit and in form from what it was in the eighteenth century. The original balance of power in the federation has been in constant flux and it has responded to the changing winds of economic, political and social fortune. There has been over the past century and a half an increasing tendency towards greater governmental powers.

As the role of the federal government has grown that of the states has diminished. Possibly it can no longer be said that the federal government rules "By Consent of the States ...." But it may be that the characteristics of a federal system of government as envisioned by the Founders of the Republic should continue to be valued by American society today.

The Constitution established a government of shared sovereignty between the federal and state governments, with ultimate authority residing in the people. Thus the central government and the states entered into a partnership of governing. The responsibilities for the various governmental functions could shift within the partnership. Alexander Hamilton believed that most powers should rest centrally if a strong economy was to be built. On the other hand, Thomas Jefferson thought the central government should govern as little as possible, allowing for maximum local decision-making. It was a feature of American federalism that these different theories could be accommodated according to circumstances.

The thirteen original colonies were initially independent entities but at the time of the Declaration of Independence the colonies united. The conduct of war necessitated a coordinated and unified government. In 1781, the Articles of Confederation officially established the United States of America and its governing body, the Congress of the Confederation. This government was characterized by a decentralization of power. Because central authority was mistrusted, the Articles guaranteed the sovereignty of the states and limited severely the powers of the new Congress. For example, Congress could not levy taxes or regulate trade. During the 1780's this document was increasingly criticized and a mode of strengthening the union was sought.

In 1787 the Constitutional Convention was convened in order to strengthen he Articles of Confederation. The major question before this Convention was to what degree power should be further centralized. The Virginia Plan, promoting a strong central government, was introduced by those most critical of the Articles — the Federalists. But forming a complete union was considered too extreme a step for thirteen different states accustomed to their independence. Thus the Virginia Plan was rejected, at least in the form in which it was introduced. The Convention proceeded to modify the Plan: the states were guaranteed a role in the formation of a central government and the control of important areas of governing; and, the Congress was granted only certain specified powers. These modifications resulted in the Constitution, which provided for a system of government significantly more centralized than had been the case under the Articles. Many at the Convention desired as centralized a government as possible, allowing only those changes necessary to gain the support of politicians concerned with state sovereignty.

Much debate between the supporters of each type of federalism preceded ratification of the Constitution. Federalists were the contingent favoring as much centralization as possible with Alexander Hamilton, John Jay, and James Madison the public spokesmen for this position. They published a remarkable series of essays, now known as *The Federalist,* which defended the new Constitutional system. These arguments combined a powerful practical sense with a subtle understanding of classical political questions. They shared several basic concerns: the maintenance of order; the mutual defense of the nation; the protection of property; and, the regulation of commerce. All these needs would be fulfilled, they claimed, by the new Union. In addition, government by the few, insured in a highly centralized system, would guarantee rule by the most able citizens. It was assumed that the country would benefit from a national unity under this capable leadership. Underlying this political preference was the belief that human nature cannot be trusted and therefore is in need of some control. This mistrust also called for insulation of the government from the individual. A central government with great authority and limited responsiveness to the popular will was the alternative supported by the Federalists.

The oppositon — the Antifederalists — preferred to adhere to the principles expressed in the Articles of Confederation as closely as possible, making only those changes necessary to insure the military survival of the states. To them, the Constitution was too radical. The Federalists had placed emphasis on order; the Antifederalists believed that, above all, tyranny and oppression should be avoided and the guarantee of rights should be sought. Local self-rule was therefore preferable for them because the smaller governmental unit was thought to be both more responsive to the particular desires of its constituency and more effective in administering to them. Basic to this political preference was another case of mistrust — that of power. Thus their objections to the Constitution focused on the collecting of authority into centralized branches of a national government. For example, it was feared that the Federal judiciary would destroy the states' judiciaries and that the President held too many powers (veto, appointment, etc.). Further, the proposed Constitution did not contain a Bill of Rights. To institute a powerful national governmental system threatened the traditionally unrestricted prerogatives of the states. But the Antifederalists did not prevail and the Constitution was ratified by the end of 1788. Hamilton, Jay, and Madison, however, agreed to the addition of "A Bill of Particulars guaranteeing certain Rights and Freedoms."

The victorious Federalists are most remembered for the measures taken by George Washington's Secretary of the Treasury, Alexander Hamilton. He developed a threefold program, funding the national debt, establishing the first Bank of North America, and raising revenue by employing excise taxes and tariff duties. These steps were all made possible by the adoption of the Constitution.

Thomas Jefferson became a leader of the political forces objecting to these first Federalist policies — the Democratic-Republican party. Their basic tenet was that government functions should be as limited as possible, an attitude of the anti-Federalist position. Becoming the third U.S. President in 1801, Jefferson encouraged reduction in department expenditures, payments on the national debt, and removal of the Federalist excise taxes. In accordance with these measures, he worked to safeguard the rights of state governments as guaranteed in the Constitution.

As in the early years of the nation, subsequent periods have witnessed a federalism of changing character, adjusting to new needs and unfamiliar pressures. The Civil War and the slavery question resulted in a direct clash between the competing theories of federalism. A fundamental constitutional issue echoed in debates leading up to the shelling of Ft. Sumter: does the national government have a constitutional right to ban slavery in new states? The Southern states rejected this interference on the basis of a theory of the Union; sovereignty resided ultimately with the states; the Union was dissolvable by any party to it; and, the states antedated and themselves created the national government. The North rejected the philosophy of the South; by the Constitution, the national government was sovereign; the Union was permanent unless all parties agreed to dissolution; and, both the state governments and the national government emerged at the same time with the Revolution. A Union victory permanently chiseled the northern view on the face of American federalism.

This victory for national government at the conclusion of the Civil War was only a first step toward increasing central authority. The adoption of the Fourteenth Amendment to the Constitution in 1868 provided for future federal action to guarantee civil rights. Earlier, in 1833, the decision in *Barron v. Baltimore* confirmed that the Bill of Rights regulated only the central government. The Fourteenth Amendment laid the basis for its application to the states.

The growth of business in America was a further contributing factor to the increased centralization of government. Beginning with the demand for canals and roads, the Federal Government took on the new responsibilities of funding and building an expanded national system of communication and tradeways. Even Calhoun, the staunch states' righter promoted these programs, while continuing to maintain the necessity of state sovereignty was necessary to the guarantee of rights. With industrialization, urbanization, and the development of mass communication, the nation became more inevitably and irrevocably interdependent. This new unity created an atmosphere in which federal action became more acceptable and commonplace. In 1887, the Interstate Commerce Commission was established, initially to regulate the railroads and eventually to regulate all interstate commerce. Today federal regulatory agencies have mushroomed, assuming responsibilities for the regulation of all facets of the country's economic life. Representative agencies include the Federal Trade Commission, the Securities and Exchange Commission and the Federal Communications Commission. Federal power was also greatly enhanced in 1913 with the establishment of the Federal Reserve System and adoption of the Eighteenth Amendment establishing the Federal Income Tax. Necessity demanded major strides toward a central government during the New Deal era and World War II. The states were incapable of dealing effectively with the massive problems of the Depression. Federal legislation was quickly recognized as the expedient solution. World War II required both large defense expenditures and wartime economic regulation on the part of the Federal Government. Thus the national government continued to grow in importance as the role of the state government diminished.

In the decades since World War II, the demand for social programs, first spawned by the Depression, increased. But the ability of the state governments to provide effective solutions to the problems of race, poverty, and pollution has been limited. As the Federal Government steps into these areas, it becomes questionable whether the states can justify any claims to sovereignty (i.e. to self-rule). A fundamental problem is money. The financial capability of the states is severely limited. State constitutions restrict various mechanisms for increasing revenue such as the type of taxes and bonding. Large social programs such as the War on Poverty, require massive federal funding. Thus, the grants-in-aid programs, where the states match federal funds, have grown significantly. In addition, the state governments are criticized for a lack of responsiveness to these social problems. State legislatures are often dominated by the rural portions of the state, and hence are unconcerned with the plight of the heavily-populated urban centers. Therefore it has appeared that the national government is often more responsive to the majority of the U.S. population, those residing in and depending upon the cities.

Originally, the Antifederalists believed that state sovereignty was necessary to the preservation of individual rights. But recently, Federal action has been required in the form of the Civil Rights Act to insure those rights. The reluctance of states to act has meant that an increased Federal role may now be critical to the guarantee of basic rights.

Despite these criticisms aimed at the states, there has been in recent years renewed support of the federal system. It has been manifested in both Lyndon Johnson's "Creative Federalism" and Richard Nixon's "New Federalism." These programs aimed at a greater emphasis on decision-making at the local level. The power to implement local decisions requires money; the concept of revenue sharing was introduced to provide it. In revenue sharing, federal tax revenue is returned to the states and, ultimately, local government. How these funds are spent becomes a matter of local discretion. Such discretion enables each locality to be responsive to its own needs, a responsiveness not possible under uniform federal programs. Many problems remain including limitations on the amount of funding and the potential misuse of funds.

The survival of federalism depends on the ability of governmental levels to initiate, design and implement effective social programs on a cooperative basis. Whether states are creatures of America's past or have a vital role to play in her future remains to be seen.

Excerpted Documents

Concept of federalism.

Frank N. Trager, Professor of International Affairs—New York University, "On Federalism," *Why Federations Fail*, Thomas Franck, ed., 1968, p. x.

What we mean by federalism is not a fixed point on a map, but a tendency which is neither unitary nor separatist. In Aristotelean terms, it is the median between these two polar positions, and thus their true opposite. A federalized state is one in which the several units and their respective powers are constitutionally or otherwise legally united under the ultimate power of a central state and government. But it is also an essential mark of a federalized state that the subordinate units retain or have reserved some irreducible powers operative within the same territory and regulating the same population over which the federal authority also applies with respect to other matters or different aspects of the same matter.

Edward McWhinney, Professor of Law—University of Toronto, *Comparative Federalism*, 1962, p. 17.

A federal constitutional system in which the nation is dominant in relation to each and all of the member-states is Marshallian in character, after the great early Chief Justice Marshall of the United States who did so much to build a strong national authority out of the factionalism of the individual states. The Pluralist federal system, by contrast, is Jeffersonian in character, with its faith in enlightened self-government and cooperation at the local level, and its distrust of centralized power.

History of federalism.

Jackson Turner Main, Professor of History—University of Wisconsin, *The Antifederalists*, 1961, p. 120.

A fundamental conviction of nearly all Antifederalists was that the Constitution established a national, not a federal government, a consolidation of previously independent states into one, a transfer of sovereignty in which the states, once sovereign, would retain but a shadow of their former power.

Herbert Wechsler, Professor of Law —Columbia University, *Federalism: Mature and Emergent*, 1962, p. 98.

National action has thus always been regarded as exceptional in our polity, an intrusion to be justified by some necessity, the special rather than the ordinary case. The point of view cuts even deeper than the concept of the central government as one of granted, limited authority, articulated in the Tenth Amendment. National power may be quite unquestioned in a given situation; those who would advocate its exercise must none the less answer the preliminary question why the matter should not be left to the states. Even when Congress acts, its tendency has been to frame enactments on an "ad hoc" basis to accomplish limited objectives, supplanting state-created norms only so far as may be necessary for the purpose.

Edward McWhinney, Professor of Law—University of Toronto, *Comparative Federalism*, 1962, p. 3.

"The epoch of federalism is over." This epitaph was uttered on the eve of World War II, to an American audience by the distinguished English Socialist theorist, Professor Harold Laski. Professor Laski was taking stock, of course, of the balance of effective powers existing in the United States, as between nation and states, at the height of the New Deal era. What Professor Laski was saying, and these were truisms accepted by very many American liberals at the time, was that social and economic planning must be accepted as an inevitable part of government in an industrial society, and that planning required, for its effective implementation, increasingly more centralized controls. On this view, federalism with its emphasis on a pluralistic approach to community policy-making and its insistence as far as possible on the territorial dispersal of political power, would run counter to the main trends of modern society and should therefore be accepted as being obsolescent as a governmental form.

Edward McWhinney, Professor of Law—University of Toronto, *Comparative Federalism*, 1962, p. 4.

For federalism seems one of the more effective machinery devices available for ensuring that, on the whole, the demands of the planned state and the welfare state, which are so widely accepted as valid and proper, shall be harmonized with the rule of law. And federalism further offers interesting and intriguing possibilities, at a time when all the pressures of nation-wide mass communication media are towards producing a mass uniformity, of preserving and strengthening claims to a cultural diversity and intellectual experimentation.

Democractic values and federalism.

Jackson Turner Main, Professor of History—University of Wisconsin, *The Antifederalists*, 1961, p. xiv.

Because the small property holders were a majority in Revolutionary times, they wanted a government dominated by the many rather than the few, and they therefore favored democratic ideas.

Arthur W. MacMahon, Professor of Public Administration—Columbia University, *Federalism: Mature and Emergent,* 1962, p. 10.

First, when diversities are pronounced and are located with reasonable compactness, the geographical deconcentration of important powers secures greater correspondence between public policies and local majority sentiment on matters entrusted to the constituent governments. Second, by multiplying the independent legislative arenas, the system gives scope for experimentation, followed by imitation. Third, the multiplication of the bodies of elected officials who bear considerable responsibility in their own right broadens the opportunity for political participation. Fourth, the system is suitable for government over large or scattered areas. ... Fifth, federalism lessens the risk of a monopoly of political power by providing a number of independent points where the party that is nationally in the minority at the time can maintain itself while it formulates and partly demonstrates its policies and capabilities and develops new leadership.

Thomas Jefferson, First Inaugural Address, in *Thomas Jefferson and the New Nation,* 1970, p. 655.

... one essential principle of U.S. Government is ... "the support of State governments in all their rights, as the most competent administrations for our domestic concerns and the surest bulwarks against anti-republican tendencies."

Franz L. Neumann, Professor of Government—Columbia University, "Federalism and Freedom: A Critique," *Federalism: Mature and Emergent,* Arthur W. MacMahon, ed., 1962, p. 51.

Yet there is an element of truth in the theory of Montesquieu and Rousseau: the smallest territorial unit—the municipality—is potentially the most responsive to the will and interests of the people and, consequently, local self-government must be considered the indispensable cornerstone of a modern large-scale democracy.

Jackson Turner Main, Professor of History—University of Wisconsin, *The Antifederalists,* 1961, p. 11.

In order to guard against the tyranny of power and preserve popular rule, the men entrusted with power had to be kept responsive to public opinion. If they were allowed to act independently, history proved that the results were evil and the former colonials did not have to look far into the past to perceive this truth.

Herbert Wechsler, Professor of Law—Columbia University, *Federalism: Mature and Emergent,* 1962, p. 97.

In a far flung, free society, the federalist values are enduring. They call upon a people to achieve a unity sufficient to resist their common perils and advance their common welfare, without undue sacrifice of their diversities and the creative energies to which diversity gives rise. They call for government responsive to the will of the full national constituency, without loss of responsiveness to lesser voices, reflecting smaller bodies of opinion, in areas that constitute their own legitimate concern.

Jackson Turner Main, Professor of History—University of Wisconsin, *The Antifederalists,* 1961, p. 281.

As a body of political thought, Antifederalism had a background in English and American political theory long before the Constitution was drafted. Its principles were embodied in the Articles of Confederation; later they were elaborated in the controversy over the impost. Always the emphasis was on local rule and the retention of power by the people, which were democratic tenets in that age. ... [The Antifederalist position] was therefore peculiarly congenial to those who were tending toward democracy, most of whom were soon to rally around Jefferson. The Antifederalists, who lost their only major battle, are forgotten while the victors are remembered, but it is not so certain which is the more memorable.

Liberty and federalism.

Jackson Turner Main, Professor of History—University of Wisconsin, *The Antifederalists,* 1961, p. 129.

Not only did consolidation entrust men with excessive power, but it violated history's lesson that freedom could be maintained only by local governments.

E. James Ferguson, Professor of Economics—University of North Carolina, *The Power of the Purse: A History of American Public Finance, 1776-1790,* 1961, p. 111.

The Articles of Confederation expressed this Revolutionary emphasis upon defense of local rights against central authority. The Articles were designed to safeguard liberty; the Union was a league of states, presided over by a dependent Congress. Its authority was limited in many ways, but of all the restraints devised to forestall usurpation of power, the denial to Congress of the right to tax was the most fundamental. ... Under the Articles of Confederation the states remained in a position to check the arbitrary proceedings by withholding revenue from Congress.

Jackson Turner Main, Professor of History—University of Wisconsin, *The Antifederalists,* 1961, p. 79.

The most dangerous of all powers, most serious in its consequences if abuse occurred, and most likely to change a free government into an oppressive one, was control over taxation, for, as "Democritus" wrote, "Power, among people civilized as we are, is necessarily connected with the direction of public money." That the Articles of Confederation denied to Congress the right to raise money by taxation was no accident, nor a product of ignorance, but a recognition that control of the public's money could be "faithfully watched" only if the individual states had their separate treasuries.

Edward McWhinney, Professor of Law—University of Toronto, *Comparative Federalism,* 1962, p. 50.

For both nation and member-states may be actively interested in the problem of internal security but, for reasons of cultural and social diversity, may well strike the balance in rather different ways among the competing interests in national security on the one hand and speech and discussion on the other.

Effective administration and federalism.

Walton H. Hamilton, Professor of Law—Yale University, *The Power to Govern,* 1937, p. 137.

Mr. Madison, who would have the states reduced to counties or turned into administrative districts, saw "the prerogative of the General Government" as "the great pervading principle that must control the centrifugal tendency of the States; which, without it, will continually fly out of their proper orbits and destroy the order and harmony of the political system."

S.P. Aiyar, Professor of Politics—University of Bombay, *Federalism and Social Change,* 1961, p. 58.

The Federal Government's efforts to fight the depression brought it into conflict with the Supreme Court which set aside most of the New Deal legislation. But the struggle between constitutional law and the needs of society not only resulted in a new attitude towards law but deeply affected the federal principle itself. The problems created by the depression were even more complicated, because the States found it impossible to deal with many problems owing to financial inadequacy. During and after the depression the States found it necessary to rely to an increasing extent on the financial aid given by the Federal Government. This tendency has gone so far that for all practical purposes the States have been subordinated to the Federal Government.

Arthur W. MacMahon, Professor of Public Administration—Columbia University, *Federalism: Mature and Emergent,* 1962, p. 3.

Modern man is oppressed by the sense of heavy organization and distant controls; he longs to resolve things into comprehensible and manageable portions. At the same time he values the physical basis of the good life; he must take account of endless elements of interdependence; he must respect the utility of large scale methods. Parthy, too, he may be led to favor centralized political power in national states to offset centralized economic power, either by positive intervention or by measures that outlaw barriers or restrictive combinations.

Otto Eckstein, Professor of Economics—Harvard University, *Public Finance*, 1967, p. 35.

When you contrast [local] decision-making process with Washington or the state capitals — where legislators deal with a wide range of issues, many of them remote from their own experience, pressured by lobbyists seeking benefits without costs for their group, and impose uniform policies on a wide range of communities of different circumstances and desires — you see the advantage of having a federal system in which vigorous local governments handle what problems they can.

Protections and a central government.

Jackson Turner Main, Professor of History—University of Wisconsin, *The Antifederalists*, 1961, p. 73.

Congress first recommended the impost in the early spring of 1781. It was a time of great stress. The military outlook was dark; Continental and state paper currency were seriously depreciated; Congress urgently needed money to pay the army and the interest on the debt. The states were having trouble supplying their troops and meeting their financial obligations and were unable to pay Congress's requisitions.

John Adams, *A Defence of the Constitutions of Government of the United States of America Against the Attack of M. Turgot in his Letter to Dr. Price*, 1797, *in Why Federations Fail*, Thomas Franck, ed., 1968, p. xii.

Adams writes, "The former confederation of the United States was formed upon the model and example of all confederacies, ancient and modern, in which the federal council was only a diplomatic body. ... The magnitude of territory, the population, the wealth and commerce, and especially the rapid growth of the United States, have shown such a government to be inadequate to their wants; and the new system, which seems admirably calculated to unite their interests and affections, and bring them to a uniformity of principles and sentiments, is equally well combined to unite their wills and forces as a single nation."

James Madison, *The Federalist*, Number 10.

Among the numerous advantages promised by a well-constructed Union, none deserves to be more accurately developed than its tendency to break and control the violence of faction. The friend of popular governments, never finds himself so much alarmed for their character and fate, as when he contemplates their propensity to this dangerous vice. He will not fail therefore to set a due value on any plan which, without violating the principles to which he is attached, provides a proper cure for it ...

John Jay, *The Federalist*, Number 2.

With equal pleasure I have often taken notice, that Providence has been pleased to give this one connected country to one united people — a people descended from the same ancestors, speaking the same language, professing the same religion, attached to the same principles of government, very similar in their manners and customs, and who, by their joint counsels, arms, and efforts, fighting side by side throughout a long and bloody war, have nobly established general liberty and independence.

Walton H. Hamilton, Professor of Law—Yale University, *The Power to Govern*, 1937, p. 142.

The Congress might legislate "in the general interests," where the several states were "incompetent," or where separate action was a threat to the harmony of the Union. Such acts were, as is usual with nations, to take precedence over local ordinances. So a later danger was anticipated and guarded against in a single sentence of classic simplicity. "This Constitution, and the Laws of the United States which shall be made in Pursuance thereof shall be the supreme Law of the Land." A simple rule of priority was proof against dual sovereignty and jurisdictional conflict.

Daniel J. Elazer, Professor of Government—Temple University, *American Federalism*, 1972, p. 161.

Perhaps paradoxically, administrative rule-making often has a decentralizing effect that extends the powers of the states in shared programs even beyond those actually authorized by congressional legislation and interference. Good relationships that develop between federal and state (or local) administrators often allow the state people to gain even more freedom of maneuver than is given them formally by law.

The politics surrounding the administration of the cooperative grant-in-aid programs demonstrate this forcefully. It has been said that "Grants-in-aid are programs for which the states have responsibility but in which the entire nation has an interest." Through the conditional transfer of funds to the states, the federal government gains a voice in making policy in those fields aided by the grants while the states remain responsible for day-to-day administration of the programs with all that the responsibility implies in the way of actual policy-making.

Richard H. Leach, Professor of Political Science—Duke University, *American Federalism*, 1970, p. 240.

The question is not simply one of freedom achieved negatively through decentralization—it can probably be demonstrated that decentralization by itself is no absolute protection against the arbitrary use of power—but one of freedom achieved positively, through combining the power forces necessary to each instance. A case in point is the recently enacted Safe Streets and Crime Control Act. The decentralist would assure us that freedom to walk the streets safely and to be secure from the effects of riots is best achieved by letting each local unit of government handle the problem at its own discretion. The realist understands that *in this instance* a combination of federal funds and local action is required to secure the safety of persons and property and so to make freedom in city streets meaningful.

Nelson A. Rockefeller, Vice President, *The Future of Federalism*, 1968, p. 1.

The federal system, conceived by the Founding Fathers and embodied in the Constitution, is a crucial stone of our arch of liberty. For us, it has provided unity without the sacrifice of desirable diversity, strength to achieve national goals while simultaneously enhancing human dignity, and an energized environment of law and custom wherein economic and social progress is achieved through equal opportunity for free individuals rather than the totalitarian dictates of a ruling hierarchy.

Roscoe C. Martin, Professor of Government—Syracuse University, *The Cities and the Federal System*, 1965, p. 75.

The single overwhelming conclusion to be drawn from this analysis is that the states' concern for the vast new problems of metropolitan America, as measured by monetary contributions toward their alleviation, is quite casual. There is little evidence, indeed, that the states recognize these problems as anything more than very limited state responsibilities. The national government, observing the inability of the cities to meet the new challenges of urbanism alone and the unwillingness of the states to lend them effective assistance, has devised a series of new programs designed to bring the nation's resources to bear on the areas of major stress. These programs generally do not possess the vigor nor do they command the support necessary to deal most effectively with the problems they address, but they do signify a growing awareness by the federal government of the existence of strains beyond the resources of traditional city governments. Unhappily the states do not share that awareness, or share it in only limited degree.

Leonard D. White, *The States and the Nation*, 1953, p. 36.

Beyond these four functions, the strictly domestic phases of government still rest largely in local and state agencies. This is reflected in the fact that the states now spend annually about fifteen billions of dollars, whereas twenty years ago they spent about two billion. New York and California each require an annual budget of over one billion, of which a substantial part goes directly to the localities for their public services. It is a hard and stubborn fact that the states are going concerns, directly responsible for vital public services of a high order of priority. Each and every one of them is a fully organized government with its own constitution written in the form its citizens prefer, its own legislative, executive, and judicial branches, and its own law enforcement machinery.

Nelson A. Rockefeller, Vice President, *The Future of Federalism*, 1968, p. 41.

No state responsibility is more fundamental than the protection of the health, the safety, and the well-being of each and every citizen. For lack of a truly serious effort at the national level, it is a fact that our people have been vulnerable and unprotected against the hazards of possible nuclear attack. In the absence of an effective national effort to meet this gravely serious state of affairs, it was left to the states and to the Governors' Conference to take the lead—by action, by example, and by advocacy—to create the awareness and the political tensions that only now, three years after the initial efforts, have led to a proposal for an effective national program to protect our people.

Richard H. Leach, Professor of Political Science—Duke University, *American Federalism*, 1970, p. 123.

Succinctly put, the case against the states is that where action has been required they have too often been inactive; where change—has been demanded, they have offered the *status quo;* where imagination and innovation have been needed, they have seldom come up with satisfactory alternatives. The states, students have agreed, are indecisive, antiquated, timid, and ineffective, unwilling to face their problems, unresponsive, and not really interested in taking action when action is required. It is the existence of just such defects that accounts for the title of Governor Sanford's book, *Storm Over the States,* and that leads many to believe that the states have outlived their usefulness in the American constitutional system.

Roscoe C. Martin, Professor of Government—Syracuse University, *The Cities and the Federal System*, 1965, p. 70.

One concomitant, or consequence, of the allocation process is reflected in the earmarked revenues and special funds which occur in such abundance. An example is the earmarking of gasoline tax revenues for highway construction—an obeisance toward the automobile and all who derive pleasure and profit from it. To the extent that the state's revenues are prededicated to special purpose or uses, the decision-makers (governor together with legislature) are limited in the course they may pursue; they are prisoners of the society at whose hands they exercise the power (but only a limited power) of decision. Yet another aspect of the problem is seen in the limitations of both tax rate and indebtedness which are found in many state constitutions. These go back in their origin to the political process; more to the point, they reflect public distrust in the judgment or integrity of those charged with responsibility for the state's financial affairs.

Richard H. Leach, Professor of Political Science—Duke University, *American Federalism*, 1970, p. 126.

Yet the states are important. They perform vital and intimate functions for the American people, functions, it should be noted, which the national government would have a hard time undertaking by itself. The states first of all administer justice for most of us most of the time. Most crimes are state crimes and most civil cases arise in state courts. The states plan, construct (to be sure with a great deal of federal aid), and maintain most highways and roads. Police, health, welfare, education, safety are all primarily state functions (many of them, to be sure, carried on with a good deal of federal money). So are such things as registration of births, occupational examination and licensing, marriage and divorce, the disposal of bodies, and the administration of estates. If the charge be made that government is ever with us, in the United States at least it applies today as it always has with greater pertinence to state governments than to the national government.

Selected Bibliography

Aiyar, S. P. *Federalism and Social Change.* New York: Asia Publishing House, 1961.

Anderson, William. *Intergovernmental Relations in Review.* Minneapolis: University of Minnesota Press, 1960.

Anderson, William. *The Nation and the States, Rivals or Partners.* Minneapolis: University of Minnesota Press, 1955.

Arrington, W. Russell, and Dunn, Richard E. "Governmental Evolution and the Response of State Legislatures." *State Government,* 43 (Summer 1970), 174.

Beard, Charles. "An Economic Interpretation of the Constitution." *Issues in American Economic History.* Edited by Gerald D. Nash. Boston: D. C. Heath and Co., 1964.

Bennett, Walter. *American Theories of Federalism.* Alabama: University of Alabama Press, 1964.

Birch, Anthony. *Federalism, Finance and Social Legislation.* London: Oxford University Press, 1955.

Bowie, Robert, and Friedrich, Carl, eds. *Studies in Federalism.* Boston: Little, Brown and Co., 1954.

Celebreeze, Anthony J. "Cooperative Federalism for an Advancing America." *State Government,* 37 (Summer 1964), 143.

Dauer, Manning J. *The Adams Federalists.* Baltimore: Johns Hopkins Press, 1954.

Debout, John E. "The States' Best Friend." *National Civic Review, 53* (February, 1964), 70.

Earle, Valerie, ed. *Federalism, Infinite Variety in Theory and Practice.* Itasca, Ill.: F. E. Peacock Publishers, Inc., 1968.

Eisenhower, Dwight D. "State Government and Liberty in America." *State Government.* 37 (Summer 1964), 138.

Elazar, Daniel. *American Federalism: A View from the States.* New York: Thomas Y. Crowell Co., 1972.

Elazar, Daniel. *The American Partnership: Intergovernmental Co-operation in the 19th Century U.S.* Chicago: University of Chicago Press, 1962.

Elazar, Daniel, ed. *Cooperation and Conflict: Readings in American Federalism.* Itasca, Ill.: F. E. Peacock Publishers, Inc., 1969.

Elazar, Daniel, ed. *The Politics of American Federalism.* Lexington, Ma.: Heath Co., 1969.

Elazar, David. "Federal-State Collaboration in the U.S." *Political Science Quarterly,* 79 (June, 1964), 248.

Elliot, Jonathon, ed. *The Debates in the Several State Conventions on the Adoption of the Federal Constitution.* Philadelphia: J.B. Lippincott and Co., 1863.

Ferguson, E. James. *The Power of the Purse: A History of American Public Finance, 1776-1790.* Chapel Hill: University of North Carolina Press, 1961.

Franck, Thomas, ed. *Why Federations Fail.* New York: New York University Press, 1968.

Friedrich, Carl J. "Federalism and Nationalism." *Orbis,* 10 (Winter 1967), 1009.

Greene, Jack. *The Quest for Power.* New York: W. W. Norton and Co., 1963.

Hamilton, Alexander; Jay, John; and Madison, James. *The Federalist.* Edited by Benjamin F. Wright. Cambridge, Ma.: Belknap Press of Harvard University Press, 1961.

Hamilton, Walton H. *The Power to Govern.* New York: W. W. Norton and Co., 1937.

Hammett, Harold D. "What is the State's Role Today?" *American Bar Association Journal,* 58 (November, 1972), 1198.

Jensen, Merrill. *The Making of the American Constitution.* Princeton, N.J.: Van Nostrand, 1964.

Jensen, Merrill. *The New Nation, A History of the United States during the Confederation.* New York: Vintage Books, 1965.

Kerber, Linda K. *Federalists in Dissent: Imagery and Ideology in Jeffersonian America.* Ithaca, N.Y.: Cornell University Press, 1970.

Kurtz, Stephen G., ed. *The Federalists - Creators and Critics of the Union. 1780-1801.* New York: John Wiley and Sons, Inc., 1972.

Livermore, Shaw, Jr. *The Twilight of Federalism.* Princeton, N.J.: Princeton University Press, 1962.

Mackinnon, Victor. *Comparative Federalism.* The Hague: Nyhoff Co., 1964.

MacMahon, Arthur, ed. *Federalism: Mature and Emergent.* New York: Russell and Russell, Inc., 1962.

McWhinney, Edward. *Comparative Federalism: States' Rights and National Power.* Canada: University of Toronto Press, 1965.

Main, Jackson Turner. *The Antifederalists.* Chapel Hill: The University of North Carolina Press, 1961.

Marshall, Burke. *Federalism and Civil Rights.* New York: Columbia University Press, 1964.

Muskie, Edmund. "Manpower: the Achilles Heel of Creative Federalism." *Public Administration Review,* 27 (June, 1967), 193.

Peterson, Merrill, ed. *Democracy. Liberty and Property.* New York: Bobbs-Merrill Co., Inc., 1966.

Riker, William. *Federalism: Origin, Operation, Significance.* Boston: Little, Brown and Co., 1964.

Romney, George W. "A New Era of Federalism: Challenge for the U.S." *National Civic Review,* 62 (January, 1973), 7.

Sanford, Terry. "Inventing the Federal System: and Making it Work." *National Civic Review,* 62 (January, 1973), 12.

Schwartz, Bernard. *From Confederation to Nation: the American Constitution.* Baltimore: Johns Hopkins University Press, 1973.

Schwartz, Bernard. *The Reins of Power.* New York: Hill and Wang, 1963.

Smith, Herbert Arthur. *Federalism in North America.* Boston: The Chipman Co., 1923.

Stewart, Maxwell S. "Nixon's New Federalism: Is It The Answer?" *Current History,* 61 (November, 1971), 279.

Tansill, Charles C., ed. *Documents Illustrative of the Formation of the Union of the American States.* Washington: Government Printing Office, 1927.

Wildavsky, Aaron, ed. *American Federalism in Perspective.* Boston: Little, Brown and Co., 1967.

"IN CONGRESS ASSEMBLED . . .":
A REPRESENTATIVE LEGISLATURE

Introductory Essay

The Founding Fathers were determined to restrain Congress, for they feared the susceptibility of popular rule to ignorance, prejudice, and demagoguery. Alexander Hamilton warned in the Federalist Papers, No. 71, that

> The tendency of the legislative authority to absorb every other has been fully displayed and illustrated by examples in some preceding numbers. In governments purely republican, this tendency is almost irresistible. The representatives of the people, in a popular assembly, seem sometimes to fancy that they are the people themselves . . .

This viewpoint explains the Constitutional barriers to popular "tyranny" by Congress: the division of responsibilities between co-equal branches of government and a division of power between the states and the federal government, and a division of legislative duties between the popularly elected House and the indirectly elected Senate.

In retrospect, not many would deny the effectiveness of these checks and balances. 1975 should have been a bright year for Congress, as the Watergate affair illuminated the dangers of excessive concentration of federal power in the executive branch and reform-minded Congressmen were elected throughout the country. Yet, a *Washington Post* survey of the House members, conducted in June, 1975, revealed an unhappy self-portrait.

> Forge of Democracy, the people's House, the first branch of government—all of the noble cliches take on a mocking quality these days. The U.S. House of Representatives, to put the matter starkly, is not a forge, but a democratic frustration. Torn and confused, fractious, unfulfilled, the House is not functioning as an instrument of popular expression. It reflects the turbulence of American politics at this moment and the general malaise, the impotence of majorities not yet born, the timidity of political indecision and politicians who are unsure of the future.

The institutions that the Founding Fathers hoped would check the unquenchable thirst for power of Congress—the Presidency and the Courts—in recent years have tended to be more radical than the feared people's lightning rod. A review of Congressional powers and how they have been exercised may shed light on the unexpected dimming of that deliberate assemblage.

Analysis of the Congress should begin with an examination of the relevant portions of the Constitution: the powers vested in the Congress, the limitations on Congressional authority, the relationship of the House of Representatives to the Senate.

The Founding Fathers expected that the legislature would be the most powerful of the three branches of the Federal government. The Consitition, which deals with Congress in Article I, specifies numerous Congressional powers, including the famous prerogative to "make all laws which shall be necessary and proper" pursuant to its powers and duties. In addition, Article I determines qualifications for office, establishes certain election procedures, and creates various guarantees of Congressional independence. The House of Representatives, which alone among the major Federal institutions was to directly embody the popular will (until passage of the 17th Amendment to the Constitution in 1913, election of Senators was the prerogative of State legislatures), was given the sole power to originate revenue-raising legislation and the sole power of impeachment. The Senate, whose members were to be chosen for staggered six-year terms by the state legislatures, was intended to act as a sobering influence on any popular intemperance; besides its joint power with the House over legislation, it was given the sole authority to try impeachment cases, approve or reject Presidential appointments, and consent to or reject treaties with foreign governments.

After gaining an understanding of the theoretical Constitutional powers and responsibilities of the Congress, a review of the historical realization of the Congressional role should be undertaken. It will soon become apparent that the importance, internal structure, and influence of Congress, and of each House, have been far from constant. There has been a dynamic, ever-changing flow of power between the various branches of the Federal Government.

External circumstances such as war or economic catastrophe; the strengthening or weakening of power through reorganization; the force of personality found in great leaders; and many other factors have conspired to transfer power at various times between the House, the Senate, the Presidency, the bureaucracy, and the Courts.

During the first major period of Congressional history—extending from the adoption of the Constitution until about 1820—the House of Representatives was the dominant force in American government. While Presidents of the young Republic were capable and distinguished national leaders, the memories of royal tyranny worked to minimize the role of the chief executives. George Washington felt that the President should not interfere in any way with the legislative process, which meant in part that the President should not advocate detailed legislation and should not endorse any particular proposal once Congress had begun deliberations on an issue. Subsequent Presidents were not limited; Jefferson, for example, used his influence as party leader to secure nomination of a Speaker of the House and committee chairmen loyal to him. However, Washington's precedents were important in setting the tone for early administrations.

An important measure of the relative importance of a particular institution in American government is the caliber of men it attracts. Hence, it is telling to note that the House overshadowed the Senate in prestige and influence to such an extent that future President James Madison said that "as a young man and desirous of increasing my reputation as a statesman, I could not afford to accept a seat in the Senate." Additionally, in 1810 Henry Clay gave up a Senate seat in order to run for the House. He became the first great Speaker of the House; his power showed the dominance of the House in the government. As leader of the War Hawks, Clay played a major role in forcing the nation into the War of 1812; he played a pivotal role in legislation providing federal financing of highways and canals and increasing the tariff; he forced the executive to recognize new Latin American republics; his support was instrumental in the Missouri Compromise of 1820, a piece of legislation in which the White House had almost no role; and he engineered the Presidency of John Quincy Adams in 1825 after the election was thrown into the House.

During the second major period of Congressional history (1820-1860), it was paradoxically the success of the House in achieving the Missouri Compromise which helped thrust power into the Senate. The Missouri Compromise exposed the deep, factional, slave versus free state divisions that eventually led the nation into Civil War. Since the population of the North was rising much faster than that of the South, the South could not long expect to maintain a near equal hold over the House. Soon the ablest

men from each state began to be elected to the Senate, where the balance between the number of free and slave states gave the South a chance to advance states' rights. The relatively mediocre Presidents of the era were no match for Webster, Clay, and Calhoun (or later Douglas, Seward, and Sumner), who moved to the Senate during its Golden Age. Other changes enhanced the role of the Senate. The Senate opened its doors, allowing the public to hear the great debates; this action clearly increased the Senate's prestige. At the same time, the size of the House increased tremendously, from the original 65 to 242 in 1830. This decreased efficiency and decreased the power of each individual Representative. In fact, de Tocqueville in 1831 found the House "remarkable for its vulgarity and poverty of talent." The Senate alone worked hard to stave off Civil War; its efforts culminated in the Great Compromise of 1850, which delayed war for a decade.

The period from the Civil War to the end of the 19th Century was one of relative governmental dormancy. This was true largely because the nation was undergoing a process of urbanization and industrialization that outpaced the ability of politicians to understand and deal with change. Despite relatively high public interest in politics, after the struggles of Reconstruction major political institutions did very little of substance on the most important issues. Presidents from Andrew Jackson until the Twentieth Century were relatively weak. The two political parties, which were closely balanced, avoided clear-cut opposing stands. Neither chamber of Congress was distinguished by its membership. Woodrow Wilson, in his classic 1885 study of Congress, termed the House of Representatives a "disintegrate mass of joining elements." However, the influence of the House as a whole enjoyed a resurgence flowing from and charted by its Speakers. By strictly enforcing party discipline, manipulating committee chairmanships, and changing rules of procedure to increase efficiency and centralize control by the party leadership in the Rules Committee, Speakers James Blaine, Thomas Reed, and Joseph Cannon increasingly consolidated the power of the House into an effective force responsive to the will of the majority. At the same time, the Senate's efficiency was decreased by the addition of 22 members. The Senate also moved into new quarters, too vast for old-fashioned oratory.

The most important trend in American government during the Twentieth Century has been the ascendance of the executive branch. Several factors have been responsible for this development. The emergence of the United States as the world's foremost military and economic power has demanded a clear, consistent foreign policy that was not necessary in the last century. A strong executive has been necessary to guide the nation through two world wars, the reconstruction of Europe, the Cold War, and the growing interdependence of nations. Further, the voters began to demand federal solutions to modern social problems; it was natural that the executive branch should offer comprehensive solutions while the legislature, with so many loci of independent power, should find it much more difficult to construct detailed, integrated legislative packages. Since the revolt against Speaker Cannon in 1910, in which the members reclaimed power from the Speaker, it has been much more difficult for the House to speak with one voice. The executive bureaucracy, which inevitably was given considerable authority and discretion in the administration of programs, has become increasingly important. Even a century ago, the federal government did not regulate the trucking industry, the airlines, or the electronic media; fund national programs of public education, welfare, manpower training, or health care; or maintain a powerful military establishment even in peacetime.

Growth of the nation, with an increasing complexity and diversity of issues confronting lawmakers, forced changes in internal Congressional organization. The committee system, for example, evolved to its present structure during and after the Civil War period. The volume of business necessitated division of labor; better policy formulation through the development of expertise and bureaucratic oversight justified retention of specific assignments, and was reinforced by promotion to committee chairmanships through the oft-criticized but long-enduring seniority system. Only lately have these criticisms borne fruit and yet undetermined is the seedling's resilience in the variable climate of public opinion.

Congress, as a branch, has weathered many storms. The contemporary *Case Against Congress* has been recited by Drew Pearson and Jack Anderson. Conflict of interest, corruption leading to conviction, agents for powerful interests, and dereliction of duty are among the frequent charges. The allegation that throughout our history Congress has over-represented the rich and powerful—a class from which our lawyer-laden representative bodies are heavily drawn—is supported by citation of opposition to Jacksonian measures, excesses during the Gilded Age, and resistance to Presidential initiatives during the Progressive Era and the New Deal. On the other hand, a multitude of historical works, particularly biographies, have reveled in the glories of past Congressional leaders. For the current generation, John F. Kennedy's *Profiles in Courage* popularized the notion captured in its title. In addition, much progressive social legislation has been properly attributed to congressional action. Substantial evidence can be mounted for a variety of interpretations. Debate over past congressional behavior will continue.

What of the future? Is the stage set and are the lines learned for a new congressional role? Will Congress re-emerge as a central character or play an incidental part?

Excerpted Documents

The internal organization of Congress: How has it affected Congressional effectiveness?

James MacGregor Burns, Professor of Political Science—Williams College, *The Deadlock of Democracy*, 1963, p. 141.

The base of the congressional system is the one-party district, as established and protected by the state legislatures. Though we hear much about congressmen's "safe seats," it is still hard to grasp the extent of non-competition in congressional elections. Almost half of the House seats never change party hands. Another quarter, roughly, switch only on rare occasions. Aside from great sweeps such as those of 1920 and 1936, about 150 Republican seats and about the same number of Democratic seats never switch to the other party. Reasonably competitive districts number about 125 out of a total of 435. Many Senate seats are also one-party, especially in the South, but not to the same extent as in the House.

Speaker of the House Nicholas Longworth, in *Power in the House*, 1968, p. 115.

I believe it to be the duty of the Speaker, standing squarely on the platform of his party, to assist, insofar as he properly can, the enactment of legislation in accordance with the declared principles and policies of his party, and by the same token to resist the enactment of legislation in violation thereof.

I believe in responsible party government . . . Just as I stand for this, . . . I am against the European system of bloc government. I have observed its workings abroad at first hand. It works badly enough over there where legislation is generally a matter of bluster and trafficking between groups, and where governments fall overnight. Here it won't work at all, because it is un-American.

James MacGregor Burns, Professor of Political Science—Williams College, *The Deadlock of Democracy*, 1963, p. 245.

The leaders of the congressional party are, of course, men who have climbed the seniority ladders and hence the men who come from the safe, usually rural, districts. They are the chairmen, or ranking majority or minority members of the more important committees . . . The statistics are conclusive. In a recent Congress the 217 most urban districts produced 26 per cent of the House chairmen in general, while the 218 least urban accounted for 74 per cent. But the imbalance of rural-urban power becomes even more significant if one notes the relative importance of the committees rather than simply their total number.

Woodrow Wilson, *Congressional Government*, 1885, pp. 102-103.

I know not how better to describe our form of government in a single phrase than by calling it a government by the chairmen of the Standing Committees of Congress. This disintegrate ministry, as it figures on the floor of the House of Representatives, has many peculiarities. In the first place, it is made up of the elders of the assembly; for, by custom, seniority in congressional service determines the bestowal of the principal chairmanships; in the second place, it is constituted of selfish and warring elements; for chairman fights against chairman for use of the time of the assembly; . . . in the third place, instead of being composed of the associated leaders of Congress, it consists of the dissociated heads of forty-eight "little legislatures" (to borrow Senator Hoar's apt name for the Committees); and, in the fourth place, it is instituted by appointment from Mr. Speaker, who is, by intention, the chief judicial, rather than the chief political, officer of the House.

Heinz Eulau, Professor of Political Science—Stanford University, "The Committees in a Revitalized Congress," in *Twelve Studies of the Organization of Congress*, 1966, pp. 243-244.

What, then, of the seniority procedure itself? Is it the best way to select committee chairmen who will be leaders? Our answer must be generally negative. Seniority does not guarantee ability and competence; moreover, the procedure favors one-party areas and sectional interests, and it tends to make for political irresponsibility, to mention only a few items in a large catalogue of familiar complaints. Nevertheless, the practice is as lustily supported as it is attacked. Seniority, its defenders say, makes for committee stability and continuity, and it avoids the competition for office and resultant strife that would enormously harm the atmosphere of good will and conviviality that is so essential to political relations in a collegial legislature; precisely because seniority is an impersonal criterion, it assures friendly relations and harmony within Congress.

James A. Robinson, Professor of Political Science—Ohio State University, "Decision Making in Congress," in *Twelve Studies of the Organization of Congress*, 1966, p. 265.

. . . no legislator today can be an expert on more than a few policy issues. Effective and influential legislators who are successful in obtaining passage of their bills are those who carve out for themselves a particular subject on which they become expert. Each committee and subcommittee of Congress always has some members who are specialists in the field concerned, as well as a few senior members possessing long records of relevant experience.

James R. Mann, U.S. Representative from Illinois, in *The Leadership of Congress*, 1922, p. 163.

On the whole, the rules of the House are probably the best considered, most scientifically constructed and finely adjusted rules governing any parliamentary body on earth.. . .It is not true that Speaker Cannon or any other Speaker is an autocrat in the House. It is true that the present Speaker is the leader and strongest influence in the House, and that he has been so for ten years, dating back to the time before he was Speaker and from the time that Speaker Reed left the House. We may some of us revile him temporarily. Great men have been abused at all times—such is the history of mankind—but when the book of history of this generation shall have been written, together with the legislation that has been enacted, the years of the Speakership of Mr. Cannon will stand out among the most brilliant in the history of our country.

Representative Nelson of Wisconsin, in *The Leadership of Congress*, 1922, pp. 158-159.

Have we not been punished by every means at the disposal of the powerful House organization? Members long chairmen of important committees, others holding high rank—all with records of faithful and efficient party service to their credit—have been ruthlessly removed, deposed, and humiliated before their constituents and the country because, forsooth, they would not cringe or crawl before the arbitrary power of the Speaker and his House machine.... We are fighting for the right of free, fair, and full representation in this body for our respective constituencies.... We are fighting with our Democratic brethren for the common right of equal representation in this House, and for the right-of-way of progressive legislation in Congress.

Checks and balances:
How well have they worked?

David M. Levitan, "The Responsibility of Administrative Officials in a Democratic Society," *Political Science Quarterly*, 1946, pp. 562-563.

The espousal of the doctrine [of separation of powers] by the "Framers" and by the leaders on the American scene during the nineteenth century was inevitable. The very simplicity and symmetry of the threefold division of governmental functions and organs suited their rationalist approach. Most important, the doctrine fitted in well with their conception of the role of government and their analysis of its operations. The concept of separation of powers and its corollary, checks and balances, appealed to men who distrusted representative bodies, feared all-powerful executives, espoused the mechanical theory of the judicial function, and believed in *laissez-faire* philosophy—"that government is best which governs least." These political ideas suited the temper and needs of the country and especially the economically dominant groups.

Arthur M. Schlesinger, Jr., Historian, *Congress and the Presidency*, 1967, pp. 2-3.

And the result of the calculated ambiguities of the founding fathers was to design not a machine but a battleground—to create the conditions for permanent guerrilla warfare between the two branches of the national government with powers of initiative. Put this way, the proposition may sound unnecessarily provocative. But I do not imply for a moment that—in civil society at least—such a battleground is a bad thing. The inherent tension between the Congress and the President has obviously served as one of the great bulwarks of American freedom. Moreover, while it has sometimes been a sterile or even destructive tension, it has also often been a creative tension, challenging Congress to its highest qualities of intelligence, scrutiny, and conception and drawing out of Presidents indispensable skills in leadership and persuasion.

James A. Robinson, Professor of Political Science—Ohio State University, "Decision Making in Congress," in *Twelve Studies of the Organization of Congress*, 1966, pp. 262-263.

A survey of the relative importance of Congress and the presidency as initiators of legislation between 1880 and 1945 can be extrapolated in graph form from Lawrence Chamberlain's study of 90 bills enacted during that period. . . . the presidency was inactive as an initiator of legislation through 1930; its role took a strong upturn during the early 1930s, slackening off by the end of the decade. Corresponding with the decline of Congress and the emergence of the presidency respectively as an initiator of legislation during the thirties is an overlapping trend of an increase in joint initiation by Congress and the presidency that persisted into the forties. An extension of Chamberlain's study from 1945 to 1965 would show that this collaboration has now yielded to virtually exclusive initiation by the executive.

Clinton Rossiter, *The American Presidency,* 1956, pp. 60-62.

The Presidency today has the same general outlines as that of 1789, *but the whole picture is a hundred times magnified.* The President is all the things he was intended to be, and he is several other things as well....

[The Presidency today] is distinctly more powerful. It cuts deeply into the powers of Congress; in fact, *it has quite reversed the expectations of the framers* by becoming itself a vortex into which these powers have been drawn in massive amounts. It cuts deeply into the lives of the people: in fact, it commands authority over their comings and goings that Hamilton himself might tremble to behold....

The outstanding feature of American constitutional development is the growth of the power and prestige of the Presidency.

Woodrow Wilson, *Congressional Government,* 1885, pp. 270-271.

. . . it is quite evident that the means which Congress has of controlling the departments and of exercising the searching oversight at which it aims are limited and defective . . .

Even the special, irksome, ungracious investigations which it from time to time institutes in its spasmodic endeavors to dispel or confirm suspicions of malfeasance or of wanton corruption do not afford it more than a glimpse of the inside of a small province of federal administration. Hostile or designing officials can always hold it at arm's length by dexterous evasions and concealments. It can violently disturb, but it cannot often fathom, the waters of the sea in which the bigger fish of the civil service swim and feed. Its dragnet stirs without cleansing the bottom. Unless it have at the head of the departments capable, fearless men, altogether in its confidence and entirely in sympathy with its designs, it is clearly helpless to do more than affright those officials whose consciences are their accusers.

James Bryce, British Ambassador to the U.S., *The American Commonwealth,* Vol. II, 1889, p. 798.

Congress has been the branch of government with the largest facilities for usurping the powers of the other branches and probably with the most disposition to do so. Congress has constantly tried to encroach both on the Executive and on the States, sometimes, like a wild bull driven into a corral, dashing itself against the imprisoning walls of the Constitution. But although Congress has succeeded in occupying nearly all the area which the Constitution left vacant and unallotted between the several authorities it established, Congress has not become any more distinctly than in earlier days the dominant power in the State, the organ of national sovereignty, the irresistible exponent of the national will.

Arthur M. Schlesinger, Jr., Historian, *Congress and the Presidency,* 1967, p. 20.

In 1793, when Washington issued a proclamation of American neutrality in the current war between France and Great Britain, pro-French congressmen and newspapers immediately charged that this act exceeded the presidential authority and invaded the congressional prerogative. Hamilton, replying under the pseudonym of Pacificus, argued that the inherent power of the executive amply qualified him to take initiative in foreign affairs. "If, on the one hand, the Legislature have a right to declare war," he wrote, "it is, on the other, the duty of the executive to preserve peace till the declaration is made." Jefferson, though as Secretary of State he had approved the proclamation, was alarmed by Hamilton's exceedingly broad affirmation of presidential authority and begged Madison to write an answer: "For God's sake, my dear Sir, take up your pen, select the most striking heresies, and cut him to pieces." In his Helvidius letters, Madison contended that the Congress had the basic authority to determine foreign policy; the President could serve only as the channel by which congressional determinations were transmitted to foreign states.

Congress won the immediate issue, when the passage of the Neutrality Act of 1794 assured its authority over neutrality problems (insofar as it has wished since to exert that authority). But Washington gradually succeeded in transforming the executive's conceded power to serve as the organ of communication into a general power over most aspects of foreign affairs. Congress had to acquiesce in this transformation if only because the project of congressional control over foreign policy was fatally inadequate to the requirements of efficient government.

Henry Steele Commager, Professor of History—Amherst College, *Majority Rule and Minority Rights*, 1943, p. 55.

The record . . . discloses not a single case, in a century and a half, where the Supreme Court has protected freedom of speech, press, assembly, or petition against Congressional attack. . . . It reveals, on the other hand, that the Court has intervened again and again to defeat Congressional efforts to free slaves, guarantee civil rights to Negroes, to protect workingmen, outlaw child labor, assist hard-pressed farmers, and to democratize the tax system. From this analysis, the Congress and not the courts emerges as the instrument for the realization of the guarantees of the Bill of Rights.

Who does Congress really represent?

Kenneth G. Olson, Associate Professorial Lecturer in Political Science—George Washington University, "The Service Function of the United States Congress," in *Twelve Studies of the Organization of Congress*, 1966, p. 340.

The Constitution does not make explicit that members of Congress shall be servants of their constituents. But the simple logic of the requirement that members are to be locally nominated and locally elected ensures that they will serve—or else take the electoral risks of not doing so.

The total number of citizens actively doing special pleading for themselves may be small, perhaps only a fraction of a House district containing half a million persons or of a state many times larger than that. But as long as "the world's greatest publicity organ is still the human mouth," this active minority of citizens can play a critical role out of all proportion to its numbers.

Consider the calculations of a senator from a large eastern state: "During the last year and a half, I have done favors for about 3,000 persons. When you consider the word-of-mouth spread, this amounts to a substantial number of voters." Over a six-year term at this rate, favors for 12,000 persons could have the multiplier effect of informing 50,000 to 100,000 constituents about the senator's diligence.

Marian Irish and James Prothro, Political Scientists, *The Politics of American Democracy*, 4th edition, 1968, p. 341.

. . . a congressman may ultimately broaden his views, but he starts out as the representative of a particular constituency, and the problem of being re-elected by the folks back home keeps their picture bright in his mind. For that matter, his colleagues would regard him as a maverick if he forgot his constituents' special needs. Congressmen from agricultural constituencies champion price supports for farmers, those from predominantly immigrant areas favor liberal immigration quotas, those from the Deep South oppose civil rights bills. Since these stands can be taken for granted regardless of the congressman's party or personal characteristics, the constituency is an important element in policy-making.

Stephen K. Bailey, *The New Congress*, 1966, p. 18.

. . . as each state and congressional district becomes more complex in its interest group structure, it becomes more and more a microcosm of the entire nation.

Joseph S. Clark, former U.S. Senator—Pennsylvania, *Congress: The Sapless Branch*, 1964, p. 20.

. . . Congress is filled with the plea that "what's best for Podunk is best for America," while the Executive looks at his constituency and replies that "what's best for the nation helps Podunk."

John C. Calhoun, Senator from South Carolina and Vice-President to Andrew Jackson, *The Works of John C. Calhoun*, Vol. 1, pp. 68-70.

But to form a juster estimate of the full force of this impulse to compromise, there must be added that, in governments of the concurrent majority, each portion, in order to advance its own peculiar interests, would have to conciliate all others, by showing a disposition to advance theirs; and, for this purpose, each would select those to represent it, whose wisdom, patriotism, and weight of character, would command the confidence of the others. Under its influence,—and with representatives so well qualified to accomplish the object for which they were selected,—the prevailing desire would be to promote the common interests of the whole; and, hence, the competition would be not which should yield the least to promote the common good, but which should yield the most. It is thus, that concession would cease to be considered a sacrifice,—would become a free-will offering on the altar of the country, and lose the name of compromise.

Marian Irish and James Prothro, Political Scientists, *The Politics of American Democracy*, 4th edition, 1968, p. 331.

The hard facts of political power originally produced bicameralism, and chances are they will sustain it. All the talk about "states" having a "right" to an equal voice was and is a more attractive way of saying that people with extra power do not like to surrender it. The word "state" has no meaning except in terms of people. Political leaders from the less populous states enjoyed power at the national level disproportionate to their numbers before and during the drafting of the Constitution. And they refused to take part in the planning of the new government unless they were given a similar advantage in at least one branch of Congress. Delegates from the more populous states agreed to this hard bargain because they had more to lose under the Articles of Confederation (with no recognition of varying state populations) than under the new scheme.

Richard Hofstadter, Professor of History—Columbia University, *The Age of Reform*, 1955, pp. 115-116.

The rise of agrarian strength was based upon the fall in agrarian numbers. The same "relentless" advance of industrialism and urbanism that, as the pathos of agrarian rhetoric has it, "crushed" the farmer in the lasting defeat of 1896 has actually provided him with greater and greater over-representation in our legislative bodies year by year. The legislative process in the United States takes place within the framework of a constricting rotten-borough system that perennially confronts urban constituencies, both in the states and in the nation, with a rural stranglehold.

Gouverneur Morris, Founding Father from Pennsylvania, in *Modern Political Analysis*, 1963, p. 68.

The first branch [of the legislature] originating from the people, will ever be subject to precipitancy, changeability, and excess. Experience evinces the truth of this remark without having recourse to reading. This can only be checked by ability and virtue in the second branch. . . . The second branch ought to be composed of men of great and established property—an aristocracy. Men who from pride will support consistency and permanency.

J. William Fulbright, Former Chairman of the Senate Foreign Relations Committee, speech at the University of Chicago in 1946, in *The Elite and the Electorate*, 1963, p. 6.

The average legislator early in his career discovers that there are certain interests, or prejudices, of his constituents which are dangerous to trifle with. Some of these prejudices may not be of fundamental importance to the welfare of the nation, in which case he is justified in humoring them, even though he may disapprove. . . . . A sound sense of values, the ability to discriminate between that which is of fundamental importance and that which is only superficial, is an indispensable qualification of a good legislator. As an example of what I mean, let us take the poll-tax issue and isolationism. Regardless of how persuasive my colleagues or the national press may be about the evils of the poll tax, I do not see its fundamental importance, and I shall follow the views of the people of my state. Although it may be symbolic of conditions which many deplore, it is exceedingly doubtful that its abolition will cure any of our major problems. On the other hand, regardless of how strongly opposed my constituents may prove to be to the creation of, and participation in, an ever stronger United Nations Organization, I could not follow such a policy in that field unless it becomes clearly hopeless. . . .

Is Congress too large?

James Madison, *The Federalist Papers*, No. 55.

The truth is that in all cases a certain number [of legislators] at least seems to be necessary to secure the benefits of free consultation and discussion, and to guard against too easy a combination for improper purposes; as, on the other hand, the number ought at most to be kept within a certain limit, in order to avoid the confusion and intemperance of a multitude. In all very numerous assemblies, of whatever characters composed, passionnever fails to wrest the scepter fromreason. Had every Athenian citizen been a Socrates, every athenian assembly would still have been a mob.

Neil MacNeil, *Forge of Democracy: The House of Representatives*, 1968, p. 309.

The very size of the Hall of the House, and the large number of Representatives crowded into it, conspired to produce confusion and chaos. For a century and a half, until the 1930's, the members had to suffer excruciating personal discomfort. The acoustics of the old Hall, now used to exhibit statues, and of the new Hall as well were appalling. So was the ventilation. Unless a Representative had a great voice—of one loud-voiced member, John P. Hale of New Hampshire, it was said that he could stand atop Mount Washington and address his entire native state—he could not be heard beyond the immediate vicinity on the floor from which he spoke. Before the construction of the first office building for Representatives, the members had no other place to transact their business than from their desks on the floor. . . . The clatter from the slamming desk drawers, the rustling of paper, the hurly-burly of pages scampering about the Hall, and the hum of many voices raised a din through which only an exceptional voice could penetrate. "If ever anything worthwhile is said," commented a Washington reporter in 1931 on House debate, "few can hear it and still fewer pay any attention." Speaking to the House, said another reporter in 1878, was "like trying to address the people in the Broadway omnibuses from the curbstone in front of the Astor House."

How effective has Congress been?

Harold Laski, Professor of History—Harvard University, *The American Democracy*, 1948, p. 92.

. . . the Senate is an outstanding success. It is perhaps the most vital check upon the despotism an ambitious president could so easily develop. If it sometimes contains members with a narrowly parochial outlook, as a legislative assembly it transcends the sectionalism which pervades every nook and cranny of the House of Representatives. If it irritates most presidents and their cabinet colleagues, it is astonishing how often its irritation is supported by the electoral opinion of the American people. All in all, the level of its big debates is remarkably high.

Harold Laski, Professor of History—Harvard University, *The American Democracy*, 1948, p. 72.

The House of Representatives has always been the least successful of federal institutions, and it retains that unenviable characteristic.

Henry Clay, in *Congress and the Presidency*, 1967, p. 14.

We are in the midst of a revolution, . . . hitherto bloodless, but rapidly tending toward a total change of the pure republican character of the Government, and to the concentration of all power in the hands of one man. . . . If Congress do not apply an instantaneous and effective remedy, the fatal collapse will soon come on, and we shall die—ignobly die—base, mean, and abject slaves; the scorn and contempt of mankind; unpitied, unwept, unmourned!

Max Lerner, Journalist, *America as a Civilization*, Vol. 1, 1957, p. 419.

[Congressmen] resent the dominating role of the Executive in foreign policy and several times have rebelled against the lines of State Department direction. In 1948 Congress forced on the Executive the China Aid Act, which changed the whole emphasis of Far Eastern policy; in 1950 it replaced a Korean aid measure with a Formosan one. In the same year it forced a big loan to Spain, incorporating it in the ECA Act and changing the emphasis of American policy toward Spain.

Selected Bibliography

Bolling, Richard W. *Power in the House: A History of Leadership in the House of Representatives.* New York: Dutton, 1968.

Bryce, James. *The American Commonwealth.* 3rd edition. New York: The Macmillan Co., 1901.

Burnham, James. *Congress and the American Tradition.* Chicago: H. Regency Co., 1959.

Burns, James MacGregor. *Congress on Trial.* New York: Harper, 1949.

Burns, James MacGregor. *Deadlock of Democracy.* Englewood Cliffs, N.J.: Prentice-Hall, 1963.

Carrol, Holbert N. *The House of Representatives and Foreign Affairs.* Pittsburgh: University of Pittsburgh Press, 1958.

Chamberlain, Lawrence. *The President, Congress, and Legislation.* New York: Columbia University Press, 1946.

Cheever, Daniel S., and Haviland, H. Field. *American Foreign Policy and the Separation of Powers.* Cambridge: Harvard University Press, 1942.

Clark, Joseph F. *Congress: The Sapless Branch.* New York: Harper & Row, 1964.

"Congressional Reversal of Supreme Court Decisions: 1945-1957." *Harvard Law Review,* 71 (1958), 1324.

De Grazia, Alfred, ed. *Congress: The First Branch of Government. Twelve Studies of the Organization of Congress.* Washington, D.C.: American Enterprise Institute, 1966.

Follett, M. P. *The Speaker of the House of Representatives.* New York: Longmans, Green and Co., 1896.

Galloway, George B. *History of the House of Representatives.* New York: Thomas Y. Crowell, 1961.

Goodwin, George, Jr. "The Seniority System in Congress." *American Political Science Review,* 52 (June, 1959), 412.

Greider, William, and Sussman, Barry. "The House Today: A Badly Tattered People's Institution." *Washington Post,* June 29, 1975, p. A1.

Hamilton, Alexander; Madison, James; and Jay, John. *The Federalist Papers.* New York: New American Library, 1961.

Harris, Joseph. *Congressional Control of Administration.* Washington, D.C.: Brookings Institution, 1964.

Hofstadter, Richard. *The Age of Reform.* New York: Random House, 1955.

Huitt, Ralph K. "Congress, the Durable Partner." *Lawmakers in a Changing World.* Edited by Elke Frank. Englewood Cliffs, N.J.: Prentice-Hall, 1966.

Kefauver, Estes, and Levin, Jack. *A Twentieth Century Congress.* New York: Duell, Sloan, and Pierce, 1947.

Kolodziej, Edward A. *The Uncommon Defense and Congress, 1945-1963.* Columbus: Ohio State University Press, 1966.

Laski, Harold. *The American Democracy: A Commentary and an Interpretation.* New York: Viking Press, 1948.

Lees, John D. *Committee System of the United States Congress.* New York: Humanities Press, 1967.

Levitan, David M. "The Responsibility of Administrative Officials in a Democratic Society." *Political Science Quarterly,* 61 (1946), 560.

MacNeil, Neil. *Forge of Democracy: The House of Representatives.* New York: David McKay Co., 1963.

Matthews, Donald R. *U.S. Senators and Their World.* Chapel Hill: The University of North Carolina Press, 1960.

Morgan, Donald G. *Congress and the Constitution: A Study of Responsibility.* Cambridge, Mass.: The Belknap Press, 1966.

Peabody, R., and Polsby, N., eds. *New Perspectives on Congress.* Chicago: Rand McNally, 1963.

Polsby, Nelson W. *Congress and the Presidency.* Englewood Cliffs, N.J.: Prentice-Hall, 1965.

Ripley, Randall B. *Party Leaders in the House of Representatives.* Washington, D.C.: Brookings Institution, 1967.

Ripley, Randall B. *Power in the Senate.* New York: St. Martin's Press, 1969.

Robinson, James. *Congress and Foreign Policy-Making.* Homewood, Ill.: Dorsey, 1962.

Rothman, David J. *Politics and Power: Senate, 1869-1901.* Cambridge: Harvard University Press, 1966.

Schrifgiesser, Karl. *Lobbysts.* Boston: Little, Brown & Co., 1951.

Truman, David B., ed. *The Congress and America's Future.* Englewood Cliffs, N.J.: Prentice-Hall, 1965.

Wallace, Robert Ash. *Congressional Control of Federal Spending.* Detroit: Wayne State University Press, 1960.

White, William S. *The Citadel: The Story of the United States Senate.* New York: Harper, 1957.

Wilmerding, Lucius. *The Spending Power: A History of the Efforts of Congress to Control Expenditures.* New Haven: Yale University Press, 1943.

Wilson, Woodrow. *Congressional Government.* New York: Meridian, 1956.

Wilson, Woodrow. *Constitutional Government in the United States.* New York: Columbia University Press, 1908.

ISSUE V
WORKING IN AMERICA

SECTIONAL EVENT—HIGH SCHOOL ISSUE
January 31—March 6, 1976

DEBATE   Resolved: That America has significantly overemphasized social welfare at the expense
of individual rights.

PERSUASIVE   The evolution of America's work ethic: A change for the better?

EXTEMPORANEOUS   Organization of the Labor Force

1. Has organized labor increased the dignity of the individual American worker?
2. How much has organized labor increased the economic and political power of the American worker?
3. How has unionization of government employees influenced the labor movement?
4. How critical has the power to strike been in collective bargaining?
5. Have American labor unions generally represented the true interests of the worker?
6. How have mass production and automation changed the lives of American workers?
7. How has the Wagner Act affected the development of the trade union movement?
8. Thomas Jefferson believed that farming was the most uplifting, satisfying form of work. Was he correct?
9. How has the role of women in the labor force changed during the last two centuries?
10. Was a non-union labor force essential to America's industrial development?
11. Was American labor more or less radical in the past?
12. What influence has organized labor had on the social welfare of non-union labor?
13. Has American labor achieved the goals set by 19th-century trade unions?

RESOLVED: THAT AMERICA HAS SIGNIFICANTLY OVEREMPHASIZED SOCIAL WELFARE AT THE EXPENSE OF INDIVIDUAL RIGHTS.

Introductory Essay

During a *Firing Line* telecast in the early 1970's, former Secretary of Health, Education and Welfare, Elliot Richardson, and William F. Buckley, Jr., the host, addressed the proper role of the state in providing for the general welfare. The issue centered on the guarantee of medical care for all Americans, but inevitably reached the more ideological terrain in which the dispute is grounded. What are the responsibilities of the individual and the state? What are their rights? Challenged to defend a comprehensive governmental medical program, Richardson developed an approach to the problem based on an evolving governmental duty. As the capacity of the state enlarges, he argued, so do its obligations. Thus, given the inability of some within the state to provide for their medical care and the power of the state to do so, a national duty emerges. Where does such an argument ultimately lead? If the relation of the individual to the state is that of a dependent, can "individual rights" have meaning for either party? Although the strain between individual rights and social welfare is evident here, the conflict is customarily couched in economic terms. Viewed more conventionally—and in a vein less tormenting for today's social and economic liberal—should the state take from some to provide for many?

Social welfare encompasses a great many things, for most programs of government can be considered beneficial to the public at large. A mass transit program may speed commuter traffic and ease travel; defense programs may contribute to the social welfare by protecting the society, as well as providing employment in defense industries; job training programs may aid social welfare by increasing the productivity of the labor force; regulation of the stock market may prevent a few inside operators from misrepresenting investments to the general public; and so forth. Inevitably, in each of these areas there is a clash between social welfare and individual rights. Government spending programs draw resources from individuals; government transportation and construction endeavors require the procurement of private property. However, since this resolution is drawn from the American Issues Forum topic, "The Welfare State: Providing a Livelihood," the discussion will be directed toward family economic welfare and its clash with individual rights.

Like many television shows of the 1950's, *Strike It Rich* gave cash awards—but not to just anyone. Its winners had to need—really need—the money. On each show a parade of contestants would bare the facts of their unhappy lives to the nation's scrutiny and curiosity: husbands injured without insurance, eviction notices and repossessed furniture; medical needs postponed or foregone entirely. Then, if the participant was lucky enough to know, say, that Boise is the capital of Idaho, he could collect a few hundred dollars to ease his plight. Even for the unfortunate contestant whose grasp of geography or show music was incomplete, all was not necessarily lost. With luck a telephone right on stage would suddenly pulsate with light and jingle shrilly. The emcee, whose face always managed to register surprise at this turn of events, would call out "Heart-Line" and take the message from a kindly grocer that a month's supply of canned goods was on the way or that an especially moved viewer was pledging a fifty-dollar check. His wallet a little fatter but his pride a little thinner, the contestant, often in grateful tears, would shuffle off.

For all its tastelessness, *Strike It Rich* was unerring in its depiction of common American attitudes toward individualism and welfare. It seems as if we have always wanted the poor to provide their own salvation. Whether they did this by finding a job or winning a quiz was not essential; the key thing was that they earn their own way. In the event that this should prove impossible, a corollary belief insisted that private agencies—never the government—should offer assistance. For public institutions to do so seems, somehow, "un-American."

Evidence of American attitudes toward the poor can be found as early as the colonial period. The dominant Protestant theology interpreted wealth as a sign of God's favor and poverty as the manifestation of some inner depravity. The Protestant social ethic applauded thrift and industry while condemning sloth and idleness. Few disagreed with the Puritan divine Cotton Mather when he moralized that hard work could help one elude "horrible Snares" and "infinite Sins." "It is not lawful for a Christian ordinarily to live without some calling," he ordained and, in a meaner spirit, "For those who indulge themselves in Idleness. . .the Express Command of God unto us is, that we should let them starve."

With customary zeal, colonial legislators sought to practice what their ministers preached. A variety of laws and social regulations excluded the immigration of paupers and expelled those who already existed. Typical was the practice of "warning out," introduced into Massachusetts in 1655, by which those who might become indigent were simply told to leave and punished if they did not. Instead of drawing on the public treasury, some local governments in the 1700's "auctioned off" the poor to bidders gambling that the cost of their upkeep would not exceed the value of their labor. Those who could not be kept off the "welfare" rolls could at least be humiliated. Hester Prynne did not wear her scarlet letter alone. Recipients of public monies in New York and Pennsylvania were required to sew on their clothing blue or red badges symbolic of their dependence. Benjamin Franklin's maxim that the poor ought not be made comfortable in their poverty but rather should be driven out of it won wide approval.

These facts are indisputable and yet they do not tell the whole story. For the colonists were men of almost literal faith who accepted without serious challenge the Biblical prescription that the poor would always be with them. Poverty, as decreed by God's all-knowing but unknowable will, was thus no blight on the body politic nor even necessarily the product of personal vice. It was simply an objective condition requiring practical (and hopefully frugal) treatment. There is as well the paradox that the most tight-fisted and unforgiving of the early settlers, the New England Puritans, also possessed the strongest sense of community. The opprobrium which Governor John Winthrop of the Massachusetts Bay Colony heaped upon those who would "enlarge their ease and safety" by deserting their fellow was echoed in numerous speeches and sermons. Colonial records are crowded with instances of governments shouldering the burdens of those who could not support themselves. Governor Winthrop's "Journal," for example, relates a decision of the General Court in 1635, to repay, "Mr. Thatcher" from the public treasury, for losses he suffered in a tempest. The minutes of a town meeting in Hadley, Massachusetts in 1687 records a vote to provide care for "Widow Baldwin," each family being required to give her room and board for two weeks. It is even possible, with a little imagination, to find an embryonic Great Society in some social legislation: an incipient food stamp program in Boston's 1740 program to sell grain to the poor at 10 percent of cost, a prototype of Medicaid in town contracts with doctors to provide care for the indigent at town expense (the frequent complaint that these doctors overcharged only strengthens the analogy), and special tax exemptions and housing allowances.

Viewing poverty from the perspectives of theology and practical government, the colonists felt little need to dissect its nature and causes or speculate about its eradication. Aside from making a few elementary distinctions (such as between employable and unemployable poor) they scarcely thought about it in a theoretical sense at all. It was merely one of many concrete social problems and it is not surprising that the attempted solutions were often variant and contradictory.

Between the time of the Revolution and the Civil War, attitudes about the poor shifted decisively. The assumption became widespread that the poor were the source of their own distress. The nature of the change is illustrated by the refusal of the Philadelphia Guardians of the Poor in 1834 to replace an almshouse "treadmill" operated by human labor with a steam engine. Once, the poor had been tolerated as community members whose lot was unfortunate but, in many or most cases, somehow inevitable; the new approach berated the poor for their sinfulness, slothfulness, and violence. The poor had become the object of fear and retribution; they deserved the treatment accorded common criminals and lunatics. At the very least, working a treadmill would show the poor of Philadelphia that public charity was harsh medicine—and hopefully it would persuade them to seek regular employment in the open labor market, where they belonged. The prevalence of this viewpoint is suggested by the most common form of support for the poor at this time: an expansion of the earlier practice of "auctioning off" poorhouse labor to the highest bidder.

What produced this shift to an almost exclusively anti-poor attitude? The ideologies that germinated before the Revolution and flowered in its aftermath explain a good deal. The dominant philosophies upon which the nation was founded accepted the need to restrain the popular exercise of too much governmental power, relying instead on the individual citizen to fulfill his own destiny. The core of the Jefferson view was, as expressed in the Declaration of Independence, that all men are created equal. Because government power erodes liberty and individual responsibility, it must be checked; hence the dictum, that government is best which governs least. The Federalists and their heirs, identified with some of the wealthier segments of society, saw an inherent antagonism between the interests of men of property and the poor. They supported checks and balances on the exercise of popular "tyranny," and "mob rule," although the Federalists desired government support of ventures to facilitate commerce and increase the national wealth. The meaning of the American Revolution, however, for all groups was that the individual should exercise individual freedom in so far as possible. There was no hereditary class structure: no aristocracy would provide patronizing support to the poor, and the poor could move up in rank through their own initiative. The Protestant ethic, celebrating work and its fruits, for the individual and society, won near-universal acceptance. The heady stream of successes for the young nation instilled smug faith in the nation's progress. The evidence of increasing political and social equality was everywhere to be seen—in wage levels that were the highest in the world, in the presidency of Jackson, in general social mobility. There seemed no reason for poverty in America, given the shortage of labor, the abundance of land, and the relative equality of individual opportunity. If there was poverty, American society was blameless; was the social order not constructed according to natural law? If poverty was to be found, the poor themselves must be faulted with moral weakness and depravity.

It was disturbing, even frightening, when the poor were rediscovered in the 1820's. Reports commissioned by several states investigated the extent of poverty, its causes, and the nature of relief efforts. In 1817, one-seventh of the population of New York City was on relief. The state (population 1.4 million) as a whole had 22,000 paupers in 1824, while Philadelphia maintained 1,000 persons permanently on relief. These figures are not shocking in light of today's percentages, yet they were very unsettling to those who saw no reason for any poverty. Many of the true causes of poverty were not seen so clearly at the time. Periodic economic downturns created involuntary unemployment in 1819, 1837, and 1857. In 1819, for example, 50,000 were unemployed in Boston, New York, and Philadelphia, according to one estimate. Immigration brought a widening river of strange peoples into the country, most of whom lacked job skills or employment. They were often willing to work at whatever jobs could be obtained. And inevitably, many of the poor could not work, because they were too young, too old, too handicapped, and so on. These facts were not totally unknown, and to some extent are reflected in the recommendations of the reports to maintain some relief programs for humanitarian reasons. Yet, given the predisposition to view poverty in moral terms, causation was located primarily in the defects of individuals. A typical report from the Society for the Prevention of Pauperism in New York, listed the causes as ignorance, idleness, want of economy, imprudent and hasty marriages, and—"the cause of causes"—intemperance. (Liquor, the favorite devil of reformers throughout the century, was given as the cause of poverty for seven-eighths of the poor.)

The welfare programs of the day were overwhelmingly limited to community and private voluntary efforts. "Outdoor relief" to families in the community was gradually cut off. The poor house, which frequently also housed criminals as well as the indigent, was used to regiment behavior and exhort the poor to reform themselves and find employment. The chief means of support became public during this period, for private contributions were inadequate.

The period between the end of the Civil War and the beginning of the Progressive Era witnessed the general industrialization of the economy. The "Gilded Age," as Mark Twain called it brought glittering wealth to a few but destitution to millions. The welfare system proved seriously deficient in meeting the new needs. Immigrants, Civil War Veterans and dependents, and those physically unable to work flooded relief agencies. Prolonged depressions in 1873-1878, 1882-1886, and 1893-1897 staggered the work force. In the winter of 1873, a quarter of the New York labor force was jobless; a fifth of Boston's population was aided by relief in 1903.

At this time those opposing welfare aid and those supporting its extension drew battle lines. The Social Darwinists argued that the law of competition must be allowed to operate if society was to progress, even if this meant catastrophic consequences for the poor. At its most extreme, this system argued that the poor were genetically inferior and should be allowed to perish in disproportionate numbers, citing the prevalence of poverty in certain immigrant ethnic groups and within families. The Gospel of Wealth, as Carnegie called it, supported this view as well. Also in this age, however, the first major movements supporting an active role for government arose. The Populists, representing farmers; the Knights of Labor; and Henry George's Single Tax movement supported active government intervention in the marketplace to relieve suffering. The new rationalists were academic figures who undermined the intellectual basis for Social Darwinism and laissez-faire economics. Lester Ward, the pioneering sociologist, advanced the idea that progress and freedom have historically been the result of conscious alterations of nature and that succumbing to the raw forces of nature—competitive or otherwise—is the antithesis of civilization. The iconoclast economist Thorstein Veblen documented the breakdown of the market in an economy consisting of concentrated industry. Edward Bellamy wrote a best-seller utopian novel, *Looking Backward*, in which he advocated "Nationalism," meaning socialistic control of the means of production. Welfare programs also began to develop support among members of the clergy involved in the Social Gospel Movement and among settlement workers such as Jane Addams.

While theoretical battles went unresolved, however, the welfare programs changed very little. Congress and the states resisted pleas to become involved in relief efforts, welfare remained primarily a local affair and Almshouses the primary method of caring for the poor; outdoor relief—for those who lived in their own homes—was abandoned in city after city when rising costs convinced voters that it fostered dependency. Public works or work relief programs aided the poor, especially in hard times. Thousands of unemployed were put to work in Boston, Pittsburgh, Cincinnati, Indianapolis, St. Louis, and Milwaukee. One important development was the expansion and greater coordination of voluntary private efforts. The Charity Organization Movement, beginning in 1877, sought to reduce fraud, inefficiency, and lack of cooperation between various programs (Philadelphia alone had over 800); and to use "friendly visitors," or investigators to survey the poor and exhort them to better behavior. Such agencies generally continued to blame the poor for their plight; the Conference of Christian Charities and Correction Survey of 1881 concluded that 50 to 90 percent of poverty and crime were caused by intemperance. By now, however, some were questioning whether poverty was more nearly the cause of the others.

The Progressive era, breaking with the Nineteenth Century programs based on the Elizabethan poor laws, laid the earliest foundations of our present welfare system. The change resulted from changing public attitudes toward the poor, who were now considered to be the victims of the same economic forces that the middle class resisted. Publicity of the degrading state of living conditions aroused the public conscience. Jacob Riis' *How the Other Half Lives* was received with shock. Robert Hunter's 1904 work, *Poverty*—called by Raymond Mohl "perhaps the most careful and objective study made up to that time"—indicated that the poor were dependent because of preventable social and economic evils, not because of defective morality. The range of social welfare measures adopted during this time is broad, including programs in housing, insurance, regulation of working conditions, and others. Public assistance measures were more limited, however. Congress rejected unemployment relief during economic downturns in 1914 and 1921, unemployment insurance on several occasions, and any participation in the welfare programs of the states. A major breakthrough at the state level was the adoption of "mothers' pensions," which accepted the principle that mothers with dependent children deserved help; these had been adopted by 42 states by 1927. Less than a third of these programs were actually funded, however. Similar programs were made available for the blind in 24 states and the aged in 28 states.

The Great Depression dealt a staggering body blow to America's self confidence in general and her faith in individual enterprise in particular. As the stock market daily explored for new lows, as the factory doors closed, as the banks failed and the breadlines lengthened, the notion that an industrious honest man could not fail in America seemed more a cruel hoax than a national credo.

Some tried to invoke the old verities. Henry Ford declared in 1930 that the poor consisted almost ex-clusively of those who "refuse to work diligently." All things considered, he judged the Depression to be a "wholesome" experience. Frugality and a little belt-tightening were urged. One Congressman estimated during an appropriations debate that 11¢ a day could feed comfortably a reservation Indian child. Even thriftier, a textile executive advised his workers that they should be able to get by on 6¢ a day. President Hoover constantly reassured his countrymen that things were just not that bad. When critics flung at him reports of beggars lining Park Avenue and tramps crowding into railroad box-cars, he insisted that "hoboes are better fed than they have ever been," adding with unconvincing familiarity, "why one hobo in New York got ten meals in one day."

So deeply had individual responsibility penetrated the national consciousness that some Americans were persuaded. Rather than accept relief, a blind black man in Georgia hitched himself to a plow and tilled farmland. In a John Steinbeck novel, a young father of unyielding pride refused to accept from hoboes the milk he could not afford for his infant. The baby died. And the story was more than fictional hyperbole. In Youngstown, Ohio a family of four refused to turn to charity and starved slowly to death.

Most Americans, however, were no longer listening to their former sages. They derisively responded to the President's pleas for self-reliance by attaching his name to the physical evidences of the Depression: Hoover flags were empty pockets turned inside out, Hoovervilles the makeshift shanties of cardboard and tin boxes that sprang up in vacant lots, Hoover hogs the jackrabbits shot by farmers to supplement their families' diets. (One popular example of Depression black humor held farmers could no longer afford to shoot jackrabbits and instead caught and milked them and set them loose. When a Steinbeck character sees a jackrabbit with no one chasing it, he theorizes that the Depression must be over. No such luck, his companion responds, it's just one that has gone dry.)

Men, women, and children rooted in the refuse of garbage dumps for scraps of food; a third of the labor force trudged the streets in weary and vain search of work; some families assigned individual members different days of the week for eating. Thinking Americans could not help but realize that they were in it together. Dorothy Parker spoke for a nation: "There is no longer I. There is WE. The day of the individual is dead."

Franklin Roosevelt's New Deal resoundingly confirmed Miss Parker's insight. As never before the Federal Government admitted that many individuals could not adequately provide for their own needs. In the "100 days" programs, a Civilian Conservation Corps provided subsistence wages for 250,000 engaged in forestry work; the Public Works Administration pumped $6 million into the economy in six years; and the Federal Emergency Relief Act pumped in $3 billion of direct relief—the first substantial federal program of direct relief to the needy. By the winter of 1934, 20 million people, or one-sixth of the entire population, was on the dole. Yet it is important to understand that no important figure from the President to the Congress to the Private sector wanted continued direct relief efforts. When the worst of the economic slump had passed, the relief efforts were abruptly terminated and the unemployed were turned back to the labor market despite the continued recession and hence lack of jobs. Examination of the New Deal and the War on Poverty of the 1960's has led Frances F. Piven and Richard A. Cloward to a provocative thesis:

> The chief function of relief arrangement... is to regulate labor, and they do that in two ways. First, when mass unemployment leads to outbreaks of turmoil, relief programs are ordinarily initiated or expanded to absorb and control enough of the unemployed to restore order; then, as turbulence subsides, the relief system contracts, expelling those who are needed to populate the labor market... Some of the aged, the disabled, the insane, and others who are of no use as workers are left on the relief rolls, and their treatment is so degrading and punitive as to instill in the laboring masses a fear of the fate that awaits them should they relax into beggary and pauperism.

Other New Deal programs of importance in the welfare area included the Social Security Act and housing assistance.

The decades of the 1940's and the 1950's were quiet ones for welfare. The 1960's were another story. While AFDC rolls had increased only 17 percent during the 1950's, they increased 107 percent between December 1960 and February 1969. This is explained by the disorders of the mid-60's in black ghettoes, by federal programs designed to make poor people aware of their opportunities and power, and by increased funding for welfare. One myth about welfare was apparently disproven: that rising employment will necessarily reduce welfare rolls. During the decade, while unemployment was cut in half, AFDC rolls increased by two-thirds in the number of recipients and doubled in funding. A new type of pressure was mounted at this time, as welfare recipients organized to protest restrictions on benefits and surveillance on those awarded money. George Wiley's National Welfare Rights Organization (NWRO) since 1966 had led most welfare protest activity. It aims at mounting pressure at the local level, where welfare recipients are often a potent political force. Another pressure group was the Poor People's Campaign of 1968, which established "Resurrection City" in Washington to pressure for greater benefits.

A possible new direction for welfare in the 1970's was outlined by President Nixon in an address on welfare in 1969. Suggesting that "America's welfare system is a failure that grows worse every day," he made several indictments of existing arrangements and proposed a Family Assistance Plan that would heavily stress legal and economic incentives to work, but would be financed by the federal government at uniform benefit levels nationwide. The program appears to have died in Congress. Yet, there are now 14 million poor who receive cash, food, and/or housing assistance from government, and the rolls continue to rise. There is a reservoir of 11 million poor who do not receive benefits because they are too proud, unaware of, or ineligible for programs in their area.

While some argue for an increase in the level and coverage of welfare programs, critics counterattack. Paying for our staggering welfare load has been a source of fiscal difficulty for more than one jurisdiction. Not insignificantly, those who find their incomes redistributed through government taxation raise strong objections. Denying welfare's efficacy, sociologists point to evidence that we may be creating permanent cultures of poverty in our society. Apart from questions of desirability, some theorists contend that these efforts are beyond the scope of proper state action. They maintain that economic welfare is not an individual right. In any case, the extent of our current welfare efforts has obscured the traditional distinction between "social welfare" and "individual rights" in the economic sphere.

Excerpted Documents

Individualism and social welfare.

Clair Wilcox, Professor of Political Economics—Swarthmore College, *Toward Social Welfare*, 1969, p. 86.

Social provision for security, unlike private provision, involves action by government. It is based upon a a recognition that self-reliance and private charity are not adequate to meet all human risks, that the community, in common decency, cannot permit people to die of starvation or exposure; that society, in its own interest, cannot deny its members the minimum support they need in order to subsist.

Sidney Fine, Professor of History—University of Michigan, *Laissez Faire and the General-Welfare State*, 1969, p. 374.

In a democratic state, the critics of laissez faire asserted, government is not something apart from the people but is merely their agent and is employed by them to accomplish such purposes as they have in view. Popular resort to state action, therefore, partakes of the nature of self-help and is not to be construed as paternalism.

Clair Wilcox, Professor of Political Economy—Swarthmore College, *Toward Social Welfare*, 1969, p. 86.

It [social welfare] is based, too, upon a recognition that the misfortunes that may befall an individual or a family are the result in large measure of conditions for which society as a whole is responsible . . . A part, at least, of the burden should be borne by the community as a matter of public policy.

Harold Faulkner, Professor of History—Smith College, *The Decline of Laissez Faire, 1897-1917*, 1951, p. 366.

Generally speaking, the masses brought no pressure on government to restrict or supervise the operation of private business until the conduct of such business became obviously disastrous or dangerous to the public welfare.

President Woodrow Wilson, *First Inaugural Address*, 1913.

Our thought has been, "Let every man look out for himself, let every generation look out for itself," while we reared giant machinery which made it impossible that any but those who stood at the levers of control should have a chance to look out for themselves. . .

President Woodrow Wilson, *First Inaugural Address*, 1913.

Society must see to it that it does not itself crush or weaken or damage its own constituent parts. The first duty of law is to keep sound the society it serves.

Lester Ward, 19th Century Sociologist, *Psychic Factors of Civilization*, 1894, pp. 261-262.

We are told to let things alone, and allow nature to take its course. But has intelligent man ever done this? Is not civilization, with all it has accomplished, the result of man's not letting nature take its course? This iron law of nature, as it may appropriately be called, was everywhere found to lie athwart the path of human progress, and the whole upward struggle of rational man. . .has been with this tyrant of nature—the law of competition.

Sidney Fine, Professor of History—University of Michigan, *Laissez Faire and the General-Welfare State*, 1969, pp. 30-31.

Those who in the industrial order that was emerging in the United States after the Civil War continued to advocate the laissez-faire brand of liberalism tended to establish economic freedom as an end in itself rather than as a means to an end, and were out of harmony with the true spirit of liberalism. They were blind to the compelling necessity for social and economic reform and refused to recognize that some positive action on the part of the state was essential to assure the effective liberty of the individual.

Emmette Redford, Professor of Government—University of Texas, *Democracy in the Administrative State*, 1969, p. 181.

Money is the usual means of economic balloting and the lack of it deprives many of the ability to vote. Anyone who looks. . .can make an extensive inventory of functions of government that have arisen because of inadequacies of the ballot in the market place. Man has turned to politics and to creation of the administrative state because his ballot in the market place did not satisfy all of his interests.

Henry Steele Commager, Professor of History—Amherst College, *The American Mind*, 1950, p. 211.

"Modern society," wrote [Lester] Ward, "is suffering from the very opposite of paternalism— from under-government. . . The true function of government is not to fetter but to liberate the forces of society; not to diminish but to increase their effectiveness." . . . "Individual freedom," Ward insisted, "can come only through social regulation," and like so many of the reformers of his generation he belied that true liberty could flourish only where the state interposed itself between the strong and the weak . . .

Henry Steele Commager, Professor of History—Amherst College, *The American Mind*, 1950, pp. 207-208.

The notion of the "survival of the fittest," which dazzled a whole generation, Ward repudiated as either meaningless or pernicious. For "fit" is not an absolute but a conditional term: fit for what? Assuredly, said Ward, mere fitness to survive is no criterion that civilization can accept, and here he echoed Huxley's statement that "social progress means a checking of the cosmic process at every step. The more advanced a society becomes the more it eliminates the struggle for existence."

Henry Steele Commager, Professor of History—Amherst College, *The American Mind*, 1950, p. 207.

Laissez faire, [Lester] Ward argued, was incoherent, fragmentary, insincere, and futile, scarcely consistent with the law of nature and wholly inconsistent with the law of man. It repudiated the past and condemned the future, denied scope to the creative faculty of man and barred the road to calculated progress. For civilization, as we know it, is the triumph of man over the blind forces of nature and the deliberate application of human genius to the task of emancipating man from the tyranny of those forces.

John S. Patterson, *Reforms: Their Difficulties and Possibilities*, 1884, p. 213.

This battle between State-interference and *laissez-faire* is now upon us; it will be waged through all the near future.

The rhetoric of government-sponsored reform.

Senator William Borah, Idaho, *Boston Herald*, July 5, 1934, p. 1.

Of all the forms of government which has ever been permitted to torture the human family, the most burdensome, the most expensive, the most demoralizing, the most devastating to human happiness and the most destructive of human values is a bureaucracy.

Harold Faulkner, Professor of History—Smith College, *The Decline of Laissez Faire, 1897-1917*, 1951, p. 269.

The motive behind (private corporate-sponsored) welfare projects varied widely. In some cases it was the humanitarian impulse of an influential member of a firm; in other cases an effort to discourage unionization.

Sometimes it was the desire to obtain favorable publicity. More usually it was the hope of developing loyalty and obtaining greater steadiness of employment by reducing absence from illness, labor turnover, and strikes. Primarily it was the hope of "greater production at less cost." Welfare work was "good business."

William Graham Sumner, *In The American Mind*, 1950, p. 202.

If we do not like survival of the fittest, we have only one possible alternative, and that is the survival of the unfittest. The former is the law of civilization; the latter is the law of anti-civilization.

Henry Steele Commager, Professor of History—Amherst College. *The American Mind*, 1950, p. 202.

His (Sumner's) position was neatly put by Edward L. Youmans in a conversation with Henry George about the corruption of New York politics. "What do you propose to do about it?" asked George. "Nothing," said Youmans. "You and I can do nothing at all. It's all a matter of evolution. Perhaps in four or five thousand years evolution may have carried men beyond this state of things."

President Grover Cleveland, *Message on the Veto of the Texas Seed Bill*, February 16, 1887, *The Writings and Speeches of Grover Cleveland*, 1892, p. 586.

I do not believe that the power and duty of the general government ought to be extended to the relief of individual suffering which is in no manner properly related to the public service or benefit. A prevalent tendency to disregard the limited mission of this power and duty should, I think, be steadfastly resisted, to the end that the lesson should be constantly enforced that, though the people support the government, the government should not support the people.

Ray Lubove, Professor of History and Social Work—University of Pittsburgh, *The Nation*, May 23, 1966, p. 609.

Private relief and charitable agencies (of the 19th Century) attributed poverty in a land of opportunity to character defects—notably, to improvidence, ignorance and intemperance.

Ray Lubove, Professor of History and Social Work—University of Pittsburgh, *The Nation*, May 23, 1966, p. 609.

The main thrust of social work, especially before the 1930s, must be understood in the context of the American work culture and a commitment to private and voluntary support of charitable enterprise. These decisively influenced the response of social work to the poor, and blocked efforts to deal with poverty as an issue of income maintenance and redistribution.

Sidney Fine, Professor of History—University of Michigan, *Laissez Faire and the General-Welfare State*, 1969, p. 3.

In theory at least, Americans (through most of the 19th century) had adhered to the view that although government was, unfortunately, a necessity, its functions should be reduced to a minimum. Free individuals, left to their own devices, could solve the problems that confronted them without the aid of the state. The state might wage war, protect property, and administer justice, but in the everyday life of the people it was not to interfere.

John Dos Passos, *Growth and Rights of Aggregated Capital*, 1899, p. 5.

Every law that you make is, as it were, a nail in the coffin of natural liberty. The object of government is not to make laws, the object of government is to avoid making laws.

William Graham Sumner in *The American Mind*, 1950, p. 201-202.

All experience is against state regulation and in favor of liberty. The freer the civil institutions are, the more weak or mischievous state regulation is. . .Projects to abolish poverty are worthy of an age which has undertaken to discuss the abolition of disease. Why not abolish death and be as gods once and for all—why trifle with details. If these agencies can get us anything they can just as well get us everything.

Harold Faulkner, Professor of History—Smith College, *The Decline of Laissez Faire, 1897-1917*, 1951, p. 366.

Whatever the main business of representative government may have been in the United States, it has generally responded to the demands of the most powerful economic groups. Those groups never followed laissez faire when anything could be gained by government action; they extolled the theory only when they wanted to be let alone.

President Franklin D. Roosevelt, *New York Times*, June 8, 1935, p. 1.

Government must try to increase the security and the happiness of a large number of people in all occupations of life and in all parts of the country; to give them more of the good things of life; to give them a greater distribution, not only of wealth in the narrow terms but of wealth in the wider terms. . .

Clair Wilcox, Professor of Political Economy—Swarthmore College, *Toward Social Welfare*, 1969, p. 90.

Establishment of this system [Social Security Act of 1935] marked the beginning of comprehensive social insurance in the United States. The law was attacked in the national campaign of 1936 by Alfred M. Landon, the Republican candidate for the presidency, who thereupon carried the states of Maine and Vermont. Since that time, the program has had bipartisan support.

Henry Stimson and McGeorge Bundy, *On Active Service in Peace and War*, 1948, p. 63.

Government should be an affirmative agency of national progress and social betterment, and it should not be considered a mere organized police force, a necessary evil.

Outlook and problems of present social welfare.

Richard Cloward, Professor—Columbia University School of Social Work, and Richard Elman, *The Nation*, February 28, 1966, p. 230.

In America, we continue to define poverty as resulting from all manner of personal devils which must be exorcised with commensurate autos-da-fe. . .Our welfare state is accordingly characterized by a lawlessness, a discrimination by class and race, a disregard for human rights and dignity, and a niggardliness that are recurrent, often routine, if not institutionalized. And if our social welfare system is regularly unjust, it is because American public opinion about the poor makes it so.

Ray Lubove, Professor of History and Social Work—University of Pittsburgh *The Nation*, May 23, 1966, p. 609.

Far from dedicating itself to the goal of economic security, American social work throughout most of its existence has embraced a deterrent psychology which expected work motivation to arise from fear and the "despair of unemployment, disease and underfeeding." As a social worker at the turn of the century observed: "The working classes are willing to provide for themselves if an unwise charity does not offer a bonus for incompetence."

Editorial, *Saturday Evening Post*, April 8, 1967, p. 90.

It has long been part of the American mythology that no honest man would accept handouts from the Government. The corollary is that anyone who does take Government handouts is probably shiftless and immoral.

None of this applies, of course, to the middle classes, who accept Government handouts with perfectly clear consciences. The professor with a grant for scientific research, the wheat rancher getting Federal subsidies, the war veteran with a monthly pension—all manner of Americans consider themselves entitled to receive Government doles. Only the poor are patronized or condemned for doing the same thing.

New York Times, June 16, 1968, p. 47.

A majority of Americans opposes a guaranteed annual income that would provide each family with a minimum income of $3,200 a year, according to the Gallup Poll. But they overwhelmingly support a plan that would guarantee each family enough work to provide this amount of money.

Pendleton Herring, President—Social Science Research Council, *Public Administration and the Public Interest,* 1967, p. 3.

When a democratic government undertakes to alleviate the maladjustment of the economic system it stirs up a greed that it may lack power to control. The "voice of the people" sometimes suggests the squeal of pigs at the trough.

Richard Cloward & Frances Fox Piven—Columbia University School of Social Work, *The Nation,* May 2, 1966, p. 511.

Because the ideal of individual social and economic mobility has deep roots, even activists seem reluctant to call for national programs to eliminate poverty by the outright redistribution of income. Instead programs are demanded to enable people to become economically competitive. But such programs are of no use to millions of today's poor. For example, one third of the 35 million poor Americans are in families headed by females; these heads of family cannot be aided appreciably by job retraining, higher minimum wages, accelerated rates of economic growth or employment in public works projects. Nor can the 5 million aged who are poor, nor those whose poverty results from the ill health of the wage earner.

New Republic, May 11, 1968, p. 4.

The rich stay rich in the United States and the poor, poor, and the gulf between them hardly changes. America's disparity of income is the single most significant and sinister social fact in the nation. There has been no important change in this disparity since 1945. Everything comes back to that.

Richard Edwards, Union for Radical Political Economics, *The Capitalist System,* 1972, p. 251.

From the English Poor Laws of the sixteenth century to the Family Assistance Plan, welfare programs have simply kept the poor from becoming *too* poor, that is, from becoming *rebelliously* poor.

Pendleton Herring, President—Social Science Research Council, *Public Administration and the Public Interest,* 1967, p. vii.

Under democracy the public interest is based not upon the welfare of one class but upon a compounding of many group interests. We assume the possibility of achieving a balance of forces, social and economic. Whether this process becomes anything more than political jugglery depends upon the standards of justice that are accorded general acceptance by the community. Will social responsibility and loyalty to the democratic process outweigh opportunism and immediate self-interest?

Emmette Redford, Professor of Government—University of Texas, *Democracy in the Administrative State,* 1969, p. 182.

The administrative state will continue to expand because politicians see that people have interests that can be fulfilled only by public policy and its public administration.

Selected Bibliography

Abbott, Edith, ed. *Pioneers in Social Welfare*. New York: Russell & Russell, 1937.

Betten, Neil. *"American Attitudes Toward the Poor: A Historical Overview."* Current History, 65 (July 1973).

Blau, Joseph L. *Men and Movements in American Philosophy*. New York: Prentice-Hall, 1952.

Blau, Joseph L, ed. *Social Theories of Jacksonian Democracy*. New York: Hafner Publishing Co., 1947.

Bremner, Robert H. *From the Depths: The Discovery of Poverty in the United States*. New York: NYU Press, 1956.

Commager, Henry S., ed. *Lester Ward and the Welfare State*. Indianapolis: Bobs-Merrill, 1967.

Davis, Kenneth S. *The Paradox of Poverty in America*. New York: H.W. Wilson, 1969.

Davis, Lance E., and Legder, John. "Government in American Economy, 1815-1902." *Journal of Economic History,* 26, (1966), 514.

Donovan, John. *Politics of Poverty*. Indianapolis: Pegasus, 1973.

Ellis, Edward Robb. A Nation in Torment: *The Great Depression, 1929-1939*. New York: Capricorn Books, 1971.

Fabricant, Solomon, and Lipsey, R.E. *Trend of Government Activity Since 1900*. New York: National Bureau of Economic Research, 1952.

Fainsod, Merle, and Gordon, Lincoln. *Government and American Economy*. New York: Norton, 1959.

Faulkner, Harold U. *The Decline of Laissez Faire, 1897-1917*. New York: Rinehart, 1951.

Faulkner, Harold U. *The Quest for Social Justice, 1898-1914*. New York: Macmillan, 1931.

Fine, Sidney. *Laissez Faire and the General-Welfare State*. Ann Arbor: University of Michigan Press, 1956.

Feagin, Joe R. *Subordinating the Poor*. Englewood Cliffs, N.J.: Prentice-Hall, Inc., 1975.

Forcey, Charles. *Crossroads of Liberalism*. New York: Oxford University Press, 1961.

Gallaway, Lowell E. "Foundations of 'War on Poverty.' " *American Economic Review,* 55 (1965), 122.

Harrington, Michael. *The Other America: Poverty in the United States*. New York: Macmillan, 1962.

Herring, Pendleton. *Public Administration and the Public Interest*. New York: Russell & Russell, 1967.

Hyneman, Charles. *Bureaucracy in a Democracy*. New York: Harper, 1950.

Larner, Jeremy, and Howe, Irving, eds. *Poverty: Views from the Left*. New York: Morrow, 1968.

Levine, Daniel. *Jane Addams and the Liberal Tradition*. Madison: State Historical Society of Wisconsin, 1971.

Lubove, Ray. "The Welfare Industry: Social Work and the Life of the Poor." *Nation,* 202 (May 23, 1966), 609.

Mann, Arthur. "British Social Thought and American Reformers of the Progressive Era." *Missippi Valley Historical Review,* 42 (1956), 672.

Mann, Arthur. *The Progressive Era: Liberal Renaissance or Liberal Failure?* New York: Holt, Rinehart, and Winston, 1963.

Mann, Arthur. *Yankee Reformers in the Urban Age*. Cambridge: Belknap Press of Harvard University Press, 1954.

Mohl, Raymond A. *"Three Centuries of American Public Welfare: 1600-1932."* Current History, 65 (July 1973).

Noble, David W. *Paradox of Progressive Thought*. Minneapolis: University of Minnesota, 1958.

Noble, David W. *The Progressive Mind, 1890-1917*. Chicago: Rand McNally, 1970.

Rothman, David. *The Discovery of the Asylum*. Boston: Little, Brown and Company, 1971.

Schlesinger, Arthur M. *The Age of Roosevelt*. Boston: Houghton-Mifflin, 1957.

Schlesinger, Arthur M. *The American as Reformer*. Cambridge: Harvard University Press, 1950.

Seligman, Ben B. *Permanent Poverty: American Syndrome*. Chicago: Quadrangle Books, 1963.

Sproat, John G. *Best Men: Liberal Reformers in the Gilded Age*. New York: Oxford University Press, 1968.

Steiner, George A. *Government's Role in Economic Life*. New York: McGraw-Hill, 1953.

Steiner, Gilbert Y. *The State of Welfare*. Washington: Brookings Institution, 1971.

Veblen, Thorstein. *Theory of the Leisure Class*. New York: Macmillan, 1899.

Wellborn, Charles. *Twentieth Century Pilgrimage: Walter Lippmann and Public Philosophy*. Baton Rouge: Louisiana State University Press, 1969.

Wilcox, Clair. *Toward Social Welfare*. Homewood, Illinois: Richard D. Irwin, 1969.

Wilensky, Harold L., and Lebeaux, Charles N. *Industrial Society and Social Welfare*. New York: Russell Sage Foundation, 1958.

THE EVOLUTION OF AMERICA'S WORK ETHIC: A CHANGE FOR THE BETTER?

Introductory Essay

The work ethic, which calls all men and women to a life of serious labor, has been more firmly and widely upheld in America than elsewhere. Although American civilization derives from and shares many characteristics with Western European civilization, our attitudes toward work have differed decidedly. European (especially Mediterranean) nations have been much more likely to view work chiefly as a means to the end of leisure. The goal of the corporate executive has been to make enough money to retire early and comfortably; the hereditary aristocracy has made a virtue of idle wealth. The roots of such attitudes may be traced to classical Greece, where intellectual pursuits were reserved for the morally and socially superior man; manual labor was the province of slaves and lower class freemen. Americans, on the other hand, have prized physical work more than contemplation. A vast, undeveloped continent, a booming economy, and a general spirit of progress beckoned all citizens to do something for themselves and, incidentally, for the nation. American heroes have been people who get things done—the farmer, the business tycoon, the general—rather than contemplative religious or academic figures. Even the main contribution of America to philosophical thought has been a call for practicality and action. Pragmatism, developed by John Dewey, William James, and others, considered philosophical disputes meaningless if not potentially relevant to the material world. A general conclusion has been reached by one student of the history of work. "Except for the slave-owning areas of the American South," Walter S. Neff judged, "no country has been as work-oriented as the United States."

In recent decades, there have been signs of change in the attitudes of the Old World and the New. In America, there is now a concern that the work ethic may be losing its hold. Leisure time has become more abundant, while increased education and the mass entertainment industry have awakened the interest of the populace to the pleasures of leisure. The blue-collar worker now frequently feels a lack of social respect, yet the white-collar worker is not content with his work either. Many have worried about the development of a hedonistic youth subculture that, in the words of the President's Commission on Campus Unrest, "found its identity in a rejection of the work ethic, materialism, and conventional social norms and pieties." Others feel that the work ethic will be rendered obsolete because automation will reduce cybernetics or will eliminate the human element in work altogether. Is the work ethic losing its hold on America? If so, is this a development we should welcome or resist?

The historical context of the "the work ethic" requires comment for it refers to a rather specific constellation of beliefs and values. Usually it is termed "the Protestant work ethic," not because Catholics or Jews fail to accept it, but because the Protestant Reformation created it in Europe during the 16th century. Protestantism rejected the older paternalistic order, in spiritual life by breaking with the papacy and in temporal life by sanctifying the pursuit of wealth (though paradoxically, not the pleasure of its disposal). The Protestant revolt stressed individual responsibility for one's own salvation, an end that necessitated a moral life of labor in one's chosen field of endeavor. Sublimation of the gratifications of idleness was necessary to avoid temptation and sin. Hard work provided the alternative. Furthermore, Calvinism (which was the basis of most American Protestantism) equated success in one's "calling" with proof that one had been elected by God for salvation. Sacrifice, thrift, and work were necessary in order to merit grace.

The work ethic has held unequal sway in disparate parts of the nation; in the South in particular, the evolution of the work ethic has taken a unique course. The institution of slavery caused by far the most rigid class structure in the country. At the top of the social pyramid were the large land and slaveholders, who never needed to engage in physical labor and who could cultivate leisurely pursuits. The identification of hard work with slavery and idleness with success was also shared by the poorer whites who had no choice but to work hard, for it was unthinkable to associate their lot with that of the black slaves. The somewhat feudal arrangement of society was recognized by Southerners, who cultivated a chivalrous manner, avidly read such books as Sir Walter Scott's *Ivanhoe*, and encouraged military schooling and training. The Civil War abolished slavery, broke up many of the old plantations, and destroyed much of the social order. However, romanticizing the antebellum period, the South avoided conversion to the otherwise national work ethic.

Today, that region's accelerating industrialization portends a future conformity.

From the time of the first colonial settlements until about 1880, American norms were Protestant in politics, economics, and daily life. This does not overstate the piety of Americans or the extent of their formal religious practice, for as the noted historian Henry Steele Commager has suggested, Americans have treated their churches like aged relatives whose claims to "support" are "vague but inescapable." Yet the most fundamental political, social, and economic assumptions of the nation were largely Protestant in origin. American behavior prompted de Tocqueville to call the U.S. the most Christian nation on earth. Even Thomas Jefferson, a deist, built a political philosophy on Protestant premises—individual responsibility, personal freedom, and natural law. It was generally assumed that laws of divine order governed human conduct, including political conduct. The Declaration of Independence invoked "the Laws of Nature and of Nature's God" to justify revolt against British rule. Democratic government, preserved by checks and balances against the corrupting influences of power, placed political responsibility on the shoulders of the individual citizen. The economic ideal of laissez faire assumed that man was rational, calculating, and self-interested. Further it argued that by relying solely on the independent decisions of individuals, unaltered by government action, the natural law of supply and demand would adjust values in such a way as to maximize satisfaction of rational needs and desires throughout the economy. The relation of these ideals to Protestant morality was not incidental. For example, Emerson made an explicit link in "Wealth": "The countingroom maxims liberally expounded are laws of the universe. The merchant's economy is a coarse symbol of the soul's economy. It is to spend for power and not for pleasure. It is to invest income."

The national ideology was thoroughly infused with the Protestant ethic, but this ideology was accepted by Americans because it squared with their experience. The fruits of the work ethic were apparent for all to see. Everywhere the forest was transformed into farmland, small towns sprang up across the landscape, and economic growth brought wealth and trade to the far corners of the nation. Decades of successes in westward expansion and internal economic development seemed to prove that the American nation as a whole was destined for salvation. It was, in fact, commonly assumed that America had a special role to play in history, and that this role was protected by divine providence. Other factors also encouraged acceptance of the work ethic. The nation was dominated for nearly a century by those employed in occupations that provide the greatest satisfaction with hard work—independent farming, self-employed merchants, frontiersmen.

The nation was 95 percent rural as late as 1790, and actually most Americans did not live in large cities until the Twentieth Century. No aristocracy arose to reduce social mobility; everyone had the opportunity to become rich (though of course some groups had far greater opportunities than others). The chance for wealth was not the least important stimulus to acceptance of the work ethic, as the popular literature suggests. Benjamin Franklin's Poor Richard was a fountain of aphorisms on these topics. School texts like *McGuffey's Reader* inculcated the spirit in youngsters: "All that other folks can do, why, with patience, should not you: Only keep this rule in view; Try, Try Again."

The climate began to change with the extensive industrialization of the continent in the decades after the Civil War, however. One of the major reasons for this development was that the nation ceased to be overwhelmingly Northwest European and Protestant. Waves of immigrants swelled the cities with millions of desperately poor Southern and Eastern European and other ethnic groups. As historian Richard Hofstadter pointed out, the value system of the immigrants was founded upon "their unfamiliarity with independent political action, their familiarity with hierarchy and authority, and upon the urgent needs that so often grew out of their immigration." The rise of the boss and the urban political machine seemed to symbolize the threat to the whole Protestant ethic. Moreover, the traditional ethic claimed that poverty was the result of the moral inferiority of the poor; the new "gospel of wealth" and Herbert Spencer's Social Darwinism similarly argued that the deserving individual would succeed. The self-evident destitution of the new groups thus seemed to require their conversion to the "true morality." It is interesting to note that the process of assimilation of ethnic groups into the mainstream of American life was marked by the acceptance of the work ethic by the new groups.

Another pivotal force in the evolution of the work ethic was the changing nature of work following industrialization. The factory came a long way during the course of the nation's history. Early Nineteenth Century factories were reasonably comfortable and pleasant places, where frequently young girls of respectable families would work for a few years before marriage. By the 1870's the factory job had become a hard living of long, boring hours performing routine, highly specialized tasks or tending often dangerous machinery. Occupational boredom and monotony were more serious still following the widespread adoption of the management techniques of Frederick Taylor, whose time and motion studies and *Principles of Scientific Management* sought to increase production to the maximum through the elimination of inefficiencies in job tasks. The maximally efficient factory worker, however, became more and more like the machines he operated. In addition, concentration of capital and industry influenced the work ethic by reducing the potential for self-employment. Just how quickly this operated is indicated by the percentage of workers who are compensated by wages and salaries (most others are self-employed): in the mid-1800's, less than half of all workers were in this category, but by 1950 the figure had reached 80%, and by 1970 it had reached 90%.

A whole range of complex societal dislocations and difficulties accompanied industrialization—vast disparities of wealth, urbanization, increasing dependence on collective instruments of societal power. These too had their influence on the work ethic. At about the turn of the century, the pioneering economist Thorstein Veblen studied the new leisure class in America, an aristocracy of wealth that rejected work as undignified. At the same time, labor unions were beginning to bring the collective power of the workers to bear on the power of the large corporation; by the early 1900's their membership reached several million. The unions were intimately concerned with questions related to the work ethic, such as working hours and working conditions as well as salary. Business leaders expressed concern about the implications of labor's most pressing demand—shorter working hours—on the willingness of workers to exchange a fair day's toil for a fair day's pay, although the unions advocated the 8-hour day as a means of increasing employment. Early national organizations such as the Knights of Labor attempted to organize all workers, skilled and unskilled, into industry-wide unions on the grounds that craft distinctions had been virtually eliminated by the extensive use of machinery. They also hoped to enable workers to control their own economic destinies through cooperative industrial enterprises, in effect making entrepreneurs out of the workers; these efforts were generally unsuccessful, however. The American Federation of Labor represented a more enduring, totally different approach. Forsaking the organization of unskilled workers as hopeless, the AFL concentrated on the skilled workmen whose relative scarcity in the labor market and pride in craftsmanship gave them a better chance to succeed in struggles with management. The AFL ignored the pursuit of social goals and the potential of government intervention in labor's behalf, instead advocating "pure and simple unionism"—higher wages and a shorter working day. More than 24,000 strikes and lockouts between 1880 and 1900 testified to the determination of labor to improve its position.

The Populist and Progressive movements embarked upon what can only be termed a crusade to return to the Protestant values of an older America. The Populist movement of the 1890's was the culmination of years of agrarian discontent, expressed in such movements as the Grange and the Greenback

Party; the Progressive movement appealed in addition to the urban middle class of professionals and small businessmen. These groups were concerned about the gravitation of power toward growing collective forces—corporations, the banking and financial system, and political machines—which threatened to remove the individual's control over his own life. The Progressive conscience was also shocked by the condition of the urban poor, who were the victims of the nation's preoccupation with unrestrained and unprincipled pursuit of wealth. The overriding ethical impulse behind these movements is shown in the moral absolutism of their rhetoric as well as in their neglect of structural reforms to meet grievances. Populism and Progressivism were an exhortation to return the faith of the fathers, including the work ethic. Railroad regulation, antitrust legislation, steps to increase citizen access to government, and financial reform were ways to make the work ethic meaningful, increasing opportunity for all citizens to share in the national prosperity. These measures were not designed to redistribute wealth, but to make the economy once again a moral system that rewarded virtue and punished evil. It was characteristic of the evangelical fervor of the age that the reforms were oversold, but in any event their objectives were fairly limited.

The ethical spirit of Progressivism was caricatured during the 1920's. The nation's rejection of internationalism after World War I included a reaction against the crusading style of leadership that had induced participation in the conflict. Government during the decade generally acceded to the popular wish that it remain aloof from the exercise of power. A notable exception was Prohibition, which vainly attempted to use the power of the state to increase the morality of the populace. The Eighteenth Amendment is often regarded as the effort of waning, old-fashioned rural Protestantism to save the nation (and especially the sinful cities) through a moral challenge to thrift, productive use of leisure, and hard work.

The Great Depression and the New Deal resulted in a realignment of American values in many areas, among them the nature of the work ethic. Though there were many elements of Populism and Progressivism in the New Deal programs, the differences are striking. The New Deal was the first liberal reform movement to begin in hard times; Jefferson, Jackson, Theodore Roosevelt, and Woodrow Wilson presented idealistic challenges in prosperous times. Franklin Roosevelt fought economic catastrophe by broad scale social and economic experimentation, which conservatives resisted with appeals to traditional values. The New Deal programs altered the older work ethic in several ways. First, it recognized a responsibility of the federal government to promote employment opportunities and to provide relief to those who could not find employment in difficult times. This is not to suggest an abandonment of the work ethic through these programs, for they employed men productively. For example, the Works Progress Administration built or improved over 2500 hospitals, 13,000 playgrounds, 5900 school buildings, and 1000 airport landing fields. Furthermore, Roosevelt eliminated the makeshift Civil Works Administration after less than a year of operation partly because he feared its "narcotic" effect on able-bodied workingmen. A second way in which the work ethic was transformed was the federal government's assumption of responsibility for many social services, including housing, pensions, and disability and unemployment insurance, that had previously been budgeted for and purchased by the worker. Finally, the New Deal accepted as inevitable the increased importance of large, impersonal forces in American life. Corporate conduct was regulated, as through the National Recovery Administration and the Securities and Exchange Commission, but antitrust efforts were all but abandoned. Countervailing power to the corporations, in the form of unions, was greatly stimulated by the Wagner Act. In sum, the meaning of the older work ethic changed as the New Deal acknowledged that the nation was no longer composed of truly independent economic men—that the forces of government, unions, and big business were here to stay.

Among the most important post-war developments was the sharp accentuation of developing trends in the composition of the work force. As attitudes about the value of older workers have become more negative and social security and pension plans have been extended, the percentage of workers aged 65 and over has declined from two-thirds in 1900 to one-half in 1947 to less than one-third today. More women work today than ever before; 90% of all young women will work at some time in their lives. About twice as high a percentage of men as compared to women are in the work force, but five times as many men worked in 1900. As education has become more extensive, fewer teenagers work; the work rate for teenage boys has dropped one-third since 1900. At the turn of the century, when 30% of jobs required no skills, non-white groups had higher levels of employment than whites, but this has reversed as education and skill acquisition among non-whites has lagged behind a change in the available jobs. Now about one-third of non-whites are unemployed, irregularly employed, or have given up looking for work.

Another development has been a shift in the character of work. The flow from farm to city employment that has been going on for over a century accelerated after World War II with increased mechanization. At least 200,000 fewer farm workers were needed each year between 1947 and 1969. Today less than four million American farmers feed this nation and, through farm surpluses, a good bit of the rest of the world. Factory work was once the bedrock of non-farm employment. Increased use of efficient machinery has reduced the need for factory workers also, however; this has been especially true since the advent of automation (a term coined by Ford Motor Co. in the 1940's) virtually removed the need for human direction of production in some industries. Factories employed 40% of non-farm wage and salary workers in 1919; 33% in 1949; and 29% in 1970. More importantly, Bureau of Labor Statistics data indicate that only 2% of workers are now employed in the most alienating work, such as on the assembly line, which is physically and emotionally debilitating. As farm and factory employment have declined, government and service sector employment have increased greatly. Today, in fact, over 60% of wage and salary workers are employed in service industries; just twenty years ago it was 50 percent. Government, which once needed relatively few people, now employs 15% of the work force.

These changes in occupational distribution have signaled a shift toward white-collar employment, in government, the professions, and parts of industry and the service sector. Although white-collar jobs have been accorded greater prestige and advanced educational requirements, the routine and repetition of office work often leads employees to speak of "paper factories." One survey of a cross-section of office employees conducted by a group of management consultants found that they were producing at only 55% of their potential; boredom was considered an important factor.

A crucial change has been the reduction of the average workweek from over 70 hours before 1900 to 40 hours by 1940, where it has remained; in the meantime paid vacations and holidays have become standard. Something of a saturation in leisure may have temporarily been reached today, for there are few calls for a shorter workweek. While labor took 70% of its increased benefits in the form of greater leisure in the period 1910-1920, in the two decades following the Second World War almost 90% of increased benefits were in the form of wages and other financial benefits. In a way, we are all part of a leisure class—free waking time occupies more of our week than work. The response of Americans to this development has been a major challenge to the work ethic. At one time, even leisure was widely used to promote individual advancement. As sociologist Nels Anderson suggests, the "American idea. . . was 'Dr. Eliot's Five-Foot Shelf of Books,' a once popular set of volumes supposed to contain all the wisdom of the world, as uttered by great men. One could become learned by reading fifteen minutes a day. One packed gems of thought away to be brought out for display on surprising occasions." Today a substantial portion of the population views leisure as the real time in which to promote personal growth and development, as reflected in greater interest in reading, cultural activities, volunteer work, political participation, and so on. But other uses of leisure time have become more important in relative terms. Conspicuous consumption has become a favorite American pastime, now that we have the time to shop and the money to spend. And a whole leisure industry has arisen to provide recreation and entertainment for the average citizen. Has all of this devalued work? Does the typical worker neglect his job, waiting absently for the workday to end so that his pleasure, idle or otherwise, may begin? There is much concern about what we will do that is interesting or meaningful with more free time; the unhappiness of the retired people and even the unemployed are disturbing omens. Do we need to plan our free time in new types of organized activities, or does this violate the spirit of leisure?

Clearly, the work ethic is now a somewhat different creature than it was in 1750 or 1850. The nation is no longer comprised primarily of agrarian and business entrepreneurs and potential entrepreneurs, striving single-mindedly to gain a comfortable piece of the rapidly expanding national wealth. In a sense, the Protestant ethic was destroyed by its own success. Entrepreneurs built the wealthiest economy on earth, but in the process concentrated opportunity and power to such an extent that individual striving meant less. Most people could no longer direct their own enterprise; most worked at hard, unsatisfying jobs created by the new technology and its consequent endeavors. In reaction, unions, government, and other collective instruments restored for the common man some of the competitive advantage he had lost and protected him against many catastrophic consequences of competition—but at the price of further reductions in the individual's responsibility for his own economic, and perhaps moral, salvation.

Today the benefits of the industrial revolution have been enormously increased and diffused, and only a relatively small part of the population fails to share in the fruits. More strikingly, the efficiency of production has allowed men to work fewer and fewer hours. The psychologist Abraham Maslow has proposed that human needs are hierarchical, in that meeting lower level needs results in the pursuit of other, higher needs. Well, the basic needs (food, clothing, shelter, safety, security) of the vast majority are met in more than acceptable fashion, and Americans more and more have turned to look for self-esteem and self-actualization (the full realization of individual potential) as best they can. This explains in part our greater willingness to speak out against the employer, as well as other sources of authority; greater interest in leisure pursuits, including a sometimes intense search for fun; and greater interest in education for its own sake.

Yet what becomes of the work ethic as this process evolves? We must answer for ourselves a basic question: Why do human beings work? Is it because they must earn a living, or because they don't know what else to do with their time, or because they want to create, achieve, or satisfy their conscience? One poll has found that fully 80% of Americans say they would work even if they inherited enough to live on comfortably without working. Yet other polls show most Americans would start all over again in a new occupation if they could. Studs Terkel's impressive volume of interviews, *Working,* adds a human dimension to such figures. In case after case, the typical man (or woman) on the street is dissatisfied with his job, sometimes tragically, more often in a vague and restless way. Throughout, the paradox becomes clearer that although the nation wants to work in a meaningful way, it does not and does not know how. Three years ago, a Special Task Force to the Secretary of Health, Education, and Welfare suggested in its report, *Work in America,* that the nation should move toward extensive employee participation in management as a way of humanizing work and providing workers with more control over their own destinies. It cited a number of studies in which workers had been given autonomous control of their work and work conditions in settings ranging from janitorial work to clerical work to the assembly line; the success of these efforts in increasing both worker satisfaction *and* productivity is truly startling. Will this be the new direction for the nation? If so, it seems fair to say that we would be returning to the individual primary responsibility for his own behavior, and requiring him to accept the consequences of his decisions—in short, restoring much that has been lost in the work ethic.

How important has Protestantism been in encouraging the work ethic?

Stanley R. Parker, *The Future of Work and Leisure*, 1971, p. 35.

Calvin developed these ideas further with his concept of predestination. Only a small part of mankind shall know everlasting life; idleness and luxury are deadly sins, and dislike of work a sign that 'election' is doubtful. All men, even the rich, must work because it is the will of God. But they must not lust after the fruits of their labour. From the paradox—the command to ceaseless effort, to ceaseless renunciation of the fruits of effort—the motive power and ideological justification of modern business derives.

Cotton Mather, Puritan Preacher, *A Christian at His Calling: Two Brief Discourses, one Directing a Christian in his General Calling; Another Directing Him in his Personal, 1701, in The American Gospel of Success, Moses Rischin, ed.,* 1965, p. 24.

To be without a *Calling* as 'tis against the *Fourth Commandment*, so 'tis against the Eighth Commandment; which bids men seek for themselves a comfortable Subsistence: How? But in the way of some good Occupation. And as a man is *Impious* towards God, if he be without a *Calling*, so he is *Unrighteous* towards his *Family*, towards his *Neighbourhood*, toward the *Commonwealth*, I. he follow no *Calling* among them . . . Yea, a *Calling* is not only our *Duty*, but also our *Safety*. Men will ordinarily fall into horrible *Snares*, and infinite *Sins*, if they have not a *Calling*, to be their preservative . . . . Tho' it were part of the *Curse* brought in by *Sin, In the Sweat of thy Face thou shalt eat Bread*, the *Curse* is become a *Blessing*, and our *Sweat* has a tendency to keep us from abundance of *Sin*. Ordinarily no man does *Nothing*: If men have *nothing* to do, they'l soon do *Too much*; do what they ought not. The Temptations of the *Devil*, are best Resisted by those that are least at *Leisure* to Receive them. An *Occupation* is an *Ordinance of God* for our safeguard against the *Temptations* of the Devil. A Bird on the *Wing* is not so soon catch'd by the *Hellish Fowler*. A man is upon the *Wing*, when he is at the *Work*, which God hath set him to do . . . .

Walter Neff, New York University, "Work and Human History," *The Social Dimensions of Work*, Clifton Bryant, ed., 1972, p. 49.

From the beginnings of colonial America, work has been persistently glorified as something intrinsically good in itself. . . . the bulk of the original white settlers of North America were already convinced advocates of the Protestant Ethic. In the second place, the conditions they encountered were highly uncongenial to the establishment of any kind of agrarian feudalism, except under the special circumstances of black slavery in the South. . . . Although attempts were made to introduce the manorial system, based on white indentured labor, they could not succeed. The abundance of open land, the extreme scarcity of labor, the early preoccupation with manufacturing and trade, combined with the general anti-aristocratic opinion which many settlers brought with them—all these factors very early established North America as the land where the path to success and security was through hard work.

Donald B. Meyer, *The Protestant Search for Political Realism, 1919-1941,* 1960, p. 27.

The gospel of wealth, the gospel of stewardship, and even the gospel of service that was to appear in the 'twenties, were all efforts to preserve the fabric, or at least the illusion, of a society unified by morality, of a culture informed by religious meaning and morale.

Industrialism, however, called all apologies into question more vividly than had the economies of the past. The great labor strikes of the seventies, eighties, and nineties testified to the breakdown of harmony, to the rise of forces beyond containment. The early articulate reaction of Protestant spokesmen to the labor strife of that period concentrated upon its violence and disorder. This was anarchy, and it was to be dealt with according to the moral logic of social order. Let the strikers be taught patience, humility, thrift, diligence, and, above all, good order. If necessary, let them taste force. This response came from orthodox quarters—though not from all orthodox quarters—in what seemed a perfectly logical application of traditional views of sinful human nature. It came also from liberal quarters.

Robert Lee, *Religion and Leisure in America,* 1964, p. 160.

[D]iversion was encouraged as healthful and helpful, but to keep it so the activity must be done in moderation. "Seasonable merriment" was the phrase the Puritans often used to describe the kind of recreation that was approved—merriment governed by the appropriate season.

The biggest criticism the Puritans had of immoderate, unseasonable diversion was based on its being "a waste of time." A man should gain refreshment from his recreation, and if, instead, he found the activity made him more tired and disgruntled it was wrong to do. Furthermore, if the activity required time and energy it should yield results which made it worth the effort. Edmund Morgan gives a delightful description of John Winthrop's argument for giving up shooting. It was against the law, exhausting, time-consuming, dangerous, expensive, and—the final point—he never hit anything anyway.

Benjamin Colman, Boston Puritan, *The Government and Improvement of Mirth,* 1707, in *The Puritans,* 1938, p. 392.

We daily need some respite & diversion, without which we dull our Powers; a little intermission sharpens 'em again. It spoils the *Bow* to keep it always bent, and the *Viol* if always strain'd up. Mirth is some loose or relaxation to the labouring Mind or Body, it lifts up the hands that hang down in weariness, and strengthens the feeble knees that cou'd stand no longer to work; it renews our strength, and we resume our labours again with vigour. 'Tis design'd by nature to chear and revive us thro' all the toils and troubles of life . . .

Christian Century editorial, June 12, 1928, p. 38.

Organized labor has won practically every gain made by labor since the industrial revolution began. Its aim should be, of itself, to bring about a social revolution equal in its gain for humanity to that brought by the industrial revolution. That thing it cannot do unless it challenges the whole regime of capitalism by offering, as steps in social progress, a program of fraternal cooperation without the dogmas of Marx, an application of the principles of democracy to industrial organization, a ringing challenge to laissez-faire and the whole system that rests on profits first, and a contribution to an era of world peace wrought out on the basis of humanity first. This it cannot do by becoming orthodox, socially respectable, bureaucratic, and a mere factor in a capitalistic society. Capitalism is only a phase in social progress; it is no more permanent than was feudalism. The rise of the third estate put an end to feudalism; the rise of the fourth estate should profoundly modify capitalism by inaugurating an era of industrial democracy, and cooperative leadership in this direction belongs to labor.

Nels Andersen, *Dimensions of Work: The Sociology of a Work Culture,* 1964, p. 157.

As the public-school system spread westward with the frontier, it became part of the educational credo of success. One grew up with the understanding that success had to be worked for, and one had to be able to walk alone or to stand alone. As Adams puts it, the doctrine was one of "root, hog, or die," and the American was supposed to know how to do his rooting. In other words, it became deeply ingrained in our outlook on life that not only must a man work but that he must know *how,* and that if he did not do either—work or know—it was his own fault. Today something of that thought is expressed in "know-how," the slogan term of American foreign aid, and people in the easygoing lands who could never understand "that mad dog of an Englishman" now find that the dedicated American also goes out in the noonday sun.

Have the poor and unemployed shared the work ethic?

Matthew Carey, *Appeal to the Wealthy of the Land,* 1833, p. 12.

Let it not be for a moment supposed, that I carry my defence of the poor to such an extravagant and ill-judged length, as to contend that all their distresses and sufferings arise from inadequate wages, or that they are all faultless: far from it. I know there are among them, as among all other classes, worthless persons—and some supremely worthless. Among the heavy sins of the class are intemperance, and desertion by some of them, of their wives and children, or, what is at least as bad, living in a state of idleness on the earnings of their wives.

Walter S. Neff, New York University, *Work and Human Behavior*, 1968, p. 248.

A good case can be made that the male child of the very poor faces considerable difficulty in acquiring the components of the positive work personality. . . . If he is a child in a fatherless family, being brought up by his mother and an array of female relatives, then he will have difficulty imagining the role of the male breadwinner.

Leonard Goodwin, Brookings Institution, *Do the Poor Want to Work?*, 1972, p. 114

The background characteristics of the average welfare mother—only ten years of education, three children, no husband, and various chronic illnesses—do not encourage the hope that many of them can achieve economic independence. Despite this, considerable government effort has gone into the attempt to train welfare recipients for jobs . . . The WIN program was successful in getting jobs for only about 2 percent . . . of the total eligible welfare population; this during a period when welfare rolls for the whole country were rising by about 40 percent. The median wage for the employed WIN women was around $2 and hour, hardly sufficient to support a family of four adequately.

Orestes Brownson, "The Laboring Classes," *Boston Quarterly Review*, 1840, p. 10.

The laborer at wages has all the disadvantages of freedom and none of its blessings, while the slave, if denied the blessings, is freed from the disadvantages. We are no advocates of slavery, we are as heartily opposed to it as any modern abolitionist can be; but we say frankly that, if there must always be a laboring population distinct from proprietors and employers, we regard the slave system as decidedly preferable to the system of wages . . . Even in seasons of general prosperity, when there was only the ordinary cry of "hard times," we have seen hundreds of people in a not very populous village, in a wealthy portion of our common country, suffering for the want of the necessaries of life, willing to work, and yet finding no work to do . . . .

Report of a Special Task Force to the Secretary of Health, Education and Welfare, *Work in America*, 1973, p. 8.

. . . unemployed workers progress from optimism through pessimism to fatalism. Attitudes toward the future and toward the community and home deteriorate. Children of long-term unemployed and marginally employed workers uniformly show poorer school grades. . . . "There are so many unconscious and group needs that work meets," Winick writes, "that unemployment may lead not only to generalized anxiety, but to free-floating hostility, somatic symptoms and the unconscious selection of some serious illnesses."

Is there an intrinsic human need for work?

Barbara Terwilliger as interviewed by Studs Terkel, *Working*, 1972, p. 424.

Everyone needs to feel they have a place in the world. It would be unbearable not to. I don't like to feel superfluous. One needs to be needed. I'm saying being idle and leisured, doing nothing, is tragic and disgraceful. Everyone must have an occupation.

Love doesn't suffice. It doesn't fill up enough hours . . . Human beings must work to create some coherence. You do it only through work and through love. And you can only count on work.

Arthur M. Ross, Commissioner—U.S. Bureau of Labor Statistics, "Work and Leisure in the Round of Life," *Labor in a Changing America*, **William Haber, ed., 1966, p. 194**

A case in point is found in the thirteen-week "sabbatical leaves" recently negotiated for employees in the basic steel industry as a device for spreading work opportunity and perhaps providing a realistic foretaste of retirement. . . .Some of the early beneficiaries of the program during the winter of 1963-1964 were described as staring moodily out the window and remarking that thirteen weeks is a long, long time. It was not difficult to predict that the employers and the union would soon engage a corps of social workers and vacation planners to assist the steelworkers in making better use of the time. And if thirteen-week vacations are to be offered, organized programs of recreation, travel and adult education do seem indispensable.

Marie Jahoda, "Notes on Work," *Psychoanalysis: A General Psychology*, **Rudolph Lowenstein and others, eds., 1966, pp. 623-628.**

In my own studies bearing on the meaning of work for the individual . . . I was helped by an almost casual remark Freud made in a footnote in *Civilization and Its Discontents*. . . . He said that work is man's strongest tie to reality. . . . I shall begin by turning Freud's statement around: that is, if work is man's strongest tie to reality, then the absence of work should leave him less solidly in touch with reality. This is indeed the case, as several studies of unemployment have demonstrated. . . . Work encourages the continuous action necessary to maintain objective knowledge of reality; work permits the pleasurable experience of competence; work adds to the store of conventional knowledge.

Stanley R. Parker, *The Future of Work and Leisure*, **1971, p. 12.**

Some people look on leisure and work in the same way as the hedonist philosophy looks on pleasure and pain —the one to be eagerly sought after and the other to be avoided like the plague. But experts in the various social sciences agree that both work *and* leisure are necessary to a healthy life and a healthy society, though whether these two spheres need to be as separate as they are for most people today is debatable. The idea that work cannot be made a source of interest and even fulfillment for the mass of people, and therefore that we should pin our hopes on leisure, is as one-sided as the view that work is the real business of life and leisure is just a waste of time. Maximum human development in both work and leisure spheres requires that they be complementary rather than one be regarded as 'good' and the other 'bad.'

Lyndon Johnson, "Message to the Congress of the United States," January 23, 1968, in *Manpower Report of the President*, **April 1968, p. xv.**

Our society as a whole will benefit when welfare recipients become taxpayers, and new jobholders increase the Nation's buying power. These are dollars and cents advantages. But there is no way to estimate the value of a decent job that replaces hostility and anger with hope and opportunity. There is no way to estimate the respect of a boy or girl for his parent who has earned a place in our world. There is no way to estimate the stirring of the American dream of learning, saving, and building a life of independence.

Karl Mannheim, Sociologist, *Freedom, Power, and Democratic Planning*, **1950, p. 269.**

Leisure, besides being the natural balance in man's work, becomes increasingly the place for personality development and self-expression. While pre-industrial societies shaped individuals at their work, impersonal work in a machine age has lost this function, which is now confined to leisure-time pursuits. These had never before served such ends. For the majority, leisure instead of work has become the road to civilization.

Thorstein Veblen, Economist—University of Chicago, *The Theory of the Leisure Class*, **1899, p. 44.**

[For the leisure class] abstention from labor is not only an honorific or meritorious act, but presently comes to be a requisite of decency . . . Abstention from labor is the conventional evidence of wealth and is therefore the conventional brink of social standing; and this insistence on the meritoriousness of wealth leads to a more strenuous insistence on leisure . . . prescription presently seizes upon this conventional evidence of wealth and fixes it in men's habits of thought a something that is in itself substantially meritorious and enabling; while productive labor at the same time and by a like process becomes in a double sense instrinsically unworthy . . . .

John Kenneth Galbraith, Professor of Economics—Harvard University, *The Affluent Society*, 1958, p. 345.

The New Class is not exclusive. While virtually no one leaves it, thousands join it every year. Overwhelmingly the qualification is education. . . .

There can be little question that in the last hundred years, and even in the last few decades, the New Class has increased enormously in size. In early nineteenth century England or the United States, excluding the leisure class and considering the New Class as a group that lived on what it has carefully called earned income, it consisted only of a handful of educators and clerics, with, in addition, a trifling number of writers, journalists, and artists. In the United States of the eighteen-fifties it could not have numbered more than a few thousand individuals. Now the number whose primary identification is with their job, rather than the income it returns, is undoubtedly in the millions.

William E. Leuchtenburg, *Franklin D. Roosevelt and the New Deal*, 1963, p. 124.

The dole, Rossevelt told Congress, was "a narcotic, a subtle destroyer of the human spirit. . . . I am not willing that the vitality of our people be further sapped by the giving of cash, of market baskets, of a few hours of weekly work cutting grass, raking leaves or picking up papers in the public parks," he declared. "The Federal Government must and shall quit this business of relief."

Has the work ethic become less important in America?

Arthur M. Ross, Commissioner—U.S. Bureau of Labor Statistics, "Work and Leisure in the Round of Life," *Labor in a Changing America*, William Haber, ed., 1966, p. 186.

Recent developments indicate that work-oriented values are not receding but are being generalized throughout the whole population. . . . Poverty is no longer the predominant human condition, but has become a form of moral turpitude. . . . One of the most widely discussed books in recent years—*The Feminine Mystique* by Betty Friedan—contends that homemaking and motherhood can no longer be considered a satisfactory career for an intelligent, well-educated woman. At the same time, approximately 4,000,000 Americans are holding two or more jobs, and overtime work opportunities are eagerly prized.

Willis Harmon, "Key Choices of the Next Two Decades," Address before the White House Conference on the Industrial World Ahead, February, 1972.

The shape of the future will no more be patterned after the hippie movement and the Youth Revolution than the Industrial Age could have been inferred from the "New Age" values of the Anabaptists.

Report of a Special Task Force to the Secretary of Health, Education, and Welfare, *Work in America*, 1973, p. 48.

Today's youth believe in independence, freedom and risk—in short, they may have the entrepreneurial spirit of early capitalism. Certainly they are more attracted to small and growing companies, to small businesses and to handicrafts, than to the bureaucracy, be it privately or publicly owned . . . On the other hand, their parents share a managerial ethic that reflects the need for security, order, and dependence that is born of hard times. Of course, this is being a bit unfair to the older generation and a bit over-generous with our youth, but it serves to get us away from the simplistic thinking that the "Protestant ethic has been abandoned."

David Riesman, Professor of Sociology—Harvard University, "The Uncommitted Generation," *The American Gospel of Success*, **Moses Rischin, ed., 1965, p. 376.**

. . . it has become fashionable to speak of one's work or other activities in deprecatory terms and to adopt a pose of relative indifference to the larger goals of an organization . . . I think we are witnessing a silent revolution against work on the part even of those relatively privileged groups who have been free to choose their work and to exercise some freedom in the doing of it. This reflects, in part, the fact that much work is meaningless per se, save as a source of income, prestige, an sociability; but it also indicates . . . that people too readily accept their work as it comes, without hope of making it more meaningful.

Hannah Arendt, *The Human Condition*, **1958, p. 147.**

This is the advent of automation, which in a few decades probably will empty the factories and liberate mankind from its oldest and most natural burden, the burden of laboring and of the bondage to necessity. Here, too, a fundamental aspect of the human condition is at stake, but the rebellion against it, the wish to be liberated from labor's "toil and trouble," is not modern but as old as recorded history. . . . What we are confronted with is the prospect of a society of laborers without labor, that is, without the only activity left to them. Surely, nothing could be worse.

Judson Gooding, Associate Editor—*Fortune*, **"Blue Collar Blues on the Assembly Line,"** *Fortune*, **July 1970.**

The central fact about the new workers is that they are young and bring into the plants with them the new perspectives of American youth in 1970. At the beginning of this year, roughly one-third of the hourly employees at Chrisler, General Motors, and Ford were under thirty. . . They are restless, changeable, mobile, demanding, all traits that make for impermanence—and for difficult adjustment to an assembly line. The deep dislike of the job and the desire to escape become terribly clear twice each day when shifts end and the men stampede out the plant gates to the parking lots, where they sometimes actually endanger lives in their desperate haste to be gone.

Max Lerner, Professor of American Civilization—Brandeis University, *America as a Civilization: The Basic Frame*, **Volume 1, 1957, p. 240.**

One might say that the old work ethic died because the work became dehumanized and joyless, but this would miss the fact that joylessness in itself might strengthen the Puritan work ethic, making work an end in itself. What did happen was that, with the growth of the big corporation, work became depersonalized; and with the change in the immigrant experience and composition, hard work became associated with the foreignborn, the Negroes, the illiterates, and the underlying social strata. The atmosphere of the Big Money and the knowledge that so much of the income comes by way of what the workers consider "easy rackets," all conspired to strip work of its incentives. In the thinking both of the corporate employers and the trade-union members work came to be expressed mainly in money terms. It was cut off from a sense of creativeness and lost much of its dignity and meaning.

Government.

Richard Hofstadter, Professor of History—Columbia University, *The Age of Reform*, **1955, p. 307.**

Even before F. D. R. took office a silent revolution had taken place in public opinion, the essential character of which can be seen when we recall how little opposition there was in the country, at the beginning, to the assumption of the New Dealers that henceforth, for the purposes of recovery, the federal government was to be responsible for the condition of the labor market as a part of its concern with the industrial problem as a whole.

Report of a Special Task Force to the Secretary of Health, Education, and Welfare, *Work in America*, 1973, p. 86.

Albert Camus wrote that "Without work all life goes rotten. But when work is soulless, life stifles and dies." Our analysis of work in America leads to much the same conclusion: Because work is central to the lives of so many Americans, either the absence of work or employment in meaningless work is creating an increasingly intolerable situation.

Studs Terkel, *Working*, 1972, p. xi.

For the many, there is a hardly concealed discontent. The blue-collar blues is no more bitterly sung than the white-collar moan. "I'm a machine," says the spot-welder. "I'm caged," says the bank teller, and echoes the hotel clerk. "I'm a mule," says the steelworker. "A monkey can do what I do," says the receptionist. "I'm less than a farm implement," says the migrant worker. "I'm an object," says the high-fashion model. Blue collar and white call upon the identical phrase: "I'm a robot," "*There is nothing to talk about,*" the young accountant despairingly enunciates. It was some time ago that John Henry sang, "A man ain't nothin' but a man." The hard, unromantic fact is: he died with his hammer in his hand, while the machine pumped on.

David Riesman, Professor of Sociology—Harvard University, *Individualism Reconsidered*, 1954, p. 204.

I'm not sure but that the hue and cry against Puritanism isn't beginning to be overdone, and that we won't come to realize that our moral seriousness—in fact, our fun-morality—is not wholly negative.

Selected Bibliography

Andersen, Nels. *Dimensions of Work: The Sociology of a Work Culture*. New York: David McKay, 1964.

Arendt, Hannah. *The Human Condition*. Chicago: University of Chicago Press, 1964.

Best, Fred, ed. *The Future of Work*. Englewood Cliffs, N.J.: Prentice-Hall, Inc., 1973.

Blauner, Robert. *Alienation and Freedom: The Factory Worker and His Industry*. Chicago: University of Chicago Press, 1964.

Bryant, Clifton D., ed. *The Social Dimensions of Work*. Englewood Cliffs, N.J.: Prentice-Hall, Inc., 1972.

Commager, Henry Steele. *The American Mind*. New Haven: Yale University Press, 1950.

DeGrazia, Sebastian. *Of Time, Work, and Leisure*. New York: Twentieth Century Fund, 1962.

Galbraith, John Kenneth. *The New Industrial State*. Boston: Houghton Mifflin, 1972 (rev. ed.).

Goldthorpe, J.H.; Lochwood, D.; Bachofer, F.; and Platt, J. *The Affluent Worker: Industrial Attitudes and Behavior*. New York: Cambridge University Press, 1968.

Goodwin, Leonard. *Do the Poor Want to Work? A Social-Psychological Study of Work Orientations*. Washington, D.C.: Brookings Institution, 1972.

Haber, William, ed. *Labor in Changing America*. New York: Basic Books, 1966.

Heron, Alexander R. *Why Men Work*. Stanford: Stanford University Press, 1948.

Hertzberg, Frederick. *Work and the Nature of Man*. Cleveland: World Publishing, 1966.

Hofstadter, Richard. *The Age of Reform*. New York: Random House, 1955.

Lee, Robert. *Religion and Leisure in America: A Study in Four Dimensions*. New York: Abingdon Press, 1964.

Lerner, Max. *America as a Civilization*. New York: Simon and Schuster, 1957.

Leuchtenburg, William E. *Franklin D. Roosevelt and the New Deal*. New York: Harper and Row, 1963.

Levenstein, Aaron. *Why People Work: Changing Incentives in a Troubled World*. New York: Crowell-Collier Press, 1962.

Meyer, Donald B. *The Protestant Search for Political Realism, 1919-1941*. Berkeley: University of California Press, 1960.

Neff, Walter S. *Work and Human Behavior*. New York: Atherton Press, 1968.

Nosow, Sigmund, and Form, William H., eds. *Man, Work and Society*. New York: Basic Books, 1962.

Parker, Stanley R. *The Future of Work and Leisure*. New York: Praeger Publishers, 1971.

Report of the President's Commission on Campus Unrest. Washington, D.C.: U.S. Government Printing Office, 1970.

Riesman, David. *Individualism Reconsidered*. Glencoe, Ill: The Free Press, 1954.

Riesman, David. *The Lonely Crowd.* New Haven: Yale University Press, 1950.

Rischin, Moses, ed. *The American Gospel of Success.* Chicago: Quadrangle Books, 1965.

Rosen, R.A. Hudson. "The Hard Core and the Puritan Ethic." *Manpower,* 2(January 1970), No. 1.

Roszak, Theodore. *The Making of a Counter Culture.* New York: Anchor Books, 1969.

Schumpeter, Joseph A. *Capitalism, Socialism, and Democracy.* London: Unwin University Books, 1954.

Smigel, Erwin O., ed. *Work and Leisure: A Contemporary Social Problem.* New Haven: College and University Press, 1963.

Special Task Force to the Secretary of Health, Education, and Welfare. *Work in America.* Cambridge: MIT Press, 1973.

Stein, Leon, and Taft, Philip, eds. *Religion, Reform, and Revolution: Labor Panaceas in the Nineteenth Century.* New York: Arno and the New York Times, 1969.

Terkel, Studs. *Working.* New York: Pantheon Books, 1972.

Veblen, Thorstein. *The Theory of the Leisure Class.* New York: Macmillan Co., 1899.

Weber, Max. *The Protestant Ethic and the Spirit of Capitalism.* New York: Scribner, 1958.

Weiss, Robert, and Riesman, David. "Some Issues in the Future of Leisure." *Social Problems.* 9 (Summer, 1961), No. 1.

Wolfbein, Seymour. *Work in American Society.* Glenview, Ill.: Scott, Foresman and Co., 1971.

Yukl, Gary A., and Wexley, Kenneth N. *Readings in Organizational Psychology.* New York: Oxford University Press, 1971.

ORGANIZATION OF THE LABOR FORCE

Introductory Essay

Franklin Roosevelt declared in a speech before the Teamsters Union in 1940:

It is one of the characteristics of a free and democratic nation that it have free and independent labor unions. . . . When union workers assemble with freedom and independence in a convention . . . it is proof that American democracy has remained unimpaired; it is a symbol of our determination to keep it free.

Today as in 1940, there are those who dispute the idea that the ability of workers to organize into unions is a defining characteristic of democracy. For a good deal of American history the right of unions to exist was unknown. The relatively recent widespread acceptance of labor unions doubtless reflects a changed perceptual set. In the face of extensive industrialization and the concentration of economic power in the hands of a limited number of giant corporations, the American dream has changed. Many Americans no longer expect that one day they will become entrepreneurs—that is, small businessmen or independent farmers. Instead, most people realize that they are and, until retirement, will remain wage earners. The public has become more sympathetic to unions as workers have come to identify more with fellow employees, and less with employers. In addition, the economy is no longer generally regarded as a fine timepiece ticking to natural laws of supply and demand. Instead, the public regards as desirable the ability of unions, government, and other institutions to transfer resources from producers (increasingly seen as *them*) to consumers (meaning *us*). It has been estimated that unionization alone increases wages 10 to 15%, a consequence that has endeared union membership to its organizations and has lately led nonindustrial groups—teachers, police and firemen, farmworkers, nurses, and many others—to bargain collectively. Even for nonunion workers, there appears to have been a substantial indirect upward push on wages as a result of union gains.

During the colonial period and the early days of the Republic, a chronic shortage of labor was the most important condition affecting the organization of the work force. Indentured servants provided one important solution to labor needs. Slavery was an answer to the labor shortage south of Pennsylvania. However, nearly everyone was expected to do his share. Thus when factories arose, it was only natural that women and children should be tapped to operate the machinery, which required less strength than farming or manual labor. By 1820, in fact, half the cotton textile factory workers were under age 16. The labor shortage meant opportunity for the typical wage-earner. Undercompensation or mistreatment by one employer would only encourage a worker to go elsewhere. The ease with which an individual might solve his own problems made collective solutions less necessary. There were occasional labor disturbances before 1800, but the only real organization of the labor force was in the form of social and mutual welfare societies which were unconcerned with economic questions. The Typographical Society of New York printers and the Union of Shoemaker Journeymen in Philadelphia were representative of these societies—limited geographically to a local area, and in membership to a single craft.

The period from 1800 until the end of the Jacksonian Era witnessed the arrival of the Industrial Revolution and the first national workingmen's organizations. Factories could produce goods much more quickly and cheaply than craftsmen working by hand. Furthermore, the developing transportation systems—roads, canals, and railroads—forced producers to compete on a regional and even a national basis. Soon the Northeast became the center of most U.S. manufacturing.

At first, such developments seemed to benefit consumers through lower prices without doing serious harm to workingmen. Factories used those outside the normal labor force, such as women, children, and unskilled immigrants, to operate their equipment. The famous Waltham system seemed to prove that factory work could be a decent means even for proper young New England ladies to find employment. The Waltham textile manufacturers paid up to three dollars for a seventy-hour workweek and provided company dormitories, which regulated the girls' social and moral behavior in a paternalistic fashion (e.g., no card-playing or drinking, and compulsory church attendance on Sundays). Despite the long workweek, foreign and domestic observers including Charles Dickens commented favorably upon the overall environment and the attitude of the girls. Elsewhere, factory hands were relatively well-paid. Typical wages for unskilled workers in 1825 were one dollar a day, one-third to one-half higher than in England, while skilled workers could expect nine dollars per week.

However, the decline of the apprentice-journeyman-master craftsman system signalled new problems. No longer could the worker easily foresee the day when he would own a shop and control his own economic destiny. In addition, the skill and creativity of the workman meant little in the factory, where no man produced more than a fraction of any finished good. In response to such pressures, workingmen began to organize. In 1827, the first city-wide union across trade lines was organized, the Mechanics Union of Trade Associations representing fifteen Philadelphia associations. The union's strike for a ten-hour workday led to the appearance of similar organizations in a dozen major cities. Political activity also began with the organization of the Workingman's Party in Philadelphia in the next year. Demands of the party were numerous and suffered from a lack of coherence. They included the ten-hour day, restriction of child labor, abolition of competition from convict labor, free universal public education, and the abolition of imprisonment for debt.

The extent of labor's influence over political developments at this time is the subject of continued historical controversy. There is little doubt, however, that this was the first time that labor's influence was felt at the national level.

The organization of workingmen was stoutly resisted by employers and most of the general public. Laissez-faire expressed the economic ideal as most saw it, and unions deliberately attempted to interfere with the "natural law" of supply and demand for labor. Thus strikes were held to be unlawful conspiracies under common law, and the closed shop was considered an illegal restriction of employment. The judge in a case involving the Philadelphia cordwainers (shoemakers) in 1806 expressed the prevailing sentiment:

A combination of workingmen to raise wages can be considered from a two-fold point of view: one is to benefit themselves; the other is to injure those who do not join their society. The rule of law condemns both.

The Massachusetts case, *Commonwealth v. Hunt* (1842), finally established the legality of worker organizations. Even after this case, however, all the means by which unions might exert power — strikes, boycotts, and the closed shop — could be found illegal and halted by court injunction.

By the Civil War, the labor market had changed dramatically in character. Most importantly, the chronic labor shortage was largely alleviated. Immigration brought 1.5 million people to the U.S. in the 1840's and 2.5 million in the 1850's.

Often desperate for work, the immigrants depressed industrial wages and discouraged organization of the work force; although the cost of living rose 10% during this generation, wage levels rose only half that amount. That poverty was widespread in the industrial cities is made manifestly clear by many documents from the period. The situation worsened during the Civil War, for prices doubled while wages lagged behind.

Some gains in labor organization were made at this time, however. Five nationwide unions appeared during the 1850's, including the Typographical Union and the Stone Cutters Union. During the Civil War, the number of union locals in the U.S. increased from 80 to 300. In addition, the workday declined from twelve hours to ten or eleven in most factories. However, the fragile nature of such advances was manifested by the fate of workers' movements under the pressure of economic downturns. Depressions in 1837 and 1857 destroyed the national organizations.

Economic growth before the Civil War was, in percentage terms, the most rapid in our history. But compared with the sustained expansion from the end of the Civil War until the early Twentieth Century, the earlier growth had a far shallower impact. Change erupted in America during the late 19th century, making the nation over into an industrial, urban, pluralistic giant. Labor's response was confused at first, but the outlines of modern unionism were clearly to be seen by the end of the period.

The most important problems of the Gilded Age had been suggested by developments in an earlier day. As work became more fixed to increasingly powerful and dangerous machinery, labor alienation from its efforts likewise magnified. Pride in craftsmanship was becoming a memory; hopes of self-employment faced ever larger obstacles in the world of large-scale, concentrated industry. Working conditions remained beyond the control of the worker, even if he belonged to a union. A tidal wave of cheap immigrant labor (25 million between 1866 and 1915) suppressed wages and made unionization more difficult. Government, particularly the judiciary, seemed to favor business reflexively. In sum, workers began to feel that they were as much a commodity as the machinery they operated—that impersonal forces beyond their control governed their compensation and the nature of their work.

Not suprisingly in light of these conditions, labor unrest prevailed throughout the period, becoming especially serious following financial panics and depressions in 1873, and 1893. In the last two decades of the century alone, the Bureau of Labor Statistics recorded 24,000 strikes involving 6.6 million workers. In many cases, full-scale violence resulted from labor-management strife. Rioting and looting by rail workers who had received wage cuts shut down two-thirds of the track mileage in the country in 1877 before federal troops were summoned. The Molly Maguires, a secret society of Pennsylvania coal miners, organized terrorist violence. In the Homestead Steel strike, a gun battle killed men on both sides as strikers fought Pinkerton detectives.

New nationwide labor organizations attempted to constructively channel worker energies during the period. The first two attempts shared many similarities. The National Labor Union was founded in 1866 by the dynamic leader of the Iron Molders, William Sylvis. The powerful Noble Order of the Knights of Labor was founded in 1869 by Uriah Stephens and others representing Philadelphia garment workers. Both the NLU and the Knights advocated an eight-hour day and higher pay for workers. Both resisted use of strikes, considered to be "acts of private warfare," in favor of arbitration of wage disputes. Both organizations hoped to replace the wage system by cooperative industries which would allow worker capitalism and decisionmaking. The Knights actually established over 135 enterprises in such fields as mining, cooperage, and shoe manufacture. The cooperative experiments of both organizations ended in failure, however.

Both the NLU and the Knights worked for broad-based political reforms. The NLU helped form the comet-like National Labor Reform Party in 1872. The Knights were somewhat more successful, electing one member to the U.S. Congress and many to state legislatures and successfully lobbying for the 1885 bar on the importation of contract labor. Their political concerns were broad — encompassing currency reform, nationalization of natural resources, curbs on land speculation, and restrictions on child labor.

The NLU passed quickly from the scene after achieving at its peak a strength of 300,000 in 1872; the untimely death of Sylvis, internal dissension, the collapse of the experimental workers' cooperatives, the utter failure of the National Labor Reform Party in the 1872 elections, and a depression beginning in 1873 all contributed to its demise.

The Knights of Labor had a greater impact before fading from influence. An outbreak of walkouts in the 1880's led to an influx of membership, despite the official stand of the Knights against strikes. The sudden increase in membership—from less than 10,000 in 1879 to 729,000 in 1886—was catastrophic for the Knights. The leadership soon lost control of the local organizations, resulting in a number of poorly executed strikes. Twice as many strikes were recorded in 1886 as in any previous year. While these were only partly the work of the Knights of Labor, the public identification of the nation's best-known labor organization with these industrial

difficulties was strong. Then, in May 1886, the infamous Haymarket Square bombing shook the nation. Chicago had been embroiled in bitter eight-hour day strikes for some time when unusually violent speeches were delivered at a rally by several radical figures. A bomb thrown into a crowd of policemen, killing seven, led to a swift and frenzied public reaction. (Eventually four radicals were hanged, though the bomb-thrower was never discovered and no direct connection was demonstrated between the bombing and the acts of the radicals.) The Knights soon ceased to be a major force in the labor movement under the weight of these events.

The American Federation of Labor (AFL), founded during the "Great Upheaval" of 1886, turned the labor movement to a new course.

It abandoned the attempts of previous national organizations to recruit the unskilled laborers comprising 90% of the labor force. Furthermore, the national AFL office made no attempt to direct the policies of individual affiliated unions from a national office. Rather, the national office attempted to expand the movement, arbitrate conflicts, and later to lobby for federal support of pro-labor legislation.

The driving force behind the new Federation was Samuel Gompers, who was the president of the AFL from 1886 until his death in 1924 except for the year 1895, when the Socialists headed a successful move to unseat him. Under Gompers' leadership, the AFL membership rolls swelled steadily. From an initial total of 150,000 in 1886, membership increased to 550,000 in 1900 and over 1.5 million in 1910.

The AFL was the first major national labor organization to accept the necessity of working within the capitalist system. That body entertained no visions of workers escaping the wage system through cooperative industrial enterprises. Instead, the AFL dedicated itself to "pure and simple" unionism—an eight-hour day, higher wages, and other strictly economic benefits to be gained through collective bargaining.

Attempts to use the unions as instruments of social reform or ideology were deemed a "betrayal of unionism."

The AFL attitude toward political action was expressed by the principle of "voluntarism," which essentially called for a government policy of laissez-faire. The AFL in fact opposed for decades some fairly basic governmental measures which might have accomplished union ends, such as a legislated reduction in working hours, unemployment compensation, and minimum wage laws. Gompers considered it the union's responsibility to bargain for these advantages. Furthermore, he felt that there was much to lose from government action. Rank and file workers might come to rely on government action to the detriment of union power, and the government might unpredictably take pro-business as well as pro-labor stands. The anti-union bias of the judiciary also threatened to overturn any legislative action.

The AFL began to take economic action upon its formation in 1886, leading a general move involving several hundred thousand workers to secure an eight-hour day—a demand closer to labor's heart than any other throughout the entire period. Nearly 200,000 workers won either an eight or nine hour day as a result of threatened or actual strikes. The next serious labor unrest followed another financial disaster for the nation in the early 1890's. In 1892, a wage reduction by the Carnegie Steel Company in Homestead, Pennsylvania, led to a strike over the right of the workers to organize into a union. As a result of the failure of the strike, unionization of the steel industry was delayed for many years. The next major AFL-led assault occurred from 1901 to 1905. During these years, strikes were unusually successful, due to the ability of business to absorb higher labor costs during prosperous times. Unions won the eight-hour day as the standard for most skilled occupations, as well as significant wage increases.

The Progressive era brought major gains to organized labor. This was not due to any great love for unions permeating the reform spirit. "Bosses" of every stripe — including unions leaders — were resisted. Labor was, however, given room to grow, partly in recognition of the problems workers faced in bargaining with concentrated industry, which was seen as a far greater menace than labor.

In 1902, the United Mine Workers carried out a long but disciplined strike in order to win higher wages and union recognition. Arrogant statements by some mine owner spokesmen and a contrasting conciliatory spirit by the UMW gained much public sympathy for the union cause. President Theodore Roosevelt personally intervened on behalf of the union, inducing business to arbitrate and grant substantial wage increases. The UMW, organized along industry-wide lines open to both unskilled and skilled workers, offered an organizational contrast to the AFL. The UMW success stimulated greater industrial unionization of the railroad and building industries.

The Department of Labor brought Cabinet-level status to federal efforts in the labor field in 1913. The Clayton Act (1914) was at first received enthusiastically by labor, for it exempted unions from antitrust laws. Unfortunately, corporate lawyers found it "solid as Swiss Cheese," and judicial action against unions continued.

World War I worked to labor's advantage in general. As in the Second World War, labor exchanged a no-strike pledge for government assistance from the agencies set up to regulate the wartime economy. Woodrow Wilson became the first President to appear before an AFL convention in 1917. Total union membership doubled from two million in 1914 to four million in 1920 as a result of such factors.

Only the radical portion of the labor movement— the International Workers of the World (Wobblies) and the Socialist Party—suffered as a result of the war. Both groups accepted the doctrine of class struggle and adamantly opposed the war as a capitalist venture fought by and at the expense of workingmen. Spectacular mass trials decimated IWW ranks, which had included some of the most desperate elements of the labor force—western miners, lumber workers, and migrant workers. The IWW had gained much notoriety in its brief history, advocating "direct action" to establish "industrial democracy," a form of anarcho-syndicalism in which workers controlled the means of production. The Socialist party was led by Eugene V. Debs, who had become increasingly radical since government and the courts had cooperated with business to crush his American Railway Union's boycott of Pullman cars in 1893, following a strike in response to severe wage cuts by the company.

The post-war period sent labor reeling. In 1919-1920, four million strikes greeted the end of government regulation of the economy. Business responded with a counter-offensive that managed to cut union membership in half, using such tactics as the "Yellow Dog" contract. This type of contract required employees to agree not to join a union.

The Boston Police Strike in 1919 foreshadowed today's public service disputes. When about two dozen policemen were suspended for joining the AFL, 1117 of 1544 policemen struck. Troops were called in to break the strike in the wake of looting and violence. The Governor of Massachusetts, Calvin Coolidge, gained national prominence when he firmly told Gompers that there was "no right to strike against the public safety by anybody, anywhere, anytime."

The dislocations of the Great Depression brought a realignment of political and economic forces in America. In the course of this process, organized labor grew faster than at any other time. The 2.9 million unionist in 1933 had become nine million six years later; by 1945, about a third of the labor force (15 million) was organized, a proportion not exceeded to this day. This astounding growth was in large measure the result of federal legislation. The Norris - La Guardia Act (1932) eliminated "government by injunction." The National Labor Relations Act, or the Wagner Act, gave organized labor federal protection in collective bargaining, established the National Labor Relations Board to arbitrate disputes, and eliminated certain "unfair practices" of employers. Another factor spurring union growth was competition between the AFL and the Committee (later Congress) for Industrial Organization, which broke away from the older body in 1935 under the leadership of the colorful John L. Lewis of the UMW. The CIO was set up on an industry-wide basis, like the UMW and unlike other AFL craft unions. By 1945, the CIO had achieved major breakthroughs in the steel and auto industries, and had nearly as large a membership as the AFL. Many of the unionization struggles at this time were bitterly and violently fought. Senate investigations discovered massive use of union spies by business; Pinkerton alone had spies in 35 cities, with 100 holding union offices at one time.

As in the previous world war, labor agreed to abide by a no-strike agreement in World War II; and as before, the end of the war brought widespread labor strife when controls were lifted. Strikes by four and a half million workers in 1946 — including those in such vital industries as steel, autos, electrical, railroads, and coal — were a major factor in the passage of the Taft-Hartley bill in 1947. This provided a means of invoking the public interest to delay certain strikes during cooling-off periods and arbitration. A decade later, further legislation restricted labor following Senate investigations of union corruption. The AFL-CIO was forced to admit the existence of this problem when it expelled the Teamsters, Bakery and Confectionary Workers, and Laundry Workers for violations of the code of ethical practices. The Landrum-Griffith Act (1959) attempted to safeguard union funds and the fairness of elections through monitoring and reporting measures.

The most important post-war labor development was the merger of the AFL and the CIO in 1955 under the leadership of George Meany and Walter Reuther. The 15 million membership of the AFL-CIO included most important unions, excluding the UMW, a few railroad brotherhoods, and some others. The merger was agreed to only after expulsion from the CIO in 1949 of several Communist-dominated unions.

In the '60's, the United Auto Workers under Reuther broke away from the AFL-CIO to join with the Teamsters under the Alliance for Labor Action. Reuther hoped to reinvigorate a labor movement that he felt was losing sight of social goals. The effort stagnated, however, after Reuther's death in a plane crash in 1970.

When the ancient world created architectural wonders on a grand scale, the feats were accomplished with armies of slaves. Bertolt Brecht has asked

Who built the seven towers of Thebes?
The books are filled with the names of kings.
Was it kings who hauled the craggy blocks of stone? . . .
On the evenings when the Chinese wall was finished
Where did the masons go? . . .

Today we mass-produce industrial miracles, but self-organized and free men share in the rewards of their labor.

Excerpted Documents

Early labor unions, 1827-1897.

John Dunlop, Labor Economist—Harvard University, "The Development of Labor Organization: A Theoretical Framework," in *Insight Into Labor Issues*, 1948, p. 186.

[One reason for difficulty in labor organization in our early history was that] . . . this was a period in which man believed that individual advancement was to be achieved solely by work, where leisure was a vice, where economic destiny depended solely upon one's ability to work and save, where poverty could only be the reward of sloth, where the poor deserved their fate, and where the public care of the impoverished was regarded as encouragement of idleness.

Foster Dulles, Historian, *Labor in America*, 1955, p. 61.

The [1830s] proposal for a ten-hour day, one newspaper declared, "strikes the very nerve of industry and good morals by dictating the hours of labour . . . .To be idle several of the most useful hours of the morning and evening will surely lead to intemperance and ruin."

Foster Dulles, Historian, *Labor in America*, 1955, p. 75.

When the manager of one mill at Holyoke, Massachusetts found his hands "languorous" because they had breakfasted, he ordered them to come before breakfast. "I regard my work-people," an agent of another factory said, "just as I regard my machinery. So long as they can do my work for what I choose to pay them, I keep them, getting out of them all I can."

Henry Ward Beecher, in *Labor in America*, 1955, p. 122.

God intended the great to be great and the little to be little . . . I do not say that a dollar a day is enough to support a working man. But it is enough to support a man! Not enough to support a man and his children if a man insists on smoking and drinking beer . . . But the man who cannot live on bread and water is not fit to live.

Foster Dulles, Historian, *Labor in America*, 1955, p. 205.

The wage earner could find a satisfaction in membership in such a meaningful social organization as a labor union that was denied him as one among many thousands of depersonalized employees.

Albert Blum, Michigan State University, *Labor History*, Winter 1968, p. 52.

To secure "more" for their members, the business unionists who were so active in the American Federation of Labor looked toward collective bargaining rather than toward politics. In fact, they came close to viewing extensive political activity as the opiate of the masses. It dissipated the energies of a growing vital labor movement, business unionists believed, and their opinion was shared by many scholars.

Herbert Spencer, British Philosopher, *Social Statics*, 1897, p. 150.

It seems hard that an unskillfulness which with all his efforts he cannot overcome should entail hunger upon the artisan. It seems hard that a labourer incapacitated by sickness from competing with his stronger fellows, should have to bear the resulting privations. It seems hard that widows and orphans should be left to struggle for life or death. Nevertheless, when regarded not separately but in connexion [sic] with the interests of the universal humanity, these hard fatalities are seen to be full of beneficence—the same beneficence which brings to early graves the children of diseased parents, and singles out the intemperate and the debilitated as the victims of an epidemic.

Max Lerner, Professor of American Civilization—Brandeis University, *America as a Civilization: Volume 1, The Basic Frame*, 1957, p. 239.

The American factories in the early nineteenth century were very different from their European counterparts; the early factory owners tried to avoid the excesses of the English and European experience, including long hours, child labor, poor pay, and scabrous working and living conditions. Eli Whitney's factories were relatively comfortable places, with decent housing provided for the workers in the vicinity. The Lowell mills were models of comfort, and the girls who came to work in them were drawn to work in preference to the less interesting and more menial jobs of doing domestic work and teaching . . . .

The idea behind the early American factories, as Mitchell Wilson has pointed out, was that the American worker was a dignified human being entitled to decent treatment.

Howard and Ralph Wolf, *Rubber: A Story of Glory and Greed*, 1936, p. 499.

[The early twentieth century in the rubber industry was] an era of dust and soapstone loading the lungs; of workers nodding drunkenly in the benzene vapors above cement tanks; of unventilated calender rooms below the street level where men withered in the heat and the skin peeled from their bodies; of hell-hole pits where the toilers slipped about in wet underfoot.

Eugene V. Debs, during the Pullman strike of 1894, in *Labor in America*, 1955, pp. 173-174.

The struggle has developed into a contest between the producing classes and the money power of the country. We stand upon the ground that the workingmen are entitled to a just proportion of the proceeds for their labor.

B. L. Weber, Chorus to I.W.W. song, "A.F. of L. Sympathy," *Industrial Worker,* December 29, 1910, p. 2.

All we got was sympathy;
  So we were bound to lose you see;
All the others had craft autonomy,
  Or else they would have struck with glee
  But I got good and hungry,
  And no craft unions go for me.
Gee! Ain't it hell in the A.F. of L.
  All you get is sympathy.

Thomas Hagerty, Catholic Priest and I.W.W. Organizer, McClure's Magazine, May 1904, p. 49.

That railroad is yours; those large business blocks and office buildings down town that bring in big rent are yours; if you want them, go and take them.

San Diego Tribune Editorial on the I.W.W., March 4, 1912, in *Labor in America*, 1955, p. 214.

Hanging is none too good for them, they would be much better dead, for they are absolutely useless in the human economy; they are the waste material of creation and should be drained off into the sewer of oblivion. . . .

Rexford G. Tugwell, Historian, *Survey,* July 3, 1920, p. 472.

. . .one who has seen the glow of the great Wobbly dream light the faces of the lumberjacks has seen the unforgettable, the imperishable. . .they plan a new order they will never know. . .they can dream and dreaming, be happy.

August Spies, Chicago Anarchist hanged for the Haymarket riots, Address to the Court, October 7, 1866, in *Famous Speeches of the Eight Chicago Anarchists in Chicago,* 1910.

If you think that by hanging us you can stamp out the labor movement—if this is your opinion, then hang us! Here you will tread upon a spark, but here and there and behind you and in front of you, everywhere flames will blaze up. It is a subterranean fire. You cannot put it out. The ground, upon which you stand, is on fire. You don't believe in the magical arts, as your grandfathers did, who burned witches at the stake, but you believe in conspiracies. . .You want to 'stamp out the conspirators'—the 'agitators?' Ah, stamp out every factory lord who has grown wealthy upon the unpaid labor of his employees. Stamp out the landlord who has amassed fortunes from the rent of overburdened workingmen and farmers. Stamp out every machine that is revolutionizing industry and agriculture, that intensifies production, ruins the producer that increases the national wealth, while the creator of all these things stands amidst them, tantalized with hunger.

Woody Guthrie, "Union Maid," in *Songs of Work and Freedom,* 1960, p. 17.

  There once was a union maid
  She never was afraid,
  Of goons and ginks and company finks

And the deputy sheriffs that made the raid;
She went to the Union Hall
When a meeting it was called,
And when the company boys came 'round
She always stood her ground.

Chorus:
    Oh, you can't scare me, I'm sticking to the union
    I'm sticking to the union, I'm sticking to the union.
    Oh, you can't scare me, I'm sticking to the union,
    I'm sticking to the union till the day I die.

The advance of labor: Clayton Act and the New Deal.

Section 6, *Clayton Anti-Trust Act,* 1914.

The labor of a human being is not a commodity or article of commerce. Nothing contained in the anti-trust laws shall be construed to forbid the existence and operation of labor organizations instituted for the purposes of mutual help. . .

Arnold Rose, *Union Solidarity: The Internal Cohesion of a Labor Union,* 1952, p. 14.

. . . the essential fact is that many workers felt [in the mid 1930s], probably for the first time, an impelling need for an organization that would represent their interests in the manipulation of economic power. They realized they were too weak individually to get for themselves the security they craved, and they found in the trade union an instrument by which many of their needs could be satisfied.

Julius Rezler, Labor Historian—Loyola University, *Union Growth Reconsidered,* 1961, p. 8.

It was the philosophy and practice of the Democratic administrations and their receptive attitude toward unionism which primarily accounted for the spectacular growth of the unions during the two world wars and the Great Depression and not the wars and Depression themselves.

Foster R. Dulles, *Labor in America,* 1960, p. 289.

Said AFL President William Green of Lewis: "He raised the voice of dualism and disunity, a voice which while pretending to unite sought to disrupt."
Said [CIO President John L.] Lewis of Green: "Alas, poor Green. I know him well. He wishes me to join him in fluttering procrastination, the while intoning O tempera, O mores."

Eugene V. Debs, 4-time Presidential Candidate for the Socialist Party of America, *The Writing and Speeches of Eugene V. Debs,* 1948, pp. 324-325.

The workers must organize their emancipation to achieve it . . . They must unite in one and the same industrial union and one and the same political party. And the union and the party must be managed by themselves, not from the top down but from the bottom up . . . The workers and the producers . . . are the creators of society and the conservators of civilization, and when they come to realize it they will conquer in the struggle for supremacy and people the earth with a race of free men.

Union democracy.

Philip Taft, Professor of Economics—Brown University, *The Structure and Government of Labor Unions*, 1954, p. 243.

There is no proof whatsoever that members are afraid to protest the conduct of their officers . . . How can one explain the numerous appeals on job issues such as seniority, lost time, and the handling of grievances? Does this indicate fear to question local officers?

Philip Taft, Professor of Economics—Brown University, *The Structure and Government of Labor Unions*, 1954, p. 246.

The elections in local unions, the numerous complaints of various kinds against local officers, are manifestations of democracy at the "grass roots" level where it is of most importance. Far from perfect, unions fundamentally reflect the will of their members.

George W. Brooks, Research and Educational Director—International Brotherhood of Pulp, Sulphite, and Paper Mill Workers, *Proceedings of the Ninth Annual Meeting, Industrial Relations Research Association*, December 28-29, 1956, p. 36.

The great change in American labor unions during the last twenty years has been a general shift in power and control from the members to the leaders. The change was far-reaching. Within the foreseeable future, it appears to be permanent.

Philip Taft, Professor of Economics—Brown University, *The Structure and Government of Labor Unions*, 1954, p. 238.

By and large unions have resisted Communist infiltration and have played an important role in reducing Communist influence. American unionism has, in the main, been inhospitable to all forms of collectivism, and this lack of enthusiasm goes back before the Russian Revolution.

Adolph Strasser, AFL Leader, *History of Labour in the United States*, Vol. 1, p. 16.

I look first to the trade I represent . . . the interest of the men who employ me to represent their interests. We have no ultimate ends. We are going from day to day. We fight only for immediate objects—objects that will be realized in a few years . . . we are all practical men.

Union corruption.

John Hutchinson, Labor Historian—U.C.L.A., *The Imperfect Union*, 1970, p. 8.

Corruption is neither simple in origin nor easy to repair . . . It is probably too much to expect the early disappearance of all the major factors which produce trade union corruption; but if patience is required, the labor movement should not in the interim be selected for punishment irrelevant to conditions, for which, in any case, it bears only a limited responsibility.

John Hutchinson, Labor Historian—U.C.L.A., *The Imperfect Union*, 1970, p. 98.

Resistance (to labor racketeers) was dangerous. In 1937, six ILA (International Longshoremen's Association) locals in Brooklyn—once controlled by the Camarda family—came under the control of Albert Anastasia, the alleged executioner for *Murder Inc.*, chief enforcement agency of the American underworld. A young longshoreman by the name of Pete Panto led an insurgent movement against the locals and its leader, claiming in due course 1000 supporters among the members of the new local. In 1939 he disappeared, his body was found a year later in a lime pit in Ohio.

Collective bargaining: Potential harms.

James Hodgson, Secretary of Labor, *Collective Bargaining: Survival in the '70's?*, 1972, p. 6.

. . . we increasingly see collective bargaining being cast in the devil's role by the public. Today, bargaining results too often in a long and publicized struggle between giants who seem not to care who gets hurt in the process. The public is concluding it is they who suffer. When the economic system is crippled, it is the public that suffers. When inflation results from high wage settlements, it is the public that suffers. So the clamor mounts.

Franklin D. Roosevelt, quoted in *Saturday Review*, December 7, 1968, p. 30.

A strike of public employees manifests nothing less than an intent on their part to prevent or obstruct the operations of government until their demands are satisfied. Such action, looking toward the paralysis of government by those who have sworn to support it, is unthinkable and intolerable.

Jerry Wurf, President—American Federation of State, County, and Municipal Employees (AFL-CIO), *Wall Street Journal*, September 15, 1967, p. 18.

We live in a country with undreamed of wealth, a staggering productive capacity, and the most advanced technology known to man. But, we pay public employees at levels that would qualify them for welfare supplements. Yet public employee efforts to improve wages and working conditions have been regarded as arrogant and unbridled self-interest and treated in manner more appropriate to major insurrections.

Women in the work force.

Evelyn Harrison, U.S. Civil Service Commission, *Public Administration Review*, June 1964, p. 79.

In the United States there are nearly 24 million women employed in the nation's labor force, comprising over 1/3 of the total work force . . . Of all married women, more than one in three are working. Of all single women between the ages of 24 and 64, 75% are working.

Evelyn Harrison, U.S. Civil Service Commission, *Public Administration Review*, June 1964, p. 80.

A study made by the Civil Service Commission showed that more than half of the requests to fill positions above the lowest four grades (of the Civil Service) were for men only, and 94% to fill positions at the three highest grades (GS-13, 14, 15) were restricted to men . . . After agencies were required to submit supporting reasons less than one percent of the requests received specified one or the other sex.

The future of unions.

Albert Blum, Michigan State University, *Labor History*, Winter 1968, p. 39.

The concern about whether labor will grow or decline also fascinates scholars. At present, there are those who argue that workers have been organized to as great an extent as they are ever likely to be. Then there are those who believe that the historical trend indicates a gradual and steady growth in the labor movement. The former school has been labeled "saturationist"; the latter has been called by its leading exponent, Irving Bernstein, the historical school.

Irving Bernstein, Associate Director—Institute of Industrial Relations, U.C.L.A., *Labor History,* **Spring 1961, p. 157.**

The growth of the labor movement is inextricably linked to the growth of the economy. If union membership expands in the future, it will do so only as part of an expanding economic system.

Thomas Brooks, Labor Historian, *Toil and Trouble,* **1971, p. xxiii.**

Roughly one out of four union members is under 30, and there is evidence that younger workers are largely responsible for the increased frequency with which rank and file union members rejected contracts negotiated by union leaders at the end of the 1960s.

Walter Reuther, President—United Auto Workers, *New Republic,* **July 21, 1958, p. 12.**

I agree that the original labor movement was basically pure and simple trade unionism—bargaining for wages and for hours and for working conditions. But, the labor movement cannot carry out its historic mission if it continues to be no more than that. As the problems of our modern society become more complex or interwoven, their solution cannot be economic or political—the solution has got to be economic *and* political.

Walter Reuther, President—United Auto Workers, *New Republic,* **July 21, 1958, p. 16.**

The thing that bothers me is that the fellow working in the Cadillac Motor Company making the Cadillac motorcar can be a part of making that Cadillac, and yet when he looks at it he gets no sense of creative achievement. In an earlier technology, a craftsman—no matter what he made—there was a little bit of him in what he made. There was a sense of creation. And when God made us in his own image, he also gave to us some creative capacity. That is being starved.

A. H. Raskin, Labor Correspondent—*New York Times, Toil and Trouble: A History of American Labor,* **1971, p. vi.**

Organized labor, at the zenith of its economic and political strength, peers timorously into an automated future that may leave it an impotent pigmy. The proud boast of the American labor movement is still *Labor Omnia Vincit.* But no sense of triumph buoys the laders of labor as they struggle to adapt the techniques of collective bargaining to the dizzying new challenges of an era of rapid technological change.

Selected Bibliography

Abbot, William L. *The American Labor Heritage.* Honolulu: Industrial Relations Center, University of Hawaii, 1967.

Alinsky, Saul. *John L. Lewis.* New York: G.P. Putnam's Sons, 1949.

Barbash, Jack. "American Unionism: From Protest to Going Concern." *Journal of Economic Issues,* (March 1968), 45.

Barkin, Solomon. *The Decline of the Labor Movement.* Santa Barbara, Calif.: Center for the Study of Democratic Institutions, 1961.

Beard, Mary. *A Short History of the American Labor Movement.* New York: Greenwood Press, 1968.

Bell, Daniel. *Work and Its Discontents.* New York: League for Industrial Development, 1960.

Bernstein, Irving. "The Growth of American Unions, 1945-60." *Labor History,* 2 (1961), 131.

Bernstein, Irving. *The Lean Years: A History of the American Worker 1920-1933.* Boston: Houghton-Mifflin Company, 1960.

Blum, Albert A. "Why Unions Grow." *Labor History,* 9 (1968), 39.

Brooks, Thomas R. *Toil and Trouble: A History of American Labor.* New York: Delacorte Press, 1971.

Cohen, Samford. *Labor in the United States.* Columbus, Ohio: Charles E. Merrill Publishing Co., 1970.

Commons, John R., and Associates. *History of Labour in the United States.* New York: Macmillan, 1921.

Derber, Milton, and Young, Edwin, eds. *Labor and the New Deal.* Madison: University of Wisconsin Press, 1957.

Dubofsky, Melvyn. *We Shall Be All: Industrial Workers of the World.* Chicago: Quadrangle Books, 1969.

Dulles, Foster, R. *Labor in America.* New York: T.Y. Crowell Co., 1955.

Dunlop, John T., and Healy, James J. "The Collective Bargaining Process." *Collective Bargaining: Principles and Cases.* Honewood, Illinois: Richard D. Irwin, Inc., 1953.

Estey, Martin. *The Unions: Structure, Development, and Management.* New York: Harcourt, Brace, and World, Inc., 1967.

"Fifty Years of Progress in American Labor." *Monthly Labor Review,* 71 (1950), 1.

Foner, Philips S. *History of the Labor Movement in the United States.* New York: International Publishers, 1962.

Fuchs, Estelle. *Pickets at the Gates: A Problem in Administration.* New York: Free Press, 1966.

Goldberg, Arthur. *AFL-CIO, Labor United.* New York: McGraw-Hill Book Company, 1956.

Gompers, Samuel. *Seventy Years of Life and Labor.* 2 vols. New York: E.P. Dutton and Company, 1934.

Greenstone, David J. *Labor in American Politics.* New York: Knopf, 1969.

Grob, Gerald N. "Reform Unionism: The National Labor Union." *Journal of Economic History,* 18 (1958), 176.

Harrison, Evelyn. "The Working Woman: Barriers in Employment." *Public Administration Review,* 24 (1964), 78.

Howe, Irving, and Widick, B.J. *The UAW and Walter Reuther.* New York: Random House, 1949.

Hutchinson, John. *The Imperfect Union: History of Corruption in American Trade Unions.* New York: Dutton, 1970.

Kampelman, Max. *The Communist Party vs. the CIO.* New York: Frederick A. Praeger, 1957.

Kutler, Stanley I. "Labor, Clayton Act, and Supreme Court." *Labor History,* 3 (1962), 19.

Leiserson, William. *American Trade Union Democracy.* New York: Columbia University Press, 1959.

Levy, B.H. "Collective Bargaining." *Harvard Business Review,* 26 (1948), 468.

Lipset, Seymour Martin; Trow, Martin A.; and Coleman, James S. *Union Democracy.* New York: Doubleday and Company, Inc., 1962.

Marx, Herbert L., Jr. *Collective Bargaining for Public Employees.* New York: H.W. Wilson Company, 1969.

Mayer, Thomas. "Some Characteristics of Union Members in 1880s and 1890s." *Labor History,* 5 (1964), 57.

Murray, Robert K. "Public Opinion, Labor, and Clayton Act." *Historian,* 21 (1959), 255.

Pelling, Henry. *American Labor.* Chicago: University of Chicago Press, 1960.

Peterson, Florence. *American Labor Unions.* New York: Harper and Row, 1963.

Rayback, Joseph G. *History of American Labor.* New York: Macmillan, 1959.

Rowan, Richard L. *Collective Bargaining: Survival in the 70s?* Philadelphia: University of Pennsylvania Press, 1972.

Seidman, Joel. *American Labor from Defense to Reconversion.* Chicago: University of Chicago Press, 1953.

Taft, Philip. *The AF of L in the Time of Gompers.* New York: Harper and Brothers, 1959.

Taft, Philip. *The AF of L from the Death of Gompers to the Merger.* New York: Harper and Brothers, 1959.

Ware, Norman J. *The Industrial Worker, 1840-1860: The Reaction of American Industrial Society to the Advance of the Industrial Revolution.* Boston: Houghton-Mifflin, 1924.

Yellen, Samuel. *American Labor Struggles.* New York: Russell and Russell, Inc., 1956.

ISSUE VI
THE BUSINESS OF AMERICA. . .

SECTIONAL EVENTS—COLLEGE AGE ISSUE
January 31—March 6, 1976

DEBATE   Resolved: That governmental policy towards the American economy has benefitted
                consumers at the expense of producers.

PERSUASIVE   Advertising—the vernacular of America?

EXTEMPORANEOUS   Private Enterprise in the Marketplace

1. Has the business of America always been business?
2. The small businessman: What does his decline mean to the American economy?
3. Antitrust: Has it been a boon to the American economy?
4. Cartel, monopoly, and oligopoly: Are today's enemies yesterday's benefactors?
5. What has been the impact of the profit motive and free enterprise system on our natural resources?
6. When should the business of business be government?
7. What was the role of American enterprise in the American revolution?
8. How has concentration of economic power affected the American psyche?
9. Has economic concentration historically been inflationary?
10. Has America ever had a free-market economy?
11. Has American industry been overregulated during the 20th century?
12. The planned economy during two World Wars: How well did it work? Would it work as well in peacetime?
13. Would the Tennessee Valley Authority represent a better model for government energy policy than the regulatory agency approach?

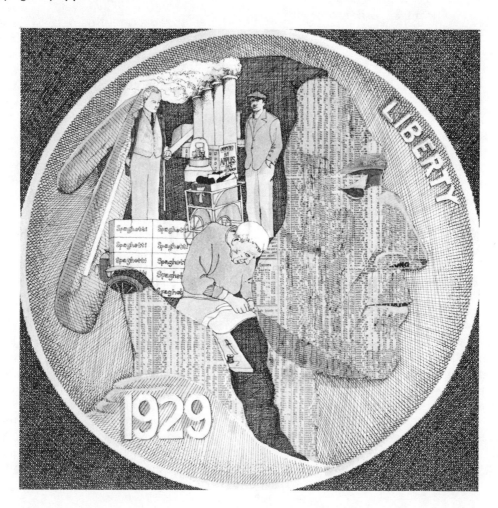

RESOLVED: THAT GOVERNMENTAL POLICY TOWARDS THE AMERICAN ECONOMY HAS BENEFITTED CONSUMERS AT THE EXPENSE OF PRODUCERS.

Introductory Essay

Adam Smith's *The Wealth of Nations* has sometimes been referred to as "the businessman's Bible." The ideas presented within it have become a large part of the theoretical justification for a laissez-faire economic policy for government. Smith's writings, however, contain a warning of what could be expected from uncontrolled business power.

> The interest of the dealers . . . in any particular branch of trade, or manufacturers, is always in some respect different from, and even opposite to, that of the public. To widen the market and to narrow the competition, is always the interest of the dealers . . . The proposal of any new law or regulation of commerce which comes from this order . . . comes from an order of men . . . who have generally an interest to deceive and even to oppress the public, and who accordingly have, upon many occasions, both deceived and oppressed it.

The American government has always recognized some need for regulation of industry, although the type and scope of regulation has changed drastically over time. The appropriateness of the various governmental responses to business practices through our history is raised in the issue, "Resolved: that governmental policy towards the American economy has benefitted consumers at the expense of producers."

The consumer movement is of relatively recent origin in the United States, but it appears to have become a permanent institution. The widespread public respect for consumer advocates like Ralph Nader, the favorable reception of dozens of consumer exposé paperbacks, and the establishment in 1970 of the Consumer Protection Agency are all indications of a groundswell of public opinion generated almost entirely in the 1960's. The topic is not limited to discussion merely of these most recent consumer trends, however, nor even of legislation dating from the "muckraking" period of social reform in America. Rather, a broad range of governmental activities spanning most of the history of our nation

fall within its purview; taxation, licensing, tariffs, quotas, and antitrust legislation, as well as the more obvious areas of health, safety, and marketing practices all deserve analysis. Congressman Benjamin Rosenthal has estimated that there are approximately 50 federal agencies and bureaus performing some 200 or 300 functions affecting the consumer. Since it would be virtually impossible to adequately study and evaluate the work of all these bodies, it becomes necessary to focus on broad historical trends and general characteristics of government regulation, with specific examples for illustration.

The government's approach to the consumer and producer interests may be divided into several periods. The first of these extended from the founding of the country to the Civil War. In general, it could be characterized as a period of laissez-faire economics, emphasizing a minimum of government intervention. Legally, the common law principle of caveat emptor (Let the buyer beware) prevailed. In large part, this was justified. The United States was primarily an agrarian society, with little need for government regulation. Goods and products were generally of such a nature that their value could be established before purchase. The seller of a product was generally known to the community and maintained his reputation by the quality of goods produced. The courts had little sympathy for the man who failed to exercise elementary caution when making a purchase. What little governmental economic policy existed could be found mainly in tariff provisions, which tended to be fairly high during this period, in an attempt to protect domestic industry from foreign competition.

After the Civil War, a different attitude slowly developed. The rapid growth of the nation reduced the opportunity to buy from a personally known seller. The materialistic, "get-rich-quick" attitude encouraged by the settlement of the frontier created a business outlook that boded ill for the consumer. Henry O. Havemeyer, president of the "Sugar Trust," summarized this point of view. "Let the buyer beware; that covers the whole business. You can not wet-nurse people from the time they are born until the time they die. They have got to wade in and get stuck, and that is the way men are educated and cultivated."

It was industrialization, however, which sparked the radical transformation of official governmental relations to the business communities. The Civil War represented a watershed; manufactured goods became the staple of the nation's taste. Gone were the halcyon days of the individual craftsman. The period from 1860 to 1900 was one of incredible growth for business interests. Capital investments in industry increased from one-half billion in 1850 to $44 billion in 1920, while the value of manufactured products showed an equally spectacular rise. By 1890, manufacturing had replaced agriculture as the most important sector of the national economy. With increased industrialization came the rise of corporations. These were no new phenomena; but the desire to operate on a large scale, combined with lax state laws, vastly expanded the use of the corporate entity. By 1904, though only 24% of all manufacturing establishments were incorporated, they produced nearly 74% of the total value of all manufactured products. Even greater concentration of economic control was brought about by the elimination of smaller competitors, as well as the establishment of trusts—whereby persons holding only a small percentage of a corporation's stock were able to control its operation. This system of absentee ownership and corporate anonymity worked to reduce personal responsibility and concern for the consumer, making a revised attitude toward government's responsibility inevitable.

The first manifestation of this new role came with the Mail Frauds Statute of 1872; and in 1886, the creation of the Interstate Commerce Commission. The railroad had become integral to the development of the West. With no easy alternative for shippers and near-monopolies in many areas, the railroads were in a position to dictate their own terms. Farmers began to complain about absurdly high rates, differential rates for long-haul as opposed to short-haul shippers, and special rates for favored customers. The establishment of the ICC constituted a recognition of the fact that the "invisible hand" of competition could not be relied upon in rail transport.

At about the same time an extensive campaign to regulate food had begun. Beginning in 1879, over one hundred bills were introduced in Congress for the regulation of various foods and drugs. The demise of caveat emptor was evident, as is reflected in testimony by the state veterinarian of Minnesota on the 1891 meat inspection act:

It is impossible for the masses to acquire this particular knowledge (detecting diseased meats) in the other engagements of life. Individual self-protection seems impossible; consequently it falls upon the government, State or general, to provide a protection for our health and life alike in this direction.

Government action was prodded by the efforts of a group of investigative journalists and writers, called "muckrakers" by their detractors. The most famous single work, Upton Sinclair's *The Jungle*, described the appalling conditions in the Chicago stockyards. Widespread public indignation prompted remedial legislation; Sinclair's revelations provided impetus for the Food and Drug Act of 1906, as well as the Agricultural Meat Inspection Act of 1907.

This period also produced the first attempt to regulate the basic structure of the market itself: the Sherman Anti-Trust Act of 1890. Riddled with loopholes, the Act was a failure, and had to be corrected by later legislation. But its significance lies largely in the fact that it was passed at all. The lobbying efforts of industry were able to modify, but not kill the bill. The Sherman Act enjoyed wide, bi-partisan support.

Mention might also be made of the Federal Reserve System, created in 1913. Although not established primarily for consumers, it served the purpose of encouraging competition by curbing the power of the great bankers. J. Pierpont Morgan's notorious remark, "I owe the public nothing," was doubtless familiar to the framers of this legislation. Federal loans for businessmen and farmers also helped to create a more competitive situation.

The third period in consumer history extends from the First World War to the Depression. In general, it was a period of lethargy, punctuated by attempts at consolidation. The defects of the Sherman Act were ameliorated by the Clayton Act and the establishment of the Federal Trade Commission, both enacted in 1914. The FTC was given a broad legal mandate—it was empowered to prohibit any "unfair methods of competition." A conservative Supreme Court neatly emasculated the meaning of this provision, however, by defining "unfair methods" only as practices already prohibited by the common law or another statutory provision.

The Transportation and Water Power Acts of 1920 created the Federal Power Commission, originally designed only to manage hydroelectric power in the public interest. Through the years, this body has gradually been assigned so many additional duties that it now ranks as one of the most important consumer agencies in government. The Sixteenth Amendment, passed in 1913, provided the basis for corporate income tax which, coupled with various excises already imposed on industry, provided the government with powerful redistributive tools.

During the postwar period there was also some tariff experimentation. An attempt was made to lessen the effect of protective tariffs on the American consumer—by providing that tariffs on foreign goods should represent only the production cost differential between them and domestic goods—and thus allow for possible competition, expressed legislatively in 1922 as the Fordney-McCumber Tariff Act. Manufacturing interests favoring high tariffs were quick to rally, however, and by 1930 had a response in the form of the Smoot-Hawley Act, which reinstated tariffs at an all-time high.

The fourth general period of consumer history began with the Depression-New Deal era and extended to about 1950. This period marked a great expansion in the powers of the Federal Trade Commission. In 1938, the Wheeler-Lee Act expanded the FTC's mandate beyond actions against unfair methods of competition to include "unfair or deceptive acts or practices in commerce," giving the Commission direct authority for consumer protection. In addition to this general mandate, Congress provided more specific imperatives in the form of the Wool Products Labeling Act of 1940 and the Fur Products Labeling Act of 1951. In 1938, the regulatory ability of the Food and Drug Administration was also greatly enhanced by passage of the Food, Drug and Cosmetics Act, which added some new areas to FDA control, most notably the use of cosmetics which could cause disfigurement, blindness, and paralysis.

A more rational tariff system also came about in this period as a result of the "trade war" caused by the Smoot-Hawley Act. The Reciprocal Trade Agreements Act of 1934 established a system of bilateral agreements to adjust tariffs to promote both the interests of the exporting and importing nations. In 1947, this system was made multilateral by the General Agreements on Tariff and Trade (GATT). Signatory nations hold periodic conferences to discuss and compromise on tariff issues. The system is by no means perfect, but it has prevented the resumption of trade wars, and has consequently benefitted consumers.

The period from 1950 to the present began rather mildly. One commentator in 1959 likened it to the period of dormancy prior to the Depression. A series of legislative enactments in the 1960's, however, have led some to refer to these years as "The Decade of the Consumer." In 1962, the Kefauver-Harris Amendments provided significant reform in the labeling of prescription drugs and the testing of new drugs. The Fair Packaging and Labeling Act was passed in 1966, as was legislation on tire and automobile safety. Many other measures affected the consumer, the most significant being the Consumer Protection Agency's establishment in 1970. The broad appeal of consumerism (in President Kennedy's words: "Consumers, by definition, include us all"(makes it likely that this trend will continue.

Wartime periods have been passed over in this historical survey, since they are by nature atypical of the normal trends in business. During war years, the government has emphasized production, even to the extent of operating plants and mandating output levels, while restricting consumption through such means as rationing. Wartime measures have not generally been considered as beneficial to either consumers or producers, but rather as necessary actions to meet the demands of the national defense.

In the prevailing public atmosphere, it seems almost unthinkable to suggest that the consumer interest might be outweighed by business considerations. Yet there is considerable merit to this position. Consumer advocates tend to sensationalize their findings, often at the expense of the truth.

Consider the widely-quoted figure of $200 billion as the cost of consumer abuse, suggested by Senator Hart and popularized by Ralph Nader. The figure seems to be a strong argument for consumer reform, until one realizes, as Ralph K. Winters, professor of law at Yale, points out, that $200 billion is substantially in excess of total profits for all businesses and almost quadruple total corporate profits. Consumer advocates often argue their cases from spectacular examples, with little hard data to show general abuse. And the public, consciously or unconsciously, often places other values higher than "consumerism": buying a sports car rather than a safer model, spending $100 for a label on a suit, or paying twenty dollars for a nutritionally imbalanced meal.

Many examples are available of legislation that may protect consumer interests, but only at the expense of other potentially greater interests. FPC interconnection of power lines for consumer benefit, for example, has exacerbated the problems of power blackouts. Stricter federal pollution standards can impose severe costs on industry for marginal benefits to the public. Legislation relating to agricultural production and prices has contributed to many of the problems of the American farmer. Even attempts at protectionist policies have often hurt industry. Adverse foreign reaction to the Smoot-Hawley tariffs and the resulting trade war caused nearly a 75% decline in American exports.

In the antitrust area, it appears that substantial industrial losses are incurred to provide greater competition. Fear of collusion charges may have inhibited the development of safety features on automobiles, as well as generally placing U.S. manufacturers at a disadvantage with foreign competitors whose governments often encourage research collaboration among industries. Large and concentrated industries do not always charge higher prices (some reputable economists claim that they generally offer lower prices), but it is clear that large concerns enjoy substantial economies of scale in plant size as well as managerial efficiency.

A more recent example might be the 1962 Kefauver-Harris Drug Amendments, which required that any prescription drug on the market must not only be safe, but effective. The rationale for eliminating useless drugs is appealing, and Dr. Donald Brodie of HEW estimated annual consumer savings in the range of one to two billion dollars. The new regulations, however, exacerbated an already lengthy process of drug approval, producing an overall negative impact on medicine. The *Medical Tribune* reported that a commission of experts in 1972 concluded that "the FDA's policies since 1962 have brought about a stifling of scientific creativity, escalation of research costs, and a continuing decline in the number of new drugs entering the market in this country."

In a different vein, one might wish to examine legislation that originally may have been useful, but which has been rendered harmful by changing circumstances and bureaucratic inertia. An example might be the ICC. Originally there was a real need for the Interstate Commerce Commission to regulate railroads. They held a monopoly on a public service and were abusing monopoly power. Today, railroads argue, there is substantial competition from different forms of transportation: trucks, water transport, and air. ICC rate regulation today, then, is not controlling a monopoly but hampering any attempts at competition.

An additional illustration might be Federal Power Commission regulation of natural gas prices. Originally, inadequate state regulation forced the federal government to control interstate transmission and wellhead prices. With the energy crisis and increased environmental awareness, pollution-free natural gas is now at a premium, and federal regulation has had perverse results. Regulated prices kept at a chronically low level have discouraged development of new gas fields, and differential interstate-intrastate prices have hampered fuel allocation in times of shortage.

Consideration can also be given to the possible adverse effects governmental policing or ownership of business can have. Certainly government firms which operate at a loss or at low-profit levels will offer traditional business interests severe and likely damaging competition. From the point of view, in short, of privately owned and operated utility companies, for example, the TVA is less than desirable competition. The same fundamental clash of economic assumptions is to be seen in such enterprises as public transit, the parcel activities of the Postal Service, and other, governmentally subsidized businesses. But, of course, a defense of such a governmental role in economic affairs is not difficult to imagine. One has only to recall that much of what stands today as government regulation was a direct, though not always speedy, consequence of widespread abuses of the public interest by private concerns. For instance, the Pure Food and Drug Act was passed only after public revulsion at the conditions revealed in *The Jungle*. The Food, Drug, and Cosmetics Act of 1938 might have died on the floor of the House had it not been for the publicity occasioned by the Elixir of Sulfanilamide catastrophe, and the 1962 amendments were passed after a narrow escape from a thalidomide disaster. Similarly, antitrust activity can be traced to public outrage at a series of business abuses.

Further, some of the purely protectionist policies toward business through history may be detailed. Tariffs, subsidies, and tax exemptions abound. Hidden subsidies for airlines through mail contracts, government underwriting of construction costs for the merchant marine, "strategic" stockpiles of surplus commodities might be singled out for analysis.

The administration of regulatory agencies offers a further area for analysis. Judge Campbell in the *Thill Securities* case noted that historically regulatory agencies have usually become protective of the interests they were designed to regulate. Members of the ICC and the FPC with disturbing regularity, for example, find jobs with the transport or energy industry after their commission terms expire. Since most of the people with sufficient expertise to regulate an industry are members of that industry, it is not surprising that these persons, when serving as regulators, are sympathetic to the industry position.

Finally, one should address the assumption that the interests of industry and the consumer necessarily differ. Although high tariffs benefit some segments of industry at the expense of the consumer, they usually harm other parts of the producing sector, notably exporters, multinationals, and firms dependent on imported raw materials. And while shoddy business practices might help the unscrupulous, they also cause public distrust of the reputable businessman. For this reason, it is not surprising to find that some of the strongest lobbying for the Fur Products Labeling Act came from the Master Furriers' Guild.

The appropriateness of governmental policy toward business is not an easy issue to resolve. At any given point in time, some elements of the government have espoused consumer policies, others emphasized business welfare, and often each worked in direct contravention of the other. Some legislation has favored both consumers and producers, and some, regrettably, has favored neither. Nor is there an easily identifiable "consumer" or "producer" position, since the tastes of consumers and the interests of producers may vary markedly. Therefore, an analyst must distill basic trends as well as extract specific elements to formulate a coherent position on governmental regulation of the economy.

Excerpted Documents

Do the interests of consumers and producers necessarily differ?

David Hamilton, *The Consumer in Our Economy*, 1962, p. 330.

This concept of the role of the conumser was but one-half of a nineteenth century economic philosophy which held *laissez faire* to be a proper economic policy for government. On the supply side the government should stay out of the way of private free enterprise, of producers seeking their own self-interest. On the demand side the government should allow a self-seeking consumer, a person believed to know what he wants and how he can best get it, to follow the dictates of his own conscience.

Elmer E. Smead, *Governmental Promotion and Regulation of Business*, 1969, p. 179.

It should not be concluded that the government always had to resort to coercion in enforcing the law. To the contrary, many concerns sought information from the bureau and made deliberate efforts to carry out its regulations. Some even spent money, at times considerable amounts, to make changes in their equipment and methods of production. Some helped to strengthen enforcement of the law by reporting violators.

On numerous occasions, government and industry cooperated. For example, when the canners of catsup and tomato sauce were unable to eliminate decomposed materials, the bureau developed a method of determining the amount of objectionable matter in the finished product and the industry, using this technique, reorganized its methods of canning. The case of Maine blueberries is another illustration. At one time, canned berries were so heavily infested with worms that the very existence of the industry was threatened. The experts of the bureau thereupon developed a piece of machinery which eliminated the unfit berries before they were canned. Instead of destroying the livelihood of canners and farmers by suppressing interstate shipment of the fruit, the industry and the government cooperated to the end of protecting the consumer and saving the industry.

Bolton Hall, *Game of Life*, in Upton Sinclair's *The Cry for Justice*, 1915, p. 710.

"Times are hard," said the Picked Chicken.
"Why," said the Rat, "this is an era of prosperity; see how I have feathered my nest."
"But," said the Picked Chicken, "you have gotten my feathers."
"You must not think," said the Rat, "that because I get more comfort you get poorer."
"But," said the Picked Chicken, "you produce no feathers and I keep none—" . . .
"Without consumers like me," said the Rat, "there would be no demand for the feathers which you produce."
"I shall vote for a change," said the Picked Chicken.
"Only those who have feathers should have the Privilege of voting," remarked the Rat.

Has business misused market power?

Alexis de Toqueville, in *Life in America*, 1951, p. 550.

I am of the opinion . . . that the manufacturing aristocracy which is growing up under our eyes is one of the harshest that ever existed in the world; but at the same time it is one of the most confined and least dangerous. Nevertheless, the friends of democracy should keep their eyes anxiously fixed in this direction; for if ever a permanent inequality of conditions and aristocracy again penetrates into the world, it may be predicted that this is the gate by which they will enter.

Harold Faulkner, *The Decline of Laissez Faire, 1897-1917*, 1951, p. 373.

Government interference in railroad transportation did not come until developing monopoly practices had curtailed what little competition remained. The transformation of the American railroad systems from a conglomeration of hundreds of independent lines to seven or eight huge combinations took place largely after 1897. Where such consolidations did not achieve an area monopoly, the railroads, as in New England, often reached out to control other types of transportation. Despite the fact that the railroads were admittedly consolidating to eliminate competition that endangered efficiency and profits, the Hepburn Act showed little interest in the strictly monopolistic aspects of the problem.

Ralph Nader and Mark Green, *Corporate Power in America*, 1973, pp. vii-viii.

As law professor Abe Chayes has written, "the modern business corporation emerged as the first successful institutional claimant of significant unregulated power since the nation-state established its title in the sixteenth and seventeenth centuries." Our large corporations are unparalleled as buffers shielding their executive decision-makers from public inquiry and accountability. A supposed democracy should not suffer the exercise of such uncontrolled power.

***First Annual Report of the Interstate Commerce Commission*, December 1, 1887, p. 5.**

Those who have controlled the railroads have not only made rules for the government of their own corporate affairs, but very largely also they have determined at pleasure what should be the terms of their contract relations with others, and others have acquiesced, though oftentimes unwillingly, because they could not with confidence affirm that the law would not compel it, and a test of the question would be difficult and expensive. The carriers of the country were thus enabled to determine in great measure what rules should govern the transportation of persons and property; rules which intimately concerned the commercial, industrial, and social life of the people.

Elmer E. Smead, *Governmental Promotion and Regulation of Business*, 1969, p. 175.

The market (before 1908) was flooded with nostrums which contained alcohol, opium, cocaine or morphine. Hence, such "medicines" as painkillers, headache powders, and soothing syrups for infants gave relief but produced no cures and sometimes even created the drug habit. Some alleged cures were worthless. For example, numerous "medicines" for the treatment of cancer were on the market. People were being led to undertake self-medication until it became too late for effective medical treatment by reputable and competent physicians. Also, some medicines were below standard in strength or purity according to the American Pharmacopoeia and thus did not have the remedial effects to be expected in the treatment of illnesses. Doctors could not always rely upon the drugs they were prescribing for their patients.

***First Annual Report of the Interstate Commerce Commission*, December 1, 1887, p. 8.**

The abuses of corporate authority to the injury of the public were not the only reasons operating upon the public mind to bring about the legislation now under consideration; some other things which in their direct effects were wrongs to stockholders only had their influence also, and this by no means a light one. The manner in which corporate stocks were manipulated for the benefit of managers and to the destruction of the interest of the owners was often a great scandal, resulting sometimes in the bankruptcy and practical destruction of roads which, if properly managed, would have been not only profitable but widely useful. This in its direct results might be a wrong to individuals only, but in its indirect influence it was a great public wrong also.

Elmer E. Smead, *Governmental Promotion and Regulation of Business*, 1969, p. 175.

Investigations produced much evidence to the effect that the limited scope of governmental regulation was failing to protect consumers. In the first place, some products on the market were injurious to health. For example, in the attempt to retard spoilage the food manufacturers used preservatives. In so far as these prevented the contamination of food by decomposition, the public health benefited. Unfortunately, however, some of the preservatives were injurious chemicals, such as boric acide, borax, and formaldehyde. Canned fruits and vegetables were laced with dangerous copper and aluminum salts. In the attempt to make foods more attractive, artificial coloring was used and sometimes proved to be deleterious. For example, investigators discovered canned cherries which had been picked green, bleached with acid and then colored with a poisonous analine dye to give the desired redness.

"Commodore" Cornelius Vanderbilt, in *The American Pageant*, 1956, p. 525.

"Law! What do I care about the law? Hain't I got the power?"

Thomas A. Bailey, Stanford University, *The American Pageant*, 1956, pp. 532-533.

Rockefeller's oil monopoly did turn out a superior product at a relatively cheap price. It achieved important economies, both at home and abroad, by its large-scale methods of production and distribution. This, in truth, was the tale of the other trusts as well. The efficient use of expensive machinery called for bigness, and consolidation proved more profitable than ruinous price wars.

William H. Vanderbilt, 1882, in *The American Pageant*, 1956, p. 519.

The railroads are not run for the benefit of the dear public. That cry is all nonsense. They are built for men who invest their money and expect to get a fair percentage on the same.

Senator Warren Magnuson and Jean Carper, *The Dark Side of the Marketplace*, 1967, p. 125.

One hundred thousand persons will be mangled or killed while operating power mowers, countless others by tools in the workshop. About 100,000 persons will be cut, disfigured or fatally injured while walking through glass doors. Twelve thousand persons will die, and 150,000 will suffer excruciating pain and often lifelong scars from fires, resulting from a match or lighted cigarette dropped on flammable clothing or upholstery. At least 1,000 will be electrocuted and many more burned and injured by faulty electrical equipment. Babies will strangle in ill-designed cribs; women will be poisoned by the noxious fumes of cleaning fluids; whole families will be asphyxiated by carbon monoxide from faulty heaters; youngsters will be cut, blinded and killed by dangerously designed toys. The list could go on almost endlessly.

Ralph Nader, *Consumerism: Search for the Consumer Interest*, 1971, p. 58.

The consumer movement is still a feeble force in American power politics. The interests of consumers are low on the list of election issues; the government's expenditures to protect those interests are negligible. Some would argue that this situation will inevitably prevail in view of the overwhelming power of American corporations in and out of government. But, as I have tried to show, new approaches to judging and influencing corporate behavior have begun to emerge in the last few years. It seems possible that people may begin to react with greater anger to the enormity of their deprivation . . . What the consumer movement is beginning to say —and must say much more strongly if it is to grow—is that business crime and corporate intransigence are the really urgent menace to law and order in America.

Has government regulation been effective?

William Graham Sumner, Professor of Sociology and Anthropology—Yale University, 1883, in *Problems in American History*, 1958, p. 408.

The consequence is that men lose the true education in freedom which is needed to support free institutions. They are taught to rely upon government officers and inspectors. The whole system of government inspectors is corrupting to free institutions. . . . social regulation by boards, commissioners, and inspectors consists in relieving negligent people of the consequences of their negligence and so leaving them to continue negligence without correction.

James E. Anderson, *The Emergence of the Modern Regulatory State*, 1962, p. 9.

Regulation was regarded by many as the middle way, as a moderate, yet adequate solution for the economic problems of the era. It avoided the unacceptable extremes of laissez faire and socialism. This idea was well-expressed by the editor of *The Outlook*, Lyman Abbott: "It is true that there is a danger in strong government, but there is a greater danger in weak government; true that there is a danger in a bureaucracy; but there is greater danger in private monopoly immune from legal control. The remedy for evils of such monopoly is not to be found in the disorganization of industry. It is not to be found in the ownership and operation of the organized industries by the State. As is so often the case, the remedy is to be found in a pathway between the two extremes. It lies neither in unrestricted individualism or State socialism. It lies in subjecting the combinations of labor and commerce to governmental regulation and control. It lies in the frank adoption and consistent application of that principle which is fundamental to all social order . . . liberty under law."

August Bolino, American University, *The Development of the American Economy*, 1966, p. 361.

The decision in the Knight case strengthened the optimism of the trust barons in their belief that the Sherman Act was impractical and unenforceable. In fact, the act worked in favor of the manufacturers since it could be applied against the unions. In the strike of the American Railway Union, the government obtained an injunction against Eugene Debs, and subsequently contempt proceedings were brought against him and the union. In this case, the Federal Circuit Court declared that the Sherman Act was meant to include not only combinations of capital, but also any type of combination restraining trade.

Roger G. Noll, Research Associate—The Brookings Institution, *Reforming Regulation*, 1971, p. 54.

Most observers believe the FDA could be far tougher in dealing with the drug industry. The agency often takes a strangely neutral stance, as though the burden of proof should be on users or the medical profession to show that a drug is unsafe or ineffective. A 1971 case involving contaminated glassware containing liquids for intravenous feeding illustrates the attitude. The FDA did not place even a temporary embargo on use of the product until an investigation could be made even though the investigation was to take only a few days.

Roger G. Noll, Research Associate—The Brookings Institution, *Reforming Regulation*, 1971, p. 57.

The FDA shares the problem of most regulatory agencies that most of the job opportunities available to their employees after they leave government service are in the regulated industry. This is bound to raise the suspicion that staff members are overly responsive, or at least subconsciously sympathetic, to the needs and claims of the industry simply because in the long run they will probably be working in the industry.

Louis M. Kohlmeier, Jr., *The Regulators*, 1969, p. 195.

Soon after President Kennedy took office, he drubbed the FPC for its "incredible backlog" of some four thousand gas rate increases adding up to more than $500 million a year. The new President's adviser on regulatory agencies, James Landis, slapped hard at the FPC for taking six years in deciding how to regulate producers' prices, claiming, "The recent action of the commission in promulgating area rates . . . has come far too late to protect the consumer. The Federal Power Commission," Jim Landis added, "without question represents the outstanding example in the Federal government of the breakdown of the administrative process."

Roger G. Noll, Research Associate—The Brookings Institution, *Reforming Regulation*, 1971, p. 57.

The [Antitrust] division has . . . had a few periods when its performance is regarded as having been especially bad. For example, its performance during the last part of the Eisenhower administration receives generally good marks; but the marks are very low for the early Eisenhower period. When the Republicans took office in 1953, a number of extremely important and far-reaching antitrust cases were in process. Virtually all were settled through consent decrees that did not go as far as had been intended when the cases were opened.

George Soule and Vincent P. Caroso, *American Economic History*, 1957, p. 470.

During World War I the antitrust laws were temporarily in abeyance. Soon afterwards, the Republicans achieved power and were not eager to prosecute. In the three Republican administrations from 1921 to 1932 an average of only 14 cases a year were begun, and a number of these were against labor. The era was marked by new mergers and holding company formation notably in electric utilities, railroads, retail stores, and other distributive services. It was also marked by the growth of already existing corporations to great size as in automobiles, and by the disappearance of many of the smaller competitors.

Has governmental subsidization of business harmed consumers?

Thomas A. Bailey, Stanford University, *The American Pageant*, 1956, pp. 519-520.

Congress . . . began to advance liberal loans to two favored companies in 1862, and added enormous donations of acreage paralleling the tracks. All told, the Washington government rewarded the railroads with 155,504,994 acres, while the western states contributed 49,000,000 more—a total area much larger than Texas . . . in some cases the profits from the sale of lands more than paid the cost of laying the rails. Loud criticisms, especially in later years, were leveled at the lavish disposal of so valuable a birthright to greedy corporations. But critics were prone to overlook the fact that the land was virtually useless until the railroads could open it up to people and industry. Besides, the government itself received certain valuable services from the subsidized lines, including preferential rates for military purposes.

Douglas C. North, American University, *Growth and Welfare in the American Past*, 1966, pp. 101-103.

Did the government, in fact, realize these differences—that is, was the government a wise investor? The investment of New York State in the Erie Canal immediately comes to mind. This was a brilliant venture that yielded handsomely to society. But in the same breath, we can mention the Pennsylvania Main Line Canal, a rather spectacular and costly failure. When we assess the total investment in canals, the results are still inconclusive. Some, such as the Ohio canals in which the state government invested substantially, may or may not have been successful ventures and worthwhile for society. Others were clear failures and indeed went bankrupt very shortly.

George Soule and Vincent P. Caroso, *American Economic History*, 1957, p. 474.

By 1933 the federal government was actually lending money to embarrassed railroads, through the Reconstruction Finance Corporation. In the same year the Railroad Emergency Act attempted to come to their rescue by setting up a Federal Railroad Coordinator who, with the assistance of committees from the carriers, was to initiate the reorganization of railroad finance and so reduce their fixed charges, to avoid waste in the railroads' operation and to improve their credit. Under the guidance of Coordinator Joseph B. Eastman, an able ICC commissioner, numerous companies finally, in this emergency, squeezed the water out of their capitalization. The Act, far too late, brought railroad holding corporations under the control of the Interstate Commerce Commission. By that time virtually all the profit that could be made out of railroad mergers had been amassed and much of it had disappeared as well.

Who benefits from government policies in international trade?

D.G. Harriman, *American Tariffs from Plymouth Rock to McKinley, A Complete and Impartial History*, 1892, p. 25.

Henry Clay, speaking in the United States Senate in 1832 about this period, said: "On a general survey we behold cultivation extended; the arts flourishing; the face of the country improved; our people fully and profitably employed; the public countenance exhibiting tranquility, contentment and happiness; its public debt of two wars nearly redeemed; and, to crown all, the public treasury overflowing. If the term of seven years were to be selected of the greatest prosperity which this people has enjoyed since the establishment of their present Constitution, it would be exactly that period of seven years which immediately followed the passage of the Tariff of 1824."

Howard R. Smith, Professor of Economics—University of Georgia, *Economic History of the United States*, 1955, pp. 105-106.

By the end of 1807 much of America had become aroused to a point of high excitement by the continued impact of the war abroad, an excitement much enhanced by an attack on an American vessel by a British ship. Seeking a method of retaliation short of a war the nation did not yet want, and remembering the success of the restrictions used against England in the years prior to the Revolution, Jefferson's administration in December declared an embargo against the departure of any ship bound for a foreign port.

Many exaggerated accounts of the results of America's restrictive policy have been given. It is certain that grass did not grow on the wharves of Boston, but it is true that the policy was more damaging to American interests than to the interests of those it was intended to injure.

. . . domestic exports fell more than 80 per cent, re-exports more than 75 per cent, and domestic imports almost 50 per cent—all in a single year . . . the most important fact about America's restrictive policy is that its burden fell most heavily on the commercial classes.

Elmer E. Smead, *Governmental Promotion and Regulation of Business*, 1969, p. 47.

Tariff advocates do not base their case solely upon protection for specific interests. They also invoke general concepts. Hence, they have claimed that by making business, labor, and agriculture more prosperous American tariffs foster a higher standard of living for all Americans and thereby promote the general welfare of the whole country. Also, it has been claimed, tariffs make the country stronger in national defense. By protecting American business, labor, and agriculture, the government is fostering the development of the skills and the capacity to produce which are necessary to make the country strong in time of war; restrictions on foreign imports make the United States independent of foreigners who might shut off the supply of vital goods.

D.G. Harriman, *American Tariffs from Plymouth Rock to McKinley, A Complete and Impartial History*, 1892, p. 23.

England saw that she must act promptly and crush out these young American industries, or her American market would be forever lost, and her manufacturing industries permanently crippled. So she resolved to flood this country with her goods then on hand, many of which were old and out of fashion, far below cost. It was a matter of so much importance that it was discussed in Parliament, and Mr. (afterward Lord) Brougham declared in the House of Commons in 1816: "It is well worth while to incur a loss upon the first exportation, in order, by the glut, to stifle in the cradle those infant manufacturers in the United States, which the war has forced into existence."
This policy was decided upon, and Great Britain poured her fabrics and acculmulated [sic] stocks of goods into our markets in an overwhelming torrent and far below cost. The tariff of 1816 was intended as a barrier against this inundation, and under ordinary circumstances would have proved such. But it was a matter of life or death with the English manufacturers, and so they continued to pour in their goods upon us at prices far lower than we could make them; and true to British custom they perservered [sic] in this policy till our own industries were very nearly ruined.

Howard R. Smith, Professor of Economics—University of Georgia, *Economic History of the United States*, 1955, pp. 125-126.

American mythology has it that the tariff of 1816 was a protectionist measure enacted under the impetus of America's newly found nationhood. This is only half right at best. Certainly it was enacted by men sincerely professing protectionist sentiments. Certainly also it was intended to be protectionist legislation. But that in the context of its time it was *not* protectionist, there can be no doubt. In the face of an import level causing much discomfort to American manufacturing concerns, men who sincerely claimed to be protectionists did in fact reduce the tariff. Only by raising duties to a level high enough to choke off both imports and revenue could the inconsistent requirements of increased protection and decreased revenue have been met in 1816. Such a step, so well understood in later stages of the tariff controversy, was not a part of men's thinking at this time.

Selected Bibliography

Aaker, David A., and Day, George S. *Consumerism: Search for the Consumer Interest.* New York: The Free Press, 1971.

Anderson, James E. *The Emergence of the Modern Regulatory State.* Washington, D.C: Public Affairs Press, 1962.

Beard, Miriam. *A History of the Business Man.* New York: Macmillan, 1938.

Bolino, August C. *The Development of the American Economy.* Columbus, Ohio: Charles E. Merrill, 1966.

Brown, Keith C., ed. *Regulation of the Natural Gas Producing Industry.* Baltimore: Johns Hopkins University Press, 1972.

Cary, William L. *Politics and the Regulatory Agencies.* New York: McGraw-Hill, 1967.

Cochran, Thomas C., and Miller, William. *The Age of Enterprise—A Social History of Industrial America.* New York: Macmillan, 1942.

Cushman, Robert E. *The Independent Regulatory Commissions.* New York: Oxford University Press, 1941.

Faulkner, Harold U. *The Decline of Laissez Faire, 1897-1917.* New York: Rinehart & Co., 1951.

Fite, Gilbert C., and Reese, Jim E. *An Economic History of the United States.* Boston: Houghton Mifflin Co., 1959.

Graham, George Adams, ed. *Regulatory Administration, An Exploratory Study.* New York: J. Wiley and Sons, 1943.

Guskill, Nelson Burr. *The Regulation of Competition.* New York: Harper and Brothers., 1936.

Hamilton, David. *The Consumer in Our Economy.* Boston: Houghton Mifflin Co., 1962.

Harris, Seymour E. *American Economic History.* New York: McGraw-Hill, 1961.

Kirkland, Edward C. *History of American Economic Life.* New York: Appleton-Century-Crofts, 1951.

Kohlmeier, Louis M., Jr. *The Regulators.* New York: Harper and Row, 1969.

Krislow, Samuel, and Musolf, Lloyd D. *The Politics of Regulation: A Reader.* Boston: Houghton Mifflin Co., 1964.

Lane, Robert Edwards. *The Regulation of Businessmen: Social Conditions of Government Economic Control.* New Haven, Conn.: Yale University Press, 1954.

MacAvoy, Paul W. *The Crisis of the Regulatory Commissions.* New York: W.W. Norton & Co., 1970.

Magnuson, Warren G., and Carper, Jean. *The Dark Side of the Marketplace.* Englewood Cliffs, N.J.: Prentice-Hall, Inc., 1967.

Mintz, Morton. *Therapeutic Nightmare.* Boston: Houghton Mifflin Co., 1965.

Nash, Gerald D. *Issues in American Economic History.* Boston: D.C. Heath & Co., 1964.

Noll, Roger D. *Reforming Regulation.* Washington, D.C.: Brookings Institution, 1971.

North, Douglass C. *Growth and Welfare in the American Past.* Englewood Cliffs, N.J.: Prentice-Hall, 1966.

Pegrum, Dudley F. *The Regulation of Industry.* Chicago: R.D. Irwin, 1950.

Posner, Richard A. *Regulation of Advertising by the FTC.* Washington, D.C.: American Enterprise Institute for Public Policy Research, 1973.

Purdy, Harry L.; Lindahl, Martin L; and Carter, William A. *Corporate Concentration and Public Policy.* Englewood Cliffs, N.J.: Prentice-Hall, Inc., 1950.

Redford, Emmette S. *American Government and the Economy.* New York: The Macmillan Company, 1965.

Salomon, Leon I. *The Independent Federal Regulatory Agencies.* New York: Wilson, 1959.

Slichter, Sumner H. *Economic Growth in the United States: Its History, Problems, and Prospects.* Baton Rouge, La.: Louisiana State University Press, 1961.

Smith, Howard R. *Economic History of the United States.* New York: The Ronald Press Co., 1955.

Soule, George, and Carosso, Vincent P. *American Economic History.* New York: The Dryden Press, 1957.

Thorelli, Hans B. *The Federal Antitrust Policy, Origin of an American Tradition.* Baltimore, Md.: The Johns Hopkins Press, 1955.

Toussig, F.W. *The Tariff History of the United States.* New York: G.P. Putnam's Sons, 1931.

Wilson, Stephen. *Food and Drug Regulation.* Washington, D.C.: American Council on Public Affairs, 1942.

Winter, Ralph K., Jr. *The Consumer Advocate Versus the Consumer.* Washington, D.C.: American Enterprise Institute for Public Policy Research, 1972.

Woll, Peter. *American Bureaucracy.* New York: Norton, 1963.

ADVERTISING — THE VERNACULAR OF AMERICA?

Introductory Essay

In one sense, advertising is an agent of egalitarian democracy in the marketplace. Advertising messages are simple enough for everyone, including children, to understand: "Coke is the real thing." and "Wheaties are the breakfast of champions." Ads beckon the rich and poor, women and men, and members of every religious and ethnic group to get their clothes "whiter than white," to "join the Pepsi generation," and to "fly the friendly skies." To be sure there are appeals to special interests—"Trix are for kids," and one brand of beer is appropriate "when you're having more than one." Yet, Americans in every part of the land can share the same dreams at exactly the same moment through the magic of television commercials, which return us to Marlboro country, encourage us to double our pleasure, and entice us to "take it all off." Advertising feeds on the American vision of success, which exhorts all citizens to attain material prosperity in the form of a late-model car, fashionable clothes, a new house, a stereo and a color television. Stanford University historian David Potter has drawn attention to the peculiarly American character of advertising.

If we seek an institution that was brought into being by abundance, without previous existence in any form, and, moreover, an institution which is peculiarly identified with American abundance rather than abundance throughout Western civilization, we will find it, I believe, in modern American advertising.

Advertising permeates our daily existence, beginning, or course, with the morning newspaper. In fact, ads predominate in many newspapers and magazines. They can also be seen in buses and subway stations, on trash bins and telephone poles. Roads and highways have traditionally served as a medium for advertising. Fence post boards along country roads were once pasted with posters. In the Twentieth Century, roadside ads had to be readable from moving automobiles. Burma Shave put imaginative limericks on a series of signs as one way of increasing its sales. (One example: "By the school house//Please go slow//Let the little Shavers grow//Burma Shave.") Today, gigantic billboards set far from the highways sell all types of products. Elaborately decorated wagons advertising goods once traveled city streets, perhaps the inspiration for the Goodyear blimp that now travels overhead. Most significant today is the repeated intrusion of advertising in radio and television programming. The growth of advertising, measured by the dollars spent, has been large and rapid. In 1867, expenditures amounted to 50 million dollars, but by 1900, they had increased tenfold to 500 million dollars; finally, in 1972, 22.4 billion dollars were spent to create and direct consumer demand.

Advertisements themselves have often become part of the cultural pattern. From the beginning people could quote the Sapolio proverbs. Advertising campaign slogans, with constant repetition, can enter into the colloquial language. Many persons have claimed, since Avis did, that "We Try Harder." But also the figures associated with products are universally familiar. Americans once had great affection for the "small yawning boy, who, with the candle in his hand and a Fisk tire over his shoulder," was about to re-*tire*. The Morton Salt girl with her umbrella still sits on every kitchen shelf with the reminder "When it rains, it pours." And now the face and antics of Ronald MacDonald are becoming fixed in the minds of American children.

P.T. Barnum was a master of American advertising. In his *Autobiography,* he attributed his upward climb to the fact that "I thoroughly understood the art of advertising, not merely by means of the printer's ink, which I have always used freely, and to which I confess myself much indebted for my success, but by turning every possible circumstance to my account." For example, Barnum once paid for a man's breakfast in order to have him take bricks with him and then, after eating, to lay them one by one on the sidewalk making a trail to Barnum's American Museum. Of course, the curiosity of the crowd led them right to the entrance. Over and over again Barnum defrauded the American public; they knew it, and they loved it. Though on a lesser scale than that of Barnum, exaggeration or "tall talk" continued as the vogue in American advertising. The ad men knew that they need only "Promise them anything!" Hence the identification of products with the pleasant, prosperous, all-American way of life has not failed to hold the attention of this population. Indeed much of advertising has a very human appeal. James Wood appropriately concluded: "If all the emotions advertising has stirred, all the actions it has provoked, all the hypnotism it has exerted, and all the gullibility it has evoked could be added up, the sum would approximate the dimensions of total human nature."

The beginnings of American advertising were quite simple in contrast to the flamboyant phrases and appealing figures of today's ads. In colonial times, straightforward paragraphs, listed in the newspaper, were the major medium for advertising. They were simply colloquial attempts by men to convey information to all in the neighborhood. Just as present ads reflect the mass consumption society, these colonial ads, in their own way, reflected the society of small merchants at that time. Wood summarized their manner of advertising:

> Colonial newspaper advertising was informed by briskness and vitality. It spoke not only of the busyness of small enterprise, the practical considerations of merchants and the purveyors of services, but also of the feelings, beliefs, and prejudices of people in New England and the Middle Colonies. The devious ways of free publicity had not yet been perfected. Men announced their attitudes and opinions in paid advertising. Public relations had not yet taught the importance of moving softly. These advertisers said what they meant and meant what they said.

However, what they said was often doubtful. Unlike Ivory Soap, the claims of our ads have never been 99 44/100% pure. For example, wild claims about the newest patent medicines were always appearing in the pages of dailies. The publishing business was consequently criticized for accepting objectionable ads. The defense was always the same: newspapers needed advertising to survive financially. Benjamin Franklin, considered the father of American advertising, characteristically added a touch of his wit to the defense. He noted that it would be rare if one of those objecting to an advertisement were willing to pay him more not to publish it than he was paid to publish it.

Newspaper advertising continued to consist of dull and monotonous columns into the Nineteenth Century. It was generaly believed that large ads were unfair to the small daily advertisers. James Bennett of the *New York Herald* claimed that an advertiser should gain advantage only from what he said. Thus an agate-type rule was the custom. But the ingenious advertiser circumvented the restrictions by arranging the small agate letters in formation (like the members of a marching band) to spell words. In addition, the quantity of advertising was restricted. Only a century ago, *Harper's* refused $18,000 from Howe Sewing Machine Company for its backcover. A comparable refusal would be quite unusual at the present time.

The effects of the westward movement were apparent by the end of the last century. New railroads, mines, and business had been established. With the improved network of transportation available, a national market, rather than the small local markets, was possible. And the national market required large-scale national advertising.

But further, the industrial revolution brought changes to advertising as it did to all facets of American life. The growth of the industrial system generated the capacity to produce more than was demanded—an abundance of physical goods. There took place a critical shift from a production to a consumption economy. This shift required that advertising induce mass consumption. Growth became the economic goal, a goal achievable only if consumers spent their incomes. Thus the nature of the ads changed from that of providing information to that of appealing for consumer demand. As Charles Reich noted in *The Greening of America*, the constant command in our society is "buy."

Manufacturers began to produce increasingly similar products with industrialization. Resultant competition required the use of distinctive brand names and advertising. With the advent of these brand names, producers began to advertise directly in the marketplace. Formerly, they had mailed advertisements to the distributors, who in turn advertised in the community the availability of products, not specific brands. By World War I, national brands of gum, hats, breakfast food, watches, pianos, and razor blades were being sold. Consumers began to ask for Ivory rather than soap.

The physical appearance of advertisements also changed at this time. The page spread replaced the small paragraph. Department stores were the pioneers of modern newspaper displays. Macy's and Lord and Taylor first used large type and double columns in the New York dailies. Only two decades after the Civil War, both Montgomery Ward and Sears Roebuck had built up businesses using the famed catalog advertising. Finally, magazines gave in to the demand to advertise. *Harper's*, which had limited advertising in 1882, was leading all periodicals in 1890. By the turn of the century, America already had its schools to teach people to write advertisements.

Modifications at the time of World War I brought further attention and publicity to this medium of persuasion, and advertising became an even more vital component of the American economy. The United States had become a consumption society and its survival now seemed tied to the materialistic values portrayed in the ads. Daniel Boorstin, Director of the National Museum of History and Technology, claimed that the elaboration of advertising and its central place in the consciousness of the community were both new and American.

Eventually advertising played a role in the political arena of America. In 1837, the *Boston Daily Times* suggested an idea one hundred years ahead of its time: that political parties use paid advertising to air their ideas. Presently, the concern is to control the amount of television time allocated to political candidates. The ultimate in mixing modern advertising techniques with politics came in Richard Nixon's 1968 campaign for the Presidency. The "supercampaign" is described in Joe McGinniss's book *The Selling of the President 1968*. The now commonplace dependence upon Madison Avenue techniques in a political campaign reflects the preoccupation of the American voter with the appealing personality.

The Twentieth Century has recorded new developments in advertising induced by changing societal concerns. Recently, consumerism has had a significant impact on the methods of advertising. The complaint is voiced that the consumer is paying for advertising that he does not want. The honesty, too, of advertising has been under attack. Passage of the Truth in Advertising Act along with other bills designed to protect the consumer has been a part of the response. The Federal Trade Commission (FTC) has exercised stricter control of standards for advertisements: the television commercials of an iron tonic pill must include a statement saying that most people do not need it; 25 percent of the advertising budget for one year (for a bread which had been advertised as diet) had to be spent in a disclaimer that the bread would not help one lose weight; and, cigarette commercials are banned from television. And Ralph Nader has been warning consumers about products they should not buy.

Inclusion of Blacks and women in advertisements recognized the quest for equality and, probably more important, available consumer dollars. Women's liberation shows up in the slogan "You've come a long way, baby." Blacks appear as consumers in more television commercials and magazine ads, a significant change from the Negro servant-like Aunt Jemima and Uncle Ben. Also the demands of ecological responsibility and conservation have become staples of present-day advertising. Whether these messages are simply bravado on the part of American companies is another issue; it is clear that advertising has been affected by these concerns of the consuming public.

There has been a revolution in the advertising world, referred to as a creative explosion, making it a highly professional field. Its beginning has been described in these words:

The lone voice in the wilderness was that of Bill Bernbach, who in 1948 had helped start an agency called Doyle, Dane, Bernbach. Rather than hero-worshiping the product, he treated it as an anti-hero. Like the consumer, he took a slightly irreverent view of the product. He admitted that not every product was perfect (remember the advertisement showing a picture of a shining Volkswagen with the word "Lemon" underneath?). He recognized that for the consumer, "biggest" didn't always mean "best" (remember Avis's "We're number two" campaign?).

Mary Wells is another contributor to the new form of persuasion. In 1967, she began the famous advertising campaign for Benson and Hedges. Creative advertising involves not only better commercials but also a change in attitudes about the clients. Bernbach, in 1957, turned down one of the nation's largest advertisers because he did not like the way the company did business.

Despite reforms in advertising, its role and influence have been scrutinized. Some view it as the expression of the democratic concept of free enterprise and consumer freedom of choice. But others see advertising as a means of social control. The object of an ad is said to be the creation of "wants" and "desires" not existing prior to the ad. In other words, advertising encourages "consumption man" for this consumption society. As an institution, it reinforces in the consumer the materialistic value of seeking and accumulating more physical wealth. J.K. Galbraith has repeatedly argued that economists have been naive in failing to integrate advertising into the theory of consumer demand. Against his critique, defenders of the use of advertising point to the benefits of the information provided. Information, they remind us, is the best foundation for choice. Still, advertising has been accused of social irresponsibility in its exaltation of consumption. Specifically, Galbraith and others have submitted that the growth of public goods has not kept pace with that of private goods. American preferences for private wealth have been shaped by commercial advertising; the public sector is not similarly promoted and therefore is not given preference. Galbraith has contended that the consequent imbalance is detrimental to American society.

Advertising has been decried as an unhealthy impetus to conformity with emulation and imitation outgrowths of idealized scenes. Individualism—except in the stereotyped Marlboro man—is not an articulated value.

Hence a uniform society of followers, it is argued, emerges—a society comprised of indistinguishable faces, ready to be agreeable consumers. On the other hand, it has been suggested that the eventual success of advertising must be predicated on some desire for the goods or services in question. It remains possible, of course, for Americans to reject the message of any advertisement. Martin Mayer offers an encouraging observation in *Madison Avenue, U.S.A:*

Advertising is essentially a surface phenomenon, a wind that can stir still water. But, as the poet observed, there are tides in the affairs of men. When the wind blows with the tide, it seems to create an elemental motion; when it blows against the tide, it blows in vain.

Somewhat less encouraging, however, are the observations of a few Americans and a growing number of visitors to this country. The style of advertising, the "adman's psychology" (from hard sell to the smooth operator) seems to define more and more facets of our culture: education, religion, all manner of institutions, and even social relationships. America justly claims credit for the creation of advertising; now let her ward off the creation lest she be consumed. For no one—not even P.T. Barnum—should accept America and Advertising as One.

Excerpted Documents

Advertising in American history.

James Playsted Wood, Editor—Marketing Research Practice, *The Story of Advertising,* 1958, p. 46.

He is also, and with sufficient reason, hailed as the father, or at least the patron saint, of American advertising. Advertising and public relations, especially self-advertising and publicity, were as natural to Franklin as his curiosity, restless intelligence, and practicality. Printer, politician, philosopher, moralist, scientist, propagandist, Franklin, in all his roles and on behalf of all his varied activities, was always the untiring promoter. He put advertising before editorial in the masthead of the first issue of the *Pennsylvania Gazette* which, with Hugh Meridith as partner, he bought from his old employer, Samuel Keimer, and began to publish October 1, 1729: "Philadelphia: Printed by B. Franklin and H. Meredith at the New Printing Office near the Market, where Advertisements are taken in, and all Persons may be supplied with the paper at Ten Shillings a Year."

Daniel Boorstin, Director—The National Museum of History and Technology, *The Americans, The Democratic Experience,* 1973, p. 137.

While advertising was not, of course, a modern invention, the American elaboration and diffusion of advertising, and its central place in the consciousness of the community, were new. The proportion of the national ingenuity, energy, and resources that went into advertising was unprecedented. We have seen how, within two decades after the end of the Civil War, Montgomery Ward and Sears, Roebuck, among others, had built their vast communities of consumers on the advertising in their skillfully composed catalogues. This advertising went to millions of readers, not sandwiched between news or fiction, but exclusively to offer specific merchandise in the best light, and so to persuade people to buy. Even before advertising had become a major American art and a developed American science, Sears, Roebuck's Big Book had become the characteristically American book.

David M. Potter, Professor of History—Stanford University, *People of Plenty,* 1954, p. 168.

... advertising created modern American radio and television, transformed the modern newspaper, evoked the modern slick periodical, and remains the vital essence of each of them at the present time. Marconi may have invented the wireless and Henry Luce may have invented the news magazine, but it is advertising that has made both wireless and news magazines what they are in America today.

Joe McGinniss, *The Selling of the President,* 1969, p. 132.

This was no time for unnamed, unseen forces, antagonisms, yearnings which did not show up on radar, which could not be factored into their binary equations, to soil the record. No wonder they were bitter as well as scared. The American people had been presented with the supercandidate, the supercampaign, yet—even faced with the sweaty, babbling alternative of Humphrey—they showed signs of discontent.

The language of advertisements.

Daniel Boorstin, Director—The National Museum of History and Technology, *The Americans, The Democratic Experience*, 1973, p. 144.

Advertising, with its spreading power and its new freedom from pedantic and typographic bonds, was already evolving a democratic genre of literature. Within the next century, advertising would shape the American language, would make new demands of writers and would offer a kaleidoscope of bizarre and staccato trivia to listeners and readers.

E. S. Turner, *The Shocking History of Advertising*, 1953, p. 142.

Instead came the age of slogans, backed by the "reason why" copy. A slogan was an effective way of clinching the message. Kodak's "You press the button, we do the rest" was one of the most admired ... For a slogan to become a household word it was unnecessary for it to have wit, rhythm, aptness, or alliteration. Primarily it had to have a backer who was willing to repeat it for a generation or more. By sheer weight of expenditure, and nothing else, an indifferent slogan can become a part of the language.

James Playsted Wood, Editor—Marketing Research Practice, *The Story of Advertising*, 1958, p. 247.

There were those in business in the 1890's who disdained advertising as not quite respectable, yet some of it—always a happy circumstance when it can be achieved—was beginning to delight the public. People might cavil at the advertising which stained the white cliffs of Dover and insist it be scrubbed away. They might rise up and pass laws when "St. Jacob's Oil" was smeared in large letters on the rocks at Niagara, but they quoted Sapolio proverbs with gusto, reveled with the happy folk of Spotless Town, breathlessly followed the adventures of Phoebe Snow, as later they followed the Perils of Pauline, and were to fall in love with a small boy yawning his way to bed with a lighted candle and a Fisk tire over his shoulder. With an innocence, a gaiety and a gusto that have long since vanished from advertising, the copywriters shared their fun with the workaday world.

James Playsted Wood, Editor—Marketing Research Practice, *The Story of Advertising*, 1958, p. 156.

P. T. Barnum made himself a compelling figure. He made showmanship, with advertising as part of it, big business. He opened the eyes of the public not only to his exhibitions and entertainments, but also to what advertising and publicity could accomplish. He made American folk figures of Jenny Lind, Tom Thumb, and Jumbo. He made an even more heroic figure of himself as the most typical of all typical American go-getters. Some of the European idea of the American, and some of the American's idea of himself reflect the character, deeds, and writings of P. T. Barnum. If Americans will good naturedly tolerate shams, applaud the swindler and admire the duplicity of public figures, provided they are successful at it, it is in large part because Barnum taught them the entertainment value in such things; and taught them, too, that their own credulity and acceptance were amusing and somehow admirable. He defrauded them again and again and let them share in his enjoyment of the joke.

Daniel Boorstin, Director—The National Museum of History and Technology, *The Americans, The Democratic Experience*, 1973, p. 145.

In the new literature of advertising, alongside the tradition of forthright plain talk, another American tradition flourished anew. This was the tradition of Tall Talk. Boosters for new consumption communities discovered extravagant possibilities in the language of the commonplace. Advertising men, like the publicists for imaginary Western towns, freely used the language of anticipation, and they, too, were seldom inhibited by the fact that something had not yet "gone through the formality of taking place." Any Western tall-talker would have been proud to call a shampoo "Halo" or to name an automobile the "Fury."

E. S. Turner, *The Shocking History of Advertising*, 1953, p. 14.

In his essay on truth, Francis Bacon wrote: "A mixture of a lie doth ever add pleasure. Doth any man doubt, that if there were taken out of men's minds vain opinions, flattering hopes, false valuations, imaginations ... and the like, but it would leave the minds of a number of men poor shrunken things, full of melancholy and indisposition, and unpleasing to themselves?"

Robin Wight, *The Day The Pigs Refused To Be Driven To Market*, 1974, p. 162.

If the advertising were selling something important (like health insurance, for example), hollering and shouting might be tolerable. But to simply dispose of what may be regarded as the flotsam and jetsam of the industrial state, the bombardment of persuasion is just too much. It isn't only the screams that upset the consumers, it's the way the advertiser always seems to be talking about things that are meaningless to the consumer, and talking about them in a way which gives the product a ludicrously overimportant role in somebody's life. The detergent (Daz) that will make the neighbors think more of you when they see your nice white washing on the line. Or in America, Fab, the detergent "that will help these girls to get married" (a detergent)? The bedtime drink (Horlicks) that can turn a Weary Willy into a superman by the quaffing of flavored malted milk every night. And always there is the suggestion that by swallowing some chemical you can solve the sort of problems that would have baffled Freud.

Daniel Boorstin, Director—The National Museum of History and Technology, *The Image*, 1962, p. 222.

In fast-moving, progress-conscious America, the consumer expects to be dizzied by progress. If he could completely understand advertising jargon he would be badly disappointed. The half-intelligibility which we expect, or even hope, to find in the latest product language personally reassures each of us that progress *is* being made: that the pace exceeds our ability to follow.

Henry Sampson, *A History of Advertising From the Earliest Times*, 1874, p. 558.

Still, without wishing to impute anything like iniquity to American newspapers generally, it must be admitted that the vast majority of them have rather lax notions of propriety, and their motto being "Get money," they are apt to ignore the existence of ill in any advertisement, provided the presenter of it has his "pile" ready, and will "come down handsome."

John Kenneth Galbraith, Professor of Economics—Harvard University, *The Affluent Society*, 1969, p. 173.

In a society where virtuosity in persuasion must keep pace with virtuosity in production, one is tempted to wonder whether the first can forever keep ahead of the second. For while production does not clearly contain within itself the seeds of its own disintegration, persuasion may. On some not distant day, the voice of each individual seller may well be lost in the collective roar of all together. Like injunctions to virtue and warnings of socialism, advertising will beat helplessly on ears that have been conditioned by previous assault to utter immunity.

Robin Wight, *The Day The Pigs Refused To Be Driven To Market*, 1974, p. 155.

You only need to look at the special television stars like Johnny Carson, Dick Cavett or Mike Douglas and compare their *style* with the style of the advertisements that slice up their shows. What has happened is that advertising has used the undoubted power of the television medium to *force* attention, when perhaps it should have used it to *invite* involvement and participation.

David M. Potter, Professor of History—Stanford University, *People of Plenty*, 1954, p. 181.

What this means, in functional terms, it seems to me, is that the newspaper feature, the magazine article, the radio program, do not attain the dignity of being ends in themselves; they are rather means to an end: that end, of course, is to catch the reader's attention so that he will then read the advertisement or hear the commercial, and to hold his interest until these essential messages have been delivered. The program or the article becomes a kind of advertisement in itself—becomes the "pitch," in the telling language of the circus barker. Its function is to induce people to accept the commercial, just as the commercial's function is to induce them to accept the product.

Jerry Della Femina, Advertiser, *From Those Wonderful Folks Who Gave You Pearl Harbor*, 1970, p. 26.

One of the first ads to come out for Volkswagen was the first ad that anyone can remember when the new agency style really came through with an entirely different look. That ad simply said, "Lemon." ... No one had ever called his product a lemon before. It was the first time anyone really took a realistic approach to advertising. It was the first time an advertiser ever talked to the consumer as though he was a grown-up instead of a baby. ... It was handled in such a way that somebody was talking directly to the consumer in a language which the consumer was dying to hear. It was a tremendous success.

Robert Glatzer, Advertiser, *The New Advertising*, 1970, p. 10.

The beginning of the so-called new advertising can be dated quite precisely. In 1949, two extremely talented advertising men founded their own agencies and began making ads based on a respect for their audiences and a respect for their own talents, two attitudes that had been notably lacking prior to that date. In that year, David Ogilvy formed Hewitt, Ogilvy, Benson & Mather (now Ogilvy & Mather), and William Bernbach founded Doyle Dane Bernbach. Realizing that a good advertisement must have some intrinsic value, some virtue, of its own, they maintained that if an advertisement served as nothing more than a flack for the product, puffing it up rather than dealing with it, it would never be good at selling that product. "Treat the consumer as if she were your wife," said Ogilvy, "because she is. Don't talk down to her." If what Ogilvy and Bernbach did could be put in one sentence, it would be that they removed the exclamation point from advertising.

James Playsted Wood, Editor—Marketing Research Practice, *The Story of Advertising*, 1958, p. 192.

Horatio Alger had written the American story. From rags to riches, from the log cabin to the White House was the way it was supposed to be; and the riches was a social compulsion as strong as the rags and cabin were admirable. Fierce aggressiveness, sanctioned by indestructible Victorian materialism, drove men and business into uncontrolled competition, and advertising was a way to compete.

Daniel Boorstin, Director—The National Museum of History and Technology, *The Americans, The Democratic Experience*, 1973, p. 147.

Of course, "communities" of Uneeda Biscuit buyers and of other brand-name consumers were held together by much thinner, more temporary ties than those that had bound earlier Americans. But they drew together in novel ways people who might not otherwise have been drawn together at all—people who did not share a religious or political ideology, who were not voyaging together on the prairie nor building new towns. The peculiar importance of American consumption communities made it easier to assimilate, to "Americanize," the many millions who arrived here in the century after the Civil War. Joining consumption communities became a characteristic American mode of acculturation.

John Kenneth Galbraith, Professor of Economics—Harvard University, *The New Industrial State*, 1967, p. 209.

[The industrial] system requires that people will work without any limiting horizon to procure more goods. Were they to cease to work after acquiring a certain sufficiency, there would be limits on the expansion of the system. Growth could not then remain a goal. Advertising and its related arts thus help develop the kind of man the goals of the industrial system require — one that reliably spends his income and works reliably because he is always in need of more.

Charles Reich, Professor of Law—Yale University, *The Greening of America*, 1970, p. 165.

The most powerful, the loudest, and the most persistent command in our society is the command to buy, to consume, to make material progress, to "grow." The voice of advertising urges us to buy, buy, buy—and it never lets up. And the voice of advertising is only the most obvious of the forces that include the mass media's portrayal of a "way of life" in their programs and stories, the rhetoric of businessmen and politicians praising economic "progress" and "growth," and the overwhelming influence of American high schools and colleges in portraying a materialistic way of life as a desirable form of existence, individually and nationally.

Giancarlo Buzzi, Advertiser, *Advertising, Its Cultural and Political Effects*, 1968, p. 99.

Comfort, pleasure, prestige, security, the beauty of the calculating machine and of synthetic resins, of kitchen cabinets, cars, and shoes — all for humanity at large: this is the promise of neocapitalism, technocracy, and their advertising. It is an earthly promise, which beneath its superficial, active optimism is a pessimistic view of reality and human nature. It implies its laziness and its rejection of the hard work of looking for the truth.

David M. Potter, Professor of History—Stanford University, *People of Plenty*, 1954, p. 177.

And at least two of these institutions, the church and the school, have been very self-conscious about their roles as guardians of the social values and have conducted themselves with a considerable degree of social responsibility.
In contrast with these, advertising has in its dynamics no motivation to seek the improvement of the individual or to impart qualities of social usefulness, unless conformity to material values may be so characterized. And, though it wields an immense social influence, comparable to the influence of religion and learning, it has no social goals and no social responsibility for what it does with its influence, so long as it refrains from palpable violations of truth and decency. It is this lack of institutional responsibility, this lack of inherent social purpose to balance social power, which, I would argue, is a basic cause for concern about the role of advertising.

John Kenneth Galbraith, Professor of Economics—Harvard University, *The Affluent Society*, 1969, p. 131.

While public services have been subject to these negative attitudes, private goods have had no such attention. On the contrary, their virtues have been extolled by the massed drums of modern advertising. They have been pictured as the ultimate wealth of the community. Clearly the competition between public and private services, apart from any question of the satisfactions they render, is an unequal one. The social consequences of this discrimination — this tendency to accord a superior prestige to private goods and an inferior role to public production — are considerable and even grave.

Advertising and the creation of wants.

John Kenneth Galbraith, Professor of Economics—Harvard University, *The New Industrial State*, 1967, p. 203.

Thus a certain amount of advertising, that of the classified ads and the department store displays, has no great purposes beyond that of conveying information — of advising the public that a particular person or enterprise has a particular item for sale and at what price. Such advertising is seized upon to show that the function of advertising is merely to convey information although, as I have noted on other occasions, only a gravely retarded citizen can need to be told that the American Tobacco Company has cigarettes for sale.

Charles Reich, Professor of Law—Yale University, *The Greening of America*, 1970, p. 165.

If the people would not dominate the forces that were changing their country, then those forces would dominate the people. Consciousness I, losing its own roots but holding tight to its myths, was ready game for manipulation by the organized forces of society. These Americans could be sold a colonial war in the name of national honor. They could be sold hundreds of billions of dollars' worth of military technology in the name of American independence. They could be sold governmental irresponsibility in the name of the old American virtue of thrift. They could be sold an ignorant and incapable leader because he looked like the embodiment of American virtues. Worst of all, perhaps, they could be sold artificial pleasures and artificial dreams to replace the high human and spiritual adventure that had once been America.

John Kenneth Galbraith, Professor of Economics—Harvard University, *The Affluent Society*, 1959, p. 149.

The even more direct link between production and wants is provided by the institutions of modern advertising and salesmanship. These cannot be reconciled with the notion of independently determined desires, for their central function is to create desires—to bring into being wants that previously did not exist. ... A broad empirical relationship exists between what is spent on production of consumer goods and what is spent in synthesizing the desires for that production.

Daniel Boorstin, Director—The National Museum of History and Technology, *The Americans, The Democratic Experience*, 1973, p. 546.

When the unexpected and the miraculous were expected, what comfort or security was there in expectation? When invention became the mother of industry, invention soon became the mother of necessity. Americans would have to look about them at the state of technology, and read the advertisements in their paper or watch the commercials on television to discover their "needs."

Giancarlo Buzzi, Advertiser, *Advertising, Its Cultural and Political Effects*, 1968, p. 15.

The conclusion is almost mandatory: needs are undefinable and impossible to grasp. They are infinitely expandable and, more important, only apparently increasing. In fact, it is not needs that are increasing, but the complexity of human relations, as a result of the growth of population and the increased inventiveness of the human mind. The boundary separating the so-called basic needs from unreal or artificially created ones is so narrow that the most reasonable conclusion is that no boundary exists.

Giancarlo Buzzi, Advertiser, *Advertising, Its Cultural and Political Effects*, 1968, p. 140.

All those who try to justify advertising (and there are many) by applying a moral yardstick find themselves in trouble. Advertising is neither licit or illicit, good or evil in itself, but only relative to a context, to values, to a choice (or group of choices), to an ideology, a vision of life. The only yardstick it can be measured by is *social morality*. Persuading men to change their ties every day is perfectly licit — in fact, quite understandable and even necessary in a neocapitalistic society inhabited by "consumption man," as Edgar Morin calls him. But it would be illicit in Communist China.

David Ogilvy, Advertising Executive, *Confessions of an Advertising Man*, 1964, p. 150.

Franklin Roosevelt said:
"If I were starting life over again, I am inclined to think that I would go into the advertising business in preference to almost any other. . . . The general raising of the standards of modern civilization among all groups of people during the past half century would have been impossible without the spreading of the knowledge of higher standards by means of advertising."

David Ogilvy, Advertising Executive, *Confessions of an Advertising Man*, 1964, p. 159.

Does advertising make people want to buy products they don't need? If you don't think people need deodorants, you are at liberty to criticize advertising for having persuaded 87 per cent of American women and 66 per cent of American men to use them. If you don't think people need beer, you are right to criticize advertising for having persuaded 58 per cent of the adult population to drink it. If you disapprove of social mobility, creature comforts, and foreign travel, you are right to blame advertising for encouraging such wickedness. If you dislike affluent society, you are right to blame advertising for inciting the masses to pursue it.

E. S. Turner, *The Shocking History of Advertising*, 1953, p. 13.

In the last resort the public's only defence against high-powered suggestion is its own common sense. Unfortunately that bulwark, though strong, cannot always be depended on to withstand the pounding and insinuating sea.

Robin Wight, *The Day The Pigs Refused To Be Driven To Market*, 1974, p. ix.

First came Orwell, then Vance Packard, then Galbraith to preach the same gospel: that the predestination of persuasion had replaced the free will of perfect competition. And growing fat on this mythology were the golden-fingered admen, who, whatever private doubts they may have had about these immense powers, were not going to repudiate this unsolicited testimonial to their skills.

Robin Wight, *The Day The Pigs Refused To Be Driven To Market*, 1974, p. 17.

The operating principles of second-generation consumerism as practiced by Nader and Banzhaf are very different from the pedantic fairness of the early consumer pioneers. The gentlemanly concept of recommending best buys becomes replaced by a newer one: the concept of worst buys. Nader seldom tells people what to buy; he merely tells them what not to buy, or, at best, what they could buy if companies used all the technology available to them.

Giancarlo Buzzi, Advertiser, *Advertising, Its Cultural and Political Effects*, 1968, p. 12.

Advertising, or more accurately, the increase in the cost of advertised products, is said to be paid for in the last analysis by the consumer, who finds himself burdened with this unjust expense and is made to bear the responsibility for a service that has no social utility, that he has not asked for and that he would, in fact, refuse if he could freely do so.

F. S. Turner, *The Shocking History of Advertising*, 1953, p. 13.

The public at large little suspects the extent to which advertising, on both sides of the Atlantic, has been cleaned up in recent years. The briefest glance at the newspaper and magazine files of between the wars will show what a tightening up there has been. Many of those advertisements wore so shifty a face that the advertising profession and the publishers have agreed voluntarily to renounce them; others, if published today, would result in prosecutions all around.

Robin Wight, *The Day The Pigs Refused To Be Driven To Market*, 1974, p. 19.

. . . in the five years 1965 to 1971, twenty consumer bills managed to get past the business lobbyists, the batteries of special-interest lawyers, and eventually onto the Statute Book of Congress. But of even more importance, in practical terms, have been the changes forced on the federal regulatory bodies. In fact, there are now thirty-three U.S. government agencies engaged in approximately three hundred consumer-protection activities.

Martin Mayer, Freelance Writer, *Madison Avenue, U.S.A.*, 1958, p. 324.

A client cannot turn down a Doyle Dane Bernbach advertising campaign any more than he can turn down a lawyer's brief; if he doesn't like it, he can go get himself another boy. . . . The future of advertising must lie in this direction. With the conception of himself as a professional offering a trained creative intelligence, the advertising man can face his critics calmly. He can face his clients courageously and he can face himself in the morning.

Robert Glatzer, Advertiser, *The New Advertising*, 1970, p. 15.

By that standard, it would be hard to deny that Doyle Dane Bernbach is the best advertising agency in the United States. It created the advertising for Volkswagen, Polaroid, Avis Rent A Car, the Jamaica Tourist Office,

Ohrbach's department stores, Colombian Coffee (Juan Valdez), Sony television, and many other famous campaigns. Its standard of work is consistently higher than that of any other agency, large or small, and its work has been the greatest single influence on advertising in this country since World War II. Client requests—at other agencies—for "a Doyle Dane Bernbach ad" have become a joke in the business. One advertising commentator, the head of a rival agency, wrote that "Doyle Dane Bernbach, in fact, is a major sociological force today. It has persuaded millions of people to act, and its economic influence on the American scene can only be measured in the billions of dollars. There never was such a 'tastemaker' in the history of this country."

Selected Bibliography

"Ad World Gets Its Back Up in Washington." *Broadcasting*, 84 (February 5, 1973), 23.

"Advertising and Society; Social, Political and Educational Roles." *Advertising Age*, 44 (November 21, 1973), 156.

"Advertising's Creative Explosion." *Newsweek*, 74 (August 18, 1969), 62.

Boorstin, Daniel J. *The Image.* New York: Atheneum, 1962.

Boorstin, Daniel J. *The Americans, The Democratic Experience.* New York: Random House, 1973.

Borden, Neil H. *Advertising in Our Economy.* Chicago: Richard D. Irwin, Inc., 1945.

Boyce, Howard H. "Advertising and Publishing in Colonial America." *American Heritage*, (Spring 1954).

Buzzi, Giancarlo. *Advertising, Its Cultural and Political Effects.* Minneapolis: University of Minnesota Press, 1968.

Cherington, Paul T. *The Consumer Looks at Advertising.* New York: Harper and Brothers, 1928.

Commager, Henry Steele. *The American Mind.* New Haven: Yale University Press, 1950.

Evans, W. A. *Advertising Today and Tomorrow.* London: George Allen and Unwin Ltd., 1974.

Femina, Jerry Della. *From Those Wonderful Folks Who Gave You Pearl Harbor.* Edited by Charles Sopkin. New York: Simon and Schuster, 1970.

Galbraith, John Kenneth. *The Affluent Society.* Boston: Houghton Mifflin Company, 1969.

Galbraith, John Kenneth. *The New Industrial State.* Boston: Houghton Mifflin Company, 1967.

Glatzer, Robert. *The New Advertising.* New York: The Citadel Press, 1970.

Harris, Ralph, and Seldon, Arthur. *Advertising and the Public.* Great Britain: Rowan Press Ltd., 1962.

Key, Wilson Bryan. *Subliminal Seduction.* Englewood Cliffs, N.J.: Prentice-Hall, Inc., 1972.

Kirkpatrick, Miles W. "Advertising and the Federal Trade Commission." *Journal of Advertising*, 1 (November 1, 1972), 10.

Knauer, Virginia H. "Advertising and Consumerism." *Journal of Advertising*, 2 (November 1, 1973), 6.

McGinniss, Joe. *The Selling of the President 1968.* New York: Trident Press, 1969.

McLuhan, Herbert Marshall. *The Mechanical Bride: Folklore of Industrial Man.* New York: Vanguard Press, 1951.

Maggard, John P., and Wise, Gordon I. "The Role and Responsibilities of Advertising in a Decade of Challenge: Quo Vadis?" *Miami Business Review*, 44 (November, 1972), 1.

Mayer, Martin. *Madison Avenue, U.S.A.* New York: Harper and Brothers, 1958.

O'Gara, J.V., ed. "New World of Advertising." *Advertising Age*, 44 (November 21, 1973), 1.

Ogilvy, David. *Confessions of an Advertising Man.* New York: Atheneum, 1964.

Packard, Vance. *The Hidden Persuaders.* New York: David McKay Co., Inc., 1957.

Posner, Richard A. *Regulation of Advertising by the FTC.* Washington: American Enterprise Institute for Public Policy Research, 1973.

Potter, David M. *People of Plenty.* Chicago: The University of Chicago Press, 1954.

Powledge, Fred. "Judgment on Madison Avenue." *Money*, 2 (September, 1973), 82.

Presbrey, Frank S. *The History and Development of Advertising.* New York: Doubleday and Company, 1929.

Reeves, Rosser. *Reality in Advertising.* New York: Knopf, 1961.

Reich, Charles A. *The Greening of America.* New York: Random House, 1970.

Sampson, Henry. *A History of Advertising From the Earliest Times.* London: Chatto and Windus, Piccadilly, 1874.

Sokolsky, George E. *The American Way of Life.* New York: Farrar and Rinehart, Inc., 1939.

Turner, E. S. *The Shocking History of Advertising.* New York: E. P. Dutton and Company, Inc., 1953.

Tyler, Poyntz. *Advertising in America.* New York: H. W. Wilson, 1959.

Warner, Daniel S., and Wright, John S. *Speaking of Advertising.* New York: McGraw-Hill Book Company, Inc., 1963.

Weiss, E. B. "Creative Advertising Moves Toward the New Society." *Advertising Age*, 44 (July 2, 1973), 27.

Weiss, E. B. "Advertising Meets Its Era of Social Accountability." *Advertising Age*, 43 (October 23, 1972), 71.

Wight, Robin. *The Day The Pigs Refused To Be Driven To Market.* New York: Random House, 1974.

Wood, James Playsted. *The Story of Advertising.* New York: The Ronald Press Company, 1958.

PRIVATE ENTERPRISE IN THE MARKETPLACE

Introductory Essay

Adam Smith postulated that an "invisible hand" could effectively guide an economy and eliminate the need for governmental intervention. Although Americans throughout history have remained loyal to this concept of *laissez-faire*, the close association between government and business has been a major theme in American history. In part, the American Revolution was a battle to free the colonial economy from hostile foreign interference. After the battle was won, however, the new government did not trust the "invisible hand" to build an industrialized nation but, instead, promoted and encouraged new businesses. By the close of the nineteenth century, market pressures and government aid had created a business monster, the "trust," which could only be tamed through government regulation and, occasionally, government ownership, and as time passed, the government found more and more weaknesses in the competitive market that could only be corrected by government intervention.

Opposition to British mercantilism was a major force leading to the Revolutionary War. Under the mercantilist philosophy the American colonies existed primarily to benefit the mother country; the colonies were an abundant source of raw materials needed in British manufacturing and a new market for British products. Major British legislation of the time manifests this mercantile philosophy. Great Britain strictly regulated colonial imports and exports. Under the Enumerated Products Act of 1660, certain American commodities such as tobacco, sugar, cotton and indigo could be shipped only to England; by the outbreak of the Revolution the list had expanded to include every American export except fish and barrel staves. The act denied the colonies the best available export markets; many of the colonial commodities shipped to Europe under the act were resold in European markets at a tremendous profit to British merchants. The Middleman's Act of 1663 prohibited importation of goods into the colonies unless they were first sent to Great Britain to be taxed. Through high tariffs on non-British colonial imports, Britain was able to gain a monopoly in the colonial import market. The Woolen Act of 1699, the Hat Act of 1732 and the Iron Act of 1750 prohibited colonial merchants from exporting certain commodities in competition with British industries. The Tea Act of 1773 was passed to save the British East

India Tea Company from bankruptcy. Under the act, England refunded a duty which the company had paid on seventeen million tons of surplus tea, thus lowering the price for the product. Moreover, the company was allowed to sell through its own agents, thus eliminating colonial middlemen. As a result, the British company was able to undersell colonial merchants who had purchased tea at a higher price. The Molasses Act of 1733, which became the Sugar Act in 1764, levied prohibitive duties on rum, molasses and sugar imported to the colonies from the French and Dutch West Indies. In addition, Great Britain attempted, through legislation, to raise revenue in the American colonies to help pay a large national debt. The Stamp Act of 1765 required the colonists to purchase stamps for legal documents, newspapers and pamphlets. The Townshend Revenue Act imposed additional duties on paint, paper, lead, glass, and tea. The colonists began to learn the burdens of their divided loyalties to their new home and mother England.

Their reaction to the British trade regulation was at first indecisive. Initially, the merchants ignored most of the laws. The customs commissioners were supervised from London; as a result, enforcement was lax and bribes were commonplace. This strategy was thwarted when, in 1767, Great Britain established a Board of Customs Commissioners to sit in Boston with instructions to seize any ships in violation of the Sugar Act. Rioting broke out in Boston in 1768 when John Hancock's ship, the "Liberty," was seized: a scrupulous customs official had refused a bribe and had been stowed below deck while the contraband was unloaded. American merchants also organized colonial boycotts. In response to the Stamp Act, one thousand merchants from New York, Boston, and Philadelphia signed an agreement banning the purchase of European goods; the result was a drastic decline in British exports to the American colonies and repeal of the Stamp Act. Later boycotts were not as effective, however, as Great Britain found new export markets in Northern Europe, the Mediterranean, and the East Indies. Delegates to the First Continental Congress formed an "association" which called for nonimportation of British goods and nonexportation of colonial goods to the mother country. By 1775 the association, including vigilantes equipped with tar and feathers, was in operation in twelve colonies. Shortly thereafter the first shots were fired at Lexington and the Revolutionary War began.

Throughout the war the American colonies were heavily dependent upon their own entrepreneurs, particularly in the area of finance. Historically, wars had been financed from "war chests" — great chests of gold that traveled with the troops like a piece of artillery. The colonies had no such accoutrements, and had to rely upon the support of private financiers such as Haym Solomon. Solomon handled bills of exchange, aided in securing loans from Holland and France, and advanced his own funds to help finance the revolution. Shortly after the war, Solomon went into bankruptcy, and at his death he owed over forty-five thousand dollars. The United States owed Solomon over six hundred thousand dollars, none of which he ever received. His countenance appears today on a commemorative postage stamp.

Following the Declaration of Independence, the states banded together under the Articles of Confederation—a loose union which allowed the states to retain their sovereignty and did not grant the national government any significant power over the economy. The American economy quickly began to suffer from too little governmental involvement, and the sometimes indiscriminate powers of certain states. The states engaged in commercial rivalry and erected barriers to interstate trade. Without a treaty-making power centralized in the national government, the young nation could not promote foreign commerce. The national government had no direct taxation power and was forced to rely upon state legislatures for revenue through taxation. In addition, the national government had no authority to regulate currency. As a result, eager entrepreneurs and debtors successfully pressured for the issuance of more currency, which created inflation and speculation.

The delegates who gathered to write the Constitution knew from these experiences that a weak national government could not foster economic development. The document which they produced evidences this concern for governmental promotion of business. The new Constitution gave the federal government the power of direct taxation, thus enabling the federal government to pay its debt in full, to the benefit of those who held public securities. The Constitution granted the new federal government a war power to be used to force open foreign markets and protect business interests from debtors' rebellions, and the new government was given the power to eliminate commercial interstate rivalries and shelter domestic industries through the foreign and interstate commerce powers, and to encourage western development through its power to establish standards for a territory's admission to the Union. That the new economic powers were to rest in the hands of a national government was apparent from the fact that the Constitution prohibited states from issuing currency or impairing contractual obligations.

As the United States grew in the early nineteenth century, its policies were governed by the belief that an autonomous economy would be self-adjusting and that the economy could progress more rapidly through competition and profit incentives. Yet legal historian James Willard Hurst argues that public policy of this era "involved a good deal less of simple laissez-faire than has often been claimed for it." The first half of the nineteenth century was characterized by "a complicated affirmative use of law to furnish instruments and procedures" designed to facilitate the release of private individual and group energies. Alexander Hamilton contended that the infant industries of the United States would never be able to compete in world markets against the European industries which were subsidized and protected by government unless the new United States government was willing to take a dynamic role in the promotion of industry. Similar sentiment was expressed in the halls of the Congress whose first major act was a tariff, and until the Civil War almost all federal revenue came from the collection of import duties. Congress inaugurated patent legislation in 1790 and continually liberalized the issuance of patents and the scope of their protection. Many states which had originally granted charters for incorporation for only internal improvements began to break down, and by the 1830's incorporation charters were granted liberally.

By the end of the nineteenth century this special bland of laissez-faire had begun to produce undesirable results, and repeatedly, the government found that it had to intervene to correct the defects of the competitive marketplace. Three types of government intervention are of special interest: antitrust, regulation by independent commission, and government ownership. But, clearly, the arena of government involvement in the economy was extensive. Direct subsidies, quotas, wartime controls, and regulation of the money supply are all areas for examination.

In 1875 many businessmen were dissatisfied with the results of competition through small business, and consequently they began to band together in giant pools, trusts, and holding companies. Increased productivity had given business the capacity to overproduce, but small competitive businesses were unable to balance production with consumption. Production of oil frequently outstripped refining and the manufacture of goods often exceeded consumer demands for the products. Prices reflected the feast or famine nature of the economy; in 1862 the price of oil fluctuated between a low of ten cents a barrel and a high of $2.25 per barrel. Price wars, business failures, and waste were common. In addition, further development required large amounts of capital which small businesses could not provide. "Robber Barons" such as John D. Rockefeller, Cornelius Vanderbilt, James J. Hill, and Andrew Carnegie organized great empires in oil, transportation, steel and finance in order to remedy these defects of competition. Businessmen first attempted to coordinate their efforts through pools; a pool was a combination of independent businessmen who voluntarily sought to control prices or limit output by dividing the market. Another popular device was the trust; when a trust was formed the owners of stock surrendered their stock and voting rights to a small group of trustees, and, in return, they received trust certificates entitling them to dividends. When the Supreme Court of Ohio ordered Standard Oil to dissolve its Ohio oil trust, the Robber Barons turned to the holding company; the holding company dominates other companies by purchasing large amounts of their stock, thus placing several companies under the ownership of a single holding company.

The corporate giant created new problems for the American economy, including high prices and cutthroat competitive practices, and Congress responded in 1890 with the Sherman Act. The act provided that "Every contract, combination in the form of trust or otherwise, or conspiracy, in restraint of trade among the several states, or foreign nations is. . .illegal."

The subsequent history of antitrust reveals both inconsistent approaches to enforcement of the laws and repeated attempts to patch up the loopholes of the Sherman Act. President Theodore Roosevelt, who believed that monopolies were more efficient than small businesses and should be regulated in the public interest, a philosophy labeled "New Nationalism." Roosevelt, despite popular misconceptions, however, did little to effectively regulate the monopolies. In 1900 there were 185 manufacturing companies in the United States with a total capitalization of over three billion dollars. In 1905 at the close of Roosevelt's first administration there were 308 companies with seven billion dollars in capitalization, and U.S. Steel had become the world's first billion dollar holding company. Woodrow Wilson announced that "Private monopoly is indefensible and intolerable" and demanded a return to pure competition through his "New Freedom" program. In 1914 Congress passed the Clayton Act which prohibited practices that substantially tended to lessen competition, including interlocking directorates, price discrimination, and tying contracts. During the Wilson presidency Congress also created the Federal Trade Commission, an organization with authority to investigate monopoly and unfair trade practices and aid the Justice Department in enforcement of antitrust laws. The Harding, Coolidge, and Hoover administration made little progress in the antitrust field. These administrations were dominated by conservatives with a "standpat" view of antitrust. In addition, the Supreme Court restricted the scope of antitrust laws through its Rule of Reason decisions, first announced in 1911. Under the Rule of Reason, the Court reserved the authority to conclude that an industrial combination was a "reasonable" restraint in trade and, hence, not in violation of the antitrust laws. In 1920 the Supreme Court decided that U.S. Steel was a reasonable restraint in trade, although the company controlled fifty percent of steel output in the United States. In 1922 the Court concluded that United Shoe Machinery was a reasonable restraint in trade although the concern controlled ninety-five percent of the market. FDR's New Deal represented a mixture of "New Nationalism" and "New Freedom." Roosevelt began his presidency with a "New Nationalism" philosophy under the National Industrial Recovery Act. Under the authority of the NIRA, businesses prescribed "codes" for fair competition which were approved by the President. Six hundred codes eventually went into operation governing business practices, prices, wages, and hours. The great failing of the codes was that they were written by the very businesses which the government sought to control. In 1938 after the NIRA had been declared unconstitutional, Roosevelt turned to a "New Freedom" philosophy, and from 1939-43 the government instituted 230 antitrust suits, more than had been brought in the entire history of the Sherman Act. In 1950 Congress tried to remedy the ills of antitrust laws through the Celler-Kefauver Act. Previously, antitrust laws had prohibited only acquisition of the stock of a competitor. The Celler-Kefauver Act prohibited any merger if the effect was to substantially lessen competition. The law has been effective in preventing horizontal mergers, the acquisition by one company of one of its competitors. The antitrust laws have been ineffective, however, in controlling conglomerate mergers. For example, CBS has owned a book company, the New York Yankees, a toy company, a guitar firm and two film companies.

In some industries the government has been willing to accept economic concentration and has relied upon regulation by independent commissions to force these industries to act in the public interest. This essay will discuss government regulation of public utilities and the railroads. The BYD participant should also be aware of the activities of the Civil Aeronautics Board, the Securities and Exchange Commission, and the Atomic Energy Commission.

Public utilities, including electric power generation, telephone, and telegraph have been subject to extensive federal regulation. Public utilities are frequently classified as natural monopolies; the large capital outlays required for their development and the economies of scale which these industries can achieve indicate that the most efficient utility company should be in a monopoly position'. The municipalities were the first to regulate public utilities through restrictions on quality, quantity, and price of service in charters of incorporation. Regulation by state commission became popular in the 1830's and continued for approximately one hundred years. Gradually a need for federal regulation became apparent. Constitutionally, the states were limited in their authority to control the retail rates of electricity within their individual states; they were powerless to control the wholesale rates of electricity transmitted across state lines. Although many major cities were served by interstate networks of natural gas supply, the states had been unable to coordinate their activities. The Federal government entered the field of public utility regulation in 1935 with the Federal Power Act. The goal of the act was to achieve planned coordination in the sale and transmission of electricity, and the act established the Federal Power Commission with authority to mandate interconnection of transmission lines and to regulate wholesale rates of electricity. Under the Natural Gas Act of 1938, the FPC acquired jurisdiction over the transport and sale of natural gas and the authority to lower natural gas rates, order extension of service, and prevent abandonment of facilities. The Communication Act of 1934 created the Federal Communications Commission with authority to prescribe rates, mandate interconnection, and permit construction of new lines for all interstate operations of telephone, telegraph, and cable companies.

The defects of competition also led to federal involvement in the railroad industry. The competitive climate of the early nineteenth century produced a "get rich quick" spirit in the railroad industry and massive speculation without regard to national needs. Railroad mergers increasingly meant poor service and rate discrimination to eliminate competitors. The Interstate Commerce Act of 1887 established the Interstate Commerce Commission, prohibited rate discrimination in rail transportation, and mandated that all rail charges must be "just and reasonable." Under the Hepburn Act of 1906 the ICC acquired explicit authority to prescribe maximum rates and issue binding orders. By 1920 many railroads faced bankruptcy and to meet this problem the Transportation Act of 1920 empowered the ICC to set minimum rates that would enable the railroads to receive a "far return for fair value of property."

The independent regulatory commissions have generally been a poor substitute for competition in the marketplace. Commissions were established to provide expertise and independence from partisan pressure in the regulation of industry. In reality, commission members have very often been seduced by the very industries which they were intended to regulate; and the case-by-case apporach of commissions has been slow and inefficient. The railroad industry has complained that the ICC has maintained railroad rates at an artificially high level, and, as a result, the railroads are unable to compete with other less expensive forms of transportation. Electric companies and natural gas companies complain that the FPC has kept their rates so low that they are unable to return the profit required for expansion.

Finally, government has become involved in the marketplace through ownership of industry. In 1933, in an effort to develop the industry and agriculture of the Tennessee Valley, the federal government created the Tennessee Valley Authority. The authority relied upon electric power generation to avoid waste of waterpower and to help finance the project. Many municipalities acquired electric power plants under Public Works Administration grants of the New Deal. Both the TVA and the Bonneville Power Administration, another government enterprise, produce a surplus of electric power and resell the power to other electric companies. Because these government projects give preference in sale of electricity to publicly owned enterprises, many municipalities have acquired electric power plants of their own. There is strong evidence to indicate that the TVA has successfully developed the Tennessee Valley by increasing the use of electricity in the area. But there is no conclusive evidence to demonstrate that the project has been self-supporting or that government ownership has enabled the Valley to receive electric power at an unusually low price.

Throughout American history there has been a presumption that the ideal economy is one of pure competition, and the government has only intervened when free enterprise was inadequate to accomplish the tasks which it faced. As industrialization of our economy has progressed, the failures of *laissez-faire* have become more frequent. Government involvement in the economy has grown, and the problems of bureaucracy have replaced the problems of monopoly and excessive competition.

Excerpted Documents

The extent of government involvement in the economy.

Louis M. Hacker, Professor of History, *Issues in American Economic History*, 1964, p. 56.

We shall not understand the character of the American crisis of 1763-1775 unless we are prepared to hold ever in mind the fact that every imperial administration program, whether in the economic or political realms, was designed to further this end: to utilize the colonies as an economic appendage of the mother country. Thus, as early as 1726, a member of the Board of Trade wrote:

> Every act of a dependant provincial government ought therefore to terminate in the advantage of the mother state unto whom it owes its beginning and protection in all its valuable privileges. Hence it follows that all advantageous projects or commercial gains in any colony which are truly prejudicial to and inconsistent with the interests of the mother state must be understood to be illegal and the practice of them unwarrantable, because they contradict the end for which the colony had a being and are incompatible with the terms on which the people claim both privileges and protection . . .For such is the end of the colonies, and if this use cannot be made of them it will be much better for the state to be without them.

Clarence H. Cramer, Professor of History, *American Enterprise: Free and Not So Free*, 1972, p. 71.

During most of the colonial period the British were lax and lenient about the enforcement of their mercantile system. Certainly the English version of mercantilism was less restrictive and brutal than that of other countries; France and Spain, as examples, embraced mercantilist principles completely and enforced them ironhandedly. In the American colonies, smuggling, in violation of trade and other acts, was so common that it became respectable; it was like buying booze in the 1920's or like stretching deductions on a current income tax report. The best people were involved. Probably 9/10's of colonial merchants were smugglers; one-quarter of the signers of the Declaration of Independence were bred to contraband trade.

Clarence H. Cramer, Professor of History, *American Enterprise: Free and Not So Free*, 1972, p. 72.

The entire mercantilist system was contrary to the principle of *laissez-faire* that was dominant on the frontier; there settlers had been practicing it for at least a century before Adam Smith formulated the theory. Later Smith himself would agree with them, and would urge independence of the American colonies.

Friedrich List, *Outlines of the American Political Economy*, reprinted in *The Government and the Economy, 1783-1861*, edited by Carter Goodrich, 1967.

Government, sire, has not only the right, but it is its duty to promote everything which may increase the wealth and power of the nation, if this object cannot be effected by individuals. So it is its duty to guard commerce by a navy, because the merchants cannot protect themselves; so it is its duty to protect the carrying trade by navigation laws, because carrying trade supports naval power, as naval power protects carrying trade; so the shipping interest and commerce must be supported by breakwaters—agriculture and every other industry by urnpikes, bridges, canals and rail roads—new inventions by patent law—so manufactures must be raised by protecting duties if foreign capital and skill prevents individuals from undertaking them.

Clarence H. Cramer, Professor of History, *American Enterprise: Free and Not So Free*, 1972.

In the United States there was not time when business enterprise was completely free from governmental regulation, but by 1875 such regulation was nominal, finding expression largely in foreign commerce, Indian affairs, and land policies. By 1875 the *laissez-faire* philosophy had become a secular religion in the United States.

Leverett S. Lyon and Victor Abramson, The Brookings Institution, *Government and Economic Life*, 1940, p. 616.

Government regulation has been a recognized and accepted feature of the supply of public utility services for so long and in such a degree that one no longer thinks of them apart from the governmental associations. Government control of the affairs of the industries is almost axiomatic, and withdrawal of the government from the field on any considerable scale is only remotely conceivable.

Clarence H. Cramer, Professor of History, *American Enterprise: Free and Not So Free*, 1972, p. 467.

. . .a number of witnesses before the Celler Committee in 1950 warned that if the nation permits Big Business to exist, it will be accompanied by Big Government and Big Labor. Adolph Berle said that when business "threatens to engulf the State—it forces the State to engulf business." Morris L. Ernst, the prominent lawyer and civil libertarian, reminded the committee of the situation in Germany during the 1930's—where cartels became too big, leading to rigid government control; he also recalled Great Britain in the same period where combinations got too large and the state took them over.

The role of small business in the economy.

Ross M. Robertson, Professor of Business Economics—Indiana University, *The Vital Majority*, 1974, p. 35.

The number of retail firms, which comprise such a large proportion of small business, has declined remarkably little over the last 30 years or so, and the decline that is evident has been at the very small end of the size spectrum where vulnerability of the small firm is notoriously great.

Clarence H. Cramer, Professor of History, *American Enterprise: Free and Not So Free*, 1972, p. 467.

[Donald A.] Schon [who is an industrial consultant with experience both in private industry and the Federal Bureau of Standards] observed that independent inventors and small companies are responsible for a remarkable percentage of the important innovations and inventions of this century. These include, *inter alia,* the following: the air conditioner, power steering, xerography, cyclotron, cotton picker, helicopter, FM circuits, automatic transmissions, zipper, Polaroid camera, cellophane, continuous hot-strip rolling of steel, and the oxygen steelmaking process.

J. K. Galbraith, Professor of Economics—Harvard University, *American Capitalism*, 1952, p. 91.

There is no more pleasant fiction than that technical change is the product of the matchless ingenuity of the small man forced by competition to employ his wits to better his neighbor. Unhappily, it is a fiction. Technical development has long since become the preserve of the scientist and the engineer. Most of the cheap and simple inventions have, to put it bluntly, been made.

Eliot Jones, Professor of Economics—Stanford University, *The Trust Problem in the United States*, 1923, p. 535.

During the period that preceded the trust movement, American manufacturers were notable for their willingness to discard even good machinery and equipment in order to install improved facilities that promised to reduce the costs of productions. It was this policy that made the Carnegie steel properties the most efficient in the country—so efficient that Mr. Carnegie could snap his finger at the various steel trusts, notwithstanding their reputed economies.

Ross M. Robertson, Professor of Business Economics—Indiana University, *The Vital Majority*, 1974, p. 29.

Just the possibility of going into business, the hope of pecuniary gain in the form of profits—the share of the total product that is the reward of successful venturing—has always offered an escape from the penury to those who could not meet the requirements of education and temperament for law, medicine, teaching, and the other professions. Moreover, for young people of considerable talent, blessed with the trading temperament, small business provides a rapid means to substantial wealth, often shortening by years of decades the safer and more certain route to fortune of moving slowly up the corporate ladder. Because it has offered involvement to great numbers of people, and by association to their families and other relatives, small business has provided political support for the business community as a whole, support that serves as a tremendous protective mechanism against the assaults of those who persistently clamor for fundamental changes in the "system."

Ross M. Robertson, Professor of Business Economics—Indiana University, *The Vital Majority*, 1974, p. 36.

There are and there always will be only a few who can achieve remarkable success in the business world, large or small. To suppose otherwise is wishful thinking. But it is precisely this kind of thinking that relieves the burdens of the world, that lightens the darkness of mediocrity in any kind of endeavor. So long as the *possibility* of success remains for those who just *may* have the trading temperament, who have the courage to risk life itself in the hope of gain, an economic system will prevail that puts the allocation of resources beyond the power of one Big Office of Marx and Lenin. So long as the possibility remains, the American business system will retain political support for its centuries-old role.

Attitudes of Americans toward business.

Clarence H. Cramer, Professor of History, *American Enterprise: Free and Not So Free*, 1972, p. 417.

Have the 'trusts' limited competition? Economists and statesmen differ in their answers to this question. What does the American public think—what is its philosophy of what business life should be? A few years ago Elmo Roper polled the citizenry of the United States on this issue. His findings revealed, first, that the vast majority of the people believe in and want a system of private ownership and operation. At the same time they are not willing to place property rights above human rights, or to regard dividends as more sacred than wages. Second, he found that a great many people believe that too much of business is at best amoral and at worst greedy. Finally, it was evident that—because they know they cannot do it themselves—many people want someone to keep an eye on business, and their candidate for that 'someone' is government.

Ross M. Roberston, Professor of Business Economics—Indiana University, *The Vital Majority*, 1974, p. 34.

Indeed, the public's lack of enthusiasm for antitrust laws, ambiguously drawn up by legislators and largely enforced by judges sympathetic to big business, suggests the lack of concern about 'the problem of monopoly'. Only when large *retail* units appeared in the form of local outlets for the mail order houses and horror of horrors, as units in great chains of grocery, drug, hardware, and variety stores, was popular resentment apparent, for the 'chain stores' spread tentacles that would ultimately strangle the 'independent retailer.'

The impact of economic
concentration upon the economy.

Wendell Berge, former Assistant Attorney General of the United States, *Cartels: Challenge to the Free World*, 1944, p. 11.

In general, cartels restrict rather than promote trade. Cartels typically engage in such practices as dividing fields of operation add market areas between members so as to eliminate competition, restricting production by agreement, and fixing prices so as to avoid competition. They also promote various kinds of patent licensing contracts which enable them to control and limit the use of new inventions and thus restrict the benefits of technological advance. The effects of these practices include reduced production and employment, retarded spread of technological improvements, and lower standard of living.

Wendell Berge, former Assistant Attorney General of the United States, *Cartels: Challenge to the Free World,* **1944, p. 11.**

The conduct of cartels before and during this war has been one of the tragic pages of our history. The shortages of aluminum resulting from cartel restrictions force us to strip the kitchens of America and scar our public squares with scrap piles. The scarcity of rubber is a never ceasing threat to our productive effort. Our armed forces plead with us to contribute our binoculars. The lack of vital drugs and medicines has jeopardized our men fighting in fever stricken areas. In fact, almost wherever there was a cartel there was a shortage.

George J. Stigler, Walgreen Professor of American Institutions—University of Chicago, *Monopoly Power and Economic Performance,* **1974, p. 5.**

Those tobacco companies did not act competitively, but with a view to extermination, against the 10c brands in the 1930's, nor have they engaged in price competition in decades . . . The steel companies, with all their salesmen, abandoned cartel pricing via base-point prices only when this price system was judged a conspiracy in restraint of trade in cement.

Eliot Jones, Professor of Economics—Stanford University, *The Trust Problem in the United States,* **1923, p. 261.**

One of the earliest and most powerful trusts was the Standard Oil Company. The prices charged for oil by this company formed the subject of an unusually elaborate study by the Bureau of Corporations, as the result of which the Bureau was able to speak with confidence and authority concerning the effect of the oil trust on prices. The Standard Oil Company, so the Bureau notes, had repeatedly claimed that it had reduced the price of oil; that it had been a benefit to the consumer, and that only a great combination like the Standard could have furnished oil at the prices that had prevailed. "Each one of these claims," said the Bureau, "is dissproved by this report."

Clarence H. Cramer, Professor of History, *American Enterprise: Free and Not So Free,* **1972, p. 459.**

For a variety of businesses they [mergers] have provided four advantages: avoidance of bankruptcy, benefits from diversifications, savings on taxes, and utilization of surplus capital.

Clarence H. Cramer, Professor of History, *American Enterprise: Free and Not Só Free,* **1972, p. 415.**

The reason Big Business has not enslaved us, as Galbraith sees it, is that at least four other power centers have expanded to match the power of Big Business. The countervailing powers are Big Labor, Big Agriculture, Big Distribution, and Big Government. Examples of such countervailing powers are:

  If major tire companies of Big Industry wanted to boost their prices—Sears (Big Distribution) stood ready to make its own tires.
  If General Foods (Big Industry) wanted to increase the prices of breakfast food—A and P (Big Distribution) stood ready to provide its own.
  If U.S. Steel (Big Industry) wanted to increase prices—John F. Kennedy (Big Government) stepped in and stopped the increase.

Allen Solganick, Professor of History—University of Maryland, "Robber Baron Concept and Its Revisionists," *Science and Society,* **1965, vol. 29, p. 264.**

The Hepburn Committee in 1879 found that 90 per cent of all refiners in the country acted in harmony with Standard Oil and in 1892 the Supreme Court of Ohio declared that the object of the Standard Oil Company was to "establish a virtual monopoly of the business of producing petroleum, and of manufacturing, refining, and dealing in it and all its products throughout the entire country, and by which it might not merely control the production, but the price, at its pleasure."

Allen Solganick, Professor of History—University of Maryland, "Robber Barons Revisited," *Science and Society,* **1965, vol. 29, p. 264.**

It was the belief of the Industrial Commission in 1902, after a most exhaustive study, 'that in most cases the combination has exerted an appreciable power over prices and in practically all cases it has increased the margin between raw materials and finished products. Since there is no reason to believe that the cost of production over a period of years has lessened, the conclusion is inevitable that the combinations have been able to increase their profits."

Allen Solganick, Professor of History—University of Maryland, "Robber Barons Revisited," *Science and Society,* **1965, vol. 29, p. 267.**

We find that the average dicennial rate of growth of fixed capital was much higher during the period 1839-1859 than it was in the period 1869-1899.

Allen Solganick, Professor of History—University of Maryland, "Robber Barons Revisited," *Science and Society,* **1965, vol. 29, p. 268.**

Another relevant study was done by W. Paul Strassman, who examined four industries: iron and steel, textiles, machine tools, and electric power. His conclusions are radically different from those which revisionists would have us believe. He found that "the vast majority of innovations, which seemed hazardous to people at the time were not, in fact, risky and that for most sweeping changes in manufacturing methods, 'the process of innovation was already a safe and even predictable routine."

Antitrust.

Clarence H. Cramer, Professor of History, *American Enterprise: Free and Not So Free,* **1972, p. 421.**

. . . enforcement of the Sherman Act over the years has been unimpressive. Because of the language and lack of enforcement machinery, economist Stuart Chase once called the act "a sheet of tissue paper across Niagara Falls. Because of the numerous loopholes it is sometimes referred to as the 'Swiss Cheese Act.' Emanuel Celler, the longtime chairman of the House Judiciary Committee, once called it a "horse-and-buggy statute applied to a jet propelled era." Justice Holmes was probably closest to the truth: he called it a "brooding omnipresence in the sky."

Clarence H. Cramer, Professor of History, *American Enterprise: Free and Not So Free,* **1972, p. 419.**

During the 11 years before TR became president only 18 antitrust suits were brought before the courts, and 4 of these were against Labor Unions.

Independent regulatory commissions.

Bernard Schwartz, former chief counsel — House Subcommittee on Legislative Oversight, *The Professor and the Commissions,* **1959, p. 118.**

"Thanks to C. Northcote Parkinson," states Robert Bendiner in a *Reporter* article on the FCC, "most of us are now aware of the natural law that bureaucracies expand rather like rabbit warrens. Closer observers of governmental phenomena are familiar with Bruce Catton's Progressive Law of Ossification, by which an administrative agency reaches full manhood and relatively complete impotence at the same time."

Bernard Schwartz, former chief counsel — House Subcommittee on Legislative Oversight, *The Professor and the Commissions,* **1959, p. 120.**

Perhaps its [ICC] most severe critic was Alfred E. Smith, "I find little in recent history to justify the continuance of the ICC as now organized," he declared in 1933. "What we need is a new transportation system, not endless hearings on a system that does not work."

Marver H. Bernstein, Professor of Economics, *Monopoly Problems in Regulated Industries: Airlines,* **Hearings, Antitrust Subcommittee of the House Judiciary Committee, 84th Congress, 2d session, 1957, part 1, p. 59.**

It is impossible to avoid the conclusion that regulation of particular industries by independent commissions tends to destroy rather than promote competition. The historical tradition of the commissions is anticompetitive. Their basic methods, especially their reliance upon a case by case approach, place small business firms at a disadvantage. The growing passivity of the commissions' approach to regulation and the inconveniences of dealing with large numbers of firms strengthen the commission tendency to identify their view of the public interest with the position of the dominant regulated firms. In short, regulation of particular businesses by independent commission stacks the cards against the small competitive firm and weakens the force of competition.

Bernard Schwartz, former chief counsel — House Subcommittee on Legislative Oversight, *The Professor and the Commissions,* **1959, p. 127.**

Robert E. Lee, a few years ago, began his term as a member of the FCC with the categorical declaration: "I don't believe in government regulation." His attitude has been shared by other commissioners. George C. McConnan Grey, appointed as the FCC chairman in 1954 sounded the theme of his tenure with the statement that he was "pretty much on record as believing in as few controls of business as possible."

Bernard Schwartz, former chief counsel — House Subcommittee on Legislative Oversight, *The Professor and the Commissions,* **1959, p. 139.**

According to it [a 1913 Report of the Minnesota Home Rule League] the companies regulated "have used their influence upon the appointing power to name men of the right minds on the commission; have sought to influence the attitude and to control the action of the commissioners after appointment."

Government ownership.

Dissenting Report, *Report of the Joint Committee Investigating the T.V.A.,* **Appendix B, 1939, p. 289.**

The electric power operations now planned and as planned for the future, and at rates now prevailing, inevitably must result in a loss which must be made up by the government.

Annual Report of the T.V.A., **1938-39, p. 77.**

The past few years have seen the demand for power in the Valley states increase at a rate more than double that for the United States as a whole.

Annual Report of the Federal Power Commission, **1939, p. 13.**

Comparison of the rates, by classes of service according to community size groups of the two types of ownership disclosed that the average typical bills charged in 1937 by privately owned utilities were, with but one exception, higher for all quantities of electricity in all communities of 2,500 or more population. The one exception was that bills of privately owned systems for 250 kilowatt hours per month residential service in communities of 2,500 to 10,000 were reported as being 2 per cent lower than those of publicly owned utilities. For communities of less than 2,500 population the privately owned utilities were reported as having lower average bills for residential service. However, for other services, such as commercial light and commercial power, in communities of 2,500 or more population and industrial service in communities of 10,000 or more, the 1937 average typical bills of the publicly owned system in every case were lower than those of the privately owned utilities.

Leverett S. Lyon and Victor Abramson, The Brookings Institution, *Government and Economic Life*, 1940, p. 740.

In its more recent report the Authority announced that its power operations for 1939 provided a net income 'of more than $1,478,000 after all expenses, including direct power expenses (management, operation of power-house, substation, and transmission system, promotion, etc) and allocated expenses incurred jointly in the operation of the multipurpose dams . . and after provision of approximately $1,736,000 for depreciation calculated on a straight-line basis.' Too, the Joint Committee (investigating the T.V.A. accepted as 'reasonably conservative' the estimates that revenues from the sale of power would not only pay all power costs, but would also cover the annual expenses of navigation and flood control and return the total investment in these programs in about 50 years.

Selected Bibliography

Abramson, Victor, and Lyon, Leverett S. *Government and Economic Life,* Washington, D.C.: The Brookings Institution, 1940.

Adams, Walter, and Gray, Horace M. *Monopoly in America: Government as Promoter,* 1955.

Adelman, M. A. "Effective Competition and Anti-trust Laws." *Harvard Law Review,* 61 (1948), 1289.

Anderson, James E. *The Emergence of the Modern Regulatory State.* Washington, D.C.: Public Affairs Press, 1962.

Berge, Wendell. *Cartels: Challenge to a Free World.* Washington, D.C.: Public Affairs Press, 1944.

Bornet, Vaughn D. "Those 'Robber Barons.'" *Western Political Quarterly,* 6 (1953), 342.

Callender, Guy Stevens. *Selections from the Economic History of the United States, 1765-1860.* New York: Augusts M. Kelley, Bookseller, 1965.

Carson, Deane, ed. *The Vital Majority: Small Business in the American Economy.* Washington, D.C.: Government Printing Office, 1974.

Chamberlain, John. *Enterprising Americans: Business History.* New York: Harper and Row, 1963.

Cochran, Thomas C. "Legend of Robber Barons," *Pennsylvania Magazine of Historical Biography,* 74 (1950), 307.

Cramer, Clarence H. *American Enterprise: Free and Not So Free.* Boston: Little, Brown and Company, 1972.

Cushman, Robert E. *The Independent Regulatory Commissions.* New York: Oxford University Press, 1941.

Fabricant, Solomon, and Lispey, R.E. *Trend of Government Activity Since 1900.* New York: National Bureau of Economic Research, 1952.

Flugel, Felix, and Faulkner, Harold. *Readings in the Economic and Social History of the United States.* New York: Harper and Bros. Publishers, 1929.

Goodrich, Carter, ed. *The Government and the Economy, 1783-1861.* New York: The Bobbs-Merrill Co., Inc., 1967.

Hacker, Louis M. *The Course of American Growth and Development.* New York: Wiley, 1970.

Handler, Milton. *Antitrust in Perspective.* New York: Columbia University Press, 1957.

Hession, Charles H., and Sardy, Hyman. *Ascent to Affluence: History of American Economic Development.* Boston: Allyn and Bacon, 1969.

Jones, Eliot. *The Trust Problem in the United States.* New York: The Macmillan Co., 1923.

Jones, Peter D., comp. *Robber Barons Revisited.* Boston: Heath, 1968.

Josephson, Matthew. *Robber Barons: Great American Capitalists, 1860-1901.* New York: Harcourt, Brace, and Co., 1934.

Kohlmeier, Louis M., Jr. *The Regulators.* New York: Harper and Row, 1969.

Michelman, Irving S. *Business at Bay: Critics and Heretics of American Business.* New York: A.M. Kelley, 1969.

Miller, William, ed. *Men in Business: Essays on the Historical Role of the Entrepreneur.* Cambridge: Harvard University Press, 1962.

Nash, Gerald, ed. *Issues in American Economic History.* Boston: D.C. Heath and Co., 1964.

Nash, Gerald. *State Government and Economic Development, 1849-1933.* Berkeley: Institute of Governmental Studies, 1964.

Nelson, Ralph L. *Merger Movements in American Industry, 1895-1956.* Princeton, N.J.: Princeton University Press, 1959.

North, Douglas C. *Growth and Welfare in the American Past.* Englewood Cliffs, N.J.: Prentice-Hall, 1966.

Phillips, Almarin, ed. *Perspectives on Antitrust Policy.* Princeton, N.J.: Princeton University Press, 1965.

Phillips, Joseph D. *Little Business in the American Economy,* Urbana, Ill.: University of Illinois Press, 1958.

Schwartz, Bernard. *The Professor and the Commissions.* New York: Alfred A. Knopf, 1959.

Solganick, Allen. "Robber Baron Concept and Its Revisionists." *Science and Society,* 29 (1965), 257.

Stocking, George W., and Watkins, Myron W. *Monopoly and Free Enterprise.* New York: Twentieth Century Fund, 1951.

Tennessee Valley Authority. *Annual Report of the T.V.A.* Washington, D.C.: Government Printing Office. 1939.

Whitney, Simon N. *Antitrust Policies: American Experience in Twenty Industries.* New York: Twentieth Century Fund, 1958.

ISSUE VII
AMERICA IN THE WORLD

REGIONAL EVENTS—COLLEGE AGE ISSUE
March 20—April 24, 1976

DEBATE   *Resolved: That American foreign policy has wrongly violated the basic principles of the Declaration of Independence.*

PERSUASIVE   *Can America afford a foreign policy based on moral principle?*

EXTEMPORANEOUS   *A Nation Among Nations*

1. *American isolationism: Will it return?*
2. *Management of the world's resources: Has America been a guardian or a despoiler?*
3. *Has America subordinated her self-interest to the need for world order and stability?*
4. *Foreign allies in the Revolution: Could we have succeeded without them?*
5. *Multilateral Agreements: How have they developed in America's foreign policy?*
6. *What role have the two great oceans played in America's foreign affairs?*
7. *American colonialism: How deeply ingrained?*
8. *Military manpower: The United States in Europe today versus Europe in the Americas in the Eighteenth century. What are the similarities and differences?*
9. *How did America come to be a superpower?*
10. *Latin America: American fiefdom or good neighbor?*
11. *Has American foreign policy traditionally underemphasized the importance of Asia?*
12. *Has America's prosperity become too dependent upon the world economy?*
13. *Has America traditionally underemphasized its responsibility to aid underdeveloped nations?*
14. *Should America attempt to be the defender of Western civilization?*
15. *How much of America's postwar military and diplomatic strength has been dependent upon nuclear weaponry?*
16. *How has dependence on foreign energy sources altered American foreign policy in the postwar period?*

RESOLVED: THAT AMERICAN FOREIGN POLICY HAS WRONGLY VIOLATED THE BASIC PRINCIPLES OF THE DECLARATION OF INDEPENDENCE.

Introductory Essay

When Thomas Jefferson took pen to record the reasons why the colonists felt impelled to take the drastic step of independence, he recognized that a "decent respect for the opinions of mankind" made such an explanation necessary. And so from the beginning, the Founding Fathers understood that they were part of the world's affairs. The creation of a nation-state was seen to have international implications.

In its two centuries, America's relations with the rest of the world have taken almost every conceivable form. We have waged war and made peace; formed alliances and shunned them; opened our ports to foreign trade and raised barriers to trading partners; signed treaties, compacts, and executive orders and protocols. We have extended diplomatic recognition to the weakest and most struggling of new states, and pretended that some of the world's most populous nations did not exist. At various times we have pronounced the quarrels of other nations none of our business, while other occasions have seen us enter into powerful international associations, or cast ourselves in the role of world policeman. Through it all, both those who have made history and those who have sought to understand it have looked back to test the nation's actions against those ideals made eloquent in Jefferson's words. The conformity of America's actions with her revolutionary precepts has prompted a rich and stimulating debate. On balance, has American foreign policy wrongly violated the principles of the Declaration of Independence? Although the Declaration does not provide a tidy blueprint for specific international policies, it does assert certain principles which may nonetheless dictate precedents or standards against which her diplomacy may be judged.

The essence of the first principle is alive in the political philosophy at the very core of our national being. Its expression stirs us yet: "We hold these truths to be self-evident, that all men are created equal, that they are endowed by their Creator with certain unalienable Rights, that among these are Life, Liberty, and the pursuit of Happiness." It is compelling that these rights were both "self-evident" and "unalienable" — that they were automatic and irrevocable. Thus the Declaration called for a profound respect for the rights of all peoples of the world. Therefore, apart from considerations of ex-pediency, American diplomacy may be held accountable to these higher values. Whether U.S. foreign policy-makers have taken seriously this particular precept of the Declaration is disputable, and historical evidence is readily available for both positions. The new nation's "Manifest Destiny" to rule the continent often took precedence over the Indians' right to the pursuit of happiness. Expansionists claimed that white men, rather than "primitive savages," were naturally entitled to the lands. Their contention was contrary to at least our current understanding of the doctrine of equality of all men. Further, the equality of the natives of the Philippines and their right to liberty were denied; judged unfit to govern themselves, they were barred from self-government. Use of the atom bomb against civilian populations in Japan and the slower but no less devastating assault on the people of Vietnam are, for many, acts that evidence a lack of respect for the right to life.

While pragmatism has often dominated policy decisions, idealism and an adherence to fundamental principles are not lacking in documentation. Outrage at stories of bloodshed and concentration camps in Cuba rallied public opinion behind the Spanish-American War. There were idealistic strains in our participation in both World Wars: we sought to "Make the World Safe for Democracy," and responded to international fascism. American relief efforts at the conclusion of the wars, likewise, sought to aid national recovery and strengthen democratic tendencies. Resolution of this expediency-principle issue requires an assessment of motive: has a commitment to the "unalienable rights" of other peoples influenced American foreign policy?

The Declaration's insistence that governments derive "their just powers from the consent of the governed" offers a second standard for measuring American foreign policy. A corollary right to revolution is posited:

> But, when a long train of abuses and usurpations, pursuing invariably the same Object, evinces a design to reduce them under absolute Despotism, it is their right, it is their duty, to throw off such Government and to provide new Guards for their future security.

The prerogative of a people to change a regime which forfeits their consent is not only granted, but demanded. Such language raises important questions about the conduct of foreign affairs, especially with respect to revolutionary activity in other countries. Contradictory interpretations may be defended. If one argues that only the people of a nation can provide "the consent of the governed" and "it is their right, it is their duty," then involvement in the internal affairs of other states is a violation of self-determination. If, on the other hand, one argues that a people are oppressed by their own or another government, then the defense of democratic states and the support of wars of liberation are the honoring of a commitment to self-determinism.

President Washington's parting admonition to avoid foreign entanglements and President Jefferson's desperate attempts to maintain neutrality reflect their isolationist stances. Henry Cabot Lodge, at the beginning of this century, argued for the same course when he opposed membership in the League of Nations; he maintained that the United States could best serve the world as an example of democracy. John Foster Dulles' rollback doctrine represents—though certainly in a radical fashion—the desire of some of our foreign policy-makers who have favored a leadership role for America in world affairs. Wilson claimed that our involvement in foreign affairs was unavoidable. The course dictated by the principle "consent of the governed" may be laid out, and our adherence to it or deviation from it may be measured only with an appreciation of motive. To ponder why, however, invites complexity.

Very likely several different influences induced the announcement of the Monroe Doctrine, closing the Western Hemisphere to further European colonization. President Monroe declared to the world community in 1823:

> With the existing colonies or dependencies of any European power we have not interfered and shall not interfere. But with the Governments who have declared their independence and maintained it, and whose independence we have, on great consideration and on just principles, acknowledged, we could not view any interposition for the purpose of oppressing them, or controlling in any other manner their destiny, by any European power in any other light than as the manifestation of an unfriendly disposition toward the United States.

The idealism of the message is evident in its recognition of the value of self-government in the Latin American nations. But principles took a back seat to enlightened pragmatism; President Monroe's wording clearly gives primacy to the denial of European colonies which were viewed as contrary to our national self-interest. Considerations of expediency, in fact, have largely governed the Doctrine's operation. Protection of vital trade routes in the Caribbean was on original impetus for it. Later, action by both France and Britain contrary to the Doctrine's tenets was ignored by the U.S., presumably because no American interest was directly threatened. Napoleon III was quickly removed, however, when the Bonaparte Monarchy in Mexico was deemed an impingement on U.S. security. This sporadic application suggests the presence of another, stronger current. A relationship between our strength and willingness to act may also be seen. Accordingly, announcement of the Roosevelt Corollary was intended to justify U.S. actions to promote stability in the Dominican Republic and Nicaragua; essentially, it gave the United States police power in this hemisphere.

President Wilson's Fourteen Points, delineated in a speech to Congress in 1918, revealed his plan to make the world "fit and safe to live in." The guarantee of self-determination was a central theme; the holding of plebiscites to determine frontiers struck a new and consonant note.

In the Cold War period, the Truman Doctrine shaped our response to the Soviet Union. Substantively, it requires that the United States oppose Communist expansion; practically, it is responsible for the American policy of intervention in the internal affairs of other nations. If it is assumed that the establishment of Communist regimes denies the right to government by the "consent of the governed," then their prevention may be viewed as consistent with our national purpose as embodied in the Declaration. An alternate hypothesis, namely, that Communist governments are perceived as a serious threat by this nation and that we are acting in our own self-interest leaves us without so obvious an appeal to high purpose. For, the result of interference by this nation can then be the denial of a people's aspirations for a particular form of government. The Twentieth Century has witnessed several instances of American military intervention to prevent revolutionary overthrows of admittedly tyrannical regimes. In recent years, American support of such dictators as Batista in Cuba and Trujillo in the Dominican Republic has not been easily reconciled with our national faith in democracy. The recent American distaste for revolution contrasts sharply with the eagerness of our early government to recognize new governments following the French Revolution and the revolt in Hungary. Perhaps the American willingness to recognize the right to revolution, which we so confidently took for ourselves, has waned over the past two centuries.

Jefferson's text provides an illustrative litany of the gross violations of the foregoing basic principles—unalianable rights and consent of the governed—by the King of England. Several illustrations are applicable to the present conduct of American foreign affairs and hence provide further potential subjects for debate. For example, the King was cited "For quartering large bodies of armed troops among us." Presently, United States military bases span the globe, sometimes despite the disapproval of the host. Only recently, Turkey requested that American troops be removed from her territory. Further, Jefferson accused George III on the grounds that "He has plundered our seas, ravaged our Coasts, burnt our towns, and destroyed the lives of our People." What of Hiroshima? How might the Vietnamese describe our use of mines, bombs and chemical defoliants? As a final example of the colonists' objections, the King is also named for "transporting large Armies of foreign Mercenaries." Can the United States escape this criticism in Southeast Asia? These are only a few from the lengthy list of examples of injuries caused by Britain which can presently provide a basis for the evaluation of American diplomacy.

It can, of course, be countered that these particular infringements cited against the British throne were not the "principles" of the Declaration, but merely the occasion which prompted the act of severance. Were this done, however, one must then be prepared to compare other general statements of principles with the specific instances out of which the policy arose. Thus, shall we distinguish Woodrow Wilson's high moral purpose to secure "the future of democracy" from his Fourteen Points, the particulars on whose foundations he assumed his grander goal would be realized?

To decide whether or not the United States has measured up to the high ideals expressed in Jefferson's words clearly requires more than isolate examples. That question can be answered only by offering sufficient examples to illustrate broad patterns of action, maintained consistently over time. Upon such patterns rests the legitimate interpretation of what generally characterizes U.S. foreign policy: expediency or principle.

Making that determination of fact, however, is not the whole answer. The doctrines of the Declaration of Independence are scarcely infallible and strict adherence to them as dogma is not required. Competing values may be introduced. A denial, in fact, that U.S. violations of the principles of the Declara-

tion have been wrong, would constitute a rejection of the resolution. One might argue that morality should not be the proper guide of diplomacy. Instead, a concern for national self-interest — for economic advancement, for military security, for political prestige — should be our goal, and policies should be chosen that will accomplish it. Basically, the position holds, the first obligation of a government is to meet the needs of its domestic constituency. This approach to foreign policy — known as the "realist" school of thought—can be isolated in such policies as the Mexican War which won the resources of California and the Southwest or our acquisition of land in Panama for an inter-ocean canal. The "idealist" position on foreign policy stands in opposition. Its major tenet is that the natural law governing all nations should take precedence over a particular nation's interests. One or the other of these philosophies must play a secondary role.

Finally, the distinction between idealism and realism is often clouded. Did we send troops to South Korea to protect that nation from aggression or to maintain a favorable balance of power in the Far East? Was Woodrow Wilson's request for a declaration of war against the Kaiser's Germany a crusade for self-determination, a reluctant response to submarine warfare, or a recognition that our economic and military future was not secure with Germany preeminent on the European Continent? In some cases, both morality and *Realpolitick* were clearly components of a single policy: we opposed Nazi Germany by force of arms both out of revulsion for Hitler and fear for our long-term survival. The emphasis on either idealism or realism has shifted with the tone of succeeding administrations. However, in many cases, the separation of the rhetoric of altruism from an inner motivation of gain is a delicate operation.

Still these analytical tasks, while difficult, are important ones to attempt. Current epithets of "neo-isolationism" notwithstanding, it is clear that the United States will play a critical role in the world in her third century as a nation. What that role should be is a question that we cannot escape. And one wonders: How true will our exchanges with other countries be to our revolutionary past?

Excerpted Documents

The democratic experiment.

Henry M. Wriston, Former Diplomat, *Diplomacy in a Democracy*, 1956, p. 78.

In our concentration upon Soviet aggression we are likely to overlook the fact that democracy, also, has been expansive, and in its American manifestation at least, inherently so. We developed a recognition policy which equated *de facto* with *de jure*; it was designed to facilitate revolutions such as that which had won our freedom. We sought to propagate democratic institutions in Latin America; we watched the "liberal" efforts at revolution in Europe in 1848 with earnest hopefulness. The eagerness of our government to recognize Kossuth, the Hungarian revolutionist, brought a protest from the Austrian Chargé Hülsemann. Daniel Webster responded with an eloquence which breathed the spirit of confidence in our future; he made the point that, without attempting intervention, we were deeply concerned with "the fortunes of nations struggling for institutions like our own." We never acquiesced in tyranny, we never accepted absolutism or statism. We always protested them.

Norman A. Graebner, Professor of History — University of Illinois, *Empire on the Pacific*, 1955, p. 16.

Jacksonian democracy had cast a spell over the land. Americans in the early forties viewed their political system with a Messianic consciousness, convinced that they held the future of republican government in their hands. Andrew Jackson in his Farewell Message asserted that Providence had selected the American people to be "the guardians of freedom to preserve it for the benefit of the human race." Soon John L. O'Sullivan attached this democratic faith to the ideal of national expansion. "We are the nation of human progress," he charged in 1839, "and who will, what can, set limits to our onward march?" Americans possessed a mandate to spread throughout the world their four freedoms—"freedom of conscience, freedom of person, freedom of trade and business pursuits, universality of freedom and equality."

Henry M. Wriston, Former Diplomat, *Diplomacy in a Democracy*, 1956, p. 76.

Abraham Lincoln said that our Declaration of Independence "gave liberty not alone to the people of this country, but hope to all the world, for all future time."

Roger Hilsmar, Professor of International Affairs—Columbia University, *To Move a Nation*, 1964, p. 582.

But above all else, President Kennedy had a vision of the future and a capacity for communicating it to the world's peoples. Kennedy was an idealist, but not an ideologue; the old ikons were being broken on all sides, and Kennedy's gift was to approach the world in new words and new sincerity. As he said over and over again in the election campaign of 1960, he wanted to get America moving not only for its own sake but so that it could provide the "inspiration and leadership" to get the world moving, too.

Richard J. Barnet, Institute for Policy Studies, *Intervention and Revolution* 1968, p. 78.

Yet America has always tried to explain its relations to the rest of the world in terms of ideological principles which transcend parochial economic or military interests. There is a messianic idea running through American history that this nation has something to give the world beyond the example of the Affluent Society and that the spread of American civilization abroad is the ultimate vindication of the American political experiment. From the earliest involvement of the Republic in foreign adventures, Americans have wrapped the desire for more land, more power, more respect, more bases, more raw materials, and more markets in an ideological mantle. So also the postwar effort to push ever farther from our own shores the ramparts of Fortress America.

Charles L. Sanford, Professor of Language and Literature—Rensselaer Polytechnic Institute, *Manifest Destiny and the Imperialism Question*, 1974, p. 9.

Thus, while Americans generally expected to exert a favorable influence over the rest of mankind, they often disagreed on the means employed. Their messianic heritage encompassed two rather different courses: one being the path of activistic proseletyzing that led by degrees to various forms of coercion, not excluding the use of military force; and the other relying on the quiet force of exemplary conduct. The strictures of Presidents Washington and Jefferson against entangling alliances belong to the *messianic example*—more popularly known as "isolationism." President Theodore Roosevelt's invocation of a police power over Latin America as a corollary to the Monroe Doctrine converted that doctrine into an expression of *messianic intervention*—sometimes confused with enlightened internationalism.

"Unalienable rights."

Charles L. Sanford, Professor of Language and Literature — Rensselaer Polytechnic Institute, *Manifest Destiny and the Imperialism Question*, 1974, p. 8.

Once colonial subjects of England, their very survival threatened by rival European powers, Americans have traditionally opposed imperialism both for themselves and for other nations, as a wicked European game. Yet John Adams predicted in 1787 that the 13 new American republics were "destined to spread over the northern part of that whole quarter of the globe . . . in favor of the rights of mankind." His son, John Quincy Adams, in formulating the Monroe Doctrine, told the British ministry straight away that everyone must consider all of North America to be controlled by the United States. An outspoken critic of European imperialism, President Jefferson was responsible for the largest acquisition of territory in American history, the Louisiana Purchase.

Dexter Perkins, Professor Emeritus of American Civilization — Cornell University, *American Approach to Foreign Policy*, 1952, p. 71.

The refusal of the President to recognize the blood-stained regime of Victoriano Huerta was based squarely upon principle, and ironically enough this insistence on principle came very near leading to intervention. No doubt Wilson's policy came in for very sharp criticism from some of those who described themselves as realists, but it was, none the less, resolutely adhered to, and it led, of course, to the fall of the Mexican dictator.

Dexter Perkins, Professor Emeritus of American Civilization — Cornell University, *American Approach to Foreign Policy*, 1952, p. 80.

The same sense of moral reprobation with regard to aggression showed itself in the American attitude towards Hitler. Not only dislike of totalitarian political forms, but indignation at the aggressions of the National Socialist regime, not only fear of consequences, but moral indignation at the methods of aggrandizement, played a part in the steadily mounting tide of feeling against the Third Reich. By the end of the thirties, too, the American people were coming to a conviction that is more and more influencing policy, the conviction that the use of force for the purposes of domination is inherently immoral and intolerable.

Senator J. William Fulbright, *The Arrogance of Power*, 1966, p. 13.

For all our noble intentions, the countries which have had most of the tutelage in democracy by United States Marines have not been particularly democratic. These include Haiti, which is under a brutal and superstitious dictatorship; the Dominican Republic, which languished under the brutal Trujillo dictatorship for thirty years and whose second elected government since the overthrow of Trujillo is threatened, like the first, by the power of a military oligarchy; and of course Cuba, which, as no one needs to be reminded, has replaced its traditional right-wing dictatorships with a communist dictatorship.

"The consent of the governed."

Dexter Perkins, Professor Emeritus of American Civilization—Cornell University, *American Approach to Foreign Policy*, 1952, p. 69.

The moral factors in diplomacy, the sympathy with the democratic ideal, was again expressed in the European revolutions of 1848. The American government acted promptly, almost precipitately, in recognizing the Second French Republic in 1848. The Hungarian revolt was followed with intense enthusiasm by many Americans, and the Taylor administration sent an American representative to Hungary, with instructions to hold out assurances of recognition, if the circumstances warranted

Senator Albert Beveridge, *Congressional Record*, January 9, 1900.

The Declaration of Independence does not forbid us to do our part in the regeneration of the world. . . .
It was written by men who, for a century and a half, had been experimenting in self-government on this continent, and whose ancestors for hundreds of years before had been gradually developing toward that high and holy estate. The Declaration applies only to people capable of self-government. How dare any man prostitute this expression of the very elect of self-governing peoples to a race of Malay children of barbarism, schooled in Spanish methods and ideas? And you, who say the Declaration applies to all men, how dare you deny its application to the American Indian? And if you deny it to the Indian at home, how dare you grant it to the Malay abroad?

Howard K. Beale, Professor of History — University of Wisconsin, *Theodore Roosevelt and the Rise of America to World Power*, 1956, p. 455.

In his more mature years, Roosevelt became troubled over the relation of democracy to empire. How a democracy was to rule colonial peoples under democratic machinery was a problem that worried him as he gained experience. The colonials he felt were not ready for democratic forms of government and so he believed rule by a great power benefited them. But could the imperial power itself maintain democracy at home and at the same time rule a colonial empire?

William Jennings Bryan, Speech Accepting the Democratic Nomination for President, August 8, 1900, *Speeches of William Jennings Bryan*, 1909, p. 24.

Those who would have this Nation enter upon a career of empires must consider, not only the effect of imperialism on the Filipinos, but they must also calculate its effects upon our own nation. We cannot repudiate the principle of self-government in the Philippines without weakening that principle here.

Dexter Perkins, Professor Emeritus of American Civilization—Cornell University, *American Approach to Foreign Policy*, 1952, p. 73.

That the peace should rest upon the will of the peoples concerned was clear to him, clear to him even before the United States entered the war, set forth in some detail in the famous address of the 22nd of January, 1917. This idea was reenunciated again and again after America entered the conflict; it is one of the dominating conceptions in the famous Speech of the Fourteen Points. And, of course, it plays an important part in the negotiation of the treaty of peace. It was respect for this principle that made Wilson fight tenaciously French ambitions for the annexation of the Saar, and that led to the setting up of an international regime in that important region, with provision for a plebiscite at the end of a fifteen year period; it was on the basis of this principle that the President contested French designs to detach the Rhineland from Germany. . . .

Thomas Bailey, Professor of History—Stanford University, *The Art of Diplomacy*, 1968, p. 86.

During World War II Franklin Roosevelt, imbued with Wilson's idealism, put pressure on his hard-pressed allies to liquidate their colonial empires. His heart went out to subject peoples. Thanks in part to Roosevelt's

217

prodding during the war and after, Britain pulled out of India, with a resultant bloodbath and the creation of a geographical absurdity in Pakistan. The British likewise abandoned their bases in Egypt, with the consequent ascendancy of Nasser and the Suez flareup of 1956, which came close to triggering World War III. The Dutch were squeezed out of Indonesia, with the subsequent rise of Sukarno and outbreaks of wholesale slaughter. The Belgians were forced out of the Congo prematurely, with frightful atrocities and more international time-bombs of a most explosive nature.

American policy in every case was largely motivated by a high-minded regard for the self-determination of colonial peoples. But in a number of instances a wholesome regard for realities might have dictated a more cautious approach

Richard J. Barnet, Institute for Policy Studies, *Intervention and Revolution*, 1968, p. 10.

In recent years the pace of both insurgent activity and U.S. intervention has been stepped up sharply. In 1965 an American expeditionary force was sent to Vietnam and Marine divisions landed in the Dominican Republic to prevent insurgents from taking power. Such major commitments demanded a clearer articulation of U.S. policy. "Revolution in any country is a matter for that country to deal with," President Johnson declared as he ordered the Marines to Santo Domingo. "It becomes a matter for hemispheric action only when the object is the establishment of a communist dictatorship.

Denna Frank Fleming, Professor Emeritus of International Relations — Vanderbilt University, "Manifest Destiny in Vietnam," in *Manifest Destiny and the Imperialism Question*, 1974, p. 151.

It followed that after world War II the people of Vietnam could not be permitted to win their war of independence from France, because they had Communist leaders. We therefore poured nearly $3 billion worth of military and economic aid for France into Vietnam, and Secretary of State Dulles did all that one utterly determined man could do to prevent France from making peace. When he failed he refused to accept the Geneva settlement of 1954, which divided Vietnam purely for the temporary purpose of liquidating the war, and our government worked to make the division permanent.

This had three effects: (1) it frustrated independence for the South Vietnamese; (2) it reimposed a feudalistic social system on the South Vietnamese peasants, involving the restoration of hated landlord rule; and (3) our Mandarin tyrant Diem plunged the country into bitter and widespread revolt.

Idealism.

Paul A. Varg, Professor of History — Michigan State University, *Foreign Policies of the Founding Fathers*, 1963, p. 4.

In the years since World War II it has become fashionable to speak of a moralistic approach to foreign policy. The moralistic approach consists of making the ends and means of foreign policy consistent with a preconceived ideal. The predominance of the ideals associated with the Declaration of Independence led the founding fathers to conceive of a world of international relations radically different from the existing system. They believed that a nation, no less than the individual, had a set of rights that had their basis in the natural order. The determination to approach foreign relations in terms of the ideal rather than in terms of existing realities predominated during the Revolution, . . . lost much of its hold during the Washington administrations, and regained prominence with the election of Thomas Jefferson.

Paul A. Varg, Professor of History—Michigan State University, *Foreign Policies of the Founding Fathers*, 1963, p. 304.

Like the later arguments in behalf of manifest destiny, Wilson's Fourteen Points, and Franklin Roosevelt's war for the Four Freedoms, the founding fathers' rhetoric was a force in itself. Rather than a mere cloak for achievement of national goals, the ideology was a dynamic force, a propellant perhaps quite as strong as land hunger, trade, profits, or national pride.

218

Dexter Perkins, Professor Emeritus of American Civilization — Cornell University, *American Approach to Foreign Policy*, 1952, p. 70.

The theme of democratic idealism runs through the whole history of Pan-Americanism, which began to find expression in positive form with James G. Blaine. The economic determinist will doubtless discover ulterior motives behind the calling of the Latin-American conference of 1889; and such motives there undoubtedly were. But would it have been possible to weld together the nations of the New World in so close an association on the basis of a trade infinitely less significant than that with Europe? Is it not certain that the belief, whether justified or not, that there existed a similarity of institutions between the states of North and South America had something to do with the success of this important movement? And have not Pan-American conferences again and again asserted the validity of democratic principles, and paid tribute to the democratic ideal?

Ernest R. May. Professor of History—Harvard University, *The World War and American Isolation, 1914-1917*, 1966, p. 48.

For Wilson, of course, it was not always sufficient that a policy be profitable and popular; it had also to be justified on legal and moral grounds. Despite his own feeling and despite the evidence of public approval, he still asked for lawyers' opinions on the policy, and he continued to meditate it within his own conscience.

Henry M. Wriston, Former Diplomat, *Diplomacy in a Democracy*, 1956, p. 115.

To what conclusion do we come? Situations of strength are still essential; a reasonable estimate of the relationship of commitments to potentialities is ordinary prudence. But armaments, economic strength, alliances are not enough. Policy must also be based upon moral considerations as well as the more tangible factors. The human spirit cannot be entered upon a balance sheet, nor weighed, nor measured, nor counted. Yet it remains the most potent force in all the world. Plain people know this instinctively; they respond to its manifestations wherever they appear throughout the globe.

Paul A. Varg, Professor of History — Michigan State University, *Foreign Policies of the Founding Fathers*, 1963, p. 304.

This moralism did not inhibit a hard-headed pragmatic approach to foreign policy. The founding fathers made the best of both worlds, appeal to justice and energetic defense of national interest. Alexander Hamilton stood alone in frankly basing foreign policy on national self-interest. Thomas Jefferson and James Madison were no less energetic in supporting national interests, but they clothed their demands in terms of moral justification. This was not a devious employment of rhetoric but a sincere expression of their honestly held views.

Realism.

Thomas Bailey, Professor of History — Stanford University, *The Art of Diplomacy*, 1968, p. 82.

If self-interest is not the primary motivation in shaping foreign relations, it ought to be. A government is not a charitable institution; it exists as the trustee of its people. Its first duty is to them, and it has no moral right to give away the assets of its constituency without at least some kind of equivalent.

Norman A. Graebner, Professor of History — University of Illinois, *Empire on the Pacific*, 1955, p. 228.

American triumphs in Mexico were essential to the success of the expansionist program, but they had no bearing on administration goals. These had been defined by Polk and his cabinet before the war was hardly under way. Manifest destiny revealed itself in the Mexican War only when it clamored for the whole of Mexico, but even that final burst of agrarian nationalism was effectively killed by the Treaty of Guadalupe Hidalgo. Polk's objectives, clear and precise, were ever limited to two ocean ports. Victories along the road to Mexico City were important only in that they eventually brought to the President the opportunity to secure what he had once hoped to achieve by diplomacy alone.

William A. Williams, Professor of History — Oregon State University, *The Roots of the Modern American Empire*, 1969, p. 4.

The expansionist, imperial foreign policy adopted by the United States at the end of the nineteenth century was largely formulated in industrial terms by men who were leaders and spokesmen of that part of the political economy. They were primarily concerned with obtaining markets for surplus manufactured goods and venture capital, and with acquiring reliable access to cheap raw materials needed by the American industrial system. That industrial orientation of American foreign policy became increasingly clear during the twentieth century as American leaders struggled to build and maintain an international system that would satisfy the interrelated economic, ideological, and security needs and desires of the United States as they defined those objectives.

Walter LaFeber, Professor of History—Cornell University, *The New Empire*, 1963, p. 408.

In 1898, however, the United States annexed Hawaii and demanded the Philippines from Spain. These acquisitions were not unheralded. Seward had pushed his nation's claims far out into the Pacific with the purchase of Alaska and the Midway islands.

One striking characteristic tied these acquisitions to the new territory brought under American control in 1898 and 1899, immediately after the war with Spain. The United States obtained these areas not to fulfill a colonial policy, but to use these holdings as a means to acquire markets for the glut of goods pouring out of highly mechanized factories and farms.

William A. Williams, Professor of History — Oregon State University, *The Roots of the Modern American Empire*, 1969, p. 452.

Those men and women embraced imperialism in the name of freedom, as well as in the practice of expanding the marketplace. Heresy though it may be, it seems very likely that radicals must accept the truth that there is a broad area in which every people is an island unto themselves. Imperialism in the name of community—at home or abroad—is a vastly more horrible travesty than imperialism in the name of the free marketplace.

Richard J. Barnet, Institute for Policy Studies, *Intervention and Revolution*, 1968, p. 276.

The preceding discussion has assumed that the primary motivation behind America's crusade against revolution is an altruistic desire to save the people of Asia, Africa, and Latin America from the terrors of Stalinism. No doubt a few members of the national-security bureaucracy have been passionately concerned about this. But the primary allegiance of national officials in any country is to their own populations. Such considerations as the fear of $16 billion in corporate assets invested in Asia, Latin America, and the Near East as a result of expropriation by radical regimes influence policymakers at least as much as the urge to rescue undeveloped countries from one particular form of totalitarianism.

Selected Bibliography

Armstrong, Hamilton Fish, ed. *Fifty Years of Foreign Affairs.* Washington: Council on Foreign Relations, 1971.

Armstrong, Hamilton Fish, ed. *The Foreign Affairs Reader.* New York: Published for the Council on Foreign Relations by Harper, 1947.

Bailey, Thomas A. *The Art of Diplomacy.* New York: Appleton, Century, Crofts, 1068.

Bailey, Thomas A. *A Diplomatic History of the American People.* New York: Appleton, Century, Crofts, 1974.

Bailyn, Bernard. *Ideological Origins of the American Revolution.* Cambridge: Belknap Press of the Harvard University Press, 1967.

Barnet, Richard J. *Intervention and Revolution.* New York: The World Publishing Co., 1968.

Beale, Howard K. *Theodore Roosevelt and the Rise of America to World Power.* Baltimore: The Johns Hopkins Press, 1956.

Becker, Carl. *Declaration of Independence.* New York: Peter Smith, 1940.

Chomsky, Noam. *American Power and the New Mandarins.* New York: Pantheon Books, 1969.

Ekirch, Arthur A. Jr. *Ideas, Ideals, and American Diplomacy.* New York: Appleton, Century, Crofts, 1966.

Gilbert, Felix. *To the Farewell Address.* Princeton: Princeton University Press, 1961.

Graebner, Norman A. *Empire on the Pacific.* New York: The Ronald Press Co., 1955.

Graebner, Norman A. *Ideas and Diplomacy.* New York: Oxford University Press, 1964.

Graebner, Norman A. *Manifest Destiny.* New York: The Bobbs-Merrill Co., Inc., 1968.

Hilsman, Roger. *To Move a Nation.* New York: Dell Publishing Co., 1964.

Kennan, George F. *Realities of American Foreign Policy.* Princeton: Princeton University Press, 1954.

LaFeber, Walter. *The New Empire.* Ithaca, N.Y.: Cornell University Press, 1963.

Leopold, Richard W. *Growth of American Foreign Policy.* New York: Knopf, 1962.

May, Ernest R. *Imperial Democracy.* New York: Harcourt, Brace and World, 1961.

May, Ernest R. *The World War and American Isolation, 1914-1917.* Chicago: Quadrangle Books, 1966.

Merk, Frederick; Morrison, Samuel Eliot; and Freidel, Frank. *Dissent in Three American Wars.* Cambridge, Mass.: Harvard University Press, 1970.

Merk, Frederick. *Manifest Destiny and Mission in American History.* New York: Knopf, 1963.

Merk, Frederick. *The Monroe Doctrine and American Expansionism, 1843-1849.* New York: Knopf, 1966.

Merli, Frank J., and Wilson, Theodore A., eds. *Makers of American Diplomacy.* New York: Scribner's, 1974.

Morgenthau, Hans J. *In Defense of the National Interest.* New York: Knopf, 1951.

Osgood, Robert E. *America and the World, from the Truman Doctrine to Vietnam.* Baltimore: The Johns Hopkins Press, 1970.

Osgood, Robert E. *Ideals and Self-Interest in America's Foreign Policy.* Chicago: University of Chicago Press, 1953.

Osgood, Robert E. *Retreat from Empire?* Baltimore: The Johns Hopkins Press, 1973.

Perkins, Dexter A. *The Evolution of American Foreign Policy.* New York: Oxford University Press, 1966.

Perkins, Dexter A. *Foreign Policy and the American Spirit.* Edited by G.G. Van Deusen and Richard Wade. Ithaca, N.Y.: Cornell University Press, 1957.

Perkins, Dexter S. *A History of the Monroe Doctrine.* Boston: Little, Brown, 1955.

Rappaport, Armin. *Issues in American Diplomacy.* New York: The Macmillan Co., 1965.

Sanford, Charles L., ed. *Manifest Destiny and the Imperialism Question.* New York: John Wiley and Sons, Inc., 1974.

Schlesinger, Arthur M. Jr. *The Bitter Heritage.* Boston: Houghton Mifflin, 1968.

Van Hoogstrate, Dorothy J. *American Foreign Policy: Realists and Idealists.* St Louis: B. Herder, 1960.

Varg, Paul A. *Foreign Policies of the Founding Fathers.* East Lansing: Michigan State University Press, 1963.

Welch, Richard E. *Imperialists vs. Anti-Imperialists.* Itasca, Ill.: F. E. Peacock Publishers, Inc., 1972.

Williams, William Appleman. *The Roots of the Modern American Empire.* New York: Random House, 1969.

Williams, William Appleman. *The Tragedy of American Diplomacy.* New York: Dell Publishing Co., 1972.

Wriston, Henry M. *Diplomacy in a Democracy.* New York: Harper, 1956.

CAN AMERICA AFFORD A FOREIGN POLICY BASED ON MORAL PRINCIPLE?

Introductory Essay

Soon after the outbreak of the Spanish-American War in 1898, Commodore George Dewey led a US. naval squadron against the Spanish fleet stationed at Manila Bay, the Philippines. The destruction of the enemy fleet was accomplished without the loss of a single man, and the islands quickly passed into American hands. But what was to be done with the Philippines? Should they be returned to Spain? Given their independence? Annexed as a colony to the United States? The fate of the islands became the subject of a fascinating debate, one that revealed a good deal about the place of morality in American foreign policy.

Among the ardent expansionists favoring the annexation of the Philippines was Senator Henry Cabot Lodge. His position had been set forth in an important speech three years previously: "The modern movement is all toward the concentration of people and territory into great nations and large dominions . . . It is a movement which makes for civilization and the advancement of the race. As one of the great nations of the world, the United States must not fall out of the line of march." Now he saw "a vast trade and wealth and power," with greater opportunity "than anything that has happened . . . since the annexation of Louisiana," in the control of the Philippines. Concurring was Senator Albert Beveridge, who saw America as a "conquering race" whose destiny was "to obey her blood and occupy new markets, and if necessary new lands" because "in the Almighty's Infinite Plan . . . debased civilizations and decaying races must give way before the higher civilization of the noble and more virile type of man." The claim of moral and practical benefits to be gained from the annexation of the islands was countered by competing claims of morality and practicality advanced by foes of annexation. The influential Senator George F. Hoar spoke of "vassal states" and "barbarous archipelagoes" which could only be obtained by "trampling on our own great Charter, which recognizes alike the liberty and the dignity of individual manhood." Darker reasons played a role for some spokesmen. "I strenuously oppose," said Georgia's "Pitchfork Ben" Tillman, "incorporating any more colored men in the body politic." The leader of the organized labor movement, Samuel Gompers, feared that annexation would bring working-

men into competition with vast numbers of "the Chinese, the Negritos, and the Malays" hungry to enter the new parent nation. President McKinley prayed for a divine guidance in resolving the problem and one night the following came to him:

(1) That we could not give (the Philippines) back to Spain—that would be cowardly and dishonorable; (2) that we could not turn them over to France or Germany—our commercial rivals in the Orient—that would be bad business and discreditable; (3) that we could not leave them to themselves—they were unfit for self-government . . . . and (4) that there was nothing left for us to do but to take them all, and to educate the Filipinos, and uplift and civilize and Christianize them, and by God's grace do the best we could by them.

Congress agreed, and we began a slow process of readying the islands for independence. Hence, in the end we could not ignore responsibilities thrust upon us by chance, nor could we bring ourselves to act in a nakedly selfish manner. Instead, America determined to Westernize the Philippines—a course which we paternalistically assumed to be in their own best interests.

The debate over annexation of the Philippines is illustrative of a wider question: Can America *afford* a foreign policy based on moral principles? Viewed in a kindly light, the national decision to guide the Filipinos along the path to democratic self-rule may be admirable, but it was a decision that levied an enormous toll on our nation—with an initial payment in the form of a bitter, bloody insurrection pitting American Marines against the forces of nationalist leader Emilio Aguinaldo, and the balance extracted by Japanese military planners who could see no place for an American protectorate in their envisioned "Co-Prosperity Sphere."

Philosophers have devoted endless hours and dedicated enormous tomes to questions of definition; an attempt to determine what basic moral principles would be most applicable in the intercourse of nations invites an extension of their art. One could judge the morality of foreign policy by examining intentions: requiring pure motives or "good intent" for the assessment of an act as moral. Another approach to the study of ethics focuses on the consequences of acts. Did the policy do the greatest good for the greatest number? Finally, we could test the morality of our acts by our willingness to see them universalized. A version of the Golden Rule: would we be willing for other nations to do unto us as we have done unto them? Any moral system is subject to inquiry and criticism, but that our standards are raised by an attempt at morality can be little questioned. While we are doubtless doomed to an imperfect achievement of an imperfect system, much can be claimed for the endeavor.

We may also choose to treat moral principles in more concrete terms. Our nation could publicly and irrevocably declare for the principle of national self-determination; we could sanction intervention to protect the unalienable rights of the individual under any system of government, with its concurrent concern for the sanctity of human life and individual liberties; the preservation and promulgation of democratic principles; the notion of "fair play," enjoining secret treaties and clandestine actions; or any combination of these, as well as a multitude of alternatives.

Deciding whether America can afford a joining of morality and diplomacy should not suggest that the two have been divorced in the past. Morality has been a recurring theme in America's international dealings, and righteous indignation an almost constant refrain. Yet our approach to decisions has not always followed consistent principles, our actions have often been colored by self interest, and philosophic bases for the changes wrought by our diplomacy have sometimes been proposed long after the policy has been set.

Conflicts over the place of moral principle in foreign policy began early in the history of the Republic. During the Revolution, France's support for America led to a treaty of mutual support in 1778. In 1793, a revolutionary French regime made war against Britain, while America, under Washington's tutelage, remained a neutral bystander. The common element in each policy was self-interest. Friendless against the world's most powerful nation, American rebels found solace and material support from a monarchic state. Young and relatively impotent among the world's nations, the newly minted United States stood aside from a European dispute. To intervene and assist a people who, like herself, had overthrown a monarch, would have been seemingly consistent with the democratic precepts announced in her own Declaration of Independence. But her vulnerability at England's hands was a higher risk than disavowal of principled alliance with her French compatriots in rebellion. The movement toward alliance and intervention were tempered by isolation's greater rewards.

Alarmed by the dispute between those supporting either Britain or France, Washington presented in his Farewell Address one of the most memorable statements ever made on American foreign policy. "It is our true policy," he indicated, "to steer clear of permanent alliances with any portion of the foreign world. . . ." He was particularly concerned about involvement in European affairs, for "Europe has a set of primary interests which to us have none or a very remote relation." Washington saw an interrelationship between the moral conduct of foreign affairs and practical advantage to be gained by such a policy:

> It will be worthy of a free, enlightened, and at no distant period a great nation to give to mankind the magnanimous and too novel example of a people always guided by an exalted justice and benevolence. Who can doubt that in the course of time and things the fruits of such a plan would richly repay any temporary advantages which might be lost by a steady adherence to it?

American foreign policy has been shaped by many considerations, but there has been a persistent element of morality since Washington's time—reflected in both successes and failures—which derives from the nations' self-image as a divinely protected beacon of freedom to the world.

Jefferson as President was forced to deal with hostile maritime acts by Britain and France, who were at that time embroiled in the Napoleonic wars. The seizure of hundreds of U.S. vessels on the high seas and the impressment of thousands of American sailors compelled Jefferson to retaliate to protect the nation's honor. The obvious military weakness of the young nation, however, dampened any notions of employing the sword. Instead, Jefferson persuaded Congress to pass the Embargo Act in 1807, which in effect prohibited exports. Virginia's John Randolph suggested that this measure was like trying to "cure the corns by cutting off the toes," and indeed the impact on foreign trade and the American economy was crippling. The nation avoided war, but only at the cost of self-inflected injury.

The smoldering and unresolved resentments against the British over maritime incidents, coupled with a covetous interest in the expansion of American borders to Canada and Florida, prodded the nation into the War of 1812. The War Hawks in Congress, led by Henry Clay, admitted to both the moral and the pragmatic reasons in favoring armed conflict.

As the nation turned toward expansion across its vast undeveloped territories, it attempted to translate Washington's injunction against involvement in European affairs into a workable principle of foreign policy. The Monroe Doctrine (1823) added to Washington's warning against our meddling in Europe that Europe must not meddle in the affairs of the Western hemisphere. The Doctrine was aimed at

Russia, which claimed territory far down the Pacific coast of the continent, and at European nations seeking advantages in Latin American nations, almost all of which had won independence from Spain in the previous six years. "The American continents," claimed Monroe, "by the free and independent condition which they have assumed and maintain, are henceforth not to be considered as subjects for future colonization by any European powers." European attempts to retake parts of the Western hemisphere were warned to be "the manifestation of an unfriendly disposition toward the United States," a threat to the nation's peace and safety. For its part, America promised not to interfere in the affairs of Europe or her existing colonies. The statement was enthusiastically received at home, but was considered an empty declaration by the European nations, who noted that the United States lacked the power to enforce any part of the policy. In 1854, for example, the British Foreign Secretary frankly concluded that the Monroe Doctrine was "only the dictum of the distinguished person who announced it, and not an international accord which ought to regulate the conduct of European states." Yet, the doctrine did set an important precedent referred to by numerous presidents once America became a power. In the most dramatic example, President Kennedy cited the Monroe Doctrine as part of his justification for carrying this nation to the brink of nuclear exchange in the Cuban Missile Crisis.

American foreign policy for the half century after the Monroe Doctrine was, in the main, preoccupied with continental expansion. "Manifest Destiny," a term coined by Democratic journalist John O'Sullivan, expressed a whole set of values rather than simply a rapacious appetite for conquest. A chosen people was fated by divine providence to create a great model of democracy and freedom and wealth in an immense area, continental in scope. Whether this idea was moral or immoral is not a simple question. The moral trappings may have been a thin disguise for greed, and yet there is every reason to believe that the ideals behind the concept of Manifest Destiny were fervently held. Still, in the course of expansion, the rights of those in our path received little attention. The Indians, for example, received outrageous treatment; westward moving whites broke treaties at their own convenience. Even presidents expressed racist views, as when Andrew Jackson announced in his message to Congress on removal of Southern Indians to Indian Territory (now Oklahoma), that it was "an established fact that they cannot live in contact with a civilized community and prosper"; he spoke at length of the steps taken to control the "overwhelming appetite" of the Indians for liquor. Such views gained greater sophistication in later years when one could allude to respectable Social Darwinist thought. Whatever the motivation, moral or otherwise, it was not until Americans had overrun the territory between the great oceans that they were again willing to look aggressively toward the rest of the world.

The place of morality in American foreign policy is illustrated in the process by which the United States came to accept the role of Manifest Destiny in distant lands. The transition was abrupt. Just a few years before, President Benjamin Harrison had expressed the prevailing opinion—that the United States was and should remain "a nation apart." Isolation was only briefly threatened by the opportunity to acquire Hawaii in 1893. President Cleveland not only refused to acknowledge a provisional government largely composed of American settlers, he ordered an investigation of the U.S. role in the revolt and tried to reinstate Queen Liliuokalani. Historian Richard Hofstadter explained the reason for a changed attitude just two years later.

Issues of profit and loss, no matter how inflated with grandiose images of national pride, could not make expansionism a popular cause. When emotion colored the issues, however, Americans responded with enthusiasm. Emotion was amply provided after 1895 by publicity given to the treatment of Cubans by Spain during a new flare-up of chronic Cuban rebellion.

Outrage at events in Cuba, fully reported and exaggerated by the "yellow journalism" which flourished at this time, generated a cry for war that could not be stilled. At the cost of only 5,000 lives, the U.S. had gained the Philippines and Puerto Rico and had secured independence for Cuba.

Theodore Roosevelt added the "Roosevelt Corollary" to the Monroe Doctrine. It provided that the United States would exercise international police power to insure order in the Western hemisphere, thus making it unnecessary for European colonial powers to intervene. The most offensive implementation of this idea was the aid given to Panama's struggle for independence from Columbia, negotiations for the Panama Canal, and the building of the Canal. Roosevelt asked War Secretary Elihu Root whether or not he, Roosevelt, had defended himself, after referring to the Columbians as "dagoes" and insisting that "the interests of collective civilization" had been served by thwarting "their criminal error." Root replied: "You certainly have, Mr. President. You have shown that you were accused of seduction and you have conclusively proved that you were guilty of rape." Other examples of expanded U.S. interest in world affairs at the time were the Open Door policy in China; President Taft's theory of dollar diplomacy, which suggested that expanded economic influence of U.S. companies would increase stability in underdeveloped nations; Roosevelt's mediation of the Russo-Japanese war, for which he received a Nobel Peace Prize; and Wilson's intervention in Mexico.

The nation was unprepared for involvement with the European powers, however, despite increased exercise of power in Asia and Latin America. The nation hoped to avoid embroilment in a European struggle, re-electing the President who had "kept us out of war." Unrestricted German submarine warfare, a shift in the balance of power, and our economic and social ties with Great Britain brought us into World War I. Our involvement in the war was couched in terms of high moral purpose, "to make the world safe for democracy," to fight "the war to end all wars," to gain "peace without victory." At the conclusion of the war, however, the nation remained unwilling to recognize interdependence; the League of Nations and foreign involvements, in general, were rejected in the period before World War II.

With World War II, this policy was reversed. Franklin Roosevelt moved as quickly as popular support would permit to aid the allies against Hitler, taking such steps as approving the Lend Lease program to arm the British navy and declaring a state of unlimited emergency. Like Wilson, whose Fourteen Points set out ideals to fight for, Roosevelt advanced the Four Freedoms to motivate our efforts: freedom of speech and expression throughout the world, freedom of worship, freedom from want, and freedom from fear. The U.S. emerged from the war as the world's most powerful nation. That America was now ready to assume a role of leadership in world affairs is shown by the Truman Doctrine, which acknowledged a responsibility to defend freedom everywhere in the world against totalitarian power, and by the Marshall Plan, a commitment to the rebuilding of European economies from the ruins of war.

Foreign policy in the post-war period was guided by a new moralism, the fight against Communism. The hysteria over the "loss" of China showed how much attitudes had changed. We assumed that China was "ours" to lose, and that the Communists must have come to power without popular support. The Korean War and the Vietnam War forced a reexamination of our Cold War ideology. We were forced to admit that our objectives were limited, that the means we would employ to obtain them were limited, and painfully, in Vietnam, that with these limitations we were not invincible. More recent developments seem to portend a less ideological, more pragmatic foreign policy: the recognition of the People's Republic of China and arms limitation negotiations with the Soviets.

Consistent and virtuous behavior in the diplomatic arena offers an appealing alternative in a world that has had its fill of self-serving actions and pointless quarrels, a world whose most ambitious attempt at international cooperation and mediation has of-

ten been debased by power politics and propaganda maneuvers. The words of Woodrow Wilson, who believed that "the only people who are going to reap the harvest of the future are the people who can entertain ideals, who can follow ideals to the death," bear for many a haunting ring of truth. Examination of the harsh ground-rules of international existence, however, demands answers to many questions: Can moral principles be meaningfully applied in a world order where actions are rarely black and white, but only varying hues of gray? Can a change in the behavior of one nation accomplish lasting change? In an increasingly interdependent world, would acts of national self-denial impose unacceptable costs?

Perhaps most fundamental, can a consistent moral policy be maintained in a democratic nation? Commitment to principle requires its maintenance over extended periods of time and under differing circumstances. A democratic society, however, requires a responsiveness to the ever changing will of the people. Franklin Roosevelt's Secretary of State, Cordell Hull, observed that "Since the time when Thomas Jefferson insisted upon a 'decent respect to the opinions of mankind' public opinion has controlled foreign policy in all democracies." More recently, Henry Kissinger agreed that "the acid test of a policy is its ability to obtain domestic support." If anything can be learned from a review of history, surely to rely on the consistency of public opinion is a fanciful hope, at best. More than a century ago, Alexis de Tocqueville drew the obvious conclusion, that fluctuations in the popular mandate make it difficult for democracies "to coordinate the details of a great undertaking and to fix some plan and carry it through in spite of obstacles." For those who find morality in intervention and involvement, the reality of the popular will may be a swift and deadly undercurrent. Our commitment to foreign aid may not hold firm in the face of economic crisis at home or even a modest reduction in our standard of living. Likewise, we may be willing to defend a state under communist assult only until our own loss of life exceeds an acceptable limit. Untrue to Kennedy's pledge that "we shall pay any price, bear any burden, meet any hardship," the public will ride an uncomfortable principle only so far. The refusal to continue the trek may, however, be merely a needed reminder that the resources of any state are limited.

Even if one were to assume unchanging moral principles at the helm of our foreign policy, could they not be subjected to varying interpretations? The clash of Woodrow Wilson and Henry Cabot Lodge on the issue of the League of Nations is instructive. President Wilson believed that the United States should promote the democratic form of government—as did Lodge. Wilson felt that this could best be served by the nation's service as a model democracy—Lodge agreed. Wilson, however, felt that America could best set an example by supporting the League—Lodge, that the same end was far better served by splendid isolation.

One must also ask the advantage of one nation promoting moral integrity in an immoral world community. Would other nations emulate our example, or would they employ it as an opportunity for gain? One of history's most pragmatic and controversial political theorists, Niccolo Machiavelli, had little doubt on the subject.

> For the manner in which men live is so different from the way in which they ought to live, that he who leaves the common course for that which he ought to follow will find that it leads him to ruin rather than to safety. For a man who, in all respects, will carry out only his professions of good, will be apt to be ruined among so many who are evil. A prince therefore who desires to maintain himself must learn to be not always good, but to be so or not as necessity may require.

Certainly, this is painted in its darkest aspect. One can hope that good acts will follow good acts. Beyond hope, acting in concert, nations have formulated principles and sought to abide by them. That we have failed in the past points to the difficulty of the undertaking and not—as some would argue—to the inevitability of failure. Before we are overtaken and consumed by pragmatism, perhaps we should ask: Can America afford a foreign policy *not* based on moral principle?

Excerpted Documents

Moralism in foreign policy.

Howard K. Beale, Professor of History—University of Wisconsin, *Theodore Roosevelt and the Rise of America to World Power*, 1956, p. 80.

In his expansionism [Theodore Roosevelt] had to use economic forces and the greed of his fellow-men. Material force could strengthen a nation, but material considerations remained to him merely means. Economic prosperity must be kept the servant of more important values. His ends were associated with the courage, the virility, the power, the greatness of his country.

Woodrow Wilson, Address to the Senate, July 10, 1919, in *American Foreign Policy*, 1963, p. 161.

There were persons amongst us at home who looked with deep disapproval and avowed anxiety on such extensions of our national authority over distant islands and over peoples whom they feared we might exploit, not serve and assist. But we have not exploited them. We have been their friends and have sought to serve them. And our dominion has been a menace to no other nation. We redeemed our honor to the utmost in our dealings with Cuba. She is weak but absolutely free; and it is her trust in us that makes her free. Weak peoples everywhere stand ready to give us any authority among them that will assure them a like friendly oversight and direction. They know that there is no ground for fear in receiving us as their mentors and guides.

Henry M. Wriston, Former Diplomat *Diplomacy in a Democracy*, 1956, p. 100.

It is striking, therefore, that the most decisively successful piece of diplomacy since the war—The Marshall Plan — was based neither on power politics nor geopolitics nor economics alone; one of its chief characteristics was a profound moral commitment. Public acceptance of the Marshall Plan depended upon the conviction that the virtues of freedom are supreme, that freedom is indivisible, and that we bear a heavy responsibility not only for its survival but also for its spread to the rest of the world.

President Lyndon Baines Johnson, Acceptance of the National Freedom Award, February 23, 1966, in *Representative American Speeches, 1965-1966*, p. 15.

Our purpose in Vietnam is to prevent the success of aggression. It is not conquest; it is not empire; it is not foreign bases; it is not domination. It is, simply put, just to prevent the forceful conquest of South Vietnam by North Vietnam.

Senator J. William Fulbright, Former Chairman of the Senate Foreign Relations Committee, *The Arrogance of Power*, 1966, p. 257.

There are many respects in which America, if she can bring herself to act with the magnanimity and the empathy which are appropriate to her size and power, can be an intelligent example to the world. We have the opportunity to set an example of generous understanding in our relations with China, of practical cooperation for peace in our relations with Russia, of reliable and respectful partnership in our relations with Western Europe, of material helpfulness without moral presumption in our relations with developing nations, of abstention from the temptations of hegemony in our relations with Latin America, and of the all-around advantages of minding one's own business in our relations with everybody.

Dexter Perkins, Professor Emeritus of American Civilization—Cornell University, *American Approach to Foreign Policy*, 1952, p. 66.

Before we examine, however, the moralistic overtones in American diplomacy, we must pause to remark that these overtones do not necessarily and inevitably mean that American foreign policy is necessarily "better" than the diplomacy of other nations, even if we maintained, which we do not, that the difference was one in kind and not in degree. For one thing, the over-simplification of the issues which results from an appeal to moral principle may or may not be desirable in practice. The conviction, for example, that democratic government is the best of all governments may lead us to try to impose it on others, without success, and with the result that international irritation ensues.

Realism in foreign policy.

James Buchanan, Minister to England, John Mason, Minister to France, and Pierre Soule, Minister to Spain, in letter to Secretary of State William L. Marcy, October 18, 1854, in *Readings in American Foreign Policy*, 1971, p. 79.

Self-preservation is the first law of nature, with States as well as with individuals. All nations have, at different periods, acted upon this maxim. . . .
After we shall have offered Spain a price for Cuba far beyond its present value, and this shall have been refused, it will then be time to consider the question, does Cuba, in the possession of Spain, seriously endanger our internal peace and the existence of our cherished Union?
Should this question be answered in the affirmative, then, by every law, human and divine, we shall be justified in wresting it from Spain if we possess the power; and this upon the very same principle that would justify an individual in tearing down the burning house of his neighbor if there were no other means of preventing the flames from destroying his own home.

Senator Arthur H. Vandenberg, "American Foreign Policy," *Congressional Record*, January 10, 1945, pp. 169-173.

Now, I am not so impractical as to expect any country to act on any final motive other than self-interest. I know of no reason why it should. That is what nations are for. I certainly intend that intelligent and loyal American self-interest shall be just as vigilantly and vigorously guarded as is amply obvious, from time to time, in their own behalf by the actions of our allies.

Senator J. William Fulbright, Former Chairman of the Senate Foreign Relations Committee, *The Arrogance of Power,* **1966, p. 250.**

Throughout our history two strands have coexisted uneasily—a dominant strand of democratic humanism and a lesser but durable strand of intolerant puritanism. There has been a tendency through the years for reason and moderation to prevail as long as things are going tolerably well or as long as our problems seem clear and finite and manageable. But when things have gone badly for any length of time, or when the reasons for adversity have seemed obscure, or simply when some event or leader of opinion has aroused the people to a state of high emotion, our puritan spirit has tended to break through, leading us to look at the world through the distorting prism of a harsh and angry moralism.

Carl Parrini, Historian-Economist, *Heir to Empire,* **1969, p. 1.**

By 1916 American political and business leaders had reached the conclusion that in order to market the goods and services which the American economy was producing they had to change the rules governing world trade and investment. Their shorthand expression for that goal was called the Open Door.

Thomas A. Bailey, Professor of History—Stanford University, "The Myth-Makers of American History," *The Journal of American History,* **June 1968, p. 5.**

The men of 1776 thought they were fighting for liberty; the revisionists of the twentieth century played up economic motivations. . . .
The men of 1812 believed they were fighting for a free sea; the revisionists of the 1920's had them fighting for Canada. . . .
The men of 1861, including Lincoln, assumed that slavery was the principal villain in the coming of the war. In the 1920's Beard and others shifted emphasis to the North's alleged industrial imperialism. . . .
The men of 1917 concluded that the submarine plunged us into hostilities with imperial Germany. The revisionists of the 1930's blamed the financiers, the "munitioneers," the "propagandeers," and the "sloganeers."

Anglo-American, pseudonym, *National Review,* **May 1938, p. 602.**

There are two American "foreign policies," distinct and diametrically opposed; one congressional and one administration. Congressional foreign policy is based on the assumption that the United States should not concern itself with moral issues; it should maintain an impartial attitude toward treaty breakers and treaty keepers; both aggressors and victims of aggression should be placed on the same footing. Administration foreign policy is based on the opposite assumption; that the United States is most essentially concerned with moral issues, must bring moral pressure to bear upon treaty breakers and play an active part in upholding the rule of international law.

Michael Kammen, Professor of History—Cornell University, *People of Paradox,* **1974, p. 279.**

The Bald Eagle on the green side of your one dollar bill holds a clutch of deadly arrows in one clenched claw, and an olive branch in the other. Americans like to remind themselves, and others, that the United States emerged from a Revolution, an act of colonial self-emancipation. Nevertheless, they also like to emphasize that they stand for stability and order, balanced growth, constitutional procedures, and legitimacy. Americans like to speak the language of power and "talk tough," all the while stressing the need for a language of community and harmony. A form of double-entry bookkeeping seems to account for our efforts at international misunderstanding. We stress the need for nations to behave as equals, and to subordinate particular interests to the common cause of peace. At the same time, however, we insist that our very disinterestedness and worldwide responsibilities entitle us to the privilege of interpreting and vouchsafing the common good.

Dexter Perkins, Professor of American Civilization—Cornell University, *Foreign Policy and the American Spirit*, 1957, p. 3.

First of all, and above all, we must emphasize the extraordinary degree to which American foreign policy is derived from public opinion, rather than from the secret deliberations of the diplomats. Of course there is some control of diplomatic action in virtually every democratic nation today. But in no other country is the tradition of popular participation in these matters so long or so strong as it is here.

Alexander Hamilton, *The Federalist*, 1788, Number 71.

The republican principle demands that the deliberate sense of the community should govern the conduct of those to whom they intrust the management of their affairs; but it does not require an unqualified complaisance to every sudden breeze of passion, or to every transient impulse which the people may receive from the arts of men, who flatter their prejudices to betray their interests.
When occasions present themselves, in which the interests of the people are at variance with their inclinations, it is the duty of the persons whom they have appointed to be the guardians of those interests, to withstand the temporary delusion, in order to give them time and opportunity for more cool and sedate reflection.

Dexter Perkins, Professor of American Civilization—Cornell University, *Foreign Policy and the American Spirit*, 1957, p. 9.

. . . there is a danger that a diplomacy influenced by public sentiment may be less pliant than that of the professional diplomats. The record of the United States does not demonstrate this; but the special circumstances of our own time, the very sharpness of the contrast between democracy and totalitarianism, suggest that we may here encounter a real danger. To embroider this point, however, would lead us into the field of prophecy, not of history.

Walter Lippmann, in *Issues in American Diplomacy*, Vol. I, 1965, p. 37.

The unhappy truth is that the prevailing public opinion has been destructively wrong at the critical junctures. The people have imposed a veto upon the judgments of informed and responsible officials. They have compelled the governments, which usually knew what would have been wiser, or was necessary, or was more expedient, to be too late with too little, or too long with too much, too pacifist in peace and too bellicose in war, too neutralist or appeasing in negotiation or too intransigent. Mass opinion has acquired mounting power in this century. It has shown itself to be a dangerous master of decisions when the stakes are life and death.

Dexter Perkins, Professor Emeritus of American Civilization— Cornell University, *American Approach to Foreign Policy*, 1952, p. 76.

Take for example, the ill-timed attempt of President Grant to establish a protectorate over the Dominican Republic in 1870. The attempt was no doubt absurd, a kind of shoddy deal, with overtones of land speculation, with a government that could only maintain itself by a treaty with a stronger neighbor; but what is interesting is the strong moral reprobation which the enterprise aroused in the breast of Charles Sumner, and the refusal of the Republican majority, in days of strong partisanship, to go along with the President.

Erich Fromm, *The Art of Loving*, 1956, p. 20.

The lack of objectivity, as far as foreign nations are concerned, is notorious. From one day to another, another nation is made out to be utterly depraved and fiendish, while one's own nation stands for everything that is good and noble. Every action of the enemy is judged by one standard—every action of oneself by another. Even good deeds by the enemy are considered a sign of particular devilishness, meant to deceive us and the world, while our bad deeds are necessary and justified by our noble goals which they serve.

Isolationism.

George Washington, Farewell Address, September 17, 1796, in *Messages and Papers of the Presidents*, Vol. I, 1897, p. 214.

It is our true policy to steer clear of permanent alliances with any portion of the foreign world, so far, I mean, as we are now at liberty to do it; for let me not be understood as capable of patronizing infidelity to existing engagements. I hold the maxim no less applicable to public than to private affairs that honesty is always the best policy. I repeat, therefore, let those engagements be observed in their genuine sense. But in my opinion it is unnecessary and would be unwise to extend them.

Thomas Paine, "Thoughts on the Present State of American Affairs," 1775, in *Common Sense*, 1776, in *Foreign Policy and the American Spirit*, 1963, p. 26.

Any submission to, or dependance on, Great Britain, tends directly to involve this Continent in European wars and quarrels, and set us at variance with nations who would otherwise seek our friendship, and against whom we have neither anger nor complaint. As Europe is our market for trade, we ought to form no partial connection with any part of it. It is the true interest of America to steer clear of European contentions, which she never can do, while, by her dependance on Britain, she is made the makeweight in the scale of British politics.

Senator Henry Cabot Lodge, *Congressional Record*, August 12, 1919, p. 411.

...there is a wide difference between taking a suitable part and bearing a due responsibility in world affairs and plunging the United States into every controversy and conflict on the face of the globe. Be meddling in all the differences which may arise among any portion or fragment of humankind we simply fritter away our influence and injure ourselves to no good purpose. We shall be of far more value to the world and its peace by occupying, so far as possible, the situation which we have occupied for the last 20 years and by adhering to the policy of Washington and Hamilton, of Jefferson and Monroe, under which we have risen to our present greatness and prosperity.

Herbert Hoover, "The Nine Horsemen and America," *Liberty Magazine*, June 5, 1940, in *American Foreign Policy*, 1963, pp. 175-176.

If we join in these wars we would start with the already great exhaustion of ten years of our depression. Then we will further exhaust our economic strength. And that exhaustion will be to a far greater degree than in the few months we participated in the last war. And when the war was over we shall need devote our remaining resources to support our wounded, our maimed, our orphaned and our destitute. We shall need every resource to rebuild our farmers and workers from our own misery and impoverishment. And our sympathies will be justly limited to suffering at home....
But if we remain out of war, we might, if we have the will to do so, use our unimpaired resources, our courage, our moral strength to do mankind infinite service.
By that service we could allay the destruction of war, and the ravages of Famine and Pestilence. That service of compassion could go far to save civilization, and restore hope to men. Free of Hate we could exert an insistent voice of reason in the making of peace.

Thomas Bailey, Professor of History—Stanford University, "American Emergence as a World Power: The Myth and the Verity," *Pacific Historical Review*, February, 1961, p. 1.

The United States was the only first-rate nation that until recent times could afford the luxury of a third-rate army.

Henry Kissinger, *American Foreign Policy*, 1969, in *Readings in American Foreign Policy*, 1971, p. 181.

No country can act wisely simultaneously in every part of the globe at every moment of time. A more pluralistic world—especially in relationships with friends—is profoundly in our long-term interest. Political multipolarity, while difficult to get used to, is the precondition for a new period of creativity. Painful as it may be to admit, we could benefit from a counterweight that would discipline our occasional impetuosity and, by supplying historical perspective, modify our penchant for abstract and "final" solutions.

Anti-isolationism.

Theodore Roosevelt, *The Strenuous Life,* 1899, p. 325.

We cannot sit huddled within our own borders and avow ourselves merely an assemblage of well-to-do hucksters who care nothing for what happens beyond. Such a policy would defeat even its own end; for as the nations grow to have ever wider and wider interests, and are brought into closer and closer contact, if we are to hold our own in the struggle for naval and commercial supremacy, we must build up our power without our own borders.

Woodrow Wilson, Address to the Senate, July 10, 1919, in *American Foreign Policy,* 1963, p. 162.

Our participation in the war established our position among the nations and nothing but our own mistaken action can alter it. It was not an accident or a matter of sudden choice that we are no longer isolated and devoted to a policy which has only our own interest and advantage for its object. It was our duty to go in, if we were indeed the champions of liberty and of right. . . . It is thus that a new role and a new responsibility have come to this great nation that we honor and which we would all wish to live to yet higher levels of service and achievement.

Felix Morley, Editor—*Washington Post,* "How Can the United States Aid in Maintaining Peace?" Annals of the American Academy, July 1937, p. 113.

Neither our political structure of democratic government nor our social and economic structure of free enterprise and individual freedom under law could long survive the material and spiritual decay which national isolation would inescapably impose upon the nation. Like the individual who would seek safety and security for himself thru escape from the responsibilities of organized society into hermitlike isolation, a nation pursuing a similar course—even if it were to succeed for a time in avoiding assault by and conflict with other nations—would soon find its dream of safety and security a bitter illusion.

Richard W. Leopold, Professor of History—Northwestern University, *The Growth of American Foreign Policy,* 1962, p. 622.

"We must begin the great task that is before us," Roosevelt told the nation on December 9, 1941, "by abandoning once and for all the illusion that we can ever again isolate ourselves from the rest of humanity," Thus did the President proclaim the abandonment of isolationism as a diplomatic policy. Just as the terrifying months from the fall of France to the enactment of Lend-Lease had witnessed the repudiation of neutrality, so did the agonizing years from the attack on Pearl Harbor to the surrender in Tokyo Bay mark the beginning of permanent alliances. Such engagements, traditionally banned as a means of promoting the national interest, became a reality as the republic first joined the United Nations and later signed a network of security treaties and executive agreements embracing the New World, the North Atlantic, the Pacific, Southeast Asia, and the Middle East.

Senator Arthur H. Vandenberg, "American Foreign Policy," in *Congressional Record,* January 10, 1945, p. 169.

I do not believe that any nation hereafter can immunize itself by its own exclusive action. Since Pearl Harbor, World War No. 2 has put the gory science of mass murder into new and sinister perspective. Our oceans have ceased to be moats which automatically protect our ramparts.

Thomas Bailey, Professor of History—Stanford University, "American Emergence as a World Power: The Myth and the Verity," *Pacific Historical Review,* **February 1961, p. 1.**

The point is often missed that during the nineteenth century the United States practiced internal colonialism and imperialism on a continental scale. When the Western European nations expanded, they had to go overseas; when we expanded, we had to go west. We self-righteously preened ourselves on not becoming an imperialistic power until 1898, when we acquired Spanish real estate in the Philippines, Guam, and Puerto Rico. Yet hundreds of Spanish place names pepper the land from California to Texas, all of which, curiously enough, somehow managed to come under our nonimperialistic flag a half century earlier.

Richard J. Barnet, Institute for Policy Studies, *Intervention and Revolution,* **1968, p. 79.**

From the earliest days of the Republic expansionists and anti-expansionists struggled with each other over the proper role of force in spreading American civilization. During the Revolutionary War there was strong sentiment for the invasion and annexation of Canada. "We shall never be on a solid footing." Samuel Adams demanded, "till Britain cedes us what Nature designs we should have, or till we wrest it from her." The "natural" requirements of security also extended to Nova Scotia and Florida. The dispossession of the Indians was justified, as Indiana's Governor Harrison put it, because "one of the fairest portions of the globe" could not remain "the haunt of a few wretched savages" when "it seems destined by the Creator to give support to a large population and to be the seat of civilization, of science, and of true religion."

James W. Angell, Professor of Economics—Columbia University, *Financial Foreign Policy of the United States,* **1933, p.5.**

The term imperialism is itself used so loosely, and to describe such a wide variety of factual situations, that it is difficult to assign it any precise meaning at all. If the term be used, however, to connote a deliberate and self-seeking policy of territorial or financial aggrandizement deliberately practised by the United States government without any particular regard for the prior rights, interests and desires of the foreign peoples affected—as was true of much of the expansion of the European countries in Africa—then the term is used erroneously, when applied to the generality of our relations with the Latin American regions.

Charles L. Sanford, Professor of Language and Literature—Rensselaer Polytechnic Institute, *Manifest Destiny and the Imperialism Question,* **1974, p. 9.**

The major United States example of European imperialism has been the Philippines, which was finally granted independence in 1916. All other American acquisitions have been either by annexation, as with Hawaii, by purchase as with Louisiana and Alaska, or by cession as with Guam and Puerto Rico. The European pattern of military conquest and political domination does not seem to hold for the United States.

Woodrow Wilson, Speech before the Southern Commercial Congress, October 23, 1913, in *The Messages and the Papers of Woodrow Wilson,* **1924, p. 35.**

I want to take this occasion to say that the United States will never again seek one additional foot of territory by conquest. She will devote herself to showing that she knows how to make honorable and fruitful use of the territory she has, and she must regard it as one of the duties of friendship to see that from no quarter are material interests made superior to human liberty and national opportunity.

Senator J. William Fulbright, Former Chairman of the Foreign Relations Committee, *The Arrogance of Power,* **1966, p. 119.**

The basis of my criticisms of American policy in Southeast Asia and Latin America is a belief that American interests are better served by supporting nationalism than by opposing communism, and that when the two are encountered in the same political movement it is in our interest to accept a communist role in the government of the country concerned rather than to undertake the cruel and all but impossible task of suppressing a genuinely nationalist revolution.

Selected Bibliography

Adler,Selig. *Isolationist Impulse: Twentieth Century Reaction.* New York: Abelard-Schuman, 1957.

Adler, Selig. *Uncertain Giant: American Foreign Policy: 1921-1941.* New York: Macmillan, 1965.

Anderson, George L., ed. *Issues and Conflicts: 20th Century American Diplomacy.* Lawrence, Kansas: University of Kansas Press, 1959.

Angell, James Waterhouse. *Financial Foreign Policy.* New York: Council on Foreign Relations, 1933.

Armstrong, William M. *Godkin and American Foreign Policy, 1865-1900.* New York: Bookman Associates, 1957.

Beale, Howard K. *Roosevelt and the Rise of America to World Power.* Baltimore: Johns Hopkins Press, 1956.

Bell, Coral. *Negotiation from Strength! Study in Politics of Power.* New York: Knopf, 1963.

Bemis, Samuel F. *American Secretaries of State and Their Diplomacy.* New York: Knopf, 1927.

Bemis, Samuel F. *Latin American Policy of the United States.* New York: Harcourt Brace, 1943.

Bohlen, Charles E. *The Transformation of American Foreign Policy.* New York: W.W. Norton & Co., 1969.

Bowles, Chester. *The Conscience of a Liberal.* New York: Harper and Row, 1948.

Brown, Seyom. *The Faces of Power: Foreign Policy from Truman to Johnson.* New York: Columbia University Press, 1968.

Bryan, William Jennings. *Speeches of William Jennings Bryan.* New York: Funk and Wagnalls, 1909.

Buehrig, Edward H. *Woodrow Wilson and Balance of Power.* Bloomington, Indiana: Indiana University Press, 1955.

Burton, David H. *Theodore Roosevelt: Confident Imperialist.* Philadelphia: University of Pennsylvania Press, 1968.

Coudert, Frederic R. *Half Century of International Problems: A Lawyer's Views.* New York: Columbia University Press, 1954.

DeConde, A., and Rappaport, A., eds. *Essays Diplomatic and Undiplomatic of Thomas A. Bailey.* New York: Appleton-Century-Crofts, 1969.

Dulles, Foster R. *America's Rise to World Power.* New York: Harper, 1955.

Duroselle, Jean Baptiste. *From Wilson to Roosevelt: Foreign Policy.* Cambridge: Harvard University Press, 1963.

Ferrell, Robert H. *American Diplomacy in the Great Depression, 1929-1933.* Hamden, Conn.: Anchor Books, 1969.

Fulbright, J. William. *The Arrogance of Power.* New York: Random House, 1966.

Gardner, Lloyd C. *Economic Aspects of New Deal Diplomacy.* Madison, Wis.: University of Wisconsin Press, 1964.

Goldwin, R.A., and Clor, H.M. *Readings in American Foreign Policy.* New York: Oxford University Press, 1971.

Guerrant, E.O. *Roosevelt's Good Neighbor Policy.* Albuquerque, New Mexico: University of New Mexico Press, 1950.

Hoover, Herbert. *The Ordeal of Woodrow Wilson.* New York: McGraw Hill, 1958.

Kennan, George F. *American Diplomacy, 1900-1950.* New York: New American Library, 1951.

La Feber, Walter. *New Empire: American Expansion, 1860-1898.* Ithaca, New York: Cornell University Press, 1963.

Langer, William L. *Diplomacy of Imperialism, 1890-1902.* New York: Knopf, 1951.

Leopold, Richard W. *Growth of American Foreign Policy.* New York: Alfred A. Knopf, 1962.

Link, Arthur S. *Wilson the Diplomatist.* Baltimore, Maryland: Johns Hopkins University Press, 1957.

Lycan, Gilbert L. *Alexander Hamilton and American Foreign Policy: A Design for Greatness.* Norman: University of Oklahoma Press, 1970.

May, Ernest R., ed. *American Foreign Policy.* New York: G. Braziller, 1963.

May, Ernest R. *Imperial Democracy: Emergence of America.* New York: Harcourt Brace & World, 1961.

McCarthy, Eugene J. *The Limits of Power.* New York: Holt, Rinehart and Winston, 1963.

Merk, Frederick. *Manifest Destiny and Mission.* New York: Knopf, 1963.

Myers, William Starr. *Foreign Policies of Herbert Hoover.* New York: C. Scribner's Sons, 1970.

Nevins, Allan. *The New Deal and World Affairs.* New Haven: Yale University Press, 1950.

Osgood, Robert E. *America Armed.* Chicago: Rand McNally, 1963.

Osgood, Robert E. *Ideals and Self Interest in America's Foreign Relations.* Chicago: University of Chicago Press, 1953.

Paolino, E.N. *The Foundations of the American Empire.* Ithaca, New York: Cornell University Press, 1973.

Parrino, Carl. *Heir to Empire: United States Economic Diplomacy, 1916-1923.* Pittsburgh: University of Pittsburgh Press, 1969.

Perkins, Dexter. *Evolution of American Foreign Policy.* New York: Oxford University Press, 1948.

Perkins, Dexter. *Foreign Policy and the American Spirit.* Ithaca, New York: Cornell University Press, 1957.

Pletcher, David M. *Awkward Years: American Foreign Relations Under Garfield and Arthur.* Columbia, Mo.: University of Missouri Press, 1962.

Rappaport, A., ed. *Issues in American Diplomacy.* New York: Macmillan, 1965.

Rostow, Walter. *The United States in the World Arena.* New York: Simon and Schuster, 1969.

Spanier, John W. *American Foreign Policy Since World War II.* New York: Praeger, 1960.

Tyler, Alice Felt. *Foreign Policy of Blaine.* Minneapolis: University of Minnesota Press, 1927.

Van Alstyne, Richard W. *American Crisis Diplomacy.* Stanford: Stanford University Press, 1952.

Vandenberg, A.H. *The Trial of Tradition.* New York: G.P. Putnam's Sons, 1926.

Varg, Paul A. *Foreign Policies of the Founding Fathers.* East Lansing: Michigan State University Press, 1963.

Weinberg, A.K. *Manifest Destiny.* Baltimore: The Johns Hopkins Press, 1935.

Wood, Bryce. *Making of Good Neighbor Policy.* New York: Columbia University Press, 1961.

A NATION AMONG NATIONS

An Introductory Essay

The voice of American power has alternately been that of an aggressive imperialist, a stern dispenser of international justice, a reluctant referee, and a weary policeman. Though some observers claim they hear a single voice in all expressions of American policy, the history of our foreign relations reflects the changing fortunes and growth of a fairly recent "Nation Among Nations." In America's double role as powerbroker and evangelistic missionary, we have tried to bestow our ideas, institutions, and religious beliefs as often as our technology, weapons, and food upon those nations we thought were less well endowed. At times we have been so firmly convinced of the worth of our own ways, we have imposed them upon the subjects of our munificence. Clearly, we have yet to adequately reconcile the competing claims made upon our conscience by our twin roles as global power and global benefactor.

Two hundred years ago, however, we were too concerned with the immediate problems of national survival to worry about the weighty questions of how to use a power which did not yet exist. Though our Founding Fathers earnestly desired that we remain aloof from European quarrels, at the beginning of our history we could not avoid the intimate connections either with our reluctant and estranged British parent or the French midwife. Indeed, our first initiatives in foreign policy were designed to gain a French alliance. Our success in this endeavor was due in large part not to any ideological sympathy but rather to the belief of French policymakers that a war with England, their traditional rival, was inevitable, and that it would be best to enter the war with an American ally before any possible Anglo-American reconciliation could be effected. The American success at Saratoga in 1777 encouraged the French to finally conclude the alliance in 1778. Although the significance of the French intervention is still controversial, it is clear that without the French naval blockade there could have been no siege of Yorktown and that French infantry provided needed stiffening to a Revolutionary army which was still weak in both numbers and experience.

These early connections with France and Britain led to factional disputes in American politics when the Federalists and Republicans split over the issue of support for the French Revolution. However, such preoccupation with European events soon faded as America began to take advantage of her geographic isolation. Throughout the Nineteenth Century we coveted that distance.

Forays into international affairs were the product of domestic interests; protection of American trade; the prospect of American continental expansion; and a statement of firm resistance against any European intrusions in the Western Hemisphere.

American commercial interests were vital to the young nation's economy and this importance was also reflected in political action. To protect this trade we proclaimed neutrality in the Napoleonic Wars. But French raids on American shipping brought us to the brink of full-scale war with our former ally. More comprehensive and effective seizures of American ships and sailors by the British fleet precipitated an ineffectual embargo and, finally, coupled with injured national honor and a desire for Canada, brought to America a nearly disastrous war. Nevertheless, America has continued to insist on the commercial rights of neutrality, an insistence which again led to war more than a century later.

At the same time that the United States asserted its claim to fair commercial rights on the high seas, the country was also involved in a headlong absorption of North America. American bellicosity engendered boundary disputes with Spanish Florida, French/Spanish Louisiana, British Canada, and a newly independent Mexico. We purchased Florida and Louisiana, negotiated with Britain over Oregon, and fought a successful war with Mexico.

Further, extending its own territorial hold on the North American continent, America also sought to insure that there would be no European claims in Latin America. To achieve this end President Monroe, in 1823, promulgated the Monroe Doctrine, which proscribed further European colonization in the Western Hemisphere. Early threats to the Doctrine were warded off more by British warships than by any American military might, as Britain's own interests were enhanced by an independent Latin America. The first true test of the Doctrine came when France took advantage of the Civil War to establish a puppet regime in Mexico. At the war's end, however, French forces were withdrawn in the face of a million American bayonets. Not only was this withdrawal fatal to Maximilian, it was also a mortal blow to any future European territorial aspirations in the New World.

While America had possessed sufficient resources to play a greater part in world affairs, she had never sought to maintain a permanent military force nor did she presume to intervene actively in affairs outside the Western Hemisphere. This reticence was set aside with America's adventures against Spain in Cuba and the Philippines. The unexpected windfall of hitherto Spanish territories, and the coup of a handful of Americans in Hawaii, precipitated a nationwide debate on imperialism which climaxed in the election of 1900. Some, unashamedly imperialistic, argued that we should follow the precedents of European colonization and reap commercial and strategic benefits. Others argued that it was our moral duty to uplift those unfortunate souls who had "become our burden," thus raising to the fore America's role as a bestower of modern ways and democratic institutions. McKinley won the election of 1900, marking short-term imperialists success, but those policies could not be sustained against a resurgent isolationist tradition. America, however, had come of age as a world power. Yet, she still refused to take an active part in European affairs; although Theodore Roosevelt, a man quite at home in power politics, secretly mediated at the Algeciras Conference of 1906 which helped postpone the coming European war. The United States did not, however, show the same reluctance in Far Eastern affairs. With the Open Door policy in China of commercial equality and national integrity, the U.S. again assumed the public role of moral benefactor. This paternal policy toward China (expressed in its ultimate form by Senator Wherry's comment that, "we will lift Shanghai up and up and up until it is just like Kansas City") became a hallmark of U.S. foreign policy and placed America in steadily increasing opposition to Japan—a competition which was to have far-reaching consequences.

The United States also embarked on a policy of active intervention in Latin America. While Roosevelt's corollary to the Monroe Doctrine asserted a right to intervene to insure the stability of these countries in order to forestall the actions of European creditors and to protect American commercial interest, Wilson managed to conceive this as an injunction to protect our southern "neighbors" from themselves. Ironically this led Wilson, apostle of democracy, to invade Mexico on two occasions and send troops into several other Central American and Caribbean nations. It remained for Franklin Roosevelt to promise a "Good Neighbor" policy which has since been at least the theme of our Latin American policy.

Events in Europe finally shook America from her strong sense of complacency in world affairs. The shifting balance of power demanded American intervention in World War I, as Germany's defeat of Russia enabled her to shift two million troops to the Western Front. Losses to unremitting German submarines added personal reasons to political considerations. But, despite the necessity to preserve the balance of power, most Americans saw the war as a moral crusade to stamp out German militarism. At war's end Americans felt that they had "saved the world for democracy" and could now disband the army. The defeat of the League of Nations was attributable in part to this isolationist spirit. The war had drastically changed the European balance of power, and the world's as well. Treatment of Germany—war indemnities and punitive occupation—sowed the seeds of future discord. Throughout, America failed to play a decisive role either in the reconstruction of a war-scarred Continent or the establishment of a new world environment. At the outbreak of World War II, America's options had been narrowed by the shortcomings of her Asiatic and European diplomacy. There were by then three totalitarian regimes prepared once again to contest ownership of Europe and the larger world. The holocaust which followed was, of course, a truly worldwide conflict. From the ashes of that massive confrontation, America and her Russian ally emerged as unparalleled powers. America, once again, had to confront the use of power within the expectations set by her democratic heritage. The Cold War had begun.

Some argue that Russian expansion forced the commitment of an American counterweight both directly in Europe and on a limited scale in Korea, to "contain" the Soviets; yet, it is also argued that America herself generated the Soviet hostility with attempts at economic domination and encircling alliances. One fact is clear: The United States had assumed responsibility for the protection of Europe and the global containment of world Communism. Faced with an imminent European economic collapse, America responded with the Marshall Plan, a comprehensive and costly aid program that revitalized Europe. At the same time America responded to threats of Soviet-inspired aggression in Greece, Iran, Turkey, and Korea. After a Soviet-sponsored coup in Czechoslovakia and the Berlin blockade, the U.S. worked to establish the North Atlantic Treaty Organization and sponsored the rearmament of West Germany. The U.S. still maintains large numbers of troops in Europe, a reminder of commitment to act as a nuclear guarantee against any invasion of Europe.

But the inadequacies of a complete reliance on nuclear retaliation to forestall aggression were demonstrated when the Korean conflict heralded the problems of limited wars. The policy of "brinksmanship" the threat of massive retaliation against any aggressor, was conceived by Eisenhower and his Secretary of State, John Foster Dulles, as a way of reducing military expenditures while preventing any violation of world peace. The policy failed to accomplish either goal. The Communists realized America's unwillingness to invest unlimited lives for relatively obscure foreign policy objectives, and proceeded with their own expansionist schemes, undeterred by public protestations from Washington and NATO allies. Concurrently, American foreign policy analysts became ever more committed to viewing the world as a battlefield between competing ideologies. The Cold War was in part the consequence of frozen perceptions.

Korea was a dramatic and prolonged example of the fixedness of the opposing camps. The United States, with minimal United Nations support and much patriotic sloganeering, attempted to combat its arch rival by military means. The war had no victor, but the lives and years lost served to reinforce attitudes.

With Cuba, America suffered competing claims of conscience. Surely she could not tolerate a communist regime a mere ninety miles from Miami. Our military adventure in 1961 proved a deep embarrassment. A short year and a half later, however, the Russians, too, had a setback. America emerged from the potentially grave dangers of the Cuban Missile Crisis a toughened, if slightly sobered, power. Vietnam, of course, has been the most sustained and vivid testament to the difficulties of wielding power in the late Twentieth Century. In the wake of America's debacle in Indochina, strong currents of isolationism have reappeared. And while we may stay clear of military engagements for a time, our position in the world will not admit of a Nineteenth Century style disengagement. However, our actions —both as benefactor and power—will be subjected to far greater domestic scrutiny. The fact of our involvement is immutable; only the particulars of that involvement are amendable.

Excerpted Documents

Foreign allies in the Revolution.

Nelson M. Blake and Oscar T. Barck, Jr., Professors of History — Syracuse University, *The United States in Its World Relations,* 1960, p. 12.

Because neither France nor Spain was ready to risk war with England, elaborate precautions were taken to deceive the British with professions of friendship while aid to the Americans was transmitted through secret channels. With characteristic ingenuity, Beaumarchais organized a fictitious commercial firm, Roderigue Hortalez & Company, to serve as a front for these transactions. Hortalez & Company in Paris was soon engaged in mysterious communications with "Mary Johnston" in London—and Mary Johnston was none other than Arthur Lee [an American emissary]. This was the situation when Silas Deane, whom the Committee of Secret Correspondence had sent abroad to seek aid, arrived in Paris on July 7, 1776 . . . . Within a few months a steady stream of gunpowder, guns, cannon, and other supplies was crossing the Atlantic. These munitions were the main reliance of the Continental armies during the critical campaigns of 1777.

John R. Alden, Professor of History—Duke University, *A History of the American Revolution, 1969,* p. 376.

Also useful to the Patriots were military technicians furnished by the French government, including Louis Le Begue de Presle Duportail, who rendered splendid service and became the first chief engineer of the American army. The young Marquis de Lafayette, a captain in the French army, slipped away to America with the connivance of French officials, performed faithfully as a Patriot major general, and became a romantic and legendary figure among the Americans. Other French and foreign officers preceded and followed Duportail and Lafayette into the Continental army, including the Baron von Steuben, Thaddeus Kosciusko, the Count Pulaski, and others less distinguished.

General Washington, Letter to Rochambeau, December 14, 1782, in *When the French Were Here,* 1945, pp. 229-230.

I cannot permit you, my dear General, to leave this country without again expressing to you the high appreciation I feel for the services you have rendered America—by the close attention you have always shown in her

Frederick Merk, Professor of History — Harvard University, *Manifest Destiny and Mission*, 1963, p. 231.

In the late 1880s and the 1890s major changes occurred in the life of the nation, and with them came a revival of agitation for expansion. The nation's economy reached maturity. . .By the mid 1890s farm prices in the United States were at their lowest levels since the black days of the 1840s. Industry also generated surpluses and corresponding price declines. The urban economy dropped from relative prosperity in the 1880s to a level comparable, after the panic of 1893, to that of agriculture. The economy as a whole sank into a prostration unparalleled since the formation of the Constitution. The sobering fact that the youthfulness of the nation had slipped away and needed somehow to be restored, was recognized by politicians of all parties. The restoratives were principally of the home variety. Republicans, however, listed expansion among the restoratives. They considered it good in principle. It would restore youth and, by generating trade, would remove surpluses.

Ernest May, Diplomatic Historian, *Imperial Democracy*, 1961, pp. 252-253.

In a famous interview with a delegation of Methodist clergymen in 1899, McKinley explained that his conclusion (about the Philippines) had come to him almost in a flash of revelation. . ."There was nothing left for us to do but to take them all, and to educate the Filipinos, and uplift and Christianize them, and by God's grace do the very best we could for them, as our fellow-men for whom Christ also died."

Ernest May, Diplomatic Historian, *Imperial Democracy*, 1961, pp. 269-270.

In the 1890s the United States had not sought a new role in world affairs. Issues in Hawaii, China, Turkey, Venezuela, and Cuba had intruded almost of their own accord. Statesmen and politicians dealt with them according to their judgment of domestic, not foreign, conditions. . .Some nations achieve greatness; the United States had greatness thrust upon it.

Moralistic diplomacy: Theodore Roosevelt and Woodrow Wilson.

George Kennan, Former Head — State Department Policy Planning Staff, *American Diplomacy, 1900-1950*, 1951, p. 47.

So far as I can judge from such evidence as I have seen, it was assumed by American statesmen that whatever was uttered or urged in the name of moral or legal principle bore with it no specific responsibility on the part of him who urged it, even though the principle might be of questionable applicability to the situation at hand and the practical effects of adherence to it drastic and far-reaching.

George Kennan, Former Head — State Department Policy Planning Staff, *American Diplomacy, 1900-1950*, 1951, pp. 52-53.

We see a distinct difference between our policy toward this (Far East) area and our policy toward Europe (in the pre-World War 2 period). We see in our approach to the Orient a lack of those inhibitions which long affected us in our approach to the affairs of the European continent. We find ourselves more willing to accept involvement in oriental affairs, less inclined to dismiss them as of no moment to us.

Henry Clay, March 24, 1818, in *A History of the Monroe Doctrine*, 1955, pp. 3-4.

The independence of Spanish America is an interest of primary consideration. Next to that, and highly important in itself, is the consideration of the nature of their governments. That is a question, however, for themselves. They will, no doubt, adopt those kinds of governments which are best suited to their condition, best calculated for their happiness. Anxious as I am that they should be free governments, we have no right to prescribe for them. They are and ought to be the sole judges for themselves.

237

interests, by the order and discipline you have invariably maintained in the army corps under your command, and by your promptness on every occasion to facilitate the joint operations of the combined armies.

The Washington Lafayette Institution, *Our Debt to France,* 1926, p. iii.

The being of the United States as a free and independent nation is due largely to the men and substance sent by France, in the darkest hour of our struggle for liberty. This is beyond cavil. France sent her Lafayette, de Rochambeau, de Grasse; they came with her armies, her ships, and money. Without them there could have been no Yorktown.

Wayne S. Cole, University of Maryland, *An Interpretive History of American Foreign Relations,* 1968, p. 41.

Most European leaders had no sympathy for the Americans and had not the slightest intention of recognizing the independence of the new state. The efforts of American agents failed in most European countries. For example, Arthur Lee's attempts to win recognition from Frederick the Great of Prussia in 1777 met with no success. South Carolina's Ralph Izard had identical results as commissioner to the Grand Duchy of Tuscany. William Lee tried his talents on Austria in 1778—and failed.

Nineteenth Century isolationism.

John Adams to the British peace negotiator Oswald, November 18, 1781, *Works of John Adams,* edited by Charles Francis Adams, 1856, Volume 3, p. 316.

It is obvious that all the powers of Europe will be continually maneuvering with us, to work us into their real or imaginary balances of power. They will all wish to make of us a makeweight candle, while they are weighing out their pounds. . .I think it ought to be our rule not to meddle.

Thomas Bailey, Professor Emeritus of History—Stanford University, *Pacific Historical Review,* February 1961, p. 8.

We did not want to become one of the great powers of Europe, not so much because we were weak as because we thought it prudent to take full advantage of our unique geographical location and our phenomenal fecundity. Lord Castlereagh was quoted as saying that the fortunate Americans won their victories not on the battle-field but in the bedchamber. Certainly to play for time, to avoid unnecessary entanglements, to fatten as feeders while the Europeans famished as fighters—all this was statesmanship rather than timidity.

Thomas Bailey, Professor Emeritus of History — Stanford University, *Pacific Historical Review,* February 1961, p. 7.

Even so acute an observer as James Bryce, writing in 1901, could refer to the United States in 1834 as follows: "Already a great nation, it could become a great power as soon as it cared to spend money on fleets and armies." An unwillingness to recognize the power position of the United States did not negate that power, as Mexico learned to her sorrow in the war of 1846-1848.

Imperialism.

Albert Beveridge, 1898, in *Beveridge and the Progressive Era,* 1932, p. 67.

Our institutions will follow our flag on the wings of commerce. And American law, American order, American civilization, and the American flag will plant themselves on shores hitherto bloody and benighted but by those agencies of God henceforth to be made beautiful and bright.

Dexter Perkins, Historian, *A History of the Monroe Doctrine,* 1955, p. 269.

Thus did Woodrow Wilson, prophet of democracy and friend of self-determination, commit himself to the principles of the Roosevelt corollary (to the Monroe Doctrine), and to a doctrine of intervention in the affairs of independent states. When the United States entered the World War in 1917, American marines had been installed on the soil of three of the New World republics; in one of these the native government had been completely suppressed; in another it was subservient to a high degree to the wishes of the authorities in Washington; in a third it existed by virtue of American arms. . .the Roosevelt corollary had led directly to the coercion of the very states it was intended to protect.

Dexter Perkins, Historian, *A History of the Monroe Doctrine,* 1955, p. 270.

That the occupation of Nicaragua, of Haiti, of Santo Domingo, resulted in some gains is undoubted. In all of these states communications were improved. In all of them something was done for education. In all of them, it can be argued, the masses of the population were better off under American control than they were under a native dictator, subject to less exploitation, more secure in the protection of their lives and properties, if they had properties.

America as superpower: World War II and postwar.

Andre Tardieu, French Philosopher, *Notes Sur Les Etats-Unis,* 1908, p. 9.

A nation of 90 million souls, which sells wheat to the universe, coal, iron, and cotton, cannot isolated itself. . .Its power creates for it a right. The right turns itself into a pretension. The pretension becomes a duty — to pronounce upon all those questions that hitherto have been arranged by agreement only among European powers. . .The United States intervenes thus in the affairs of the universe. It is seated at the table where the great game is played, and it cannot leave it.

John Spanier, Historian, *American Foreign Policy Since World War II,* 1973, p. 15.

. . .they (the Americans in World War I) believed they were fighting a war for freedom and democracy, conducting a crusade to destroy German despotism and militarism and to banish power politics forever. It is hardly surprising, therefore, that, once the war had burned out this crusading spirit, the American public, still blissfully unaware of the relationship between American independence and the balance of power, should again wish to retire into its prewar isolationist state. . .Americans refused to face the responsibility that attended the possession of great power.

Herbert Butterfield, Historian — Cambridge University, *The Review of Politics,* April 1950, pp. 151-152.

Behind the great conflicts of mankind is a terrible human predicament which lies at the heart of the story. . .Contemporaries fail to see the predicament or refuse to recognize its genuineness so that our knowledge of it comes from later analysis. It is only with the progress of historical science on a particular subject that men came really to recognize that there was a terrible knot almost beyond the ingenuity of man to untie.

George Kennan, Former Head — State Department Policy Planning Staff, *American Diplomacy, 1900-1950,* 1951, pp. 84-85.

If it cannot be said that the Western democracies gained very much from these talks with the Russian (Moscow, Teheran, Yalta), it would also be incorrect to say that we gave very much away. The establishment of Soviet military power in eastern Europe and the entry of Soviet forces into Manchuria was not the result of these talks; it was the result of the military operations during the concluding phases of the war.

Alexis de Tocqueville, 1835, in *Imperial Democracy,* 1961, p. 3.

Their (America and Russia's) starting point is different, and their courses are not the same; yet each of them seems marked out by the will of Heaven to sway the destinies of half the globe.

Henri Martin, French Philosopher, *La Russie et L'Europe*, 1866, p. 316.

If Europe does not unite, the continent will fall under the yoke of an Asiatic despotism; England will disappear, smothered between Russia and America, and there will be but two powers on earth and it will be partitioned into light and darkness.

George Kennan, Former Head — State Department Policy Planning Staff, *American Diplomacy, 1900-1950*, 1951, p. 3.

A half-century ago people in this country had a sense of security vis a vis their world environment such as I suppose no people had ever had since the days of the Roman Empire. Today that pattern is almost reversed — our national consciousness is dominated at present by a sense of insecurity greater even than that of many of the peoples of Western Europe who stand closer to, and in a position far more vulnerable to, those things that are the main source of our concern.

Winston Churchill, speaking at Fulton, Missouri, 1946, in *American Foreign Policy Since World War II*, 1973, p. 33.

The Russians do not desire war. What they desire is the fruits of war and the indefinite expansion of their power and doctrines. Our difficulties and dangers will not be removed by more waiting to see what happens; nor will they be relieved by a policy of appeasement.

John Spanier, Historian, *American Foreign Policy Since World War II*, 1973, p. 43.

Hostile Soviet behavior was the reason for the gradual shift of American policy and public opinion from amity to enmity; American policy was not the product of a virulent and pre-existing anti-Communist ideology. . . the role of anti-Communism in American policy was essentially to mobilize Congressional and public support for the policy once it had been decided upon.

J. H. Huizinga, Dutch Social Historian, *New York Times Magazine*, January 26, 1969, p. 22.

When they (Americans) could no longer see their country as the noble, disinterested guardian on the ramparts of freedom, when the competitive pursuit of security could no longer be glamorized as a fight for the highest values, many sought refuge in the old illusion that one only has to recognize the beam in one's own eye to remove the splinter from that of one's opponent and thus live happily together forever after.

President Dwight D. Eisenhower, *Second Inaugural Address*, January 20, 1957.

The mutual dependence of nations makes isolation an impossibility. . .No nation can longer be a fortress, lone and strong and safe. And any people, seeking such shelter for themselves, can now only build their own prison.

Walter LaFeber, Historian, *American, Russia, and the Cold War, 1945-1971*, 1972, pp. 291-292.

The U. S. multinational corporation formed the 3rd greatest economic power in the world, behind only the American domestic economy and economy of the Soviet Union. . .The top 20 multinational organizations produced an amount equal to the entire gross national product of Great Britain. The top four could finance Belgium's governmental budget from their profits alone. Europe was being gripped by what one French author called, "the American Challenge." When asked whether Belgium was in danger of becoming an American colony, a Belgian economic affairs minister replied, "We already are."

The United States and Europe.

Henry A. Kissinger, *The Troubled Partnership*, 1965, p. 6.

Faced with a ravaged Europe, the United States came to deal with its Allies paternalistically. This has involved a certain self-righteousness and impatience with criticism. American policymakers often act as if disagreement with their views is due to ignorance which must be overcome by extensive briefings and insistent reiteration. They are less inclined to inquire whether there may be some merit in an opposing view than in overwhelming it with floods of emissaries, official and semi-official. As a result, the United States and Europe have too often conducted their dialogue over the technical implementation of a blueprint manufactured in America.

Harald von Riekhoff, *NATO: Issues and Prospects*, 1967, p. 10.

. . .various psychological cleavages torment the Alliance. The European members of NATO are heirs to a long tradition of membership in various alliances. This tradition includes, among others, a record of broken alliance commitments and faulty alliance management under far less critical conditions than those which may be anticipated in a future crisis. The present European suspicion about the future of the American guarantee, vexing and unfounded as this may appear to the chief guarantor, cannot be divorced from this historical experience. The United States, on the other hand, has become historically conditioned to its role as unilateral guarantor through the tradition of the Monroe Doctrine, and having previously avoided alliance commitments and consequent disappointments, Americans are less inclined to question the reliability of alliance guarantees than their European partners.

Henry A. Kissinger, *The Troubled Partnership*, 1965, p. 3.

The most constructive American foreign policy since the end of World War II has been the development of Atlantic relationships. Through a series of far-sighted and bold measures starting with the Greek-Turkish aid program and the Marshall Plan, the United States helped Europe recover from the economic dislocations of six years of war. When the Communist coup in Czechoslovakia and the Berlin blockade raised fears about Soviet aggressiveness, the United States organized the Atlantic Alliance to insure the security of Europe. Every administration since then has promoted European recovery, Atlantic cooperation and joint defense. As a result, Europe has become more prosperous than ever and it feels safe from invasion.

Nuclear power and diplomacy.

Nelson M. Blake and Oscar T. Barck, Jr., Professors of History — Syracuse University, *The United States in Its World Relations*, 1960, p. 755.

In January, 1954, Secretary of State John Foster Dulles warned potential aggressors that they could not count on prescribing battle conditions to suit themselves. To deter troublemakers, the United States would "depend primarily upon a great capacity to retaliate instantly, by means and at places of our choosing." In pronouncing this policy of "massive retaliation," Dulles was serving notice to the Communist world that the Eisenhower administration did not intend to dissipate national energies in a series of Korea-type conflicts. Repudiating the Truman-Acheson policies as unduly timid and negative, he threatened destructive punishment to any transgressor.

Wayne S. Cole, University of Maryland, *An Interpretive History of American Foreign Relations*, 1968, pp. 480-481.

America's many military commitments could involve the United States in local conflicts encouraged by the greater nationalism and independence of the many states. The proliferation of nuclear weapons among additional states will make the unstable situation even more dangerous. In such an environment any talk of American isolationism would be purely academic and hypothetical. The only question was what form American involvement would take and what kind of involvement would be most likely to have the best results. Efforts to

241

guard peace and security in that explosive world atmosphere spectacularly expanded United States power and influence over much of the earth during and after World War II.

Lawrence H. Chamberlain, Associate Professor of Government — Columbia University, and Richard C. Snyder, Assistant Professor of Politics — Princeton University, *American Foreign Policy*, 1948, p. 472.

Rather clumsily used, the bomb has proved a diplomatic liability. Continued production and stock-piling in the absence of any threat to the United States, coupled with the Marxian theory of "capitalist war," has, justifiably or not, given ground for the suspicion that the U.S.S.R. is being subjected to subtle blackmail. The Russian people are obviously unaware of the significance of the bomb and no appeal can be made to them.

Wynfred Joshua and Walter Hahn, Center for Strategic and International Studies — Georgetown University, *Nuclear Politics: America, France, and Britain*, 1973, p. 73.

The European quest for nuclear hardware under European possession and control had intensified in the period of the "missile gap" (roughly 1958-1961), when the American strategic deterrent seemed thoroughly discredited by an assumed Soviet primacy in space and missile power. Yet, the ensuing years and their intelligence yield disproved such beliefs. The American strategic nuclear panoply, although compromised by Soviet advances, continued supreme into the latter part of the sixties.

Foreign aid.

Reginald Mauding, Chancellor of the Exchequer, *Speech to the House of Commons*, September 17, 1963.

It is to my mind impossible for the industrial societies to live easily with their consciences while the indigent societies are just over their garden fence. . .We must recognize that overseas aid is a great and growing burden on our resources. Our reactions should not be. . .to cut back on the aid, but rather to regard this as a source of inspiration.

Andrew Westwood, Brookings Institution, *Foreign Aid in a Foreign Policy Framework*, 1966, p. 4.

Aid has offered only to supply the extra margin, missing component, or additional inducement needed for success. The more characteristic situation in underdeveloped countries has been the absence of a whole range of the elements necessary for success. Were only financial difficulties the things that made a government precarious, aid could well meet these difficulties. But the problem rarely has been that simple.

Lessons of the past and questions for the future.

Walter LaFeber, Historian, *America, Russia, and the Cold War, 1945-1971*, 1972, p. 299.

The question was not whether the United States had sufficient power or whether American officials were courageous enough to apply enough power. The crux of the problem was whether the American system could delineate the ends for which that power could most properly and profitably be used. . .this dominance of power had led American officials and public opinion to believe in a military solution for primary, unsolvable problems.

Reinhold Niebuhr, Philosopher, *Christian Century*, December 31, 1969, p. 1662.

Perhaps there is not much to choose between communist and anti-communist fanaticism, particularly when the latter, combined with our wealth, has caused us to stumble into the most pointless, costly and bloody war in our history.

Senator J. W. Fulbright, Former Chairman — Senate Foreign Relations Committee, 1968, in *American Foreign Policy Since World War II*, 1973, p. xi.

If we do not (change), it will not be because history assigned to us an imperial role. It will be because we *chose* to believe such pompous nonsense, because power went to our heads like a superdose of LSD, leading us to betray our history and the purposes for which this nation was founded.

Lionel Gelber, Canadian Historian, *Yale Review*, Fall 1967, p. 934.

I have yet to hear of any viable alternative to what the United States has been doing on the world stage. Even if free countries wished to reject American leadership in theory they could not do so in practice; the United States herself cannot throw it off. For the American role is shaped by the nature of the world in which we live.

John Spanier, Historian, *American Foreign Policy Since World War II*, 1973, p. 273.

The crucial and decisive question for the future conduct of American foreign policy, therefore, is whether, in the absence of anti-Communism, the United States would "dirty" its hands by playing straight and unadorned power politics. The real test of its international role will therefore come *after* Vietnam.

Selected Bibliography

Adler, Selig. *Uncertain Giant: American Foreign Policy, 1921-1941.* New York: Macmillan, 1965.

Alden, John R. *A History of the American Revolution.* New York: Knopf, 1969.

Bailey, Thomas A. *Woodrow Wilson and Lost Peace.* New York: Macmillan, 1944.

Bailey, Thomas A. "America's Emergence as a World Power." *Pacific Historical Review,* 30 (1961), 1.

Baldwin, David A. *Foreign Aid and American Foreign Policy.* New York: Praeger, 1966.

Beale, Howard K. *Theodore Roosevelt and Rise of America to World Power.* Baltimore: Johns Hopkins Press, 1956.

Blake, Nelson M., and Barck, Oscar T. Jr. *The United States in Its World Relations.* New York: McGraw-Hill, 1960.

Bohlen, Charles E. *The Transformation of American Foreign Policy.* New York: Norton, 1969.

Bonsal, Stephen. *When the French Were Here.* Garden City, New York: Doubleday, 1945.

Brown, Seyom. *The Faces of Power: Foreign Policy from Truman to Johnson.* New York: Columbia University Press, 1969.

Callahan, J.M. *American Foreign Policy in Mexican Relations.* New York: Macmillan, 1932.

Callcott, Wilfrid H. *The Caribbean Policy of the United States, 1890-1920.* Baltimore: Johns Hopkins Press, 1942.

Cole, Wayne S. *An Interpretive History of American Foreign Relations.* Homewood, Ill.: Dorsey Press, 1968.

Coletta, Paolo E. "Bryan, McKinley and the Treaty of Paris." *Pacific Historical Review,* 26 (1957), 131.

Corwin, Edward S. *French Policy and the American Alliance.* New York: B. Franklin, 1916.

Council on Foreign Relations. *United States in World Affairs.* 1931.

Deconde, Alexander, ed. *Isolation and Security: Twentieth Century American Foreign Policy.* Durham, North Carolina: Duke University Press, 1957.

Divine, Robert A. *Reluctant Belligerent: American Entry into World War II.* New York: Wiley, 1965.

Donovan, J.C. "Congressional Isolationists and the Roosevelt Foreign Policy." *World Politics,* 2 (1951), 299.

Feis, Herbert. *Road to Pearl Harbor.* Princeton: Princeton University Press, 1950.

Feis, Herbert. *Churchill, Roosevelt, Stalin: The War They Waged and the Peace They Sought.* Princeton, New Jersey: Princeton University Press, 1957.

Feis, Herbert. *Foreign Aid and Foreign Policy.* New York: St. Martin's Press, 1964.

Gardner, Lloyd; Schlesinger, Arthur Jr.; and Morgenthau, Hans J. *The Origins of the Cold War.* Waltham, Massachusetts: Ginn-Blaisdell, 1970.

Goodell, Stephen. "Woodrow Wilson in Latin America." *Historian,* 28 (1965), 96.

Grenville, John, and Young, George B. *Politics, Strategy, and American Diplomacy, 1873-1917.* New Haven: Yale University Press, 1966.

Hyneman, Charles S. *First American Neutrality: Neutral Obligations During the Years 1792-1815.* Porcupine Press, (Reprint 1975), 1934.

Israel, Jerry. "For God, for China, and for Yale — Open Door in Action." *American Historical Review,* 75 (1970), 796.

Kennan, George F. *American Diplomacy, 1900-1950.* Chicago: University of Chicago Press, 1951.

Kissinger, Henry A. "American Strategic Doctrine and Diplomacy." *Theory and Practice of War: Essays presented to Captain B. H. Liddell Hart.* Edited by Michael Howard. New York: Praeger, 1965.

Kissinger, Henry A. *The Troubled Partnership; A Re-appraisal of the Atlantic Alliance.* New York: McGraw-Hill, 1965.

LaFeber, Walter. "Mercantilistic Imperialism: of Alfred Thayer Mahan." *Mississippi Valley Historical Review,* 39 (1952), 483.

LaFeber, Walter. *America, Russia, and the Cold War, 1945-1971.* New York: Wiley, 1972.

Link, Arthur S. *Wilson the Diplomatist.* Chicago: Quadrangle Books, 1957.

Liss, Sheldon B. *The Canal: Aspects of United States-Panamanian Relations.* South Bend, Indiana: University of Notre Dame Press, 1967.

Mason, Edward S. *Foreign Aid and Foreign Policy.* New York: Harper & Row, 1964.

May, Ernest R. *American Imperialism.* New York: Atheneum, 1968.

Mecham, John L. *United States and Inter-American Security, 1889-1960.* Austin: University of Texas Press, 1961.

Merk, Frederick. *Manifest Destiny and Mission.* New York: Knopf, 1963.

Montgomery, John D. *Foreign Aid in International Politics.* Englewood Cliffs, New Jersey: Prentice-Hall, 1967.

Morris, Richard B. *Peacemakers: Great Powers and American Independence.* New York: Harper & Row, 1965.

Munro, Dana G. *Intervention and Dollar Diplomacy in the Caribbean, 1900-1921.* Princeton, New Jersey: Princeton University Press, 1964.

Osgood, Robert E., et al. *America and the World: Truman Doctrine to Vietnam.* Baltimore: Johns Hopkins Press, 1970.

Perkins, Dexter. *A History of the Monroe Doctrine.* Boston: Little, Brown, 1955 (rev. ed.).

Pratt, Julius W. *Challenge and Rejection: United States and World Leadership, 1900-1921.* New York: Macmillan, 1967.

Ritcheson, Charles R. *Aftermath of Revolution: British Policy Toward the United States 1783-1795.* New York: Norton, 1969.

Spanier, John W. *American Foreign Policy Since World War II.* New York: Praeger, 1973 (6th rev. ed.).

Sumberg, Theodore A. *Foreign Aid as a Moral Obligation?* Beverly Hills, California: Sage, 1973.

Van Alstyne, Richard W. *American Crisis Diplomacy.* Stanford: Stanford University Press, 1952.

Van Alstyne, Richard W. *Empire and Independence: American Revolution.* New York: Wiley, 1965.

Van Tyne, Claude H. "Influences which Determined the French Government to Make the Treaty with America, 1778." *American Historical Review,* 21(1916), 528.

Varg, Paul A. *Making of a Myth: United States and China, 1879-1912.* East Lansing: Michigan State University Press, 1968.

Westwood, Andrew. *Foreign Aid in a Foreign Policy Framework.* Washington: Brookings Institution, 1966.

Wood, Bryce. *Making of Good Neighbor Policy.* New York: Columbia University Press, 1961.

ISSUE VIII
GROWING UP IN AMERICA

REGIONAL EVENTS—HIGH SCHOOL ISSUE
March 20—April 24, 1976

DEBATE   Resolved: That American public education has emphasized socialization to the detriment of intellectual development.

PERSUASIVE   The American Family: A Past with a Future?

EXTEMPORANEOUS   "In God We Trust" and A Sense of Belonging

1. *What role has membership in a community played in the lives of Americans?*
2. *Does increasing mobility spell the loss of community as America has known it?*
3. *Can we recover the "sense of community" experienced in the early days of the Republic?*
4. *Did the plantation provide a necessary community in the antebellum South?*
5. *Ethnic communities: Are they "Unamerican?"*
6. *Discrimination in America: Has the ideal American community been white Anglo-Saxon Protestant?*
7. *What was the role of early political parties in American communities?*
8. *Was the Constitutional separation of church and state an overreaction to religious oppression in Europe?*
9. *"In God We Trust": Has America ceased to be one nation under God?*
10. *Have America's churches been a major force for progressive change?*
11. *What was the role of religion in the expansion of the American frontier?*
12. *Has American public education been impoverished by an underemphasis on religion?*

RESOLVED: THAT AMERICAN PUBLIC EDUCATION HAS EMPHASIZED SOCIALIZATION TO THE DETRIMENT OF INTELLECTUAL DEVELOPMENT.

Introductory Essay

President Washington, in a 1790 address to a joint session of the Congress, suggested that:

> There is nothing which can better deserve your patronage than the promotion of science and literature. Knowledge is in every country the surest base of public happiness. In one, in which the measures of government receive their impression so immediately from the sense of the community, as in ours, it is proportionately essential.

Washington's comments exemplify the continuing commitment of Americans to education through our nation's history. This general and near-universal agreement, however, sometimes obscures widespread disagreement on particulars. Should our nation's primary commitment be to equality of educational opportunity or to individual excellence? Can public education be best carried out by religious or secular bodies? Is the role of education to accustom the student to societal mores, or should it help to develop an intellect capable of objective evaluation of that society? Should educational philosophy be child centered, allowing a maximum of creative freedom, or is it better that the child be guided along the path of development most beneficial to society? And most importantly, are these goals mutually exclusive, or can they be complementary? All of these questions are given play in the topic "Resolved: That American public education has emphasized socialization to the detriment of intellectual development."

Socialization generally means "to fit or train for a social environment." In a sense, all education contains elements of socialization, since all learning contributes to knowledge or understanding of one's surroundings. Emphasis on socialization, however, is generally exhibited in more overt forms: reinforcement of attitudes and moral precepts held desirable by the group, training for vocational areas of which society has special need, or indoctrination into religious beliefs acceptable to the community. Intellectual development need not be antithetical to these ends, but would generally involve the presentation of more abstract forms of knowledge. Studies in classical literature, the more esoteric realms of mathematics and philosophy, have been considered by many to be purely intellectual pursuits.

Colonial education was a patchwork affair. The South had no educational system to speak of. Tutors were hired by the wealthy plantation owners, some common schools developed in the heavily-populated areas, and an overseas education was available for those willing to pay, but for most, education was provided by members of the immediate family, or in some cases, the apprenticeship system.

Puritan New England, however, developed a system of public education very early. The Puritan theocratic state, particularly in the Massachusetts Bay Colony, regarded education as a tool to insure religious conformity and obedience to the laws of the Commonwealth. The initial education legislation in Massachusetts (often referred to as the "old deluder" act) set forth in 1647 the primary motive for promoting literacy.

> It being one chiefe project of ye ould deluder, Satan, to keep men from the knowledge of ye Scriptures, as in former times by keeping ym in an unknowne tongue, so in these latter times by perswading from ye use of tongues, yt so at least ye true sence and meaning of ye originall might be clouded by the false glosses of saint seeming deceivers. . .It is therefore ordered, yt evry towneship in this jurisdiction, aftr ye Lord hath increased ym number to 50 householdrs shall then forthwth appoint one wth in their towne to teach all such children as shall resort to him to write & reade. . .

This mandate was reflected in the choice of teachers. One author notes that "The certification of the elementary teacher was based primarily on the candidate's religious and political orthodoxy" and only secondarily on specific teaching skills. Generations of children who used the *New England Primer* learned their A B C's through a series of moral rhymes:

A   In Adam's Fall
     We Sinned All.

B   Thy life to Mend
     This Book Attend.

Not only religion, but respect for the Crown was also allotted its share of the alphabet. The *Primer* also provided Puritan children with a list of the books of the Bible and an uplifting account of the burning at the stake of a Protestant martyr.

The children of the social and religious elite, however, pursued a different course of study. Aided by private tutelage, they might enter a Latin Grammar school, and eventually Harvard. An idea of the rigorous studies necessary to attend that institution may be gained from the "Laws, Liberties, and Orders" of Harvard College in 1642.

> When any scholar is able to read Tully, or such like classical Latin author *extempore*, and make and speak true Latin in verse and prose *suo (ut aiunt) Marte,* and decline perfectly the paradigms of nouns and verbs in the Greek tongue, then may he be admitted into the College, nor shall any claim admission before such qualifications.

While socialization was the avowed purpose of the lower schools, Harvard was designed to create an intellectual elite in the New England community. The basically religious nature of instruction, however, was also set out "Every one shall consider the main end of his life and studies, to know God and Jesus Christ, which is eternal life; John xvii.3."

Even before the establishment of the Constitution, the national government recognized the value of education; the Ordinance of 1785 set aside land in the Northwest Territory of which the income was to be applied toward education, and the Ordinance of 1787 recognized education as "necessary to good government and the happiness of mankind." Two prominent Revolutionary figures indulged in theorization on educational systems. Thomas Jefferson, who ranked his founding of the University of Virginia equal with his role in the Declaration of Independence and the Virginia Bill of Rights, advocated a system which contained both democratic and elitist provisions: democratic in that it provided for at least some education for all white children; elitist in that it was intended to produce government by an aristocratic upper class. Benjamin Franklin favored a more utilitarian system. He included several vocational skill areas, emphasized English rather than classical languages, and proposed practical rather than theoretical mathematics.

> Thus instructed, Youth will come out of this School fitted for learning any Business, Calling or Profession, except such wherein Languages are required; and tho' unacquainted with any ancient or foreign Tongue, they will be Masters of their own, which is of more immediate and general Use...

Although neither system was acutally put into use, both reflected currents of educational thought of that time. Jefferson's proposal suggested the growing shift from a religious to a secular viewpoint, and both his and Franklin's systems exhibited a conviction of the strong relationship between education and the political and social structure.

An increased interest in schooling grew largely out of a sense of injured national pride, provoked by the custom of educating children in Europe. Conscious of the socializing effect of education, Noah Webster, a prominent educator, warned "Let ten American youths be sent, each to a different European kingdom, and live there from the age of twelve to twenty, & each will give the preference to the country where he has resided." The Virginia House of Delegates called for the establishment of a national university, while the Georgia legislature responded by temporarily revoking some of the privileges of citizenship for foreign-educated students. In 1795, George Washington expressed his concern over the situation, and urged, "The time is ...come, when a plan of Universal education ought to be adopted in the United States..." Numerous private colleges sprang up across the country, and several state colleges were established. Plagued by poor staff, wretched locations, and unprepared students, most led a rather anemic existence. First of a new breed was the University of Virginia, chartered in 1819. Non-sectarian, publicly supported, and offering a high level of instruction in scientific (rather than classical) subjects, the University of Virginia was emulated in various aspects by other state institutions prior to the Civil War.

The democratic spirit of the period permeated all facets of national life, and educational thought was no exception. Opposed to any kind of superiority of one citizen over another, this egalitarian mood deemphasized the bright student. J. Merton England noted this tendency among textbook authors of the Jacksonian period. "Their opposition to aristocracy extended even to an aristocracy of brains. They valued creativity less than uniformity, trained intelligence less than spreading useful knowledge and the cultivation of virtue." In 1833, the Tennessee legislature even opposed appropriations for the maintenance of West Point, objecting to the selective nature of the Academy.

> ...a few young men, sons of distinguished and wealthy families, through the intervention of members of Congress, are educated at this institution, at the expense of the great body of the American people, which entitled them to privileges, and elevate them above their fellow citizens who have not been so fortunate as to be educated under the patronage of this aristocratical institution.

It was only natural that this national sentiment should result in demands for free and universal education. Various innovations in school systems were examined, including Sunday schools, infant schools, and the Lancastrian system of instruction. The latter, developed by two Englishmen, Lancaster and Bell, involved a master instructor, who taught a group of students designated as "monitors," who in turn taught other students. This system enjoyed brief popularity, mainly because of the attractive per-pupil cost, but its obvious educational difficulties forced its reassessment and ultimate rejection.

The drive for the common school was more successful. Spearheaded by the American Lyceum movement, and aided by the editorial skill of Henry Bernard's *Connecticut Common School Journal* and Horace Mann's *Common School Journal,* the movement gained momentum. In 1827, Massachusetts became the first state to support the school system by compulsory finance. Other New England states and the Midwest quickly followed, with the South and some border states following much later. The common schools were usually elementary, emphasizing literacy and citizenship.

Horace Mann and other advocates of universal schooling used numerous arguments to support their reforms. Chiefly, they expanded on Washington's view of the close relationship between education and a democratic form of government. Children not only needed to be educated in the appreciation of democratic principles, but an educated populace was also the only guarantee of a workable democratic system. Some of Mann's visions of the benefits of education as a socializing influence scaled the heights of prose and reached pinnacles of metaphorical oratory.

> Without money and without price, it throws open its doors, and spreads the table of its bounty, for all the children of the State. Like the sun, it shines, not only upon the good, but upon the evil, that they may become good; and, like the rain, its blessings descend, not only upon the just, but upon the unjust, that their injustice may depart from them and be known no more.

Critics attacked the common school for lowering all students to the level of the worst, and many objected to the payment of school taxes. Mann cleverly addressed himself to the latter by pointing out that the socializing effects of free schooling were in the self-interest of the rich. "Without a sense of the inviolability of property, your deeds are but wastepaper. Without a sense of the sacredness of person and life, you are only a watchdog whose baying is to be silenced, that your house may be more securely entered and plundered."

Nineteenth Century textbooks followed the trend of attempting to inculcate proper attitudes through the education process. Willard's *Abridged History of the United States* modestly admitted that "We have, indeed, been desirous to cultivate the memory, the intellect and the taste. But much more anxious have we been to sow the seeds of virtue." Ruth Miller Elson noted in *Guardians of Tradition: American Schoolbooks of the Nineteenth Century* that the authors of many texts made large claims for the efficacy of moral instruction. One wrote: "The mind of the child is like the soft wax to receive an impression, but like the rigid marble to retain it." Noah Webster suggested that teachers use his book because it would enable them "to instil into their [the children's] minds, with the first rudiments of the language, some just ideas of religion, morals, and domestic economy." The socialization practiced by schoolbooks was not entirely beneficial. Elson found that in addition to such patriotic themes as glorification of America's place in the world and unstinting adulation of the Founding Fathers, a more ominous melody could be heard: Roman Catholicism was inherently evil, and dangerous to the principles of the Republic; the Caucasians were innately superior to all other races; and a poor man could be in that state only because of some inner failing.

During the first half of the century, the emphasis of the colleges on classical curricula drew increasing criticism from many citizens. There was an unfilled need for education and research in industrial and agricultural subjects. In 1862, Congress passed the Morrill Act, establishing "land grant" colleges and universities focusing on these neglected areas. President Buchanan had originally vetoed the bill on Constitutional grounds, but Lincoln looked more favorably upon the measure. Although the Act was aimed at correcting deficiencies in practical education, it did not ignore the more traditional "intellectual" areas, which Buchanan cited in his veto message as one of the more pleasant aspects of the proposal.

> Under this bill it is provided that scientific and classical studies shall not be excluded ... Indeed, it would be almost impossible to sustain them [the universities] without such a provision, for no father would incur the expense of sending a son to one of these institutions for the sole purpose of making him a scientific farmer or mechanic.

The late Nineteenth and early Twentieth Centuries brought major changes in educational institutions. In the period from 1880 to 1920 the American high school was largely college preparatory, offering mostly "strong" academic courses. At the same time, however, a group of American educators challenged the dominance of high schools by colleges, arguing that they should appeal to a wider-based student clientele. The high school gradually became less selective; in 1880, they enrolled slightly over 100,000, and by 1920, well over two million. On the college level, the closing years of the century saw the infusion of characteristics of the German university system, which stressed scholarship and research. Beginning at Johns Hopkins in 1876, the German method spread rapidly to other graduate schools. In time, the American university became a hybrid institution, with the professional schools and rigorous graduate studies imposed on the pre-existing undergraduate liberal arts programs. Robert Hutchins, in *Higher Learning in America,* 1936, attacked the university system as being overspecialized, with various professors working in such a rarified atmosphere and such small fields that they could not adequately communicate with each other —in spite of the fact that a university is often referred to as a community of scholars. Hutchins also criticized the emphasis on monetary matters and sports as detracting from a suitable intellectual environment.

In the early 1900's, American schools served as socialization tools in the purest sense, helping to assimilate a massive influx of immigrants. Clarence J. Karier observed that during the "first half of the century, schools were organized to educate the immigrants away from their un-American traditions, and the children of immigrants away from the ways of their un-American parents, and toward Anglo-Saxon standards." Although there is considerable doubt currently as to whether this was a wise decision, the schools at that time were perceived as fulfilling an essential public role. Gregory Mason, in a 1916 article in *The Outlook* entitled "An Americanization Factory," reminded readers that

> Hyphenated citizenship is as dangerous to a republic as a cancer to the human body. Education is the knife to use in cutting out the hyphen, and the public schools of Rochester are a laboratory in which it has been proved that the operation can be done.

Schools also became more careful about who was teaching children—not their qualifications, but their political views. The "red scare" of the 1920's prompted state legislation requiring loyalty oaths from teachers. This particular concern quieted after a while, and in 1937 the Congress repealed a provision of the District of Columbia statutes relating to the teaching or advocacy of communism, "*Provided, however,* that nothing herein shall be construed as permitting the advocating of communism."

The national commitment to educational programs emphasizing the needs of the business market was strengthened by the 1917 Smith-Hughes Vocational Education Act, which provided federal funds to the states for training programs. President Hoover detailed the value of such education in a 1924 speech.

> Expenditures on account of [vocational] ... education [are] in the nature of an investment which will yield large dividends from year to year through the progressive increase of labor, skill and industrial efficiency.... There is, in fact, no better economy than the economy of adequate training for the pursuits of agriculture, commerce, industry, and the home.

Critics of the increasing emphasis on vocational education have suggested, however, that machine work is best learned in professional machine shops, and that vocational education classes are not "schooling" in any realistic sense.

By far the most controversial educational issue of this century has been the value of "progressive" education. John Dewey's educational philosophy sought to unify the child's personality with the social environment. He criticized the fragmentation of existing teaching systems as

> ... so-called cultural education which tends to be academic and pedantic, and in any case aloof from the concerns of life, and an industrial and manual education which at best gains command of tools and means without intelligent grasp of purposes and ends.

The first three Principles of Progressive Education, as published in April of 1924, were: "1. Freedom to develop naturally; 2. Interest, the motive of all work; and 3. The teacher a guide, not a task-maker." A split in progressive education occured in the 1930's when George S. Counts published *Dare the School Build a New Social Order?* One wing of the movement remained child centered, while the other wing advocated the accomplishment of social reform through the schools.

Many of progressivisim's pedagogical reform suggestions were adopted by schools, but agreement with their philosophy was by no means universal. Prominent educators who felt that the main purpose of teaching was the transmission of knowledge and analytical skills found much of the progressive program objectionable— "soft pedagogy" —and were morally repulsed by the idea of using their discipline as a tool to promote social change.

Criticism of progressive education reached its zenith in the 1950's. The successful Russian Sputnik satellite launching, eclipsing U.S. space efforts, demanded an explanation, and our educational system seemed the likely culprit. Russia, with a more "traditional" approach to teaching, was reportedly turning out twice as many scientists as America. Critics pointed out that the public school system's emphasis on equality was discouraging intellectual development, and that classroom instruction was maintained at the lowest common denominator. A number of books criticizing the schooling system appeared, with titles suggestive of their message: *Educational Wastelands, The Restoration of Learning, Schools Without Scholars, Suffer Little Children. Life* magazine suggested that "surely the history of the Crusades can give a young American a better idea of the problems implicit in the UN or NATO than dressing up as a Pakistani delegate at an imitation UN assembly in school." In 1957, Admiral Hyman G. Rickover roundly condemned the entire system.

> This inelasticity. . . is the direct result of the sentimental attachment we hold for the concept of a comprehensive school in which all children—stupid, average, talented and bright—march sedately up to the eighteenth year, absorbing so little real education that it takes another four years at college before the preprofessional stage of education is completed.

In 1958, the Congress passed the National Defense Education Act, providing financial assistance for educational efforts in science, mathematics, and foreign languages.

Defenders of progressive education cited statistical research denying the claims of the system's detractors. They suggested that the nation should have a strong commitment to equality of opportunity as well as excellence, and noted that any problems were merely a result of student overload which could be easily solved with an increased financial commitment. In 1958, James B. Conant, former President of Harvard University, presented a relatively unbiased view. With a combination of hard data and insight, he refuted the more extreme charges against public education and made helpful suggestions for change in areas of deficiency.

Controversy over the relevance of public school curricula is by no means stilled. Richard Hofstadter, in his 1964 book, *Anti-Intellectualism in American Life*, questions the intellectual legitimacy of such required public school courses as "Home and Family Living," in which classroom discussions cover such topics as "Developing School Spirit," "My Duties as a Baby Sitter," and "Clicking With the Crowd."

In another arena, the Supreme Court has shown a willingness to use the school as a socializing lever to promote racial equality. In the landmark 1954 decision, *Brown v. Board of Education of Topeka*, the Court noted that education "is a principal instrument in awakening the child to cultural values, in preparing him for later professional training, and in helping him to adjust normally to his environment." Most Americans agree that the elimination of race discrimination is a highly desirable social goal, but many question whether the school system is the proper vehicle for reaching that goal, pointing out the detrimental intellectual effects of classroom racial strife and long-distance busing.

Francis Keppel, former U.S. Commissioner of Education, has spoken of two educational revolutions—quantitative and qualitative. The first is largely resolved, as educational opportunity has been extended to the great majority of Americans. The second, qualitative revolution, he suggests, is still underway. Through the years, the resources that Americans have been willing to devote to education have been limited. Whether those resources have been wisely allocated, providing both for the intellectual rights of the individual and the legitimate expectations of society, remains one of the more perplexing questions in the history of American public education.

Excerpted Documents

Is socialization possible or desirable?

John D. Russell and Charles H. Judd, *The American Educational System* 1940, p. 11.

Throughout this book the view deliberately adopted and defended is that the school is a socializing as well as a social institution. The school was established originally to meet a social need, and its continued existence is justified only by its service to the social order in which it is maintained. Another and perhaps more instructive way of emphasizing the idea here expressed is to say that the major purpose of the school is to make available to the pupil all the experience which the race has accumulated, that is, to prepare him for civilized life.

National Educational Association, Associated Press Dispatch, Berkeley, California, June 12, 1949.

The National Education Association affirms that the foundations of our American system of government are built in our free public schools. The Association strongly asserts that all schools have an obligation to teach the rights, privileges, and the responsibilities of living in a democracy.

The responsibility of the schools is to teach the superiority of the American way of life, founded as it is on the dignity and worth of the individual; therefore, our youth should know it, believe in it, and live it continuously.

Marion Brown, "Is There a Nationality Problem in Our Schools?" *National Education Association Proceedings,* **1900.**

As Rome brought order, peace, and personal freedom to the various nationalities in her borders, so today must the teacher endeavor for each of the ethical microcosms that we call American children; bring them to the Anglo-Saxon standard, train them to self-control that means freedom, the love of country that foreshadows the brotherhood of man, the developing personality that can take only justice and right as its standard, a consumation possible only thru knowledge of the mazes of inherited tendencies, by sympathy with the soul struggling in shackles of ancestral bondage.

Glenn Frank, President—University of Wisconsin, Address at the Dedication of a University Extension Building, Milwaukee, September 18, 1928.

Perhaps the most influential part of a man's education comes not from the school he attends but from the community in which he lives and from the work by which he makes his living. Schools cannot make men better citizens than their communities demand and their working lives determine. The school can, for a time, lure an individual student beyond the standards of his community, but, save with the expectional person, the community will sooner or later get him. The community has its schools, but the community is itself a school. And our education is the product of all of our experiences, not merely of our classroom experiences. All this means, I think, that we must revise our ancient notion of the relationship between school and society. The school and the social order must be saved together or they will sink together.

Address of the Trustees, Society for Establishing a Free School in the City of New York, for the Education of such Poor Children as do not Belong to, or are not Provided for by, any Religious Society, May, 1805, in *History of the Public School Society of the City of New York,* 1870.

Children. . .brought up in ignorance, and amidst the contagion of bad example, are in imminent danger of ruin; and too many of them, it is to be feared, instead of being useful members of the community, will become the burden and pests of society. Early instruction and fixed habits of industry, decency, and order, are the surest safeguards of virtuous conduct; and when parents are either unable or unwilling to bestow the necessary attention on the education of their children, it becomes the duty of the public, and of individuals, who have the power, to assist them in the discharge of this important obligation.

George Washington, 1795, in *The Writings of George Washington,* 1940, p. 149.

It is with indescribable regret, that I have seen the youth of the United States migrating to foreign countries, in order to acquire the higher branches of erudition, and to obtain a knowledge of the Sciences. Altho' it would be injustice to many to pronounce the certainty of their imbibing maxims, not congenial with republicanism; it must nevertheless be admitted, that a serious danger is encountered, by sending abroad among other political systems those, who have not well learned the value of their own.

The New York Times, April 22, 1920.

There has been only too much evidence of the success of the Socialists in imparting their fatal doctrines to young and ductile minds. It is incredible that the State should allow schools or teachers whose teaching is for the express purpose of destroying the State. The danger is not that any loyal teacher will be disqualified, but that disloyal teachers will profess loyalty.

Abraham Flexner, in the Foreward to Henry Simon, *Preface to Teaching*, 1938.

In recent years professors of education have frequently taken themselves far too seriously. Aware of the fact that the world is changing—by the way, it has always been changing—they have assumed that, having in charge the younger generation, it is their business to change the world according to their conception of what it should be. Though I cannot pretend to an exhaustive knowledge of recent educational literature, Professor Simon represents a quite different standpoint. He recognizes frankly that the schools are of this world and that, though within a limited range they can do something to mould character and instil ideas, the outlook of children will nevertheless be mainly determined by the families to which they belong and the companions with whom they associate, not to mention a thousand other factors, the influence of which may or may not be considerable.

Does intellectual development deserve greater emphasis?

William F. Russell, *Annual Report of the Dean of Teachers College*, New York, 1930.

Increasing numbers of secondary schools yield increasing numbers of graduates who are content only with positions in the already overcrowded fields of professional life and government service, the "white-collar" jobs. Many are doomed to disappointment, and thus there develops a discontented and unhappy "educated proletariat," a floating population which becomes the source of sedition, revolution, and unrest. "Sound educational theory," according to Professor Monroe, would include the restriction of cultural secondary education and the establishment of far more vocational and practical education.

John F. Kennedy, January 23, 1963, in *An Historical Introduction to American Education*, 1970, p. 120.

Now a veritable tidal wave of students is advancing inexorably on our institutions of higher education, where the annual costs per student are several times as high as the cost of a high school education, and where these costs must be borne in large part by the student or his parents. Five years ago the graduating class of the secondary schools was 1.5 million; 5 years from now it will be 2.5 million. The future of these young people and the nation rests in large part on their access to college and graduate education. For this country reserves its highest honors for only one kind of aristocracy—that which the Founding Fathers called "an aristocracy of achievement arising out of a democracy of opportunity."

Horace Mann, *Tenth Annual Report* to the Massachusetts State Board of Education, 1846.

In later times, and since the achievement of American independence, the universal and ever-repeated argument in favor of free schools has been that the general intelligence which they are capable of diffusing, and which can be imparted by no other human instrumentality, is indispensable to the continuance of a republican government.

Glenn Frank President—University of Wisconsin, Address at the Dedication of a University Extension Building, Milwaukee, September 18, 1928.

. . . mere literacy is not the vital education upon which a valid democracy depends. We might see to it that every man, woman, and child in the United States could read and write and still be a grossly illiterate people. There is an illiteracy of the literate—political illiteracy, economic illiteracy, religious illiteracy, and social illiteracy—that stands like a wall between us and an increasing rational and realistic social order. This generalization is more than obvious when we break it up into some of its elements.
We must not assume that if we teach everybody to read and write we shall thereby eradicate crime from the United States. The mere tools of education are no guaranty of character. A man may carry a kit of burglar's tools and a doctor's degree at the same time. The conquest of illiteracy of this elementary sort leaves us still challenged to evolve an education that will more and more effectively help character to keep pace with the new powers and the new perils of modern civilization. . . .

John W. Gardner, *Excellence: Can We be Equal and Excellent Too?* 1961, p. 37.

Despite the foresight of men such as William James, the critical importance of human resources in modern society did not force itself to public attention until very recently, when the nation began to experience dramatic shortages in strategic professions such as medicine, teaching, engineering and physics.

As each profession faced shortages, each laid cool and aggressive plans to capture a bigger share of the oncoming stream of talent. Then it became apparent that the total stream was limited, . . . Our kind of society must make maximum use of the talent available. It needs desperately to find and train able individuals at many levels, and to an increasing degree modern educational systems are designed to accomplish that result. To the extent that they are not well fitted to achieve that end, they are not modern.

Glenn Frank, President—University of Wisconsin, Address at the Dedication of a University Extension Building, Milwaukee, September 18, 1928.

A merely conventional schooling indifferently pursued does not necessarily make the schooled man materially different from the unschooled man. I have seen a distinguished scientist vie with a ward-heeler in bringing passion, prejudice, and partisanship to a political campaign. I have seen eminent scholars join hands with emotional fanatics in labeling and libeling as dangerous men who choose to challenge the judgment of the herd. I have seen whole faculties of universities, with here and there a heartening exception, grow drunken on the wine of war-time hysteria and join the witch-burners. I have seen men think scientifically about the bacillus of a fever and sentimentally about the basis of a foreign policy within the same twenty-four hours. . . .

Robert M. Hutchins, "Why Go to College?" *The Saturday Evening Post*, January 22, 1938.

Some three hundred college and university presidents recently answered a questionnaire in which they were asked to list, in the order of importance, what they regarded as the purposes of their institutions. Mental discipline, which ranked first sixty years ago, according to a recent analysis of the college catalogues of that day, now ranks twenty-second among the twenty-five avowed purposes of our institutions of higher learning. It is preceded by such objects of higher education as good manners. "Good manners" have no place in the program of higher education. "Personality" has no place in the program of higher education. "Character" has no place in the program of higher education. College develops character by giving young people the habits of hard work and honest analysis. If it tries to teach character directly, it succeeds only in being boring.

Alfred North Whitehead, Professor of Philosophy—Cambridge, *The Aims of Education and Other Essays*, 1929, p. 1.

Culture is activity of thought, and receptiveness to beauty and humane feeling. Scraps of information have nothing to do with it. A merely well-informed man is the most useless bore on God's earth. What we should aim at producing is men who possess both culture and expert knowledge in some special direction.

Alexander Meiklejohn, President—Amherst College, *Journal of Proceedings and Addresses*, National Education Association, 1914, pp. 102-103.

It is sometimes said that the task of the liberal college is simply to train boys to think to give them intellectual method, and that hence it makes very little difference what they think about, what courses they take, during the college years. But if thinking is worth doing, those four years should not be wasted. There are certain essential and fundamental interests to which any liberally educated man should give attention; and no man is liberally educated unless he has in some way or other dealt with them in his own experience. Finally, the liberal college is not merely an institution for training "scholars," men who are to be by profession "investigators" in some field of learning. In a democratic society the liberal college is seeking, not merely the intellectual boy, but also the average American boy, and it proposes to train him for life whatever his profession or calling may be.

Anonymous, Open Letter in *The Raleigh (North Carolina) Register*, November 9, 1929, in *Readings in American Educational History*, 1951, p. 340.

[Note: The editors regard the letter as a possible satire or hoax.]

The University has already cost the people not a little; and the good it has accomplished thus far is extremely doubtful; if I might not rather allege it to have been productive of mischief. College learned persons give themselves great airs, are proud, and the fewer of them we have amongst us the better. I have long been of the opinion, and trust you will join me in it, that establishments of this kind are aristocratical in their nature, and evidently opposed to the plain, simple, honest matter-of-fact republicanism, which ought to flourish among us. The branches of learning cultivated in them are, for the most part, of a lofty arrogant and useless sort. Who wants Latin and Greek and abstruse mathematics in these times and in a country like this? Might we not as well patronize alchymy, astrology, heraldry and the black art?

Has the pursuit of equality been at the expense of excellence?

Daniel Webster, Address Delivered at Madison, Indiana, 1838.

Among the planets of the sky of New England—the burning lights which throw their intelligence and happiness on her people—the first and most brilliant is her system of common schools. I congratulate myself that my first speech on entering public life was in their behalf. Education, to accomplish the ends of good government, should be universally diffused. Open the doors of the schoolhouse to all the children of the land.

Horace Mann, *Tenth Annual Report* to the Massachusetts State Board of Education, 1846.

I believe in the existence of a great, immortal, immutable principle of natural law, or natural ethics,—a principle antecedent to all human insulations, and incapable of being abrogated by any ordinance of man,—a principle of divine origin, clearly legible in the ways of Providence as those ways are manifested in the order of nature and in the history of the race, which proves the *absolute right* to an education of every human being that comes into the world, and which, of course, proves the correlative duty of every government to see that the means of that education are provided for all. . .

William F. Russell, *Annual Report of the Dean of Teachers College*, New York, 1928.

Those who favor quantity are extending educational facilities and welcoming the hordes of students who flock to the doors of our schools and colleges. Those who think first of quality are restricting attendance in order to do their best for small numbers. If it were possible to give a satisfactory education to large numbers in big institutions under conditions of reasonable economy, the results would be of utmost importance. After all, it is a question of the possibility of quantity production of quality in education.

Charles W. Eliot, *Proceedings of the National Education Association*, 1892.

We all know that children, like adults, are not alike, but infinitely different; that the object of education, as of life, is to hang out the innate powers and to develop to the highest possible degree the natural and acquired capacities of each individual. An education or training, therefore, which at the end of four years, ten years, or twenty years leaves the subjects of it alike in skill, capacity, or power of service must have been ill directed.

Henry S. Pritchett, *Sixth Annual Report*, Carnegie Foundation for the Advancement of Teaching.

The colleges, for example, have to a large extent discarded the old compulsory classical training, which at least had the merit of discipline and thoroughness. In adopting a much broader and in many ways a more sensible curriculum they have not yet had time to reach any such stage of thoroughness as was attained under the old form.

Charles W. Eliot, *Proceedings of the National Education Association*, 1892.

In any room of a perfectly graded grammar school we find, in the fall, a single class of from forty to sixty children who are supposed to have had the same preparation for the coming year's work; who have had the same lessons, in the same books, at the same times, under the same teacher, throughout the year; who are to make as nearly as possible the same progress every day in each subject, and to submit to the same tests at the same intervals. They are all kept together, day by day, so far as is possible. The bright ones never work to their utmost, and are frequently marking time; the slow ones are urged forward at a rate which drives some of them to despair; and the ideal of the class is that of equal preparation, equal capacity, equal progress, and equal attainments. If, at the beginning of the year, the children are obtrusively unequal in capacity or attainments, it is an inconvenience to be regretted. The teacher will not be able to "handle her class" so easily as she could if they were all of the same mental size and strength. If, at the end of the year, they have not been pretty well evened up, the teacher has been less successful than she could have wished. This is an extreme statement of the most undesirable uniformity in schools. This is the sense in which close grading is an educational curse.

What has been the role of school texts?

J. Merton England, *American Quarterly*, 1963, p. 191.

From Noah Webster in the 1780s to Emma Willard in 1860, the authors of American school textbooks emphatically believed that there was such a thing as national character and that they had a duty to help form and preserve it. They set out to create a usable past for republican America - an agreed-upon national myth, we might say now. Fundamental elements in the canon they constructed were the enduring shibboleths of the American democratic faith - liberty, equality, morality.

Ruth Miller Elson, *Guardians of Tradition: American Schoolbooks of the Nineteenth Century*, 1964, p. 87.

From his description in all Geography books, the African Negro is clearly regarded as the most degraded of the races. Southerners, who by 1830 justified slavery on the grounds that the Negro was incapable of improvement, could find ample evidence for their attitudes in the schoolbooks used at the time in both North and South. "They [Negroes] are a brutish people, having little more of humanity but the form"; or, "Their mental powers, in general, participate in the imbecility of their bodies"; or, "Africa has justly been called the country of monsters. . . . Even man, in this quarter of the world exists in a state of lowest barbarism." At best Africa is distinguished as the land where "Human nature is nowhere exhibited in a more rude and disgusting attire than in this portion of the globe."

Reverend Jedidiah Morse, Preface to *American Universal Geography*, 1793.

No national government holds out to its subjects so many alluring motives to obtain an accurate knowledge of their own country, and of its various interests, as that of the United States. By the freedom of our elections, public honors and public offices are not confined to any one class of men, but are offered to merit, in whatever rank it may be found. To discharge the duties of public office with honor and applause, the history, policy, commerce, productions, particular advantages and interests of the several States, ought to be thoroughly understood. . .
It is to be lamented that this part of education has been so long neglected in America. Our young men, universally, have been much better acquainted with the geography of Europe and Asia than with that of our own States and country. The want of suitable books on the subject has been the cause. . . of the shameful defect in our education.

Ruth Miller Elson, *Guardians of Tradition: American Schoolbooks of the Nineteenth Century*, 1964, p. 338.

Unlike many modern schoolbooks, those of the nineteenth century made no pretense of neutrality. While they evade issues seriously controverted in their day, they take a firm and unanimous stand on matters of basic belief. The value judgment is their stock in trade: love of country, love of God, duty to parents, the necessity to develop habits of thrift, honesty, and hard work in order to accumulate property, the certainty of progress, the perfection of the United States. These are not to be questioned.

Richard Mosier, *Making the American Mind,* **1965, p. 167.**

Textbook compilers may contribute to the shaping of the basic ideas and values of their culture, and their part in the educative process can be crucial and strategic.

Is the concept of "progressive" education anti-intellectual?

Progressive Education: A Quarterly Review of the Newer Tendencies in Education, **Vol. I, No. 1, April, 1924, p. 2.**

The conduct of the pupil should be governed by himself according to the social needs of his community, rather than by arbitrary laws. Full opportunity for initiative and self-expression should be provided, together with an environment rich in interesting material that is available for the free use of every pupil.

Richard Hofstadter, *Anti-Intellectualism in American Life,* **1964, pp. 353-354.**

One group of educationists, looking forward to the day when "the aristocratic, cultural tradition of education [will be] completely and finally abandoned," had this to say of pupils who showed unusual intellectual curiosity: "Any help we can give them should be theirs, but such favored people learn directly from their surroundings. Our efforts to teach them are quite incidental in their development. It is therefore unnecessary and futile for the schools to attempt to gear their programs to the needs of unusual people." In this atmosphere, as Jerome Bruner puts it, "the top quarter of public school students, from which we must draw intellectual leadership in the next generation, is perhaps the group most neglected by our schools in the recent past." This group has indeed been neglected by many educators and looked upon by some not as the hope or the challenge or the standard of aspiration for the educational system, but as a deviant, a side issue, a special problem, at times even a kind of pathology.

Alfred North Whitehead, Professor of Philosophy—Cambridge, *The Aims of Education and Other Essays,* **1929, p. 3.**

Whenever a text-book is written of real educational worth, you may be quite certain that some reviewer will say that it will be difficult to teach from it. Of course it will be difficult to teach from it. If it were easy, the book ought to be burned; for it cannot be educational. In education, as elsewhere, the broad primrose path leads to a nasty place.

Marc Raeff, Professor of History—Clark, *New York Times Magazine,* **September 8, 1957, p. 10.**

Perhaps the most serious failure of the American educational system has been its tendency to produce intellectual passivity. It has not helped to develop active, critical, inquisitive minds.

Howard G. Spalding, High School Principal, *U.S. News and World Report,* **May 16, 1958, p. 99.**

For years, public-school seniors have consistently outranked seniors in private schools on the achievement examinations of the College Entrance Examination Board, although the private schools, being selective in character and emphasizing academic curricula, closely resemble the schools that Professor Bestor advocates.

Arthur Bestor, Professor of History—Illinois, *U.S. News and World Report,* **January 24, 1958, p. 69.**

An educational system that refuses to single out for high and exceptional honors those who demonstrate in fair competition their brilliance and their willingness to work is not a democratic school system at all. It is simply an anti-intellectual school system. And it is no excuse to say that society as a whole has relatively little respect for intellectual achievement. In this matter the school has got to be the leader. If schools, whose business is intellectual training, do not really respect it, how can one expect society as a whole to do so?

Editorial, *Life*, March 31, 1958, p. 32.

"We agree," Dewey once said, "that we are uncertain as to where we are going and where we want to go, and why we are doing what we do." In a kind of country club existentialism, Dewey and his boys genially contended that the traditional ends of education - and indeed of human life - like God, virtue and the idea of "culture" were all debatable and hence not worth debating. In their place: enter life adjustment. The alternative to educating the individual thus became, as John Keats puts it in his excellent new book, *Schools without Scholars*, "to bring the individual by a process of conditioning, to a realization of his functional role in society."

Selected Bibliography

Bailyn, Bernard. *Education in the Forming of American Society: Needs and Opportunities for Study.* Chapel Hill: University of North Carolina Press, 1960.

Berkson, I.B. *Education Faces the Future: An Appraisal of Contemporary Movements in Education.* New York: Harper & Brothers, Publishers, 1943.

Butts, R. Freeman, and Cremin, Lawrence A. *A History of Education in American Culture.* New York: Holt, 1953.

Calhoun, Daniel, ed. *The Educating of Americans: A Documentary History.* Boston: Houghton Mifflin Company, 1969.

Callahan, Raymond A. *Education and the Cult of Efficiency: A Study of the Social Forces That Have Shaped the Administration of the Public Schools.* Chicago: The University of Chicago Press, 1962.

Cohen, W.J. "Changing Influences in American Education." *Current History*, 63 (August, 1972), 49.

Conant, James Bryant. *Slums and Suburbs.* New York: McGraw-Hill Book Company, 1961.

Counts, George S. *Education and American Civilization.* Westport, Conn.: Greenwood Press, 1952.

Cremin, Lawrence A. *Transformation of the School: Progressivism, 1876-1957.* New York: Knopf, 1961.

Cubberley, Ellwood P. *The History of Education.* Boston: Houghton Mifflin, 1920.

Curti, Merle. *Social Ideas of American Educators.* Paterson, N.J.: Pageant Books, 1959.

Dewey, John. *Intelligence in the Modern World.* Edited by Joseph Ratner. New York: Alfred A Knopf, 1947.

Ebel, R.I. "Command of Knowledge Should Be the Primary Objective of Education." *Today's Education*, 60 (March, 1971), 36.

Edwards, Newton, and Richey, Herman G. *The School in the American Social Order: The Dynamics of American Education.* Boston: Houghton Mifflin, 1947.

Elson, Ruth M. *Guardians of Tradition: American Schoolbooks of the Nineteenth Century.* Lincoln: University of Nebraska Press, 1964.

England, J. Merton. "Democratic Faith in Schoolbooks, 1783-1860." *American Quarterly*, 15 (1963), 191.

Fischer, J.H. "Education and the Democratic Dilemma." *Vital Speeches*, 39 (May 15, 1973), 467.

Frankena, William K. *Philosophy of Education.* New York: Macmillan, 1965.

Franklin, John Hope. *From Slavery to Freedom: A History of Negro Americans.* New York: Alfred A. Knopf, 1947.

Gardner, John W. *Excellence: Can We Be Equal and Excellent Too?* New York: Harper & Brothers, Publishers, 1961.

Greene, Maxine. *The Public School and the Private Vision: A Search for America in Education and Literature.* New York: Random House, 1965.

Greenstein, Fred I. *Children and Politics.* New Haven: Yale University Press, 1969.

Grieder, C. "Have the Schools Failed Society?" *Educational Digest*, 38 (November, 1972), 35.

Gutek, Gerald L. *An Historical Introduction to American Education.* New York: Thomas Y. Crowell Company, 1970.

Gross, Neal. "Critical Questions for Contemporary Education." *Intellect*, 102 (October, 1973), 24.

Hofstadter, Richard. *Anti-Intellectualism in American Life.* New York: Alfred A. Knopf, 1963.

Jencks, Christopher, and Riesman, David. *The Academic Revolution.* Garden City, N.Y.: Doubleday, 1968.

Karier, Clarence J., ed. *Shaping the American Educational State.* New York: The Free Press, 1975.

Keats, John. *Schools Without Scholars.* Boston: Houghton Mifflin Company, 1958.

Kilpatrick, William H. "Progressive Education: A Debate." *New York Times Magazine*, (September 8, 1957), 25.

Knight, Edgar W., and Hall, Clifton L., eds. *Readings in American Educational History.* New York: Appleton-Century-Crofts, 1951.

McClellan, Grant S., ed. *America's Educational Needs.* New York: H.W. Wilson, 1958.

Mosier, Richard D. *Making the American Mind: McGuffey Readers.* New York: Russell & Russell, 1965.

Myrdal, Gunnar. *An American Dilemma: The Negro Problem and Modern Democracy.* New York: Harper & Brothers, Publishers, 1944.

Neill, A.S. *Summerhill: A Radical Approach to Child Rearing.* New York City: Hart Publishing Company, 1960.

Pierce, Bessie L. *Public Opinion and the Teaching of History.* New York: Knopf, 1925.

Rippa, S. Alexander. *Educational Ideas in America: A Documentary History.* New York: D. McKay Co., 1969.

Schultz, Stanley K. *The Culture Factory: Boston Schools, 1789-1960.* New York: Oxford University Press, 1963.

Silberman, Charles. *Crisis in the Classroom.* New York: Random House, 1970.

Skinner, B.F. *Walden Two.* New York: The Macmillan Company, 1948.

Welter, Rush. *Popular Education and Democratic Thought in America.* New York: Columbia University Press, 1962.

THE AMERICAN FAMILY—A PAST WITH A FUTURE?

Introductory Essay

Their critics accuse the New England Puritans of many things, but indecisiveness is rarely one of them. For what the Puritans believed, they preached uncompromisingly and practiced with uncommon discipline and thoroughness. And of few judgments were they more certain than that a well ordered family was the only secure foundation of society, the building block from which larger institutions could be shaped.

Accordingly the early New England towns enticed bachelors with the promise of free land upon marriage and penalized those who resisted with higher taxes. For the most stubborn, Connecticut resorted to the direct approach: the government simply singled out a stable household of worthy influence and ordered the unattached male to move in. Divorce was rare and widowed spouses prompt to remarry. Children rash enough to challenge their parents invariably (and literally) felt the consequences. If a father hesitated to wield the rod himself, a town official would. More than a mere breach of etiquette, filial disobedience had been made a civil crime. Massachusetts statutes — never models of restraint — actually prescribed the death penalty in severe cases. Institutions which might encroach on the family's prerogative were discouraged; most early efforts to establish schools foundered on the belief that education was a family responsibility. When a child did leave home to learn a trade, his father made certain he was apprenticed to another good Puritan family where the domestic virtues would be constantly before him.

As in most matters, in the theory and practice of family life the Puritan colonists were more articulate and systematic than their Anglican or Quaker neighbors. Still the difference was one of degree. In the Southern and Middle colonies as well as New England, custom, law and rhetoric all decreed that the family would provide the foundation for society.

Today many profess to see in the family an archaic and dying institution. One in four American marriages ends in divorce with the rate creeping toward one in three. A subculture of "swinging singles" recognizes the dating-bar rather than the home as the hub of social life. Zero Population Growth advocates argue that bringing children into the world is no longer fair — either to the children or to the world. Feminists question the possibility of finding "fulfillment" in being a wife and mother. There is a vogue of alternative life styles — ranging from communes to gay liberation — in which the family is, at least, peripheral and, at most, biologically impossible. The most sensitive barometer of American popular culture, television, may have been trying to tell us something when child-rearing passed from the hands of Ozzie and Harriet to Eddie's Father and when Mrs. Madison and Mrs. Unger shipped out Oscar and Felix to become the "Odd Couple."

Somewhere along the way, something has happened. The first unambiguous evidence that the colonial family order had changed appears in the journals and travel reports of European visitors to America just after the Age of Jackson. They dwelt on a basic theme: the American father had lost his authority. For the earliest Americans that authority had been unchallenged. As texts and sermons on the family explained, the husband would decide, command, and lead; his wife would concur, obey, and follow. As for their children, more than one reader of the documents has found it difficult to distinguish their duties from those of the domestic servants. Nineteenth Century visitors painted a sharply contrasting picture. One British traveler, for example, told of watching in amazement as a three-year-old boy defied his father's orders to come into the house. Commands, bribes, threats were all unavailing. Most dumb-founding of all was the father's response. "A sturdy Republican, sir," he laughed with a wink for his visitor. Democracy and the rhetoric of egalitarianism, as de Tocqueville was to argue, had its effects upon home life as well as the body politic.

It should be no surprise that the first significant decline in the stern superiority of the man of the house was balanced by some improvement in the lot of his wife. "It was in the 1830's and 1840's," one historian wrote, "that women in America first began to be spoken of as 'restless'; and as everyone knows, they have been restless ever since." Too much should not be made of this. No one was called a male chauvinist just yet. But the first movement for female suffrage, demands that women be granted more educational opportunity and the extra-familial activities of reformers like Dorothea Dix: each of these suggested that the traditional subordinate role of woman was not immutable. Articles in women's magazines like *Ladies Companion* still urged the acquisition of domestic skills and demure behavior, but their emphasis had changed. Earlier the tone had been self-righteous and assured, reflecting a firm belief on the necessity and glory of women's inferior role; now it was coy, even contrived, hinting that inferiority was a useful social tactic rather than an absolute condition.

Paralleling the decline of the father within the family was the diminished role played by the family in society. The industrial revolution was decades away from its full impact, but the home had already begun to relinquish its role as the basic economic unit. With the spread of common schools, education was no longer a major family function. The encroachment of other institutions upon the once sovereign family had begun.

The triple revolution of industrialism, immigration, and urbanization which transformed America in the late Nineteenth Century weakened the patriarchal family still further. That immigration should have had this effect is distinctly ironic. Profoundly conservative, closer to Old World ways, presuming the continuity of generations and venerating the father, the immigrant family seemed a force for stability, not for change. There may have flickered in the breasts of immigrant fathers the hope — so fundamental to the American myth — that their children would have a better life, but few fathers would have interpreted better to mean different.

Almost from the day he left Ellis Island for a new home — most likely a crowded urban tenement — forces beyond his control loosened the father's grip on his family. In Italy or Poland or Greece, the father had been the transmitter of wisdom, the explainer of tradition. But in the swirling urban world the immigrant family entered, the wisdom seemed less meaningful, the traditions increasingly out of place. In the old country, the father's authority had its roots in the economic and physical security he provided his family. In America, his skills were often obsolete or irrelevant to an industrialized economy; his wife and children were pressed into work to supplement his earnings. The police, the city political machine, the settlement house, institutions he had never heard of, assumed his traditional protective functions. Less bound by tradition, more adaptable to a new language and novel manners, his children were soon better able to cope with the new life than he. Increasingly, he began to define his own worth in terms of what he could help them accomplish. The irony of this reversal was not lost on a perceptive Russian immigrant girl named Mary Antin who saw both tragedy and ultimate triumph in the immigrant fathers doing American's urban dirty work:

You see them shuffle from door to door with a basket of spools and buttons, or bending over sizzling irons in a basement tailor shop, or rummaging in your trash can, or moving a push cart from curb to curb, at the command of the burly policeman.... What if the crosslegged tailor is supporting a boy in college who is one day going to mend your state constitution for you? What if the rag-picker's daughters are hastening over the ocean to teach your children in the public schools?... the greasy alien on the street was born thousands of years before the oldest living American; and he may have something to communicate to you...

Not all immigrant children shared Mary Antin's vision and compassion. Some sneered at their parents' anachronistic manners and inability to "assimilate" or "Americanize." Others still, out of parental control altogether, took to the streets to join the gangs of "Street Arabs" that terrorized passers-by and even attacked policemen. The immigrant family's experience differed only in degree from that undergone by other American families as they moved from town to city and from farm to factory. An investigation by the State of Massachusetts revealed that only half of the skilled workers and less than one unskilled worker in ten could support a family without help from another member. Even among managerial personnel one in four men required assistance from a working wife or child.

For most women from lower class homes, getting out of the house was anything but liberation. Their jobs were mind-numbing and back-breaking — operating factory machines or stitching cheap clothing and rolling cigars in poorly lit and ill-ventilated tenements. That their rescue depended finally on elaborate programs of government-sponsored social legislation during the Progressive Era and the New Deal was yet one more indication that the family and its head could no longer play the traditional protective role.

For women from middle class homes, the situation was more promising. In the last decades of the Nineteenth Century a man named Remington began to manufacture an invention of a man named Sholes. Today, asking a female job applicant, "Can you type?" is a symbol of oppression; then, it was an invitation to freedom. Along with school teaching and the opening of many women's colleges (by 1894, 84,000 women were enrolled), the new secretarial and clerical positions available for skilled typists offered a novel and welcome alternative to the kitchen or factory. Encouraged by the possibility of independence from fathers or husbands, women renewed pressure for a wide variety of legal and social reforms. Their new strength was symbolized in the winning of the vote by a Constitutional Amendment in 1920.

Children were less capable of lobbying for their interests. Literally millions of them were evading compulsory-school laws to quench the thirst of industry for cheap labor, sometimes working for a penny an hour or less. Theodore Roosevelt called a White House Conference on Children in 1909 to dramatize the problem. As reformer Lillian Wald wrote,

> The national sense of humor was aroused... that whereas the federal government concerns itself with the conservation of hogs and lobsters... citizens who desire instruction and guidance for the conservation and protection of children have no responsible governmental body to which to appeal.

Three years later a U.S. Children's Bureau was established to fill that need. Since then, the Federal government's role in the health and welfare of its youngest citizens has grown steadily and once each decade a White House Conference renews its commitment.

The New Deal and the Progressive Era stand as ironic landmarks in family history. Probably not since the colonial era had so many laws dealt with the role of the family in society. Still there was a profound difference. The early statutes had recognized the fundamental strength of the family and its head and reinforced that strength. The modern legislation was based upon the understanding that the family and the father were often incapable of handling the pressures and demands of a complex industrial state and that public surrogates had become necessary.

The "average" American family had lived in a small town or on a farm in the Nineteenth Century and in a big city at the turn of the Twentieth. In the course of the next fifty years it pulled up stakes and moved again — to the suburbs.

It lived in a split-level house among a hundred or so other split-level houses stamped from an identical mold on a street named something like "Cherry Hill Lane" in a "development" called something like "Meadowbrook Acres." The father carried an attaché case or lunch pail, spent an hour fighting traffic to get to his job in the city, and belonged to a country club (attaché case) or bowling league (lunch pail). The mother joined a garden-club, played bridge with the "girls" twice a week and may or may not have appreciated the vacuum cleaner, garbage disposal, pop-up toaster and other miraculous gadgets which freed enough of her time to do so. The son moved from his paper route to Little League practice to — modern rite of passage — his first driver's license. The daughter seemed to spend a large portion of her adolescence in braces and on the phone. Each evening, all four clustered in the *family* room in front of the most marvelous gadget of all and watched the Nelsons run through all the possible permutations of "Hi Mom, Hi Pop, Hi Dave, Hi Rick."

From today's perspective, this stereotyped image evokes a curious amalgam of scorn and nostalgia. At the time, however, suburbia seemed to offer a rebirth of traditional family values in modern trappings. The divorce rate fell sharply after 1946, and a "baby boom" signaled a trend to larger families. Fathers—as portrayed in popular novels and on television—were more available for counsel and family outings. Egged on by advertising and a do-it-yourself fad, mothers took a renewed interest in redecorating their homes and cooking and making their own clothes. When the novelist Sloan Wilson said that "modern man needed an old-fashion woman around the house," many Americans agreed.

But, as in politics and race relations and foreign affairs, the quietude of the fifties was deceptive. Under the surface, the move to suburbia stimulated rather than quelled the long-term weakening of the family in society and the father's role within it. Work and commuting kept fathers away from home much of the time. (The television dramas blithely ignored this uncomfortable fact; Ozzie Nelson had no visible means of support and not even a trivia expert could tell you what "Beaver's" father did for a living.) Lore that fathers once passed on to sons was now provided by Little League coaches, scout leaders and guitar teachers.

More than ever before, these factors gave the mother new authority within the home. This phenomenon and the rhetoric which glorified it alarmed observers of varying credibility. A decade earlier, Philip Wylie had decried the excesses of mother-worship in the country and coined a new term — momism. Other societies, he wrote, had paid due filial respect to mothers. "But I cannot think offhand of any civilization except ours in which an entire division of living men has been used, during wartime, or at any time, to spell out the word 'mom' on a drill field." More dispassionate observers, such as the noted psychoanalyst Erik Erikson, rejected Wylie's sensationalism but conceded that one case history after another had established the domineering mother as a significant historical phenomenon in American society, posing psychological dangers which could not be viewed without concern.

Others thought the emphasis on "mom" misplaced; the new power in the home was really the once downtrodden figure — the child. With the demise of the family as an economic unit, with its protective responsibilities yielded largely to the state, with its recreational and educative functions substantially diminished, its remaining role was one of raising children. An index of how seriously this role was taken may be deduced from the biographies of two books. *Infant Care*, a federal government pamphlet, was first printed in 1916; thirty years later Benjamin Spock wrote *Baby and Child Care*. The two publications have sold fifty-nine and twenty-two million copies respectively—one copy for virtually every first child born to an American family in each book's lifetime. The sales, many thought, were an index to the obsession of American families with their children. Sociologists wrote of the "child-centered home" and alarmists of a "cult of the child." Conservatives grumbled about the lack of discipline and warned that widespread catering to children would destroy the old values.

The latent concerns of the fifties emerged full-blown as the public crises and movements of the sixties and seventies. Increasing numbers of young people feeling their new strength within the family discovered that they could not "communicate" with their parents. "Don't trust anyone over thirty" grew from watchword to cliché. The generation gap was born.

Women more emphatically than ever before rejected the idea of social inferiority. Homemaking, they insisted, was *a* career, not *the* career. Organizing interest groups, exuding a new militancy, they demanded changes both symbolic (call me "Ms.") and substantive (equal pay for equal work).

Perhaps most significantly of all, the nation's leading thinkers and most powerful institutions reinforced these trends. Jurists and philosophers began to develop theories of children's rights. The White House which had sponsored conferences *about* children and youth in 1970 organized one *of* young people who conducted their own discussions and passed their own resolutions. A Constitutional Amendment lowered the voting age to eighteen.

The nation's judiciary awarded women many of their most vigorously sought goals. Economic discrimination in such disparate forms as job advertising by sex and unequal salary scales—was severely limited by a series of decisions. In an historic judgment, the Supreme Court declared anti-abortion legislation unconstitutional. Women had won the "right to regulate their own bodies." More comprehensively, the proposed Equal Rights Amendment seems likely of passage.

These developments have as much relevance for the position of the family within society as they do for the interrelationships of the family members themselves. To the extent that their lives could be defined and their worth established independent of the family, women and children had less need for it. It is now a sociologist's commonplace that the family has lost all its functions except the "affective" and "socializing" ones. Now it seems possible that even these can be provided by alternatives: communes, "living together," singles clubs, day care centers, and so on.

What does it all portend? Many commentators feel safe in predicting that the American family, its functions totally obsolete, will deteriorate and disappear. Certainly, the trend over centuries has been one of undeniable decline. Caution, however, is in order. For what appear as novel, irresistible forces are often old problems, long successfully withstood, in new guise. The generation gap, for example, seems a strikingly modern phenomenon. But Puritan and Quaker parents fretted that their offspring were abandoning the old ways. College students of the 1830's seized campus buildings for causes they defended. Immigrant children did not trust their parents. A half-century ago, F. Scott Fitzgerald defined a generation as a reaction against fathers that occurs three times a century.

Despite its weakening, the family has been a sturdy and resilient entity. Assaulted by vast impersonal economic and technological forces, challenged by powerful political institutions, it nonetheless survives. With all that has happened to it in two centuries, it remains the life style chosen by nine of every ten Americans. Printing its obituary may well be premature.

Excerpted Documents

The colonial and revolutionary family.

Arthur M. Schlesinger, Sr., late Professor of American History—Harvard University, *The Birth of the Nation*, 1968, p. 17.

Although colonial life was woven of many strands—English, Scotch-Irish, Dutch, French, German, and so on— all the new groups, whatever their ethnic differences, shared the common belief that the family was, in Franklin's phrase, the "sacred cement of all societies." As Cotton Mather put it in 1693, "*Families* are the *Nurseries* of all Societies; and the First Combinations of mankind. *Well-ordered Families* naturally produced a *Good Order* in other Societies."

Edmund S. Morgan, Professor of History—Yale University, "The Puritans and Sex," 1952, in *The American Family in Social-Historical Perspective,* 1973, pp. 291-292.

The courts,. . .were not satisfied with mere cohabitation; they insisted that it be peaceful cohabitation. Husbands and wives were forbidden by law to strike one another, and the law was enforced on numerous occasions. But the courts did not stop there. Henry Flood was required to give bond for a good behavior because he had abused his wife simply by "ill words. . ." On another occasion the court favored the husband: Jacob Pudeator, fined for striking and kicking his wife, had the sentence moderated when the court was informed that she was a women "of great provocation."

Max Lerner, Professor of American Civilization—Brandeis University, *America as a Civilization, Vol II: Culture and Personality,* 1957, p. 561.

Americans today sometimes idealize the life of the child in colonial and early agrarian America. Actually there was a struggle of parents and children with the hobgoblins of Original Sin, a continuing war with the Devil, and an adamant effort by parents and clergy to repair the child's ignorance and willfulness by catechisms and prepare him early for the trials and duties of life and the deliverance of death. It is easy to note in the history books the recorded successes of this method of child-rearing and to forget the obscure failures, the "lives of quiet desperation" that Thoreau saw around him, the wild outbursts of family rebellion.

Benjamin Franklin, writing to a friend, in *The Family: Past and Present,* edited by Bernhard Stein, 1938, p. 208.

It is the Man and Woman united that make the complete human Being. Separate, she wants his Force of Body and Strength of Reason; he, her Softness, Sensibility and acute Discernment. Together they are more likely to succeed in the World. A single Man has not nearly the value he would have in the State of Union. He is an incomplete Anima. He resembles the odd half of a Pair of Scissors. If you get a prudent, healthy Wife, your industry in your Profession, with her good Economy, will be a fortune sufficient.

Gilman Ostrander, Professor of History—University of Michigan, *American Civilization in the First Machine Age, 1890-1940,* 1970, p. 17.

The signers of the Declaration of Independence were not not demonstrably concerned about the unalienable rights of women—although some of the wives, Abigail Adams, for instance, were—and nobody supposed that children should think and act for themselves. Bachelors were eligible for the rights of man but only grudgingly so; colonial legislation had in some instances treated them virtually as outlaws. The true basis for a libertarian republican government was an electorate composed of property-owning husbands and fathers representing their households at the polling booths.

Gilman Ostrander, Professor of History—University of Michigan, *American Civilization in the First Machine Age, 1890-1940,* 1970, pp. 238-239.

The American wilderness had not been subdued under God's law as had the English countryside, and the head of the family often had to share his authority under new and trying circumstances, with the pioneer wife and with the children. Far more subversive than this, however, was what Frederick Jackson Turner called "the hither edge of free land," encouraging independence in boys and girls as well.

The democratic family in the age of the common man.

Michael Paul Rogin, Professor of Political Science—University of California, Berkeley, *Fathers and Children: Andrew Jackson and the Subjugation of the American Indian,* 1975, pp. 63-64.

A split had opened between family and society by the Jacksonian period. The family lost functions to other institutions—schools, workplaces, asylums, markets. Schools grew to supplement or replace informal education in the home; other social institutions—hospitals, prisons, factories, poorhouses—also carried out functions and cared for people once accommodated within the household. . . .

As the family lost functions to society, it became the reserve of natural feelings. Tocqueville observed, "The natural bond is drawn closer in proportion as the social bond is loosened." Emotion was withdrawn from social ties, bolstered by extended family connections, and concentrated within the conjugal unit.

Arthur W. Calhoun, Sociologist, *A Social History of the American Family*, 1917, Vol II, p. 37.

The advent of male political democracy consequent on the free life of the frontier went hand in hand with an intense individualism akin to anarchism. . .The progress of individualistic democracy was quite consistent with the reduction of social control over marriage, as in the abolition of banns and the dropping of the requirement of publicity as if the union of the individuals were their own exclusive affairs concerning no one else.

Alexis de Tocqueville, *Democracy in America*, 1848, edited by J.P. Mayer, translated by George Lawrence, 1969, pp. 587-588.

[In a democratic family, a father's] orders might be ill-received, but his advice is usually weighty. He may not be surrounded with formal marks of respect, but at least his sons address him with confidence. There is no recognized formula of address, but they talk to him constantly and freely consult him every day. The master and magistrate have vanished; the father remains. . . .Among democratic nations every word a son addresses to his father has a tang of freedom, familiarity, and tenderness all at once, which gives an immediate impression of the new relationship prevailing in the family.

Barbara Welter, Historian, "The Cult of True Womanhood: 1820-1860," 1966, in *The American Family in Social-Historical Perspective*, edited by Michael Gordon, 1973, pp. 237, 241.

The magazines were filled with domestic tragedies in which spoiled young girls learned that when there was a hungry man to feed French and china painting were not helpful. According to these stories many a marriage is jeopardized because the wife has not learned to keep house.

. . . If any woman asked for greater scope for her gifts the magazines were sharply critical. Such women were tampering with society, undermining civilization. Mary Wollstonecraft, Frances Wright and Harriet Martineau were condemned in the strongest possible language—they were read out of the sex. "They are only semi-women, mental hermaphrodites." The Rev. Harrington knew the women of America could not possibly approve of such perversions and went to some wives and mothers to ask if they did want a "wider sphere of interest" as these nonwomen claimed. The answer was reassuring. 'NO!' they cried simultaneously, 'Let the men take care of politics, *we will take care of the children!*'

Oscar Handlin, Professor of American History—Harvard University, *Facing Life: Youth and the Family in American History*, 1971, p. 128.

An incident at the University of Virginia was . . . not unrepresentative. Fear of student violence had long kept the faculty on edge. But in 1836 the boys organized an independent military company and announced that they would resist the tyrannical order to remove all arms from the campus. The teachers out of desperation or boldness then voted a substantial number of expulsions. Two days of rioting ended in compromise: the appearance of the militia upheld the majesty of the law and the retreat of the faculty readmitted the offending students. Ironically, four years later a student shot to death the professor who had engineered the compromise.

Immigrant and native American families in an industrial age.

Leonard Covello, Educator, *The Heart is the Teacher*, 1958, in *Children and Youth in America: A Documentary History*, 1971, edited by Robert Bremner, 1971, Vol. II, pp. 59-60.

With a weary expression my father glanced over the marks on the report card and was about to sign it. However, he paused with the pen in his hand.

263

"What is this?" he said. "Leonard Covello! What happened to the *i* in Coviello?"... "What difference does it make?" I said. "It's more American. The *i* doesn't help anything." It was one of the very few times that I dared oppose my father. But even at that age I was beginning to feel that anything that made a name less foreign was an improvement.

For a moment my father sat there, bitter rebellion building in him. Then with a shrug of resignation, he signed the report card and shoved it over to me.

Hutchins Hapgood, *The Spirit of the Ghetto*, 1898-1902, in *Children and Youth in America: A Documentary History*, edited by Robert Bremner, 1971, Vol. II, p. 61.

The orthodox parents begin to see that the boy, in order to "get along" in the New World, must receive a Gentile training...The growing sense of superiority on the part of the boy to the Hebraic part of his environment extends itself soon to the home. He learns to feel that his parents, too, are "greenhorns." In the struggle between the two sets of influences that of the home becomes less and less effective. He runs away from the supper table to join his gang on the Bowery, where he is quick to pick up the very latest slang; where his talent for caricature is developed often at the expense of his parents, his race and all "foreigners"; for he is an American, he is "the people"...

Hutchins Hapgood, *The Spirit of the Ghetto*, 1898-1902, in *Children and Youth in America: A Documentary History*, edited by Robert Bremner, 1971, Vol. II, p. 62.

In Russia the father gives the son an education and supports him until his marriage, and often afterward, until the young man is able to take care of his wife and children. The father is, therefore, the head of the house in reality. But in the New World the boy contributes very early to the family's support. The father is in this country less able to make an economic place for himself than is the son. The little fellow sells papers, black boots, and becomes a street merchant on a small scale. As he speaks English, and his parents do not, he is commonly the interpreter in business transactions, and tends generally to take things into his own hands. There is a tendency, therefore, for the father to respect the son.

Harvey Wish, Professor of History—Western Reserve University, *Society and Thought in Modern America*, 1962, p. 136.

In the seventies, for example, New York city debated the question of what to do with an estimated ten thousand homeless boys who wandered about the streets and often moved in gangs and beat up policemen and poorly protected citizens. In 1890, Jacob Riis, a Danish-born journalist of New York, sardonically reported the reform of Hell's Kitchen. "The gang rarely beats a policeman nowadays and it has not killed one in a long while." Gangs usually sprouted in city slums, especially in poor immigrant neighborhoods where adolescents frequently broke from parental control and imitated the worst traits of "Americanized" youngsters.

Harvey Wish, Professor of History—Western Reserve University, *Society and Thought in Modern America*, 1962, p. 138.

Rather ironically, the effective defense of mistreated children had to await the more humane treatment of animals. Henry Bergh of New York, who had founded in 1866 the Society for the Prevention of Cruelty to Animals, decided almost a decade later to sponsor the Society for the Prevention of Cruelty to Children. His society vigorously prosecuted callous parents, removed children from brutal environments, and inspired the growth of similar societies elsewhere. After 1883 a movement began in Illinois to shift dependent children from orphanages and other institutions to private foster homes at the expense and under the supervision of the states.

Robert and Helen Lynd, Sociologists, *Middletown in Transition*, 1937, in *The Family Past and Present*, edited by Bernhard Stein, 1938, pp. 316-317.

As one stood at the emergency commissary watching young and old family members in a long queue waiting for their food doles, one again felt the shock of something new in this enforced mass parading of family extremity. One found oneself speculating as to what this public advertisement of family inadequacy was doing to the face-to-face living of the families in their homes: Who was goading whom to "go down and stand in line—it's *your* turn"? What were the hot retorts from men defending a battered personal status against the sharp words of reproachful wives and children?. . .One knew, too, that in the less exposed homes, behind the brave, solid front that local canons of respectable competence require a family to present to its neighbors, difficult problems were being faced in augmented numbers: mortgage foreclosures, the postponement of having children, the shattering of plans for financial security, the crumbling of affection under the hard hand of disappointment and worry, the decision not to send children to college, and the answering low drumbeat of a frustrated younger generation.

The American family at mid-century.

Philip Wylie, Novelist and Social Critic, *Generation of Vipers*, 1942, pp. 185-186.

Mom is everywhere and everything and damned near everybody, and from her depends all the rest of the U.S. . . . .Men live for her and die for her, dote upon her and whisper her name as they pass away and I believe she has now achieved, in the hierarchy of miscellaneous articles, a spot next to the Bible and the Flag, being reckoned part of both in a way.

Betty Friedan, Feminist Leader, *The Feminine Mystique*, 1963, in *The American Woman: Who Was She?*, edited by Anne F. Scott, 1971, pp. 171-172.

By the end of the nineteen-fifties, the average marriage age of women in America dropped to 20, and was still dropping, into the teens. Fourteen millions girls were engaged by 17. The proportion of women attending college in comparison with men dropped from 47 percent in 1920 to 35 percent in 1958. A century earlier, women had fought for higher education; now girls went to college to get a husband. By the mid-fifties, 60 percent dropped out of college to marry, or because they were afraid too much education would be a marriage bar. Colleges built dormitories for "married students," but the students were almost always the husbands. A new degree was instituted for the wives—"Ph.T." (Putting Husband Through).
. . .Statisticians were especially astounded at the drastic increase in the number of babies among college women. Where once they had two children, now they had four, five, six. Women who had once wanted careers were now making careers out of having babies. So rejoiced *Life* magazine in a 1956 paean to the movement of American women back to the home.

Betty Friedan, Feminist Leader, *The Feminine Mystique*, 1963, in *The American Woman: Who Was She?*, edited by Anne F. Scott, 1971, p. 173.

In the fifteen years after World War II, this mystique of feminine fulfillment became the cherished and self-perpetuating core of contemporary American culture. Millions of women lived their lives in the image of those pretty pictures of the American suburban housewife, kissing their husbands goodbye in front of the picture window, depositing their stationwagonsful of children at school, and smiling as they ran the new electric waxer over the spotless kitchen floor. They baked their own bread, sewed their own and their children's clothes, kept their new washing machines and dryers running all day. They changed the sheets on the beds twice a week instead of once, took the rug-hooking class in adult education, and pitied their poor frustrated mothers, who had dreamed of having a career. Their only dream was to be perfect wives and mothers; their highest ambition to have five children and a beautiful house, their only fight to get and keep their husbands. They had no thought for the unfeminine problems of the world outside the home; they wanted the men to make the major decisions. They gloried in their role as women, and wrote proudly on the census blank: "Occupation: housewife."

Max Lerner, Professor of American Civilization—Brandeis University, *America as a Civilization*, Vol II: *Culture and Personality*, 1957, p. 562.

The entire family plan, especially on the middle-class level, centers around the child. It is dressed up, coddled, socialized early. In an effort to set the stage for what Margaret Mead calls the "expected childhood experience," the parents sometimes squeeze themselves dry of spontaneous emotion. They watch the stages of the child's growth against the statistical norms of Gesell or (on a lower-class level) the traditional folklore of expected growth. They brood over the moot questions of child-rearing: the child's thumb-sucking, the choice of feeding and the time for weaning, its toilet training, its bed-wetting, its temper tantrums: and later its speech and reading difficulties, lying, stealing.

Margaret Mead, Anthropologist, *And Keep Your Powder Dry*, 1942, pp. 89-90.

Each civilization conveys different things to its children. . .and as the Balinese baby learns that the unknown is always to be avoided, and the Iatmul baby learns to play at being strong, the American baby learns that its parents' love—even if they are his parents and he isn't adopted—is conditional upon the way in which he compares with others. "He's such a poor eater. I don't know what to do with him. I just can't get him to eat like other children." His mother thinks he isn't listening, as he digs with his shovel under the park bench, but the "won't eat" and the depreciating tone in which she says it gets through to him—she is not worrying because her beloved child does not take the food which she has lovingly prepared for him, but because he is showing himself inferior at being a growing child. At his next meal he looks guiltily at his carrots. If he rejects them again that same depreciatory note will recur tomorrow in his mother's voice.

James Joslyn and John Pendleton, "The Adventures of Ozzie and Harriet," *Journal of Popular Culture*, 1973, pp. 23, 32.

The names Ozzie and Harriet Nelson evoke images of a simpler past for most Americans old enough to remember them on television. Recollections of "America's favorite family," however, range from the nostalgic to the cynical.
. . .Nostalgia, which literally means homesickness, best describes the emotional response that the stable Nelson television family has kindled in the minds of its admirers. But for the other, primarily young, viewers, Ozzie and Harriet seemed to represent the false reality of middle class stability that television has generally portrayed. The demise of "The Adventures of Ozzie and Harriet" in 1966 coincided with an acceleration of a lifestyle revolution among many young, affluent Americans. The increasing currency of words such as "alienation" and "counter-culture" testified to the growing tendency to attack the traditional family structure as an outdated, irrelevant and unhealthy institution. . .
Ozzie and Harriet received thousands of annual letters from adult viewers who admired the show as a pillar of strength for the sagging family institution and from children requesting to be adopted by the congenial couple.

The family today and tomorrow: Generation gaps and women's liberation.

Gael Greene, Contributing Editor—*New York Magazine*, "A Vote Against Motherhood," 1963, in *Pronatalism: The Myth of Mom and Apple Pie*, edited by Ellen Peck and Judith Senderowitz, 1974, p. 264.

I don't want to have any children. Motherhood is only a part of marriage, and I am unwilling to sacrifice the other equally important feminine roles upon the overexalted altar of parenthood. Instead of condemning myself to the common syndrome of the unhappy creature who is mother first, wife second, woman third and human being last, I champion the wondrously satisfying love of a woman and her husband, two adults enjoying the knowledge and mystery of each other, tasting dependence, accepting responsibility, yet individual and free.

Betty Rollin, NBC Correspondent, "Motherhood: Need or Myth," 1970, in *Pronatalism: The Myth of Mom and Apple Pie*, edited by Ellen Peck and Judith Senderowitz, 1974, p. 147.

The notion that the maternal wish and the activity of mothering are instinctive or biologically predestined is baloney. Try asking most sociologists, psychoanalysts, biologists—many of whom are mothers—about motherhood being instinctive; it's like asking department-store presidents if their Santa Clauses are real. "Motherhood—instinctive?" shouts distinguished sociologist/author Dr. Jessie Bernard. "Biological destiny? Forget biology! If it were biology, people would die from not doing it."
"Women don't need to be mothers any more than they need spaghetti," says Dr. Richard Rabkin, a New York psychiatrist. "But if you're in a world where everyone is eating spaghetti, thinking they need it and want it, you will think so to."

J. Anthony Lukas, *New York Times* Correspondent, *Don't Shoot—We Are Your Children*, 1971, pp. 448-449.

Today's adults, too, depend heavily on drugs—alcohol, tobacco, the amphetamines and barbiturates. But the values these drugs symbolize are still covert. When the father downs three martinis coming home on the club car he rarely admits to himself he is seeking pleasure; he says he needs the drinks to relax after a hard day's work and to recharge his batteries for the next day. When his son smokes marijuana he openly proclaims that he turns on for "kicks," or pleasure. One generation's forbidden fruit becomes the daily bread of the next.

In turn, this may influence the parents' and the older generation's view of youthful behavior. If the germ of that behavior is there—but suppressed—in the older generation, its uninhibited appearance in the young may stir up no little guilt in the parents. And guilt is rarely an aid to understanding or compassion. There is an old saying: "The most effective way to punish your parents is to imitate them"; if so, many parents today are being subtly tortured by their own children.

Leontine Young, Executive Director of the Newark Child Service Association, *The Fractured Family*, 1973, pp. 135-136.

Some people believe that the family, as a vital human institution, is finished. Its power gone, it will slowly or speedily deteriorate into another historical dust heap. Others believe it will transform itself into a totally different kind of institution; still others believe it may renew itself and fulfill its ancient functions with new meaning and strength.

Those who foresee great change in family structure observe correctly that we are already traveling in the direction of a peer-group society. People associate with their own age groups and regard other groups with a strange mixture of suspicion and hopeful fantasy or, as with the very old and the very young, don't regard them much at all.

Max Lerner, Professor of American Civilization—Brandeis University, *America as a Civilization*, Vol. II: *Culture and Personality*, 1957, p. 551.

With all its weaknesses and excesses the American family is a going concern reflecting less the disintegration of the culture than its mobility and genius for innovation.   For that reason it is a pain to moralists, traditionalists, religious absolutists, bourgeois-baiting Marxists, and professional cultural pessimists. If the American family system is sick, then the class system must also be sick, and the whole economy, the democratic idea, the passion for equality, the striving for happiness, and the belief that there can be free choice and a future of hope. For it is on these that the American family is founded. You may feel varying degrees of approval or disapproval of the American institutions and ideas I have listed, but the point is that the American family is part of the totality and reflects its virtues as well as its weaknesses.

The Black family in slavery and freedom.

Eugene Genovese, Professor of History—University of Rochester, *Roll, Jordon, Roll*, 1974, p. 482.

According to the slaveholders, slave men had little sense of responsibility toward their families and abused them so mercilessly that Ole Massa constantly had to intervene to protect the women and children. Skeptics might wonder how these allegedly emasculated men so easily dominated the strong-willed and physically powerful women of the matriarchal legend, but the slaveholders never troubled themselves about such inconsistencies.

Eugene Genovese, Professor of History—University of Rochester, *Roll, Jordan, Roll*, 1974, p. 494.

What happened to a slave boy who witnessed, as many did, his father's being whipped by a white man, or worse, his father's standing by helplessly while his mother was being whipped? Clearly, the moment had to be traumatic and the boy's confidence in his father had to be shaken. Children apparently did not often witness such scenes: most masters preferred to discipline their slaves at times and in places unavailable to the children, and the slave parents conspired to keep their children ignorant. As for those children who saw and suffered, many possibly never got over the shock. But there is no evidence that many despised their fathers, especially since their mothers tried to explain the acquiescence and instruct their children in the ways of survival. Nor do we know how many children reacted like that Mexican peasant boy who saw his father collapse helplessly in tears when a treacherous landowner expropriated his land. Emiliano Zapata did not despise his father. He swore vengeance.

...Peter Poyas, Denmark Vesey's lieutenant in the abortive rising of 1822, is remembered as the man who showed his troops how to face execution: "Do not open your lips; die silent, as you shall see me do." He might also be remembered for his restrained comment to the judge who sentenced him to death: "I suppose you'll let me see my wife and family before I die?"

John W. Blassingame, Professor of History—Yale University, *The Slave Community*, 1972, p. 103.

Although it was weak, although it was frequently broken, the slave family provided an important buffer, a refuge from the rigors of slavery. While the slave father could rarely protect the members of his family from abuse, he could often gain their love and respect in other ways. In his family, the slave not only learned how to avoid the blows of the master, but also drew on the love and sympathy of its members to raise his spirits. The family was, in short, an important survival mechanism.

John W. Blassingame, Professor of History—Yale University, *The Slave Community*, 1972, pp. 102-103.

The degree to which slaves were able to give their children hope in the midst of adversity is reflected in the attitudes the black autobiographers held toward their parents. Fathers were loved and respected because of their physical strength, courage, and compassion. Austin Steward described his father as "a kind, affectionate husband and a fond, indulgent parent." James Watkins admired his father because he was "a clever, Shrewd man." James Mars stood in awe of his father who "was a man of considerable muscular strength, and was not easily frightened into obedience."
...Slave mothers, were, of course, held in even greater esteem by their children. Frequently small children fought overseers who were flogging their mothers. Even when they had an opportunity to escape from bondage, many slaves refused to leave their mothers.

Robert Abzug, Professor of History—University of California, Berkeley, "The Black Family During Reconstruction," in Key *Issues in the Afro-American Experience*, edited by Nathan Huggins, et al., 1971, Vol II, pp. 32-33.

When the war finally ended and all slaves were free, it was not surprising that many made the reuniting of their scattered families the first order of business. "Ask almost any one what they are going to do this winter," a white traveler reported from South Carolina in 1865, "and they will answer you. 'I'se got a sister'—a wife or mother, as the case might be—'in Virginia, and I'm going to look her up and fetch her home.'"

Robert Abzug, Professor of History—University of California, Berkeley, "The Black Family During Reconstruction," in *Key Issues in the Afro-American Experience*, edited by Nathan Huggins, et al., 1971, Vol II, p. 38.

. . . education and immediate economic advancement conflicted for the post-Emancipation family, since children otherwise able to do farm labor were sent to school. No long-range promises could cure the financial ills many families faced because they sent their children to school instead of to work. "My stepfather," wrote Booker T. Washington of his pre-Hampton days, "had discovered that I had a financial value, and so when the school opened, he decided that he could not spare me from my work." It was Washington's mother who finally saved her child from oblivion in the salt furnaces of the Kanawha Valley and let him go to school.

Dick Gregory, *Nigger: An Autobiography*, 1964, in *The American Woman: Who Was She?*, edited by Anne F. Scott, 1971, pp. 32, 35.

Like a lot of Negro kids, we never would have made it without our Momma. When there was no fatback to go with the beans, no socks to go with the shoes, no hope to go with tomorrow, she'd smile and say: "We ain't poor, we're just broke." Poor is a state of mind you never grow out of, but being broke is just a temporary condition. She always had a big smile, even when her legs and feet swelled from high blood pressure and she collapsed across the table with sugar diabetes. You have to smile twenty-four hours a day, Momma would say. If you walk through life showing the aggravation you've gone through, people will feel sorry for you, and they'll never respect you. She taught us that man has two ways out in life—laughing or crying. There's more hope in laughing.

Daniel Moynihan, U.S. Ambassador to the United Nations, *The Negro Family: The Case for National Action*, 1966, in *The Moynihan Report and the Politics of Controversy*, edited by Lee Rainwater and William L. Yancey, 1967, p. 62.

When Jim Crow made its appearance towards the end of the 19th century it may be speculated that it was the Negro male who was most humiliated thereby; the male was more likely to use public facilities, which rapidly became segregated once the process began, and just as important, segregation, and the submissiveness it exacts, is surely more destructive to the male than to the female personality. Keeping the Negro "in his place" can be translated as keeping the Negro male in his place: the female was not a threat to anyone.
Unquestionably, these events worked against the emergence of a strong father figure. The very essence of the male animal, from the bantam rooster to the four-star general, is to strut. Indeed, in 19th century America, a particular type of exaggerated male boastfulness became almost a national style. Not for the Negro male. The "sassy nigger" was lynched.
In this situation, the Negro family made but little progress toward the middle-class pattern of the present time.

Booker T. Washington, "Education Will Solve the Race Problem: A Reply," 1900, in *Children and Youth in America: A Documentary History*, edited by Robert Bremner, 1971, Vol II, p. 39.

The negro has not had time enough to collect the broken and scattered members of his family. For the sake of illustration, and to employ a personal reference, I do not know who my own father was; I have no idea who my grandmother was; I have or had uncles, aunts and cousins, but I have no knowledge as to where most of them now are. My case will illustrate that of hundreds of thousands of black people in every part of our country. Perhaps those who direct attention to the negro's moral weakness, and compare his moral progress with that of the whites, do not consider the influence of the memories which cling about the old family homestead upon the character and aspirations of individuals.

E. Franklin Frazier, Sociologist, 1950, in *The Moynihan Report and the Politics of Controversy*, edited by Lee Rainwater and William L. Yancey, 1967, p. 94.

As the result of family disorganization a large proportion of Negro children and youth have not undergone the socialization which only the family can provide. The disorganized families have failed to provide for their emotional needs and have not provided the discipline and habits which are necessary for personality development....Since the widespread family disorganization among Negroes has resulted from the failure of the father to play the role in family life required by American society, the mitigation of this problem must await those changes in the Negro and American society which will enable the Negro father to play the role required of him.

Selected Bibliography

Abzug, Robert H. "The Black Family During Reconstruction." *Key Issues in the Afro-American Experience.* Edited by Nathan Huggins, et al. 2 vols. New York: Harcourt-Brace-Jovanovich, 1971.

Bailyn, Bernard. *Education in the Forming of American Society.* Chapel Hill: University of North Carolina Press, 1960.

Blassingame, John W. *The Slave Community.* New York: Oxford University Press, 1972.

Bremner, Robert, ed. *Children and Youth in America: A Documentary History.* 3 vols. Cambridge: Harvard University Press, 1971-75.

Broffenbrenner, Urie. *Two Worlds of Childhood: US and USSR.* New York: Basic Books, 1970.

Calhoun, Arthur W. *A Social History of the American Family.* 3 vols. Cleveland: The Arthur H. Clark Company, 1917.

Chafe, William H. *The American Woman: Her Changing Social, Economic and Political Roles, 1920-1970.* New York: Oxford University Press, 1972.

Cole, Arthur H. "The Price System and the Rites of Passage." *The American Culture.* Edited by Hennig Cohen. Boston: Houghton-Mifflin Company, 1968.

Damos, John. *A Little Commonwealth: Family Life in the Plymouth Colony.* New York: Oxford University Press, 1970.

Ditzion, Sidney. *Marriage, Morals, and Sex in America: A History of Ideas.* New York: Octagon Books, 1969.

Erikson, Erik H. *Childhood and Society.* New York: W.W. Norton and Company, Inc., 1963.

Frost, J. William. *The Quaker Family in Colonial America.* New York: St. Martin's Press, 1973.

Genovese, Eugene. *Roll, Jordon, Roll.* New York: Random House, 1974.

Gordon, Michael, ed. *The American Family in Social-Historical Perspective.* New York: St. Martin's Press, 1973.

Handlin, Oscar, and Handlin, Mary F. *Facing Life: Youth and the Family in American History.* Boston and Toronto: Little, Brown and Company, 1971.

Joslyn, James, and Pendleton, John. "The Adventures of Ozzie and Harriet." *Journal of Popular Culture,* 1973.

Lerner, Max. *America as a Civilization. Vol. II: Culture and Personality.* New York: Simon and Schuster, 1957.

Lukas, J. Anthony. *Don't Shoot—We Are Your Children.* New York: Random House, 1968.

McLaughlin, Virginia Yans. "Patterns of Work and Family Organization: Buffalo's Italians." *The Family in History: Interdisciplinary Essays.* Edited by Theodore K. Rabb and Robert I. Rotberg. New York: Harper and Row, 1973.

Mead, Margaret. *And Keep Your Powder Dry.* New York: William Morrow and Company, 1942.

Morgan, Edmund S. *The Puritan Family.* New York: Harper and Row, 1966.

Morgan Edmund S. *Virginians at Home: Family Life in the Eighteenth Century.* Williamsburg, Virginia: William Byrd Press, 1952.

O'Neill, William L. "Divorce in the Progressive Era." *American Quarterly, 17 (1965), 203.*

Ostrander, Gilman M. *American Civilization in the First Machine Age, 1890-1940.* New York: Harper and Row, 1970.

Peck, Ellen, and Senderowitz, Judith. *Pronatalism: The Myth of Mom and Apple Pie.* New York: Thomas Crowell, 1974.

Rainwater, Lee. "Crucible of Identity: The Negro Lower-Class Family." *Daedalus,* 45 (Winter, 1966), 172.

Rainwater, Lee, and Yancey, William L., eds. *The Moynihan Report and the Politics of Controversy.* Cambridge, Mass: MIT Press, 1967.

Rapson, Richard L. "The American Child as Seen by British Travelers, 1845-1935." *American Quarterly,* 17 (1965), 520.

Riesman, David. *The Lonely Crowd.* New Haven: Yale University Press, 1950.

Rogin, Michael Paul. *Fathers and Children: Andrew Jackson and the Subjugation of the American Indian.* New York: Alfred A. Knopf, 1975.

Rosendorf, Sidney, "Youth Has its Say in the Rockies." *Children,* 18 (1971), 122.

Saveth, Edward. "The Problem of American Family History." *American Quarterly,* 21 (1969), 311.

Schlesinger, Arthur M. Sr. *The Birth of the Nation.* New York: Alfred A. Knopf, 1968.

Schlesinger, Elizabeth Bancroft. "Cotton Mather and His Children." *William and Mary Quarterly,* 3rd series, 10, 181.

Scott, Anne Firor, ed. *The American Woman: Who Was She?* Englewood Cliffs, New Jersey: Prentice Hall, Inc., 1971.

Sennett, Richard. *Families Against the City: Middle Class Homes of Industrial Chicago, 1872-1890.* Cambridge: Harvard University Press, 1970.

Stern, Bernhard J., ed. *The Family: Past and Present.* New York: Appleton, 1938.

Sunley, Robert. "Early Nineteenth-Century Literature on Child Rearing." *Childhood in Contemporary Cultures.* Edited by Margaret Mead and M. Wolfenstein. Chicago: University of Chicago Press, 1963.

de Tocqueville, Alexis. *Democracy in America.* Edited by J. P. Mayer. Translated by George Lawrence. Garden City, New York: Doubleday and Company, 1969.

Walzer, John E. "A Period of Ambivalence: Eighteenth-Century American Childhood." *The History of Childhood.* Edited by Lloyd de Mause. New York: Harper and Row, 1974.

Welter, Barbara. "The Cult of True Womanhood: 1820-1860." *American Quarterly,* 18 (1966), 151.

Wish, Harvey. *Society and Thought in Modern America.* London: Longman's, 1962.

Young, Leontine. *The Fractured Family.* New York: McGraw-Hill Book Company, 1973.

"IN GOD WE TRUST" and A SENSE OF BELONGING

Introductory Essay

Man seeks community. Ray Ginger writes, "He seeks a sense of safety and security. . ., He wants to feel that he belongs to some group, to identify himself with it, to know that others accept him and that he accepts them. . . . He wants to know that he is making a reality of the potentialities that he was born with, . . .He wants to know that he is a personal force in the world." Men are united into communities by the bonds of kinship, religion, language; by territorial proximity, subjection to the same government; by common social institutions; by common responsibilities, experiences or interests, ideals and goals. When all of these combine together, a strong, vital, and complete community emerges.

In the United States, three major forces help forge the bonds of community: churches, local government and schools.

Economic status, differences in religious and ethnic background, and the division between urban and rural modes of life add further diversity to the kinds of communities which appear in America. In some times and in some places, these boundaries are transcended altogether and a special community is realized. But for the most part, Americans find a "sense of belonging" as members of a homogeneous group.

The Puritans of New England consciously sought to establish a community wherein political, religious and social interests served as its foundation. They believed that whatever excellence man may attain requires community and encouragement from others. John Winthrop, Puritan leader, wrote, "We must delight in each other, make others' conditions our own, rejoice together, mourn together, labor and suffer together; always having before our eyes our commission and community in the work, our community as members of the same body." Community was fostered by intense religious commitment to one another and to God, and received additional nourishment from local self-governnment. The town meetings involved the participation of every individual in discussions and decisions. Thus each man exerted a force in shaping the affairs of the community and thereby increased his commitment to it. By teaching the Puritan doctrine and the principles of democracy, the schools reinforced loyalty to the township.

The Puritans laid out their settlements as compact villages with surrounding farms in order to form a geographic nucleus for community. In contrast, the Englishmen of Virginia spread themselves out upon the banks of the tidewater rivers for the sake of the money-crop tobacco. The county system was adopted; the destiny of the South as predominately rural and consequently isolated was determined. By the 1760's, the "First Families of Virginia" dominated the political and economic life of the state. The small farmers, the yeomen and the slaves who composed the lower classes were doomed to isolation; but the aristocracy escaped, for their presence was not essential to the plantation. They developed social customs and a community based on class identification. The tradition of the 'Southern gentlemen' was established.

A community also reflects the values of its members. For the Puritans, community was a spiritual value which required commitment and hard work for its creation and maintenance. Consequently their community was vigorous and included all those who lived in the township. The Virginians chose tobacco, giving first priority to wealth; community was an unintentional by-product. It is no surprise that the community which did emerge was based on economic position. One aspect of the history of community in America is the conflict between materialistic and social values. Religion is a gauge for the values of a nation and, as a consequence, this conflict is visible in the experience of American religious institutions. The seeds of the conflict were present at the outset. The explorers came with two words upon their lips, "God" and "gold." "God" suffered by association with "gold": the name of God was used to justify greed rather than the creation of a spiritual community among men. In the 1830's, de Tocqueville remarked, "The American preachers are constantly referring to the earth. . . . It is often difficult to ascertain from their discourses whether the principle object of religion is to procure eternal felicity in the other world, or prosperity in this." And in the 1920's, in *The Man Nobody Knows*, Bruce Barton pointed out that for some Jesus had become "a backslapping businessman, a right thinker about the things of this world." On the other hand, the Biblical tradition advocates community as a value. In the Old Testament, a man is considered primarily a member of his clan or tribe, not an individual. And in the New, all are members united in the body of Christ. The result of the conflict of values is a compromise. In America our communities are often defined by class interests, but within that class the religious institutions hold fast to the principle of community. This is illustrated in the division of Southern denominations along class lines. Regardless of the compromises that religion has been compelled to make with class structure, historically it has remained a major force for community.

At the same time as the South was extending the plantation system and developing its traditions, the Puritan's vision of community was being threatened. In the seaports of New England the well-to-do merchants and lawyers slowly replaced the leadership of the clergy. The separation of church and state discouraged the complete integration of political, religious and social institutions as modeled in the Puritan township. De Tocqueville remarked, "In several states the law excludes them [the clergy] from political life; public opinion excludes them in all." This was a loss, for though the Biblical tradition endorses the value of community, its power to bind people together is weak without the support of political institutions. In addition, as the towns became cities, local government could not involve everyone. Politics became the work of the few and the burden of sustaining community was transferred almost entirely to the church.

In rural areas the church has always been marked by a special intensity and vitality. The early frontier set the pattern when the "camp meeting" revivals gave much needed relief from the loneliness and emotional deprivation experienced by many on isolated farms. The church tamed the frontier personality, providing a morality to civilize the rowdy Westerners; the rural church filled a great emptiness, in it people found warmth, friendship and community. Country religion provided a psychological and sometimes physical catharsis through personal revelation, impassioning a soul that was weary with the drudgery of farm life. For hundreds of years the church was the center of community social life. And although rural life has been dramatically changed by the automobile and the telephone, in 1966, seventy percent of the social participation of a sample of rural people in North Carolina was still centered in their churches. When industrialization transplanted many farmers into the mill towns, the church eased the adjustment. Mill towns were planned for profit and though the absentee owners controlled the economic life of the towns, they wanted no responsibility for social life. Early mill towns were not self-governing, therefore there were no roots for political community, but the church had accompanied the workers and resumed its familiar role as the center for community.

"America was born in the country but she grew up in the city." Young cities were rising everywhere in the Nineteenth Century. Increasing population brought all of the "modern" problems: housing was shoddy and over-crowded, crime was common, and family bonds were loosened. By 1822, Boston had to abandon the traditional town form of government. The last vestige of a completely united community, the town meeting, could not survive substantial increases in population. In the city, accordingly, a new kind of community evolved. Such communities may exist over an extended geographic area or may float without territorial definition — not a nomadic group but associations of men from various locations who share certain interests. These are formed for the fulfillment of a variety of goals while establishing a basis for much needed social interaction. Such associations built upon special interests flourish in the city, where people find access to one another, and the neighborhood alone cannot be a focus for the spiritual and intellectual life of the individual.

The small village bound people of different classes, provided a social center for outlying farmers, and its government brought people of various religions together. But the city became more than a single community; it was a collection of communities. The rich had churches and societies distinct from those of common people who found their social life in taverns. At the lowest level of the economic ladder, the immigrants tried to duplicate the village life from which they had come. A common cultural heritage of language, myths, customs, and religion united them at a time when resentment of foreigners was far more common than it is today. In Philadelphia, Benjamin Franklin gave voice to the native American's recurring hostility to the ethnic community. "Why should the Palatine boors be suffered to swarm into our settlements, and by hording together establish their language and manners to the exclusion of ours?" The community insulated the immigrant from painful slights by the natives. Some immigrants reacted to hostility by becoming ardent nationalists. They resisted the assimilation process and made every effort to preserve their customs and beliefs. Like the Puritans, they held that their community and the sense of belonging which they derived from it required commitment and hard work. They chose isolation from the mainstream of American life in order to protect their traditions. Gradually most immigrants changed their language and their customs, but the one thing they rarely changed was their religion. Will Herberg writes, "At home the church (or synagogue) had been, for most of them, the meaningful center of life, the repository of the sacred symbols of community existence." It becomes the only tie to the past and remains as a way of identifying oneself in society. Where the ethnic neighborhood survives, it is one of the rare places in the city where one may still find the fathers in rolled-up shirt sleeves playing with the children and dozens of people chattering on porches and along the sidewalk.

Like the separation of church and state, public education has weakened religion's power to instill the conviction that community, itself, is a value. The notion "brotherhood of man" rests upon a belief in a common Father who created a set of obligations beyond physical necessity. American public school curricula have steered clear of religious questions. Originally, the churches dominated education, but reformers pressured the various states, until, by the turn of the last century, the nation had fully established secular public education. The local school has emerged as a device for welding a diversity of people into a single neighborhood; it has compelled children and parents of various ethnic backgrounds to rub cultures with one another. Sometimes the result has been warmth and a sense of belonging, sometimes frictions have sparked to fire. But the neighborhood patterns are not always such that the local school must play the role of "melting pot." More often it is simply another institution that augments community feelings within a homogeneous group.

Industrialization has placed special pressures on the individual and his sense of community. There were attempts to re-establish psychological identity through the labor union. Prior to industrialization, the worker knew his place. Apprentice or craftsman, he was an invaluable member of his community. But now he had lost his uniqueness — a measure of identity; he had to re-establish his relation to society in some other way. Samuel Gompers claimed that, "In the trade union. . . the workers could obtain another variety of the sense of community." The union offered a promise of a "sense of belonging" to the alienated worker. John Mitchell of the Mine Workers said that the union "stands for fraternity, complete and absolute." People fighting to make the labor unions shared an ideal and a goal. The songs, the stories of workers' heroism, and the excitement of dreams of universal and unending solidarity among working people, served to encourage men who might otherwise have been alienated from modern society. This spirit survives in the struggle for rights that continues in those places where labor remains unorganized; but for the most part, the early days of the union are looked upon as a period of youthful idealism. There are times when a local union seems to be just another social club, if members bother to keep contact at all. The union alone could not salvage community. Ethnic distinctions remained more significant in the worker's life and competed against union claims of class consciousness.

Nineteenth Century reformers also exhibited a youthful idealism. They endeavored to establish communities which would stand as models for a re-organization of American society at large. These utopias (literally, "no places") were considered dreams. Dream or not, they served to criticize the superficiality of the communities man had accepted. Most of the utopias relied upon uniform religious beliefs for their unity; but Brook Farm, founded by Unitarians, was tolerant of all sects and creeds. Its founders attacked the problem of worker alienation by trying to combine the worker and the thinker into one. George William Curtis wrote that "The weeds were scratched out of the ground to the music of Tennyson and Browning." Here was a tiny world in which every member might realize the potentials of both mind and body. All were required to perform manual labor and those who came without education attended a school based upon complete freedom of intercourse between students and faculty. This freedom harkened back to the early democratic townships of New England. It was hoped that cooperation rather than competition would become an American goal. The most important characteristic of Brook Farm was that it was the happiest of the utopias. Unfortunately, it was financially unstable, and costly fire brought an end to its short life of six years. Yet, Hawthorne wrote of it with the words, "I feel we struck upon what ought to be a truth, posterity may dig it up and profit by it."

Industrial workers were not alone in seeking community through organizations intended to promote economic interests. In the 1870's, the Granger movement was the farmer's response to both economic and social crises of the industrial era. Officially called The Patrons of Husbandry, it was the farmer's equivalent to the union and offered the same promise of a "place to belong." The political cooperation in the Grange, the Farmer's Alliance, and similar organizations supplied a network for the spread of a fuller sense of community in rural areas. In Garland's novel, *A Spoil of Office*, Ida Wilbur gave voice to the farmer's hopes:

> I see a time when the farmer will not need to live in a cabin on a lonely farm. I see the farmers coming together in groups. I see them with time . . . to visit their fellows . . . . I see them gather like the Saxons of old upon the green at evening to sing and dance. I see cities rising near them with schools, and churches, and concert halls. I see a day when the farmer will no longer be a drudge and his wife a bond slave. . . when the boys and girls will not go west nor to the city; when life will be worth living.

Technological advance brought a twisted fulfillment to a part of Ida Wilbur's dream. By the 1930's, the automobile gave half of America's rural population access to the city. But this release from isolation had its price. Country life became "citified." The cheap thrills of bright lights and movie theaters replaced the pleasures of dancing on the village green and quiet evenings on the family homestead. The radio disseminated urban values over the countryside, planting the seeds of discontent into the hearts of the most isolated country children; and the boys and girls kept fleeing the farms in a mass migration to the cities. It is disputable whether the life they found there was as "worth living" as advertised. Some are prepared to advance this cynicism in telling argument. For the concentrated population of the city is a false promise for human contact. As early as 1890, crusading clergyman Josiah Strong wrote, "In the city there is no sense of neighborhood. You may be separated from your next neighbor by only a few inches, and yet for years never see his face or learn his name. Mere proximity does not imply social touch." He added that the first thing young people from the country experience is "their own utter loneliness, which often seems unendurable." The reaction to the thin walled apartment's destruction of privacy is this strange city-isolation, accompanied by averted eyes in even the most innocuous social situations. The childless apartment dwellers have no need for a local community; and for many urban dwellers, the essential function of the neighborhood is to provide a house lot and a way to get to it.

The lack of community life in the city made suburbia desirable; universal car ownership, the expanding highway system, the availability of cheap land, cheap homes, and cheap financing after World War II made it possible; and the status which came to be associated with it made it essential. By 1969, one third of the nation was living in the suburbs. What is suburbia? Wilson Cary McWilliams writes that it is "our best contemporary example of the neighborhood," And Max Lerner observed:

> The suburbanites found new roots for their lives in a new sense of neighborhood which was closer than anything in previous American experience except college dormitories or fraternities or the communal settlements of the early nineteenth century.... New comers were expected to be "outgoing" and to "join the gang".... There was intensive "joining" in club work and community participation, including greatly increased church membership.... (T)here was an enforced intimacy so that everyone's life was known to everyone, and no one had to face his problems alone.

Many a suburban dweller has been made to feel discomfort by the unflattering stereotypes which have been popularized: "warrens of young executives on the way up"; "perfectly homogeneous"; "the elysian fields of community action"; "child centered and female dominated." Unfortunately it is true that divisions of class and ethnic background are prominent in the suburbs; but the higher participation in local government, church membership, and the importance of the school reflect a greater feeling of community than in the city. On the other hand, the frequent appearance of the moving van evokes the suspicion that it is superficial. McWilliams points out that the desire to recapture the close atmosphere of the small town motivated the suburban development, but that this remains impossible without economic autonomy. Changes in economic circumstances force people to move to "where the jobs are" and it is hard for the roots of community to grow. When people do move, the standardization of American life makes it possible to find a very close approximation to the previous community. The church, the school, and the local form of government are duplicated along with the monotony of "ranch houses," split-levels, picture windows and shopping centers. The uniformity has often made suburbia an object of derision; and the frequency with which people move brings the charge of superficiality. America has become increasingly standarized and the relations among men are charged with impermanence.

What prospects remain for community in America's Third Century? Her past bears the mark of hopes which have too often refused to flower, and there are those who have given up the quest. It may be a fundamental hunger, this yearning for a sense that one is not alone — that man is as Donne wrote—"a piece of the continent." The circumstances of an increasingly complex industrialized society may render this yearning futile. Aristotle long ago observed that no city of men is possible with less than ten nor more than one hundred thousand. We may be amused at the arbitrary bounds, but the fundamental question may yet be one of magnitude. Perhaps a community, whatever else its character, has limits beyond which much of America has irrevocably passed.

A sense of community.

Will Herberg, Professor of Judaic Studies and Social Philosophy—Drew University, *Protestant-Catholic-Jew*, 1960, p. 12.

"What am I?"
This question is perhaps the most immediate that a man can ask himself in the course of his social life. Everyone finds himself in a social context which he shares with many others, but within this social context, how shall he locate himself? Unless he can so locate himself, he cannot tell himself, and others will not be able to know, who and what he is; he will remain "anyonymous," a nobody—which is intolerable. To live, he must "belong"; to belong, he must be able to locate himself in the larger social whole, to identify himself to himself and to others.

Warren H. Wilson, Former Secretary of Agriculture, in *The Rural Community*, 1932, p. 9.

The average man would define the community as "the place where we live." This definition contains every essential element, locality, personal and social relations, and vital experiences. The community is that complex of economic and social processes in which individuals find the satisfactions not supplied in their homes. The community is the larger social whole outside the household; a population complete in itself for the needs of its residents from birth to death. It is a man's home town.

Carl C. Zimmerman, Harvard University, *The Changing Community*, 1938, p. 20.

To have a web of common experiences, any community must have some rootage in the past. Nowhere is this necessary attribute of the community more clearly evident than in the history of American colonization. With the exception of numerous Massachusetts and New Hampshire towns which were legislated into existence by absentee landowners, no community was recognized until the pioneer fringe had developed a local cohesiveness and a collective will strong enough to demand and receive that recognition. In the West, as well as in the South, efforts to legislate towns into existence failed. The settlers in those regions were pioneers who disdained the communal organization of New England settlements. It was not until these adventurous spirits had developed a web of common experience that they were ready to live as community members. Hence communities, in the South and West particularly, were built upon a rock of common belief fashioned by time.

Alexis de Tocqueville, *Democracy in America*, 1835, Vol. I, p. 71.

The native of New England is attached to his township because it is independent and free: his co-operation in its affairs ensures his attachment to its interests; the well-being it affords him secures his affection; and its welfare is the aim of his ambition and of his future exertions. He takes a part in every occurrence in the place; he practices the art of government in the small sphere within his reach; he accustoms himself to those forms without which liberty can only advance by revolutions; he imbibes their spirit; he acquires a taste for order, comprehends the balance of powers, and collects clear practical notions on the nature of his duties and the extent of his rights.

Phillips Bradley, "An Historical Essay," *Democracy in America*, 1945, Vol. II, p. 462.

The shift in the scale of the economy from local to national has, then, inevitably modified the natural parochialism of popular opinion. When people buy in chain stores most of the things they need—that is, products, advertised nationally and manufactured by a company with plants in a dozen states—localism does not flourish. When the individual's job depends on decisions taken in distant offices and as the result of considerations that have little or nor relation to the community where he lives, he does not look homeward for his security. Strong as the pull of community feeling still is, even in economic matters, the integration of our present-day economy has done much to temper if not to obliterate it.

Warren H. Wilson, Former Secretary of Agriculture, in *The Rural Community,* 1932, p. 8.

The country community is defined by the team haul. People in the country think of the community as that territory, with its people, which lies within the team haul of a given center.
. . .Social customs do not proceed farther than the team haul. Imitation, which is an accepted mode of social organization, does not go any farther in the country than the customary drive with a horse and wagon. The influence of leading rural personalities does not extend indefinitely in the country, but disappears at the boundary of the next community. Intimate knowledge of personalities is confined to the community and does not pass beyond the team haul radius. Within this radius all the affairs of any individual are known in minute detail; nobody hopes to live a life apart from the knowledge of his neighbors; but beyond the community, so defined, this knowledge quickly disappears. Men's lives are housed and their reputations are encircled by the boundary of the team haul.

Carl N. Degler, Historian, *Out of Our Past,* 1959, p. 329.

By the turn of the century, however, the great national farm magazines . . . carried fiction of the same type and locale as the urban periodicals. Rural folk, like the people of the city, were now reading stories based on urban assumptions and depicting the life of the city. In the twentieth century, the telephone, the mass newspaper, the mailorder catalogue, the automobile, improved highways and roads, rural free delivery, the radio, the movies, and, most recently, television have advanced still further the farmer's emulation of urban ways. And where the farmer himself might be slow to respond to such simulti, his more worldly-wise and adaptable children added to the pressure.

Lewis Mumford, *City Development,* 1945, p. 21.

Civic life, in fine, the life of intelligent association and common action, a life whose faded pattern still lingers in the old New England town, is not something that we daily enjoy, as we work in an office or a factory. It is rather a temporary state that we occasionally achieve with a great deal of time, bother, and expense. The city is not around us, in our little town, suburb, or neighborhood: it lies beyond us, at the end of a subway ride or a railway journey. We are citizens occasionally: we are suburbanites (*denizens, idiots*) by regular routine.

William Dobriner, *The Suburban Community,* 1958, p. 152.

The widespread belief that the central city teems with wickedness and moral degradation has also contributed to the suburban vision. The simple virtues of the countryside have long been a part of the American stereotype, but for many persons these attractions paled in the sparkling glitter of neon lights which symbolize the technological advantages of urban life responsible for the urban migration. The suburb offers a compromise in which all the conveniences of the city may be achieved while retaining the simple virtues of the countryside without its inconveniences.

Community in the antebellum South.

Carl N. Degler, Historian, *Out of Our Past,* 1959, p. 162.

The great majority of the southern white people held no slaves at all and therefore had no direct interest in or even connection with the institution. Out of a total of some 1.6 million white families in the South in 1860, only 384,000 owned the four million slaves. . . .
Such census statistics should destroy any lingering illusion that the planter and his hundreds of slaves were typical or even commonplace figures in Dixie. Indeed, the Southerner with any slaves at all, let alone hundreds, was in the distinct minority, a curiosity amid the millions of plain people who owned no slaves at all and

who, perhaps, rarely saw one. Statistically, the small yeoman farmer, working his land unassisted by the labor of black men, was the typical white Southerner in the ante-bellum era.

Wilson Cary McWilliams, *The Idea of Fraternity in America*, 1973, p. 260.

In fact, that absence of group loyalty was responsible for some of the equalitarian feelings of Southerners. Upper and lower classes alike developed no loyalty to class, no special bonds to set one group of men off from another. Equality may grow out of such relations, but it is an equality in which all men are equally irrelevant to the self, not one in which they are brothers.

Wilson Cary McWilliams, *The Idea of Fraternity in America*, 1973, p. 265.

The real bond, however, was negative: white unity was aroused by the menace of the Negro. Whiteness became salient in a sea of black, an ocean always disturbed by resentment against slavery; the threat of insurrection and the motive of status were the cement of white "fraternity." Jefferson Davis admitted as much, conceding that white brotherhood was united largely by the "presence of a lower race." That alone suggests the spuriousness of white "brotherhood"; it lacked unity in either value or joy and was no more than an alliance of individuals driven by fear and hostility into a semi-permanent confederacy.

Ethnic communities.

Will Herberg, Professor of Judaic Studies and Social Philosophy—Drew University, *Protestant-Catholic-Jew*, 1960, p. 14.

The ethnic group, because it was for so many millions of Americans the primary context of identification and social location, entered as a major factor into the economic, social, and political life of the total community, and into the most intimate personal and social relations of the "ethnics" themselves. Social-class structure, marriage selection, "availability" of political candidates, church and religious forms, all reflected the profound influence of the ethnic groups into which American reality had organized the bewildered immigrants.

Michael Harrington, *The Other America*, 1962, p. 140.

That flood of human vitality came to an end after World War I when the nation established quota systems [of immigration], but the tradition of the ethnic groups survived for a generation. Symbolically, the tenements in which these newcomers lived had been built for them and had not trickled down after the middle class found them inadequate. The neighborhoods were dense and the housing was inadequate, yet the people were not defeated by their environment. There was community, there was aspiration. . . .
Now the incredible American adventure of the ethnic slums is coming to an end.

Wilson Cary McWilliams, *The Idea of Fraternity in America*, 1973, p. 589.

The demand for racial recognition is, in fact, a demand that others honor one's home and origin, which is not an assertion of racial fraternity but an essential precondition of genuine fraternity based on common values. Home and origin, after all, are part of what a man is; he can hardly be our brother if we are blind to them, still less if he seeks to blind himself.
Much of the struggle of black America, in fact, has been an effort to establish a home, a place of security and pride in which personal development can begin, a first covenant which is the precondition of fraternity.

Wilson Cary McWilliams, *The Idea of Fraternity in America*, 1973, p. 102.

For racial minorities and immigrant groups, "community" has served as a solace amid exclusion, a retreat from slights and prejudice (and too often, this has made it only the mark of failure, something resented for all its helps). The "assimilated," however, may find something lacking in their greater abundance; permanent insecurity and lack of warmth seem characteristic of life, and those whose lives seem communal and affectionate are envied. Americans have passed through alternating cycles in their attitudes toward the ethnic culture of immigrants and the "simpler ways" of racial minorities. From fear and hatred, they pass to nostalgia and romanticism.

Associations: political, fraternal, and the labor union.

Alexis de Tocqueville, *Democracy in America*, 1840, Vol. II, p. 117.

Feelings and opinions are recruited, the heart is enlarged, and the human mind is developed only by the reciprocal influence of men upon one another. I have shown that these influences are almost null in democratic countries; they must therefore be artificially created, and this can only be accomplished by associations.
As soon as several of the inhabitants of the United States have taken up an opinion or a feeling which they wish to promote in the world, they look out for mutual assistance; and as soon as they have found one another out, they combine. From that moment they are no longer isolated men, but a power seen from afar.

Mosei I. Ostrogoskii, *Democracy*, 1910, p. 4.

Another description of the Caucus, dating from February, 1763, is given in the journal of John Adams, who was himself about to become one of its most important members: "this day learned that the Caucus club meets at certain times in the garret of Tom Dawes, the Adjutant of the Boston regiment. He has a large house and he has a movable partition in his garret which he takes down, and the whole club meets in one room. There they smoke tobacco till you cannot see from one end of the garret to the other. There they drink flip, I suppose, and they choose a moderator who puts questions to the vote regularly; and selectmen, assessors, collectors, fire-wards, and representatives are regularly chosen before they are chosen in the town."

Fortescue Cuming, Scotch Traveller, in *Cities in American Life*, 1971, p. 60.

There are two parties, which style themselves Federal republicans, and Democratic republicans, and call each Federalists and Democrats. . . .[T]heir opinions. . .are argued with more warmth and are productive of more rancor and violence in Pittsburgh than perhaps in any other part of America. There are very few neutrals, as it requires a bold independence of sentiment to prevent a person from attaching himself to one or the other party. . . .[B]esides, to a man who has not resources for the employment of time within himself, the alternative of not being of one or the other party is insupportable, as he is shunned equally by both and in this populous town lives, with respect to society, as though he were in a desert.

Wilson Cary McWilliams, Historian, *The Idea of Fraternity in America*, 1973, p. 380.

It was the great age of the fraternal orders which sprang up across America in the townsman's search for some safe retreat from his daily life of competition, insecurity, and hostility.
. . . The private world of affection which the lodges provided made bearable much of the townsman's life which would otherwise have been intolerable and allowed him to cling, in his public life, to the individualistic creed and the established mores.
. . . Allowing the individual a faint, romantic echo of fraternity, they also suggested that in the gigantic and expanding nation he was not alone and insignificant, but one of a band of brothers with lodges about the land. It was some comfort, but too feeble to do more than quiet tension. The communities were passing, men were becoming small units of a great system, and more than passwords and regalia were required to remove anxiety.

Wilbart E. Moore, *Industrialization and Labor*, 1951, pp. 311-312.

What is the most general explanation that may be given (for) the pervasive strength of the industrial system in subverting social systems and surmounting or penetrating the natural barriers that a balanced nonindustrial system possesses?. . .A tentative generalization may be hazarded; it is the positive, institutionally sanctioned, and structurally necessary prescription of *mobility* that is at once the source of productive efficiency of the industrial system and the source of disruption of nonindustrial systems. The beginnings of the institutionalization of mobility are fraught with difficulties almost as various as the societies encountered.

Carl N. Degler, Historian, *Out of Our Past*, 1959, p. 262.

The union is a training ground for democracy and provides "daily object lessons in ideal justice; it breathes into the working classes the spirit of unity", but above all, it affords that needed sense of community. The labor union "provides a field for noble comradeship, for deeds of loyalty, for self-sacrifice beneficial to one's fellow-workers. In the trade union, in short, the workers could obtain another variety of that sense of community, of comradeship, as Gompers put it, which the acid of individualistic capitalism had dissolved.

Religion in America.

Richard Hofstadter, Professor of American History—Columbia University, *America in 1750*, 1971, p. 180.

Perhaps the most striking fact about the organized religious life of the colonials in the eighteenth century is the large number of people who were left out of it. Whether they had lost their faith before migrating or had been torn loose from church life in the business of moving, or whether they resented the authority of the dutiful ministers or the loose ways of the less dutiful, or were lost through the inability of the churches to establish viable church-community life in the open spaces and diffused settlements of America, surprisingly large numbers in the English continental colonies enjoyed little or none of the amenities and comforts of a religious community, and many seemed not to be trying very hard to get them.

Alexis de Tocqueville, *Democracy in America*, 1840, p. 142.

Although the desire of acquiring the good things of this world is the prevailing passion of the American people, certain momentary outbreaks occur when their souls seem suddenly to burst the bonds of matter by which they are restrained and to soar impetuously towards heaven.

Ray Ginger, Professor of History—University of Calgary, *Altgeld's America*, 1958, pp. 235-236.

Thorstein Veblen had another explanation. Religion, he wrote was "a survival from an earlier phase of associated life—a mark of arrested spiritual development." Industrial workers would increasingly spurn all forms of supernaturalism because contact with modern industry tended to breed the habit of thinking in terms of material impersonal causes. The most devout groups were the groups least exposed to this influence: Southern Negroes, lower-class immigrants who had not yet penetrated the factories, much of the rural population, "the leisure class proper", and "the lower-class delinquents."

Samuel S. Hill, "The Uses of Religion in the South," *Cross Currents*, Summer 1966, p. 346.

. . .the often disquieting challenge of adjustment to life in congested communities has perhaps figured in the retention of church loyalty by many, and acted as a catalyst toward a serious religious involvement on the part of some.

Martin E. Marty, *The New Ordeal of Christianity*, 1957, p. 110.

American culture, in this urbanized period into which we have moved, is no longer Protestant. It has never been and is not now, Roman Catholic. It is not religious at all. We still like to employ religious symbols, but actually we are living in a secular culture. Secularism has taken over the United States.

Wilson Cary McWilliams, *The Idea of Fraternity in America*, 1973, pp. 580-581.

In institution, idea, and symbol, religion became the common bond, the thread uniting Negroes in America. . . . Politically, religion had value in the fact that it spoke both to black hopes and white guilts. And in human affairs, hope and guilt are closely related; the guilts of whites were hopes which had been buried or put aside. Religious thought argued for a community in which material things were adapted to the needs of men, a political order organized to develop and educate the self. All men can feel the power of such ideas; but to American Negroes, they were also the soberest common sense. Living in a "dusty desert of dollars and smartness," DuBois wrote, the "vast ideal of brotherhood," which for others was only an abstraction was, for most Negroes, the most immediate aspiration and the most pressing of their interests.

Will Herberg, Professor of Judaic Studies and Social Philosophy—Drew University, *Protestant-Catholic-Jew*, 1960, pp. 56-57.

Naming oneself a Protestant, a Catholic, or a Jew carries with it a distinctive attitude to "one's" church, an attitude that is definitely favorable. . . .There does not seem to be any real question that the restructuring of American society that emerges with the third generation has been a major factor in the turn to a religion so characteristic of our time. Religion has become a primary symbol of "heritage," and church membership the most appropriate form of "belonging" under contemporary American conditions.

Martin E. Marty, *The Pro and Con Book of Religious America*, 1975, pp. 16-17.

Something has to be going on in a nation where three out of five people list themselves as church members two hundred years after most of their original states removed all legal sanctions for religion. No threat of hell or punishment goes with neglect of worship, and society has few positive goods to pass out to the faithful. Yet after all that time over 60 percent of the people want to be found among the religious, just as over nine out of ten of them are quite clear in telling pollsters that they believe in God.
Membership can be very casual, and can reflect little more than old habits. More significant is the fact that two out of five Americans can be found at worship every weekend.

Louis B. Wright, Historian, *Culture on the Moving Frontier*, 1955, pp. 196-197.

Crude and lawless many Western communities were—at first. But with amazing rapidity the churches and church folk began to operate in most of these communities, and they rarely gave up until they had routed the Devil and at least some of his works. Their notions of conquering the powers of evil did not stop with victory in the realm of morality. . . .The churches always fought to re-establish traditional civilization and their conservatism usually prevailed.

Separation of church and state.

Gustave Myers, *History of Bigotry in the United States*, 1943, p. 46.

"Why," wrote Thomas Jefferson, presumably in 1776, "have Christians been distinguished above all people who have ever lived for persecutions? Is it because it is the genius of their religion? No, its genius is the reverse. It is the refusing *toleration* to those of a different opinion which has produced all the bustles and wars account of religion." In the Virginia Bill of Rights, drawn under his inspiration, all men, according to their reason and conviction, were declared equally entitled to the free exercise of religion, and people were exhorted "to practice Christian forbearance, love and charity toward each other."

Alexis de Tocqueville, *Democracy in America*, 1840, Vol. II, pp. 321- 322.

As long as a religion rests only upon those sentiments which are the consolation of all affliction, it may attract the affections of all mankind. But if it be mixed up with the bitter passions of the world, it may be constrained to defend allies whom its interests, and not the principle of love, have given to it; or to repel as antagonists men who are still attached to it, however opposed they may be to the powers with which it is allied. The church cannot share the temporal power of the state without being the object of a portion of that animosity which the latter excites.

Religion and public schools.

Robert M. Healey, *Jefferson on Religion in Public Education*, 1962, p. 268.

The role of religion in public education is to be determined by the need to make public education as effective a tool as possible in continuing and fostering the functioning of democracy and the development of a free society. The goals of instruction with respect to religion in public schools should grow out of and be properly related to the general purposes of education. If the purpose of democratic public education is to develop adults who can deal creatively and responsibly with the clash of values that inevitably accompanies cultural pluralism, then perhaps the very controversiality of religion may make it a must in education for democratic citizenship. The effect of religion upon the development of human culture cannot be denied. It has had a profound influence upon law, morality, the fine arts, literature, economics, and history. It continues to be a potent political force.

Vivian Trow Thayer, *The Attack Upon the American Secular School*, 1951, p. 219.

The secular school is neither anti-religious as some charge, on the theory that he who is not aggressively for me is against me, nor is it dedicated to the promotion of any one religious viewpoint or final philosophy of life. Properly conceived, the secular school represents the most recent state in the evolution of an institution which originated to serve the interests of a narrowly sectarian and homogeneous community and has learned to meet the growing needs of young people who must live in a rapidly changing and heterogeneous society.

Marvin Braiterman, *Religion and the Public Schools*, 1958, p. 35.

Advocates of programs of moral and spiritual values in the public schools seldom give careful attention to the host of practical realities. For example: are there materials and textbooks for public schools which deal with all religious faiths impartially? Are public school teachers trained and equipped to handle religion without partiality toward their own religious commitment? What of the teacher who has no religious faith? Is he to be excluded? Are we to impose a religious test upon our public school teachers? And what of the child of non-believing parents? Is he to be subjected to a kind of compulsory public school religion? Is the American school prepared for the intrusion of church authorities on the content of the public school curricula?. . .
America's religious tradition, on the other hand, stands for the protection, and even the enhancement, of differences, without threats or intimidation or a predilection to a nation-wide orthodoxy.

Report of the Committee on Religion and Education of the American Council on Education, April 1947, pp. 44-45.

We believe the religious structure of society, that is, the institutions of religion, are at least as essential to the permanent maintenance of religious faith and mood of mankind as other institutions are to the perpetuation of the interests they serve. . . . The schools aid the church today by giving to youth an appreciation of fundamental spiritual values to which we have referred. They might aid it much more by giving to youth an orientation toward the specifically religious phases of human culture. And they might remove a definite disservice to the church which results from the devaluation of religion that is implicit in ignoring it.

Selected Bibliography

Aubrey, Edwin E., *Secularism A Myth: Spiritual Values in Secular Culture.* New York: Harper, 1954.

Beggs, David W., and McQuigg, R. Bruce, ed. *America's Schools and Churches: Partners in Conflict.* Bloomington: Indiana University Press, 1966.

Blassingame, John W. *The Slave Community; Plantation Life in the Antebellum South.* New York: Oxford University Press, 1972.

Borden, Morton. *Parties and Politics in the Early Republic.* New York: Cromwell, 1967.

Braiterman, Marvin. *Religion and the Public Schools.* New York: Commission on Social Action of Reform Judaism, 1958.

Bryce, James. *The American Commonwealth.* New York: Macmillan, 1913.

Degler, Carl N. *Out of Our Past: The Forces That Shaped Modern America.* New York: Harper and Row, 1959.

Dobriner, William. "The Natural History of a Reluctant Suburb." *The Yale Review.* (Spring 1960), p. 399.

Dobriner, William, ed. *The Suburban Community.* New York: Putnam, 1958.

Duverger, Maurice. *Political Parties.* New York: Wiley, 1951.

Fantino, Morio D. *Community Control and the Urban School.* New York: Praeger Publishers, 1970.

Fauset, A. H. *Black Gods of the Metropolis.* Philadelphia: University of Pennsylvania, 1944.

Frazier, E. Franklin. *The Negro Church in America.* New York: Schoken, 1963.

Gans, Herbert, *The Urban Villages.* New York: Free Press, 1962.

Ginger, Ray. *Altgeld's America.* New York: Funk and Wagnalls Co., 1958.

Goodman, Percival, and Goodman, Paul. *Communitas.* Chicago: The University of Chicago Press, 1947.

Green, Phillip, and Levinson, Sanford, eds. *Power and Community.* New York: Pantheon, 1970.

Handlin, Oscar. *The American People in the Twentieth Century.* Cambridge: Harvard University Press, 1954.

Handlin, Oscar. *The Uprooted: The Epic Story of the Great Migrations That Made the American People.* New York: Grossett and Dunlap, 1961.

Harrington, Michael. *The Other America.* New York: Macmillan Co., 1962.

Healey, Robert M. *Jefferson on Religion in Public Education.* New Haven: Yale University Press, 1962.

Herberg, Will. *Protestant, Catholic, Jew; an Essay in American Religious Sociology.* Garden City, New York: Doubleday, 1955.

Hill, Samuel S. "The Uses of Religion in the South." *Cross Currents.* West Nyack, N.Y.: Cross Currents Corporation, 1966, 16, 3, p. 339.

Jones, Charles O., and Hoppe, Layne D., eds. *The Urban Crisis.* Washington: Washington National Press, Inc., 1969.

Marty, Martin E. *The Pro and Con Book of Religious America, a Bicentennial Argument.* Texas: Word Books, 1975.

McWilliams, Wilson C. *The Idea of Fraternity in America.* Berkeley: University of California Press, 1973.

Miller, Perry. *Errand into the Wilderness.* Boston: Harvard University Press, 1956.

Moehlman, Conrad. *School and Church: The American Way.* New York: Harper, 1944.

Moore, Wilbert E. *Industrialization and Labor.* Ithaca, New York: Cornell University Press, 1951.

Morgan, Edmund. *Virginians at Home.* Williamsburg, Pa.: Colonial Williamsbug, 1952.

Morison, Samuel Eliot. *The Oxford History of the American People.* New York: Oxford University Press, 1965.

Mumford, Lewis. *The Story of Utopias.* New York: Boni and Liveright, Inc., 1922.

Myers, Gustave. *History of Bigotry in the United States.* New York: Capricorn Books, Random House, 1960.

Nichols, Roy F. *Invention of the American Political Parties.* New York: Macmillan, 1967.

Niebuhr, H. Richard. *The Kingdom of God in America.* Chicago: Willet, 1937.

Noll, Bishop John F. *Our National Enemy No. 1, Education Without Religion.* Huntington, Indiana: Our Sunday Visitor Press, 1942.

Ostrogorski, Mosei I. *Democracy and the Party System in U.S.* New York: Arno Press, 1974.

Pell, Roy V. *Political Clubs of the City of New York.* New York: Putnam, 1935.

Phares, Ross. *Bible in Pocket, Gun in Hand: The Story of Frontier Religion.* Garden City, New York: Doubleday, 1964.

Phillips, Ulrich Bonnell, ed. *Plantation and Frontier 1649-1863.* New York: B. Franklin, 1969.

Pierson, George Wilson. *The Moving American.* New York: Knopf, Inc., 1973.

Shannon, James P. *Catholic Colonization on Western Frontier.* New Haven: Yale University Press, 1957.

Sims, Newell Leroy, ed. *The Rural Community; Ancient and Modern.* New York: Charles Scribner's Sons, 1920.

Stein, Maurice R. *The Eclipse of Community.* Princeton: Princeton University Press, 1960.

Thayer, Vivian T. *Attack on American Secular School.* Westport, Connecticut: Greenwood Press, 1970.

de Tocqueville, Alexis. *Democracy in America.* Translated by Henry Reeve, revised by Francis Bowen, edited by Philips Bradley. New York: Vintage Books, 1945.

Tyler, Alice Felt. *Freedom's Ferment; Phases of American Social History to 1860.* Minneapolis: University of Minnesota Press, 1944.

Wade, Richard C. ed. *Cities in American Life.* New York: Houghton Mifflin Co., 1971.

Whyte, W. F. *Street Corner Society.* Chicago: University of Chicago Press, 1955.

Williams, Robin M. *Strangers Next Door: Ethnic Relations in American Communities.* Englewood Cliffs, New Jersey: Prentice-Hall, 1964.

Wright, Louis B. *Culture on the Moving Frontier.* Bloomington, Indiana: University Press, 1955.

ISSUE IX
LIFE, LIBERTY AND THE PURSUIT OF HAPPINESS

NATIONAL EVENT
June 1-4, 1976

DEBATE *Resolved: That the history of America has been the history of a decline in the importance of the individual.*

PERSUASIVE *The American Bicentennial: Has age bred wisdom?*

EXTEMPORANEOUS *The Dream of Success*

1. *Is the Horatio Alger story typical of the American dream of success?*
2. *Was slavery an outgrowth of economic necessity?*
3. *The growth of organized labor: Could the individual worker have done as well on his own?*
4. *Has the growth of governmental taxation decreased the opportunity of each individual to succeed on his own?*
5. *Is America still a "land of opportunity" for most of its citizens?*
6. *The first 50 years: Would America have grown as quickly as a colony as she did as a nation?*
7. *The poor in the land of opportunity: An American nightmare?*
8. *How have welfare programs evolved in American history?*
9. *"Yankee ingenuity": How much of America's success has been honestly achieved?*
10. *Has success in America too often been equated with economic wealth?*
11. *How will sex roles change by the twenty-first century?*
12. *The welfare state: Will it destroy the work ethic?*
13. *How has the dream of success changed throughout American history?*
14. *How have those who haven't "made it" promoted social and political change?*

RESOLVED: THAT THE HISTORY OF AMERICA HAS BEEN THE HISTORY OF A DECLINE IN THE IMPORTANCE OF THE INDIVIDUAL.

Introductory Essay

It was once widely believed that to be an American was to participate in a great adventure. The ideas of progress, democracy, political freedom, Manifest Destiny, and general prosperity were some of the important elements of this belief. Central to all of these concepts was a faith in the capability and sovereignty of the individual. The individual, generally unimpeded (though sometimes aided) by government or institutions, was released to conquer a continent. Today many of the ideals that motivated the pioneer individualist no longer seem as special or important. America no longer appears to be so noble an experiment in democracy; democratic freedom has spread to many parts of the world, and the shortcomings of our own government are seen more clearly. Individuals today seem less certain of themselves than in past ages when the nation yearned for power and glory, yet America has been the richest and most militarily powerful nation on earth for a considerable number of decades. Individuals are less sure of their own values and of the essential rightness of the American way of life, but are more tolerant of the values and ways of others. Everywhere the modern American seems to be told that one is not responsible for one's actions: people are poor because the economic system cannot operate safely at full employment or because the poor are old, young, sick, or raising children, rather than because they are weak and lazy; murders are committed by reason of insanity; workers need not plan for retirement because Social Security, medical care, and housing will be waiting in any event as a result of government programs. Is the individual less important today for these reasons? The pace and diversity of modern life place much greater strain and responsibility on the individual than in previous times. Does this mean that the individual is just as important as before, although in different ways?

An investigation of the meaning of "the importance of the individual" can uncover the central issues behind the proposition. Several perspectives are useful here. First, is "the individual" the same person as "the common man?" Our creed declares that all men are created equal. If this is so, the degree and significance of the freedom of the average American becomes a central issue. We would prefer political, social, and economic systems which guarantee that the common man will remain paramount; an example would be Jefferson's agrarian ideal of a rural nation of independent farmers. Alternatively, we may believe that men are inherently unequal, and that society's duty is to foster an equality of opportunity that will permit the superior individual to rise to an unequal prominence. In this case, we would not disapprove a social system which permits an Andrew Carnegie or a John D. Rockefeller to amass great wealth at the expense of many common men.

A second question must be analyzed. By what standard do we measure the importance of the individual? One potential standard would involve placing high value on independence and freedom from the interference of others; the individual is considered important because he thinks and acts for himself. Applying such a standard to our times, the individual may have become less important, since he is today more dependent than his pioneer ancestor on collective forces such as corporations, government, and peer groups for the successful fulfillment of needs. In contrast, we may decide that the individual becomes more important as his choices multiply and yet maintain that interdependence is good because it frees him from the basic needs to grow food, make clothing, build a house, and so forth. On this account, the individual within a complex society acquires a range of choices not hitherto available. The possibilities of leisure and work have multiplied, and hence his opportunities to develop "individuality," have been enormously increased. Self-reliance and freedom of choice, in short, remain values that can be defended in several ways as the basis of the individual's importance.

A final perspective examines the possible conflict between the individual's importance and collective exercise of power. Does the expansion of governmental authority come only at the expense of the individual? An urban renewal program, for example, decreases individual power in that it requires support through taxation, sets collective standards for housing at a higher level than that set by property owners in the renewal area, and acquires land that individual landowners may not wish to sell. Yet government power can also be viewed as a means of enhancing individual power through removal of barriers to equality and the performance of desirable functions that increase individual choice. If some individuals lose by urban renewal, others gain; wise and democratic policies seek to distribute social benefits with equity.

The origins of the American emphasis on the individual can be found in British and French political philosophy, in Calvinist religious doctrines, and in the geography of the American continent. America's political philosophy, as reflected in the substance of the Declaration of Independence, was frankly borrowed from John Locke. All men are born equal; men have a natural right to freedom (which includes the freedom to own property); government which seriously infringes on natural rights is tyrannical, and can justly be dissolved and replaced by government more in harmony with natural law. Among the moral implications of a belief in man's equality was the belief that government should not favor particular individuals at the expense of others; together with the danger posed by government's tendency toward tyranny, this led to the view that collective government power was something to be restricted wherever possible. The influence of Calvinist religion, particularly Puritanism, on American character can be overstated, but it seems clear that many of its tenets were either widely praised or left unquestioned. In particular, the individual's responsibility for his own salvation, the duty of the individual to lead a life of honest toil rather than idle pleasure, and the importance of self-reliance were taken for granted. The moral tone of Benjamin Franklin's *Poor Richard,* the folksy personification of Americana, is suggestive of popular belief: "The sleeping fox catches no poultry," "what maintains one vice would bring up two children," and "the used key is always bright." Geography guaranteed the practice of these philosophical and religious beliefs. It was difficult for a traditional European aristocracy to develop in America; few would voluntarily remain to serve a lord when a vast and virgin land called on everyone to seek out an individual destiny. The loneliness and challenge of the frontier demanded a character type able to get along at times entirely on his own resources. This required steady goals as well as the forebearance and imagination to pursue them. Characters such as the cowboy, the prospector, and the homesteader have become folk heroes.

The manifestations of this outlook in historical events are numerous. The Bill of Rights, the gradual extention of the franchise to most adult freeman, and legislated restraints upon government: each led to the cultivation of the most pervasive practice of democracy by a major nation that history had seen. Laissez-faire, which placed supreme reliance on individual decision-making, found acceptance as the nation's economic ideology throughout most American history, even as government's role in controlling the marketplace grew apace and thus contradicted its pure rhetoric of non-interference in the private sector. Just as natural law was the basis for a governmental theory, another "natural law," that of supply and demand, became the basis for economics. One illustration of reliance on the private sector was banking and currency policy. After Andrew Jackson successfully fought the rechartering of the bank of the United States (largely because it gave special privilege to the wealthy), no effective national banking system existed until Woodrow Wilson's administration eight decades later. Territorial expansion often began as an individual matter, as when American settlers who had moved into Mexican territory in Texas became embroiled in rebellion. Eventually America found herself at war with Mexico; a war which resulted in the annexation of the present southwest corner of the United States.

The industrialization of the nation, especially following the Civil War, was an earthquake in the midst of American civilization. It transformed the United States in the nation's first century from an almost entirely rural seaboard country into the greatest industrial power in the world. A handful of men changed the face of the emerging nation. The story of their rail, steel, oil, and financial empires is well known. These men became the heroes of their age.

The dominant ideology of the period was Social Darwinism, a theory first championed by the English thinker Herbert Spencer. The natural law of society was held to be "survival of the fittest"; unrestrained competition continually worked toward progress by elevating superior individuals above inferior ones, creating a more advanced race and a better society. Government and other collective action taken to aid the weak would only jeopardize this "splendid march toward mankind's just reward." Hardship and poverty were unfortunate, but inevitable, by-products of progress.

Opposition to such theories grew stronger and more incisive as reform movements gathered momentum and as the real plight and circumstances of the industrial poor became publicized. It was pointed out that pure individual competition was an unknown ideal in American capitalism. Government had often offered valuable assistance to politically powerful businesses; the transcontinental railroads, for example, might never have been built despite their profitability without government grants of millions of dollars worth of land to the rail companies. Furthermore, monopoly power in many crucial industries foreclosed any real competition.

As a counterweight to such monopolies, the federal government began to intervene in the marketplace in the general interest, first by regulating the railroads (1887) and secondly by the Sherman Antitrust Act (1890) and its application. Such action was continued in the administrations of Theodore Roosevelt and Woodrow Wilson, although the judiciary acted as a major restraining force against abandoning laissez-faire until the New Deal. Many private groups did not wait for government action. Most prominently, the unions, led by the American Federation of Labor, built a countervailing collective power in many industries which became capable of challenging even the established power of the largest corporations.

Still other attacks on Social Darwinism were raised by new students of the social sciences. Thorstein Veblen's economic studies cast serious doubt on the superiority of the wealthy. The new leisure class was exposed as a largely unthinking model of conformity, bigotry and complacency. Furthermore, the daring entrepreneur had ceased to direct American business by the turn of the century. The new breed of executives was more likely to have been trained in specialized fields like financial management and the new technologies; such technocrats were interested in maximizing profits, but avoided the dangers of risk-taking wherever possible. The pioneering sociologist Lester Ward suggested that most of man's civilized and creative acts, from developing hybrid strains of vegetables to manufacturing steel to building homes, were violations of "the natural order." He argued that society could be intelligently managed without contradiction of any universal laws. Finally, some groups (especially the more radical) challenged material competition as a basis for organizing society; they claimed that individualism was being stifled by a preoccupation with material gain.

Such ideas fueled reform movements from Populism to Progressivism to the New Deal. A pervasive rhetorical strategy was to show the manner in which reform would enhance opportunity for the individual. Important political reforms of the Progressive era were designed to increase the participation of average citizens by the political process. Adoption of the referendum, initiative, and recall in several states, direct election of Senators, and adoption of a constitutional amendment granting the vote to women followed quickly upon one another. A great deal of practical municipal reform was also undertaken, as corrupt bosses were voted out in many cities and slum conditions began to be seen in the cold light of public disclosures.

The reforms of the Roosevelt administration during the Great Depression, however, finally confirmed that a fundamental shift in the citizens' relationship with government had occurred. Government was clearly part of everyone's life. The range of new federal services and responsibilities is indicated by the new programs: the Social Security Act; the Wagner Act, which greatly spurred the growth of unions; agricultural price supports, the Rural Electri-

fication Administration, and the Tennessee Valley Authority, which did much to improve the quality of rural life; the Federal Housing Administration, which aided middle-class homebuyers; and the Securities and Exchange Commission, regulating the financial markets. This trend has not abated.

What, then, of our individual? Has modern society altered our conception of the individual? One contemporary study — David Riesman's The Lonely Crowd — suggests that it has. He distinguishes two kinds of social persons and roles. Unlike the "inner-directed" individual of an earlier day, who adhered firmly to internalized principles and goals, the "other-directed" individual, increasingly prominent in America, has internalized only the need for approval from others. His values are loose and shifting, he is friendly but shallow, and he has little capability to go it alone.

A multitude of forces has increased and decreased individual importance over the course of our history. Political forces have worked to some extent in both directions. Perhaps the most important political development has been an evolution of political thought resulting from the nation's industrialization. The early decades of the nation were remarkable for the universality of accepted political values. Traditional liberal thought had been produced by a European middle class seeking freedom to create wealth and to carve out a place of dignity for itself within the post-feudal social order. In Europe, however, the aristocracy fought all attacks on its own dominant position, while in turn the middle class resisted as irresponsible the claims of the petty bourgeois and property-less laborers and industrial workers. A rich and powerful aristocracy never arose in America, and at least initially no upper-middle class aristocracy of wealth was able to assume an analogous role. Although in the early South, particularly, certain families assumed a special role in the politics and manners of their region, it has been said that we were a nation of Jacobins—independent farmers and shopkeepers. The rough economic equality nurtured a belief in the virtue of individual self-reliance and government non-interference that remained almost unchallenged into the twentieth century, although the nation had long since become economically stratified. What once was called "liberal" became "conservative," a defense of the old values, by the time that the New Deal shifted the individual's relationship to government. Government policy no longer assumed that individuals could fairly compete in society without government assistance to disadvantaged groups and without oversight of the marketplace. While rejecting radical programs that would have redistributed income in such a way as to produce economic equality, the new liberalism sought to foster equality of opportunity and to protect outright some of the weakest individuals in society. The trend toward collective government action in all phases of life has continued since the 1930's.

Whether or not this shift has threatened the importance of the individual depends upon prior judgments and beliefs about the very idea and value of an "individual." If individual initiative and independence, unrestrained by government taxation, social services, or regulation of the economy, are valued highly, then clearly the individual has become less important as the collective exercise of government power has increased. If government policies and services are viewed as a means to dismantle societal barriers to individual opportunity, then the importance of the individual has not suffered and may have increased.

Certain political reforms have apparently increased the importance of the individual in the political process. The vote has been extended to the propertyless, to blacks, and to women. Slavery, which in a fundamental manner denied the humanity of a major part of the Southern population, has been abolished. In one sense, the individual citizen has probably assumed more responsibility and awareness of political issues and candidates, especially since the introduction of the electronic media. Furthermore, printed and electronic media have increased the access of diverse viewpoints to the political process. Muckrakers such as Lincoln Steffens were prominent in stimulating reforms of the Progressive era but Ralph Nader's success today has been largely made possible by the media.

Other factors, suggest a decline in the importance of the individual. The rigidity and inertia of the two-party system, a post-Civil War phenomenon, has suppressed representation of minority viewpoints in government. Of course "third parties" are not uncommon and while Populists, Socialists, or George Wallaces may find it more difficult to gain power than they would have had party lines not been ossified, there have been increasing opportunities for them to make know their views.

Industrial development and its companion, technological change, have had mixed effects also. Many have seen threats to the individual in the impersonality of the large corporation; the ever increasing interdependence of local, national, and international economics; the fragmentation of work into specialized tasks bearing dim relation to some finished products; the advent of the computer; and the identification of masses of individuals with abstract numbers. The story of conformity and confusion in the face of change presented in the Lynds' study of *Middletown* during the 1920's has continued to account for much of American experience in subsequent decades. The more recent picture of the modern businessman presented by William Whyte's *Organization Man* is one in which individuality has been surrendered in the name of faceless success. Where today are the Andrew Carnegies of an earlier America? How many people could name the individual who heads General Motors or Exxon? Urbanization, too, one of the consequences of industrialization, has loosened traditional religious and family supports for the individual while simultaneously increasing stress through vastly multiplied confrontations with other individuals, a depersonalization of the living environment, a loss of the sense of community, and greater economic dependence. And so, as related earlier, many social problems, including some types of crime, juvenile delinquency, and mental illness, have been viewed as mere consequences of the individuals's inability to cope with the impersonality of the urban world.

The individual has not necessarily been buried by these forces, however. Industrialization and the productivity generated by technological developments have been accompanied by increased leisure time for the average worker. The average work week declined from just under sixty hours in 1890 to below fifty in the 1920's to a current standard of forty. Greater available leisure time for recreational, intellectual, and cultural pursuits of course does not insure individual development of unique talents and potentials. And yet Americans have always exhibited an appetite for self-improvement, manifested in the early development of public schools, the success of the Chautauqua movement, and the current repopularity of adult education. There is little question that the interests of today's average citizen and his tolerance for variety are far greater than in previous ages. Furthermore, a loss of individual leadership in business and general economic self-reliance have been balanced by a greater concern for the mass. The capricious swings of the business cycle, which have always been beyond the control of the average citizen, no longer threaten him to the same extent, due to unemployment compensation and government regulation of the economy in general and the financial markets in particular. While the individual may be more insulated in some ways today, the rapidity of technological change has meant that in certain fields an individual's impact may be felt more swiftly and pervasively. Scientific breakthroughs often receive immediate application. Witness the discovery by Jonas Salk of a vaccine for polio, which virtually wiped out a dreaded childhood disease within a few years of its introduction. In addition, though specialization of work and the diversity and complexity of urban life have threatened to overwhelm the individual at times, these forces have doubtlessly increased the opportunity of the individual to choose his own way. The enforced contact of urban dwellers with a multitude of people from diverse backgrounds has also encouraged increased consciousness of the needs and desires of others. This has often resulted in tensions. Racial and ethnic relations remain a testing ground for the honored, if not always practiced, American creed.

Another two-headed blessing is found in the increasing application of the social sciences. A great increase in knowledge about the individual and social behavior of the human organism has been made possible by turning so-called "scientific techniques" to the study of the individual and society. Critical issues are thus raised by the prospect of deliberate engineering of new patterns of behavior in individuals. The applications of such techniques have involved the succesful treatment of a great range of mental disorders, the advertising of products ranging from soap to political candidates, and the design of more productive work environments. The potential of behavioral engineering appears to be enormous. Will they crush the individual by granting nearly unlimited power to the state, as George Orwell's *1984* warns? Or is the behavioral psychologist B. F. Skinner's optimistic vision in *Walden Two* more accurate? There, government structures life around reinforcements consonant with both productivity and satisfaction. The question of government utilization of manipulative techniques aside, a loose movement in the discipline of psychology centering on the individual has arisen during recent decades. Representatives of the new "humanistic" approaches, such as Abraham Maslow and Carl Rogers, have concluded that individuals may consciously choose to act in an autonomous, independent, creative, and, to a large extent, free manner. Generally they agree with other psychologists who have found that most individuals fail to overcome the forceful but often irrational and destructive dictates of parental training, inheritance, and the environment. The therapeutic techniques of their theory seek to overcome these impediments to the individual's control of his own destiny. It is felt that the new psychological knowledge offers modern man unique opportunities, since it may be possible to apply it generally; in previous ages, only those individuals with a rare and fortuitous combination of experiences were able to act in a genuinely autonomous manner.

Finally, cultural achievement may be viewed as an index of individual importance for several reasons. It celebrates individual artistic accomplishment; it offers models and raises the possibility of self-expression in those for whom art is simply an avocation; and it multiplies the opportunities of the individual to develop creative awareness and more refined and encompassing tastes. Art, in this sense, fashions life. If culural achievement is accepted as a measure of individual importance, it may be said that American history has seen greater individual importance in this respect over the course of time.

During the early progress of American civilization, foreign observers such as de Tocqueville took special note of the lack of indigenous art and speculative activity in general. The most common interpretation, encouraged by American writers for many years, was that the American was so preoccupied with external life (chiefly, material success) that he left no time for pleasures that could not easily be assigned a value. Sinclair Lewis won a Nobel prize in literature for *Babbitt,* his portrayal of the American lifestyle in such terms. Yet it is fair to note that the culture the Europeans took pride in was largely limited to the upper classes, which had the leisure time and the money to pursue cultural interests; it is far from clear that the typical European was more culturally advanced than the typical American. One might, indeed, argue that the development of a leisure class of wealth in the United States coincided with an increased interest in art and patronage of artists. Today America's contributions to world culture, if perhaps not commensurate with the nation's power in economic or military fields, are unquestioned. The United States, and especially New York, has become the dance center of the world, particularly for the modern forms of dance. American jazz, rooted in the African music of the slaves, has gone through many stages of development; today it is one of the most important and vital musical forms. In painting, Americans like Jackson Pollack made major contributions to the abstract expressionist movement of the 1940's.

The motion picture was an American invention; the average citizen has supported this medium throughout its brief history. Although the mass of movies produced may have more entertainment than artistic merit, the almost unrestricted freedom of today's directors and producers has undoubtedly made film a major art form. Technological breakthroughs have brought stereo music, inexpensive paperback books, and television to most homes. For all the possible banality of these media, they have nevertheless, increased the access of Americans to at least the idea of culture; millions of people who would otherwise miss the experience are introduced to fine drama on television, good literature through paperbacks, and music through radio and recordings.

Has the individual, then, become less important in American history? Whether "the individual" is the hero or the man on the street, whether "important" means free from restraints, free to grow or something else entirely — these considerations have much to do with one's reply.

Excerpted Documents

Has collective action become more necessary or desirable in American society?

Harry McPherson, Aide to President Johnson, "Many Indians, No Chiefs," *Washington Post*, December 8, 1974, p. B5.

Leaders call upon, and ultimately focus, the energies of the rest of us. It is safe to say that none of our national problems can be successfully tackled unless we act to some degree collectively, upon the recommendations of genuine leaders. It is likely that without leaders, art tends to decay into incoherence, legislative politics into mere log-rolling, the executive into deviousness, electoral politics into promotional schemes, business into timorousness and fast buck manipulations, labor into preoccupation with narrow interest, and so on.

Alexis de Tocqueville, *Democracy in America*, 1835, p. 114

The political associations which exist in the United States are only a single feature in the midst of the immense assemblage of associations in that country. Americans of all ages, all conditions, and all dispositions, constantly form associations. They have not only commercial and manufacturing companies, in which all take part, but associations of a thousand other kinds—religious, moral, serious, futile, extensive or restricted, enormous or diminutive. The Americans make associations to give entertainments, to found establishments for education, to build inns, to construct churches, to diffuse books, to send missionaries to the antipodes; and in this manner they found hospitals, prisons, and schools. If it be proposed to advance some truth, or to foster some feeling by the encouragement of a great example, they form a society.

Milton Friedman, Professor of Economics—University of Chicago, *Capitalism and Freedom*, pp. 3-4.

The great advances of civilization, whether in architecture or painting, in science or literature, in industry or agriculture, have never come from centralized government. Columbus did not set out to seek a new route to China in response to a majority directive of a parliament, though he was partly financed by an absolute monarch. Newton and Leibnitz; Einstein and Bohr; Shakespeare, Milton, and Pasternak; Whitney, McCormick, Edison, and Ford; Jane Addams, Florence Nightingale, and Albert Schweitzer; no one of these opened new frontiers in human knowledge and understanding, in literature, in technical possibilities or in the relief of human misery in response to governmental directives. Their achievements were the product of individual genius of strongly held minority views, of a social climate permitting variety and diversity.

Government can never duplicate the variety and diversity of individual action.

Woodrow Wilson, *The New Freedom*, 1913, pp. 197-198.

I do not want to live under a philanthropy. I do not want to be taken care of by the government, either directly, or by any instruments through which the government is acting. I want only to have right and justice prevail, so far as I am concerned. Give me right and justice and I will undertake to take care of myself. If you enthrone the trusts as the means of the development of this country under the supervision of the government, then I shall pray the old Spanish proverb, "God save me from my friends, and I'll take care of my enemies."

John Mitchell, President—United Mine Workers, *Organized Labor and Its Ideals*, 1903, p. 2.

Trade unionism starts from the recognition of the fact that under normal conditions the individual, unorganized workman cannot bargain advantageously with the employer for the sale of his labor. Since the working-man has no money in reserve and must sell his labor immediately, since, moreover, he has no knowledge of the market and no skill in bargaining, since, finally, he has only his own labor to sell, while the employer engages hundreds or thousands of men and can easily do without the services of any particular individual, the workingman, if bargaining on his own account and for himself alone, is at an enormous disadvantage. Trade unionism recognizes the fact that under such conditions labor becomes more and more degenerate, because the labor which the workman sells is, unlike other commodities, a thing which is of his very life and soul and being. In the individual contract between a rich employer and a poor workman, the laborer will secure the worst of it. . . .

Charles Francis Adams, Jr., *Chapters of Erie and Other Essays*, 1871, p. 12.

. . . already our great corporations are fast emancipating themselves from the State, or rather subjecting the state to their own control, while individual capitalists, who long ago abandoned the attempt to compete with them, will next seek to control them. In this dangerous path of centralization [Cornelius] Vanderbilt has taken the latest step in advance. He has combined the natural power of the individual with the factitious power of the corporation. The famous "L'etat, c'est moi" [I am the state] of Louis XIV represents Vanderbilt's position in regard to his railroads. Unconsciously he has introduced Caesarism into corporate life. He has, however, but pointed the way which others will tread. The individual will hereafter be engrafted on the corporation—democracy running its course, and resulting in imperialism; and Vanderbilt is but the precursor of a class of men who wield within the state a power created by the State, but too great for its control. He is the founder of a dynasty.

Samuel P. Hays, Professor of History—University of Pittsburgh, *The Response to Industrialism: 1885-1914*, 1957, p. 48.

Businessmen, farmers, and workers individually could not cope with the impersonal price-and-market network, but they soon discovered that as organized groups they could wield considerable power. Individual economic enterprise, therefore, gave way to collective effort. Producers joined to control the conditions under which they sold their commodities; distributors combined to wield influence over marketing and transportation; workingmen formed trade unions to bargain with management over wages, hours, and working conditions; farmers and industrial consumers joined to reduce purchasing costs.

Walter Lippman, Journalist, *The Method of Freedom*, 1934, p. 48.

. . . the vital defect of individualism . . . is that the multitude of individual decisions is not sufficiently enlightened to keep the economy *as a whole* in working order. Regulation is essentially negative. In the main it merely forbids this or that. But it is not possible to prohibit by laws the cumulative errors which produce the cycles of boom and depression. The state cannot make laws against the excessive optimism of prosperity or the panic pessimism of the ensuing crash. Yet it is in this cycle that the supreme danger arises. For the social order has now become so intricate that any serious breakdown in its economy will unloose forces that may destroy it.

Has American individualism concentrated too heavily on material gain?

Francis X. Sutton, Seymour E. Harris, Carl Kaysen, and James Tobin, Economists, *The American Business Creed*, 1956, p. 102.

The notion that businessmen go into business primarily to make money in order to increase their personal consumption has been widely resisted in this country. American businessmen express surprise at their European colleagues who seem indeed to go into business in the hope of accumulating sufficient means to get out of it as soon as possible. To W.J. Cameron, those who retire when they have "made enough" are "deserters." Mr. Queeny criticizes high salaries in good Puritan fashion; they may encourage extravagant living at the expense of devotion to work and duty. Such statements confirm a general impression that American businessmen do not really work for money alone; for an adult male American, having a job is so much the expected pattern that there is little place for the wealthier man of leisure. The feeling that a man should go on working even though his wealth would permit him to retire at an early age is certainly not restricted to a few unreconstructed Puritans in our society but is very widely accepted.

Calvin Coolidge, *Foundations of the Republic: Speeches and Addresses of Calvin Coolidge,* 1926, p. 317.

[Business] is something far more important than a sordid desire for gain. It could not successively succeed on that basis. It is dominated by a more worthy impulse; it rests on a higher law. True business represents the mutual organized effort of society to minister to the economic requirements of civilization. It is an effort by which men provide for the material needs of each other. While it is not an end in itself, it is the important means for the attainment of a supreme end. It rests squarely on the law of service. It has for its main reliance truth and faith and justice. In its larger sense it is one of the greatest contributing forces to the moral and spiritual advancement of the race.

David C. McClelland, Professor of Psychology—Harvard University, *The Achieving Society,* 1961, pp. 233-34.

If we can assume, as all our evidence indicates, that Western capitalists were actually motivated primarily by the achievement motive, we can now understand why they were so interested in money and profit, although not, paradoxically, for its own sake. Money, to them, was the measure of success. It gave them the concrete knowledge of the outcome of their efforts that their motivation demanded.

Herbert Hoover, *American Individualism,* 1922, p. 32.

That high and increasing standards of living and comfort should be the first of considerations in public mind and in government needs no apology. We have long since realized that the basis of an advancing civilization must be a high and growing standard of living for all the people, not for a single class; that education, food, clothing, housing, and the spreading use of what we so often term nonessentials, are the real fertilizers of the soil from which spring the finer flowers of life.

Max Lerner, Professor of American Civilization—Brandeis University, *America as a Civilization: Volume 1, the Basic Frame,* 1957, p. 179.

I don't mean that Suburbia, U.S.A., is a conformist society. Its outer aspects are standardized and its ways of life tend to be uniform; yet this is different from conformism. The social intimacy that prevails in the suburb is partly a quest for roots, partly (as I have said) a flight from the temporariness and the loneliness of American life. To some extent it is also an effort to mitigate the bleakness of spending one's life within the confines of the same corporate "organization" and in pursuit of the same technical or sales proficiency. The chance to be intimate with people of different backgrounds, to share with them the experience of building a new community, and to take part in group action is an appealing one to those who have absorbed the cultural ideals and stereotypes of America.

Thomas C. Cochran, University of Pennsylvania, "The Role of the Business Leader," *Problems in American History,* 1957, p. 400.

A telling criticism of nineteenth-century businessmen was that many not only failed to be more responsible and circumspect, but that, as a whole, they also failed to recognize any obligation to do so. This, to be sure, was in keeping with the popular Social Darwinian philosophy of the time, the belief that individual success, even by ruthless means, inevitably led to social progress. The ordinary businessman seems to have felt that most of his duty to society was discharged by working hard to make money, raising a family, and supporting a church. Even when very big businessmen such as Rockefeller, Carnegie, or Hill recognized certain social obligations attaching to their wealth and power, the realization does not seem greatly to have affected their business policies.

Harold Laski, British Scholar of American History, *The American Democracy: A Commentary and an Interpretation,* 1948, p. 746.

A careful study was made of 500 films produced in 1930. While the main ambition of the chief characters is success in love, it is closely followed by financial success in some form or another; but revenge or rivalry, whether in love or business, are also very frequent. Even when the idea of fulfilling some social obligation is the major theme of a film, it appears to be stressed as an individual fulfillment in which what is important is not the outcome for the community, but the outcome for the hero or the villain of the piece. The overwhelming major theme is the principle of individualism—the idea that everyone works for his own advantage and that "success" mean attaining this result. The successful lover, the man who wins his way to wealth, the girl who makes a successful marriage, the detective who "gets" his man, these are the ideas round which the industry builds the stories its translates into pictures.

Moses Rischin, *The American Gospel of Success: Individualism and Beyond,* **1965, p. 3.**

Indeed, perhaps nowhere else in the world has a seemingly materialistic cult been so uninhibitedly transformed into a veritable gospel that has been called a dream. Even Walt Whitman could write, in *Democratic Vistas,* "I perceive clearly that the extreme business energy, and this almost maniacal appetite for wealth prevalent in the United States are parts of amelioration and progress, indispensably need to prepare the very results I demand. My theory includes riches, and the getting of riches." And Whitman, America's uncrowned laureate, but echoed Emerson, the nation's folk philosopher, and of course Franklin, the nation's grandfather —and all three bespoke the sentiments of the American. When William James labeled success "the American bitch-goddess," he was simply paying unwitting tribute to the American dream.

John Dewey, Philosopher and Educator, *Individualism—Old and New,* **1950, pp. 62-63.**

It is probably easy to exaggerate the extent of the decadence of religion in an outward sense, church membership, church going and so on. But it is hardly possible to overstate its decline as a vitally integrative and directive force in men's thought and sentiments. Whether even in the ages of the past that are called religious, religion was itself the actively central force that it is sometimes said to have been may be doubted. But it cannot be doubted that it was the symbol of the existence of conditions and forces that gave unity and a center to men's views of life. It at least gathered together in weighty and shared symbols a sense of the objects to which men were so attached as to have support and stay in their outlook on life.

Religion does not now have this result. The divorce of church and state has been followed by that of religion and society. Wherever religion has not become a merely private indulgence, it has become at best a matter of sects and denominations divided from one another by doctrinal differences, and united internally by tenets that have a merely historical origin, and a purely metaphysical or else ritualistic meaning. . . . Religion is not so much a root of unity as it is its flower or fruit. The very attempt to secure integration for the individual, and through him for society, by means of a deliberate and conscious cultivation of religion, is itself proof of how far the individual has become lost through detachment from acknowledged social values.

Does the exercise of government power interfere with or enhance individualism?

Lester Frank Ward, Pioneering American Sociologist, *Glimpses of the Cosmos,* **Volume IV, p. 42.**

The great economic principle is that civilization depends entirely upon the intelligent control of natural forces, including the social forces, and their direction into channels of human advantage. These forces left to themselves always run to waste, often become hostile to man. Such is the case with fire, water, steam, wind, electricity, etc. It is only by controlling, regulating, and directing them that they become the servants of man. The same can be shown to be true of the vital forces in vegetable and animal life. The valuable products of either kingdom are those which have been brought to perfection by thought, labor, and skill. It is also true of the social forces which have proved susceptible of control, regulation, and intelligent direction through the application of the same principle as that which has reduced the rest of nature to subjection.

Andrew Carnegie, "The Gospel of Wealth," *North American Review,* **June 1889, p. 653.**

[The law of competition] is here; we cannot evade it; no substitutes for it have been found; and while the law may be sometimes hard for the individual, it is best for the race, because it insures the survival of the fittest in every department. We accept and welcome, therefore, as conditions to which we must accomodate ourselves, great inequality of environment, the concentration of business, industrial and commercial, in the hands of a few, and the law of competition between these, as being not only beneficial, but essential for the future progress of the human race.

William Graham Sumner, Professor of Sociology—Yale, *The Forgotten Man and Other Essays*, 1918, p. 480.

There is an apparently invincible prejudice in people's minds in favor of state regulation. All experience is against state regulation and in favor of liberty. The freer the civil institutions are, the more weak or mischievous state regulation is. The Prussian bureaucracy can do a score of things for the citizen which no governmental organ in the United States can do; and, conversely, if we want to be taken care of as Prussians and Frenchmen are, we must give up something of our personal liberty.

Henry David Thoreau, "Civil Disobedience," *Writings*, 1893, p. 170.

The progress from an absolute to a limited monarchy, from a limited monarchy to a democracy, is a progress toward a true respect for the individual. Is a democracy, such as we know it, the last improvement possible in government? Is it not possible to take a step further towards recognizing and organizing the rights of man? There will never be a really free and enlightened state, until the state comes to recognize the individual as a higher and independent power, from which all its own power and authority are derived, and treats him accordingly.

Has American capitalism been truly compatible with individualism?

Joseph A. Schumpeter, Professor of Economics—Harvard, *Capitalism, Socialism and Democracy*, 1950, p. 134.

Since capitalist enterprise, by its very achievements, tends to automatize progress, we conclude that it tends to make itself superfluous—to break to pieces under the pressure of its own success. The perfectly bureaucratized giant industrial unit not only ousts the small or medium-sized firm and "expropriates" its owners, but in the end it also ousts the entrepreneur and expropriates the bourgeoisie as a class which in the process stands to lose not only its income but also what is infinitely more important, its function. The true pacemakers of socialism were not the intellectuals or agitators who preached it but the Vanderbilts, Carnegies, and Rockefellers. This result may not in every respect be to the taste of Marxian socialists . . . . But so far as prognosis goes, it does not differ from theirs.

Oswald Knauth, Economist, *Managerial Enterprise*, 1948, p. 66.

The qualities that lead a person to found a business and bring it to maturity and those that make a good manager are quite different—the former calls for innovation, the latter for statesmanship. Such terms as "rugged individualist" and "economic royalist" describe the owners of the preceding century better than they do the managers of the present. Managerial enterprise is entwined with the national economy. Its acts are important, not only to itself but also to others and often to the community. It has to succeed or it disintegrates, yet its success cannot be at the expense of the community. No codes of behavior or ethics to cover these, at times conflicting, responsibilities have yet been formulated. Political discernment as well as business sagacity is required.

John Dewey, Philosopher and Educator, *Individualism—Old and New*, 1950, pp. 54-55.

The most marked trait of present life, economically speaking, is insecurity. It is tragic that millions of men desirous of working should be recurrently out of employment; aside from cyclical depressions there is a standing army at all times who have no regular work. We have not any adequate information as to the number of these persons. But the ignorance even as to numbers is slight compared with our inability to grasp the psychological and moral consequences of the precarious condition in which vast multitudes live. Insecurity cuts deeper and extends more widely than bare unemployment. Fear of loss of work, dread of the oncoming of old age, create anxiety and eat into self-respect in a way that impairs personal dignity. Where fears abound, courageous and robust individuality is undermined.

293

Harold Laski, British Scholar of American History, *The American Democracy: A Commentary and an Interpretation,* **1948, p. 744.**

A mainly agrarian America, in which farmers owned and tilled their own soil, and the independent mechanic applied his own tools and skill to the craft he practised, these, for him, were the primary constituents of democracy. Men such as these had little need of government, save for the maintenance of order and defence against oppression. Yet within a decade of Jefferson's death the validity of his individualism was doubtful. Not only were American workingmen, like Skidmore and Evans, urging that America might well repeat the tragedy of the European proletariat; but Emerson and Channing and Parker were warning their readers against a materialism which might destroy the free individual by destroying social equality. . . . The Jeffersonian ideal ceased to have any decisive relevance to American conditions round about the time of the depression of 1837. But what Turner called the "pioneer ideal of creative and competitive individualism" enjoyed a kind of prolonged Indian summer of romantic influence until the last frontier had been reached.

John Dewey, Philosopher and Educator, *Individualism—Old and New,* **1930, p. 18.**

Meanwhile our institutions embody another and older tradition. Industry and business conducted for money profit are nothing new; they are not the product of our own age and culture; they come to us from a long past. But the invention of the machine has given them a power and scope they never had in the past from which they derive. Our law and politics and the incidents of human association depend upon a novel combination of the machine and money, and the result is the pecuniary culture characteristic of our civilization. The spiritual factor of our tradition, equal opportunity and free association and intercommunication, is obscured and crowded out. Instead of the development of individualities which it prophetically set forth, there is a perversion of the whole ideal of individualism to conform to the practices of a pecuniary culture. It has become the source and justification of inequalities and oppressions. Hence our compromises, and the conflicts in which aims and standards are confused beyond recognition.

Selected Bibliography

Arieli, Yehoshua. *Individualism and Nationalism.* Cambridge: Harvard University Press, 1964.

Berman, Marshall. *Politics of Authenticity: Radical Individualism and the Emergence of Modern Society.* New York: Atheneum, 1970.

Bettleheim, Bruno. *The Informed Heart: Autonomy in a Mass Age.* New York: Free Press, 1960.

Cawelti, John G. *Apostles of the Self-Made Man.* Chicago: University of Chicago Press, 1965.

Cooley, Charles H. *Human Nature and the Social Order.* Glencoe, Illinois: The Free Press, 1956.

Dewey, John. *Individualism-Old and New.* New York: Minton, Balch, and Co., 1930.

Dewey, John. *The Public and Its Problems.* Chicago: Swallow Press, 1927.

Green, Theodore P. *America's Heroes: The Changing Models of Success in American Magazines.* New York: Oxford University Press, 1970.

Hacker, Louis H. *The Triumph of American Capitalism.* New York: Simon and Schuster, 1950.

Hague, Gabriel. *Is the Individual Obsolete?* Pittsburgh: Carnegie Institute of Technology, 1964.

Hartz, Louis. "Individualism in Modern America." *Texas Quarterly,* 6 (1963), 100.

Hays, Samuel P. *The Response to Industrialism: 1885-1914.* Chicago: University of Chicago Press, 1957.

Hofstadter, Richard. *Social Darwinism in American Thought.* Boston: Beacon Press, 1955.

Hoover, Herbert. *American Individualism.* Garden City, New York: Doubleday, Page & Co., 1922.

Kallen, Horace M. *Individualism: An American Way of Life.* New York: Liveright, Inc., 1933.

Lippman, Walter. *The Method of Freedom.* New York: Macmillan, 1934.

Locke, John. *Two Treatises of Government.* Edited by Peter Laslett. Cambridge: Cambridge University Press, 1960.

Lynd, Robert, and Lynd, Helen. *Middletown.* New York: Harcourt, Brace, 1929.

Lynn, Kenneth S. *Dream of Success: The Modern American Imagination.* Boston: Greenwood Press, 1955.

McClelland, David C. *The Achieving Society.* Princeton: D. Van Nostrand Co., 1961.

McPherson, Harry, "Many Indians, No Chiefs." *Washington Post,* December 8, 1974, p. B1.

Meyer, Donald. "The Dissolution of Calvinism." *Paths of American Thought.* Edited by Arthur M. Schlesinger, Jr. and Morton White. Boston: Houghton Mifflin, 1963.

Miller, David L. *Individualism: Personal Achievement and the Open Society.* Austin: University of Texas Press, 1967.

Miller, William. "The Recruitment of the American Business Elite." *Quarterly Journal of Economics*, 64 (May 1950), 329.

Mills, Gordon, ed. *Innocence and Power: Individualism in Twentieth-Century America*. Austin: University of Texas Press, 1965.

Morley, Felix, ed. *Essays on Individuality*. Philadelphia: University of Pennsylvania Press, 1958.

Riesman, David. *The Lonely Crowd*. New Haven: Yale University Press, 1950.

Rischin, Moses. *The American Gospel of Success: Individualism and Beyond*. Chicago: Quadrangle Books, 1965.

Rogers, Carl R. *On Becoming a Person: A Therapist's View of Psychotherapy*. Boston: Houghton Mifflin, 1961.

Rozwenc, Edwin C., ed. *The Meaning of Jacksonian Democracy*. Boston: D.C. Heath and Company, 1963.

Ruitenbeek, Hendrick Marinus, ed. *The Dilemma of Organizational Society*. New York: Dutton, 1963.

Ruitenbeek, Hendrick M. *The Individual and the Crowd: A Study of Identity in America*. New York: Thomas Nelson & Sons, 1964.

Russell, Bertrand. *Authority and the Individual*. New York: Simon and Schuster, 1949.

Schlesinger, Arthur M. Jr. *The Age of Roosevelt: The Coming of the New Deal*. Boston: Houghton Mifflin Co., 1959.

Schneider, Herbert W. *The Puritan Mind*. Ann Arbor: The University of Michigan Press, 1958.

Skinner, B.F. "Freedom and the Control of Men." *American Scholar*, 25 (1955-56), 52.

Spencer, Herbert. *The Man versus the State: a Collection of Essays by Herbert Spencer*. Edited by Truxton Beale. New York: M. Kennerly, 1916.

Tebbel, John W. *From Rags to Riches*. New York: MacMillan, 1963.

Veblen, Thorstein. *The Theory of the Leisure Class*. New York: MacMillan, 1899.

Whyte, William H. Jr. *Organization Man*. New York: Simon and Schuster, 1956.

Wood, Ellen Meiksins. *Mind and Politics: An Approach to the Meaning of Liberal and Socialist Individualism*. Berkeley: University of California Press, 1972.

Wyllie, Irvin G. *The Self-Made Man in America: The Myth of Rags to Riches*. New Brunswick, N.J.: Free Press, 1954.

THE AMERICAN BICENTENNIAL: HAS AGE BRED WISDOM?

Introductory Essay

At the end of "General Electric Theater," a popular television show during the boom years of the late 1950's and early 1960's, Ronald Reagan, then its host, would always conclude the telecast with the words: "Remember, at General Electric, progress is our most important product." This sublime self-confidence is a supremely American motto; something like an unstated amendment to the Declaration of Independence's stirring assertion about the "the pursuit of happiness." The conviction lies too deep within our national conscience to require formal enactment. Ours is a nation founded amidst high expectations; politics was conceived as the tool by which human freedom would be guaranteed. This faith, despite recurrent crises, has stuck fast to the marrow of our political record. Everhopeful, Americans have viewed the future as the province of accomplishments soon to be theirs.

But what that future would truly be like and of what progress itself consists have been questions for keen debate. For many, progress has been conceived in intimate union with technology and growth. The key to the good life, according to this view, consists in continued acquisition and the development of material production. More, quite simply, is better. But there is a tradition standing against this cult. There are dangers in overdevelopment just as with impoverishment; and in any case, there is more to life than increased bread alone. The argument cuts twice. Not growth alone is questioned, but its direction and character. Clearly many things can be built and the lives of many remain much in need of material improvement. Accordingly, some dissenters from the commonplace adoration of growth, measured by numbers and the GNP alone, do not charge that technology or invention are themselves evil. Rather, they raise compelling admonitions about the purposes to which knowledge and power are to be put. A simplistic rejection of material progress as conventionally measured is, in short, no more satisfactory than a mindless celebration of quantitative growth. They recite the motto of the Sierra Club: "opposition to blind progress, not blind opposition to progress." For them, America has too often been like Doctor Faustus, enamored of the fruits his power promises. Theirs is the voice of caution; for while much is possible, the question remains whether the possible is the desirable. And

indeed, whether the feasible is also the wise. What measures wisdom, and how shall we record progress? One unavoidable standard is to be found in the documents which first proclaimed the Nation's birth, and asserted its principled intentions and high desires. Jefferson's Declaration is anchored in proud phrases: "life, liberty, and the pursuit of happiness." These have always been stern taskmasters for those who would champion democracy.

The pursuit of happiness is thus part of the canon of our political heritage. But it is an often elusive doctrine, shaped to no single standard and described by no simple rule. If there is wisdom in age, then the history of that gift must be understood. But just as ingenuity can seduce, so too does history have its charms and deceptions. The pursuit of happiness, in other words, travels a difficult terrain: its landmarks are the mixed scars and rewards of the Nation's inheritance. Its meaning cannot legitimately be severed from its roots in our economic and social histories.

American society in the Eighteenth Century functioned not unlike a feudal system. From Maine to Georgia life, according to Robert Nisbet, was rooted in the land and centered around the family. Eight out of every ten colonists made their living from farming during this period and the acquisition of property automatically meant improved social and economic standing in the community. The vast quantity of unoccupied land also afforded a perfect opportunity for those colonists who differed with the will of the majority to solve their problems by separation rather than accommodation. Institutions, in Eighteenth Century society, grew locally to serve individual communities and in politics, law enforcement, religion and education the intrusion of any central authority was deeply suspect. As Michael Zuckerman has written about politics in Eighteenth Century Massachusetts: "Effective authority in the Eighteenth Century was local authority and a Governor had to accede to it if he wished to rule effectively." So it is not surprising that the Founding Fathers, who most feared the encroachment of natural rights by the central authority, envisioned an ideal community which consisted of "independent freeholders, each tilling their own plot of land and enjoying the fruits of their own labor." Thomas Jefferson, in extolling the life of the farmer, wrote, "Dependence begets subservience. It suffocates the germ of virtue and prepares fit tools for the design of ambition." Fearing the subordination of man to man in a highly organized and industrial social structure, Reinhold Niebuhr explains, the Founding Fathers were confident of the future virtue of America only in so far as it remained predominantly agricultural.

The watchword of the new society of the Nineteenth Century was rapid change and Americans altered their ideas concerning the frontier and institutions to fit these new circumstances. While the average American still sought land, above all, to farm he also now envisioned it as a source of credit and speculation, and a route of trade. This was, above all, a century of unparalleled economic expansion and its distinctive features were industrialization and urbanization. The natural elite of the Eighteenth Century was replaced at the top of the social heap by the self-made entrepreneur. "With startling speed a nation of farmers" and artisans, writes Sigmund Diamond, was transformed by a method of production, based on the factory and machine, that made use of ever increasing supplies of capital and labor. By the end of the Nineteenth Century the United States had become both the world's largest producer of food and raw materials and the largest manufacturer. Although small town life remained the norm, the revolution in transportation made it more and more difficult to maintain local autonomy and that sense of separation which had been so important a century earlier. The urbanization of Nineteenth Century America was no less rapid. In 1860, less than a quarter of the population lived in urban areas; by 1890, the figure had climbed to a third; by 1910, nearly half. The population of the great cities grew more than twice as fast as that of the country as a whole during these years and by 1890 New York, Chicago and Philadelphia all had populations of over one million. And what seemed on the surface to be a period of the fragmentation of American society was, in truth, an age of unusual community strength. Political parties, religious denominations, and the numerous reform movements of the period all stressed similar values and ideals that enabled individuals on the frontier and in the growing urban areas to go about their lives with a common sense of purpose.

In Twentieth Century America an individual's occupation became more important than where he lived. As Robert Wiebe has written: "Just as citizens had once contested boundaries across space, they now competed along the borders of occupational privilege and the antagonists were determined by business specialties, professions and labor skills rather than by communities, . . . and the economic ambitions that these units of nineteenth century society had supported." Whereas in the earlier period almost anyone with incentive could be successful or acquire the skills of a profession, now,

according to Wiebe, in order to succeed, individuals had to concentrate on a single specialty, and, in order to survive, they had to rely upon specialists in those many areas beyond their knowledge. What had originated in the Nineteenth Century as a way of organizing work and responsibilites was now the pattern of life in the Twentieth Century. While the shift of labor out of agriculture has continued during this century two other equally important changes have been taking place. First, the white-collar experience of the office has become increasingly more typical than the factory or farm; and second, the proportion of the working force employed within large scale units has increased dramatically. "We have become a nation of employees," John Coleman has written, "Today more than four-fifths of the labor force are paid employees, only 7 per cent are employed in agriculture and fewer, still are what might be called 'independent farmers'." Government, the most feared institution in the Eighteenth and Nineteenth Centuries, has become America's largest employer, with over ten million Americans working for federal, state or local governments. Not only its size, but the role of government has also dramatically expanded. Since the Progressive Era there has been a consensus among the American public that the government should perform a wide range of economic functions designed to guarantee equality of opportunity, and, more recently, equality of status to the less advantaged groups in the society.

So within the space of two centuries American society made the transition from a small, intimate agricultural community to a vast, impersonal national system—not envisioned by the Founding Fathers, even in their wildest nightmares. As the late philosopher and theologian Reinhold Niebuhr has written: "There is a special irony in the contrast between the course of American history toward the development of large-scale industry and Jefferson's belief that democracy was secure only in an agrarian economy. America has become what Jefferson most feared." By the 1960's a number of critics, and by no means all foreign, were pointing to the disparity between the values Americans proclaimed allegiance to and the ones they practiced. American rhetoric was of a humane world mission and an egalitarian society, the record was one of imperialism, racism and oppression. What others had described as evidence of cooperation and accommodation, these critics interpreted as usurpation and the calculated abuse of power. And the failure of our revolutionary heritage and tradition to correct these abuses just proved how bankrupt American society had become.

What had happened? Some blamed it on the absence of community and the disintegration of the family. "Modern living," Charles Reich declared, "has obliterated place, locality, and neighborhood, and given us the anonymous separateness of our existence. The family . . . has been ruthlessly stripped to its functional essentials. . . . The great organizations to which most people give their working day . . . are equally places of loneliness and alienation." Others pointed to the artificiality of work and culture and to uncontrolled technology and the destruction of the environment. Had the rate of change accelerated beyond the human capacity to manage it? Had organization and bureaucracy begun to dictate how we live our lives and had the logic of organization taken precedence over any other values? The more strident critics helped fuel the fires of this general indictment of Twentieth Century American society by revealing those responsible for its betrayal. The corporate class, who, controlling the instruments of public power, was responsible for America's social and moral bankruptcy. But what these expressions of betrayal and hypocrisy failed to provide, a noted American historian has observed, was a framework capable of comprehending modern American society and so their criticisms were assimilated into a complex social system that continued to function in the mid-1970's much as it had a decade before. "Filling an American chamber of horrors with hypocrisies judged an accumulation of evidence without explaining it . . . . [I]t encouraged the delusion that to formulate a problem was to answer it. . . ."

The blanket indictments of modern American society not only failed to revolutionize it, but rather convinced the majority of the population that they had been right all along and toughened their resistance. Some were compelled to explain why they felt that age had, indeed, bred wisdom, instead of premature senility as the critics of the 1960's had claimed. In explaining "how this great experiment in government . . . has been able to survive under the conditions of the Twentieth Century," Herbert von Borch wrote that "the looseness and elasticity of the American political system acts as a shock-absorber in serious conflicts" preventing the profound social upheavals of the last century from developing into political ones. Von Borch credits the elastic nature of our political system to the extreme fragmentation of authority among our political institutions on the part of the Founding Fathers: ". . . in their hostility to power, the settlers were also concerned with obstructing government as such, with splitting and neutralizing the exercise of power, by means of a multiplicity of safeguards. The government was set up as a permeable structure, as a transparent organism through which the energies of society would be able to flow freely and unimpeded." Its elasticity and looseness, then, can be attributed to the system of checks and balances, which hinder the abuse of political power and promote enlightened public policies.

But the flexible nature of the American political system has as much to do with our political style,
which since the Nineteenth Century has been characterized by populism and anti-elitism, as with the formulations of the Founding Fathers. In the Eighteenth Century there were no organized political parties and professional politicans in today's sense of those words because established lawyers, merchants and planters held the major offices and perceived of their political tenure as part of the responsibility of their elevated social status. The disappearance of this older social hierarchy and its traditional belief in elite rule in the Nineteenth Century made possible and necessitated the creation of modern political organizations. Gordon Wood has written, "Individuals, cut loose from traditional ties to the social hierarchy, were now forced to combine in new groups for political ends. Political office no longer was set by social ascription, but rather was won by political achievement within the organization of a party and through winning of votes." By vying for political leadership and competing for votes, new men were fed into the political process and were successful not because of their elevated social standing but because they knew how to appeal to the people. The rise of egalitarian politics, as Gordon Wood calls it, during the Nineteenth and Twentieth Centuries, has made the American political system more responsive to the will of the people and, in this day of unprecedented governmental interference in our lives, acts as a check on the government's abuse of its power, particularly in the area of foreign affairs, where the Founding Fathers saw fit to limit management to only the President, his closest advisers and the members of the Senate.

Our special faith in egalitarian politics has sparked much of the heightened interest in political and voting rights during the past couple of decades and a belief that political integration through voting is the best means of solving social problems. Voting rights acts and the anti-poll tax amendment of the mid-1960's were based on the deeply rooted belief that no nation with our heritage could in conscience exclude any of its citizens from the political process. The same logic underlay the Supreme Court's decision to apply the idea of "one man, one vote" to congressional and state legislative electoral redistricting and the adoption of the Twenty-sixth Amendment granting eighteen year olds the right to vote. And, more recently, large and unequal campaign contributions have caused so much concern because they seem to do violence to equality of participation in the political process. In fact, interest in the actuality and equality of consent has never been greater than it is today and it bespeaks and underlying confidence in the processes of egalitarian politics and in suffrage as the sole criterion of representation, which surface events and news headlines frequently obscure.

One test of the wisdom of public policy, of course, are the consequences it reaps. The arena in which decisions affecting national life are made is a tangled environs where political actions confront community problems, expectations stall in the face of compromise, and the public at large is left to bear the often shallow finale. Human actions, in short, comprise a web of tangled dependents. If coal companies, for example, strip-mine hills, a cheap source for needed electricity is supplied. But acreage is ruined for agricultural purposes. Similarly, if more expensive natural resources are relied upon to produce required energy, costs skyrocket and some may be unable to acquire essentials. As with men, so too political decisions: no law or policy is an island unto itself.

To measure wisdom, therefore, is to judge maturity. How much, then, has America learned by its past? How deeply are the lessons writ upon its political and cultural imagination? Do we do better today what yesterday we doubted or feared? How far have we come? These questions can be painted across a broad canvas of national concerns. For example, are our political tools today more refined and effective than those of our forbears? How and by whom are our decisions made? Does our foreign policy display greater appreciation for the use and abuse of military and economic power? What is the state of individual liberties? Is this today a Nation of finer culture? And what improvements may we boast of in the care and protection of our fundamental resources, our land and our people? Such questions are as numerous as our Nation's character is ample and diverse.

To tell if our aging has made us wiser, we must probe what we have been and where we are tending. To know if we are wise, we must understand why we have done what we have and what we are likely to do. To measure our age we need only count the years; wisdom is not such easy stuff to know.

Excerpted Documents

The democratic ideal.

Seymour Martin Lipset. Professor of Government—Harvard University, "Opportunities and Welfare in the First Nation." 1974, pp. 7-8.

Much of the social history of the United States, then, may be read in terms of an attempt to elaborate on the egalitarian promise of the Declaration of Independence. The United States led other nations in expanding its suffrage to cover all white males (slavery was its great exception and horror, and continued racism its Achilles' heel). It also led in providing education to its inhabitants. The census of 1840 indicated that over 90 percent of whites were literate. The figure was undoubtedly an exaggeration. Yet, then and later, this country spent a greater share of public funds on education than other societies. From the nineteenth century down to the present, a much larger percentage of the appropriate age population has attended secondary schools and institutions of higher education here than elsewhere. In other words, education has been more equally distributed in the United States than in other countries for a century and a half. Further, a myriad of foreign observers—Tocqueville, Martineau and Bryce among them—have commented on the emphasis in social relations on symbolic equality. They have noted that, in effect, no man need doff his cap to another, that the symbols of rank so prevalent in Europe have been absent here. Populism and anti-elitism have characterized America's political style.

Ray Allen Billington, *America's Frontier Heritage*, 1966, p. 157.

Just as vestiges of frontier individualism remain to distinguish the social attitudes of modern America from those of modern Europe, so do remnants of pioneer democracy. The United States is no longer a country free of class distinctions and so wedded to egalitarianism that manifestations of wealth arouse public resentment. But its social democracy does differ from that of older nations, marked by its relative lack of class awareness, and by the brash assurance of the humble that they are as worthy of respect as the elite. The house painter who addresses a client by his first name, the elevator operator who enters into casual conversation with his passengers, the garage mechanic who condescendingly compares his expensive car with your aging model, could exist only in the United States. Their counterparts are unknown in England or on the Continent partly because America's frontiering experience bred-into the people attitudes toward democracy that have persisted down to the present.

Gordon Wood, Professor of History—Brown University, "Revolution and the Political Integration of the Enslaved and Disenfranchised", American Enterprise Inst., 1974, p. 3.

In the eighteenth century the legal exclusion of the propertyless from the franchise was based not on the fear that the poor might confiscate the wealth of the aristocratic few, but on the opposite fear: that the aristocratic few might manipulate and corrupt the poor for their own ends. Established social leaders expected deference from those below them, and generally got it and were habitually reelected to political office. There were no organized political parties and no professional politicians in today's sense of those words. Established merchants, wealthy lawyers, and large planters held the major offices and ran political affairs as part of the responsibility of their elevated social positions. It was rare for a tavern keeper or small farmer to gain a political office of any consequence. Men were granted political authority in accord not with their seniority or experience in politics but with their established economic and social superiority.

Herbert von Borch, *The Unfinished Society*, 1963, p. 42.

The Founding Fathers' fear of the mass rule of the majority has not been justified by events. America has become a mosaic of minorities. Not merely minorities in the usual sense of national groups (which have preserved themselves much better in the "melting pot" than was to be expected), but also in the sense of purely individual forces, representing no one but themselves, which work at the fabric of political power: lobbyists in Washington, industrial leaders, trade-union leaders (who have not long been sitting at the table of the mighty), chairmen of Congressional committees with investigatory powers (which the late Senator McCarthy, though not unpunished, could abuse), the "veto groups" which, if they cannot make their own policies prevail, are nevertheless in a position to obstruct the policies of others (as for instance the Southern senators on the racial question)—all these are tiles in the great power mosaic. The two political parties are no exception to this rule; they too are composed in mosaic fashion, representing more or less loose coalitions of groups and not homogeneous political organisms.

Gordon Wood, Professor of History—Brown University, "Revolution and the Political Integration of the Enslaved and Disenfranchised," 1974, p. 2.

We Americans have never been able to figure out why the rest of the world has had such a hard time catching up with us. Because the process of creating a republican citizenry seemed so simple for us, we have believed it ought to be simple for others. It seems to us to be merely a matter of allowing the people to vote. Because voting is the most obvious means by which the people participate in politics, we have tended to emphasize the right to vote as the necessary and sufficient criterion of democratic politics. But this is a mistake. The suffrage is clearly a prerequisite for democratic politics, but it is hardly all there is to it. It is important for us in our bicentennial celebrations to examine our Revolution and its heritage and to seek to understand the sources of our political practice and values. Only with knowledge of the conditions that underlie the principle of consent in our polity can we confront the world and the future.

Alan Westin, *Views of America*, 1966, p. 125.

In the course of the past half century the portion of the United States government in question has grown to fifty to sixty times its original size. In the last twenty years alone, the growth has been somewhere upwards of 1000 per cent. This expansion has occurred, for the most part, in a few great spurts, the two World Wars and the period of Cold War in the late forties being the principal occasions.

With this stormy growth, spelling as it did the transition from the small, intimate organization to the vast, impersonal one, there came all the normal concomitants of bigness and complexity: a greatly increased coefficient of internal friction within the governmental machinery; an elaborate cumbersomeness of the decision-taking process; a sacrifice of timeliness and incisiveness in the decisions taken; a ponderous inertia in the apparatus as a whole; a loss of flexibility; mechanical, impersonal personnel procedures, with attendant loss of efficiency in utilization of personnel.

Herbert von Borch, The Unfinished Society, 1963, p. 12.

Only in American civilization do we find the great and stirring currents of the eighteenth century projected so forcibly into the actualities of the twentieth century. Because in the second half of that century, in 1776 to be precise, a colonial venture was transformed into a free, independent society by a deliberate and well-pondered act of will, and because the Union was not so much born as made, America more than any other historical entity can be identified with a particular philosophy. Its Utopia, which the Founding Fathers wished to achieve for all time on North American soil, flowed from the religion of freedom, as Croce calls that fusion of ideas and sentiments known to the history of philosophy as enlightenment, rationalism optimism or deism. . . . But now the American nation must take leave of its Utopia. Should that Utopia be retained as an ideology without basis in reality, it could easily degenerate into a collective deception. America will finally have to bid farewell to the eighteenth century.

A changing society.

Robert Nisbet, Professor of Humanities—Columbia University,"The Social Impact of the Revolution," 1974, p. 5.

I am inclined to think that a feudal system necessarily emerges whenever a relatively small number of persons seek to live in a new territory with great expanses of land to be had by the well-off or energetic, where ties with a central authority are weak or absent, where localism is enforced by topography as well as custom, and where landed property tends to create the fundamental rights and privileges in society. Certainly by the middle of the eighteenth century the American colonies met these and other distinctively feudal criteria, no matter how loath we may be to apply these criteria to Pilgrims and others of established historical fancy who, as we are prone to believe, left not only Europe but all European history behind them when they came to the New World.

From Maine to Georgia American life was rooted in the land, in this was just as true of New England—its fisheries and manufactures, so often exaggerated in their importance, notwithstanding—as it was in other parts of America.

Richard Hofstadter, Professor of History—Columbia University, *America at 1750: A Social Portrait*, 1972, p. 168.

But of couse this was a middle-class world with a difference, which sets if off from post-industrial worlds: it was a middle-class *rural* society, peopled mainly by farmers and small planters and by those who bought from them, supplied them, worked for or slaved for them. Perhaps eight out of ten of its people made their living from farming, the rest as artisans or in extractive industries. Its middle class was based less upon shopkeeping, industry, or urban services than upon the widespread ownership of the land, which in America was easier to get and keep to work and inherit, than anywhere else in the world.

Robert Mead, *Atlantic Legacy: Essays in American-European Cultural History*, 1969, p. 252.

Jefferson saw the future security of American democracy in the individual farmer. Whether it was the physiocratic element of the soil or the frontier, one new ingredient was added: that of opportunity or its reverse, freedom from economic and social restraints. If the frontier closed, new opportunities arose in the growing industrialized cities. There is an American impatience with any restraint on activity that does not endanger the community, for the free-enterprising individual is face to face with his own fate as with his free-willing Calvinist God. This is the essence of American rugged individualism. But this very freedom of opportunity brought with it a sense of community, of collective self-help. This spirit has been transcended in contemporary America by the concept of human relations in industry, the key to increased production and the mutual interest of all engaged in rationalizing and perfecting the productive process.

Reinhold Niebuhr, Philosopher, *The Irony of American History*, 1952, p. 31.

One single note of realism runs through Jefferson's idyllic picture of American innocency. That consists in his preference for an agricultural over an urban society. Jefferson was confident of the future virtue of America only in so far as it would continue as an agricultural nation. Fearing the social tensions and the subordination of man to man in a highly organized social structure, his ideal community consisted of independent freeholders, each tilling his own plot of ground and enjoying the fruits of his own labor. "Dependence begets subservience," he wrote in extolling the life of the farmer. "It suffocates the germ of virtue and prepares fit tools for the design of ambition."

There is a special irony in the contrast between the course of American history toward the development of large-scale industry and Jefferson's belief that democracy was secure only in an agrarian economy. America has become what Jefferson most feared; but the moral consequences have not been as catastrophic as he anticipated. While democracy is tainted by more corruption in our great metropolitan areas than in the remainder of our political life, we have managed to achieve a tolerable justice in the collective relations of industry by balancing power against power and equilibrating the various competing social forces of society. The rise of the labor movement has been particularly important in achieving this result; for its organization of the power of the workers was necessary to produce the counter-weight to the great concentrations of economic power which justice requires.

Ray Allen Billington, *America's Frontier Heritage,* **1966, p. 157.**

The social democracy and frontier-type individualism that characterized America's growing period have not persisted unchanged into the twentieth century. Individualism has retreated before the advance of social cohesiveness essential in an urban-industrial society. The nation's folk hero may still be the rugged individualist, but the lone wolves of the past have found that they cannot fight the pack and that in cut-throat competition all throats are cut. At least since the 1890s the economic community had grudgingly accepted the regulation that the pioneer resisted save when it was to his advantage, and today cooperation and reliance on government are almost as commonplace in the United States as in the older countries of Europe. Yet American individualism differs from that of France or England in it's continued insistence on a degree of economic freedom that has long since vanished in those countries, and in a glorification of the individual's ability to care for himself despite daily proof that joint effort alone will succeed in a society increasingly enmeshed.

Stephan Thernstrom, Professor of History—Harvard University, "Urbanization, Migration, and Social Mobility in Late Nineteenth Century America," in *Towards a New Past,* **1968, p. 158.**

The United States, it has been said, was born in the country and has moved to the city. It was during the half-century between the Civil War and World War I that the move was made. In 1860, less than a quarter of the American population lived in city or town; by 1890, the figure had reached a third; by 1910, nearly half. By more sophisticated measures than the mere count of heads, the center of gravity of the society had obviously tilted cityward well before the last date.

The urbanization of late nineteenth-century America took place at a dizzying pace. Chicago, for instance, doubled its population every decade but one between 1850 and 1890, growing from 30,000 to over a million in little more than a generation. And it was not merely the conspicuous metropolitan giants but the Akrons, the Duluths, the Tacomas that were bursting at the seams; no less than 101 American communities grew by 100 percent or more in the 1880s.

John Coleman, ed. *The Changing American Economy,* **1967, p. 282.**

And we have become a nation of employees—"hirelings," as Blake put it. When this nation was founded, more than four fifths of the working people were independent farmers—and most of the rest were independent tradesmen or handicraftsmen. Today more than four-fifths of the labor force are paid employees; only 7 per cent are employed in agriculture and fewer still are what might be called "independent farmers."
A number of private companies are as rich as small nations. The 500 largest American industrial corporations, with assets of over $250 billion, employ more than 10 million people—three-fifths of all those who work in manufacturing and mining. There are also great corporations in the fields of retailing, transportation, utilities, finance, even publishing. Fifty-five corporations have annual sales of more than $1 billion each.
Government—the feared enemy of freedom to liberals like Jefferson—has also become a huge employer; today more than 10 million Americans work for federal, state, or local governments. Total government spending

accounts for one-fifth of national output, and government's regulatory and other activities significantly affect a still larger share of business and individual behavior.

Labor unions—almost unknown in Jefferson's day—today number more than 18 million members in their ranks. It is commonly said that this has become an organizational society.

How does the freedom of the individual fare in this land, now that the weight of big business, big labor, and big government has become so evident?

Charles Reich, Professor of Law—Yale University, *The Greening of America: How the Youth Revolution is Trying To Make America Livable,* 1970, pp. 17-18.

Work and living have become more and more pointless and empty. There is no lack of meaningful projects that cry out to be done, but our working days are used up in work that lacks meaning: making useless or harmful products, or servicing the bureaucratic structures. For most Americans, work is mindless, exhausting, boring, servile, and hateful, something to be endured while "life" is confined to "time off." At the same time our culture has been reduced to the grossly commercial; all cultural values are for sale, and those that fail to make a profit are not preserved. Our life activities have become plastic, vicarious, and false to our genuine needs, activities fabricated by others and forced upon us.

The vanishing wilderness.

John Muir, *The Yosemite,* 1912, p. 198.

Everybody needs beauty as well as bread, places to play in and pray in, where Nature may heal and cheer and give strength to body and soul alike. This natural beauty-hunger is made manifest in the little windowsill gardens of the poor, though perhaps only a geranium slip in a broken cup, as well as in the carefully tended rose and lily gardens of the rich, the thousands of spacious city parks and botanical gardens, and in our magnificent National Parks—the Yellowstone, Yosemite, Sequoia, etc.—Nature's sublime wonderlands, the admiration and joy of the world.

James Fenimore Cooper, *The Prairie,* 1826, p. 78.

America has grown, my men since the days of my youth to be a country larger than I once had thought the world itself to be. Near seventy years I dwelt in York, province and state together; you've been in York, 'tis like?"

"Not I—not I; I never visited the towns, but often have heard the place you speak of named. 'Tis a wide clearing there, I reckon. .''

"Too wide! Too wide! They schourge the very 'arth with their axes. Such hills and hunting grounds as I have seen stripped of the gifts of the Lord, without remorse or shame I tarried till the mouths of my hounds were deafened by the blows of the chopper, and then I came west in search of quiet. It was a grievous journey that I made, a grievous toil to pass through falling timber and to breathe the thick air of smoky clearings week after week as I did!

Henry David Thoreau, *Walden,* 1854.

Our village life would stagnate if it were not for the unexplored forests and meadows which surround it. We need the tonic of wildness—to wade sometimes in marshes where the bittern and the meadowhen lurk, and hear the booming of the snipe; to smell the whispering sedge where only some wilder and more solitary fowl builds her nest, and the mink crawls with its belly close to the ground. At the same time that we are earnest to explore and learn all things, we require that all things be mysterious and unexplorable, that land and sea be infinitely wild, unsurveyed and unfathomed by us because unfathomable. We can never have enough of Nature. We must be refreshed by the sight of inexhaustible vigor, vast and Titanic features, the sea-coast with its wrecks, the wilderness with its living and its decaying trees, the thunder cloud, and the rain which lasts three weeks and produces freshets. We need to witness our own limits transgressed, and some life pasturing freely where we never wander.

Chief Luther Standing Bear, *Land of the Spotted Eagle*, 1933.

The white man does not understand the Indian for the reason that he does not understand America. He is too far removed from its formative processes. The roots of the tree of his life have not yet grasped the rock and soil. The white man is still troubled with primitive fears; he still has in his consciousness the perils of this frontier continent, some of its vastnesses not yet having yielded to his questing footsteps and inquiring eyes. He shudders still with the memory of the loss of his forefathers upon its scorching deserts and forbidding mountain-tops. The man from Europe is still a foreigner and an alien. And he still hates the man who questioned his path across the continent. But in the Indian the spirit of the land is still vested; it will be until other men are able to divine and meet its rhythm.

Aldo Leopold, *The Sand County Almanac*, 1949, p. 227.

We have realized dimly, of course, that a day afield was good for the tired businessman. We have also realized that the destruction of wildlife removed the incentive for days afield. But we have not yet learned to express the value of wildlife in terms of social welfare. Some have attempted to justify wildlife conservation in terms of meat, others in terms of personal pleasure, others in terms of cash, still others in the interest of science, education, agriculture, art, public health, and even military preparedness. But few have so far clearly realized and expressed the whole truth, namely, that all these things are but factors in broad social value, and that wildlife, like golf, is a social asset.

Is technology progress?

Frank Norris, *The Octopus*, 1901, pp. 32-33

Then, faint and prolonged, across the levels of the ranch, be heard the engine whistling for Bonneville. Again and again, at rapid intervals in its flying course, it whistled for road crossings, for sharp curves, for trestles; ominous notes, hoarse, bellowing, ringing with the accents of menace and defiance; and abruptly Presley saw again, in his imagination, the galloping monster, the terror of steel and steam, with its single eye, Cyclopean, red, shooting from horizon to horizon; but saw it now as the symbol of a vast power, huge, terrible, flinging the echo of its thunder over all the reaches of the valley, leaving blood and destruction in its path; the leviathan, with tentacles of steel clutching into the soil, the soulless Force, the ironhearted Power, the monster, the Colossus, the Octopus.

Ivan Ilydr, *Energy and Equity*, 1974, p. 31.

The typical American male devotes more than 1,600 hours a year to his car. He sits in it while it goes and while it stands idling. He parks it and searches for it. He earns the money to put down on it and to meet the monthly instalments. He works to pay for petrol, tolls, insurace, taxes and tickets. He spends four of his sixteen waking hours on the road or gathering his resources for it. And this figure does not take into account the time consumed by other activities dictated by transport: time spent in hospitals, traffic courts and garages; time spent watching automobile commercials or attending consumer education meetings to improve the quality of the next buy. The model American puts in 1,600 hours to get 7,500 miles: less than five miles per hour.

Sigmund Diamond, *The Nation Transformed: The Creation of an Industrial Society*, 1963, p. 6.

Behind these changes—beneficent to some, cataclysmic to others—lay a new method of production based on factory and machine, with an increasingly refined technology that made use of ever-increasing supplies of capital and specialized labor. Regional differences remained, though, with the passage of time these tended to be more important to local-colorist writers, exploiting a nostalgia for the past, than to men-of-affairs, for whom it was the present reality of a great national market, welded together by a network of railroads and communications, that was to be exploited. And while the face of the land was itself being made over, so, too, were the millions of men and women from rural American and from Europe, who pouring into the new industrial centers of the nation, were subjected to the new discipline of factory labor. With startling speed, a nation of farmers and small-town merchants began to learn, if not wholly to master, the techniques of an industrial society.

Charles Reich, Professor of Law—Yale University, *The Greening of America: How the Youth Revolution is Trying To Make America Livable*, 1970, pp. 16-17.

Technology and production can be great benefactors of man, but they are mindless instruments; if undirected they careen along with a momentum of their own. In our country they pulverize everything in their path: the landscape, the natural environment, history and tradition, the amenities and civilities, the privacy and spaciousness of life, beauty, and the fragile, slow-growing social structures which bind us together. Organization and bureaucracy, which are applications of technology to social institutions, increasingly dictate how we shall live our lives, with the logic of organization taking precedence over any other values.

Henry David Thoreau, *Walden* 1854.

As with our colleges, so with a hundred "modern improvements;" there is an illusion about them; there is not always a positive advance. The devil goes on exacting compound interest to the last for his early share and numerous succeeding investments in them. Our inventions are wont to be pretty toys, which distract our attention from serious things. They are but improved means to an unimproved end, an end which it was already but too easy to arrive at; as railroads lead to Boston or New York. We are in great haste to construct a magnetic telegraph from Maine to Texas; but Maine and Texas, it may be, have nothing important to communicate.

Selected Bibliography

Banfield, Edward C. "The City and the Revolutionary Tradition." Distinguished Lecture Series on the Bicentennial. Washington, D.C.: American Enterprise Institute for Public Policy Research, 1974.

Bell, Daniel, ed. *Toward the Year 2000: Work in Progress.* Boston, Mass.: Beacon Press, 1967.

Bernstein, Barton J., ed. *Towards a New Past: Dissenting Essays in American History.* New York: Pantheon Books, 1968.

Billington, Ray Allen, *America's Frontier Heritage.* New York: Holt, Rinehart & Winston, 1966.

Boorstin, Daniel J. *The Democratic Experience.* New York: Random House, 1973.

Borch, Herbert von, *The Unfinished Society.* New York: Sidgwick and Jackson, 1963.

Brogan, D.W. *The American Character.* New York: Alfred A. Knopf, 1944.

Coben, Stanley, and Ratner, Lorman, eds. *The Development of an American Culture.* Englewood Cliffs, New Jersey: Prentice-Hall, Inc., 1970.

Coleman, John R., ed. *The Changing American Economy.* New York: Basic Books, 1967.

Danhof, Clarence. *Change in Agriculture, The Northern United States, 1820-1870.* Cambridge, Mass.: Harvard University Press, 1969.

Diamond, Sigmund, ed. *The Nation Transformed: The Creation Of an Industrial Society.* New York: George Braziller, Inc., 1963.

Douglas, Jack D., ed. *The Technological Threat.* Englewood Cliffs, New Jersey: Prentice-Hall, Inc., 1971.

Engler, Richard E. *The Challenge of Diversity.* New York: Harper & Row, 1964.

Ernst, Morris L. *Utopia, 1976,* New York: Greenwood Press, 1955.

Freedman, Leonard, and Cotter, Cornelius, eds. *Issues of the Sixties.* Belmont, California: Wadsworth Publishing Company, Inc., 1961.

Gabriel, Ralph H. *American Values: Continuity and Change.* Westport, Conn.: Greenwood Press, 1974.

Gross, Bertram M., ed. *A Great Society?* New York: Basic Books, Inc., 1966.

Hague, John A. *American Character and Culture: Some Twentieth Century Perspectives.* Deland, Florida: Everett Edwards Press, Inc., 1964.

Handlin, Oscar and Mary. *Facing Life: Youth and Family in American History.* Boston, Mass.: Little, Brown and Company, 1971.

Hofstadter, Richard. *America at 1750: A Social Portrait.* New York: Alfred A. Knopf, 1972.

Kaplan, Abraham. *American Ethics and Public Policy.* New York: Oxford University Press, 1963.

Kennedy, Senator Edward M. *Decisions for a Decade: Policies and Programs for the 1970's* Garden City, New York: Doubleday & Company, Inc., 1968.

Lipset, Seymour Martin. "Opportunity and Welfare in the First Nation." Distinguished Lecture Series on the Bicentennial. Washington, D.C.: American Enterprise Institute for Public Policy Research, 1974.

Main, Jackson Turner. *The Social Structure of Revolutionary America.* Princeton, New Jersey: Princeton University Press, 1965.

Marx, Leo. *The Machine in the Garden: Technology and the Pastoral Ideal in America.* New York: Oxford University Press, 1964.

Mead, Margret. *And Keep Your Powder Dry: An Anthropologist Looks at America.* New York: William Morrow & Company, 1948.

Mead, Robert. *Atlantic Legacy: Essays in American-European Cultural History.* New York: New York University Press, 1969.

Morison, Elting E., ed. *The American Scene: Essays in Value and Performance.* New York: Harper & Brothers, 1958.

Niebuhr, Reinhold. *The Irony of American History.* New York: Charles Scribner's Sons, 1952.

Nisbet, Robert A. "The Social Impact of the Revolution." Distinguished Lecture Series on the Bicentennial. Washington, D.C.: American Enterprise Institute for Public Policy Research, 1974.

Parrington, Vernon L. *American Dreams: A Study of American Utopias.* New York: Russell and Russell, Inc., 1964.

Reich, Charles A. *The Greening of America: How the Youth Revolution is Trying to Make America Livable.* New York: Random House, 1970.

Republican Committee on Program and Progress. *Decisions for A Better America.* Garden City, New York: Doubleday & Company, Inc., 1960.

Spiller, Robert, and Larrabee, Eric, eds.*American Perspectives: The National Self-Image in the Twentieth Cen-tury.* Cambridge, Mass.: Harvard University Press, 1961.

Westin, Alan F., ed. *Views of America.* New York: Harcourt, Brace & World, Inc., 1966.

Wood, Gordon S. "Revolution and the Political Integration of The Enslaved and Disenfranchised." Distinguished Lecture Series on the Bicentennial. Washington, D.C.: American Enterprise Institute for Public Policy Research, 1974.

Ziff, Larzer. *The American 1890's: Life and Times of a Lost Generation.* New York: Viking Press, 1966.

THE DREAM OF SUCCESS

Introductory Essay

The right to dream, as one American historian has noted, was America's first democratically distributed privilege and by the late Eighteenth Century a large portion of the dreams of America's early settlers were incorporated by the Founding Fathers into a single vision of an entire society. Their vision, above all, emphasized the new nation's uniqueness, distinguishing it from all others by its laws, customs and industrious citizenry. The Founding Fathers relied primarily upon negative qualities to define their vision for the settlers of the new country: their republicanism was without monarchy; their democracy was without entrenched privilege. There were to be neither castes nor classes in America and, while the Founding Fathers did not assume equal talent among the people of the new land, it was their special vision that America be the land of equal opportunities for all its citizens. In this way a complete correspondence between social status and merit would be guaranteed and America would retain its uniqueness, and thus live up to the spirit of Goethe's famous tribute to the land of opportunity in his poem, *Amerika, Du Hast Es Besser:* "America, you have it better than our old continent - no crumbling castles, no dark ruins, no useless memories and vain quarrels to trouble the soul of your vital epoch."

Over the course of the last 200 years the original vision of the Founding Fathers has undergone much transformation, but one of the things Americans have remained most proud of is the notion of a land of equal opportunities and success for all those who merit it. According to these beliefs life in America was a race open to all, regardless of social background and training. Inherited wealth and established social position were only seeming advantages because the wealthy and the privileged could occupy their superior positions in society only so long as their performance warranted it; the talented, but low born, were certain to rise to stations befitting their true worth. And it is precisely this notion that the positions at the top were open to those with talent that nurtured dreams of success, for the very reason that it implied dreams could be striven for and made real. Throughout our history, from Benjamin Franklin to Horatio Alger to Norman Vincent Peale, apostles of success have stressed that individuals in America succeed or fail, not from accident or external surroundings, but from possessing the elements of success in themselves. And it was an American statesman and politican who coined the expression "the Self-Made Man," which, unlike the French expressions *parvenu* and *nouveau riche* which emphasize only the newness of the individual's success, implies that the individual succeeded by his own exertion and bears no hint of condescension. The belief in the land of equal opportunity quickly evolved into the land of boundless success and the "small army of European visitors" who toured the United States in the early Nineteenth Century, most notably de Tocqueville, was likewise convinced from what they saw and heard that in the society of the young republic the social ladder was accessible to all and easily climbed.

That historians and sociologists, over the years, have found scant evidence of the type of success stories, talked about by both apostles of success in this country and European visitors in the Nineteenth Century, has hardly mattered. It has not detracted from either the popular conviction that the dream of success was, and to a certain extent still is, a reality; or from Americans' acceptance of this conclusion as both logical and comforting. So, one of the primary questions to be addressed when examining the role the 'dream of success' has played in the evolution of American history is its persistence. How, in other words, has it sustained itself in our imaginations as one of the fundamental underpinnings of American society and one of the finest legacies of the American Revolution?

A partial answer to that question has been suggested by one historian, who writes in this way about the myth of the self-made man: "It seems reasonable to conclude that he has persisted as a popular hero and as a central symbol of American society because Americans were able to synthesize, under his aegis, many conflicting strands of belief and aspiration." It becomes obvious, after a study of the idea of success in American life, that, in spite of a persistent devotion to the ideal of success, Americans have differed greatly in the way they have defined it over the last two centuries. Not only has the 'dream of success' meant different things to different groups within American society, but its content has also been altered to fit the changing realities of social and political life in this country.

The traditional ideal of American success, the self-made man, did not flourish until the middle of the Nineteenth Century. The image was inextricably linked to the possibilities of an emerging industrialized, urbanized America. For the early years of the Republic, however, a somewhat different model prevailed. Embedded in the roots of their classical understanding of political life, the Founding Fathers had profound reservations about the feasibility of unhampered upward mobility in American society. The success of an individual reflected more than effort alone. Some men were naturally endowed with greater skills. And yet, the hope of a democracy was that every man could, in the open field of competition and opportunity, make his own way, staking his rightful claim to the earth's abundance and society's rewards. The Constitution, designed in the wake of warfare and the deficiencies of the Articles of Confederation, delineates limits as much as opportunities. Success, though severed from the strict Old World lineage of inheritance and unearned social standing, also had a double-face: effort counted but nature could not be ignored. The Founding Fathers did not reject aristocracy as such; they intended the "rule of the best" to be grounded in individual talent and proven by the tests of freedom and initiative. In this, their vision embodied the Jeffersonian concept of a "natural elite." His ideal of the agrarian citizen was rooted in his hope that the life of the land would encourage the life of reason.

Thus, it was not wealth and self-aggrandizement for their own sakes that concerned the framers of our national political doctrines. Theirs was a vision of what constituted the good or best life; economic security, though clearly important, was not the central goal. But a new nation requires strength, and the idea of success became inevitably tied to the question of survival. Both as a nation and as individuals, the new land issued demands upon the young America: these demands, coupled with the vast possibilities of a new and largely untouched continent, became the stuff from which a changing conception of success was shaped. The rhetoric of democratic hopes was kept for special occasions; the requirements of daily living molded a new standard for worldly accomplishments. For now, during the Age of Jackson and after, the question of success and the possession of wealth and power were intimates. The acqusition of wealth, quite simply, opened doors otherwise closed. The ownership of land, too, brought privilege. Success took upon itself the clothes of enterprise.

A new class structure accompanied these developments, based on property regardless of the manner in which it was acquired. Inherited status still held importance in New England and parts of the Old South, but a less entrenched test was now increasingly available. Capital assured position, and position secured power. Democracy dealt in the franchise, and, as had been the experience of other nations, political power could be acquired by the purse.

Life in America continued to change. By the middle of the Nineteenth Century, the settlement of the frontier, the rapid growth of towns and cities, the construction of a national network of roads, canals and railroads, and the remarkable expansion of industry all served to stimulate the quest for private fortune implict in the emerging standard of success. Growth brought severe personal losses and great gains; everyone became increasingly aware of the safety to be won by wealth. For wealth, as had been true for the rooted inheritance of social classes in Europe, was a defense against the vagaries of ill fortune and the means to assert some sense of mastery over one's own world.

Famed orator Henry Clay gave brief eloquence to the mood. While defending business enterprise before the U.S. Senate in 1832, he painted the now-classic portrait: "In Kentucky, almost every manufactory known to me is in the hands of enterprising and self-made men, who have acquired whatever wealth they possess by patient and diligent labor."

Success was now perceived as entirely dependent on the will and actions of the individual and the ideal of success was now identified with the activities and pursuit of business enterprise. With the transformation in attitudes, the Jeffersonian conception of a natural aristocracy had all but disappeared; at the top of the social heap now stood the self-made entrepreneur, proud in his success.

The rewards of success were seen in a new light as well, portrayed in secular rather than religious terms. The chief goal of the socially ambitious was no longer narrowly defined as the acquisition of property, but rather the accumulation of a vast fortune. Wealth was the universally acknowledged symbol of superior status in the Nineteenth Century American society; as Francis Bowen, in his popular *Principles of a Political Economy*, observed "it is the only distinction that is recognized among us." Wealth was to be earned, not married, and a stable marriage was seen as a prerequisite for success. As one contemporary observer put it: "They are married men not because they are better off than their fellows, but are better off because they are married men." The secret to success lay in the practice of industry and economy, but almost any socially desirable quality was useful - honesty, sobriety, courage, charity, and dozen others. And finally, the Nineteenth Century apostles of the ideal of success made it clear that opportunities for making money were much better in the cities, but they also implied that a rural childhood and poor beginnings were necessary to instill the correct values for success in later life.

Not only had the content of the 'dream of success' changed to fit new circumstances, but, almost as significant, the frequency and intensity with which the philosophy of success was voiced radically changed. The literature of success became a genre in its own right. No more the inspiring maxims of prudence and caution. In their place Americans learned an ideology, expounded with a passionate intensity. This "rags-to-riches" mentality so penetrated American thought during this period that chroniclers of the wealthy invented 'poor beginnings' and even 'rural childhoods' for many who were born neither poor nor in the country. The constant repetition of these success stories nurtured the hope that opportunity was just around the corner for those who lived right and worked hard - if not now, then in a few years; if not for oneself, then for one's children. As such this Nineteenth Century 'dream of success' played a strategic role in the evolution of American social attitudes, serving in some ways to help overcome traditional hostilities toward the city and the factory and to help allay fears of many who saw urbanization and industrialization as a threat to democratic values and institutions.

Movement up the social ladder, in the style of the rags-to-riches ideology, was really quite rare, and the few restless men on the make who were fabulously successful should not be confused with the great majority of the nation's laborers and small farmers who were not in a position to take advantage of the new economic opportunities which the period offered. (Detailed historical research for the period 1830 until 1900 has shown that successful professional men, along with those who accumulated vast fortunes were, in most cases, men who depended less on innate entrepreneurial abilities than on inheritance of wealth and social standing. This was true even in the frontier city, where the local boosters advertised the great equality of opportunity on the frontier. Social distinctions, although not as obvious in Eastern cities, developed quickly and as the circle of the elite in the frontier towns became more exclusive and distinct, there was substantially less opportunity for upward social mobility. The failure of most laborers and small farmers in America to move from blue-collar to white-collar positions reminds us of the wide discrepancies which mark the story of individualism in America.) Thernstrom reports that the manual worker in Nineteenth Century cities the criterion of success now became what he saved, what he earned and whether he owned property. Most of the gains during this period registered by manual laborers and small farmers were decidedly modest; nonetheless, the 'dream of success' was as important to their lives as for those few who actually succeeded.

But major social developments in the late Nineteenth Century combined to force a further reshaping of American attitudes towards success. For as the national scene changed with the birth of diverse social, political, and economic organizations, and the wave of immigrants to her shores rose to new heights, the earlier notion of success could not bear the burden of the more varied experience of a changing people. One of the primary weaknesses of the self-made man conception of the 'dream of success' was that it explained success and failure only in terms of inner qualities, ignoring the influence of the environment, and social circumstances. By the turn of the century, many had come to appreciate the relationship between opportunity and success. The federal government soon became the principal advocate of social legislation designed to increase opportunities, both economic and social, among those groups who had not benefited from the complicated demands of American life during the early Twentieth Century. However, much of Wilson's and Roosevelt's social legislation according to Cawelti, was based on the principle of self-help. Rejecting attempts at a planned economy, Americans preferred reforms (such as a graduated income tax, social security, minimum wages and hours and aid to education) which were intended to free these groups from abject poverty and illiteracy, yet give them an opportunity to compete with those who had greater economic and cultural advantages.

The 'dream of success,' as idealized by the image of the self-made man, received yet another blow in the early Twentieth Century. For as business grew in both size and complexity, the demand for the specialist also increased. Where earlier attitudes toward success had held versatility in high regard, holding the jack-of-all trades above the expert, demands of Twentieth Century urban existence unseated those values. This meant, of course, that the two major success strategies of the Nineteenth Century - the apprenticeship system and individual entrepreneurship - were no longer economically viable. Formal education was now seen the major avenue toward the attainment of success and higher status. Wyllie notes that until 1900 the educational requirements of the business community consisted of nothing more than common school training and a business apprenticeship. But in the Twentieth Century, the successful individual did not rise from the ranks; he was hired as an executive trainee on the basis of a college degree. As one Twentieth Century observer noted, "The office boy of Horatio Alger's day might have had some hope of rising to a partnership . . . today's office boy knows that a year at the Harvard Business School will do more for his career than a lifetime of industry, economy, temperance and piety."

The success story of Twentieth Century America has largely been an account of the rapid rise in both wealth and status of professional groups, taking advantage of their educational opportunities to acquire a specialty. There is a more cynical interpretation. For the average American, it now seems that education, connections and social status are the primary avenues of success and that unless an individual has these opportunities from birth, only a miraculous intervention could place the ordinary citizen in the highest reaches of American society. But this idea, like the earlier rags-to-riches mythology, is an exaggeration. The 'dream of success' still plays an important part in the lives of those disadvantaged groups who do not entertain hopes of leaping from the bottom to the top of American society. In the last couple of decades there have been encouraging signs for minority groups, particularly Blacks and women, in their struggle for equality. For them as for others, political power has become a tool for hope. So far this realization has proven a significant incentive toward organization among minority groups in Twentieth Century America and, although most of the social gains registered by these groups have been decidedly modest - a move one notch up the occupational scale, better educational opportunities-the great majority of them have indeed 'gotten ahead', and in their eyes the 'dream of success' burns just as brightly as it continues to do among the more advantaged groups of American society.

It is indisputable that the 'dream of success' has played a large and constant role in the development of American society and culture over the last two hundred years of our history. It is equally indisputable, however, that that dream - in each of its scenarios - served many interests and purposes, not just one. During the Nineteenth Century it glorified material progress and persuaded many that happiness really meant material accomplishments. It inspired the 'common man' to defy distinctions of class and status and strive to be as successful as his talents allowed. And it helped to instill democratic values and virtues in the mind of the average citizen by honoring activity over repose, and assigning merit on the basis of achievement. Martin Luther King voiced the common hope: "I have a dream." Equality of opportunity and the right to a better life had long been a part of the nation's rhetoric; increasingly, the disadvantaged called America to task.

In the final analysis, it is apparent that the 'dream of success' has universal appeal and that in every period of American history "the disadvantaged hero struggling against odds, bearing witness to aspiration, but finally redeemed by success, is a folk hero everywhere rejoiced in. It is not surprising, therefore," given our continuing faith in the promise of our democratic past, that belief in the reality of the 'dream of success' still survives, although "edited and revised" to fit the conditions of Twentieth Century America.

Excerpted Documents

The vision of the Founding Fathers:
uniqueness and equality of opportunity.

Daniel Boorstin, Senior Historian of the Smithsonian National Museum of History and Technology, *The Image of What Happened to the American Dream*, 1962, p. 240.

A dream is a vision or an aspiration to which we can compare reality. It may be very vivid, but its vividness reminds us how different is the real world . . . the American Dream was the most accurate way of describing the hopes of men in America . . . the unprecedented American opportunities have always tempted us to confuse the visionary with the real. America has not been plagued by utopianism for the very reason that here dreams could be striven for and made real .

Seymour Martin Lipset, Professor of Government — Harvard University, and Reinhard Bendix, Professor of Political Science — University of California at Berkeley, *Social Mobility in Industrial Society*, 1959, p. 78.

We can only speculate when we attempt to assess the effects of the absence of a feudal past in America. Clearly it has not meant the absence of status distinctions . . . . But it has led to an ideological equalitarianism, which is not any less important because it has been contradicted on every side by the existence of status differences. No act is perhaps as symbolic of this ideology as Jefferson's order to have a round table replace the rectangular one at the While House because this would relieve him of the necessity of stipulating the order of preference at official receptions. This act was not a denial of the existing ranks and authority; it was rather a testimony to the belief that these were accidental, not essential attributes, of man .

Edward Pessen, Professor of History — New York University, *Riches, Class and Power Before the Civil War,* 1973, p. 87.

Contemporary writers [mid-nineteenth century], particularly the small army of European visitors who toured the United States during the era, were for the most part convinced that in the society of the young fabled republic the social ladder was easily climbed. That most of the visitors actually found little evidence of upward social movement hardly detracted either from their own conviction that such mobility was a reality or from their American audience's acceptance of a conclusion both logical and comforting. . .

Opportunities for success in
revolutionary America.

Jackson Main, Professor of History — Princeton University, *The Social Structure of Revolutionary America,* 1965, pp. 282-283.

Just as the revolutionary American could increase his wealth, he could also advance in prestige. The status order, which the colonists brought with them from Europe . . .gradually disappeared in America partly because no European aristocracy was present to perpetuate it, but largely because of the actual condition of social equality and the remarkable ease with which the colonial could improve his position. Therefore the old order was eventually replaced by one which developed out of the new economic circumstances. This indigenous class structure was based upon property rather than inherited status.

Jackson Main, Professor of History — Princeton University, *The Social Structure of Revolutionary America,* 1965, p. 119.

The chance to rise in the revolutionary era varied with the circumstances . . . Two pieces of advice could be given to the socially ambitious: the acquisition of wealth opened all doors, even in Virginia, but especially in the cities; and the ownership of land did bring with it a special prestige. Perhaps most important to the average American was the fact that class did not depend upon inheritance but upon property. Since anyone could acquire property, anyone could rise, and the poor man could and occasionally did become a wealthy esquire.

The pursuit of wealth
and the virtues of a poor and rural childhood.

Stephan Thernstrom, Professor of History — Harvard University, *Poverty and Progress: Social Mobility in a Nineteenth Century City,* 1964, p. 63.

The Nineteenth Century American seems to have found nothing offensive in the patent medicine advertisement which read: "The first object in life with the American people is to get rich; the second how to retain good health. The first can be obtained by energy, honesty, and saving; the second by using Green August Flower".

Andrew Carnegie, in *The Dream of Success: A Study of the Modern American Imagination,* 1955. p. 158.

As a rule, there is more genuine satisfaction, a truer life, and more obtained from life in the humble cottages of the poor than in the palaces of the rich. I always pity the sons and daughters of rich men.

Benjamin Franklin, *Poor Richard Improved,* 1757, in *The American Gospel of Success,* 1965, pp. 34-35.

If we are industrious, we shall never starve; for, "At the working man's house hunger looks in but dares not enter." Nor will the bailiff nor the constable enter, for "Industry pays debts, while despair increaseth them." What though you have found no treasure, nor has any rich relation left you a legacy, "Diligence is the mother of good luck, and God gives all things to industry. Then plough deep while sluggards sleep, and you shall have corn to sell and to keep."

Ralph Waldo Emerson, "Wealth," in *The American Gospel of Success*, 1965, p. 40.

Every man is a consumer, and ought to be a producer. He fails to make his place good in the world unless he not only pays his debt but also adds something to the common wealth. Nor can he do justice to his genius without making some larger demand on the world than a bare subsistence. He is by constitution expensive, and needs to be rich.

John C. Van Dyke, *The Money God*, 1908, in *The Self-Made Man in America: The Myth of Rags to Riches*, 1954, p. 4.

Every one knows that success with the great masses spells money. It is money that the new generation expects to win, and it is money that the parents want them to win. The boy will make it, and the girl, if she is not a goose, will marry it. They will get it in one way or another.

William James, Letter to H. G. Wells, September 11, 1906.

The exclusive worship of the bitch-goddes SUCCESS . . . is our national disease.

Frederick W. Farrar, *Success in Life*, 1885, p. 21.

Analyze the elements of it, and you will see that success is identified to some extent with fame; still more with power; most of all, with wealth.

Ralph Waldo Emerson, in *The Dream of Success: A Study of the Modern American Imagination*, 1955, p. 75.

There is in America a general conviction in the minds of all mature men, that every young man of good faculty and good habits can by perseverance attain to an adequate estate; if he have a turn for business . . . he can come to wealth.

Cyril N. Parkinson, *In-Laws and Outlaws*, 1962, p. vii.

Books on how to succeed, of which this is the latest and best, are seldom in disagreement about what success can be taken to mean. The expression "to make good," as colloquially used, may not appeal (and in fact doesn't appeal) to the philosopher or moralist, but it has at least the merit of being understood. We know, roughly, what is meant. We picture the successful man as one with high office, secure future, untarnished repute and a good press; all gained or improved by his own effort. Our mental image shows successively the house by the lake, the mature garden, the daughter's jodhpurs and the Georgian silver. With change of focus we picture the paneled office, the shining desk, the expensive tailoring and the silent car. A last angle shot reveals the exclusive club, the central figure of the central group, the modest disclaimer of sincere applause. For what? Victory, promotion, honors or another son? All four perhaps. That is what success commonly means and that is the sense in which the term will here be used.

John G. Cawelti, *The Apostles of the Self-Made Man*, 1965, p. 46.

Under the stimulus of economic opportunity, the methods of enterprise and the figure of the successful businessman gradually eclipsed the Jeffersonian image of the democratic community with its natural aristocracy, and the ideal of the mobile society was dominated by the apolitical ethos of individual economic advancement.

Irvin G. Wyllie, *The Self-Made Man in America: They Myth of Rags to Riches*, 1954, pp. 26-27.

The first conclusion from these facts is that a man who wishes to succeed should select a country farm for his birthplace . . . . the sturdy, vigorous, hardy qualities - the stamina, the brawn, the grit which characterize men who do great things in this world are, as a rule, country bred . . . . our successful men do not feed themselves on boyhood cigarettes and late suppers, with loafing as their only labor . . .

Edward Pessen, Professor of History — New York University, *Riches, Class and Power Before the Civil War*, 1973, pp. 88-89.

The rags-to-riches ideology had so penetrated American thought during the [Jacksonian] era that men whose own publications contradicted the thesis, nevertheless, insisted it was true, often reaching conclusions at odds with the evidence . . . . Perhaps the most Pollyannish contemporary (mis) interpreter of biographical evidence was Freeman Hunt . . . according to Hunt, Stephan Girard [a successful merchant] had left his native country . . . in the capacity of a cabin boy, without education, excepting a limited knowledge of the elements of reading and writing. From this description one would hardly guess that the great merchant's father was a shipping merchant who "piled up a good-sized fortune and left a substantial inheritance to young Girard."

The historial reality:
the myth of the self-made man, 1830-1900.

Edward Pessen, Professor of History — New York University, *Three Centuries of Social Mobility in America*, 1974, p. 92.

Whatever the ultimate explanation, it seems clear that historians' belief in the most dramatic form of social mobility — the alleged leap from the bottom to the top in one generation — is untenable. The evidence . . . . indicates that the 'self-made man' — recently shown to have been more fantasy than fact during the post Civil War decade — was similarly a creature of the imagination a generation earlier, at the very time when the great Henry Clay was asserting the phantom's corporeality and ubiquitousness.

Irvin G. Wyllie, *The Self-Made Man in America: The Myth of Rags to Riches*, 1954, p. 24.

In his study of deceased American millionaires, mostly men of the last century, Pitirim Sorokin, for example, discovered that 38.8 percent of them started life poor. Another statistical study of the American business elite showed that 43 percent of those leaders who came to maturity around the year 1870 originated in the lower classes; they encountered fewer difficulties on their road from rags to riches than earlier or later generations.

Richard Wade, *The Urban Frontier*, 1959, p. 63

. . . . local boosters talked a great deal about equalitarianism in the West, but urban practice belied the theory. In the frontier towns social lines developed very quickly and although never drawn as tightly as in Eastern cities, they denoted meaningful distinctions . . . and a heightened sense of separateness . . . the circle [of the elite] becoming tighter and more distinct.

Lyman Abbott, Late Nineteenth-Century Clergyman, in *The Self-Made Man in America: The Myth of Rags to Riches*, 1954, p. 1.

The ambition to succeed may be and always ought to be a laudable one. It is the mainspring of activity; the driving wheel of industry; the spur to intellectual and moral progress. It gives the individual energy; the nation push. It makes us at once active and restless; industrious and overworked; generous and greedy. When it is great, it is a virtue; when it is petty, it is a vice.

Edward Pessen, Professor of History — New York University, *Jacksonian America: Society, Personality and Politics*, 1969, pp. 57-58.

Has the time not come, then, to discard the label, the Era of the Common Man? Like its companion designation, the Age of Egalitarianism, it has rested on questionable assumptions . . . . The absence of a caste system has been interpreted as though it denoted the absence of a class system. It is true that, theorectically, individuals could move freely up the social ladder, actually doing so if they had talent and good fortune. But these restless men on the make should not be confused with the bulk of the nation's workingmen or small farmers . . . whatever it might have been, the era named after Andrew Jackson was neither an age of egalitarianism nor of the common man.

A more modest definition of success
for the Nineteenth Century laborer

Stephan Thernstrom, Professor of History — Harvard University, *Poverty and Progress: Social Mobility in a Nineteenth Century City*, 1964, pp. 68-69.

Through the practice of industry and economy the working man could escape poverty and attain success. But what constituted success? Two answers can be found in the ideology of mobility. The more common defined success as mobility out of the status of manual laborer. To succeed was to move into a new type of job - as foreman, clerk, manager, professional or business: owner . . . a second definition held out a more modest reward to the enterprising laborer. Instead of asserting that the laborer was perfectly able to change his occupational status, this doctrine redefined status . . . The criterion became whether or not he owned property. Saving money was a prerequisite for occupational mobility, according to the first theory; to save money was itself a change in status, according to this one.

Stephan Thernstrom, Professor of History — Harvard University, *Poverty and Progress; Social Mobility in a Nineteenth Century City*, 1964, pp. 164-65.

The ordinary workmen of Newburyport, in short, could view America as a land of opportunity despite the fact that the class realities which governed their life chances confined most of them to the working class . . . Most of the social gains registered by the laborers during these years were decidedly modest — a move one notch up the occupational scale, the acquisition of a small amount of property. Yet in their eyes these accomplishments must have loomed large . . . . The "dream of success" certainly affected these laboring families, but the personal measure of success was modest. By this measure, the great majority of them had indeed "gotten ahead."

The Twentieth Century:
the dream of success as taken up by the immigrants, labor unions, professionals and the Federal Government.

John G. Cawelti, *The Apostles of the Self-Made Man*, 1965, p. 126.

. . . . from 1865 on, more and more Americans were immediately and directly affected by the two major social developments of the nineteenth century: the creation of more complex and more centralized social organizations (cities, corporations, and political institutions); and the growing importance of groups other than the native Protestant middle class of western European background . . . . . the ideal [of success] itself was transformed as it was taken up by the new groups and revised to meet new conditions and needs.

Irvin G. Wyllie, *The Self-Made Man in America: The Myth of Rags to Riches*, 1954, p. 143.

One of the fatal weaknesses of the self-help argument was that it explained everything in terms of inner qualities and nothing in terms of the environment . . . . by the turn of the century men less astute than Ward had begun to appreciate the relationship between opportunity and success. The rise of the great trusts helped to advertise, as nothing else could, that the average man's chances for success were less than they had been in the pioneering age of business. . .

John G. Cawelti, *The Apostles of the Self-Made Man*, 1965, p. 204.

Wilsonian and Rooseveltian social legislation was frequently based on the principle of self-help. The New Deal's early attempt at a planned economy . . .failed to establish itself in American life. Instead Americans preferred more indirect forms of social legislation, fearing that politically centered planning would restrict and discourage individual achievement. A graduated income tax, social security, minimum wages and hours and aid to education were the most in line with American attitudes. This type of social legislation tried to free the individual from abject poverty and illiteracy, giving him the possibility of competing with those who had the economic and cultural advantages of higher status.

John Tipple, *Crisis of the American Dream: A History of American Social Thought, 1920-1940,* 1968, p. 160.

Social control of business was blocked by an almost sacrosanct belief in individualism. From the beginning of the nation Americans had thought in terms of the individual, had distrusted government, had celebrated the virtues of an uncontrolled and unregulated economic system. No idea was more deeply ingrained in the minds of the people than the idea that the greatness of the nation, its prosperity and progress, was inextricably bound up with the efforts of those enterprising individuals who were shrewd enough to recognize economic opportunity and strong enough to take it.

The new breed of success:
the expert and the influence of education.

Irvin G. Wyllie, *The Self-Made Man in America: The Myth of Rags to Riches,* 1954, p. 139.

Within each calling there were specialists, and the man who aimed for the highest success had to cultivate one of these. Rural America had honored versatility, cherishing the jack of all trades above the expert, but the demands of urban life reversed this system of values. As business grew in size and complexity in the years after the Civil War the highly specialized man became the darling of the success cult.

John G. Cawelti, *The Apostles of the Self-Made Man,* 1965, p. 207.

Both the apprenticeship system and individual entrepreneurship, the major success strategies of the nineteenth century, had been largely superseded by formal education. Today's self-made man does not rise from the ranks; he is hired as an executive trainee on the basis of a college degree in business administration, engineering or economics. The office boy of Horatio Alger's day might have had some hope of rising to a partnership...today's office boy knows that a year at the Harvard Business School will do more for his career than a lifetime of industry, economy, temperance and piety.

Irvin G. Wyllie, *The Self-Made Man in America: The Myth of Rags to Riches,* 1954, p. 95.

Until the last decade of the nineteenth century the educational ideal of the business community embraced nothing more than common school training and a business apprenticeship. This was an ideal that squared with the facts of life....in pre-corporate days, pioneering business age sensible men did not expect managers and engineers to come ready made from schools...

The dream of success:
is it still a reality in today's world and for what groups in American society?

Robert Wiebe, Professor of History — Northwestern University, *The Segmented Soceity,* 1975, pp. 60-61.

For example, many modern dreams of success started with the realistic premise that only a miraculous intervention could place ordinary individuals in the highest reaches of American society. Character in the nineteenth century sense no longer helped; a leap to the top now, unlike that of a Horatio Alger hero, seemed to require a repudiation of everyday values, a rejection of the prudential maxims in favor of Hollywood promiscuity or Jet Set extravagance. Education, connections and social polish marked an upward route that either began at birth or rarely proceeded very far.

315

Car Degler, "Revolution without Ideology: The Changing Place of Women in America," *The American Past: A Social Record*, edited by Irvin Unger, 1971, p. 393.

If feminism is defined as the belief that women are entitled to the same opportunities for self expression as men, then America has harbored a feminist bias from the beginning. In both the 18th and 19th centuries foreign travellers remarked on the freedom for women in America....Lord Bryce wrote that in the United States: "It is easier for women to find a career, to obtain work of an intellectual and of a commercial kind than in any part of Europe."

R. Richard Wohl, "The Rags to Riches Story: An Episode of Secular Idealism," *Class, Status and Power: Social Stratification in Comparative Perspective*, edited by Reinhard Bendix and Seymour Martin Lipset, 1953, p. 394.

The Alger saga...has universal appeal. In all ages, the disadvantaged hero, struggling against odds, bearing witness to aspiration, but finally redeemed by success is a folk hero everywhere rejoiced in. It is not suprising therefore that a story cognate to this universal theme survives. All that was required for it to survive in association with Alger's name was that it was edited and revised to fit new conditions. In its modern version the smug congruity between the altered legend and the changed circumstances is achieved. The new hero is a slum boy making his way in the modern world.

Kenneth S. Lynn, *The Dream of Success: A Study of the Modern American Imagination*, 1955, p. 253.

In the complex multiverse which is the United States in the middle of the twentieth century, Alger's version of the success myth seems primitive and naive, hopelessly inadequate to the task of ordering and interpreting our social experience to ourselves. Alger preached the gospel that hard work was the *sine qua non* of success, yet in contemporary America the "Protestant ethic" has given way to personality-selling as the classic means of rising in the world.

Irvin G. Wyllie, *The Self-Made Man in America: The Myth of Rags to Riches*, 1954, pp. 151-152.

If the success ideology is examined in relation to its uses, it is apparent that it served many interests and purposes, not just one. On its progressive side it glorified material progress and inspired men to believe that they could enjoy salvation in this life as well as in the next. It encouraged the lowly to defy inherited orders of caste and custom, and to rise as far as their talents would allow. In keeping with the democratic faith it honored activity over repose, and judged merit on the basis of achievement. But on the other side the success gospel inspired material longings that could never be satisfied, except for a fortunate few...in America self-help represented both the mighty and the lowly, but it represented them unequally; in time, like men who try to serve two masters, it came to love the one and hate the other, to despise the one and hold to the other...

Martin Luther King, Jr., Speech at the Washington Monument during the March on Washington, August 28, 1963.

I say to you today, my friends, that in spite of the difficulties and frustrations of the moment I still have a dream. It is a dream deeply rooted in the American dream.

I have a dream that one day this nation will rise up and live out the true meaning of its creed: "We hold these truths to be self-evident; that all men are created equal."

I have a dream that one day on the red hills of Georgia the sons of former slaves and the sons of former slaveowners will be able to sit down together at the table of brotherhood.

I have a dream that one day even the state of Mississippi, a desert state sweltering with the heat of injustice and oppression, will be transformed into an oasis of freedom and justice.

I have a dream that my four little children will one day live in a nation where they will not be judged by the color of their skin but by the content of their character.

Selected Bibliography

Baltzell, E. Digby. *Philadelphia Gentlemen, The Making of a National Upper Class*. Glencoe, Illinois: Free Press, 1958.

Bendix, Reinhard, and Lipset, Seymour Martin, eds. *Class, Status and Power: Social Stratification in Comparative Perspective*. Glencoe, Illinois: Free Press, 1953.

Bendix, Reinhard, and Lipset, Seymour Martin. *Social Mobility in Industrial Society*. Berkeley, CA: University of California Press, 1959.

Boorstin, Daniel. *The Lost World of Thomas Jefferson*. Boston, Mass.: Beacon, Press, 1948.

Boorstin, Daniel. *The Image, or What Happened to the American Dream*. New York: Harper and Row, 1962.

Calhoun, Daniel H. *Professional Lives in America: Structure and Aspiration, 1750-1850*. Cambridge, Mass.: Harvard Univeristy Press, 1965.

Cawelti, John G. *Apostles of the Self-Made Man*. Chicago: The University of Chicago Press, 1965.

Curti, Merle. *The Growth of American Thought*. New York: Harper Press, 1951.

Dorfman, Joseph. *The Economic Mind in American Civilization*. New York: The Viking Press, 1949.

Fogel, Robert, and Engerman, Stanley L. *Time on The Cross: the Economics of American Negro Slavery*. Boston: Little and Brown, 1974.

Foner, Eric. *Free Soil, Free Labor, Free Men: The Ideology of the Republican Party before the Civil War*. New York: Oxford Univeristy Press, 1970.

Gabriel, Ralph. *The Course of American Democratic Thought*. New York: The Ronald Press, 1940.

Greven, Philip Jr. *Four Generations: Population, Land, and Family in Colonial Andover, Massachusetts*. Ithaca, New York: Cornell University Press, 1970.

Handlin, Oscar. *Boston's Immigrants*. Cambridge, Mass.: Harvard University Press, 1941.

Handlin, Oscar. *The Newcomers: Negroes and Puerto Ricans in a Changing Metropolis*. Cambridge, Mass.: Harvard University Press, 1959.

Harrington, Michael. *The Other America: Poverty in the United States*. New York: Macmillan, 1962.

Hays, Samuel. *The Response to Industrialism, 1885-1914*. Chicago: The University of Chicago Press, 1957.

Hofstadter, Richard. *The Age of Reform*. New York: Knopf, 1955.

Huber, Richard M. *The American Idea of Success*. New York: McGraw-Hill, 1971.

Lubove, Roy. *The Struggle for Social Security, 1900-1935*. Cambridge, Mass.: Harvard University Press, 1968.

Lynn, Kenneth. *The Dream of Success*. Boston: Little and Brown, 1955.

Main, Jackson. *The Social Structure of Revolutionary America*. Princeton, N.J.: Princeton University Press, 1965.

Meyer, Donald B. *The Positive Thinkers, A Study of the American Quest for Health, Wealth, and Personal Power from Mary Baker Eddy to Norman Vincent Peale*. Garden City, New York: Doubleday, 1965.

Miller, William, ed. *Men in Business: Essays on The Historical Role of the Entrepreneur*. New York: Harper and Brothers, 1962.

Pessen, Edward. *Riches, Class and Power before the Civil War*. Lexington, Mass.: Heath, 1973.

Pessen, Edward. *Three Centuries of Social Mobility in America*. Lexington, Mass.: Heath, 1974.

Pessen, Edward. *Jacksonian America: Society, Personality and Politics*. Homewood, Ill.: University of Illinois Press, 1969.

Potter, David. *People of Plenty*. Chicago: The University of Chicago Press, 1954.

Reissman, Leonard. *Inequality in American Society: Social Stratification*. Glenview, Ill.: Scott Foresman and Co., 1973.

Thernstrom, Stephan, and Sennett, Richard. *Nineteenth Century Cities: Essays on New Urban History*. New Haven, Conn.: Yale University Press, 1969.

Thernstrom, Stephan. *Poverty and Progress: Social Mobility in a Nineteenth Century City*. Cambridge, Mass.: Harvard University Press, 1964.

Thernstrom, Stephan. *The Other Bostonians: Poverty And Progress in the American Metropolis, 1880-1970*. Cambridge, Mass.: Harvard Univeristy Press, 1973.

Tipple, John. *Crisis of the American Dream: A History of American Social Thought, 1920-1940*. New York: Pegasus, 1968.

Unger, Irvin, ed. *The American Past: A Social Record, 1607 to the Present*. Waltham, Mass.: Xerox College Publications, 1971.

Wade, Richard. *The Urban Frontier*. Cambridge, Mass.: Harvard University Press, 1959.

Warner, W. L., and Abegglen. *Occupational Mobility In American Business and Industry, 1928-1952*. New York: Harper and Brothers, 1955.

Weiss, Richard. *The American Myth of Success; from Horatio Alger to Norman Vincent Peale*. New York: Basic Books, 1969.

Wiebe, Robert, *The Search for Order, 1877-1920*. New York: Hill and Wang, 1967.

Wiebe, Robert. *The Segmented Society*. New York: Oxford University Press, 1975.

Wyllie, Irvin G. *The Self-Made Man in America: The Myth of Rags to Riches*. Rutgers, N.J.: Rutgers University Press, 1954.

PREPARING FOR BYD EVENTS

PREPARING FOR BYD EVENTS

This section is designed to offer suggestions for participation in and preparation for BYD events. You will probably find some elements more useful than others. For example, you may already be familiar with research techniques as a result of your schoolwork, or you may have experience in delivering speeches through participation in forensic contests.

There are few hard-and-fast rules to follow in public speaking. The guidelines here represent ways to research, organize, analyze, and discuss a topic. If you are more comfortable with sound alternative approaches, by all means use them.

The sections on (1) Research, (2) Organization of Speeches, (3) Delivery, and (4) Attacking and Defending Ideas apply to all events, since these processes remain much the same whether an individual participates in Lincoln-Douglas Debate, Extemporaneous Speaking, or Persuasive Speaking. (Specific advice and instructions applying to each event are offered later in this section.)

In order to illustrate in a more concrete fashion the recommendations discussed below, a topic similar to those actually used in BYD events has been devised. The topic was drawn from the broad American Issues Forum area "The Government: The Growth of the Bureaucracy."

The hypothetical Debate resolution relating to the bureaucracy issue area is: "Resolved: That in America, the federal government has traditionally delegated excessive authority to non-elected officials." The Extemporaneous Speaking version of the same hypothetical topic is: "Has the federal government traditionally delegated excessive authority to non-elected officials?" The Persuasive Speaking construction of the topic is: "Democracy and bureaucracy: Has America delegated excessive authority to non-elected officials?" (Note: In order to simplify the illustrations below, hypothetical Lincoln-Douglas Debate, Extemporaneous Speaking, and Persuasive Speaking topics were drawn from the same issue area. Normally, topics for each BYD event will be drawn from more discrete issue areas.)

RESEARCH

General Approach to the Subject Area Participants in BYD events are unlikely to have conducted advanced research in the subject areas from which topics are drawn. Hence, participants will want to begin their research efforts with general reading about the topic.

Research will be most productive if you conduct it with an open mind. BYD participants should heed the counsel of Benjamin Disraeli, who a century ago was Prime Minister of Great Britain and an eminent orator: "To be conscious that you are ignorant is a great step to knowledge." By researching the topic area without a biased frame of mind, you will discover many new ideas, gain a more sophisticated understanding of familiar ideas, and obtain entirely new perspectives for analyzing the subject area. Although new arguments and evidence should be evaluated critically, you should be careful not to reject arguments or evidence merely because you personally hold a different viewpoint. While a researcher is entitled to his own opinion, that opinion may be wrong; and it is difficult to know whether an opinion is right or wrong until conflicting evidence is weighed objectively.

Background Research: Sources Most BYD participants will wish to obtain a broad overview of America's past before conducting research on a particular subject area. One way to accomplish this is to read relevant portions of history textbooks. Examples of some of the better texts include:

Bailey, Thomas A., *American Pageant* (4th ed., 1970).
Caughey, John W., and Ernest R. May, *A History of the United States* (1974).
Garraty, John A., *The American Nation* (2nd ed., 1971).
Morison, Samuel E., Henry S. Commager, and William E. Leuchtenburg, *Growth of the American Republic* (6th ed., 2 vols., 1969).
Sellers, Charles G., and Henry May, *A Synopsis of American History* (2nd ed., 1969).

You will want to consult the subject headings in the card catalogs of your school and/or municipal library to find books written about your research topics. (On the bureaucracy topic, for example, you would check under such headings as "Bureaucracy," "History, U.S.—Bureaucracy," "Regulatory Agencies," and more specific topics related to special aspects of your research.) Try using a college or university library if possible—they usually have more material available than other libraries. Even if you do not attend such an institution and are unable to check books out, usually you can work in the library with research materials.

In order to get an overview of particular subjects and the available literature pertaining to them, you may want to use some of the following encyclopedias and bibliographic sources.

Carruth, Gorton, et al., eds., *Encyclopedia of American Facts and Dates* (4th ed., 1965).
Cochran, Thomas C., and Wayne Andrews, eds., *Concise Dictionary of American History* (1962).
Encyclopedia Americana.
Encyclopedia Britannica.
Freidel, Frank, ed., *Harvard Guide to American History* (rev. ed., 1974). Includes bibliographies on the major topics in American history.
Morris, Richard B., ed., *Encyclopedia of American History* (rev. ed., 1965).
Mugridge, Donald H., and Blanche P. McCrum, *A Guide to the Study of the United States of America* (1960). Includes bibliographies of materials published prior to 1958.
Webster's Guide to American History (1971).

In several important ways, research for BYD topics differs from research for the usual questions of policy posed in most competitive debates. Since typical debate topics involve proposed changes in current approaches to contemporary problems, they require an examination of the most recently available evidence.

On the other hand, questions of history and value have a timeless quality. Historical interpretations and a nation's values change slowly, minimizing the advantage of recency in research material. Furthermore, discussions of historical issues are rarely found in newspapers and popular periodicals—publications live by today's headlines.

Thus, such standard library resources as the *Reader's Guide to Periodical Literature* and the indexes to newspapers are less useful for those researching the historical and value questions posed by the BYD than they would be for other purposes.

Note-Taking It is recommended that participants in BYD events use the "file-card system" of note-taking. There are several advantages to this method. Facts and authoritative conclusions can quickly be found in such a file to support specific points the speaker will make in his speech. The organization of the speaker's research following the lines of analysis he wishes to employ is relatively easy, and reorganization according to new lines of analysis is also facilitated. The strengths and weaknesses of evidential support for the speaker's various arguments are readily apparent.

The following guidelines should be followed in setting up a file-card system for collection of research (see below for sample):

— Select a uniform file-card size (4" x 6" cards are most commonly used).
— Fully cite the source of the evidence on each card (1).
— Limit each card to a single analytical point documented by a single research source.
— Quote verbatim where possible; take special care not to distort the position of a source in any paraphrase (2).
— Place an idea heading at the top of the card which corresponds to the argument heading under which it is filed (3).
— Organize the cards in a file according to major and subordinate issues.

(3) →
(1) →
(2) →

> NEED FOR REGULATORY AGENCIES: RAILROADS PRIOR TO ICC
>
> John A. Garraty, Professor of History—Columbia University, *The American Nation*, 1966, p. 510.
>
> "Although cheap transportation stimulated the economy, few persons really benefitted from cutthroat competition (in the railroads). ...The instability of rates troubled even interests like the middle western flour millers who benefitted from the competitive situation, for it hampered planning...Probably the worst sufferers were the roads themselves. ...In 1876 two-fifths of all railroads were in default; three years later 65 lines were bankrupt."

Background Research: Approach Throughout your background reading, you will want to consider concepts and theories that can serve to organize your thoughts. A little practice will demonstrate that this is not as difficult as it may sound—the process will give you the framework with which to consider in a more systematic, complete, and useful fashion many of the ideas that would have occurred to you anyway.

Background research can be productively pursued through a variety of approaches; thus you need not employ the procedures described below. However, you might want to consider the same types of questions if you choose another approach. The following steps offer one thorough method of analyzing a topic through your research.

(1) *Interpretation of the topic*
    A. What are the various ways in which the topic can be interpreted?
    B. What historical problems does the topic address? (Consider categories of related ideas.)

(2) *Research into historical background*
    A. What is the factual context of the historical issue?
       Which groups of people were involved?
       Which institutions were involved?
       What were the major events?
       What were the important trends?
    B. How are these facts explained?
       Why did history happen as it did? (What causes underlie historical developments?)
       Were the causes of historical developments beyond our control?

Remember: the facts (2A) have little meaning unless you consider explanations for them (2B).

Many BYD topics will be questions of historical fact. For these topics, your primary objectives will be to (1) gain a full understanding of the topic's meaning; and (2) research into the facts and causes of facts in order to properly address these topics. If the bureaucracy debate topic were phrased, "Resolved: That the federal government has traditionally delegated *significant* authority to non-elected officials," the topic would be a question of historical fact. Since the topic was phrased "Resolved: That the federal government has traditionally delegated *excessive* authority to non-elected officials," the topic is also a question of value—it requires the speaker to identify delegation of authority which is "excessive." What is "excessive" and what is not depends upon a particular framework of values which the speaker must defend or attack. This involves the following step:

(3) *Relating value to fact*
    A. What values were responsible for the historical developments? Are different values today responsible for the perpetuation of these developments?
    B. What values justified or opposed the historical development? Do different values today justify or oppose these developments?
    C. Which value should be or should have been considered higher values?

You should be aware that the term "value" is not used in any precise technical sense here. We include within the meaning of "value" that which might be called "attitude" in other contexts. The term "value" in this *Guide* is used in a broad sense; it includes core values and the attitudes which derive from them.

Background Research: An Illustration You may wish to check whether or not you understand these analytical steps by applying them to a sample topic, such as delegation of authority to non-elected officials.

STEP 1A: Interpretation of the Topic. Look for various interpretations of the topic. Note the phrase "federal government"—this prevents consideration of the delegation of authority by state and local governments. The term "traditionally" requires that *historical* rather than chiefly contemporary delegations of authority be examined. This definition leaves questions to be resolved. Is a historical problem one that applies to every period of American history, or only to selected periods? If a problem has been prominent only during the last fifty years, or was prominent only during the 19th century, can we call it a "traditional" problem? Now consider the term "delegated." Upon checking the dictionary and thinking about common usages of the term, you would probably see that "delegated" might reasonably be considered an "active" or a "passive" term. That is, it applies to specific acts by which the federal government grants greather authority to a non-elected official; *or* it applies to cases in which the federal government fails to prevent some agent from representing the United States, whether or not a specific law or decree acknowledges this action. "Authority" embraces such distinct ideas as power, legal right, and freedom to perform certain actions. You would want to consider the extent to which these concepts overlap. For example, often the power to act in a pragmatic sense does not necessarily imply the authority to do so in a legal sense. The Defense Department (or some other agency) may have usurped power in a number of policy areas due to the inaction of elected officials, yet may never have been delegated the authority to set such policy. The term "non-elected officials" is certainly broad. It includes Cabinet-level bureaucracy—the Department of Agriculture, the Department of State, the Department of Defense, and so forth. It also includes federal regulatory agencies—the Interstate Commerce Commission, the Federal Communications Commission, the Securities and Exchange Commission, and others. Does it not also include judicial officers? and presidential and congressional staff aides? With a little imagination, you can come up with other categories.

STEP 1B: Historical Problems Addressed by the Topic. Some problems which seem to pertain to the topic are not really *historical* problems, and hence are inappropriate for speeches in BYD events. An example might be the delegation of authority to congressional and presidential staffers. While some observers feel that the great power these groups have obtained presents a serious problem for democratic government, most of the examples proving this are from the last two decades. (You would need to do a little research to verify this, of course.) The issue of judicial power, on the other hand, goes back to the early days of the Republic, when Chief Justice John Marshall and his court established the principle of judicial review. (Judicial review of constitutionality was only inferred from the Constitution—it was never explicitly mentioned as a prerogative of the courts.) Throughout American history, the Supreme Court has reached decisions which were at variance with laws passed by elected officials, frequently with significant ramifications for the nation. The bureaucracy problem is also very old—as old as the United States itself. The most serious manifestations of the bureaucracy problem have surfaced during the last century. As America began to rapidly expand her responsibilities for the social welfare of the citizenry, the size and power of the bureaucracy rose proportionately. A regulatory agency was established at about the same time to check the enormous power of the railroads; creation of other regulatory agencies soon followed.

If you planned to enter Persuasive Speaking event, at this point you could choose one of these areas (or another area entirely) as the subject of your speech. You would carry out steps 2 and 3—evaluating fact and value—just for that particular area. If you planned to enter the Extemporaneous Speaking or Debate events, you would want a broader knowledge of the topic. You would therefore conduct steps 2 and 3 for each major subject area pertaining to the topic.

STEP 2: Research into Historical Background. This research step involves a fairly detailed explanation of specific facts and explanations of facts. "Who, what, when, where, and why" questions come naturally and readily to mind even among novice researchers; these are the questions you should and would probably ask. However, in order to suggest the process involved, a sample answer will be provided to illustrate the "why" questions—the explanations behind the fact.

One explanation for the vastly increased power of the bureaucracy is the growing commitment of government to programs in specialized and technical fields. It is argued that politicians cannot possess a detailed working knowledge of all or even most of the complex technological and social problems confronting modern America. Career bureaucrats, who through training and years of experience have a much more intimate knowledge of a particular problem area, are said to be much more qualified than politicians to set policy in many areas. Hence, elected officials have felt the need to delegate more and more policy-making authority to non-elected officials.

Another explanation for the increased power of the bureaucracy is the growing role of the federal government in American life. The federal government has become deeply involved in virtually every important area of American endeavor: social services such as education, welfare, employment, police protection, and health; military security; business, industry, and trade; and countless others. How could we expect the few hundred officials elected at the federal level (the President, Vice President, and members of Congress) to directly control all of this activity? Only two alternatives could have prevented the increase in the power of non-elected officials which took place during the last century. The nation might have decided to elect thousands of officials throughout the bureaucracy (a proposal of very dubious feasibility); or we might have forced government to substantially limit its operations.

STEP 3: Relating Fact to Value. What are the competing values supporting or opposing delegation of so much power to non-elected officials? You can discover these values either by researching or by examining for yourself the assumptions behind the historical interpretations found in Step 2.

There is an assumption implicit in the first causal explanation offered above—namely, that non-elected officials should make policy because of their specialized expertise. This means that greater *effectiveness* in government programs is worth some sacrifice in democratic ideals. Can you think of arguments which could be used to attack or defend this assumption?

The second causal explanation—that an increase in bureaucratic power was necessitated by an expanded governmental role—assumes that government *commitment* to social and economic programs is worth some sacrifice in democratic principles. Let us examine this assumption in greater detail.

Some observers would not be convinced that this explanation justifies expanded power for non-elected officials. They might agree strongly with some or all of the following value statements. "Government should interfere with the lives of its citizens as little as possible." "The exercise of governmental power threatens individual liberty." "The programs of government are doomed to error and folly since man, who is imbued with natural error and folly, must run governments." "Men should be treated unequally." "It is better to reward and encourage excellence." As you can see, since these values are based on a pessimistic view of man's ability to govern others responsibly and effectively, restraint of society's power is considered desirable. The result of such a value framework would be the view that government programs are dangerous, usually unsuccessful, and based on a mistaken understanding of human nature.

On the other hand, some or all of the following value statements might be used to support the expanded role of the federal government in modern life. "Government action benefits all citizens; it is better to require a small sacrifice of individualism than to bypass the benefits of collective action." "Government must perform certain social functions because individuals cannot or will not perform them (for example, restraint of monopolistic business activity and control of the economy)." "All men are created equal." "Government should assure an equal chance for all citizens to pursue the fruits of life." "Rich and powerful groups do not maintain their power by fair means." "Government should strive to reduce the suffering and increase the happiness of its citizens." These statements view government action as a necessary and desirable method of redressing inequality and fostering benefits for most or all citizens. The proponents of such a view would support an expanded, active governmental role.

Notice that these conflicting values apply most directly to the question of whether government should be active or passive, whether policy is set by elected or non-elected officials. A further assumption is required to link this idea to the topic on delegation of authority to non-elected officials. We must assume that *active* governments always delegate vast authority to non-elected officials—that it is impractical for a truly active government to be run exclusively by elected officials.

Background Research: A Final Word It will take some thought and a little time to pose the right questions with which to consider a particular historical question of value. However, you should not be intimidated by this process—with a little practice it will become quite natural. Your effort will be rewarded many times over by greater efficiency in your research, better argumentation, and clearer thinking about the topic.

Specific Investigations within a Subject Area Once a general background has been established, specific research within the subject area can begin. This involves: (1) reformulation of the issues on the topic in light of new facts and theories you discover and (2) research into specific sub-issues to fill gaps in your knowledge and collection of evidence.

If your background questions have been properly formulated, your research will lead to a rapid expansion of your knowledge about the topic area. The next step will be to gain an understanding of the issues as they might actually be developed in a speech. This requires that you refine your background questions, adapting them specifically to the arguments you have discovered. The strengths and weaknesses of arguments will be revealed in this way. (Much of the success of your issue analysis may depend upon your familiarity with the tests of reasoning and evidence, discussed in the Attacking and Defending Ideas section.)

Consider an example from our hypothetical topic on bureaucracy. One of our background questions asked which values supported the extension of greater authority to non-elected officials. As has been indicated, one such value is expertise in government.

Your questions about this argument should examine its basic assumptions. Do politicians have expertise in the important areas of public policy? Does the Congressional committee system, for example, provide the specialization needed for politicians to deal with particular problem areas? On the other hand, is the level of expertise in the bureaucracy really so superior? In those instances in which bureaucracy was given a large measure of independence from political pressures, was public policy improved?

Furthermore, do we have methods of tapping bureaucratic expertise already? Does legislation frequently set broad guidelines for policy, while leaving many of the details of implementation to the bureaucracy? And do bureaucrats have many opportunities to air their views, in construction of the Presidential budget, in Congressional hearings, and elsewhere?

Finally, how do we balance the need for expertise in government against other values? Is it better to sacrifice democratic principles than to live with government programs that do not work very well?

The answers to many of these questions can only be found through research. You will want to concentrate your research at this point on those areas in which you need additional evidence. For example, if you have good evidence on the level of expertise in Congress and the bureaucracy, but no evidence discussing methods of tapping bureaucratic expertise, you will want to concentrate your research efforts on the latter area. This is done by looking for titles of articles and book chapters which seem likely to discuss these issues. In addition, you will not want to record evidence on arguments you can already thoroughly prove unless it is clearly superior to that which you have already recorded.

ORGANIZATION OF SPEECHES

Purpose Several purposes are served by proper organization of a speech. First, the process of organizing the speech forces the speaker to analyze his subject carefully. Second, a well-organized approach allows the speaker to communicate his theme effectively. Unlike a written essay, which the reader is at liberty to reread or to read with special care, a speech must be understood on its first hearing. In order for an oral message to be comprehensibile, its major points must be stated with simplicity, clarity, and logical consistency. Finally, organization permits the speaker to identify the points where emotional peaks can be elicited. Good organization will focus the attention of the audience on these points to provide additional emphasis and greater understanding of the overall message.

The Opening A critical function of the opening is to attract the interest of the audience to your presentation. Another important function is to introduce the topic, previewing the message that will follow. The manner in which this is done depends partly on the likelihood that your audience will accept the message. If the audience is likely to accept or be indifferent to the message, the thesis can be placed in the opening. If it is likely that your thesis will be immediately rejected, it is usually advisable to establish your credibility in the opening by emphasizing areas of agreement about ideas relevant to your thesis, while saving the thesis statement for the conclusion of your speech.

There are many types of openings suitable to the speeches delivered in BYD events. A quotation, a rhetorical question, an interesting statistic, a brief true story, or a short poem are example. A much underemphasized method of introuduction is the humorous story or statement. Humor, when appropriately and skillfully incorporated into a speech, gains the attention and interest of the audience while increasing the appeal of the message.

Body of the Speech The central purpose of organizing the body of the speech is to provide the audience with reasons to adopt your thesis. Outlining is an invaluable aid to both the speaker and the audience. An outline forces you to identify the major analytical points in your speech, together with subordinate analysis and proof. It also exposes flaws, inconsistencies, and redundancies in your reasoning, permitting you to correct these errors before you actually begin composing the speech. Most importantly, the audience is unlikely to follow your reasoning process unless the speech is presented in a variation of the outline format. Only by identifying your key points and supporting them with subordinate points can you expect an audience to understand and remember the crucial ideas in your speech. Since you will want to present your ideas in outline form anyway, you should precede the composition of the speech with construction of an outline. The techniques of outlining are not difficult to learn. Several steps are involved:

(1) *Determine the purpose of your speech.* You must know whether you are presenting a speech which primarily addresses a question of historical fact or a question of value and historical fact. Most BYD topics are questions of value and fact—they require you to use history to advance your ideas in terms of a value or values which are defended as superior to other values. Such topics ask implicitly, is X better than Y? Some BYD topics will be questions of fact; these will require that you support or attack a proposed interpretation of historical events or propose your own description of events. Such topics ask, did X occur? or, can you describe X?

(2) *Determine which main arguments about the topic are strongest.* This step is a natural extension of your research. Recall that in the Specific Investigations section of your research, you used the tools from the Attacking and Defending Ideas section to determine the merits of various arguments, and conducted supplemental research in promising areas which were inadequately supported by evidence in your file.

Now you can again determine which arguments have the greatest logical and evidential support. Remember, a speaker has an obligation to present the strongest arguments in support of his position.

For questions of value, you will want to select one or more values as a basis for your analysis as well as other arguments offering historical explanation of the merits of your value(s). For questions of historical fact, you need only to select statements of fact and explanations of fact as your main arguments.

On the hypothetical, value-laden bureaucracy topic, we might conclude that the following arguments are strongly supported in your research.

Statements of value:
Delegation of authority to non-elected officials should not be allowed to thwart the popular will.
Delegation of authority to non-elected officials should not lead to a deprivation of individual rights.
Delegation of authority to non-elected officials should not foster policies responsive only to the needs of special interest groups.

325

Statements of fact or explanation:
  Non-elected officials traditionally have not been controlled by elected officials.
  Non-elected officials set much national policy.
  Non-elected officials create policy which deprives individuals of rights to due process, privacy, and equal
    protection under the law.
  Non-elected officials often create policy which remains rigid in the face of changing needs.
  Non-elected officials create policy which increases costs for the taxpayer.
  Non-elected officials often thwart policies of elected officials.

(3) *Develop a thesis statement.* The thesis statement is a one-sentence summary of the central idea in a speech. (If you cannot summarize your speech in one sentence, the idea behind it may not be thought out well enough.) The thesis is devised by keeping in mind (a) the purpose of your speech and (b) your strongest arguments.

In the case of our hypothetical topic on the authority delegated to non-elected officials, one possible thesis statement would be: "Delegation of excessive policy-making authority to non-elected officials has interfered with the most fundamental democratic value: the responsiveness of government to the will of the majority."

(4) *Select the best 2-5 main ideas supporting the thesis.* You should choose statements at this point which are related to one another, which are related to the thesis, and which are discrete (i.e., their meanings do not overlap). A question of value requires that you defend at least one value in your presentation, while value judgments are peripheral to questions of historical fact.

Here, you must discard good ideas that are unrelated to the thesis. Solid but irrelevant ideas will only confuse the audience. They should not persuade anyone to accept your central idea.

We might choose the following main ideas on the bureaucracy question.
1. In a democracy, elected officials should make policy.
2. In America, non-elected officials have been granted vast policy-making power.
3. Policy-making by non-elected officials is harmful to democratic ideals.

Notice that the three ideas progress logically. Did you correctly identify the value statement? It was statement number one, which said that something "should" happen, whether or not it actually has happened. Statement number two is a statement of fact; number three incorporates fact and value elements.

(5) *Outline the speech.* In this step, you provide the links in reasoning behind each of the main statements. Several principles are useful in outlining. These include:

Progression of ideas— the development of a logical series of statements which, if true, lead to a particular conclusion.

Subordination—whenever more than one step or concept is used to explain or prove a main statement, these ideas are clearly identified by a statement which is assigned a letter. This gives the outline its characteristic structure (see the example below).

Discreteness—each major point should address a single idea not developed under another major point. Main arguments which violate this principle overlap in content, confusing the audience. The principle of discreteness should also be observed within each subordinate level of analysis.

Clarity—the headings (argument labels) throughout the outline should be simple, brief, and easily understandable. Many members of the audience will listen to the speeches without taking notes; it is extremely unlikely that they will remember your major arguments unless you give them clear labels. Other members of the audience will take notes while they listen. Note-takers will be much less likely to miss the major points in your speech if you label them.

Enumeration, Repetition, and Parallels—These techniques make your points much easier to understand and remember. Enumeration of several points attacking or defending the same idea is easy, since it requires no modifications in your choice of words for argument labels. Repetition of main points during a speech lends special emphasis and greatly aids note-taking. Parallels are easy to remember, since few words are changed during a progression of ideas. Parallels are often rhetorically appealing.

The Conclusion The conclusion gives you a final opportunity to convey your crucial ideas to the audience. A re-explanation of the development of your thesis or a summary of your main points, a final dramatic example supporting your thesis, or an eloquent summary statement are typical conclusions.

Below is a sample outline for a speech on the delegation of authority to non-elected officials.

Speech Outline

I. In a democracy, elected officials should make public policy.
    A. Democratic government should reflect the popular will.
    B. Democratic elections manifest the popular will.
    C. Elected officials are responsive to the popular will.

II. In America, non-elected officials have been granted vast policy-making power.
    A. Regulatory commissions have been granted statutory autonomy.
       —e.g., Interstate Commerce Commission (established in 1887).
    B. Cabinet-level bureaucracy has secured de facto autonomy.
       —e.g., Department of State.
    C. The Judiciary has usurped legislative authority.
       —e.g., Chief Justice Marshall's precedents establishing judicial review power.
       —e.g., Pattern of overturning of social legislation, 1880-1940.

III. Policy-making by non-elected officials is harmful to democratic ideals.
    A. Non-elected officials are unaccountable to the popular will.
    B. Bureaucracy responds to special interest groups.
    C. Bureaucracy thwarts the interests of the majority.

The Final Product Whether you speak from a prepared text (as in Persuasive Speaking or parts of Lincoln-Douglas Debate) or directly from an outline, you will want to remember two features of a well-constructed speech. First, you should spend proportionately more time on what you identify as critical arguments. In general, arguments which are most central to the thesis, most in conflict with popular belief, most complex and/or most in need of extensive proof may be considered critical.

Another feature of a well-constructed speech is the use of appropriate transitions. These summarize the ideas preceding the transition and identify the speaker's place in his progression of ideas.

A detailed outline is the skeleton of a speech. If you can construct a good, logical outline for your speech, you will probably find that the development of individual ideas will come easily.

DELIVERY

A style of delivery which demonstrates an authentic desire to communicate and attractive personal qualities will draw interest, facilitate understanding, and ultimately—persuade. There are no firm rules which, if followed, will result in an appealing performance. However, there are a few principles and techniques which may prove to be helpful when attempting productive oral expression.

Natural Delivery Intentionally or not, personality traits are reflected in every public address. The better speaker develops a natural mode of delivery by capitalizing on individual strengths, such as a sincere manner, an analytical mind, or a good sense of humor. On the other hand, an inappropriate style, whether it be timid or bombastic, implies that the speaker lacks self-control and will lessen the persuasive appeal of the message. An effective communicator avoids displaying these unattractive qualities without rendering a stilted recitation of information. Similarly, a good speaker avoids excessive reliance on notes or a prepared text.

You should try to present a composed, confident image to the audience. This will become easier with practice and experience. It is worth remembering that your audience is not hostile, but is inclined to accept any reasonable idea which you might submit to them. What may appear to you to be serious mistakes—short stutters or improper word choices—will hardly be noticed by listeners.

If you are well prepared and know what you want to say, then you can concentrate on sharing your ideas with the audience. By focusing your energies on the thought behind your words, you will become less nervous and your message will be more directly and honestly communicated to listeners.

A speech involves several avenues of communication. Expression occurs not only through words but through voice qualities, gestures, and eye contact. Each element of the presentation provides an opportunity to interest the audience and promote your idea. Variety is an important component of natural delivery. Utilization of the complete range of these communication channels keeps the presentation fresh and permits emphasis of major points.

Word Choice and Sentence Structure Unlike written statements, the spoken word cannot be reviewed at leisure. Instantaneous comprehension is essential. Oral communication is most readily understood when it consists of concise statements, vivid expressions, and familiar vocabulary. The audience will find a variety of expressions to be more interesting than those which are trite or clichéd; grandiose words and verbose sentences tend to confuse rather than impress. Shorter phrases and concrete terms are easier to understand and remember. For example, a speaker flaunting imaginative vocabulary in a self-defeating attempt to appear eloquent might say: "The hordes of faceless potentates haunting the corridors of official Washington have shamelessly trampled on our dearest and most sacred liberties." A more concise and informative expression of the same idea is: "Federal bureaucrats have repeatedly violated the constitutional rights of due process, privacy, and equal protection."

Metaphors, similes, epigrams, and other types of figurative language will assist in getting a point across. Consider which method in the following illustration best expresses the idea. A speaker might describe American foreign policy in the early twentieth century as a dual faceted approach which involved: (1) maintenance of low profile designed to avoid needlessly antagonizing enemies and allies alike; and (2) deterrence of other nations from interfering with American interests by threat of forceful retaliation. President Theodore Roosevelt put it more simply: "Speak softly and carry a big stick." Hopefully you have noticed that the frequent use of examples is another way of explaining abstract concepts in understandable, concrete terms.

Voice Of course it is necessary that words be clearly enunciated, but your voice can contribute much more. Key phrases can be emphasized by fluctuations in tone, volume, or the rate of speaking. Since the tone of voice expresses your interest in the topic and the audience, its effective use is a method of generating contagious enthusiasm. You might also reinforce the organization of the speech by making tonal distinctions when entering transitions or when discussing a new concept.

Dramatic impact is heightened by alterations in volume. A common device involves building to a moderately loud volume and at the peak of a dramatic climax suddenly dropping into a loud stage whisper.

Changes in the rate of delivery can bring about a similar effect. To stress a particularly critical statement, you might pause before beginning the sentence, and then speak quite slowly, taking care to pronounce completely each word. Less important parts of the address may be presented more rapidly.

However, an extreme rate or volume will be distracting if not a complete bar to reception. A successful speaker gives a varied, but balanced, presentation using reasonable fluctuations from the norm to attract and focus attention.

Gesture and Body Movement Spontaneous gestures and movements enhance the naturalness of a good delivery. Since these are not subjects of conscious attention in daily conversation, you might want to study the range and type of gestures which might be employed. Through observation of oneself and others, it should be possible to discover some comfortable gestures which can be used to accentuate a point. A few well-timed steps may also serve the same purpose.

Public speakers have a tendency to raise their hand to gesture and then not fully retract it. To avoid this distracting habit, hands should rest at your sides when not in use. Intentional gestures and motions will enhance communication, but unconscious fiddling with objects, slouching, or swaying will have the opposite effect.

Eye Contact When addressing more than a few people, the personal contact of more intimate communication is lost. One practice which minimizes this effect is the establishment of eye contact. If the audience is small, you should look at each member of it. When speaking before a large group, it is important to view each section of the audience. Try not to stare for too long at any one person. A better approach is to go smoothly from person to person, momentarily establishing contact and then moving on without recognizable pattern. In so doing you will relate to the audience on a more individual basis. Feedback is also received in this way. Perhaps listeners look puzzled because a point is not coming across. You will find out and have a chance to try another means of explanation.

A Final Note Do not forget that good delivery should enhance communication. It is not an end in itself. The audience may remember how funny you were or how dramatic your voice and language were, and still not be persuaded to accept the basic concept of your speech.

ATTACKING AND DEFENDING IDEAS

This section will discuss valid methods of reasoning; methods of reasoning used in refutation; forms of proof; and the construction of arguments.

Valid Methods of Reasoning There are at least two fundamental and distinct methods of reasoning. You have undoubtedly used both of these methods many times whether you know their names or uses.

1) *Example to Principle* This type of reasoning involves the use of specific examples to draw a general conclusion. Reasoning from the specific to the general corresponds to the method of science (called inductive reasoning).

In order to illustrate the use of this form of reasoning in BYD events, suppose you were working on the extemporaneous speaking topic from Issue III on the changing meaning of the statement, "All men are created equal." You might want to approach this topic by examining each period of American history to determine the extent to which Americans have been treated equally in the political, social, and economic spheres. You might note, for example, that property requirements for voting were eliminated and the status of the common man rose generally in the early decades of the Republic; slavery was eliminated and the first steps toward racial equality were taken after the Civil War; new ethnic groups were assimilated during the nation's industrialization in the late 19th and early 20th centuries; women were guaranteed the vote by the Constitutional amendment of 1920; the Civil Rights Movement began in the mid-1950's. From such evidence, you might reach the conclusion that America has step by step moved towards a realization of the statement, "All men are created equal," during the course of her history. This conclusion is a generalization induced from many examples.

2) *Principle to Example* This type of reasoning begins with one or more statements which are assumed to be true and deduces conclusions from them. Reasoning from the general to the specific, or from principles to other principles, corresponds to the methods of mathematics and philosophy (called deductive reasoning). This type of reasoning is employed less frequently than the first type, since few general principles are universally accepted as truth. Value statements may serve as principles from which other ideas may be inferred.

For example, "In a democracy, elected officials should make all major policy." It follows naturally from this statement that non-elected officials should not make major policy in a democracy. It also follows that democratic principles are violated when non-elected officials make major policy. Therefore, if non-elected officials have made major economic policy (for example, the Federal Reserve Board's control of money supplies and interest rates), democratic principles were violated in those instances.

3) *Combined Approach* Probably the most common method of reasoning in public speaking combines both of the previous methods. This involves proof of a general proposition and illustration of the proposition through specific examples.

For instance, the speaker may first prove the validity of the general statement, "Populist political parties have been an important progressive influence on American government." This can be proven by a quotation from authority and from an explanation of the manner in which progressive influence can be manifested. Then, the principle can be made concrete through examples of specific populist parties which have had a major impact. Without the examples, the principle would lack concreteness and force. Without proof of the principle, the examples alone might seem insufficient to prove your point.

Methods of Reasoning Used in Refutation The following methods of reasoning deserve special attention from participants in BYD events. They can be very effective persuasive tools when skillfully employed, yet these techniques are used far too infrequently by public speakers.

1) *Turning the Tables*—accepting the validity of an argument or piece of evidence and then demonstrating that the argument or evidence actually supports the opposite conclusion from that which was intended. Suppose that the affirmative speaker, in a Lincoln-Douglas debate on the bureaucracy question, claimed that non-elected officials who are granted independent policy-making authority often act against the public interest. The speaker may cite as an example the Federal Reserve Board, which has a great deal of control over the economy through manipulation of interest rates and the money supply. It might be claimed that FRB policies have thrown the nation into a recession several times. The negative speaker may decide to admit that FRB policies have caused recessions and attempt to turn the tables. First, he may offer proof that FRB policies have been necessitated by rates of inflation so high that the nation was forced to swallow the bitter medicine of recession. Second, he may suggest that the inflationary episodes were caused by the failure of elected officials to adopt unpopular anti-inflationary measures restricting government spending. In other words, the FRB example would prove that non-elected officials have acted more responsibily than elected officials in the area of economic policy.

2) *Reductio ad absurdum*—"reducing to absurdity," which means to show that an argument is foolish by carrying out its reasoning to a logical conclusion. Example: Suppose that you were delivering an extemporaneous speech on the topic, "What should be the role of compromise in Congress?" You might wish to examine

the extreme view that elected officials should never compromise their principles by reducing this belief to absurdity. Suppose each of our 535 Representatives and Senators decided to fight to the bitter end on each question of importance. Normally several, perhaps even several dozen, different bills will be introduced to deal with a given problem of current importance, and amendments will be proposed to bills reaching the floor. If every legislator felt compelled to reject every bill that in some way conflicted with his own version of the best solution, how often could enough consensus be reached to create legislation? What chaos would reign if legislators in the minority felt the necessity to block alternative approaches with all the procedural means at their disposal? Evidence showing that no initial consensus existed for many historically vital pieces of legislation would be persuasive here.

3) _Contradiction_—presentation of arguments or evidence which cannot both be true at the same time. Contradictory arguments are often made because a speaker fails to consider the meaning of an argument or piece of evidence presented in one part of his speech in the other parts of the speech. Participants in Lincoln-Douglas debate should remain aware of the opportunity to exploit an opponent's contradictions by pointing to evidence or arguments which invalidate each other.

4) _Attacking an Unstated Premise_—any argument is based on assumptions; more often than not, the assumptions are not proven. If you can identify a questionable assumption of an argument and point out that it is unproven, you can show that the argument is also unproven. For example, an affirmative speaker may claim that urbanization lowers the quality of life because it reduces man's contact with nature. The speaker may go on to prove that there is little parkland in most cities and that city-dwellers take few trips to the country. The negative speaker may legitimately require the affirmative speaker to justify his assumption that contact with nature is necessarily an ingredient of a higher quality of life. Cities, for example, provide interesting and diverse scenery as well as many recreational opportunities not available in the country.

Forms of Proof In some cases, you will be able to gain acceptance for your arguments by merely stating ideas that are so widely held that they will not be disputed. Usually, however, you will need to support your arguments with specific examples, expert testimony from authorities, or statistical evidence. Some tests for the reliability of evidence are provided below.

1) _Testimony from Authorities_ Statements from authorities are an indispensible element of proof in speeches on questions of historical fact and value. These quotations provide expert testimony supporting the accuracy of the speaker's facts and conclusions. Your use of testimony will be more effective if you adhere to the following guidelines. Give the qualifications of your source unless the source is very well known. Corroborate your conclusionary quotations with the statements of other authorities who agree with the first source. This is important for arguments that are critical to your speech: arguments that are central to your thesis, complex, or of low audience acceptability. Finally, if you exclude irrelevant material from the quotations, be careful not to distort the meaning of the authority's statement. The following tests of credibility apply especially to expert testimony:

a) Is the source qualified to speak on the subject of the quotation?
b) Is the source biased?
c) Does the source provide the reasons for his conclusions?
d) Is the source consistent in his statements?
e) Are the source's conclusions supported by an adequate level of evidence?

2) _Statistics_ Statistics, when properly employed, can lend an invaluable degree of concreteness and accuracy to your conclusions. It is useful to keep in mind some methods of presenting statistics effectively in a speech. Cite the source of the statistics; the more dramatic the statistics, the less credible they will sound in the absence of a source. Use statistics judiciously, since the audience will not be able to remember a string of numbers, and note-takers will probably have difficulty writing them down correctly. Translate the statistics if possible into a meaningful form, such as a proportion, a percentage, or a familiar unit of measurement. If the evidence does not seem believable on first hearing, it may be helpful to explain the methodology behind the statistics. The following tests of credibility apply especially to statistical evidence:

a) Is the sample from which the statistics were drawn representative of the relevant population? (For example, we cannot infer the number of immigrants who were poor from the number of poor Irish immigrants.)
b) Are the units clearly classified? (For example, If the number of poor people in America for each of several historical periods is shown, the meaning of "poverty" in each of these periods should be made clear.)

c) Are all major relevant variables considered? (The number of poor people in pre-urban America may not be meaningful if most poor people satisfied their basic needs by living off the land.)

d) Are statistical differences significant? (One percentage point's difference may mean many billions of dollars if one is discussing total output in the American economy, while it may mean little if one is discussing the price of milk by the half-gallon.)

e) Is the base of a percentage an important consideration? (The number of pupils enrolled in public education increased several hundred percent in the first half of the nineteenth century—from a very small number of students to a slightly larger number.)

3) *Examples and Historical Analogies* One of the best ways to bring an abstract idea home to the audience is to illustrate it with a good example or historical analogy. These forms of proof lend concreteness, clarity, and vitality to ideas.

Historical analogies make extended comparisons between two related examples. The more familiar example is used to provide information about the less well known example. Extemporaneous Speaking Topic 8, Issue VII, is an example of a topic which lends itself readily to a historical analogy. ("Military manpower: The U.S. in Europe today versus Europe in the Americas in the 18th century. What are the similarities and differences?") The speaker could use the current situation in Europe, with which the audience would be more familiar, as a basis for an understanding of the situation in the 18th century.

You should be careful to choose examples and analogies which are representative of the idea they support in all pertinent respects. You may attack the examples and historical analogies used by others if they overlook important differences. Also, you may attack generalizations drawn from examples for failing to meet the criteria discussed in the next section.

4) *Generalization* A generalization is a conclusion drawn from several examples. (e.g., "America has moved steadily towards greater equality of opportunity for its citizens.") In your speech, you can challenge the generalizations of others for failing to meet the following criteria:

a) Is the generalization based on adequate evidence?

b) Is the generalization consistent with all the evidence? Are there other examples which contradict the generalization? Should the generalization be qualified to incorporate contradictory evidence?

c) Does the evidence really support the generalization? Does the evidence lead to some other generalization more directly?

5) *Causal explanations* These answer the question, "Why did events happen as they did?" One possible causal explanation for America's trend towards equality might be that egalitarianism and individualism are deeply ingrained in the popular culture, and that each generation of Americans feels compelled to advance closer to a realization of the central goal of equality. The following criteria must be met if a causal explanation is to be valid:

a) Is the causal explanation based on adequate evidence?

b) Is the causal explanation consistent with all the evidence? Are there other examples which contradict the explanation? Should the explanation be qualified in such a way as to incorporate contradictory evidence?

c) Are other causes also responsible for the events as they occurred? If so, how important is the causal explanation under consideration?

d) Is the causal explanation sufficient to account for the occurrence of pertinent events? Would the events have occurred in the absence of the cause? Could the events have been predicted from the causal explanation?

Constructing Arguments There are several acceptable methods of structuring an effective argument. One method of doing this is the "S.R.E.C." (State, Relate, Evidence, Conclude) formula.

1) The speaker first *states* the title of the argument. Like their counterparts in an outline, the captions for arguments should be concise, clear, and accurate. They should be brief enough for those taking notes to record them and for those not taking notes to understand and remember them.

2) The speaker *relates* his argument by conveying a sense of its importance and its relationship to other ideas in the speech. In Lincoln-Douglas debate, rebuttal arguments include a reference in this step to the argument which is being addressed. (It is important to restate another speaker's argument fairly and accurately; misrepresentation of an opposing argument violates the purposes of rational argument and reduces your credibility.)

3) *Evidence* is discussed above in the section on Forms of Proof. It is worth reiterating here that proof (or evidence) includes reasoning as well as quotations and statistics. Whether authoritative evidence is necessary

to support your position, in addition to reasoning and generally accepted facts, depends upon the logical tests of evidence described above.

4) _Conclusion_ includes (a) a statement of the impact of the argument on your own and your opponent's main ideas and (b) a transition to the next argument or the conclusion of your speech.

For example, a speaker might make the following argument:

(State) _Regulatory Commissions have been granted statutory autonomy._

(Relate) The elected representatives of the American people play only a minor role in the development of policy in many of the most vital domestic areas. In the name of insulating policy from political interference, we have removed policy from _democratic_ interference—and hence from the influence of you, the voter.

(Evidence) In large measure, the nation's policy with respect to transportation has been formulated by the Interstate Commerce Commission and the Civil Aeronautics Board; with respect to the economy, banking, and currency, by the Federal Reserve Board; with respect to fair practice of interstate commerce, by the Federal Trade Commission. Similarly, the nation's policy in the areas of energy, the stock market, communications, and labor management relations is largely set by other independent agencies. Marian Irish of the School of International Service, American University, and James Prothro, Professor of Political Science at the University of North Carolina, discussed the nine major independent regulatory commissions when they indicated: "All are outside the executive departments and are free from direct responsibility to the President. All engage in policy making and regulatory activities, mostly in the economic sphere. All have quasi-legislative and quasi-judicial powers. Taken together, these commissions exercise tremendous authority. . ."

(Conclude) Independent commissions, then, have by law been given regulatory power in a number of pivotal areas in our society; they have been deliberately removed from popular control. But what of other areas, where nominal control of policy rests with elected officials? My next point is that:

(State) _Cabinet level bureaucracy has secured de facto autonomy_. (The speaker would then develop this point according to the same formula.)

LINCOLN-DOUGLAS DEBATE

The BYD Lincoln-Douglas Debate event is designed to stimulate advocates to define and resolve questions of historical importance. As a participant you will want to take advantage of analytic and communicative faculties to persuade the audience to your position.

Interpretation At issue are fundamental American ideals, not specific or limited policy considerations. In the first speech, the affirmative speaker should provide a reasonable interpretation of the resolution. Since the terms of the proposition derive substance from their societal context, the meaning of the topic to a reasonable member of the community furnishes an appropriate standard of interpretation. The accompanying BYD Issue Analyses indicate topical approaches to each resolution. The negative speaker is only obliged to contest unreasonable definitions and should resist making facile challenges to the appropriateness of justified analyses.

On the affirmative, you have the opportunity to focus the debate by constructing a _framework_ within which arguments on both sides of the proposition will be considered. BYD topics involve issues which are factual or combinations of fact and value. When arguing questions of value, the speaker should delineate the relevant values and offer supporting reasoning and illustrations. If the controversy is factual, the affirmative presentation pattern should include, organized by major points, sufficient data to warrant the proposition. (For additional information on affirmative structure, see the Organization section above.)

If you are on the negative, at the beginning of your presentation you should state the _negative thesis,_ and then explain how it will be developed. The negative thesis is a summary statement of the basic negative position. It is the focal point of the negative's analysis and should be a common bond unifying the major negative arguments. (See sample outline below.) After explaining the thesis, in part of your speech you might demonstrate the inability of the affirmative to defend its position. During the rest of your speaking time, you should establish alternative values and interpretations of history which warrant a negative view of the proposition. It does not matter whether denial of the affirmative case precedes or follows the negative arguments. However, it is important to let listeners know what the order of your presentation will be.

Direct refutation of the affirmative position involves identification of gaps in the reasoning or proof of the case, as well as presentation of directly contrary reasoning and evidence. Direct refutation is best understood if you follow the order of affirmative presentation and carefully identify the point that is being addressed and the method of denial. This is easily accomplished by referring to the label or title of the affirmative argument, and explaining your response to it, and then indicating the importance of the failure of the affirmative to sustain its position. (The methods of responding to arguments are considered above in Attacking and Defending Ideas.)

Prepared constructive arguments should pertain to almost any plausible interpretation of the resolution. These ideas may be outlined in advance of the debate and could be presented in your own organizational framework. Whenever your standard arguments comfortably fit the affirmative structure, they should be presented as direct refutation of particular affirmative points. It is important to realize that prepared arguments should be used only if they are relevant to the particular interpretation of the proposition which the affirmative has chosen.

Following is a sample outline of a negative speech on the hypothetical bureaucracy topic.

Negative Position: An effective democratic government delegates authority to non-elected officials.
I. The number of policy decisions to be made justifies delegation of authority.
   A. The federal government confronts a vast number of policy decisions.
   B. Elected officials lack sufficient time to make all policy decisions.
   C. Non-elected officials must make many policy decisions.
   (Politicians should not set policy since)
II. The need for expertise justifies delegation of authority.
   A. Effective government requires expertise, e.g., foreign policy, economics, education.
   B. Elected officials lack expertise. They are chosen for popular appeal, not expertise.
   C. Non-elected officials provide expertise, e.g., political scientists, economists, educators.
   (The popular will is not ignored because)
III. Non-elected officials must heed the popular will.
   A. Non-elected officials are accountable to elected officials.
   B. Elected officials are accountable to the popular will.
   C. Non-elected officials are accountable to the popular will. (The politicians who appoint bureaucrats may revise unpopular policies, or replace the experts who were unresponsive. If not, the politician is likely to be defeated at the polls and replaced with one who will make popular decisions.)

Compare the above outline to the affirmative structure presented in the Organization section. The negative position and the first argument concerning the vast number of policy decisions which the federal government must make might be presented at the beginning of the speech. The second argument—expertise in government is desirable—could be used to offset the affirmative claim that elected officials should determine policy. If used this way, the second argument would be presented in refutation of an affirmative point. The third argument—bureaucrats are indirectly responsive to the popular will—may be used to refute the affirmative contention that delegation of policy-making authority is inimical to democratic ideals.

Argument Development A good debate will center on clearly defined and well-developed issues. This will happen if the debaters carefully select the arguments they address and give full consideration to their opponents' responses.

Argument selection will have a direct bearing on the outcome of the debate. Before beginning a speech, you should decide which arguments are needed to establish your position. If an opponent's argument appears to be important, but it is not, you should explain why. You should emphasize arguments which are particularly critical to your position. Sometimes a single argument will serve to deny several opposing arguments which share a common flaw.

Cross-examination Cross-examination provides the opportunity to ask for clarification of confusing ideas, gain admissions from your opponent, and point out flaws in reasoning or evidence. Questions should have a specific purpose, and they should be asked in a logical sequence.

The following guidelines might prove helpful when questioning:
   1. Ask questions, do not make statements;
   2. Maintain a relaxed manner, try not to appear pushy;
   3. Politely cut off unreasonably long answers;
   4. Make use of admissions gained in a subsequent speech;
   5. Focus on central issues, not peripheral concerns;
   6. Ask precise questions; avoid questions which call for rambling answers.

When answering:
1. Ask for clarification of vague questions;
2. Do not argue with the questioner;
3. Qualify answers when necessary;
4. Try not to appear evasive;
5. Be confident, not defensive;
6. Refer to arguments presented in your speech in answering.

PERSUASIVE SPEAKING

The purpose of a persuasive speech is to convince the audience to accept a thesis which they had not previously held, or to reinforce a view which they had already accepted. Prior to delivery, a speech should be researched, written, and practiced. In effect, a BYD persuasive speech is an original oration which is designed to persuade the audience to your position.

The subject of your speech should reflect both the substance and the tone of the BYD Persuasive Speaking topic. This means that you shoudl select a facet of the general topic which concerns a historical question of fact and/or value that is directly related to the BYD topic. The relevance of the thesis to the general topic should be apparent from your speech.

Since the goal is to persuade, your speech should establish a viewpoint as well as provide information. Avoid choosing the topic that is so generally accepted that persuasion is unnecessary. For example, under the broad subject area "My Country Right or Wrong?" one would not pick the thesis "America sometimes makes mistakes, but often it is right." That simply is not of a controversial nature. A much more interesting speech would argue that: "To preserve what is decent about America, the law must be followed." One of the advantages of persuasive speaking is that you are free to choose your own thesis. As a result, topic selection is an important component of the speech, and a major factor in the judges' evaluation.

After the selection of your topic, you will begin to research your speech. Persuasive Speaking requires in-depth research in a narrow subject area. You need to concentrate your efforts to formulate a specific thesis; once selected, further research should be oriented to discovering the arguments that can contribute to a coherent, consistent, compelling position in support of the thesis.

Persuasive speeches should be prepared and polished in advance. You have the opportunity to select carefully your words and to plan smooth, logical transitions between your main points. Although the regulations permit you to use a manuscript, it might prove more effective to memorize the speech and use the text or an outline as a prompter. If you know your speech well, you can concentrate on communication rather than word choice. This familiarity will permit you to maintain eye contact with the audience and leads to a smoother, more controlled style.

A couple of techniques are helpful in memorization of speeches. Try to memorize the speech in terms of ideas, not just words—in this way, you will be able to forget a few words without losing your thought. Also, try to memorize your speech a section at a time in the course of several sittings; it is difficult to learn a ten-minute speech all at one time.

The conclusion should draw together the reasons for your listener to adopt the view you are advocating. You may choose to return to an introductory example or incident; you may wish to end with a recurring symbol. However, rather than forcing the use of a particular device, the conclusion should be the natural and reasonable outcome of the speech as a whole.

EXTEMPORANEOUS SPEAKING

Unlike impromptu speaking or some forms of extemporaneous speaking, the BYD Extemporaneous Speaking topics are disclosed in advance. This will allow you to explore the specific topics ahead of time in order to prepare a cogent, interesting, and articulare presentation.

If you find that the topic is ambiguous or equivocal, it will be necessary to interpret it. Having done so, the emphasis of your position should be to support, deny, or modify the assertion contained in the topic. To accomplish this without speaking vague generalities, it is useful to develop in detail one or more narrow aspects of the topic. These representative illustrations should be explained and organized in a way that expresses your position on the topic.

As with all BYD events you will want to support your ideas with analysis and evidence that the audience will find convincing. Unlike debate, which involves an examination of a general proposition, you will need to research each of the specific BYD Extemporaneous Speaking topics.

You may want to begin your speech with a humorous or memorable introduction, but be careful not to develop the introduction at the expense of the quality of the reasoning and proof presented in the body of your speech. Introductions should be pertinent and to the point. To avoid the possibility of misunderstanding, it will be a good idea to state the BYD Extemporaneous Speaking topic in the introduction.

It is not necessary to explain your organization by saying, "My first contention is. .," although, for example, you might want to tell the audience that there are "three basic ideas in my speech and they are: (1). . .(2). . .(3). . . ." Your organization can be made clear by using a varieity of communicative channels, including language, voice, and gestures. To indicate a transition, you might walk a few steps; or when introducing a major concept you would reduce your rate of delivery.

It will not be especially useful to write out an entire extemporaneous speech. As a practical matter, it would be impossible to memorize ten or more different speeches. You might want to outline speeches for each of the topics since you will be permitted to speak from notes but not from a text.

You will be asked questions by the judges. It is probable that they will ask for more information about some of the ideas you have presented. They may also inquire about your reasoning. Consequently, you should be prepared to provide more detailed information in support of your arguments. You should be as informative and lucid as possible.

Since you only have seven minutes to speak, you will need to be concise and direct. Carefully select the ideas you are discussing and present them in a clear, convincing manner. Your conclusion should tie together the central points of the message and end the speech in a positive manner.

ADDITIONAL INFORMATION

Several sources of additional information on Bicentennial Youth Debates topics are readily available. During the Bicentennial year there will be numerous media activities focusing on the American Issues Forum:

Courses by Newspaper

The publication of weekly lectures on Forum topics in selected newspapers across the country and two volumes of readings for general distribution.

George Colburn/C.A. Lewis
"Courses By Newspaper"
4901 Morena Boulevard
Suite 209
San Diego, California 92117
Tel: (714) 452-3405

AIF Reading Lists

The American Library Association has developed and distributed two reading lists—one for adults and one for young readers—on each of the weekly Forum topics.

Mr. Donald E. Stewart
American Library Association
50 East Huron Street
Chicago, Illinois 60611
Tel: (312) 944-6780

National Public Radio

NPR's nine monthly three hour forums include presentations on the issues, discussions by leading figures and call-in participation.

Dr. Jack Mitchell
Director of Informational
    Programs
National Public Radio
2025 M Street, N.W.
Washington, D.C. 20036
Tel: (202) 785-5436

A significant cross-section of national organizations are preparing materials representing their perspectives on the monthly AIF topics for distribution to their members. Materials may be requested from the organizations directly:

AFL-CIO

Mrs. Dorothy Shields
Division of Education
AFL-CIO
815 16th Street, N.W.
Washington, D.C. 20006
Tel: (202) 637-5148

NAACP

Mr. Warren Marr, II
Editor, Crisis
1790 Broadway
New York, New York 10019
Tel: (212) 245-2100

American Association for
State and Local History

Dr. William T. Alderson
Executive Director
American Association for
State and Local History
1400 Eighth Ave. South
Nashville, Tennessee 37203
Tel: (615) 242-5583

National Center for Urban
Ethnic Affairs

Msgr. Geno Baroni, Pres.
Andy Leon Harney, Editor
National Center for Urban
  Ethnic Affairs
4408 Eighth Street, N.E.
Washington, D.C. 20017
Tel: (202) 529-5400

National Council on the
Aging

Mr. Louis Hausman
NCOA - Suite 504
1828 L Street, N.W.
Washington, D.C. 20036
Tel: (202) 223-6250

National Grange

Mr. David R. Lambert
The National Grange
1616 H Street, N.W.
Washington, D.C. 20006
Tel: (202) 628-3507

National Urban League

Mr. James Williams
Director of Communications
National Urban League
500 East 62nd Street
New York, New York 10022
Tel: (212) 644-6500

Foreign Policy Association

Dr. Norman Jacobs
Director
Foreign Policy Association
345 East 46th Street
New York, New York 10017
Tel: (212) 697-2432

CALENDAR OF BYD PUBLICATIONS AND EVENTS

1975
AUGUST   BYD PARTICIPANT AND ADMINISTRATIVE GUIDE and
15   ADMINISTRATIVE MATERIALS

One copy of the BYD PARTICIPANT AND ADMINISTRATIVE GUIDE along with ADMINISTRATIVE MATERI-
ALS have been mailed to the local coordinators in each responding school and institution in the United
States. In other schools, the packet has been mailed to the "Librarian/Bicentennial Coordinator." The
GUIDE provides tournament procedures for administrators and rules and regulations for participants.
ADMINISTRATIVE MATERIALS include certification forms, instructions for moderators, and ballots for the
local event.

SEPTEMBER
27   ELIGIBILITY DEADLINE

Entrants in competitive events must be under 25 years old and not hold a bachelor's degree or its equivalent.

27
(through
Nov. 1)   ISSUES I AND II LOCAL EVENTS

Individual schools and organizations, hereafter referred to as Local, will hold contests in all three events.
The High School Program events will be based on Issue I: "A Nation of Nations," and the College Age
events will be based on Issue II: "The Land of Plenty."

OCTOBER
1   DISTRICT EVENT NOTIFICATION

Site, date and schedule for the District event forwarded to each Local BYD Coordinator with the name,
address and telephone number of the District BYD Coordinator.

5
(through 10)   BRITISH-AMERICAN DEBATES

American teams debate a British team: "Was the American Revolution a Failure?"
    October 5 - Boston, Massachusetts
    October 7 - Springfield, Illinois
    October 8 - Los Angeles, California
    October 10 - Philadelphia, Pennsylvania

(These events are co-sponsored by the Committee on International Discussion and Debate, Speech Communication Association.)

NOVEMBER   DEADLINE FOR CERTIFICATION
3   OF LOCAL QUALIFIERS

The Local Coordinator will certify to the District Coordinator and National office local debaters who have
qualified to participate in District events.

15
(through
Dec. 20)   ISSUES III AND IV DISTRICT EVENTS

High School participants will debate Issue III: "Certain Inalienable Rights" and College Age participants will debate Issue IV: "A More Perfect Union: The American Government."

1976
JANUARY   DEADLINE FOR CERTIFICATION
5   DISTRICT QUALIFIERS

The District Coordinator will certify to the Sectional Coordinator and National office debaters who have qualified to participate in Sectional events.

15   SECTIONAL EVENT NOTIFICATION

Site, date and schedule for the Sectional event forwarded to each Local Coordinator who has a participant advancing to the Sectional event.

31
(through
March 6)   ISSUES V AND VI SECTIONAL EVENTS

High School events will use Issue V: "Working in America" and College Age events will use Issue VI: "The Business of America. . ."

MARCH   DEADLINE FOR CERTIFICATION
9   OF SECTIONAL QUALIFIERS

The Sectional Coordinator will certify to the Regional Director and National office debaters who have qualified to participate in Regional events.

15   REGIONAL EVENT NOTIFICATION

Site, date and schedule for the Regional event forwarded to each Local Coordinator who has a participant advancing to the Regional event.

20
(through
April 24)   ISSUES VII AND VIII REGIONAL EVENTS

College Age participants will debate Issue VII: "America in the World" and High School participants will debate Issue VIII: "Growing Up in America."

340

MAY
1

DEADLINE FOR CERTIFICATION
OF REGIONAL QUALIFIERS

The Regional Director will certify to the National office debaters who have qualified to participate in National events.

15

NATIONAL EVENT NOTIFICATION

Site, date and schedule for the National event forwarded to each Local Coordinator who has a participant advancing to the National event.

JUNE
1-4

ISSUE IX NATIONAL EVENT

The National event will be held in Washington, D.C. Both High School and College Age events will be based on Issue IX: "Life, Liberty and the Pursuit of Happiness." Outstanding young people who have participated in the BYD program and have qualified for this event will attend a conference where they will meet with outstanding Americans including members of the BYD National Advisory Council and other American leaders, for discussion of the important issues which they have debated.

NATIONAL OFFICE

Bicentennial Youth Debates
1625 Massachusetts Avenue, N. W.
Washington, D. C. 20036
(202) 265-1070

Dr. Richard C. Huseman	Project Director
James I. Luck	Associate Project Director
Pamela A. Martinson	Project Manager
Harvey Silver	Information/Development
Marvin P. Isgur	Regional Coordinator

REGIONAL DIRECTORS

NORTHEAST: Irene Malton
Amherst High School, Triangle Street, Amherst, Massachusetts 01002, 413/549-2810
Connecticut, Maine, Massachusetts, New Hampshire, New York, Rhode Island, Vermont

MID-ATLANTIC: David Horn
Bishop McDevitt High School, 205 Royal Avenue, Wyncote, Pennsylvania 19095, 215/885-0858
Delaware, District of Columbia, Maryland, New Jersey, Pennsylvania

CENTRAL: Lannie Katzman
Toledo Start High School, 2061 Farragut Street, Toledo, Ohio 43613, 419/473-1119
Indiana, Kentucky, Ohio, Virginia, West Virginia

SOUTHEAST: John Bloodworth
University of Georgia, Department of Management, Athens, Georgia 30602, 404/542-7281
Alabama, Florida, Georgia, Mississippi, North Carolina, South Carolina, Tennessee

SOUTHWEST: John Crain
Notre Dame High School, 2821 Lansing Boulevard, Wichita Falls, Texas 76309, 817/692-7202
Arizona, Colorado, Louisiana, New Mexico, Oklahoma, Texas, Utah

MID-WEST: Steve Davis
Glenbrook North High School, Northbrook, Illinois 60062, 312/564-1246
Arkansas, Illinois, Iowa, Kansas, Missouri, Nebraska

NORTH-CENTRAL: Donald Ritzenhein
Wayne State University, Department of Speech Communication & Theatre, Detroit, Michigan 48202, 313/577-2318
Michigan, Minnesota, Montana, North Dakota, South Dakota, Wisconsin, Wyoming

PACIFIC: Dr. Louis W. Cockerham
University of Redlands, Dept. of Speech Communication, Redlands, California 92373, 714/793-2444
Alaska, California, Hawaii, Idaho, Nevada, Oregon, Washington

NATIONAL ADVISORY COUNCIL

Joseph L. Block
Chm. Nat'l. Merit Scholarship Corp.

William F. Buckley, Jr.
Editor, *National Review*

Walter Cronkite
CBS News Correspondent

Arthur J. Goldberg
Former Supreme Court Justice

Barry Goldwater
U.S. Senator, Arizona

Patricia Roberts Harris
Former Ambassador to Luxembourg

Barbara Jordan
U.S. Representative, Texas

George Meany
President, AFL-CIO

Francine I. Neff
Treasurer of the United States

Dean Rusk
Former Secretary of State

COUNCIL FOR DEVELOPMENT AND COMMUNITY INVOLVEMENT

W. A. Applegate
Executive Director
Distributive Education
Clubs of America

Alden G. Barber
Chief Scout Executive
National Council,
Boy Scouts of America

Earle B. Barnes
President
Dow Chemical, U.S.A.

Robert A. Buchler
Director of Youth Activities
Civitan International

Ruth C. Clusen
President
League of Women Voters

Cecil L. Gilliat
President
National School
Boards Association

David L. Hale
President
United States Jaycees

James A. Harris
President
National Education Asssociation

Roger W. Heyns
President
American Council on Education

Larry W. Johnson
Executive Director
Vocational Industrial
Clubs of America

Carol Kimmel
President
National Congress of
Parents and Teachers

R. Heath Larry
Vice Chairman of the Board
United States
Steel Corporation

William A. Marquard
President
American Standard, Inc.

Robert H. McBride
President
National Association of
State Boards of Education

Terrence J. McCann
Executive Director
Toastmasters International

Richard Maxwell
President
Junior Achievement

Jack P. Nix
President
National Council of Chief
State School Officers

Ted R. Osborn
President-Elect
Kiwanis International

Cecily C. Selby
National Executive Director
Girls Scouts of
The U.S.A.

Albert Shanker
President
American Federation
of Teachers

Robert Stuart
Chairman of the Board
National Can Corporation

Jean Tilford
President
National Council for
the Social Studies

Alpha Trivette
President
Future Farmers of America

Hester Turner
National Executive Director
Camp Fire Girls

E. Dean Vaughan
National Director
4-H Clubs

Robert Wedgeworth
Executive Director
American Library Association

FORENSIC LEADERSHIP COUNCIL

John E. Baird
President
Pi Kappa Delta

James Collie
President
Phi Rho Pi

Nicholas M. Cripe
President
Delta Sigma Rho- Tau Kappa Alpha

James F. Hawker
President
National Forensic League

Lucy M. Keele, Past Chairperson
Forensics Division
Speech Communication Association

Scott Nobles
President
American Forensic Association

Robert J. Prior
President
National Catholic Forensic League

James F. Weaver, Chairperson
Forensics Division
Speech Communication Association

BYD is recognized by the American Revolution Bicentennial Administration as a major national Bicentennial program and is supported, endorsed or recognized by many groups and individuals including:

American Association of Community and Junior Colleges
American Bar Association National Bicentennial Committee
American Business Communication Association
AFL-CIO
American Federation of Teachers
American Forensic Association
Ted H. Bell, U.S. Commissioner of Education
Evron M. Kirkpatrick, Executive Director,
  American Political Science Association

Freedoms Foundation at Valley Forge
National Association of Secondary School Principals
National Congress of Parents and Teachers(PTA)
National Council of Teachers of English
National Forensic League
National School Board Association
National University Extension Association Committee on Discussion
and Debate
Toastmasters International

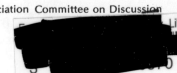